SEMIOTEXT(E) FOREIGN AGENTS SERIES

Originally published as *Sphären III. Schäume* by Editions Suhrkamp, Frankfurt.
© Suhrkamp Verlag Frankfurt am Main 2004. All rights reserved

This edition Semiotext(e) © 2016

Published by Semiotext(e)
PO BOX 629, South Pasadena, CA 91031
www.semiotexte.com

Special thanks to John Ebert.

Cover photograph by Balthasar Burkhard, Normandie 1995.
© Estate Balthasar Burkhard.

Design: Hedi El Kholti

ISBN: 978-1-58435-187-0
Distributed by The MIT Press, Cambridge, Mass. and London, England
Printed in the United States of America

SPHERES

VOLUME 3: FOAMS

PLURAL SPHEROLOGY

Peter Sloterdijk

Translated by Wieland Hoban

Contents

SPHERES

VOLUME 3: FOAMS

MACROSPHEROLOGY

Looking back century by century to remotest Antiquity, I see nothing that resembles what I see before me.

— Alexis de Tocqueville, *Democracy in America*

NOTE

The present book is the third and final part of a philosophical project that began with the publication of *Sphären I, Blasen* in 1998 and continued with that of *Sphären II, Globen* in 1999.[1] This has consequences for its legibility. The author must meet the requirement that a book which is published separately should also be separately legible and comprehensible. This applies fully to the present work. It is possible to begin with the third part of *Spheres* as if it were the first—which it is, in a certain sense, for the enterprise as a whole can only be grasped in terms of its concluding pole.

It should not impair the reading process if I preface this volume with a few comments on the connections between the parts of the trilogy. In the two previous volumes, I attempted to give the word "sphere" the status of a basic concept whose meaning can be separated out into topological, anthropological, immunological and semiological aspects. *Spheres I* suggests a description (which the author believes to be new in parts) of the human space that the close being-together of humans with humans creates an interior that has so far received too little attention. This inside is termed the microsphere and characterized as a highly sensitive and adaptive soul-spatial, or (moral, if you will) immune system. The emphasis is the thesis that compared to the individual, the couple constitutes the more real unit—which simultaneously means that we-immunity embodies a deeper phenomenon than I-immunity. In a time that swears by elementary particles and individuals, such an assertion cannot be taken for granted. I characterize human worlds of closeness as surreal spaces in order to express that even non-spatial relationships such as sympathy and understanding translate themselves into quasi-spatial relationships within which to become imaginable and livable.

In its form, the human space—as I show in seven attempts—was from the outset, literally *ab utero*, bipolar at first and pluripolar at higher levels. It possesses the structure and dynamics of, to use an old-fashioned turn of phrase, an ensouling intertwinement of life forms disposed towards closeness and sharing in each other; not infrequently, this close interlocking triggers the perverse closeness of primary aggression—for things that harbor each other can also imprison and eradicate each other. At the same time, this relationship also holds all those possibilities referred to by tradition with such sonorous words as "friendship," "love," "understanding," "consensus," *concordia* and *communitas*. Even the run-down term "solidarity" to which the inelegant left of today has attached its soul (and which currently means something like tele-sentimentality), can only be regenerated—if at all—from this source.

Humans, in so far as they are the beings that "exist," are the geniuses of the neighborhood. Heidegger articulated this in his most creative phase: if the existing exist together, they keep themselves "in the same sphere of openness [*Offenbarkeit*]." They are accessible yet transcendent to one another—an observation that dialogic thinkers never tire of underlining. Not only persons,

Pablo Reinoso, *La parole* (1998)

however, but also things and circumstances are affected in their respective ways by the principle of neighborhood. That is why "world" here refers to the connections between possibilities of access. "Dasein already brings the sphere of possible neighborhood with it; it is by nature a neighbor to…"[2] Two stones lying next to each another do not know ecstatic openness for each other.[3] One could certainly read *Spheres I* as a dive into the abyss of ontological nervousness for the co-existent, the other, the outer. On this stoic journey into the first ecological niche of humans, outlining a form of philosophical gynecology was inevitable. It is clear why that is not to everyone's taste. So much the worse for readers who will gain even less enjoyment from the theologically informed propaedeutics of intimacy with which this book of excesses closes inwards.

In *Spheres II*, conclusions are drawn from a view of the ecstatic-surreal nature of the experienced and inhabited space. This occurs in the form of a grand narrative on the expansion of the soul domain in the course of imperial and cognitive world-changings. One could now call the undertaking a philosophical novel that carries out the rounding off of the external in manageable stages. Here exaggeration proves its worth not only as a stylistic tool, but also as a method of clarifying contexts. The first chapter of the hyperbolic novel is allotted to the first volume, where the intimate constitution of the dyad and its development into simple familiality is discussed—a process that leads from duality to a five-pole structure as the minimum form of psychological attachment capability and world-openness. Starting from the basic domestic situation—its architectural symbol is the hut—the expansion program proceeds from the village to the city, to the empire and onwards to the finite universe until it loses itself in the uninhabitable boundless space. Dante's hells constitute painful branches of this radiant path; they illustrate almost all the possibilities of immersion in the worst. In this apprenticeship of inclusive feeling, one can observe how countless smaller spheres burst and occasionally regenerate themselves in larger formats. Once again: the microsphere is a space that learns and possesses the ability to grow. In it, the law of incorporation through assimilation applies; if it keeps itself in flux, it is by fleeing to the larger scale. It is a hybrid elastic space that reacts to deformation not simply with regeneration, but with expansion. The postula tion that ultimate security can be found in the largest, and only there, initiated the soul's affair with geometry. The event called metaphysics was precisely that: the insight that local existence integrates itself into the absolute orb—and the ensouled point swells up into the universal sphere. In that, the psyche believed it had found a share in the indestructible. The most uncompromising simplification paved the way to salvation.

In the course of the narrative, it should become clear why classical philosophy took form as macrospherology, as contemplation of the greatest orb and most encompassing immune structure. Wherever philosophical thought after Plato was at the necessary level, the two epitomes of totality, the world and God, were envisaged as an all-enclosing spheric volume in which countless subordinate world shells, value spheres and energy circles are concentrically embedded—extending down to the soul point, which is experienced as the light source of the I-atom. Existence is characterized by immersion in a final element—it is either "in God" or "in the world," possibly in both at once. *Tell me what you are immersed in, and I will tell you what you are.* One can gain a sense of the penetrative power of such reflections by recapitulating how much they earned the respect of the strongest Old European thinkers: from Plotinus to Leibniz, the observation of macrospheres was the authoritative form of ontology.[4] According to traditional conviction, that same "sphere of openness" encompassed both the physical cosmos and the perceiving subject. Hence the exuberant belief that it was in the nature of the human spirit to attain a form of cognizance of the first and last things; hence also the easily disappointed initial expectation of the existential debutants that they could achieve great things on earth. "I was all head; and was just as perfection and eternity represent themselves, namely circular; this gave me hope of a future [...] I set off on a global campaign."[5] According to the author's tongue-in-cheek insights, each individual determines the curve of their life with such prenatal anticipations. If reality lived

Albert Speer, design of the great hall

up to the ideal, the human spirit would not become fully grown until it had learned to grasp itself as the junior partner of the absolute. Just as the anonymous placental genius and the fetus form the first couple, God and the soul—or alternatively the cosmos and the individual intellect—form the last.

The grand narrative of *Spheres II*, which follows the catastrophe-punctuated curve from minimum to maximum, attempts to communicate why metaphysics was the continuation of animism by theoretical and political means—animism is the belief in the hyper-immune system of the soul. This explains why classical metaphysics was destined to founder on its internal contradiction. Although the legend that it was brought down by sobering critique and the better knowledge of a later order of intelligence is promoted everywhere, it was actually the inner impossibility of its aim that thwarted it. The few who were

Josiah Woodward, *Fair Warnings to a Careless World* (1707), detail

serious about it understand that to this day: it failed because it sought to defend the cause of life, which by nature only exists in the finitude of an individuated immune system, while simultaneously espousing the infinite, which denies every isolated life and ignores private immune interests. As the servant of two masters, it was doomed by the impossibility of its position—without language criticism, psychology or "deconstruction" having to lift a finger. The lessons from this endogenous failure (which also demanded to be found at an external level) were far-reaching: it manifested the conflict between infinity and immunity in which the primal dispute of modern thought, and perhaps all thought that seeks to be philosophical, takes place.

In keeping with the logic of its object, the reconstruction of the metaphysical delirium of simplification and unification closes with a brief history of the modern world—as Europe-focused as necessary and as world-philosophical as possible. Modernity here means, quite conventionally, the epoch in which the Old World broke out of metaphysical monocentrism. It saw the rupture of the magic simple circle that had once provided all living beings immunity in their One God, that is to say in the smooth totality. Anyone recounting such a history must willy-nilly provide an outline of European expansion after 1492. This eccentric movement, one-eyedly termed "globalization" in the present day (as if there were only one, not three), was traced in Chapter 8 of *Spheres II* under the heading "The Last Orb: On a Philosophical History of Terrestrial Globalization" in the style of a macrohistorical investigation. What I call "terrestrial" globalization is the variety that followed the metaphysical and preceded the telecommunicative. In its outer and inner dimensions, this section can be read as an independent publication.[6]

An anecdote related by Albert Speer in his memoirs is informative about the state of circle- and orb-related ideas—in relation to the doctrine of worlds—in the twentieth century: in the early summer of 1939, Adolf Hitler (who, along with Gandhi, was nominated for the Nobel Peace Prize that year, albeit satirically), trusting in his plans of universal domination, made a change to the model of the monumental new Reich Chancellery in Berlin, which he and Speer had designed together. Now the imperial eagle at the top of the 290-meter dome was no longer to float as planned above the Nazi symbol, the swastika. Hitler dictated:

> To crown this greatest building in the world the eagle must stand above the globe.[7]

Arkadi Schaichet, *Globe Mounted on the Central Telegraph Office in Moscow* (1928)

Is it necessary to explain why this dictum offers insight into the decomposition history of political metaphysics? This discipline, when it spoke clearly, had always expressed itself as imperial monospherology, and when Hitler replaced the swastika with the globe in his reverie, he too was a classical philosopher for one second. It is slightly harder to understand how the decomposition of the monospheric doctrine of God progressed. Its beginning could be explained with the help of the following reflection by Abbé Sieyès from 1789:

I like to conceive of the law as if it is at the center of an immense globe. Every citizen, without exception, is at an equal distance from it on the circumference of the globe, and each individual occupies an equal place. Everyone depends equally upon the law.[8]

The disintegration of the divine monosphere reveals itself in the decree that all human beings must be equidistant from the God-point. Was it not foreseeable that the democratization of the reference to God would amount to its neutralization and ultimate extinction, and would force the installation of a replacement? Diderot had already completed this change of personnel *expressis verbis* as early as 1755, in a defense of the *Encyclopédie*, declaring man the "joint center" of all things (and encyclopedia entries): "Is there some point in infinite space from which we could more advantageously originate the immense lines which we propose to extend to all other points?"[9] At the provisional end of history we encounter a radio-theoretical statement by Marshall McLuhan:

With the advent of a world environment of simultaneous and instantaneous information, Western man shifted from visual to acoustic space, for acoustic space is a sphere whose center is everywhere and whose boundaries are nowhere.[10]

On the surface, this seems to be a claim about the distribution of hearing opportunities in the radio-acoustic space of the global village. On closer inspection the statement shows its theoretical claws: the Pauline ambitions of the greatest media theorist of his time draw directly on the secrecy-shrouded theorem of Hermetic theosophy from the high medieval *Book of Twenty-Four Philosophers*[11] to invoke a last theory of the One Orb from the spirit of electronic Catholicism. With a generosity bordering on cooption, McLuhan postulates a hybrid, tribal-global information orb that encloses us all in a "single, universal membrane"[12] as happy and coerced members of the "human family" and is simultaneously round (centered, Roman) and unround (peripheral, Canadian). The machine capable of working this miracle is the computer, interpreted in the pentecostal spirit: according to McLuhan, it enables the integration of humanity into a super-tribalist "psychic community." Who could miss the fact that the unity of global village and church was being taught here once again—and who knows, perhaps for the last time?

Spheres III, Foams offers—in contrast to this—a theory of the present age from the perspective that "life" unfolds multifocally, multiperspectively and heterarchically. Its point of departure lies in a non-metaphysical and non-holistic definition of life: its immunization can no longer be thought with the tools of ontological simplification, of collection in the smooth universal orb. If "life" has a boundlessly manifold space-forming effect, this is not only because every monad has its own individual environment, but more significantly because they are all intertwined with other lives and consist of countless units. Life articulates itself on nested simultaneous stages; it produces and devours itself in interconnected workshops. What is decisive here, however, is that it always produces the space in which it is and which is in it in the first place. Just as Bruno Latour has spoken of a "parliament of things,"[13] I will make use of the foam metaphor to examine a republic of spaces.

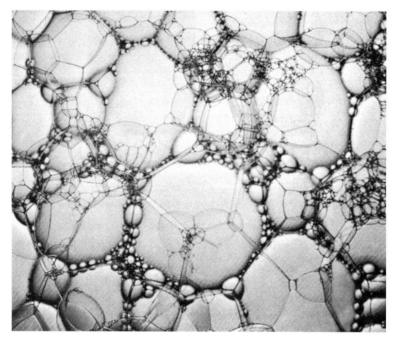

Michael Boran, *Honey*

The investigations of the third volume take up the thread at the point where the work of mourning—or rather the work of lightening—over the impossible metaphysics of the encompassing One reaches its conclusion. Its point of departure is the supposition that the cause of life was not really in good hands with either the representatives of the traditional religions or the metaphysicians. Both were dubious advisers to the indecisive life, for they ultimately never had a better solution to offer than the placebo of devotion to a heavenly simplification. If this is the case, then the relation between knowledge and life must be rethought even more comprehensively than ever occurred to the reformists of the twentieth century. Philosophy, that Old

European form of thought and life, is undeniably exhausted; biosophy has only just begun its work; the theory of atmospheres has only reached provisional consolidation; the General Theory of immune and commune systems is in its infancy;[14] a theory of places, situations and immersions is hesitantly getting underway;[15] the replacement of sociology with the theory of networks of actors is a hypothesis that has so far received little attention;[16] and reflections on the convening of a realistically composed collective to adopt a new constitution for the global society of knowledge have barely shown more than outlines. These indications do not point clearly to any shared tendency. Only one thing is clear: where losses of form were bemoaned, gains in mobility are now in evidence.

The lively thought-image of foam serves to recover the premetaphysical pluralism of world-inventions postmetaphysically. It helps us to enter the element of a manifold thought undeterred by the nihilistic pathos that involuntarily accompanied a reflection disappointed by monological metaphysics during the nineteenth and twentieth centuries. It explains once again what this liveliness is about: the statement "God is dead" is affirmed as the good news of the present day. One could reformulate it thus: "So the One Orb has imploded—now the foams are alive." When the mechanisms of cooption through simplifying globes and imperial totalizations have been seen through, this is precisely *not* a reason to abandon everything that was considered great, inspiring and valuable. Claiming that the harmful god of consensus has died means declaring which energies are required to resume work: it can only be those that were bound by metaphysical hyperbole. Once a great exaggeration becomes obsolete, swarms of more discreet upsurges arise.

Foam-Bornness

And even to me, as one who is fond of life, it seems that butterflies and soap-bubbles, and whatever is like them among humans, know the most about happiness.

— Friedrich Nietzsche, *Thus Spoke Zarathustra*,
"On Reading and Writing"[1]

Air in Unexpected Places

Almost nothing, yet not nothing. A something, if only a delicate web of cavities and subtle walls. An actual thing, but a construct fearful of contact that yields and bursts at the slightest touch. That is foam as encountered in everyday experience. Through the addition of air, a liquid or solid loses its density; what had seemed autonomous, homogeneous and solid is transformed into loosened structures. What is happening there? It is the miscibility of the most opposed elements that becomes a phenomenon in foam. The light element evidently has a cunning ability to penetrate the heavier ones and combine with them, at least ephemerally, though in some cases even for a longer time. "Earth," combined with air, results in stable and dry foam like volcanic rock or cellular glass—phenomena that only came to be termed foam in modern times, once the introduction of air chambers into materials of any hardness or elasticity had become industrial routine. "Water," on the other hand, connected to air, produces damp-fluid and fleeting foam such as sea spray or the scum on fermenting tubs. This short-term combination of gases and liquids provides the model for the established idea of foam. It suggests that, under as yet unclarified circumstances, that which is dense, continuous and massive is subject to an invasion by the hollow. Air, the misunderstood element, finds ways and means of advancing to places where no one reckons with its presence; and, more significantly, it makes space on its own strength for strange places where there were previously none. What, then, would a first definition of foam have to be? Air in unexpected places?

Foam, in its fleeting form, gives us opportunity to observe the subversion of substance with our own eyes. At the same time, one gains the experience that the revenge of the solid is not usually long in coming. As soon as the mixing agitation that ensures the introduction of air comes to a halt, the foam's glory quickly collapses. An unease remains: the thing that dares to hollow out substance, even if only for a short while—does it not have a part in what must be considered bad and suspicious, perhaps even antagonistic? That is how tradition usually viewed this precarious something, distrusting it as if it were a perversion. As an unstable fabric of gas-filled cavities that gained the upper hand over the solid as if in some nocturnal coup, foam presents itself as a mischievous inversion of the natural order in the very midst of nature. It is as if matter had gone astray and embraced the hopeless at a physical saturnalia. It is no coincidence that for an entire age, foam was assigned the flaw of having to act as a metaphor for the essenceless and untenable. Humans give credence to phantoms at night and to utopias at twilight, but once the waking world and the morning sun return, they "dissolve like mere foam."[2] It is the blown and light, the illusory and trumped-up, the unreliable and shimmering—a bastard of matter, born of an illegitimate connection between elements, an opalescent surface, a charlatanry made of air and something or other. Upsurging forces are expressed in foam that are inevitably disconcerting to friends of solid states. If dense substance willingly undergoes foaming, it can only become an illusion of itself. Matter, the fertile matron that leads a respectable life at the side of the logos, suffers a hysterical crisis and leaps into the arms of the first available illusion. The evil pearls of air perform the most dubious tricks on it. There is seething, inflation, quaking and bursting. What remains? Foam air returns home to the general atmosphere while more solid substance disintegrates into drops of dust. What is almost nothing becomes what is almost not. If solid substance gains nothing from embracing the null but phantom pregnancies, who could call that an unexpected result?

Disappointment is thus guaranteed wherever foam swells up. Just as dreams once seemed to represent no more than an empty supplement to the real which could safely be forgotten—indeed, which should be avoided at all costs—so too, if one wished to remain in the sphere of the categorical, substantial and public, foams lacked everything that could permissibly be associated with the awe-inspiring spheres of the lastingly valid. For an entire epoch, Heraclitus' warning to follow the shared (*koínon*) was perceived as a call to avoid the nocturnal and solely private, the dreamlike and foamlike, these agents of the non-shared, non-public and non-worldly.[3] Ally yourself with daylight and you will be in the right. Where the shared is experienced soberly, being behaves officially. The saying "dreams are foams"[4] equates two forms of nullity. Foam and dream—here one essencelessness rhymes with another. Even the Leipzig student Goethe still precociously scolded the "empty head that foams on its stool / Dreaming oracular sayings like Pythia." Foam is actually existing deception—the non-entity as an entity nonetheless, or a feigner of being, a symbol of the First False, an emblem for the undermining of the solid by the untenable—a ghost light, a superfluity, a mood, a swamp gas, inhabited by a dubious subjectivity.

It was not only the academics, the fundamentalists of the essential following Plato, who thought these things. A popular moral rectitude sought to give the foamy, that which was light, all-too-light, the cold shoulder. There had always been agreement between classical metaphysics and popular-ontological everyday life, despite their profound differences, that one would know the serious, responsible spirit by its contempt for foam. The verbal outpourings of the unserious: foam and buildings made of air; the mode of existence of the depraved: scum;[5] the yearning figments of romantic spirits: sickly-sweet fermentations of a hollow subjectivity within itself; the angry and empty demands of the dissatisfied from politics, or better still from the whole: speech bubbles, produced by stirring the container of collective illusions. One is no stranger to such things: wherever manifestations of hollowness come to power, they leave behind a trail of burst platitudes. Foam, like the house of cards, is where the dreamers and agitators are at home; one will never find the adults, the serious and those with measured behavior there. Who is an adult?

Someone who refuses to seek stability in the unstable. Only the seducers and impostors, biased towards the impossible, want to draw their victims into their own fathomless excitement. Foam is the going-out uniform of that *nihil* from which nothing can come, if one can still trust the words of Lucretius; it is the untenable, the "one-aged," which betrays itself through infertility and lack of action. The foamy, one hears from informed parties, exists only in empty self-reference, achieving no more than episodes and remaining eternally trapped in self-inflation and collapse. Something whose only future is disintegration is malign bloatedness, an anecdote that has come to power. Foam begets nothing, it has no consequences. With no life expectancy or next generation, all it knows is running ahead into its own bursting. Among the chaos of odd sons, therefore, foam, though not the first-born, is certainly the most contemptible.[6]

And yet: when thought broke through to polyvalence in Hegel's new logic, a positivization of the negative came into view, and with it a possible rehabilitation of foam: "Out of the ferment of finitude, before its transformation into foam, spirit rises up fragrantly."[7] Does spirit itself, the medium in which substance develops into the subject, even now owe something to foam? Does this bastard that could not be trusted transpire as the long-sought middle element in which the spiritual and the material join to form that concreteness which we call existence? Is it the third factor through which binary idiocy could be overcome? Did Aristotle foresee such amalgams when, in *Problemata physica*, he classed the illness of brilliant men—melancholy—among the "air-filled ailments," whose features include an affinity for foamable substances: black gall, which the doctors of antiquity believed to appear as an aerated mixture? If ordinary mortals wish to feel the states of the brilliant, they are helped by foamy, warm, dark wine, which puts them in a condition "in which the air-filled melancholics have always been."[8] So then the study of melancholy would be the unexpected link between anthropology and the theory of foams? Such men long for wine if it makes them as amorous as it is foamy and aerated. According to Aristotle, even male ejaculation, like erection, is a pneumatic effect—so once again we have air in unexpected places, for the "expulsion (of sperm) evidently also takes place because air pushes it from behind."[9]

Interpretation of Foam

With the change of world picture in the nineteenth and twentieth centuries, neither dreams nor foams could keep their positions in the old cosmos of essences; this—alongside numerous other reversals of conditions and surprising redeployments of powers—was one of the intimate signatures of the world form that we now, in a calmer tone of voice, call the modern one. If one rightly considers Viennese psychoanalysis one of the motors of mental modernization, despite its conservative aspects, it is primarily because it practiced a new mode of dealing with the seemingly marginal, the once-secondary and previously unremarkable. By being situated in the epistemological place where the confluence of late idealistic-Romantic philosophies of the unconscious with scientific-technological concepts of mechanisms was supposed to take place, the psychoanalytical avant-garde succeeded in formulating a concept of the sign that opened up a new perspective on the inconspicuous. By making psychological symptoms as legible as texts, Freud was able to become a "Galilei of the inner world of facts," as Arnold Gehlen put it. What had been a *quantité négligeable* became a focus of attention and something capable of gaining significance. Freud's early decision to distinguish dreams as the royal road to the unconscious displayed the "revolutionary" exchange of emphasis between the central and the peripheral. But the publication of *The Interpretation of Dreams* in 1900, as was recently evident in retrospectives of the last century, not only marked the epistemic-propagandist founding act of the psychoanalytical movement, for it was also one of the starting points for the subversion of the traditional system of seriousness and for the consciousness of the weighty as such. Something that shifts seriousness and revises decorum changes culture as a whole. Through its participation in the rehabilitation of the dream dimension, for which Romanticism had paved the way, Viennese psychoanalysis entered a context in which no less was at stake than a redistribution of emphases in the field of the primary, the validating and the meaning-giving—a process of culturally revolutionary scope: here the shockwaves from Nietzsche's intervention in metaphysical idealism came together with the confusions resulting from both the Marxist and positivist critiques of superstructure. The new art of reading for barely noticed signs of intimate and public contexts of meaning integrated the most private thoughts, tics, rashes and slips of the tongue in subversively expanded suppositions of significance. By re-drawing the boundaries between meaning and non-meaning, the serious and the unserious, this revision decisively altered the formatting of the cultural space. Now the insignificant could settle old scores with the significant. Since then, dreams have no longer been foams—at most, they indicate an endogenous foaming of mental systems and encourage the formulation of hypotheses about the laws determining the development of symptoms and the bubbling-up of inner images.

If modernity is distinguished by its shifts of seriousness, what about the other side of the equation of dreams and foams? How seriously did the twentieth century know to take foam? What status did it assign to that "air in unusual places?" In what way did it work on the rehabilitation of this fleeting phenomenon dedicated to disintegration? By what means did it attempt to do justice to the self-referential spaces, the internal spheres filled with intrinsic values, the breathable interiors and the climatic facts? The adequate response to these questions, assuming it is already possible in our time, would consist in a synopsis of modernization. It would describe a wide-range admission procedure for the coincidental, the momentary, the vague, the transient and the atmospheric—a procedure in which the arts, theories and experimental life forms are involved with their own respective stakes. The procedure's results include a fundamentally new, post-heroic formulation of decorum—the set of rules used to calibrate cultures as a whole.[10] Anyone hoping to undertake a comprehensive retelling of these processes would have to speak of a non-misrepresented Nietzsche's intentions as well as the development of Husserl's impulse; of perspectivism around 1900 as well as chaos theory around 2000; of the promotion of the surreal to a self-willed section of the real as well as the elevation of the atmospheric to theory-worthiness;[11] of the mathematization of the unfocused[12] as well as the conceptual analysis of striated structures and irregular quantities.[13] One would have to discuss a revolt of the inconspicuous whereby the small and fleeting

Jean-Luc Parant, *Livres de Jean-Luc Parant mis en boules*

secured a share in the eyesight of great theory—a science of traces that attempted to read the signs of the world event's tendencies in unassuming clues.[14] Beyond the "micrological" turn, one would have to speak of a discovery of the indeterminate that has enabled—perhaps for the first time in the history of thought— the not-nothing,[15] the almost-nothing,[16] the coincidental and the formless[17] to join the domain of theory-capable realities.

However broadly such an overview of the redistribution of seriousness to neglected, unnoticed and marginalized signs and facts might be conceived, it would confirm the finding that there had never been a convincing collection of these innovations within a shared context. The long shadow of substance-oriented thought, which has so little interest in the accidental, still covers modern theories and theories of modernity. Even in recent times, contempt for the insubstantial has characterized the thematic choices of an academicized philosophy in which the oldest inertias remain in effect. This has not prevented freer spirits from, for some time now, campaigning on the frontlines of a hazardous currentness; so far, however, their efforts have not yet led to any coherent redefinition of the situation. Even if dreams have ceased to be viewed as foams, this remains only half an achievement as long as foams have not achieved their own emancipation. The overturnings of seriousness and revisions of decorum in modernity will only have definite consequences if the interpretation of dreams is assisted by an interpretation of foam.[18] Its task would be to pay the "air in unexpected places" the tribute it deserves, at the risk of also producing theory in unexpected places—post-heroic theory that gives the fleeting, unimportant and secondary the attention reserved in heroic theory for the eternal, substantial and primary. Perhaps, in fact, the true meaning of the interpretation of dreams will only transpire after a parallel action in favor of foam. Just as Ernst Bloch, in his political ontology of the human capacity for anticipation—widely forgotten after initial successes—abandoned the bias of Freud's interpretation of dreams towards nocturnal and regressive layers of meaning, giving the daydream dignity as a utopian potency and reality-positing projective power, so too the interpretation of foams would have to constitute itself as a political ontology of animated internal spaces. Here the most fragile would be viewed as the centerpiece of the real.

In the language of this attempt, the interpretation of foam will be examined under the names "polyspherology," or "extended

Sandro Botticelli, *The Birth of Venus* (1477–78)

hothouse science." It should be clear from the start that this "reading" in foams cannot remain mere hermeneutics, nor can it stop at the decoding of signs. Only as a technological theory of humanly inhabited, symbolically air-conditioned spaces can it get to the point, that is to say as a set of engineering-scientific and political instructions for the construction and preservation of civilizatory units—an area that was previously the domain of ethics and its offshoots in political and educational science. The closest discipline to this heterodox theory of culture and civiliza-tion is presently that of manned space travel: nowhere else is there such radical enquiry into the technical conditions of possi-bility of human existence in life-sustaining capsules.[19]

The new constellation, then, is this: the serious and the fragile, or—to take the change of seriousness conditions to the extreme, which is their current position—foam and fertility. Aphrology—from the Greek *áphros*, "foam"—is the theory of

Sandro Botticelli, detail

co-fragile systems. If one succeeded in proving that the foam-like can have future promise, and can even produce offspring under certain conditions, this would deprive substantialist prejudice of its foundation. The age-old despicable-artificial, the seemingly frivolous, which exists only towards its implosion, would regain its share in the definition of the real. Then one would understands: the suspended must be understood as a special kind of foundation, the hollow as a fullness in its own right, the fragile as the place and mode of the realest, and the unrepeatable as the higher phenomenon than the serial. Nonetheless: is the notion of an "essential" foam not a contradiction in terms, hardly less on the physical than the metaphorical level? Can a construct that cannot even guarantee it will stay in shape be considered a possible enabler of life sequences and creative long-distance effects?

Fertile Foams—Mythological Interlude

The figure of fertile foams has not always been an illegitimate fiction in the history of conceptual and pictorial motifs: to prove this hypothesis, one need only go back to a time before the age of popular-ontologically and substance-metaphysically motivated contempt for foam. Among the earliest mythological instances of foam in ancient European, Indian and Near Eastern traditions, there is a close connection between the imaginative complexes of the maritime-foamlike and the mutable-indestructible. The philosophizing rhapsodist Hesiod, who lived in Boeotia after 700 BC as a shepherd and free farmer, made the liaison of foam and generative potency unforgettable for the Western tradition with his account of the goddess Aphrodite's foamy birth as the result of a Titan's castration. Through this macabre and lyrical tale, a Presocratic poetry of foam managed to keep itself in memory alongside the transience-despising metaphysics that would subsequently come to power. The sparse documentation makes it impossible to say whether this association came from Hesiod's own imagination or points back to an older mythological pictoriality. All that seems certain is that Hesiod fell prey to a fortunate etymological deception when he attributed the name of the goddess—who had been imported to the Greek pantheon from the Near East—to *áphros*, namely foam. In so doing, he connected the Hellenic goddess of love and fertility with that insubstantial substance credited with erogenous functions. Hesiod's pseudo-etymology made the Greek corruption of the Phoenician-Syrian goddess's name Astarte (or the Babylonian Ishtar) to Aphrodite productive, using it to gain a genealogical contextualization that helped foam to make a spectacular debut in the stories about the divine generations told and retold by the Greeks and their descendants.

Here the poet succeeded in creating—along with the myth of a coastal advent that enchanted Renaissance painters—the unprecedented thought-image of a foam which possesses not only power of form, but also a capacity for birth and a generative effectiveness to produce beautiful, attractive and perfect things. The foam under discussion here, admittedly, is no ordinary kind: released by the disastrous contact between the sea's waves and the genitals of the great father Uranus, cunningly severed by his son Cronos, it testifies to a far-reaching anomaly in the sequence of divine procreations:

> The genitals, he threw them out into the surging main:
> There on the waves they rose and fell and rose and fell again;
> And round about the immortal flesh white foam arose, and from
> That form a girl was born—the first to Kythera did come,
> To sacred Kythera, and thence to sea-girt Kypris came,
> And stepped upon the shore a lovely goddess with a claim
> To reverence, and grass sprang up beneath her feet; her name
> Is Aphrodite—gods and men both call her this (since from
> The *aphros* she was nurtured—yes, within the frothy foam),
> And also Kytherea, since from Kythera she was come,
> And Kyprogenia, having been on sea-washed Kypris born,
> And laughter loving, coming from the members that were torn.
> Eros walked beside her; lovely longing close behind
> Followed as soon as she was born and also when she joined
> The gods' race [...][20]

At the critical point in his song, the poet ventures an adjectival invention, *aphrogenéa*, to accompany *théa*, the goddess; from then on, it is evident that it has the potential to rise through the terminological ranks from an evocatively ornamental addition to a noun of its own. Through the description of the goddess as foam-born, aphrogenic, foam itself gains the ability to beget. By virtue of her foam-bornness—or, more precisely, her grownness-in-foam (*en aphro*)—Hesiod's Aphrodite becomes, within the horizon of Western tradition, the chief witness to the fact that foam is not entirely nothing, especially if it can be associated with the primordial god's member. Just as a later metaphysics of spirit sometimes gave the world-positing logos the attribute *spermatikós*, Presocratic poetry here already knew an *áphros spermatikós*, a foam capable of conceiving and bearing children with the properties of a matrix. What is telling about Hesiod's account is that it transposes the later Olympian goddess Aphrodite (who, in a different tradition, came from Zeus' intercourse with the oak goddess Dione) into a Titanoid context, a series of monstrous conceptions and elemental atrocities—undoubtedly influenced by the motive of embedding the mistress of lust in a cosmically very early context of primary processes, still entirely dominated by pre-rational elemental powers. Charging foam with generative potency and meanings of fertility was only possible in this context, and only with Titanic sperm was it plausible that it could transpire as erogenous, aphrogenic and theogenic. The *en aphro* fertilization of the goddess shows how foam—for one mythopoetically productive moment—could be envisaged as a uterine analogue and a matrix of far-reaching morphological formations.[21]

Similar and related things, heightened to the level of a transcendent Baroque novel, can be found in the ancient Indian

J. A. D. Ingres, *Venus Anadyomene* (1808)

myth in which the deities decide to stir up the ocean into foam to produce the nectar of immortality—a story that exists in different versions in the *Ramayana* and the *Mahabharata*, among others.[22] Common to both is the motif of how the gods, concerned about their uncertain immortality, are told by a divine adviser (Vishnu-Narayana in the *Mahabharata*) that they should churn the milky world ocean until it yields *amrita*, the elixir of death-lessness. The heavenly ones follow this advice, using the world mountain Mount Meru as a churning rod and the thousand-headed giant snake Vasuki as a churning rope. After churning the depths for a thousand years, the moment of success approaches:

> First the mild moon rose from the milk sea; then the Lady Lakshmi, bearing good fortune to men; then the smooth jewel adorning Narayana's breast; then Indra's elephant Airavata, white as clouds; then Surabhi, the white cow who grants any wish; then Parikata the wishing-tree of fragrance; then Rambha the nymph, the first Apsaras; and at last Dhanwantari the physician, robed in white, bearing a cup filled with amrita, the essence of life.
>
> Suddenly poison burst fuming from the sea, and the milk became salt water. Shiva, the Lord of Mountains and Songs swallowed the poison to save worlds. He held it in his throat and his neck turned blue, iridescent as a butterfly's wing.[23]

In the *Ramayana*, attributed to the poet Valmiki (c. 200 AD), the thousand-year churning likewise brings forth a series of appara-tions from the milky foam, albeit in a different order: here the divine physician Dhanwantari comes first of all, bearing his sublime nectar jug—containing the holy "ascetic water"—followed by an immeasurable throng of shining love maidens, the *apsaras*, sixty million in total, accompanied by countless servant girls, female beings that bring joy and "belong to everyone," as neither humans nor gods are willing to wed them. These erotic emanations of the foaming ocean are followed by Varuni, daughter of the water god Varuna, and then the supreme white horse, the divine jewel and finally the desired elixir, the essence that brings immortality, which immediately causes a fierce war for its possession between the gods and demons.[24]

What is noticeable about the Indian tales of foaming or churning the ocean is that they no longer present an anonymous elemental process, as in Hesiod, but rather an action that—in addition to alchemistic aspects—unmistakably exhibits production character. Not only has the milk foam become a matrix for the creation of further forms; the foam itself is created through a foam-forming, *aphrogenic* operation in a second sense of the word: production from foam is augmented by the production of foam. This lends the phenomenon of aphrogenia a technical element, enabling it to be read from two sides. It can rise to the conceptual level by combining formation from foam with the formation of foam in an overarching expression. However grotesque the tools—a mountain and a giant snake, joined to form a whisk beating away in the cosmic dairy—there is no doubt that we are dealing with a thought-image from the motivic context of craftsmanly observation. The parallel with the procedures of butter production is especially obvious—hardly surprising in a culture where libations of liquid butter at the sacrificial fire (*ajya*) were among the primary ritual gestures.[25] At the same time, stirring conjures up the primitive core procedure of alchemy, which has always seemed to revolve around acquiring an effective essence through filtering and reduction. Beating air into the substance serves to precipitate the most substantial component from the substance until the utmost contraction of becoming power is obtained in a single vessel, a final seminal point. It is obvious that if, as in nascent First Theory, one presupposes the unity of original power and abundance of essence, it is a small step to the radicalization of the search; one will then dare to attempt magical access to the essence of the essence in order to filter the power out from the power. In this theurgical drama, whose aim was to elevate the gods to immortality once and for all, the production of foam acts as a prelude to absolute extraction.

We should not forget that even the Egyptian creation myth know the image of a cosmogonic salivary foam: here the mouth of the god Atum is described as the first animating center crucible or primal vessel, in which *Tefnut* (moisture) and Shu (*air*) are first of all produced and intertwined, until both exit the primal mouth as a totipotent mixture to bring forth all further creatures. What is particularly notable here is that what emanates from the god's mouth are not first distinctions and "Let there be" commands, as is customary in the logocratic schema, but a foamy bimaterial *prima materia* that, like a first couple, calls everything else into existence by propagation—a supreme spitting, as it were.

These myths indicate early alternatives to the prejudice that foams are sterile; hence they can at best offer the constellation of foam and fertility a poetic plausibility. From a distance, at least, they prepare a notion of aphrogenia that encourages us to ask not only about divine procreations, but also about the genesis of

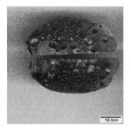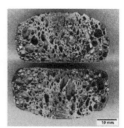

Porous iron-based materials

humans from the airy, the floating, the mixed and the inspired. In the following, it will be shown that foam—in a sense of the word that has yet to be consolidated—constitutes the matrix of human facts as a whole. *We are such stuff as foams are made on.* As we have seen, the first lesion of the interpretation of foam should turn out as a mythological excursus; the second will consist in letting the theogonic motifs rest and then, after a brief look at current scientific contributions to foam research, shifting to the anthropological register.

Natural Foams, Aphrospheres

In the physical context, foams are defined as multi-chambered systems of air pockets within solid and liquid materials whose cells are separated by film-like walls. All impulses for scientific research on foam structures stem from the Belgian physicist Joseph Antoine Ferdinand Plateau, who, around the middle of the nineteenth century, formulated one of the most important—and still valid—laws for the geometry of foams, laws that brought a minimum of order into the seeming chaos of foamy agglomerations of bubbles. Thanks to them, foams could be

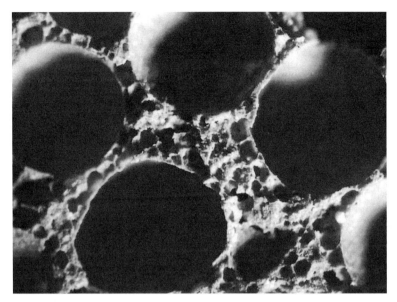

Photograph of a foam brick porosified with polystyrene and foam

precisely described as tension sculptures of film membranes. They state that the edges of a foam bubble, or rather a foam polyhedron, are formed by exactly three film walls; that two of these three walls always meet at an angle of 120 degrees; and that precisely four edges of foam cells converge on one point. The existence of soap membranes is based on the surface tension of water, which was already mentioned around 1508 by Leonardo da Vinci in his observations on the morphology of drops. The visual properties of wet and dry foams were laid out by the British physicist Charles Vernon Boys in 1890 in a popular treatise on the colors of soap bubbles.[26] As a result of his study, the marvels of the rainbow entered Victorian nurseries.

The twentieth century's most important innovation in the analysis of foam was the introduction of time. We learned that foams are processes, and that there are constant leaps, redistributions and reformattings occurring inside the multi-celled chaos. This restlessness has a direction: it leads to greater stability and inclusivity. One can recognize old foam by the fact that its bubbles are larger than in young foam—because bursting young cells die into their neighbors, as it were, bequeathing their volume to them. The wetter and younger a foam is, the smaller, rounder, more mobile and more autonomous the bubbles concentrated inside it will be; the drier and older it is, on the other hand, the more individual bubbles will already have given up the ghost, the larger the surviving cells will become, the more strongly they will affect one another, and the more Plateau's laws of neighborhood geometry will be in evidence in the mutual deformation of the magnified bubbles. An aged foam embodies the ideal of a co-fragile system in which a maximum of interdependence has been achieved. In this framework of stable-unstable, large polyhedrons, it is potentially impossible for any one cell to burst without tearing the whole construct along with it into nothingness. The processual dynamic of the foam thus provides the empty form for all stories dealing with immanently growing spaces of inclusion. These tragic geometries contain such a high degree of internal tension, or tensegrity, between the remaining co-isolated spaces that their shared existential risk can be expressed in a co-fragility formula. The large cells of a mature foam act together to achieve an extension of their existence, and they likewise disappear together at the final implosion. Let us note that there are no central cells in foams, and that the notion of a single capital would be inherently absurd.

In more recent times, the multi-chamber motif has also made a career in spatial theories in the field of physics. As a result, the

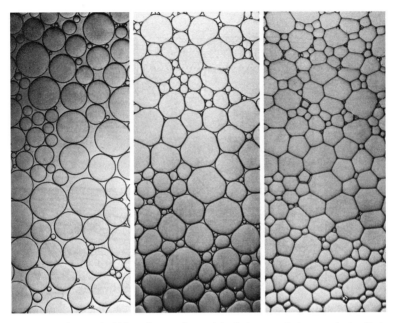

Transition from a bubble raft to a flat polyhedral network in a study by Frei Otto's group

foam metaphor is increasingly used to describe spontaneous spatial formations, both on the smallest scale and for middle-world phenomena, and finally also for processes of galactic, even cosmic proportions. The twenty-first century is virtually advertised as the "century of foam." A significant part of recent astrophysics appears in an aphrophysical guise. Some of the cosmological models currently being discussed depict the universe as a fabric of inflationary bubbles, each of which embodies a big bang system analogous to the world context inhabited by present-day humanity.[27] Numerous microphysical realities are now also being presented in terms of foam and spontaneous microspheric spatial formation. None of the current sciences, however, ascribe as large a role to the morphological potency of foam as cell biology. In the view of some biologists, the birth of life can only be explained by the spontaneous formation of foam from the murky waters of the primordial ocean:

> cell-like membranous enclosures form as naturally as bubbles when oil is shaken with water. In the earliest days of the still lifeless Earth, such bubble enclosures separated inside from outside. […]These lipidic bags grew and developed self-main-tenance. […] Probably solar energy at first moved through the droplets; controlled energy flow led to the selfhood that became cell life.[28]

In this account of cellular genesis, the round form and energetic content supposedly affected each other in such a way that a first life form, the foam-born monad, could rise from the sea, swim-ming in the water and free in it, yet also already separate from it, full of inner and own things. On the path of self-inclusion, small form-protected primal interiors viewed as the precursors to life separated off from the primordial molecular soup. In the par-lance of systemic biology, they form "semi-open systems" that process as self-sensitive and environmentally sensitive reaction spaces. The oldest fossils found on earth thus far, over 3.5 billion years old, are interpreted by paleobiologists as leftovers of primal bacteria; because of their shape and place of discovery, they are known as Swaziland microspheres. Their existence proves that the secret of life is inseparable from the secret of form, or more precisely from the formation of interiors according to spheric laws. Where unicellular organisms appear, the history of the organic begins as spheric compression and encapsulation: gathering

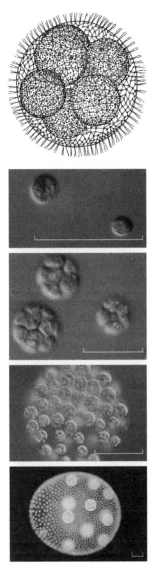

A biological coenobium with daughter colonies: the Volvox alga as an evolutionary example of the transition from colony-forming unicellular organisms to the
multicellular, globular and gender-distinct individual

under orb-shaped membranes is the *more* that will be called life. In the primitive organism, the space is on the way to the self. The first characteristic of the self is the ability to adopt a position through opposition to something external. Position, it would seem, results from folding into oneself—or from willfulness in unusual places. Should the mysterious path already lead inwards, even in the most primitive life forms?[29]

Human Foams

As impressive as the connection between the morphology of foam and primitive zoogenesis in the light of the recent life sciences may be, I only see the adventure of spatial pluralities beginning with the entry into anthropological and culture-theoretical contexts. Via the concept of foam, I describe agglomerations of *bubbles* in the sense of my earlier microspherological investigations.[30] The term stands for systems or aggregates of spheric neighborhoods in which each individual "cell" constitutes a self-augmenting context (more colloquially: a world, a place), an intimate space of meaning whose tension is maintained by dyadic and pluripolar resonances, or a "household" that vibrates with its own individual animation, which can only be experienced by itself and within itself.[31] Each one of these households, each one of these symbioses and alliances, is a hothouse of relationships *sui generis*. One could call such constructs "society in pairs"[32] (assuming one did not, as I do, intend to show later on that the term "society" is always counterproductive in such matters). Where places of this type form, the existence-towards-one-another of the closely united acts as the true agent of spatial formation; the climatization

Vito Acconci, partition. "In its original position, the walls form a box-like closed space in the middle of the hall. If someone wants to enter it, they can push one wall aside. Then, however, there is a further wall in its place…"

of the coexistential interior follows through the reciprocal extraversion of the symbionts, which temper the shared interior like a hearth before the hearth.[33] Each microsphere constitutes its own axis of the intimate. It will be shown later how this axis can be bent individualistically.

The introversion of the individual households does not contradict its conglomeration in more close-knit associations, that is to say social foams: neighborly connection and separateness can be read as two sides of the same situation. In foam the principle of co-isolation applies, meaning that one and the same dividing wall serves as a boundary for two or more spheres. Such walls, appropriated from both sides, are the original interfaces. If the individual bubble in physically real foam borders on a majority of neighboring orbs and is co-conditioned by them through partitioning, a thought-image for the interpretation of social associations can be derived from this: in the human field too, individual cells are stuck together through reciprocal isolations, separations and immunizations. One of the particularities of this region of objects is that the multiple co-isolation of the bubble households in their plural neighborhoods can be described equally aptly as a cutting-off or an openness to the world. Foam thus constitutes a paradoxical interior in which, from my position, the great majority of surrounding co-bubbles are simultaneously adjacent and inaccessible, both connected and removed.

In spherological terms, "societies" are foams in the sense of the word I have just delineated. This formulation is meant to block access as early as possible to the fantasy that was used by traditional groups to supply an imaginary interpretation of their being: the notion that the social field is an organic totality integrated into a universally shared, universally inclusive hypersphere. This is precisely what the autoplastic propaganda of empires and kingdom-of-God fictions has promoted since time immemorial.[34] In reality, "societies" are only comprehensible as restless and asymmetrical associations of pluralities of space and processes whose cells can neither be truly united nor truly separate. Only as long as "societies" hypnotize themselves as homogeneous units, for example as genetically or theologically substantial national peoples, can they view themselves as monospheres united through their origins (or by an exceptional constitution). They present themselves as enchanted spaces that profit from an imaginary immunity and a magically comprehensive commonality of essence and election—this is the sense in which Slavoj Žižek recently adopted my concept of the "sphere"

Morphosis (Thom Mayne/Michel Rotondi), Politix (retail store), Portland, Space modulator (1990)

and applied it critically to the mental state of the USA before the attacks on the World Trade Center.[35] Need it be explained why the beginning of knowledge lies in the collaboration of humans in the decision to leave the magic circle of mutual hypnosis? Anyone wishing to speak theoretically of "society" must operate outside of the "we" stupor. Once this is achieved, one can observe that "societies" or peoples themselves are of a far more fluid, hybrid, permeable and promiscuous constitution than their homogeneous names suggest.

When I speak in the following of "society," the term refers not (as in rampant nationalism) to a monospheric container that encloses a countable population of individuals and families under an essential political name or a constitutive phantasm, nor (as for some systems theorists) to a non-spatial communication process that "progressively differentiates" itself into subsystems.[36] "Society" is understood here as an aggregate of microspheres (couples, households, businesses, associations) of different formats that, like the individual bubbles in a mountain of foam, border on one another and are layered over and under one another, yet without truly being accessible or effectively separable from one another.[37] There are certainly, to quote Ernst Bloch's evocative formulation, "many chambers in the world house"—but they have no doors, perhaps even nothing except false windows with outdoor scenes painted on them. The bubbles in foam, that is to say the couples and households, the teams and survival communities, are self-referentially constituted microcontinents. However much they might purport to be connected with other and outside things, they initially round themselves off purely in their respective selves. Each of the symbiotic units is world-forming in itself and for itself—alongside neighboring groups of world-formers who do the same in their own way, and with whom they are drawn into an interactive network based on the principle of co-isolation. Their similarities seem to permit the conclusion that they are in animated communication and wide open to one another; in reality, they are usually only similar because they arise in shared

Jennie Pineus, *Cocoon Chair* (2000)

waves of imitation[38] and have analogous media facilities. Operatively, they usually have virtually nothing to do with one another.
(Consider the passengers of automobiles driving behind one
another in convoys: any driving group internally constitutes a
resonant cell, yet the vehicles are mutually isolated—which is
quite right, for communication would mean collision.) Their
attunement occurs not in a direct exchange between the cells, but
through the mimetic infiltration of each single one by similar
patterns, agitations, contagious goods and symbols. In earlier
times, the best model to demonstrate these assertions would have

been that of the nuclear family, for couples willing to procreate have always been (and will presumably continue to be) the most plausible example of growth-capable dyads. In the present day, these findings can be expanded to include childless couples, even people who live alone in their special forms of "cocooning" (for example Japanese *takotsubo* culture, the "octopus pot" autism scene).[39] I emphasize that a cell in foam is not an abstract individual, but rather a dyadic or multipolar structure.[40] Foam theory is unabashedly neo-monadological in its orientation; its monads, however, have the basic form of dyads or more complex soul-space, communal and team structures.

In media terms, foam cell "society" is a murky medium with a certain conductivity for information and a certain permeability for substances. It does not pass on outpourings of immediate truth; if Einstein lived next door, I would not know any more about the universe as a result. If the son of God and I had lived on the same floor for years, I would only learn afterwards—if at all—who my neighbor was. Every point in the foam offers glimpses of the bordering ones, but comprehensive views are not available—in the most advanced case, exaggerations are formulated inside one bubble and can be used in many neighboring ones. Messages are selectively transferable, and there are no exits into the whole. For theory that accepts being-in-foam as the primary definition of our situation, final super-visions of the One World are not only unattainable, but impossible—and, correctly understood, also undesirable.

Whoever speaks of foams in this tone has abandoned the central symbol of classical metaphysics, of the all-gathering monosphere, namely the orb-shaped One and its projection into panoptic central constructions. These would logically lead into

Alfons Schilling, *Darkroom Hat* (1984)

the encyclopedic system, politically into the imperial *urbi et orbi* space (whose fates were described in the third and seventh chapters of *Spheres II*), in police terms to the form of the surveillance panopticon, and militarily to a paranoid Pentagon ontology. Needless to say, such centralisms would now only be of historical interest. As systems of asymmetrical neighborhoods between intimacy hothouses and autonomous worlds of medium size, foams are semi-transparent and semi-opaque. Every location in the foam means a relative intertwining of circumspection and blindness that is focused on that individual bubble; every being-in-the-world, understood as being-in-foam, opens up a clearing in the impenetrable. The turn towards a pluralistic ontology was prefigured by modern biology and metabiology after they arrived—thanks to the introduction of the environment concept—at a new view of their subject:

> It was an error to think that the human world provided a shared stage for all life forms. Each life form has a special stage no less real than the special stage of humans. [...] Through this insight we gain an entirely new view of the universe: it consists not of a single soap bubble that we have blown up beyond our horizon into the infinite, but of countless millions of narrowly bounded soap bubbles that overlap and intersect everywhere.[41]

The collection of innumerable "soap bubbles" can thus no longer be envisaged as the monocosmos of metaphysics, where the abundance of existents was called together under a logos common to all. The philosophical super-soap bubble, the universal monad of the One World—whose shapes and forms I detailed primarily in the fourth and fifth chapters of *Spheres II*—is replaced by a polycosmic agglomeration. This can be described as a gathering of gatherers, a semi-opaque foam of world-forming spatial constructs. It is important to understand that these boundlessly manifold varieties of sentient existence in sense-structured environments is already developed at the level of animal intelligence—and, it would seem, there is no animal that catalogues all other animals and relates them to itself. Humans, for their part, after the end of the centric delirium (anthropo-, ethno-, ego- and logo-), will perhaps develop slightly more appropriate notions of their existence in a milieu of ontological foams. They will then understand why Herder was speaking more of the past than the future when he wrote: "Every nation has *its own inner center* of happiness, as every sphere its own centre of gravity."[42] Some very foresighted formulations by contemporary cyberspace theorists give a first idea of the elastic mode of being found in decentered world concepts. Pierre Lévy, in his essay on the semiotic productivity of the developing "collective intelligence," notes:

> In the knowledge space active exhalations work together, not to bring about some hypothetical fusion of individual beings, but to collectively inflate the same bubble, thousands of rainbow-tinged bubbles, provisional universes, shared worlds of signification.[43]

As world formations always also express themselves architecturally, or more precisely in the synergetic tension between movables and immovables, one must observe the spheropoietic processes that materialize in the form of habitats, buildings and built agglomerations. According to a statement by Le Corbusier, a building is comparable to a soap bubble:

> The bubble is perfectly harmonious if the breath is evenly applied, evenly regulated from the inside. The outside is the result of an inside.[44]

Foams in the Time of Knowledge

Delicate things become object late on: that is what they have in common with numerous seemingly self-evident things that only mature to the point of conspicuity once they are lost; and they are usually lost from the moment in which they are used for

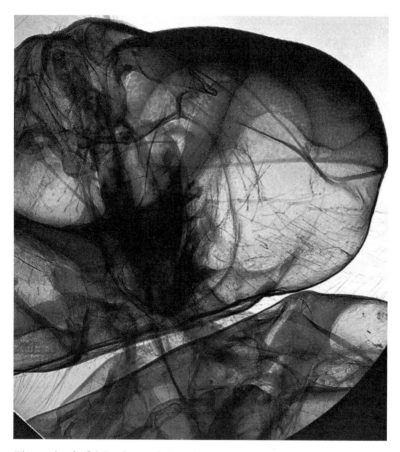

The inside of a fly's head viewed through an x-ray microscope

comparisons, which robs them of their naïve givenness. The air we thoughtlessly breathe; the mood-saturated situations in which we unknowingly exist contained and containing; the atmospheres, so obvious as to be imperceptible, in which we live, move and have our being—all of these constitute late arrivals in the thematic space because, before they could be given explicit attention, they seemed *a priori* to provide a mute background scenery to our being-there and being-here, like eternal natures or consumer goods. They are abnormalities that appear late on, only called to thematic and technical careers through their recently proven manipulability in both the constructive and the destructive senses. Previously accepted as discreet concessions from being, they had to become objects of concern before turning into objects of theory. They had to be experienced as fragile, losable and destructible before they could advance to workable task fields for air and mood phenomenologists, relationship therapists, atmosphere engineers and interior designers, and finally for cultural theorists and media technologists. They had to become unbreathable for people to learn to recognize themselves as guardians, reconstructors and reinventors of what had merely been taken for granted.

The background only breaks its silence when foreground processes exceed its burdening capacity. How many real ecological and military disasters were needed before it could be said with juristic, physical and atmotechnic precision how one can set up humanly breathable air environments? How much obliviousness to the atmospheric premises of human existence had to accumulate in theory and practice before the attention of a radicalized thought was capable of immersing itself in the nature of attunements[45]—and later extending its reach to the constitutions of being-in within encompassing milieus as such, and also to the modes of existential embeddedness in whole-based conditions[46] (for which we recently started using the term "immersion")? How far did the pendulum have to swing towards individualistic misunderstandings and autistic atrophies before the autonomous value of resonance phenomena and interpsychological intertwinements in spaces of ensoulment could be mentioned in any

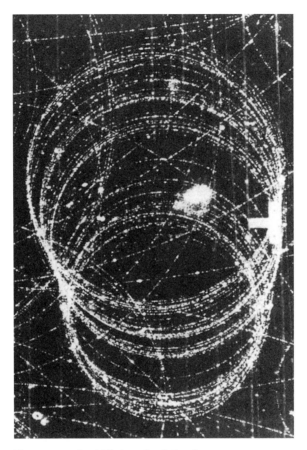

Electrons, made visible in a cloud chamber

remotely unabridged way? How much neglect, disguised as pro-gressiveness, needed to devastate human closeness relationships before the constitutive meaning of sufficiently good couple and family relationships could be described with the respect afforded to basic concepts?[47]

Anything very explicit becomes demonic. Whoever embarks on making background realities explicit, realities formerly preserved in what was tacitly thought and known—and even more in the never-thought and never-known—embraces a situation in which the scarcity of the presupposable and silenceable is already advanced and continues inexorably. Woe to those who harbor deserts: now one must rebuild artificially what once seemed given as a natural resource. One is forced to articulate with burdensome caution and at provocative length what was formerly a tacitly understood connotation. At this turn towards the explicit, the modern function of cultural science becomes manifest. It commends itself as the agent of civilizatory explications in general. It must be shown that from now on, the science of culture must always also be a science of technology and a curatorial training for work in cultural hothouses. Now that cultures—and precisely cultures—have ceased to seem given, one must see to their survival and regeneration by cultivating, redescribing, filtering, clarifying and reforming: in the age of background explication, the culture of cultures becomes the criterion for civilization.

To be absolutely contemporary, we must presuppose that there is hardly anything left to presuppose. At this point, let us begin to articulate at disconcerting length what, according to the state of the art, we can say about our being-in-the-world; let us describe (with the phenomenologists) with circumspect explicitness which encompassing states or whole-based relationships we see ourselves placed in; finally, let us design and reconstruct (with the media technologists, the interior architects, the labor medics and atmo-designers) the facilities, atmospheres and encompassing situations in which, according to our own plans and assessments, we will reside: thus these constructive and reconstructive activities are still affected by the defamiliarizations that did away with all self-evident things before permitting their return to a second givenness. When they return, they are products of explication or objects of conservational care. They are placed under the control of long-term sociopolitical concern or technical redesigning. Where there was "lifeworld," there must now be air conditioning technology.

Revolution, Rotation, Invasion

The demonic nature of the explicit is the trace of civilization history; it grows to the extent that modernity progresses in its awareness of artificiality. When things previously in the background shift to the foreground; when things unmentioned in living memory suddenly have to be thematized; when the folding of the implicit is spread out and projected into the clear surface, where every detail that was inwardly concealed now stands in equally bright visibility and equally spread out—then these processes testify to a movement in which those who know radically change their stance towards the objects now known thus, which were once known differently or not at all. In the light of such a change of stance, the worn-out metaphor of revolution as a fundamental overturning of conditions between bodies and roles can gain epistemological honor one last time (before being deposited in the archive of obsolete concepts).

What a "revolution" means can best be explained with reference to the breakthroughs of sixteenth-century anatomists, who had resolved to open the human inner body with cuts and publish it using descriptively adequate depictions. It may be true that the Vesalian "revolution" was of far greater consequence for the self-relationships of Western people than the long over-cited and

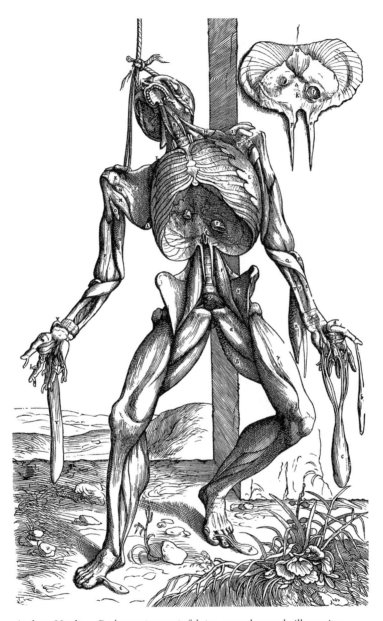

Andreas Vesalius, *De humani corporis fabrica*, seventh muscle illustration

misunderstood Copernican one. By opposing the ordinary darkness of their own corporeality with their organ maps and building plans of the newly, precisely viewed inner world of machines—it is no coincidence that the *magnum opus* of Vesalius is entitled *De humani corporis fabrica*—the anatomists of the early Modern Age tore open the image-deficient inner somatic basis of perceived selfhood, involving the independent knowledge of the portrayed bodily subjects in a turn after which nothing would be found in the same place of being and knowledge as before. Now I must look at the anatomical cards and receive their message: that is you! That is what your inside looks like as soon as those in the know examine you with their scalpels! No anti-anatomical *mauvaise foi* can help to reinstate the naïveté of existence as a bodily being when faced with the ability to operate. Whether they wanted to or not, actors of the Modern Age took part in an almost auto-surgical shift. Even those who did not have to deal with cuts into organic tissue as professional dissection artists were, as cultural participants, placed virtually at a point of knowledge and operation where they had no choice but to join in their great turn away from the old inner bodily universe. Understanding one's own corporeal interior in terms of the possibility of its anatomical externalization: this was the primary cognitive "revolutionary" result of the Modern Age, comparable only to the world picture-changing power of the first circumnavigation of the earth by Magellan and del Cano.[48]

In its cognitive habitus, cutting open the human body from all sides and graphically representing it from every perspective is the same as circumnavigating and mapping the earth. Both operations were part of the great rotation that altered the angle (*klima*) of knowledge about things and circumstances. "Making it explicit"—from the start of the Modern Age onwards, this meant taking part in overturning the corporeal world through the operative skill of the anatomists and constituting oneself as a virtual self-operator from a radically altered angle of dealing with oneself—"for an object only becomes tangible for us at an angle smaller than 45 degrees."[49] The Modern Age is the age of anatomists, the age of cuts, invasions, penetrations, implantations in the dark continent, the former Lethe.

In a much later phase, after academic abstractions had pushed the basic operative conditions of modern knowledge to an unrecognizably distant place, philosophers could find themselves thinking that making things explicit was a discursive operation, primarily a form of bookkeeping for a speaker's opinion and conviction account.[50] Would not every person who speaks therefore be a speculator at the stock exchange of assertions, and philosophy would act as the supervisory authority? The true meaning of explication lies in another field; the strong hallmark of modern knowledge conditions is not the fact that "subjects" can mirror themselves in themselves or account for their opinions in front of an audience, but rather that they operate on themselves and have the cards of their own, partly illuminated dark regions before them, which show them the potential weak points for self-surgery. One must not be deceived by the division of labor between surgeons and non-surgeons: after Vesalius, anyone who is a "subject" lived in an auto-operatively curved space, whether they had agreed to or not. In the Modern Age, I can no longer be myself authentically, that is to say congruently with the overall cultural standard, as long as I abstract from my potential operator. When people of the Modern Age tell any deeper form of lie, it virtually always comes from consciously ignoring their auto-operable constitution.[51] The fundamental "no" to operating on one's own findings and reserves is the core of bad Romanticism. Our inevitably imperfect, yet always expandable capacity to reach into our own somatic and psychosemantic inner basis characterizes the situation that we describe with the worn-out term "modern." It is obvious why we hardly encounter so-called "reification" any more at this level.

When the Implicit Becomes Explicit: Phenomenology

The system of knowledge was set in motion by the incessant invasion of the hidden via intelligence: in its standard reading, this fact—which is constitutive of all higher civilization, especially modernity—was known as "research." Where the interpretation of this restlessness became more advanced, it bore, for a distinctive period in intellectual history, the name "phenomenology": the theory of "objects" stepping forwards into appearance, and the logical acknowledgement of their existence in connection with the rest of our knowledge. Not everything is revealed to humans at once, for the arrival of objects in our knowledge is subject to the laws of a sequence, an equally strict and opaque order of earlier and later: this was the original intuition, first formulated by Xenophanes, which was later developed by evolutionary and phenomenological thought into philosophical *Bildungsromane* or intellectual histories. The core of this intuition was the observation that the relationship between the later and the earlier is often like that between the explicit and the implicit. Explications transform facts and intimations into concepts—and these transformations can be both

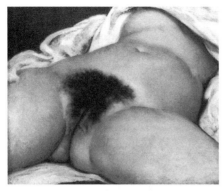

Gustave Courbet,
The Origin of the World (1866)

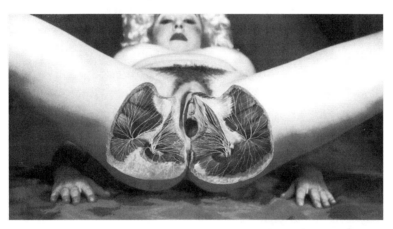

Veronika Bromová, *Views* (1996)

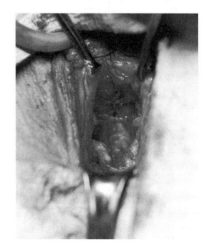

Transvaginal correction

communicated and justified. This enables the science of irreversible mental processes, which deals with invention-logically directed sequences of successive ideas (such as notions of God, concepts of soul and persons, ideas of society, construction forms and writing techniques). Phenomenology is the narrative theory of the explication of what can at first only be implicitly present. Being implicit here means: presupposed in a non-unfolded state, left in cognitive retirement, freed from the pressure of comprehensive mention and development and given in the mode of dark proximity—not already on the tip of one's tongue, not already available the next moment, not mobilized by the discursive regime and not incorporated into procedures. Becoming explicit, on the other hand, means: being swept along by the current flowing from the background to the foreground, from Lethe into the clearing, from enfolding into unfolding. The time's arrow of thought strives towards greater explicitness. Whatever can be said with a higher degree of extensive articulatedness brings about the mobilization of arguments—assuming the epistemic zeitgeist has called to action. Certainly implication is, among other things, a relationship between statements; it is traditionally understood as the containedness of the less general assertion in the more general, or as the embedding of texts in contexts; and as far as this applies, logical investigation can prove its worth as an explication procedure. Its true meaning, however, lies in the fact that the implicit indicates a place in the existent where the bud is located for the purpose of an unfolding, an articulation, an explication.[52] That is why the form of the true history of knowledge is the becoming-phenomenon of the previously unmanifested—the transition from the unilluminated to the illuminated, or the rise of shadow givens to foreground themes. Actual knowledge: that is what we call the discourses that have survived the long night of implication and now romp about in the daytime of the thematic and spread-out.

More than a few of Old Europe's most eminent minds have thought about the process of knowledge in terms of this schema—reason enough to examine the conditions of this theoretical vogue's success in the wake of its decline.[53] For almost two centuries, rigorous and edifying thinkers from different departments arrived at the conviction that everything which appears in knowledge, however heteronomous and novel it might seem, ultimately cannot be foreign to the self of those who know, and must consequently—after crises of whatever depth—enter our intimate education history (and the phrase "our history" has an air of higher cultural self, to avoid invoking the world spirit). Phenomenologists spread the good news that there is no outside without a corresponding inside; they suggest there is nothing foreign that cannot, through appropriation, be integrated into what is ours. Their belief in appropriation without boundaries rested on the claim that what later knowledge unfolds is nothing other than what was already present in the earliest implications.

The ontological foundation of this optimism was articulated in the fifteenth century by Nicolas of Cusa when he postulated the symmetry of maximum implicitness (God as contraction to an atomic point) and maximum explicitness (God as unfolding to the universal orb). Under Cusa's conditions, human thought would always be a cognitive going-along with divine expansion into the explicit, that is the realized and created, in so far as such a concurrence could succeed in the finite world. I discussed the culmination of occidental orb theology in the seemingly light-footed treatise *De ludo globi*, penned by the jovial cardinal, at length in the *Deus sive sphaera* chapter of *Spheres II*. One encounters a related cognitive optimism in Spinoza's ethics, which constitutes a great call to unfold the potential of nature: we do not yet know everything of which the dark body is capable—learn more about it, and you will gain vision and ability. With Leibniz, cognitive optimism assumed more muted forms, as the author of *Monadology* had a precise idea of the unfathomability of implications, which extend to infinity.[54] Even Hegel's construct of a circle made of circles, however, still rests on the principle that the last is merely the first, fulfilled and brought epicentrically to itself in our comprehension.

Where optimism sets the tone, it dictates the question of how the inward could ultimately become fully outward. Viewed in a positive light, human practice is nothing other than the great rotation that brings what is concealed in the dark of the lived moment before our eyes in such a way that it can be incorporated into the human treasury as a clear notion. From the perspective of consistent optimism, the history of cognition and technology would end in a final picture where the parity between inwardness and outwardness had been achieved point by point. But how would this be possible if one could show that when the implicit becomes explicit, something completely willful, foreign, different, something never intended, never expected and never to be assimilated penetrates thought? If the research that advances into liminal regions makes known something previously unknown, of which it cannot be said that a subject comes "into itself" in it? If there are new things that elude the symmetry of the implicit and the explicit, and enter the structures of knowledge as something that remains foreign, external and monstrous to the end?

The Monstrous Appears

After the expiry of the optimistic trend, one can calmly state what phenomenology *de facto* meant in its usual application: it was a rescue service for phenomena at a time when most "manifestations" no longer approached the eye or the other senses of their own accord, but were rather brought to visibility through research, invasive explications and the accompanying measurements (which means "observations" via machines and artificial sensors). It invited its adepts to participate in the attempt to defend the metaphysical precedence of observational perception over measuring, calculating and operating.[55] It devoted itself to the task of fending off the disconcerting flooding of consciousness with unassimilable insights and outlooks into cut-open bodies and the innards of machines—not to reject the new, but to integrate it into the habitual perception of circumstances or nature, as if nothing had happened after the technological caesura. Heidegger rightly taught that technology was a "mode of unconcealing" [*Weise des Entbergens*]. This at once meant that what is technologically unconcealed and made public can only possess a derived phenomenality, a hybrid publicity and an impaired affiliation with perception.[56]

Alongside the monstrous visibility of the anatomical facts that have accompanied us since the sixteenth century (and which no humanism can still integrate into a well-rounded picture of the literate human being), we are confronted with the sights enabled from the seventeenth century onwards by microscopes and telescopes, the two infernal machines for the eye. Magnification: this (alongside cartography) was the first strike capacity of explication that coerced the previously invisible

Sound waves made visible on a metal disc

world to become pictorial.[57] I am also thinking of the becoming-phenomenon of nuclear mushrooms, cell nuclei and interior views of humans, of X-ray images and CT scans, of galactic photographs—of a diffuse universe of complex, barely decipherable sights for whose emergence no human (more carefully put: ancient human) eye could have been prepared. (Let us note that the discipline of design—as the artificial production of perceptual surfaces and user interfaces through invisible functions, or as an aesthetically intentional highlighting of otherwise unnoticed functional motifs—begins from a point that is one dimension more modern than its age-mate phenomenology, assuming it already operates at the level of second perceptibility, that is to say of observation via devices and sensors.)

The phenomenologically committed, then, are those who are determined to treat the artificially achieved visibility of once naturally concealed facts and latent mechanisms or functions as if the jovial old alliance of eye and light still applied to these new arrivals in the space of the observable. In this sense, phenomenology is a restoration in favor of perception after its overtaking by mechanical observation. It consciously distracts from the question of whether the human eye can compete with the Geiger counter. As long as the distraction is effective, the suggestion remains intact that knowledge can inhabit the world as the bourgeois inhabits his villa.

First of all, one cannot deny that even the sights and depictions of the disturbing things that became visible upon cutting open human and animal bodies from manifold angles, as well as the chemical disintegration of matter, extending to nuclear epiphanies over the American desert and atomic traces in cloud chambers, entered the human perception as if these new visibilities were simply continuing the unconcealed state of the first nature by more current means. They are not. All these neo-visibilities, these penetrations of the phenomenal background, enabled by developed image-giving procedures: these unrelentingly

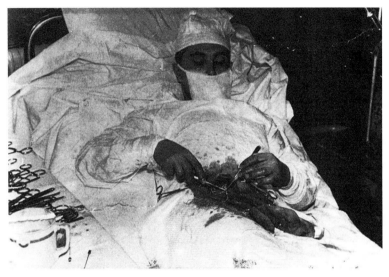

Leonid Rogozov, Novolazarevskaya Station, Antarctic, during a self-operation on the appendix in April 1961

explicit cuts through animate and inanimate bodies, these external views of naturally enclosed organs, these counterintuitive artificial views of the night and mechanical side of nature, these close-ups of exposed matter, produced with sound operational knowledge and seasoned eccentricity—they are all separated by an ontological divide from the primordial, circumspect and lenient cognitive willingness of human views in varyingly familiar horizon-immanent circumstances which, since time immemorial, have conventionally been termed "nature." Only after the auto-operative rotation did recent knowledge find itself in the position where things become phenomenal that were in no way intended for the human perceptual apparatus, at least not in its first design. What was shifted to the surface by research had to be "brought to light" or "unconcealed" in a form of cognitive mining. Modernity offers various names for the origin of these extractions: they come either from the "unconscious" or from latency, from ignorance, from concealment on the insides of the phenomenal folds or from some other framing of the cognitive not-yet.

Of no genre of "objects" is this truer than the heroic topics of the new "life sciences" that have recently advanced spectacularly into regions formerly withdrawn, non-appearing, and hence invisible. Thanks to these invasions, human brains, the human genome and human immune systems have been placed on the epistemological stage so theatrically that the public sphere of education and sensation is kept in constant suspense through their enactment and establishment, which are presented as "exploration" and "deciphering."

All three object fields can be used to explain how absurd it would be to consider disciplines of this orientation expressions or products of human reflection on existence, or even manifestations of what idealistic philosophers have called self-reflection. The turn of knowledge towards brains—where, as far as we can tell, every knowledge, even this acute knowledge of knowledge, is processed—as well as genomes and immune systems, which undoubtedly also constitute the current biological premises for the existence of these geneticists and immunologists, was not of a "reflective" or mirroring character; it only performed the auto-operative rotation after which knowledge reached behind the mirror, or to the "reverse" of subjectivities. This required forced access to the concealed, for only after breaking through to the hidden and integrating it into the illuminated space can those things which naturally existed and still exist latently, aphenomenally and without necessary relation to a cognizant

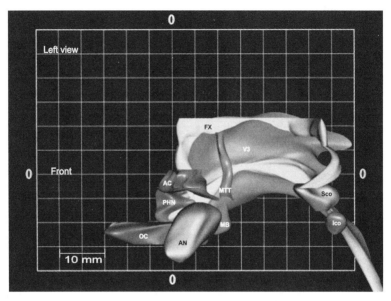

Amygdala, fornix and periventricula of the brain, three-dimensional reconstruction

consciousness become noticeable as phenomena. For genes, brains and immune systems to come under pressure to appear, Lethe-breaking procedures and instruments are indispensable—the effective tools of that rotation which brings the non-present into the position of the present.[58]

It should be emphasized that this making-present cannot retain the character of a domineering elevation over objects for ever—the new life sciences in particular allow us to predict how research is increasingly infused with insight into the advancing of the object. Whoever raises the question of what life is must begin by conceding that life has long since provided the answer. There is ever less cause to speak of an appropriation of the object by the researching subject. My brain, my genome, my immune system—in such combinations, the good old possessive pronouns sound like presentations of grammatical folklore. The new possessions could never become our property, for nothing is more foreign to us—and will always remain so—than our "own" explicated biomechanics. That the long-term attack on concealment occurs by necessity, however, and is undertaken rightfully in every respect, is—accompanied by such catchphrases as "freedom of research" or "improvement of human living conditions"—one of the primary convictions of modern civilization, convictions that for their part flow from ancient sources, for example the Aristotelian doctrine that striving for insight is part of human nature.

I shall refrain from commenting on these postulations—except to note that every foregrounding of long-latent things has a price, especially when it is the atmospheric and climatic contingencies of cultures whose erosion, and even more their intentional destruction, pushes them to become manifest. Once wounded, they are concretely present and urge operative reconstruction. This applies especially to the knowledge about cultures that was brought into an external and technological position by the great rotation.[59] One can say all manner of bad things about the twentieth century—but not that it failed to pay the price for such defamiliarizations. No other epoch displayed such advanced expertise in the art of annihilating existence from its vital premises. On the other side of these destruction procedures, the constructive preconditions for the preservation of cultural spaces become visible. Their fate will depend on the reconstructive knowledge and skill that civilizations acquire about themselves.

We Have Never Been Revolutionary

After the end of the twentieth century, it is dawning on people that it was a mistake to place the concept of revolution at the center of its interpretation—just as it was a mistake to understand the extremist ways of thinking from that time as mirroring "revolutionary" events in the social "base." One still shows complicity by lending credence to the self-mystifications of the epoch's actors. Whoever spoke of revolutions before and after 1917, whether political or cultural, almost always allowed an unclear metaphor of motion to make fools of them. At no time did the strength of the century lie in overturning. Nowhere did the top and the bottom change places; nothing that stood on its head was placed on its feet; it would be futile to search for evidence that the last became the first anywhere. Nothing was overturned, nothing circulated. On the other hand, background elements were foregrounded everywhere; things latent were brought to manifestation on countless fronts. Whatever could be uncovered through invasive hypotheses, interventions and deep drilling went into the tanks, the printed word and the business balances. The middle ground was broadened, representative functions multiplied, courts were restaffed, administrations expanded, the targets for actions, productions and publications proliferated, new positions sprouted up and the number of career chances was multiplied a thousandfold. There is a hint of all that in Paul Valéry's malicious claim that the French, and *eo ipso* the moderns, had turned the "revolution" into a "routine."

The true and real basic concept of modernity is not revolution but explication. Explication is the true name of becoming for our time—and can be followed or accompanied by the conventional modes of becoming through drift, imitation, disaster and creative recombination. Deleuze was probably articulating a related thought when he attempted to shift the event type "revolution" to the molecular level to escape the ambivalences of action in the "mass"; what counts is not voluminous upheaval but flowing, a discreet progression into the next state, the sustained flight from the status quo. At the molecular level, only small and smallest maneuvers count; anything new that leads further is operative. The visibility of true innovation simply goes back to the explication effect—what is then declared a "revolution" is usually no more than the noise that follows once the event is over. The present age does not turn things, conditions or themes over; it rolls them out. It unfolds them, it pulls them forwards, it lays them flat and takes them apart, it coerces them into manifestation, it respells them analytically and incorporates them into synthetic routines. It turns suppositions into operations; it supplies muddled expressive tensions with exact methods; it translates dreams into instruction manuals; it arms *ressentiment* and lets love play on countless, often newly invented instruments. It wants to know everything about all things in the background, folded inwards, previously unavailable and withdrawn—enough, at least, to make it available for new foreground actions, unfolding and splitting, interventions and remoldings. It translates the monstrous into the commonplace. It invents procedures for integrating the unheard-of into the register of the real; it builds the keyboard that allows users easy access to things previously impossible. It tells its own: "There is no such thing as powerlessness; whatever you cannot do, you can learn." It is rightfully called the technological age.

In the following, I will repeat a few chapters from the disaster history of the twentieth century in order to explain what struggles and traumas forced the human sojourn in breathable milieus to become an object of explicit cultivation. Once this has been understood, it only requires a small effort to show why every ethics of value, virtue and discourse remains hollow as long as it is not translated into climate ethics. Was Heraclitus exaggerating when he proclaimed that war is the father of all things? No contemporary philosopher, at any rate, would be going too far by describing terror as the father of the science of cultures.

Airquake

Breathless from the strained vigilance, breathless from the
stuffiness of the stuffy night-air...
— Hermann Broch, *The Death of Virgil* [1]

I. Gas Warfare, or: The Atmoterrorist Pattern

If one had to say in a single sentence with the most concise
formulations what the twentieth century, alongside its incommensurable achievements in the arts, had contributed to the
history of civilization in the way of unmistakably individual
qualities, three criteria would probably suffice for the answer.
Anyone who wants to understand the originality of this epoch
must consider the following: the practice of terrorism, the concept of product design and the environmental idea. The first of
these placed interactions between enemies on post-military
foundations; the second allowed functionalism to reconnect
with the perceptual world; and the third allowed life and
knowledge phenomena to be linked to an unprecedented extent.
Together, these three mark the acceleration of explication—the

revealing incorporation of latencies or background circumstances into manifest operations.

If, beyond this, one had to determine at what point the century genuinely began, the answer could be given with great precision. The same information allows us to clarify how the three primary characteristics of the age were initially connected in a shared primal scene. The twentieth century dawned in spectacularly revealing fashion on April 22, 1915, with the first large-scale use of chlorine gas as a warfare agent by a specially established "gas regiment" in the western German armies against French and Canadian infantry positions in the northern Ypres Salient. In the preceding weeks, German soldiers on that part of the front had, unnoticed by the enemy, assembled thousands of hidden gas bottles into batteries of a previously unknown kind along the edges of their trenches. At exactly 6 pm, pioneers of the new regiment under the command of Colonel Max Peterson opened 1,600 large (90 lb) and 4,130 smaller (45 lb) bottles of chlorine while a north-northeasterly wind was blowing. This "blowing off" of the liquefied substance caused the spread of some 150 tons of chlorine in a gas cloud almost four miles wide and roughly half a mile deep.[2] An aerial photograph captured the spread of the first military poison cloud over the Ypres front. The favorable wind carried the cloud towards the French positions at a speed of between six and ten feet per second; the concentration of the aerial poison was around 0.5%, which caused severe damage to the airways and lungs upon extended exposure.

The French general Jean-Jules Henry Mordacq (1868–1943), who was positioned three miles behind the front, at the time, received a field call shortly after 6:20 pm from an officer of the first Tirailleur regiment, located near the front, to report yellowish

Aerial photograph of the first German chlorine gas attack near Ypres on April 22, 1915

smoke clouds blowing towards the French positions from the German trenches.[3] When this alarm, which was initially questioned but subsequently confirmed through further calls, prompted Mordacq to set off on horseback with his adjutants to examine the situation at the front with his own eyes, he and his companions soon experienced breathing difficulties, irritations of the throat and heavy ringing in their ears; when the horses refused to continue, Mordacq's group had to approach the gassed zones on foot. Soon he found a multitude of soldiers running towards him in a state of panic, their uniform jackets open and their guns discarded, spitting blood and screaming for water. Some of them rolled about on the ground, vainly gasping for air. By 7 pm there was a gap in the French and Canadian front some four miles wide; around that time, German troops advanced and occupied Langemarck.[4] The only means of protection the attacking units had were gauze pads dipped in soda solution and a chlorine-binding liquid, which were used to cover the mouth and nose. Mordacq survived the attack and published his war memoirs in the year that Hitler came to power.

The operation's military success was never in question—only a few days after the events near Ypres, Emperor Wilhelm II granted a personal audience to the scientific director of the German chemical weapons program, the chemist Professor Fritz Haber, head of the Kaiser Wilhelm Institute of Physical Chemistry and Electrochemistry in Berlin-Dahlem, to promote him to the rank of captain.[5] At most, the opinion was voiced that the German troops, themselves surprised by the efficiency of the new method, had not exploited the triumph of April 22 energetically enough. Information about the number of victims, on the other hand, was and remains highly divergent: unofficial French sources spoke of a mere 625 soldiers injured by gas, no more than three of whom died of the poison, whereas early German reports claimed that 15,000 had been affected and 5,000 had died—numbers that were repeatedly lowered in the course of further research. Obviously, these differences point to interpretive battles which show the military and moral purpose in various lights. A Canadian autopsy report on a gas victim from one of the most heavily struck sections of the front states: "Upon removal of the lungs, a considerable amount of foaming light-yellow fluid, evidently with a high protein content, was released [ ] The veins on the brain's surface were severely blocked, and all small blood vessels were markedly standing out."[6]

While the disastrous twentieth century is currently attempting to go down in history as the "age of extremes," and

Installation of chlorine bottles in German frontline trenches

is falling victim to the growing obsolescence of its battle lines and mobilizing concepts—its scripts for world history are no less yellowed than the calls of medieval theologians to liberate the Holy Sepulcher—one of the technological patterns of this past era is manifesting itself with increasing clarity. One could call it the introduction of the environment into the battle between opponents.

For as long as there has been artillery, it has been part of the profession of shooters and warlords to aim direct shots at the enemy and their defensive shields. Anyone seeking to eliminate an enemy in accordance with the art of soldierly long-distance killing must use the barrel of a firearm to produce an *intention directa* aimed at his body, then immobilize the target with sufficiently accurate shots. From the late Middle Ages to the outbreak of the First World War, one of the defining traits of a soldier was his ability to summon and "nurture" this intentionality in himself. During that time, manliness was encoded partly in the capacity and willingness to give death to an enemy with causal immediacy—by one's own hand and with one's own weapon. Aiming at the enemy is, as it were, the continuation of the duel by ballistic means. Hence the gesture of killing from man to man remained so closely tied to the pre-bourgeois notion of personal courage and possible heroism that it even continued to remain in effect, however anachronistically, under the conditions of long-distance combat and anonymous attrition warfare. If members of twentieth-century armies could believe they were still practicing a "manly," under martial premises "honest" profession, this was based on the risk of a direct lethal encounter. The weapon manifestation of this is the bayonet-fitted rifle: if the (bourgeois) elimination of the enemy through long-distance shots should fail for some reason, this weapon indicates the possibility of returning to the (aristocratic and archaic) act of direct close-range impalement.

The twentieth century will be remembered as the age whose decisive idea was no longer to aim at an enemy's body, but rather his environment. This is the central premise of terror in the more explicit and contemporary sense. Shakespeare put its principle prophetically in Shylock's mouth: "You take my life / When you do take the means whereby I live."[7] Next to the economic means, the ecological and psychosocial conditions of human existence have now taken center stage. The new procedures for removing the preconditions for the enemy's life by targeting his environment reveal the contours of a specifically modern, post-Hegelian concept of terror.[8]

The terror of the twentieth century is considerably more than the "I am allowed to because I can" attitude with which Jacobean self-awareness trampled over those who obstructed the path of its freedom; it also differs fundamentally—despite similarities of form—from the bombings carried out by anarchists and nihilists in the last third of the nineteenth century, whose purpose was a destabilization of the bourgeois-late aristocratic social order, and which not infrequently entailed a clumsy "philosophy of the bomb" that expressed the power fantasies of destructive petty bourgeois minds.[9] It should, furthermore, not be confused in either its methods nor its aims with the phobocratic techniques of existing or burgeoning dictatorships, which use a calculated mixture of "ceremony and terror" to scare their own populations into submission. Finally, one must keep its precise concept at a distance from the countless episodes in which individual desperados appropriated modern means of destruction out of vengeful, paranoid and herostratic motives to stage isolated apocalypses.[10]

The terror of our age is a manifestation of the environment-theoretically modernized knowledge of extermination that enables terrorists to understand their victims better than they understand themselves. If the enemy's body can no longer be liquidated with direct hits, the attacker is now presented with the possibility of making their continued existence impossible by immersing them in an unlivable milieu for a sufficiently long time.

It is this conclusion that gave rise to modern "chemical warfare"—as an attack on the enemy's environment-dependent vital functions, namely breathing, regulation of the central nervous system and livable temperature and radiation conditions. This is, in fact, the point at which traditional war becomes terrorism, assuming the latter is based on a rejection of the old crossing of blades between equal opponents. Current terror operates beyond the naïve exchange of armed strikes between regular troops. Its concern is to replace classical battle forms with attacks on the enemy's environmental preconditions for life. Such a change suggests itself when very unequal opponents meet—as we perceive in the current popularity of non-state wars and the friction between state armies and non-state combatants. Nonetheless, it is entirely wrong to claim that terror is the weapon of the weak. Any glance at the history of terror in the twentieth century shows that it was the states, and the strong ones among them, that first embraced the means and methods of terrorism.

The military-historical peculiarity of gas warfare between 1915 and 1918 lies, as one sees in retrospect, in the fact that on both sides of the front, officially supported forms of environmental terror were integrated into the regular warfare conducted by legally recruited armies—in conscious violation of Article 23a of the Hague Land War Convention of 1907, which expressly rules out the use of all poisons and weapons for increasing suffering in actions against the enemy, and all the more against the non-combatant population.[11] In 1918, the Germans supposedly had nine gas battalions with roughly 7,000 soldiers and the Allies thirteen battalions of "chemical troops" with over 12,000 men. It is not without reason that experts spoke of a "war within a war." This phrase announces the liberation of exterminism from cultivated martial force. Numerous statements by soldiers in the First World War, especially professional officers of noble birth, show that they recognized gas combat as a degeneration of warfare that was degrading for everyone involved. Nonetheless, there is barely a single report of an army member openly opposing the new "law of war."[12]

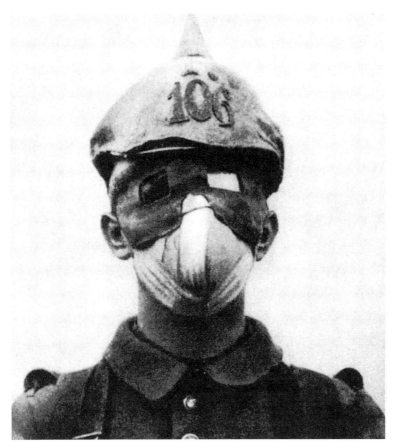

The discovery of the "environment"

The discovery of the "environment" took place in the trenches of the First World War, where soldiers on both sides had made themselves unreachable by the bullets or explosives meant for them to such a significant extent that the problem of atmospheric warfare was destined to rear its head. What was later called "gas warfare" (and even later "aerial bomb warfare") presented itself as the technical solution: its principle was to cloak the enemy in a toxic cloud of sufficient "combat concentration" long enough—which in practice meant at least a few minutes—for them to fall prey to their innate need for air. (The production of toxic psychological clouds over their own population is usually a matter for the mass media of the warring groups: they convert their need for information into an involuntary complicity by generalizing local terror on a national scale with an honest face.) These toxic clouds were practically never composed of gases in the strict physical sense so much as extremely fine particle dust released by explosions. This brought the phenomenon of a second artillery into view: it no longer aimed at enemy soldiers and their positions, but rather at the air surrounding the enemy bodies. Consequently, the concept of the "hit" started to become more hazy: henceforth, whatever was close enough to the object could be considered adequately precise and thus operatively controlled.[13] In a later phase, the explosive ammunition of traditional artillery would be replaced by the mist-spreading projectiles of the new gas artillery. There was frantic research to ascertain how one could deal with the rapid thinning of poison gas clouds above the battlefield—which was usually achieved by chemical supplements that modified the behavior of the highly volatile combat dust particles in the desired fashion. After the events of Ypres, a form of military climatology sprung up that one can plausibly acknowledge as the key phenomenon of terrorism.

The study of toxic clouds was the first science with which the twentieth century presented its identity certificate.[14] Before April 22, 1915 this statement would have been pataphysical; for the time after that, however, it must be seen as the core of an ontology of currentness. It explicates the phenomenon of the unbreathable space traditionally implied in the concept of miasma. The still unclear status of toxic cloud studies or the theory of unlivable spaces within climatology only serves to clarify that for now, climate theory has not yet broken out of its natural-scientific stupor. In reality, as we will see, it was the first of the new human sciences that resulted from the knowledge about world war.[15]

The overnight development of military breathing apparatuses (production-line gas masks were a popular item) revealed the adaptation of the troops to a situation in which human respiration was about to assume a direct role in combat activities. Fritz Haber would soon be celebrated as the father of the gas mask. When one learns from works of military history that between February and June 1916, the responsible field depot supplied almost five and a half million gas masks and 4,300 breathing apparatuses (mostly taken from the mining industry) with two million liters of oxygen to the German troops at Verdun alone,[16] it becomes evident in numbers how far "ecologized" war, a war brought into the atmospheric environment, had become a battle for the respiratory potentials of hostile parties. Combat now incorporated the biological weak points of the conflict partners. The rapidly popularized concept of the gas mask expressed how the victim of attack attempted to escape his dependence on the immediate respiratory milieu by hiding behind an air filter—a first step towards the principle of air conditioning, which is based on decoupling a defined volume of air from the surrounding air. Its counterpart on the offensive side was an escalation of the attack on the atmosphere using toxic substances intended to penetrate the enemy's respiratory devices; beginning in the summer of 1917, German chemists and officers deployed the warfare agent diphenylchlorarsine or Clark I, one of the substances that became known as Blue Cross, which was capable of overcoming enemy respirator filters in the form of extremely fine airborne particles—an effect that led its recipients to dub it "mask breaker." At the same time, the German gas artillery on the Western Front introduced the new war gas Yellow Cross or Lost,[17] which, even in the smallest quantities caused severe damage to the organism upon contact with the airways, skin or mucous membranes, especially blindness and disastrous nervous dysfunctions. One of the more well-known victims of Lost or Ypérite on the Western Front was Private Adolf Hitler, who was caught in one of the last British gas attacks of the First World War on a hill near Wervik (La Montagne), south of Ypres, in the night of October 13, 1918. In his memoirs, he wrote that his eyes had felt as if transformed into glowing coals on the morning of the 14th; he also claimed that the events of November 9 in Germany, which he experienced via rumors in the Pomeranian military hospital in Pasewalk, had caused a relapse of his Lost-induced blindness during which he made the decision to "become a politician." In the spring of 1944, faced with increasingly imminent defeat, Hitler told Speer that he feared going blind again as he had in 1918. The gas trauma stayed with him to the end as a nervous trace. One of the military-technological determinants of the Second World War, it would seem, was the fact that those events led Hitler to incorporate an idiosyncratic view of gas into his personal concept of war on the one hand, and of genocidal practice on the other.[18]

In its first appearance, gas warfare introduced the operative criteria of the twentieth century—terrorism, design-consciousness and an environmental approach—in close union. The exact concept of terror, as shown above, presupposes an explicit concept of environment, as terror constitutes the shifting of destructive action from the "system" (here the physically concrete enemy body) to its "environment"—in the present case the aerial milieu in which the enemy bodies, forced to breathe, are located. Hence terrorist action inherently and always has the character of an assassination [*Attentat*], whose definition (Lat. *attentatum*: "attempt, essay in killing") not only entails a surprise ambush, but also the malign exploitation of the victims' living habits. In gas warfare, the deepest levels of people's biological condition was incorporated into the attacks on them: the ineluctable habit of breathing is used against the breathers in such a way that they become involuntary accomplices in their own destruction—provided the gas terrorists succeed in trapping the victims in the toxic milieu long enough for them to deliver themselves up to the unbreathable environment through inevitable inhalations. Not only is, as Jean-Paul Sartre remarked, despair an act of self-assassination; the aerial assassination by the gas terrorist produces in its target the despair at being forced to participate in the extinction of their own life by the inability to refrain from breathing.

The phenomenon of the gas war introduced a new level of explication for the climatic and atmospheric premises of human existence; it provided a formal elaboration of the immersion of the living in a breathable milieu. The principle of design was incorporated into this advance of explication, as the operative handling of gas milieus in open spaces necessitates a series of atmotechnic innovations; hence military toxic clouds became a product design assignment. The forces deployed as ordinary soldiers on the gas fronts in the east and west were faced with the problem of developing routines for regional atmospheric design. The artificial production or installation of clouds of war dust demanded an effective coordination of cloud-forming factors with regard to concentration, diffusion, sedimentation, coherence, mass, extension and movement. This marked the emergence of a black meteorology that occupied itself with "precipitations" of a very special kind.

A stronghold of this special knowledge was the Kaiser Wilhelm Institute of Physical Chemistry and Electrochemistry in Berlin-Dahlem, headed by Fritz Haber, one of the most ominous theory addresses of the twentieth century; analogous institutes also existed in France and Britain. To reach the necessary military concentrations on the ground, the combat agents usually required stabilizers. Whether these toxic precipitations were applied in a continuous barrage of gas grenades or through a wind-supported "blowing off" of prepared gas bottles was, compared to definitively conceiving the principle of controlled toxic cloud production over a designated, by necessity vaguely demarcated terrain under outdoor conditions, only a relatively minor technological difference. In a Green Cross diphosgene attack by the German gas artillery at Fleury-devant-Douaumont in the night of June 22, 1916, the necessary cloud consistency for a lethal effect in an open space would have demanded at least fifty field howitzer shots or a hundred field gun shots per hectare per minute—values that were not quite reached, which is why the French "only" had 1,600 men suffering from gas poisoning and 90 fatalities on the field the next morning.[19]

The decisive aspect was that through gas terrorism, technology broke through to the horizon of a design for the immaterial—which put latent topics such as physical air quality, artificial atmospheric supplements and other climate-forming factors in human dwelling spaces under pressure of explication. Through that progressive explication, humanism and terrorism are tied together. The Nobel laureate Fritz Haber declared himself a glowing patriot and humanist throughout his life. As he asserted in his farewell letter of October 1, 1933 to his institute, he was proud to have served the fatherland in wartime and humanity in peacetime.

Terrorism suspends the distinction between violence against persons and violence against things from the environmental—it is violence against those human-surrounding "things" without which persons cannot remain persons. Violence against the air that groups breathe transforms the immediate atmospheric shell of humans into a thing whose infirmity or intactness will henceforth be subject to negotiation. Only in response to such withdrawal by terrorism can the air and the atmosphere—primary media of life, both physically and metaphorically—become objects of explicit precautions and aerotechnic, medical, legal, political, aesthetic and culture-theoretical supervision. In this sense, air theory and climate technology are not mere sediments of war and post-war knowledge, and *eo ipso* first objects of a science of peace that could only arise in the war stress shadow;[20] more than that, they are primary post-terrorist forms of knowledge. Terming them thus already means explaining why such knowledge was previously only preserved in contexts that were unstable, incoherent and lacking in authority; perhaps the idea that there could be such a thing as authentic terror experts is hubristic in itself.

Professional opponents and analysts of terror show a notable interest in misreading its nature on a grand scale—a phenomenon for which the floods of expert statements after the attack on the World Trade Center in New York and the Pentagon in Washington on September 11, 2001 provided clear evidence in their elaborated helplessness. The tenor of virtually all proclamations about this attack on the prominent symbols of the USA was that Americans had been as surprised by the events as the rest of the world, but felt confirmed in the belief that there are things against which one can never adequately protect oneself. In the "War on Terror" campaign of American television networks, which adapted their language conventions to those of the Pentagon and almost entirely switched from news to propaganda, there was not a single mention of the basic insight that terrorism is not an opponent but a *modus operandi*, a method of warfare that usually spreads to both sides of a conflict, which is why "war on terror" is a nonsensical formulation.[21] It elevates an allegory to a political enemy. As soon as one brackets the infectious imposition of taking sides and follows the central principle of peace processes, namely to listen to the other side too, it becomes evident that the individual terrorist act is never an absolute beginning. There is no terrorist *acte gratuit*, no original "let there be" of terror. Every terror attack sees itself as a counterattack in a series that is described as having been initiated by the opponent. Thus terrorism is itself of an anti-terrorist constitution; this even applies to the "primal scene" on the Ypres front in 1915—not only because it immediately led to the usual sequence of counterstrikes and counter-counterstrikes, but also because the German side could truthfully claim the prior deployment of gas ammunition by the French and British.[22] Terror does not begin with the execution of an individual attack by one side, but rather with the will and readiness of conflict partners to operate on an expanded battlefield. By expanding the combat zone, the principle of explication makes itself noticeable in warfare: the enemy is explicated as an object in the environment whose removal amounts to a survival condition for the system. Terrorism is an explication of the other in terms of their exterminability.[23] If war has always meant one's behavior towards the enemy, it is only with terrorism that its true "nature" is revealed. As soon as hostility is no longer tamed by international law, the technological relationship with the enemy takes command. By advancing the explicitness of procedures, technology militarily encapsulates the nature of enmity: it is nothing other than the will to annihilate one's opponent. Enmity made technologically explicit is exterminism. This explains why the mature style of warfare in the twentieth century was annihilation-oriented.

Stabilizing a viable knowledge of terror thus depends not only on the precise memory of its practices; it demands a formulation of the tenets that have defined terrorist action in its technological explicitness and continuing explication since 1915. One can only understand terrorism if one views it as a way of exploring the environment from the perspective of its destructibility. It exploits the fact that mere inhabitants have a user relationship with their environment, and naturally consume it first of all as a tacit precondition of their existence and nothing else. This time, however, destroying is more analytical than using: terror via isolated acts draws advantages from the asymmetry of harmlessness between the attack and the undefended object, while systematized terror creates a sustained climate of fear in which the defense expects constant attacks without being able to parry them. This means that terroristically heightened warfare increasingly becomes a competition for explication advantages in the form of weak points in the opposing environment. New weapons of terror are those that make the conditions

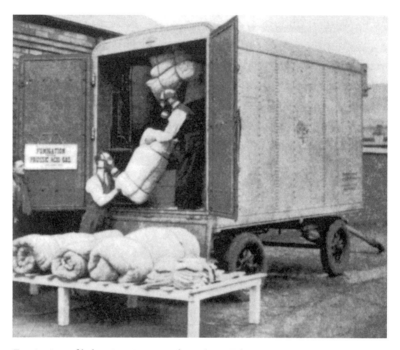

Fumigation of belongings in removal van (c. 1930)

of life more explicit; new categories of attacks reveal—in the mode of the nasty surprise—new surfaces of vulnerability. A terrorist is one who acquires an explication advantage with regard to the implicit preconditions of their opponent's life and uses it for the deed. That is why, after major terrorist turning points, one can have the feeling that something futuristic has happened; whatever breaks open the implicit and converts seeming harmlessness into combat zones has a future.

All terror is atmoterroristically constituted in its *modus operandi*. It has the form of the assassin's attack against the environmental living conditions of the enemy, starting with a poison attack on the most immediate environmental resource of the human organism, namely the air that it breathes.[24] This concedes that what, since 1793 and even more since 1915, we have called *terreur* and terror could be anticipated in every possible form of violence towards the lifeworldly conditions of human existence—think of poisoned drinking wells, which were already known in antiquity, medieval plague attacks on defended fortresses, the burning and smoking out of cities and hiding-places by the besieging troops, or the dissemination of horrific rumors and demoralizing news. But such comparisons miss the real point. Terrorism remains a child of modernity because it was not able to mature into its exact definition until the principle of an attack on the environment and the immune defenses of an organism or form of life had manifested itself sufficiently explicitly. This first took place, as described above, with the events of April 22, 1915, when the cloud of chlorine gas blown out of 5,700 gas bottles drifted on a light breeze from the German positions towards the French trenches between Bixschoote and Langemarck. In the early evening hours of that day, between 6 and 7 pm, the hand on the epochal clock leapt from the vitalist-late Romantic phase of modernity to that of atmoterrorist objectivity. There has not been any caesura of such depth since. Every one of the great disasters of the twentieth and early twenty-first centuries belongs to the explication history of what happened on the Western Front that April evening, when the surprised French-Canadian units retreated in panic and horror from the white-yellow gas cloud creeping towards them from the northeast.

Naturally, the further technical explication of the military-climatological procedural knowledge acquired in the war took a detour via its "peaceful use" after November 1918, if not earlier. With the war's approaching end, the bed bug, the common gnat, the flour moth and above all the clothes louse were targeted by the Berlin chemists. They had evidently not let the ban on all production of combat agents by the Treaty of Versailles drive out the fascination of their profession. Professor Ferdinand Flury, one of Fritz Haber's closest staff members at the Dahlem Institute, gave a programmatic lecture on the subject in September 1918 in Munich, at a conference of the German Society of Applied Entomology: "The Activities of the Kaiser Wilhelm Institute of Physical Chemistry and Electrochemistry, Berlin-Dahlem, in the Service of Pest Control." In the discussion, Fritz Haber spoke up and described the work of a "Technical Committee for Pest Control" (Tasch) he had cofounded, which concerned itself primarily with introducing (hydrogen cyanide, HCN) as an insecticide for German farmers. He noted: "The larger underlying idea, now that peace has been restored, is to make cyanide as well as the other combat agents brought about by the war available for supporting agriculture through pest control."[25] In his presentation, Flury pointed out that "when gases affect insects or mites, very different circumstances come into consideration compared to those for the inhalation of gases and vapors through the lungs of mammals, though there are parallels with their toxicity for higher animals."[26] As early as 1920, a journal of the German Society for Pest Control (Degesch), which was founded shortly before the end of the war, was able to announce that since 1917, roughly 20 million cubic meters of "building space in mills, ships, barracks, military hospitals, schools, granaries and seed stores" and the like had been fumigated according to the criteria of advanced cyanide technology (using the "vat process"). In 1920, this was augmented by a new gas product developed by Flury and others which preserved the advantage of cyanide, namely its extreme toxicity, while lacking its disadvantage, namely the dangerous imperceptibility of the gas by smell, taste or other human senses (or more precisely for a group of people, as the ability to perceive the smell of cyanide gas appears to be genetically determined). The point of the new introduction was a ten percent (later less) admixture of a highly perceptible irritant gas (such as methyl chloroformate) with the toxic hydrogen cyanide. The new product came on the market under the name "Zyklon A," and was recommended for the "disinfestation of pest-ridden living spaces." What was notable about Zyklon A was that it constituted a designer gas that perfectly demonstrated a specific task of design: the reintroduction of imperceptible or obscured product functions into the user's awareness—because its main component hydrogen cyanide, which evaporates at around 27° Celsius, is often not directly perceptible for humans, the developers considered it wise to equip their product with a highly conspicuous irritant component whose strong aversive effect would indicate the substance's presence. (In philosophical terms one would speak of a re-phenomenalization of the non-apparent.)[27] One should note that the first "large-scale disinfestation" took place almost two years to the day after the Ypres attack with the fumigation of a mill in Heidingsfeld, near Würzburg, on April 21, 1917. A mere eighty-five years passed between the death of Goethe and the introduction of the word *Grossraumentwesung* [large-scale disinfestation] into the German language; the terms *Entmottung* [de-mothing] and *Entrattung* [de-ratting] also enriched the German vocabulary from this time onwards. The mill owner went on record as saying that his business had remained "moth-free" for a long time after the fumigation.

The civil production of cyanide clouds almost exclusively concerned closed built-up spaces (an exception to this were fruit trees in open spaces, which were covered with airtight tarpaulins and subsequently fumigated). This could involve concentrations that enabled the providers of such services to claim a complete extermination of local insect populations, including eggs and nits—not least because hydrogen cyanide gas found its way into every last nook and cranny. In the early phase of these practices, the connection between the special air zone—the volume of space to be gassed—and the general air, the public atmosphere, was interpreted as unproblematic. As a result, fumigations were normally concluded with a simple ventilation—that is, the diffusion of the poison gas in the surrounding air until a "safe level" was reached. At the time, no one was concerned that the "ventilation" of the former areas would lead to the pollution of the latter ones. The negligibility of the fumigated interiors in relation to the non-fumigated outside air seemed certain *a priori* and for all time. The professional literature of the branch noted in the early 1940s, not without some pride, that 142 million cubic meters of space had meanwhile been "disinfested" using 1.5 million kilograms of hydrogen cyanide (which, one should add, were incorporated into the atmosphere without any safety measures). With the advancing environmental problem, the relationship between the surrounding air and the special air zone was reversed, for now the artificially prepared—today we call it air-conditioned—zone offers privileged air quality, while the surroundings are subject to an increased breathing risk, even to the extent of acute unbreathability and chronic unlivability.

During the 1920s, several northern German pest extermination firms offered routine Zyklon fumigations for ships, warehouses,

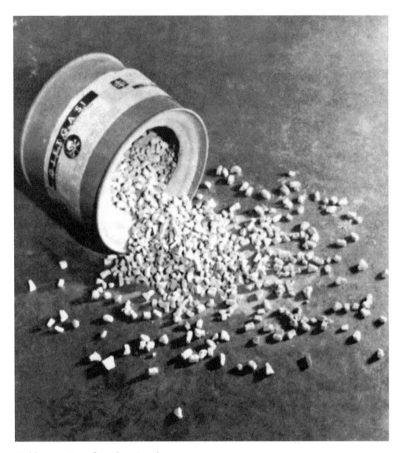

Zyklon canister found at Auschwitz

mass accommodation, shacks, railway cars and similar spaces—including, from 1924 on, the newly founded Hamburg company Tesch & Stabenow (Testa), whose top product, patented in 1926, would become known under the name Zyklon B.[28] The fact that one of the company's two founders, Dr. Bruno Tesch (b. 1890), who was sentenced to death by a British military tribunal at Hamburg's Curiohaus in 1946 and executed at

Hamelin Prison, worked at Fritz Haber's military-chemical institute from 1915–1920 and was involved in the development of gas warfare from the start, is a concrete proof of the widespread continuity of personnel and content in the new disinfestation methods beyond war and peace. The merit of Zyklon B, invented or developed further by Dr. Walter Heerdt, was that the highly volatile hydrogen cyanide was absorbed by porous dry carrier substances like diatomite, which considerably facilitated storage and transportation in comparison to the previous liquid form. It came on the market in 200 g, 500 g, 1 kg and 5 kg cans. As early as the 1930s, Zyklon B—which was initially produced exclusively in Dessau (later also in Kolin) and jointly distributed by the Testa company and the German Society for Pest Control—had achieved a near-monopoly on the world market of pest control products; the only competition came from an older sulfur gas procedure in the area of ship fumigations.[29] The practice of exterminating vermin in stationary or mobile de-mothing and "disinfestations chambers" had also been introduced by this time: here the material to be treated, usually carpets, uniforms and textiles of all kinds, as well as upholstery, was placed in the gas-filled space and aired afterwards.

After the outbreak of war in the autumn of 1939, the Testa company provided disinfection courses for both members of the Wehrmacht and civilians in the east. This also entailed demonstrations of gas chambers. The de-lousing of both troops and prisoners of war continued to be viewed as one of the most urgent tasks facing pest controllers. At the turn of 1941–42, Testa supplied their business customers, which meanwhile included both the Wehrmacht in the east and the Waffen-SS as significant factions, with a brochure entitled "The Little Testa

Handbook of Zyklon," whose language shows indications of a militarization of "disinfestations procedures"—perhaps even of a possible redeployment of hydrogen cyanide in human environments. It states that exterminating vermin "is not only demanded by prudence, but is furthermore an act of self-defense!"[30] In the medical context, this can be taken as a reference to the typhus epidemic that had broken out among the eastern forces in 1941, though barely more than 10% of those infected died—considering that the usual mortality rate with this illness was 30%, this was already a success for German hygiene, as the typhus pathogen *Rickettsia prowazekii* is transmitted by clothes lice. In the light of subsequent events, one can understand how the legal term "self-defense" anticipated the potential rapprochement between fumigation technology and the domain of human objects. It became apparent only a few months later that the atmotechnic form of organism extermination was also intended to encompass applications to human content. When, in 1941 and 1942, a number of articles by historians of chemistry within the company hailed the twenty-five-year anniversary of the introduction of hydrogen cyanide in the battle against vermin as an event that was relevant for the entire cultural world, their authors did not yet know the scale on which their opportunistic hyperbole would prove significant for the diagnostic definition of the civilizational context as a whole.

The year 1924 plays an eminent part in the drama of atmospheric explication—not only because of the founding of the Hamburg Zyklon B company Tesch & Stabenow, but also because in that year, the atmoterrorist motif of exterminating organisms by destroying their environment was introduced into

Gas chamber at Nevada State Prison, Carson City (1926)

the penal law of a democratic state. On February 8, 1924, the State of Nevada put into operation the first "civil" gas chamber for carrying out allegedly humane, efficient executions. This acted as a model for eleven other U.S. states, including California, which became famous for the two-seated, crypt-like gas chamber in San Quentin State Prison and notorious for the possible judicial murder of Cheryl Chessman on May 2, 1960. The Nevada State Legislature had already laid the legal foundation for the new method of execution in March, 1921. The first person to be executed by the new method was the twenty-nine-year-old Chinese-born man Gee Jon, who (in connection with a gang war in California in the early 1920s) had been found guilty of murdering the Chinese Tom Quong Kee. In U.S. gas chambers, the delinquents died from inhaling hydrogen cyanide

Lucinda Devlin, *The Omega Suites: Witness Room, Broad River Correctional Facility,*
Columbia, South Carolina (1991)

fumes that developed when the components of the poison
flowed into a vessel. As military-chemical research had discovered in the laboratory and tested on the battlefield, the
gas inhibits oxygen transport in the blood and causes internal
suffocation.

From the last years of the First World War onwards, the
international community of design experts for poison gas and
atmospheres was permeable enough to react within a very short
time, both cisatlantically and transatlantically, to both technical
innovations and fluctuations in the moral climate surrounding
their application. Since the establishment of the Edgewood
Arsenal near Baltimore, a huge war research complex that was
energetically expanded using large resources after America's

entry into the war in 1917, the United States had an academic-military-industrial complex at their disposal which allowed far closer co-operations between the departments for weapons development than in the corresponding European institutions. Edgewood became one of the birthplaces of teamwork—only surpassed, if at all, by the dream team of the Los Alamos National Laboratory, which began working towards the nuclear bomb in 1943 like a meditation camp for exterminism. The Edgewood teams of scientists, officers and entrepreneurs were already concerned with finding civil forms of survival because of the declining war industry after 1918. The creator of the gas chamber at Nevada State Prison in Carson City, D. A. Turner, had been a major in the U.S. Army Medical Corps during the war; his contribution was to transfer the experiences of the military deployment of hydrogen cyanide to the conditions of civil execution.

Compared to the application of poison gas in the open, its use in the chamber had the advantage of eliminating the problem of an unstable lethal concentration outdoors. Hence the gas cloud design faded into the background in favor of the chamber and gas device. That the relationship between chamber and cloud can still become problematic has not only been demonstrated by gas chamber executions in the USA, however; the very uneven sarin attacks on several lines of the Tokyo subway on March 20, 1995 demonstrated that the ideal conditions for a controlled relation between poison gas and spatial volume are empirically difficult to create.[31] This would even be the case for less unprofessional assassins than the members of the Aum Shinrikyo sect, who wrapped their prepared plastic bags of sarin in newspaper and placed them on the floor of the subway trains, then puncturing them shortly before they alighted with the sharpened metal tips of their umbrellas while the remaining passengers inhaled the escaping poison.[32]

What guarantees the Nevada judicial system a place in the history of the explication of human atmosphere-dependence is its both quick-witted and preemptive sensitivity to the modern qualities of death by gas. In this field, methods can be considered modern if they promise to combine humanity with a high degree of efficiency—in the present case, the supposed shortening of the delinquent's suffering through the rapid effect of the poison. Major Turner specifically recommended his chamber as the milder alternative to the electric chair, already notorious at the time, where severe electric shocks fry the delinquent's brain under a tight, damp rubber cap. The concept of gas execution shows that war is not the only force which makes things explicit; the same effect comes equally often from the direct humanism that has characterized American spontaneous philosophy since the mid-nineteenth century, and whose academic version becomes pragmatism. In its will to combine the effective with the painless, this mindset remained unperturbed by execution records documenting the unprecedented agony of some gas chamber delinquents—descriptions so gruesome that one could think the USA, under humanitarian pretexts, had returned in the twentieth century to the medieval torture-execution. In the public perception, death by gas would remain an equally practi-cal and humane procedure for the time being; in this respect, the Nevada gas chamber was a cult site of pragmatic humanism. Its establishment was dictated by the sentimental law of moder-nity, which states that the public space must be kept free of acts of manifest cruelty. No one has summarized the compulsion of the moderns to occult the cruel traits of their own actions as aptly as Elias Canetti: "The sum total of sensitivity in culture has become very great. [...] Today it would be harder to condemn one man publicly to be burnt at the stake than to unleash a world war."[33]

The gas chamber for executions, an innovative idea in penal technology, presupposes complete control of the difference between the lethal interior climate of the chamber and the exterior climate—a motif evident in the fitting of execution rooms with glass walls, which allow invited witnesses to observe the efficiency of atmospheric conditions inside the chamber for themselves. Thus a form of ontological difference is spatially installed—the lethal climate inside the clearly defined, fastidiously sealed "cell," and the convivial climate in the lifeworldly domain of the executioners and observers; on the outside, being and ability-to-be, and on the inside, entity and inability-to-be. In the present context, being an observer means being an observer of agony, equipped with the privilege of following, from the outside, the demise of an organic "system" through the making-unlivable of its "environment." Some of the gas chamber doors in German death camps likewise had glass sections that allowed the executioners to exercise their privilege of observation.

If the concern is to bring about death as a production in the exact sense, and hence as a rendering explicit of the procedures that result in killed bodies, then the gas chamber in Nevada constitutes one of the milestones of reasonable exterminism in the twentieth century, even if its use and imitation in numerous other U.S. states remained sporadic (the Carson City chamber was used thirty-two times between 1924 and 1979). In 1927, when Heidegger spoke in *Being and Time*, with ontological

Lucinda Devlin, *The Omega Suites: Gas Chamber, Arizona State Prison, Florence, Arizona* (1992)

circuitousness, of the existential aspect of being-unto-death, American correctional staff and execution doctors had already put into operation a machine that turned breathing-unto-death into an ontically controlled process. One cannot speak here of "running ahead" into one's own death; now it is a matter of keeping the candidate in the lethal air trap.

It is not important here to investigate in detail how the two ideas of the gas chamber that had existed alongside each other since the 1930s eventually fused. Suffice it to note that the site or processor of this fusion was a certain SS intelligentsia which, on the one hand, received advice from the German pest control industry, and could, on the other hand, be sure of its mandate from the Reich Chancellery in Berlin to use "unusual methods" after Hitler's decision to bring about the "final solution of the Jewish question," which was placed on the agenda of select SS units from the summer of 1941 onwards through a secret command passed on by word of mouth. Equipped with this assignment, which gave them considerable leeway for their own initiatives, Hitler's most loyal helpers began their rampage of duty fulfillment. Systematic killings of prisoners of war with the aid of exhaust fumes (in camps such as Belzec, Chelmno and elsewhere), as well as extensive killing of patients in German mental hospitals using gas showers in chambers set up in vans, acted as catalysts for the conceptual combination of pest control and the execution of human beings with hydrogen cyanide gas.

At this relatively advanced stage in the explication of atmospheric background realities through technologically assisted terrorism, the Hitler factor comes into play as an escalating element. There can scarcely be any doubt that the utmost exterminist escalation of German "Jewish policy" after 1941 was conveyed using the imagery of vermin, which, since the early 1920s, had been a central component of the Nazi Party rhetoric developed by Hitler, and rose from 1933 on to become a virtually official language convention in the forcibly coordinated German public sphere. The pseudo-normalizing effect of the term *Volksschädling*[34] ("public menace," covering a broad semantic area including defeatism, trafficking, jokes about the Führer, criticism of the system, inadequate faith in the future or internationalist convictions) was partly responsible for the nationalist movement's success in popularizing their idiosyncratic form of excessive anti-Semitism, or at least making it acceptable or imitable on a wide scale, as a specifically German variety of supposed hygiene. At the same time, the imagery of vermin and parasites also featured in the rhetorical ammunition of Stalinism, which produced the most comprehensive politics of camp terror without reaching the extremes of SS "disinfestation" practices.

At the heart of the industry of gas chambers and crematoria at Auschwitz and other camps lay, unmistakably, the enacted metaphor of "pest control." The phrase "special treatment" referred primarily to the direct application to human populations of procedures for wiping out insects. The practical execution of this metaphorical operation extended to the use of the most common "disinfestation" agent, Zyklon B, and to the fanatically analogous implementation of the widespread gas chamber method. In the extreme pragmatism of the executioners, the psychotic enactment of a metaphor merged almost seamlessly with the professionally indifferent carrying-out of procedures.

Holocaust research has rightly recognized the fusion of rampage and routine as the operational hallmark of Auschwitz. That Zyklon B, according to witness accounts, was often brought to the camps in Red Cross vehicles corresponds both to the hygienicizing and medicalizing tendency of the operations and to the perpetrators' need for secrecy. In the professional journal *Der praktische Disinfektor*, Jews are described by a military doctor as being almost the sole "disease carriers"—almost a conventional statement in the wider context of the time, but against the specific background a thinly veiled threat. An aphoristic diary entry from November 2 of the same year by the Reich Minister of Propaganda, Joseph Goebbels, confirms the stable association between the entomological and political fields of ideas: "The Jews are the lice of civilized humanity."[35] The entry shows that Goebbels communicated with himself like an agitator before a crowd. Like stupidity, evil is autohypnotic.

In January 1942, two gas chambers were constructed and "put into operation" in a converted farmhouse (known as "Bunker I") on the grounds of the Auschwitz-Birkenau camp. It soon became clear that a greater capacity was required; further facilities were quickly added. In the night of March 13, 1943, a total of 1,492 Jews from the Krakow ghetto who were "unfit for work" were gassed in Morgue I of Crematorium II at Auschwitz; using 6 kg of Zyklon B resulted in the concentration recommended by Degesch for de-lousing, c. 20 g of hydrogen cyanide per cubic meter. In the summer, the cellar of Crematorium III was equipped with a gas-proof door and fourteen fake shower heads. In the early summer of 1944, technical progress came to Auschwitz with the installation of an electric shortwave de-lousing system for work clothes and uniforms, developed by Siemens. In November, Reichsführer-SS Heinrich Himmler ordered the gas killings to cease. According to the lowest serious estimates, three quarters of a million people had fallen victim to the treatment by that time; the real numbers are likely to be higher. In the winter of 1944–45, camp troops and inmates were busy removing the traces of the gas-terrorist installations before the arrival of Allied forces. The companies Degesch (Frankfurt), Tesch & Stabenow (Hamburg) and Heerdt-Lingler (Frankfurt), which had delivered their products to the camps in cognizance of their application, recognized the necessity of destroying business records.

2. Increasing Explicitness

Through this information about the atmoterrorist procedures of the gas war (1915–1918) and about genocidal gas exterminism (1941), the outlines of a special climatology emerge. In this field, the manipulation of breathing air becomes a cultural matter, albeit initially only in the most destructive areas. From the start, it shows the hallmarks of design approach in which varyingly definable microclimates of death are designed by humans for humans and created *lege artis*. This "negative air conditioning" offers insights into the process of modernity as an explication of atmospheres. Atmoterrorism provided the decisive modernizing impulse for those areas of human sojourn in "lifeworld" conditions—the areas with a natural connection to the atmosphere and the detachment of those who inhabited and traveled in an unquestionably given air milieu they could blithely take for granted—that had been able to resist the transition to modern views the longest. Until then, average human being-in-the-world—likewise a modern explicatory name for the ontological "situation" after the loss of Old European certainties about the world—had so assuredly and self-evidently been a being-in-the-air, or more precisely a being-in-the-breathable, that an extensive thematization of air and atmospheric conditions could, if at all, appear in poetic forms or in physical and medical contexts, but certainly not in the everyday self-relationships of cultural participants, let alone in the definitions of their life form. One possible exception was the far-sighted intuitions of the untimely cultural theorist Johann Gottfried Herder, who, in his inexhaustible *Outlines of a Philosophy of the History of Man*, postulated a new science of "aerology" as early as 1784, as well as

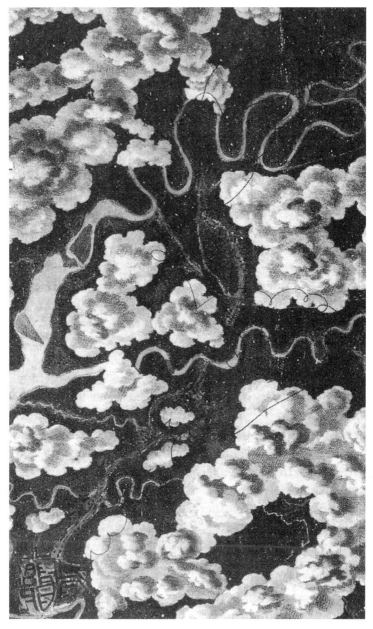

Thomas Baldwin, *Airopaidia* (1786), detail: view from the balloon above the clouds

a general study of the atmosphere as the exploration of the life-harboring "air sphere": "for man, like everything else, is a pupil of the air." If only, Herder cried out, we had an academy that taught such disciplines, we would gain a new understanding of the connection between nature and the cultural being that is man, and would be able to "see this great hothouse of nature operating a thousand changes by the same fundamental laws."[36]

These lines remind us that Herder was the force behind a large-scale anthropology in this century; here he will not be cited, once again, as the originator of the precarious doctrine of the deficient nature of humans,[37] but as the initiator of a theory of human cultures as forms of organization for existence in hot-houses. Nonetheless, his philanthropic anticipations, which float eutonically above the opposition of nature and culture, could not yet grasp the dialectical or thematogenic connection between terrorism and background explication. Even Nietzsche's well-known hypersensitivity to anything concerning climatic conditions of existence such as air pressure, moisture, wind, clouds and more or less immaterial tensions still belongs to the last twilight of an Old European faith in nature and atmosphere, albeit in a broken form. In a fit of humor, Nietzsche even recommended himself as a possible exhibit at the Paris electricity exhibition of 1881 on account of his abnormal atmospheric sensitivity—as a pataphysical voltmeter, so to speak.[38] However: what air, climate, breathing milieu and atmosphere mean in the micro- and macroclimatological sense, and all the more in culture- and media-theoretical terms, can only be learned by going through the modes and stages of exterminist-atmoterrorist practices in the twentieth century—though it is already apparent that the twenty-first is advancing to new forms of explicitness.

Airquake: as air, climate and atmospheric conditions become explicit, the primal advantage of those who exist over the primary medium of existence is challenged and exposed as naïve. Whenever in their history humans have been able to step into the open or under a roof in any given climate, relying on an unquestioning assumption of breathability with reference to the air around them—excepting miasmic zones—they made use, as one sees in retrospect, of a privilege of naïveté that was irretrievably lost with the advent of the twentieth century. Anyone living after this caesura and operating in a cultural zone synchronized with modernity is condemned to veritable climatic concern and atmospheric design, whether in rudimentary or elaborated forms. They must admit their willingness to participate in modernity by submitting to its explicatory power over what was once inconspicuously under-"lying" or environmentally surrounding-encompassing.

Before the new duty of concern for the atmospheric and climatic could become stable in the consciousness of those born later, a few further stages in the explication of atmoterrorism had to be completed. Here is an opportunity to speak in philosophical terms of the development of the modern *air force*,[39] whose name declares its responsibility for interventions in atmospheric facts. In our context it must be made clear that air weapons as such constitute a central phenomenon of atmoterrorism in its nationalized form. Military aircraft, like rocket artillery later on, act primarily as access weapons; they negate the immunizing effect of the spatial distance between army groups and force access to objects that could scarcely be reached on the ground, or only with great losses. The question of whether or not the combatants are natural neighbors thus

The start of bomb warfare: manual dropping from the air (1914)

becomes secondary. Without the explosion in range through airborne weapons, the globalization of war via teledestructive systems would be inexplicable. Because of their use, a large part of specific exterminism in the twentieth century can be classed as a form of black meteorology. This theory of man-made special precipitations will address the exploitation of the air space with flying machines and their employment for atmoterrorist and para-artilleristic assignments.

While the forms of gas terrorism manifest between 1915 and 1945 consistently operated on the ground (with the exception of the Rif War in Spanish Morocco from 1922–1927, which marked the first instance of aerochemical warfare),[40] thermoterrorist and radioterrorist attacks on enemy lifeworlds virtually always depend on air force operations for technical and tactical reasons. After the shocking attacks of German aircraft on Guernica on April 26, 1937 and Coventry in the night of November 14, 1940, it is above all the destruction of Dresden on February 13 and 14, 1945 by British bomber fleets and the annihilation of Hiroshima and Nagasaki on August 6 and 9, 1945 using two single atomic bombs dropped by American fighter planes that remain the paradigmatic examples of this. Historically, skirmishes between equally powerful groups of aircraft were usually of marginal significance, however much they occupied imaginations with tournament scenes performed by knights of the air; the notorious Battle of Britain was an exception in military history. Rather, in the domain of aerial combat, it was *de facto* the practice of one-sided, unreciprocable air strikes in which either individual aircraft carried out precision attacks on defined targets or larger fleets were deployed for carpet bombing, the latter analogous to the logic of imprecision with gas artillery: in operational terms, being close enough was as good as being accurate. What must always be taken as given is the modern exterminist approach, where victory means annihilation—air force, artillery and asepsis all follow analogous paths of development in this respect. The metaphor of the bomb carpet first invoked in the 1940s encapsulates the phenomenon in a suggestive image: extensive segments of built-up and inhabited landscapes are given a lethal floor covering by attacking air squadrons. As the NATO air strikes against Serbia in the Kosovo affair between March 24 and June 10, 1999 demonstrated, however, precision bombings can also result in the destruction of entire areas if the target density is sufficiently high.

However amenable air forces may be to a military-romantic interpretation of their functions, and however discreetly they present themselves as a neo-aristocratic branch of the armed services—the continuation of the royal branch of artillery in a freer medium, one could say—they are, in their practical tendency, the preferred organ of state-decreed atmoterrorism.[41] This confirms that state control of weapons, far from being an antidote to terrorist practices, rather effects their systematization. As the principle of terror is inherent in weapons as such, there can no longer be symmetry between attack and defense; the extermination of the attacked, whether persons or things, is intended *a priori* (but because exterminism is not allowed to appear in the self-descriptions of Western political structures, and must only serve to characterize enemy mindsets, no images showing the aftermath of American air strikes have been permitted since Operation Desert Storm, for the liberation of Kuwait, in 1990–91). That the air forces have risen to the leading weapon systems since the Second World War, especially in the numerous wars of intervention by the USA since 1945, merely testifies to the normalization of the state terrorist habitus and the ecologization of warfare.[42] When air force-based state terrorism sets the tone, the mass elimination of civilian life is taken on board; not infrequently, the alleged side effect (collateral damage) transpires as the main result. From this perspective, the demonstrations by Serbian civilians, who stood on Branko's Bridge (over the River Save) decorated as targets in the spring of 1999, was an apt commentary on the reality of aerial warfare in the twentieth and twenty-first centuries.

The warfare of state air forces—as the experiences of the Second World War in Europe and the Far East, as well as others,

Civilians on Branko's Bridge over the Sava River, Belgrade

have shown—generally applies the habitus of the assassin, as the *modus operandi* of air strikes is always that of an ambush. In addition, even when carried out as precision strikes against "facilities," they always incorporate the damaging of enemy lifeworlds, and hence *eo ipso* the risk of civilian deaths; in area attacks, this becomes the primary intention. It is no secret that the generalized "terror bombing" over the territory of the German Reich from 1940–1945 was not directed purely at military structures, but even more at the mental infrastructure of the country; that is why, because of its supposed morale-breaking effect—some spoke of "moral bombing"—it had to be defended from internal criticism among the Allies, not only from pacifists. Two entire generations would pass before military historiography could dare to explain the systematic character of the will to annihilate that motivated British and American aerial warfare on German cities.[43]

The bombing of Dresden in the night of February 13, 1945 by two Lancaster bomber fleets of the Royal Air Force followed a pyrotechnical conception whereby the flammable old city center was surrounded and strewn with a dense ring of explosive and incendiary bombs in a quadrant-shaped sector. This was intended to create a blast furnace effect over the entire area; the attackers were concerned to unify the multitude of individual fires into a total fire, the possible annihilating power of which they had established after first tests over other flammable old towns, such as those of Hamburg in July 1943 (in Operation Gomorrah) and Kassel in October of the same year. Through the great compaction of stick-type incendiary bombs, they aimed to create a central vacuum exerting a hurricane-like pull. This procedure for the systematic stoking of the firestorm—corresponding to a "principle of closed zones of annihilation"[44]—had been declared a potentially war-deciding means by the British Air Chief Marshal Arthur Harris. The desired effect in Dresden was prepared by the first bombing between 10:03 and 10:28 pm and consolidated by the second wave of attacks between 1:30 and 1:55 am, which advanced the firestorm and caused its spread to large areas of the city, especially that around the central train station, which was crowded with evacuees. The third wave of attacks, by American fleets, came down on a city already devastated. The first two attacks saw the dropping of 650,000 individual bombs, including some 1,500 tons of mines and high explosive bombs and around 1,200 tons of incendiary bombs, dropped in a fine scattering like raindrops.[45] The high proportion of incendiary bombs showed that the primary objective was the annihilation of civilian life. The assailants knew that if their concept was executed as planned, the result in a city flooded with refugees from the east would

"On the way to the goal—incendiary and explosive bombs falling earthwards onto the Nazi rail hub at Bruchsal on March 1, 1945"

inevitably result in a great number of civilian deaths. Churchill was willing, at least, to term himself a terrorist.

The success of the undertaking manifested itself in, among other things, the fact that numerous people locked inside the furnace were found dehydrated, shrunken and mummified without having come into direct contact with flames. Because of stack effects, some places of shelter were transformed into convection ovens whose inmates were boiled alive; for over 12,000, the cellars became smoke-filled gas traps. The history of applied terror before August 6, 1945 barely contains any examples of how conditions like those in a combustion chamber on a high setting could be created in a "lifeworld" as large as a city's historic district; it reached temperatures of over 1,000° Celsius. In a single night, according to the lowest estimates, 35,000 people (in fact, probably over 40,000) could be burned, carbonized, dried and suffocated: this constituted an innovation in the field of mass rapid killings.[46] Though it can be viewed as the culmination of a series of war-conditioned singularities, the night of fire in Dresden gave birth to the new archetype of extensive thermoterrorism: what took place was a thoroughly planned large-scale attack on the thermic boundary conditions of life. It was the most explicit negation of the most implicit expectation: that human being-in-the-world cannot possibly mean a being-in-fire.

It was one of the no-longer-surprising surprises of the twentieth century that this maximum proved surpassable. The explication of the atmosphere via terror did not stop at converting "lifeworlds" into gas and fire chambers. To go beyond the horrors of Churchill's furnaces, it required no less than a "world picture revolution," or more precisely—since realizing the falsity of the talk of "revolution"—an even wider unfolding of what keeps the world together in its physical and biospheric latency. A recapitulation of the shared history of nuclear physics and the nuclear weapon would be superfluous here. In the present context, it is significant that the explication of radioactive matter through nuclear power and its popular demonstration in nuclear mushrooms over arid testing grounds and inhabited cities simultaneously unlocked a new level of depth in the explication of the humanly relevant atmospheric realm. This resulted in a "revolutionary" reordering of "environmental" awareness towards the invisible milieu of waves and rays. In the light of this, a recourse to the classical clearing in which we "live, move and have our being"—whether one reads it theologically or phenomenologically—can no longer achieve anything. The (post-) phenomenological commentary on the nuclear flashes over the Nevada Desert and the two Japanese cities is this: making radioactivity explicit.

The dropping of the nuclear bombs on Hiroshima and Nagasaki not only quantitatively surpassed the events in Germany—the simultaneous eradication of (according to the most conservative estimates) over 100,000 plus 40,000 human lives[47] was the provisional culmination of the atmoterrorist explication process; at the same time, the nuclear explosions of August 6 and 9, 1945 advanced the escalation in qualitative terms because they made the transition from the thermoterrorist to the radioterrorist dimension. The radiation victims of Hiroshima and Nagasaki, who joined the heat victims of the first seconds and minutes not much later—and in countless cases with a delay of years or decades—rendered explicit the realization that human existence is embedded in a complex atmosphere of waves and rays whose reality is revealed to us at most by certain indirect effects, but not by any immediate perceptions. The direct emission of a dose of radioactivity that was acutely or chronically lethal to humans and released "behind" the primary thermic and kinetic effects of the

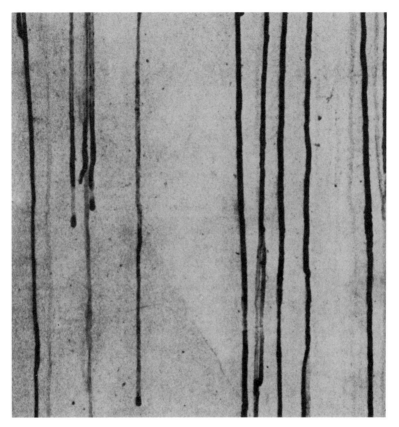

Black rain, which fell on Nagasaki and was highly radioactive (photograph: Yuichiro Sasaki).

bombs tore open an entirely new dimension of latency in the knowledge of the injured and the witnesses.

Long-concealed, unknown, unconscious, never-known, never-noticed and never-noticeable things were suddenly forced into the level of manifestation; they became conspicuous indirectly in the form of peeling skin and sores, as if an invisible fire was causing visible burn wounds. The faces of the survivors

The "mask of Hiroshima": a young woman searching for her family in Hiroshima

mirrored a new form of apathy: the "masks of Hiroshima" stared at the remains of a world that had been taken away from those caught in the storm of light; it was returned to them as a contaminated desert. These faces comment on the imposition that is being, at its dark limit. After the black rain over Japan, the nameless evil manifested itself for decades in cancerous growths of all kinds and the deepest of psychological scars. Until 1952, any public reference to the two acts of terror in Japan was forbidden by the American censors.[48]

These events show a dimensional growth in terrorist action: the nuclear attack on the enemy's lifeworld henceforth includes the terrorist exploitation of latency as such. The imperceptibility of the radiation weapon becomes a central part of the weapon's actual effect. Only after contamination does the enemy understand that they were existing in an atmosphere not only of air, but also of waves and rays. Nuclear extremism, even more than chemical extremism, which uses gas and fire, is the emergency of atmospheric explication.

With the step of nuclear explication, the phenomenal disaster becomes a disaster of the phenomenal. The advance of the physicists and the military informed by them to the radioactive level of environmental influence made it clear: there could be something in the air that the blithely breathing, naïvely context-sensitive worldlings of the pre-nuclear era, the time-honored human "pupils of the air," were unable to notice. From this caesura onwards, the coercion to expect the imperceptible was imposed on them like a new kind of law. In future one would have to distrust one's own perceptions in order to survive in toxic environments. The mode of thought and experience of the paranoids becomes part of general education—"Only the Paranoid Survive";[49] anyone who keeps up with the facts must feel stalked by the probability that the harmful wishes of distant foes will invisibly materialize.

The bioterrorists (as well as their simulators and parasites), in state and non-state contexts, also operate in the newly defined latency. They incorporate the dimension of the imperceptibly small into their calculus of attack and threaten the enemy's environment with invisible assailants. In the dimension of bio-atmospheric terrorism, Soviet military researchers in the 1970s and 80s made the most explicit advances. Among its primary scenes were the experiments with the tularemia pathogen carried out in 1982 and 1983, in which hundreds of monkeys specially imported from Africa were fastened to posts

Drawing by a survivor of the nuclear bombing of Hiroshima: the man lying in the street on his back was killed directly after the dropping of the bomb. His hand was stretched to the sky, the fingers burning with blue flames. Drops of dark liquid fell from the hand to the ground.

on a publicly inaccessible island in the Aral Sea. The subsequent dropping of newly developed tularemia bombs provided the researchers with the satisfying result that almost all test animals, though vaccinated, died within a short time of inhaling the pathogens.[50]

If Martin Heidegger often spoke in his essays after 1945 of "homelessness" as the existential watchword of humans in the age of enframing [*Ge-stell*], this referred not only to the lost naïveté of residing in country houses and the transition to existence in urban living machines. At a deeper level, the term "homeless" refers to the expatriation of humans from their natural air shell and their move to air-conditioned spaces; in an even more radical reading, the discussion of homelessness symbolizes the exodus from all possible niches of security in latency. After psychoanalysis, not even the unconscious was any longer usable as a home; after modern art, the same was true of "tradition"; and after modern biology, "life" was scarcely an option either—to say nothing of the "environment." After Hiroshima, the spectrum of these breakthroughs towards a-patrial existence included the forced revelation of the radiophysical and electromagnetic dimensions of the atmosphere. Dwelling was replaced by sojourns in radiotechnically guarded areas. The physicist Carl Friedrich von Weizsäcker, who was familiar with Heidegger's work, memorialized this when, at the height of the nuclear arms race between the USA and the Soviet Union in the 1970s, he demonstratively had a radioprotective shelter built under his house near Starnberg.

We have reason to doubt that Heidegger's evocative words on the "dwelling" of humans in a "region" [*Gegend*] that enables and calls upon them can remain the last word in matters of an existence that is now forced to explicate itself and its mission of self-development. When the philosopher praised the calm sojourn in the "region," he leapt forwards a little too quickly to the ideal of a reintegrating space with old and new implications.[51] "Region" here is the name for a zone in which an authentic existence could still succeed. It would be difficult to say how one

Nuclear fallout shelter, installation by Guillaume Bijl (1985), Place St. Lambert, Liège

might reach it if not already residing there. It would have to be a place passed over by explication, as if it only applied elsewhere; a place that had been touched by the cold wind of the outside, the locational risk of modernization, yet remained a home. Its inhabitants would know that the desert was growing—and yet they could, precisely in the place where they were, feel indebted to a wondrously immunizing "expanse" [*Weite*] and "abiding-while" [*Weile*].[52] One could speak here of high idyllics. Nonetheless, one cannot deny that the "region," for all its provisionality and provincial connotations, has an indicative force pointing to the therapeutic dimension in the art of space formation.[53]

Magdalena Jetelová, *Atlantic Wall* (1994–1995)

What is therapeutics but the procedural knowledge and the art of knowledge about the reestablishment of suitable human measures after the irruption of the measureless—an architecture for habitats after the demonstration of the unlivable? Where I part ways with Heidegger is in the historically developed and theoretically stabilized conviction that in the age of background explication, even conditions based on "region" and home, where they still succeed locally, cannot simply be accepted as gifts of Being, but rather depend on great efforts of formal design, technical production, legal support and political molding.

With these references to the unfolding, initiated by gas warfare (and reinforced by industrial smog), of the question of the conditions for the breathability of the air, then to the gas-terrorist and thermoterrorist escalations of the Second World War, and finally the explosive exposure of the radiological background dimension to human being-in-the-world, which must be constantly thematized after the events of Hiroshima and Nagasaki, I have traced a historical arc of increasing explicitness in the problematization of the human sojourn in gas and radiation milieus. A retrospective such as the one attempted here should not be taken as claiming that the history of atmospheric explication through the perfecting of nuclear weapons reached its conclusion with the end of the Cold War. After the disappearance of the Soviet Union, the last remaining world power acquired a monopoly for expanding the continuum of atmoterroristm elaborated from 1915–1990 into even more explicit and monstrous dimensions. The end of the Cold War may have put an end to nuclear intimidation; as far as the inclusion of previously undeveloped climatic, radiophysical and neurophysiological background dimensions of human existence in military projects of the world power are concerned, however, the threshold of the 1990s was more of a new beginning. From that point on, virtually unnoticed by the public, a leap to an unpredictable level in the escalation of chances for atmoterrorist intervention took place.

In a paper presented by the Department of Defense on June 17, 1996 and not classified, despite its sensitive subject matter, seven officers outlined a future ionospheric warfare to a scientific research department at the Pentagon. The project paper, presented under the title "Weather as a Force Multiplier: Owning the Weather in 2025,"[54] was commissioned by the Air Force General Staff to state the necessary conditions for the United States to assert its role as the absolutely dominant power in air and space weapons by 2025. The paper's authors assumed that within a thirty-year development period, it would be possible to make the ionosphere controllable, as one of those components of the earth's outer physical shells that are invisible to humans, in a way suitable for war—primarily through the willful production and termination of stormy weather conditions, which would guarantee "battlefield dominance" for the owner of the ionospheric weapon. According to present anticipations, the areas covered by the weather weapon are the maintenance or reduction of visibility in the air space; raising and lowering of the comfort levels (morale) of troops; reinforcement and modification of storms; denial of rainfall over enemy territories and creation of artificial aridity; intercepting and preventing enemy communications and obstructing analogous weather activities by the enemy.

With the explication of these new parameters for operative interventions of the military in the "battlespace environment," the possible future state of "battlefield shaping" and "battlefield awareness" is already planned for today. That is why the paper's summary states the following:

> A high-risk, high-reward endeavor, weather-modification offers a dilemma not unlike the splitting of the atom. While some segments of society will always be reluctant to examine controversial issues such as weather-modification, the tremendous military capabilities that could result from this field are ignored at our own peril.[55]

With these words, the authors not only make clear that they espouse the development of such weapons even in opposition to public opinion; they place themselves within a cultural environment that is only capable of anticipating a single type of war: military confrontation between the USA and "rogue" states, or states that tolerate or support military or terrorist actions against the civilizatory complex of the "West." Only in this context is the promotion of a future meteorological weapon and the entrance into an escalation of atmoterrorist practices compatible with a highly legislation-based cultural situation with an extreme sensitivity to duties of justification. A stable moral asymmetry between American warfare and any potential non-American warfare is built into the premises of weather weapons research: under no other circumstances could the investment of public funds in the construction of a technologically asymmetrical weapon of clear terrorist character be justified. To give democratic legitimacy to atmoterrorism in its advanced form, one must presuppose a concept of the enemy that renders the deployment of suitable means for its ionospheric special treatment plausible. In the American way of war, fighting the enemy also entails their punishment, as no one but manifest criminals can still be imagined as harboring armed hostility towards the United States. This standard has applied since the Cold War, in fact, during which Moscow was persistently termed the "world-base of all terrorism."[56] Hence the declaration of war is, in practice, replaced by an arrest warrant or writ of execution for the enemy. Whoever has the prerogative of interpretation to declare those fighting for a foreign cause terrorists systematically shifts the perception of terror from the methods to the beliefs of the opposing group, thus removing themselves from the picture. From that point on, warfare becomes indistinguishable from summary execution. The anticipated victor's justice is carried out not only through warfare that has been declared a disciplinary measure; it also occurs as arms research against the foes of tomorrow and the day after.

Beyond the declared interest in the weather weapon, however, the USA began work in 1993 on a related but secret program

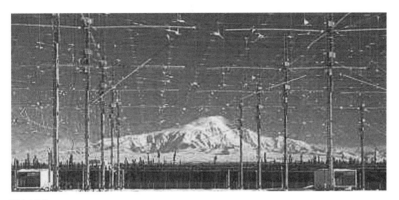

HAARP project, antennae

to investigate the aurora: the High-Frequency Active Auroral Research Program (HAARP), which could be used to derive the scientific and technological premises for a potential super wave weapon. When they cannot avoid facing the public, advocates of the program emphasize its civil character, for example its possible use for recreating the defective ozone layer and preventing whirlwinds, while its critics—not many in number—see such information as the typical camouflage for top secret military plans.[57] The HAARP project relies on a research facility in Gakona, South Central Alaska, some 300 kilometers northwest of Anchorage, consisting of a multitude of antennae that produce high-energy electromagnetic fields and radiate them into the ionosphere. By using its reflective and resonant effect, the intention is to focus energy fields above any given point on the earth's surface; emissions of this kind could be used to create an almost unlimitedly effective energy artillery. The technical premises of this facility come from the ideas of the inventor Nikola Tesla (1856–1943), who drew the American government's attention to the military possibilities of a long-range energy weapon as early as 1940.

If a system of this kind could be implanted, it would be capable of creating tremendous physical effects—extending to the production of climate disasters and earthquakes in chosen target areas. Some observers have claimed connections between the tests at the facility in Alaska and erratic blizzards and fog in Arizona, as well as other inexplicable weather phenomena in various parts of the world. As ELF (Extremely Low Frequency) waves or infrasound waves not only influence inorganic matter, however, but also living organisms—especially the human brain, which works in low frequency ranges—HAARP offers prospects of producing a neurotelepathic weapon that could destabilize human populations through long-range attacks on their cerebral functions.[58] It goes without saying that a weapon of this kind, even at a speculative level, could only be conceived if the moral asymmetry between the brains developing it and the brains to be fought with ELF waves seemed indisputable in the present and remained stable in the future. Even in the case of a non-lethal weapon, it could only be used against human incarnations of the quintessentially alien or of absolute evil. It cannot be ruled out, however, that participation in such research enterprises *per se* would entail moral complications that are disastrous for the ascertaining of such an asymmetry. If the distinction between rogue brains and non-rogue brains is blurred, the production of a wave weapon against one side of this difference could—as already evident with nuclear weapons—also have dire results for the other side through self reference.

One might consider it surrealistic to mention such prospects; it is no more surrealistic, however, than announcements of a gas weapon before 1915 and a nuclear weapon before 1945 would have been. Before the event proved that the development of nuclear weapons was a reality, most educated people in the western hemisphere would have dismissed it as a form of scientifically disguised occultism and completely denied its plausibility. The surreality effect of the real before publication is one of the side effects of progressive explication, which has always split society into a smaller group of people who participate in the breakthrough to the explicit as thinkers, operators and victims, and a different, far larger group that maintains the position of being allowed to exist in the implicit *ante eventum*, reacting to explications at best afterwards and in isolated cases. Public hysteria is the democratic response to the explicit once it has become undeniable.

The everyday sojourn in latency becomes increasingly restless. Two forms of sleepers appear: sleepers in the implicit, who continue to search for security through ignorance, and sleepers in the explicit, who know what is planned at the front and wait to be called into action. Atmoterrorist explication tears the consciousnesses of a single cultural population (whether one calls them a people or a population has long ceased to matter) so far apart that they *de facto* no longer inhabit the same world, only forming a single society in terms of citizenship. It turns one side into employees of explication, and thus—at constantly changing sections of the front—agents of a structural, albeit only rarely current terror against the background conditions of nature and culture, while the others—transformed into inner aborigines, regionalists and voluntary curators of their own untimeliness— reside in fact-free reservations with the advantage of being allowed to cling to world pictures and symbolic immune conditions from the age of latency.

3. Air/Condition

Among the offensives of modernity, that of surrealism in particular heightened the realization that the explication of culture must be the main interest of the present day. Culture is here understood—following ideas from the work of Bazon Brock, Heiner Mühlmann, Eugen Rosenstock-Huessy, Ludwig Wittgenstein, Dieter Claessens and others—as the inclusive concept of rules and mandates for action that are passed on and varied in processes between generations.

Surrealism obeys the imperative to occupy the symbolic dimensions of the modernization campaign. Its declared and undeclared goal is to make creative processes explicit and technically unlock their source regions. To this end, it immediately introduces the fetish of the epoch, the universally legitimizing word "revolution." As already in the political space (which has *de facto* never been concerned with an actual "rotation" in the sense of a reversal of above and below, but rather the proliferation of top positions and their restaffing with representatives of aggressive middle classes—which, in reality, was not possible without a partial increase in the transparency of power mechanisms, in other words democratization, and rarely without an initial phase of open violence from below), the misnomer for these processes is also evident in the cultural field. For here, it has likewise never been a matter of "upheaval," only of the redistribution of symbolic hegemony—which required a certain disclosure of artistic procedures; that is why, in this area too, there had to be a phase of barbarisms and iconoclasms. In the context of culture, "revolution" is a codeword for "legitimate" violence towards latency. It enacts the break of the new operators, who are sure of their methods, with the holisms and cozinesses of bourgeois art situations.

A reminder of one of the most well-known scenes from the surrealist offensive can perhaps explain the parallel between the atmoterrorist explications of climate and the culture-"revolutionary" attacks on the mentality of a bourgeois art audience. On July 1, 1936, Salvador Dalí—who was at the start of his career as the self-appointed ambassador from the realm of the preternatural—gave a performance-lecture at the New Burlington Galleries in London, on the occasion of the International Surrealist Exhibition, in which he intended to expound, with reference to his own exhibit, the principles of the "paranoiac-critical method" he had developed. To make it clear to his audience through his very appearance that he was speaking in the name of the other-worldly and as a representative of a radical elsewhere, Dalí had decided to wear a deep-sea diving suit for his address. According to the report in the London *Star* of July 2, the cooling plate from a car radiator was mounted above the helmet; the artist was holding a billiard cue in one hand and had two large dogs accompanying him.[59] In his self-portrayal *Comment on devient Dalí* [How One Becomes Dali], the artist relates a version of the incident that resulted from this idea:

> I had decided to make a speech at this exhibit, but from inside a deep-sea diver's suit, to symbolize the subconscious. I was put into the outfit, even including the leaden shoes that nailed me to the spot. I had to be carried up to the stage. Then the helmet was screwed and bolted on. I started my speech behind the glass facepiece in front of a microphone which picked up nothing. But my facial expressions fascinated the audience.

Dalí in a diving suit at his London lecture on July 1, 1936

Soon they saw me open-mouthed, apoplectic, then turning blue, my eyes revulsed. No one had thought of connecting me to an air supply and I was yelling out that I was asphyxiating. The specialist who had the suit on me was nowhere to be found. I gesticulated in such a way as to make friends understand that the situation was becoming critical. One of them grabbed a pair of scissors and tried in vain to cut a vent in the fabric, another tried to unscrew the helmet and, when that did not work, started banging at the bolts with a hammer. My head pounded like a ringing bell and my eyes teared with pain. I was being pulled and pushed every which way. Two men were trying to force the mask off, while a third kept striking blows that knocked me out. The stage had turned into a frenzied melee from which I emerged as a disjointed puppet in my copper helmet that resounded like a gong. At this, the crowd went wild with applause before the total success of the Dalinian mimodrama which in its eyes was a representation of the conscious trying to apprehend the subconscious. I almost died of this triumph. When finally they got the helmet off I was as pale as Jesus coming out of the desert after the forty-day fast.[60]

The scene makes two things clear: Surrealism is amateurish when it uses technical objects symbolically rather than on their own terms; at the same time, it is part of the explicitivist movement of modernity, because it presents itself unambiguously as a latency-breaking and background-dissolving method. An important aspect of background-dissolution in the cultural field is the attempt to destroy the consensus between producers and recipients in the art world in order to liberate the radical intrinsic value of the showing events. It explicates both the absoluteness of production and the willfulness of reception.

Such interventions possess combat value as clarifications directed against provincialism and cultural narcissism. It was not for nothing that the Surrealists developed the art of confusing the bourgeois as a form of action *sui generis* in the early phase of their attack wave—firstly, because it helped the innovators to distinguish between the in-group and the out-group, and secondly, because public protest could be taken as a sign of success in dismantling the traditional system. Whoever scandalizes the bourgeois declares allegiance to progressive iconoclasm. They use terror against symbols in order to break open positions of latency and reach a breakthrough with more explicit techniques. The legitimate premise of symbolic aggression lies in the assumption that cultures have too many skeletons in their closets, and that

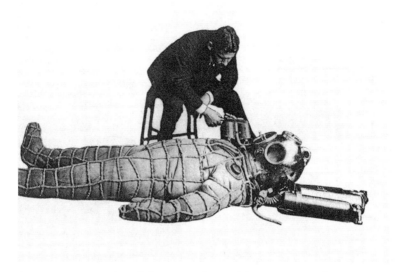

Dräger pressure suit (1915) for treating forms of decompression sickness

the time has come to blast open the latency-protected connections between armament and edification.

If the early avant-gardists fell prey to a fallacy nonetheless, it was the notion that the bourgeoisie they were meant to shock always learned its lesson much more quickly than any of the aesthetic bogeymen had foreseen. After a few turns between the provocateurs and the provoked, a situation inevitably came about in which the mass-culturally loosened bourgeoisie took the lead in the explication of art, culture and meaningfulness through marketing, design and self-hypnosis. The artists dutifully continued shocking, without registering that the time for this method had passed. (Semantic terrorism loses effect as soon as the audience understands its role; the same would also happen to criminal and military terror if the press retired from its role as accomplice.) Others were subject to a neo-Romantic turn and allied themselves once more with depth. Soon many seemed to have forgotten Hegel's precept for modern philosophy, which analogously applies to aesthetic productions: that the depth of an idea is measured alone by its capacity to be comprehensive—otherwise the claim to depth remains but an empty symbol of unmastered latency.

These findings can be verified using Dalí's failed performance, which was informative precisely in its failure: firstly, it proves that the destruction of the consensus between the artist and the audience cannot succeed once the latter has understood the rule that the expansion of the work to encompass its own surroundings must itself be read as the work's form. The enthusiastic applause Dalí received at the New Burlington Galleries illustrated how consistently the informed public followed the new contracts for art perception. Secondly, the scene showed the artist as a latency-breaker bringing the profane masses a message from the realm of otherness. Dalí's function in this game was characterized by an ambiguity that offers substantial insight into his fluctuation between Romanticism and objectivity: on the one hand he presents himself as the cool technologist of the other, for he intended in his speech, whose text has not survived but can easily be extrapolated from the title of the lecture—"Authentic Paranoiac Fantasies"—to speak of an exact procedure that made access to the "unconscious" controllable: the same paranoiac-critical method with which Dalí formulated strict instructions for the "conquest of the irrational."[61] He pledged himself to a sort of photorealism dealing with irrational images that was meant to objectify, with the precision of an old master, what had presented itself in dreams, deliria and inner observation. In a sense, the Surrealist artist is the secretary of a private beyond, producing a record of its dictations as mechanically and precisely as possible; the work consequently represents an archive of visions. Like Picasso, Dalí does not seek—he finds. And here, finding means putting on file the form that rises from the unconscious.

At that time, Dalí, like Breton and others before him, already viewed his work as a parallel campaign to what was termed the "discovery of the unconscious through psycho-analysis"—the scientific myth absorbed by many among both the aesthetic avant-gardes and the educated audience in the 1920s and 30s (and which Lacan, Dalí's admirer and rival, put back on the map between the 50s and the 70s by reanimating the Surrealist lecture form for a "return to Freud"). From this perspective, Surrealism locates itself among the manifestations of the operativist "revolution" that carries continuous moderniza-tion. On the other hand, Dalí clung in decidedly anti-critical fashion to the Romantic conception of the ambassador-artist who walks among the unilluminated as the delegate of a meaning-laden realm beyond. With this posture he exposes himself as an imperious amateur who embraces the illusion of being able to use advanced technical devices to articulate metaphysical kitsch events. This is exemplified by the user attitude, which childishly leaves the technical side of performance to "specialists" without verifying their competence. The lack of rehearsal before the appearance also betrays the artist's negatively literary approach to technical structures.

Nonetheless, there is a lucid aspect to Dalí's choice of outfit. His accident is prophetic—not only in the audience's reactions, which heralded applause for the uncomprehended as a new cul-tural habitus. That the artist had selected a diving suit reliant on an artificial air supply for his appearance as an ambassador from the deep connects him directly to the development of atmospheric consciousness that, as I attempt to show here, is at the center of cultural self-explication in the twentieth century. Even if the Surrealist only arrives at a semi-technical interpretation of the global and cultural background as a "sea of the subconscious," he postulates a competence to navigate this space with professional procedures. His performance illustrates that conscious existence must be lived as conscious context-diving. Anyone in the multi-milieu society who ventures outside of their own camp must be sure of their "diving gear," that is to say, their physical and mental immune system or social space capsule. (Marshall McLuhan wrote in the early 1960s that modern man had turned into a "frogman of the mind"—a statement that can be read as a commentary both on intercultural surfing and space travel.)[62] The accident should not be attributed to amateurism alone; it also exposes the systemic risks of atmospheric explication via technology and forced access to the other element via technology—just as the risk of poisoning one's own troops in gas warfare was already inseparable from the actions of military atmoterrorism. If Dalí's description of the incident is not an exaggeration, then he came close to going down in the cultural history of modernity as a martyr of dives in the symbolic realm.

Under the given circumstances, the accident proved its worth as a form of production. In the artist, it released the panic that had always been an inherent motor of their work. With the failed attempt to present the "subconscious" as a navigable zone, the fear of annihilation that the explication process had been set in motion to control and repress broke through to the surface. The contra-phobic experiment of modernization can never emancipate itself from its background of fear, because the latter could only manifest itself if fear could be admitted to existence as itself—which, by the nature of things, is the ruled-out hypothesis. Modernity as background explication remains trapped in a phobic circle; by striving to overcome fear through fear-producing technology, it must always fall short of its goal. Primary and secondary fear both provide the decisive boost for the continuation of the futile process; its urgency justifies the further use of latency-breaking and background-controlling violence—or, to use the dominant language conventions: it demands foundational research and innovation in permanence.

Aesthetic modernity is a procedure of applying violence neither to persons nor things, but rather to unclarified cultural circumstances. It organizes a wave of attacks on holistic attitudes like faith, love and moral rectitude, and on pseudo-evident categories like form, content, image, work and art. Its *modus operandi* is the live experiment on users of such terms. Consistently enough, aggressive modernism breaks with reverence for the classics, which, as it notes with great aversion, usually displays a vague holism—combined with a tendency to continue following a whole that is left to stand as inexplicable and undeveloped. It is with this sharpened will to explicitness that Surrealism declares war on the ordinary: it recognizes it as the opportune hiding-place for the anti-modern inertias that resist the operative development and reconstructive disclosure of folded-up precepts. Because normality is considered a crime in this war of mentalities, art—as a medium of crime fighting—can invoke unusual commands to action. When Isaac Babel declared, "banality is the counterrevolution," he indirectly uttered the principle of modernist "revolution": the use of terror as violence against normality breaks open both aesthetic and social latency and brings those laws to the surface which determine the construction of societies and works of art. Terror serves the completion of the anti-naturalist turn, which asserts the primacy of the artificial in all areas. The permanent "revolution" wants permanent terror, for it postulates a society that continually proves itself anew as a shockable, revisable one. In the *Second Manifesto of Surrealism* of 1930, André Breton writes:

> The simplest Surrealist act consists of dashing down into the street, pistol in hand, and firing blindly, as fast as you can pull the trigger, into the crowd.[63]

The new art is steeped in the arousal of the newest because it makes its appearance in terror-mimetic and war-analogous fashion—often without being able to say whether it is declaring war on the war of societies or a war of its own. The artist must constantly decide whether to advance against the public sphere as a savior of differences or a warlord of innovations. They must also explain to themselves whether they agree with the law of imitating the superior, which previous culture was built upon, or should rather join the neo-barbaric habitus of modernity in elevating the imitation of the defeated to the rule.[64] In the light of these ambivalences, what we call "postmodernity" was not entirely wrong when it articulated itself as a counter-explicit, counter-extremist and partially anti-barbaric reaction to the aesthetic and analytical terrorism of modernity.

Like all terrorism, the aesthetic variety too attacks the unmarked background against which works of art articulate themselves and lets it appear on the front stage as a phenomenon in its own right. The prototype of modern painting exhibiting this tendency, Kasimir Malevich's *Black Square* of 1913, owes its inexhaustible interpretability to the artist's decision to evacuate the pictorial space in favor of a pure dark surface. Thus its being-square itself becomes the figure which, in other pictorial situations, it underlies as a carrier. The scandal of the work is, among other things, that it asserts itself as a painting in its own right rather than simply passing the empty canvas off as something worth seeing, as would have been imaginable in the context of Dadaist art-mockery actions. It may be that the picture can be viewed as a Platonic icon of the equilateral quadrangle that pays tribute to sensuality through a minimal irregularity; at the same time, however, it is the icon of the aniconic—of the usually invisible background of a picture. That is why the black square is set off against a white background that places itself around it as a manner of frame; in *White Square* of 1914, even this difference would be almost eliminated. The basic gesture of such form-presentations is an elevation of the athematic to the thematic. The possible manifold forms of images that could appear in the background are not degraded to a single, eternally unchanging background; rather, the background as such is carried out with care and thus made explicit as the figure of the figure-carrier. The terror of purification in the longing for the "supremacy of pure feeling" is unmistakable. The work demands the unconditional capitulation of the viewer's perception to its real presence.

However clearly supremacism, with all its anti-naturalism and anti-phenomenalism, shows itself as an offensive movement on the aesthetic flank of explication, it remains indebted to the idealistic assumption that explication means attributing things sensually present to intellectual things that are not present. It is

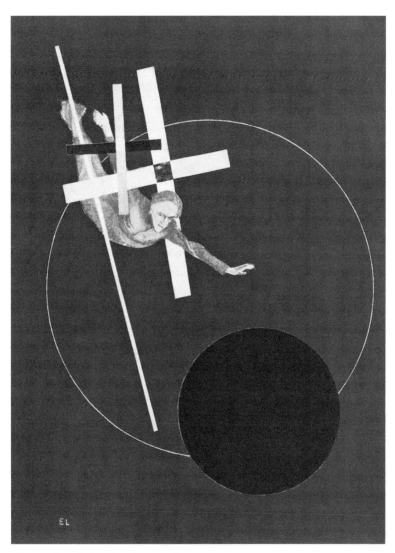

El Lissitzky, *Black Spheres* (1921–22)

tied to Old European dictates to the extent that it explains things upwards and reduces empirical forms to pure primary forms. This was not the case in Surrealism, which solidarized more with materialist explication downwards—without going so far as letting itself be called "sousrealism." While the materialist tendency remained a flirtation for the Surrealist movement, its alliance with depth psychologies, especially those of the psychoanalytical variety, revealed a unique trait. The Surrealist reception of Viennese psychoanalysis is one of numerous cases showing that Freudianism achieved its early successes among artists and members of the educated classes not as a therapeutic method, but rather as a strategy for sign interpretation and background manipulation that gave anyone interested the freedom to apply it in accordance with their own needs. Do we not tend to be most impressed by the psychoanalysis we did not undergo?

Freud's approach led to the unfolding of a special type of latency area that was given a name taken from the Idealist philosophy of Schelling, Schubert, Carus and the nineteenth-century philosophies of life, especially Schopenhauer and Hartmann: the "unconscious." It marked out a subjective dimension of non-unconcealment by bringing up inner latencies and invisibly folded preconditions for egotic states. Once edited by Freud, the term's meaning was greatly limited and sufficiently specialized to be suitable for clinical operationalization; it now referred no longer to the reservoir of dark, integrating forces in a potentially salvific and image-creating nature prior to consciousness, nor the substratum of blindly self-affirming streams of will beneath the "subject." Rather, it circumscribed a small inner container filled up by acts of suppression and subjected to neurosis-creating tension through the force of what is being suppressed.[65] The enthusiasm of the Surrealists for psychoanalysis came from their confusion of the Freudian concept of the unconscious with that of Romantic metaphysics. This creative misreading produced such proclamations as Dalí's "Declaration of the Independence of the Imagination and the Rights of Man to His Own Madness" of 1939, which contains lines such as these:

> A man has the right to love women with ecstatic fish heads. A man has the right to find lukewarm telephones disgusting and demand telephones as cold, green and aphrodisiacal as the sleep of Spanish flies, haunted by faces.[66]

The Surrealist assertion of the right to madness warns individuals of their tendency to submit to normalizing therapies; it seeks to turn ordinarily unhappy patients into monarchs who return from exile in neuroses of reason to the realm of their most personal delusions.

The fact that Dalí's performance in July 1936 ended with his helpers enabling him to return to the shared atmosphere of the London gallery by tearing off his diving helmet, though a reasonable solution in individual cases, is useless for the situation of civilization as a whole because the process of atmospheric explication permits no return to what could formerly be implicitly presupposed. The circumstances of technological civilization no longer permit the decisive aspect to be forgotten as it was in Dalí's experiment: people who momentarily or habitually stay in decidedly indoor situations must be connected to a supporting "air supply system." Advanced atmospheric explication forces sustained attention to be directed towards the air's breathability—

initially in the physical sense, then increasingly with reference to the metaphorical dimensions of breathing in cultural spaces of motivation and concerns.

After the end of the twentieth century, the doctrine of *homo sapiens* as a pupil of their air took pragmatic shape. People began to understand that humans not only are what they eat, but also what they breathe and what they dive into. Cultures are collective states of immersion in sounding air and sign systems.

The theme of the cultural sciences in the transition from the twentieth to the twenty-first century is therefore "making air conditions explicit." They practice pneumatology with an empirical approach: the science of ventilating meaning-dependent life forms through informative and imperative milieus. This program can currently only be dealt with through reconstruction and collection, for the "matter itself," the universe of influenced climates, shaped atmospheres, modified airs and calibrated, measured and juridified environments, has an almost insurmountable headstart on the formation of culture-theoretical concepts after the extremely advanced waves of explication in the scientific, technical, military, legislative-juristic, architectural and creative spaces. It therefore seems most prudent for theory to follow the most expanded forms of atmospheric description in science, namely meteorology and climatology, in a first phase of self-assurance before devoting itself to more culturally and humanly relevant air and climate phenomena in a second step.

Modern meteorology (which was given this name in the seventeenth century, based on the Greek *metéoros*, "floating in the air")—the science of "precipitations" and all other bodies that flash in the sky or float above—imposed, through its most successful publicistic form, the "weather report" (*informations*

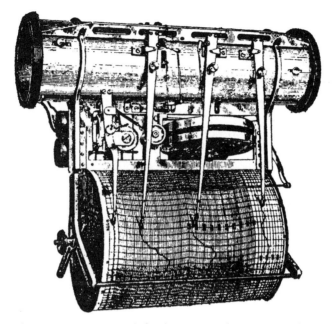

The Marvin Meteorograph for the U.S. Weather Bureau in the 1890s

météorologiques, Wetterbericht), a historically new form of conversation on the populations of modern nation-states and political media communities that is best termed a "climatological briefing." Modern societies are weather-discussing communities to the extent that an official climate information system uses the prevailing weather conditions to put the topics of social self-understanding in the citizens' mouths. Through media-assisted weather communication, large-scale modern communities with millions of members are transformed into village-like neighborhoods in which people exchange comments on how it is too hot, too cold, too rainy or too dry for the time of year. By telling national populations to compare their personal perception with the briefing and form an opinion about ongoing events, modern weather reporting molds them into spectators at a climate theater. By describing the weather as a performance given by nature for society, meteorologists gather people to form an audience of connoisseurs under a shared sky; they turn each individual into a climate reviewer who evaluates nature's current presentations according to their personal taste. In periods of bad weather, stricter climate critics fly in droves to regions where there is an adequate likelihood of a more pleasant performance— which is why Mauritius and Morocco are flooded with weather dissidents from Europe between Christmas Eve and Epiphany.

As long as meteorology presents itself as a natural science and nothing else, it can afford to leave out the question of the weather's originator. Viewed in the context of nature, climate is something that purely makes itself and incessantly processes itself from a given state into the next. Here it is enough to describe the most important climate "factors" in their dynamic effects on one another: under the influence of solar radiation, the atmosphere (gas shell), the hydrosphere (water world), the biosphere (animal and plant world), the cryosphere (ice region) and the pedosphere (mainland) develop extremely complex patterns of energy exchange that can be represented with a purely scientific stance without reference to any initially planning or later intervening intelligence.[67] An adequate analysis of these processes proves so complex that it forces the development of a new type of physics capable of dealing with unpredictable currents and turbulences. This chaos-theoretically upgraded weather physics likewise requires no recourse to a transcendent intelligence; it requires neither a global weather-maker of animist provenance nor the world watchmaker of deism to interpret its data. It stands in the tradition of occidental rationalism, which, from the start of the

Modern Age onwards, gave leave to any possible God previously responsible for weather phenomena and elevated him to supra-climatic zones. While Zeus and Jupiter hurled thunderbolts, the God of modern Europeans was a *deus otiosus* and *eo ipso* climatically inactive. The modern weather report can therefore present itself as a regional-ontological discipline that deals with causes, but not creators. It speaks of what, before any consideration of human concerns, happens the way it happens, of its own accord and on its own terms, and which is at most "mirrored" in a subjective medium as a datum of objective rank.

Nonetheless, modern meteorology is allied with a progressive subjectification of the weather, in several ways: firstly, because it increasingly relates climatic "circumstances" to the statements, calculations and reactions of populations who are becoming ever less indifferent to their atmospheric surroundings with regard to projects of their own; and secondly, because the regional and global objective climate must increasingly be described as an effect of the forms of life in industrial societies. The two aspects of this orientation of the weather towards modern humans as weather clients and weather co-instigators are closely connected. Certainly, from the perspective of older traditions, weather reporting as we know it must already have seemed like temptation to blasphemy; for it stirs humans unmistakably to the impertinence of having an opinion on a matter which, in keeping with metaphysical orthodoxy, one should merely accept in mute submission. For the ancients it was clear that like birth and death, the weather comes from God alone. In tradition, abandonment to God and abandonment to the weather are analogous indications of the willing subject's effort to minimize its hubristic difference from fate.

Even so, the modern tendency to form an "opinion" about the climate is not merely a subjective whim that deviates from a valid norm of being and is best avoided; it mirrors the fact that the polytechnically active European and Caucasian cultures themselves became climate powers from the early eighteenth century onwards. Since then, people have encountered—however indirectly—the atmospherically objectified emissions of their own industrial-chemotechnic, military, locomotive and tourist activities. Taken together, these, through many billions of micro-emissions, not only change the atmospheric balance of energy, but also the composition and "mood" of the whole air mantle. Hence the coercion to have an opinion about the climate is not so much a sign of a takeover of an anthropocentric despotism over everything that is the case in the environment. It prepares the change of basic stance that makes humans turn from supposed "lords and owners" of nature into atmospheric designers and climate wardens—not to be confused with Heidegger's guardians of Being.

In the macro-realm, the challenge of the climatic power of judgment among modern humans lies above all in a phenomenon that became known in the public debate as the anthropogenic greenhouse effect. This refers to the cumulative effects of climate-modifying emissions from human cultural and technical activities such as the running of power plants, industrial complexes, private heating, automobiles, airplanes and countless other ways of passing exhaust fumes and vapors into the surrounding air. This secondary greenhouse effect, of which we have taken notice in a diffuse form for barely two hundred years, and in an explicit formulation for just under three decades, is a historical fact that expresses itself in the energy-consuming style of the "industrial age": it is the climatic trace of a civilizatory project that rests on easier access to large amounts of fossil fuels through coal mining and oil production.[68] Access to fossil energy is the objective crutch of the frivolity without which there would be no consumer society, no automobilism and no global market for meat or fashion.[69] In the unfolding of mass demand for high-energy carbon substances, the "subterranean forest" of the Paleozoic Era is lifted to the earth's surface in solid and liquid form and converted by heat engines.[70] Consequently, the combustion product carbon dioxide (alongside methane, carbon monoxide, chlorofluorocarbons, various nitric oxides and others) quantitatively plays the most important part in enriching the atmosphere with second-order greenhouse factors. They reinforce—in almost certainly disastrous fashion—the primary greenhouse effect, without which, as climatologists cannot emphasize enough, no life would ever have become possible on our planet. The reason why the earth, a parasite of the sun—it draws a little under a billionth of the energy radiated by the sun to itself—became the birthplace of life was that water vapor and greenhouse gases in the earth's atmosphere impede the reflection of the short-wave energy from the sun in the form of long-wave infrared radiation; this enabled a warming of the earth's surface to a mean temperature of 15° Celsius, which was compatible with life. If the heat trap keeping that solar energy in the atmosphere were to fail, the earth's surface temperature would reach no more than an average of -18°: "Without the greenhouse effect, the earth would be a sprawling ice desert."[71] Life as we know it depends on the fact that the earth's surface lives some thirty-three degrees beyond its means. If humans are, to quote Herder once again, pupils of the air, the clouds were their tutors. Life is a side

Partial view of the air conditioning system in the basement of the Fondation Beyeler Museum in Rieten, near Basel, by Renzo Piano (1997)

effect of climatic pampering. The age of fossil energy shows its signature in the fact that the pampered became reckless enough to jeopardize their pampering by taking the risk of anthropogenic overwarming (or, going by different calculations, an interglacial period).[72]

Long before such far-reaching macroclimatological insights took scientific shape and received a public response, the power of climatic judgment among modern cultural participants was called upon by fairly small-scale and local phenomena—air conditioning in houses and apartments, which only became convivial islands of warmth through artificial fireplaces; the cooling effect of cellars, which permitted the storage of food and drink; the miasmic air quality of public spaces near cemeteries, knackeries and cesspools;[73] and the precarious atmospheric state of numerous workplaces such as weaving mills, mines and quarries, where organic and mineral dust led to severe pulmonary diseases. Between the eighteenth and twentieth centuries, these source areas of all manner of microclimatic air anomalies gave rise to the design-assisted "discovery of the obvious" that motivated people in the age of explication to reach a second time for what was self-evident. These fields saw the development of the concrete atmotechnics without which modern forms of existence would be unimaginable in both urban and rural contexts: the popularization of the formerly luxurious and aristocratic sunshades and umbrellas;[74] the construction of heating and ventilation systems in private houses and large-scale architectures; the artificial regulation of temperature and humidity in recreation rooms and warehouses; the installation of refrigerators in apartments and the introduction of fixed or mobile cooling chambers for food transportation and storage; the air hygiene policy for work environments in factories, mines and office buildings,[75] and finally the aromatechnic modification of the atmosphere that completed the transition to aggressive air design.

Air design is the technological answer to the belatedly recorded phenomenological insight that human being-in-the-world is always and without exception a modification of being-in-the-air. Because something is always in the air, the idea of placing it there oneself as a precaution suggested itself in the course of atmospheric explication. As soon as the human dependence on air is formulated in a fundamental tone, it demands a corresponding emancipation. It calls for and achieves the active reshaping of the element.

This is where the technical path diverges from that of the phenomenologists, who have only recently begun striving to explicate the human sojourn in overall atmospheric circumstances with the resources of a radical art of description. On this path, Luce Irigaray has even suggested bracketing Heidegger's concept of the clearing and replacing it with a mindfulness of air—airing rather than clearing.

> It is not light that creates the clearing, but light comes about only in virtue of the transparent levity of air. Light presupposes air.[76]

The author cannot emphasize enough how much air is a condition of existence that lies hidden in the unthought and unnoticed—but she barely takes into account that aerotechnic practice, including atmoterror, has long declared this supposedly unthought domain an operational area for highly explicit procedures. As a phenomenologist, she clings to the fondly held illusion that a matter has only become explicit once it has been thematized by philosophers trained in Husserlian methods. In reality, technicians were at work a hundred years earlier to take practical control of the supposedly unthought. This confirms the suspicion that on the threshold of the phenomenal world, a mode of thought which remains phenomenological for too long becomes a form of inner water color painting, finally fading away in untechnical contemplation.

By contrast, air design "faces" the air with an attitude of practical strength. It replaces the hygienically motivated, defensive stance of concern for "air monitoring," subordinating the thematized air to positive objectives—one could say that it suggests the continuation of private perfume usage by public means. Air design undoubtedly aims for mood modification among users of the air space, thus serving the declared purpose of binding air passers-by to a place through pleasant, odor-induced situational

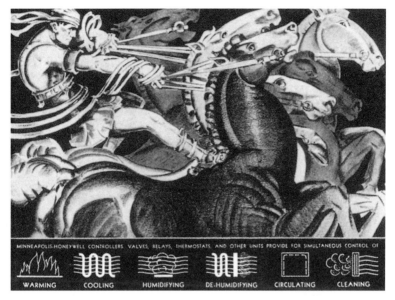

An advert for air conditioning (1934) promises control over the six indoor climate factors: warming, cooling, humidifying, de-humidifying, circulating and cleaning.

impressions and eliciting an increased product affirmation and willingness to buy.[77] The point-of-sale atmosphere becomes the center of attention as an "independent marketing tool." Commerce—especially in the field of "experience shopping"—fights to bind the customer affectively to the salesroom and the product range through an active indoor air quality policy. The legal assessment of such subliminally invasive methods to produce a "psychological compulsion to buy" is contentious. If customers interpret their "forced odorization" as an attempt to manipulate them, aversive reactions are natural and attested—in other cases, well-chosen olfactory shadings of the sales environment are perceived as welcome aspects of a comprehensive concept of client care. Through the modeling of breathing environments with psychoactive designer air—especially in shopping malls, but also clinics, trade fairs, conference centers, hotels, adventure worlds, health and wellness areas, passenger compartments and the like—the principle of interior design expands to include that otherwise imperceptible milieu of life, the gas and aroma environment. The benchmarks for such interventions can be deduced from empirical observations on the "olfactory pleasantness" of air space users. It thus becomes known that complex "olfactory ranges" are preferable to "mono-fragrances." The first commandment of the new odor ethics is that indoor essence supplements must not be used to conceal negative smells or pollutants behind an olfactory mask. The sub-trend towards an "odor-hedonistic society"[78] integrates itself into the primary trend in consumer society towards a development of experience markets and "scenes" in which atmospheres are made available as composite situations of stimuli, signs and chances for contact.[79]

Let us not forget that what we call consumer and experience society today was invented in the greenhouse—in those glass-roofed arcades of the early nineteenth century in which a first generation of experience customers learned to inhale the intoxicating fragrance of a closed inner world of commodities. The arcades constituted an early stage of urbanist atmospheric explication—an objective eversion of the "dwelling-addicted" disposition which, in Walter Benjamin's view, had seized the nineteenth century. Addiction to dwelling, Benjamin says, is the irresistible urge to "[fashion] a shell for ourselves."[80] Benjamin's theory of the interior already combined the "timeless" need for uterus simulation with the symbolic forms of a concrete historical situation. The twentieth century, admittedly, showed with its

100 Years of Air Conditioning: 1880–1980

1880:   The dining room of a New York hotel on Staten Island is cooled by passing air over ice.

1889:   Alfred R. Wolff, an American engineer, cools New York's Carnegie Hall using air blown over ice blocks. This procedure is not successful, however, because the humidity is too high. A pipeline cooling system is installed in the subways of London, Paris, New York, Boston and other large American cities.

1890:   The "great ice shortage" resulting from a mild winter leads the American ice industry to adopt mechanical cooling methods.

1904:   For the first time, a large crowd of people can enjoy the advantages of air conditioning in the Missouri pavilion at the St. Louis World's Fair.

1905:   Stuart Cramer, an American textile engineer, coins the term "air conditioning," while the Carrier company uses the slogan "manufactured weather."

1906:   Carrier acquires the first patent for a "device for treatment of air."

1922:   Carrier develops a centrifugal chiller, the first practicable method for air-conditioning large spaces.

1928:   Carrier manufactures the first air conditioning system for private homes, the "weathermaker."

1950:   After television sets, air conditioning systems display the second-largest growth in all industrial sectors.

1955:   5 percent of all American households have an air conditioner. The American government calls for the installation of air conditioning systems in state buildings.

1979:   President Carter declares an energy emergency and orders that the air temperature in state and commercial buildings go no lower than 78° Fahrenheit.

1980:   55 percent of all American households own an air conditioner.

Shopping center in Camden, New Jersey, designed in 1961 by Victor Gruen

large-scale edifices how far the construction of "shells" was driven beyond the needs of the search for a habitable interior. The large-scale containers and collectors[81] of the present day, be they office blocks or shopping malls, stadiums or conference centers, were increasingly freed from the task of simulating homeliness; the occasional encounter between the department store and the greenhouse which, with ingenious exaggeration, Benjamin believed to be the signature of modernity, had to collapse once more with the progressive differentiation of architectural forms. We still lack a study that does for the twentieth century what *The Arcades Project* had in mind for the nineteenth. With everything we know about the period today, such a work would have to be entitled *The Air Conditioning Project*.

The year 1936 features in the history of aesthetic and culture-theoretical atmospheric explication not only because of Salvador

Dalí's London accident in the diving suit; on November 1 of the same year, the thirty-one-year-old writer Elias Canetti gave a celebratory speech on Hermann Broch's fiftieth birthday in Vienna that was unusual in both content and tone; in it, he not only painted a deep portrait of the author being honored, but almost founded a new genre of laudation. The originality of Canetti's speech lay in the unprecedented way in which he posed the question of an author's connection to their era. Canetti defines the artist's sojourn in a time as a breathing connection— as a special mode of immersion in the atmospheric conditions of the present. He sees Broch as the first grandmaster of a "poetry of the atmospheric as something static"[82] (today one would speak of an immersive art); he credits him with the ability to render visible the "static breathing space," or, in our terminology, the climate design of persons and groups in their typical spaces.

> [His] involvement is always with the entire space in which he is present, with a kind of atmospheric unity.[83]

Canetti praises Broch's ability to view all people ecologically, as it were: in every person he recognizes a singular existence in its own breathing air, surrounded by an unmistakable climatic shell, integrated into a personal "respiratory economy." He compares the writer to an inquisitive bird that has the freedom to slip into all sorts of cages and take "air samples" back from them; gifted with a bafflingly alert air and "respiratory memory," it thus knows how it feels to be at home in this or that atmospheric habitat. Because Broch approaches his characters more as a poet than a philosopher, he does not describe them as abstract ego-points in some universal ether; he portrays them as embodied figures, each living in its own particular air shell and moving between a multitude of atmospheric constellations. Only with regard to these multiplicities does the question of whether a literature is possible "which takes its form from respiratory experience" lead to any fruitful insight:

> We would have to reply, above all, that the multiplicity in our world consists to a large extent in the multiplicity of our breathing-spaces. The room you are sitting in here, in a very definite arrangement, almost totally cut off from the world around us, the way each person's breath mixes into an air common to all of you... all those things, from the breather's standpoint, are a totally unique... situation. But then, go a few steps further and you will find a completely different situation of another breathing space... The big city is as full of such breathing-spaces as of individual people. Now none of these people is like the next, each is a kind of cul-de-sac; and just as their splintering makes up the chief attraction and chief distress of life, so too one could also lament the splintering of the atmosphere.[84]

In this characterization, Broch's storytelling rests on the discovery of atmospheric multiplicities: through them, the modern novel moved beyond the portrayal of individual fates. It no longer deals with individuals in their actions and experience, but rather the expanded union of the individual with breathing space—and the interweaving of several such spaces in foam-like aggregates. The plots no longer take place between people, but between respiratory economies and their inhabitants. This ecological view changes the foundations on which the alienation-critical motif of modernity rests: it is the atmospherically separate nature of humans that causes their enclosure in their own respective "respiratory economies"; their inaccessibility to the differently minded, differently enclosed and differently air-conditioned reveals itself as more justifiable than ever. The fracturing of the social world into mutually inaccessible zones of willfulness is the moral analogue to the microclimatic "splintering of the atmosphere" (which, according to the author, corresponds to a splintering of the "world of values"). Because Broch, having progressed to the individual-climatic and personal-ecological level, had almost systemically pinpointed the isolation of modern individuals, the question of the conditions for their unification in a shared ether beyond the splintering of the atmosphere had to confront him with a clarity and urgency unparalleled either in his own time or at any later moment in the history of sociological studies on the element of social cohesion—with the possible exception of Canetti's related approach in *Crowds and Power*.

In his 1936 speech, Canetti identifies Hermann Broch as the prophetic figure warning of an unprecedented threat to humanity from the atmospheric, in both the metaphorical and the physical sense:

> However, the greatest of all dangers ever to emerge in the history of mankind has chosen our generation as a victim.
>
> It is the defenselessness of breathing, which I would like to talk about in conclusion. One can hardly form too great a notion of it. To nothing is a man so open as to air. He moves in it as Adam did in Paradise... Air is the last common property. It belongs to all people collectively. It is not doled out in advance, even the poorest may partake of it...

And this last thing, which has belonged to all of us collectively, shall poison all of us collectively...

Hermann Broch's work stands between war and war, gas war and gas war. It could be that he still somewhere feels the poisonous particles of the last war... What is certain, however, is that he, who knows how to breathe better than we do, is already choking on the gas that shall claim our breath—who knows when?[85]

Canetti's emotive reflection shows how the information about gas warfare between 1915 and 1918 had been conceptually translated in the 1930s by the most intense analyst of his time: Broch had realized that after the intentional destructions of the atmosphere in chemical warfare, social synthesis itself took on the character of gas warfare in some respects, as if atmoterrorism had turned inwards. The "total war" heralded by chemical particles and political indications would inevitably take on the character of an environmental war, in which the atmosphere itself became a theater of war—more still, the air would become a form of weapon and a battlefield of its own kind. And beyond this: from the jointly breathed air, the ether of the collective, the delirious community would henceforth wage the poison war against itself. How this could happen would have to be clarified by a theory of "states of somnolence" [Dämmerzustände]—undoubtedly the most original, albeit most unfinished part of Broch's mass-psychological hypotheses.

States of somnolence are states in which humans move about as trend-followers in the trance of the normal. Because the imminent total war would essentially be waged atmoterroristically and ecologically (and thus in the medium of total mass communication), it affects the "moral" of the troops, who can hardly be distinguished from the population anymore. Combatants and non-combatants, the simultaneously gassed and the simultaneously aroused, are kept together in a collective state of somnolence by toxic communions. The modernized masses find themselves integrated into an emergency-communist unit that is meant to give them an acute sense of identity through a common threat. What transpires as particularly dangerous are the climate poisons emanating from the affected themselves as long as they stand, hopelessly aroused, under closed communication domes: in the pathogenic air conditioners of standardized and aroused public spheres, the inhabitants keep inhaling their own exhalations. Here, what is in the air is put into it through totalitarian circular communication: it is filled with the injured masses' dreams of victory and their intoxicated, far from empirical self-elevations, which are followed, as if by a shadow, by the longing to humiliate their opponents. Life in the media state is a sojourn in a gas palace animated by experiential poisons.

From 1936 onwards, Broch's views were not only based on the expectation of a new world war close ahead, one which the author assumed would be waged primarily as a universal mutual "gassing";[86] even more importantly, they came from the socio-theoretical diagnosis that mass-medially integrated modern large-scale societies had entered a phase in which day-to-day existence had come under the atmospheric and political domination of mass-psychological mechanisms. That is why the *Theory of Mass Delusion* had to become the focus of all analysis of the period; starting in 1939, Broch worked on it over an entire decade.

The constant communications from the press and the radio have been the carrier and agent of delusions in modern collectives since the 1920s. The great majority of them act as media of disinhibition in which slogans come true. The self-poisoning of "society" through mass communication is a phenomenon whose inception Broch's older contemporary Karl Kraus had persistently observed, and whose unfolding he had fought throughout his life—Kraus only gave up the fight against the "air from Sodom"[87] four months before his death in February 1936, in the last issue of *Die Fackel*. Let us note that he had invoked the tensions in Europe in the image of the worst atmospheric pollution already in 1908: "Everywhere is filled with the gases coming from the muck of the universal brain, culture cannot catch its breath."[88]

It would be an understatement if one described the effects of such media with the secularly faded, missionary-theological term "propaganda." Their aim is the immersion of entire national populations in strategically created battle climates; they are the informatic analogue of chemical warfare. Broch's theoretical intuition grasped the parallel between gas warfare, as the attempt to wrap the enemy in a poison cloud dense enough to bring about their physical annihilation, and the creation of states of mass delusion, as the attempt to immerse the population in an ecstatic atmosphere overloaded with longing for "supersatisfactions" and sufficient to bring about their self-destruction. Both cases involve cloakings that trap their victims or dwellers in a presently inescapable overall relationship: the propagandistically nationalized atmosphere temporarily functions as a "closed system"; the space of air and signs places itself trance-inducingly around its denizens as a zone of prescribed possession. Under the totalitarian dome of signs, people inhale the lies of their own that have become public opinion, moving about voluntarily yet unfreely in an opportunistic hypnosis. On the inside of such toxic atmospheres, individuals are even more emphatically recognizable as what they would still be under freer circumstances: "sleepwalkers" who move as if remote-controlled in the "social daydream"[89] of their organizations. In this scenario, journalists are assigned the role of anesthetists who ensure the stability of the collective trance. One can assume that Broch's images contain an echo of Gabriel Tarde's theses on social sleepwalking. ("I shall not seem fanciful in thinking of social man as a veritable somnambulist.")[90] The socialized sleepwalkers, equipped with their fictions of freedom and their imaginary critiques, gather under slogans and flags like co-owners of castles in the air. Canetti articulated this in a different context:

> Flags are wind made visible. They are like bits cut from clouds... Nations use them to mark the air above them as their own, as though the wind could be partitioned.[91]

In Broch's theory, intuitions with this tendency give rise to the beginnings of a new kind of atmospheric ethics whose "hygienic" part deals with the prevention of being carried away, and whose "therapeutic" part deals with bringing those seized by intoxication back into the livable rationality of an "open system"—also known as democracy, or the separation of powers into panics and hysterias.[92] Measured against the task of such an ethics of the atmospheric, it was not only the democracies of 1939 that lived in "yesterday's world";[93] even today, they are entirely blind to their acute tendency to develop closed atmospheres and aggrandize systems of victorious delusion—as if the political-psychological and moral lessons of the twentieth century had only been taught in empty classrooms.[94]

Marcel Duchamp, *Paris Air* (1919)

Marcel Duchamp spent the Christmas of 1919 with his family in Rouen. On the evening of December 27, he wanted to board the SS *La Touraine* in Le Havre and travel to New York. Shortly before his departure he went to a pharmacy in the Rue Blomet, where he persuaded the chemist to take a medium-size phial off the shelf, pour out the liquid it contained, and then close the bulbous vessel again. In New York he gave the empty phial, which he had stored in his luggage, to the collector couple Walter and Louise Arensberg as a gift, explaining that because his wealthy friends already had everything, he had wanted to bring them 50 cubic centimeters of *Air de Paris*. And so it happened that a volume of French coastal air found its way into the list of first ready-mades. Duchamp was evidently unconcerned that his ready-air object was a fake from the start, as it was filled not with air from Paris, but from a pharmacy in Le Havre; the act of naming outweighed the object's true origin. Nonetheless, the "original" was dear to him; when a neighborhood boy accidentally shattered the phial of *Paris Air* in Arensberg's collection in 1949, Duchamp obtained the same phial from the same pharmacy through a helpful friend in Le Havre.[95] Ten years later, Duchamp said in an interview in a New York hotel lobby: "Art was a dream that became unnecessary [...] I spend my time very easily, but I wouldn't know how to tell you what I do [...] I'm a *respirateur*—a breather."[96]

4. World Soul in Agony, or:
The Emergence of Immune Systems

Modernity's campaign against the supposedly self-evident realm once termed "nature" caused the air, the atmosphere, culture, art and life to come under a pressure of explication that fundamentally changed the mode of being of these "givens." What was background and saturated latency has now, with thematic emphasis, been transferred to the side of the envisioned, the concrete, the worked-out and the producible. With terror, iconoclasm and science, three latency-breaking powers moved into position whose effects cause the data and interpretations of the old "lifeworlds" to collapse. Terror explicates the environment in terms of its vulnerability; iconoclasm explicates first nature with regard to its replaceability by prosthetic devices and its integrability into technical procedures; and systems theories explicate societies as constructs that see their own vision and are blind to their own blindness.

Encompassing relationships, which could usually be experienced in the mode of devotion, participation, and communion without ulterior motives, were moved by explication into the concrete mode of givenness of the technically doable and the technically done, without people consequently being able to terminate their sojourn in these "circumstances" or "media." Distrust may grow; we are immanent in the suspicious. We are condemned to being-in, even if the containers and atmospheres that we must allow to surround us can no longer be taken for granted like good natures.[97]

These circumstantial totalities, which we cannot leave, but which we cannot simply trust anymore either, were termed "environments" from the early twentieth century onwards—a term that was introduced into the discourse of theoretical biology by Jakob von Uexküll in 1909, and has since then followed the confusing career that occasionally awaits pseudo-evident concepts.[98] The realization that life is always already life in an environment—and thus also against an environment and in opposition to many foreign environments—triggers the perpetual crisis of holism. The disposition of early humans to let oneself be captured by totalities of closeness, as if they were benevolent local gods, lost its benchmark status once the surroundings themselves became, or were recognized as, constructs. In the age of poisons and strategies, leaning quasi-religiously on the primary around oneself—whether called nature, cosmos, creation, situation, culture, home or whatever—would seem like temptation to self-endangerment. Advanced explication forces naïveté to change its meaning—more still, it makes it become increasingly conspicuous, even offensive; now, whatever invites people to sleepwalk amid present danger is naïve.

When one has become aware of the first and second greenhouse effects, living and breathing under an open sky can no longer mean what they meant in earlier times. From the immemorial homeliness of mortals in the open air, something uncanny, uninhabitable and unbreathable has set itself apart. With the appearance of the environmental question, human habitation in the primary milieu becomes increasingly problematic. Since Pasteur and Koch revealed the existence of microbes and established it in scientific publications, human existence must find explicit measures for symbiosis with the invisible—and more: for a prevention of and protection against the now precisely positioned microbic competitors. After the massive gas attacks of the Germans and the devastating counterstrikes of the Allies in 1915, the breathable air had lost its innocence; from 1919 onwards it could be given away in portions as a ready-made, and from 1924 onwards it could bring death to delinquents as execution air. After the forcible coordination of national presses during a world war, civil communication is completely exposed; the signs themselves are as if soiled, compromised by their participation in bellicistic deliria and psychosemantic arms races. Thanks to critiques of religion, ideology and language, large parts of semantic environments are designated as intellectually unbreathable zones—from that point, the only responsible choice would be to reside in spaces that have been pumped dry by analysis, refurnished and opened for critical-mobile inhabitation. The Mona Lisa also smiled differently once Duchamp had given her a moustache.

In this situation, immune systems become a central theme. If everything could be latently polluted and poisoned, everything potentially deceptive and suspicious, then whole and being-able-to-be-whole can no longer be derived from external circumstances. Integrity can no longer be envisaged as something gained through devotion to something benevolently enveloping, only as the individual contribution of an organism that actively sees to its separation from the environment. This allows the idea to unfold that life is determined not so much by opening and participation in the whole as by self-closing and a selective refusal to participate. For the organism, the largest part of its social surroundings is poison or meaningless background; it therefore settles in a zone of strictly selected objects and signals that can now be articulated as its own circle of relevance—in short, its environment. It is no exaggeration to call this the basic principle of a postmetaphysical or differently metaphysical civilization. Its psychosocial trace manifests itself in the naturalism shock with which biologically self-enlightening culture learns to shift from a phantasmatic ethics of universal, peaceful coexistence to an ethics of antagonistic interest preservation among finite units—a learning process in which the political system made an advance that has been manifest since Machiavelli.

The theme of the century emerges from the disaster that befell traditional culture and its holistic morality: making the immune systems explicit. It should be clear that the construction of immunity is far too comprehensive and far too contradictory an event to be described with medical-biochemical categories alone. In keeping with its complex nature, political, military, legal, insurance and psychosemantic or religious components contribute to its unfolding in real terms.[99] The dawn of immunity determines the intellectual lighting conditions for the twentieth century. A process of learning to distrust, unprecedented in intellectual history, colors the sense of everything that was once termed rationality. For the intellectuals in the vanguard of the development, this initiated an apprenticeship in non-devotion.

The first, widely felt yet barely conceptualized consequence of the primacy of this isolation from participation is the increasing risk affecting the inhabitants and shapers of current global scenarios since the early twentieth century. Because people in the age of background explication have ever less untouched *a priori* information to take with them about how, where and in what form they should be—unless they were born between high mountains and intactly rooted in one of the traditional cultures that are now a rarity—they are forced to adjust their orientations from implicit embedding in the background to explicit positings. Where self-evident truths became scarce, options had to take over their role. This initiated the age of elective world pictures and elective self-images. The long market cycle of so-called "identities" now began. Identity is a self-evidence hypothesis on uncertain terrain, and is crafted according to individualistic and collectivistic patterns.[100] The concept of building mental prostheses expresses both the realization and the fact that the production of vital assumptions—life-guiding "hypotheses" in

William James' sense—no longer derives primarily from cultural heritage, but increasingly becomes a matter of reinvention and ongoing reformatting. This subsequently drives the trend towards the individualization of life forms. Granted, as long as I consider it the foremost fact of my life that I am a Corsican, an Armenian or an Irish Protestant, modernisms of this kind are no concern of mine; then I can take myself as an ethnic ready-made and prepare for performances at the multicultural bazaar. If necessary, I will even take to the street to demand the preservation of fox-hunting in Britain. And if this flight to a type does not suit me, I should assure myself of the native organismic foundations that I wish to keep for the time being.

It is only in this context that the excessive interest of modern people in "health" becomes understandable: it is a cover phenomenon for an inquiry into those background certainties which, after the dissolution of their natural and cultural latencies—and the fading of the regional character colors[101]—still remain valid. The current storm on the health base—prefigured by Schopenhauer in the philosophical field—thus results from the most plausible drive. For what if not the presumed inner biological foundation should be the standard in the search for what is my own, and more still, the core of what inalienably belongs to me? Is the existence of my own body not the irrefutable proof of evolution as a success story—and can I do anything more sensible than align myself with its ability to be healthy? Nonetheless, this search for inner solidity is not without its irony. For the mass interest in biologically based selfhood draws precisely the keenest clients of the "identity through health" concept into a paradoxical de-securing—extending to the realization that health in the full sense of the word cannot exist. An aspect of the health cult of which one can lose sight is the subversive role of medical research in explicatory processes: because of the search for the last foundations of health as a minimum biological background fulfillment of existence, it was inevitable that there would be a discovery and problematization of those finely tuned, unstable structures referred to for some two hundred years as "immune systems," in the biochemical sense of the term. The forced tracing of background security in one's own bodily foundation exposes a layer of regulating mechanisms whose appearance brought into view, for the first time, the profound improbability of biosystemic integrity as such.

The thematization of endogenous immune systems radically changed the relationship between the illuminated details and the organic conditions for individual health and sickness. One must now acknowledge that there are occult battles between pathogens and "antibodies" in the human organism whose results are responsible for the status of our health. Many biologists describe the somatic self as a besieged terrain defended by endogenous border troops with varying success. The users of this hawkish terminology are opposed by a faction of biological doves who paint a less martial picture of immune processes; in this version, the self and the foreign are so interwoven at deep levels that overly primitive strategies of delineation are more likely to have counterproductive effects. What also comes to light is a tangled play of endocrinological emissions that are active on the threshold between unconscious biochemical processes and the organism's experiential surface. It is not only through their complexity that the immune systems confuse their owners' longing for security; they cause even more perplexity through their immanent paradox, as their successes, if they become too thorough, are perverted to become their own kind of reasons for illness: the growing universe of auto-immune pathologies illustrates the dangerous tendency of the own to win itself to death in the battle against the other.

It is no coincidence that recent interpretations of the immunity phenomenon exhibit a tendency to assign far greater significance to the presence of the foreign amidst the own than was intended in traditional identitary understandings of a monolithically closed organismic self—one could almost speak of a post-structuralist turn in biology.[102] In the light of this, the patrol of antibodies in an organism seems less like a police force applying a rigid immigration policy than a theater troupe parodying its invaders and performing as their transvestites. But however one chooses to summarize the biologists' dispute over the interpretation of immunity, anyone sufficiently interested in the ability to be healthy as a basic layer of personal integrity and identity will sooner or later learn so much about their functional conditions that the biochemical immune dimension as such will confusingly emerge from latency, growing into the most worrying of all foreground topics.

This has consequences for the mental immune status of "enlightened society," which now not only knows what it knows, but must also form an opinion on how it intends to live with the respective states of explication it has reached. The moderns are shown with increasing intensity that the progress of being able to know cannot be steadily converted into analogous immunity advantages. Knowledge is not simply power after all. If five hundred new illnesses are discovered or described per year, as is currently the case, this does not directly increase the safety of the inhabitants of the proud tower of civilization. Because of its increasing explicitness (and unlimited capacity for repression), developed knowledge of the security architecture of existence—from the human field via the legal to the political—often has a destabilizing effect overall. Owing to the counterproductive effects of advanced explication, latency as such, in its desired functions, is explicated too. Those who attain this knowledge come to appreciate their former ignorance in retrospect. Now it transpires that pre-enlightened or pre-explicit states as such can already be immunologically relevant—at least in the sense that the sojourn in the undeveloped temporarily and partially allows individuals to profit psychologically from certain protective effects of ignorance. This was already recognized by classical authors such as Cicero, who declares: "Undoubtedly ignorance of future ills is a more useful thing than knowledge."[103] It may be that the discovery of these connections was directly linked to the invention of the religions of salvation. Indeed, perhaps what Christian tradition called faith was initially no more than a pro-grammatic progressive-regressive change of stance from a weakening knowledge to a strengthening ignorance, combined with a beneficent illusion. The *vera religio* became successful against the background of the classical enlightenment because it could be recommended as a therapeutic course given by priests to combat the sickness of imperial realism. Through its counter-factual form, faith gave its practitioners the chance to cling to a salvific phantasm, even against one's better knowledge of the dis-astrous circumstances one now bravely calls "external."

While the enlightened consciousness today necessarily assumes explicitly imagined possibilities of failure—statistically supported references to accident risks, terror risks, business risks, cancer and heart attack risks and other dimensions of precisely quantifiable probabilities of damage—the non-alarmed life, provided it coincides vaguely with its background and can let itself be borne by traditions, occasionally retains an aura of safety in naïveté. As an enlightened person one derides it, but at times envies those who have it when one has been living in a state of constant alarm for too long. Enlightenment about enlightenment becomes management for the collateral damage of knowledge. As a result of the first stage of enlightenment, we are all—to use a phrase by Botho Strauss—"prognostically contaminated."[104]

It also becomes apparent now, however, that because of the narrowness of its thematic window, no consciousness can process more than one or two alarm motifs at the same time; this means that it must consign most of the currently explicated subjects of concern to the background as if they did not exist in reality. (In the multi-alarm society, several dozen bells ring simultaneously twenty-four hours a day, yet we usually manage to filter out a single main alarm that we can process.) The non-interruptible game of thematizing and de-thematizing risks gives rise to a tried and tested, functional substitute for naïveté: while the purveyor of primary naïveté could not adequately imagine the risk space in which they operated because of the pre-explicit constitution of their consciousness, the modern navigates the same space with a form of second naïveté, for even—and especially—in a risk-analytically treated zone, it is impossible to simultaneously consider everything that should be considered. I shall call the secondary naïve stance "re-implication"; it is the standby function of explicated, yet intermittently sidelined issues. Re-implication supplies the prosthesis for trust; its use presupposes that everything which can happen does in fact happen—albeit only occasionally, and usually in such a way that damage is done only to the others. As far as documents go, the typical place of re-implication is the archive, and in the realm of personal experience, the long-term memory in its unused state; potential alarm knowledge deposited there grants the user secondary carefreeness. Sufficiently orderly long-term memories and archives provide a formal crutch for second latency.[105] Shortly before Emil von Behring and Shibasaburo Kitasato, assistants to Robert Koch in Berlin, decisively stimulated the development of medical immunology[106] in 1890 with the joint discovery and naming of "anti-toxins," a first manifestation of antibodies, Nietzsche's foundational research into the workings of human consciousness had brought to his attention the existence of a mental defense system; he recognized the inconspicuous efficiency with which it put itself in the service of a ruling self-center and its needs for meaning. In this light, Nietzsche—after preparatory work by Mesmer, Fichte, Schelling, Carus and Schopenhauer—can be considered the true discoverer of the operative unconscious. In his moral-critical *magnum opus*, *Beyond Good and Evil*, published in August 1886, he noted:

The power of the spirit to appropriate foreign elements manifests itself in a strong tendency to assimilate the new to the old, to simplify the manifold, to disregard or push aside utter inconsistencies [...]. This same will is served by [...] a suddenly emerging resolution in favor of ignorance and arbitrary termination, a closing of its windows, an inner nay-saying to something or other, a come-no-closer, a type of defensive state against many knowable things, a contentment with darkness, with closing horizons, a yea-saying and approval of ignorance.[107]

If reflections of this kind could present themselves under the title of a "philosophy of the future," it was because they caused the breakthrough to the immunological paradigm of the critique of reason: once it had crossed this threshold, thought operated beyond the imperative of "know thyself." Hence there would seem to be what one could call semantic antibodies or idea suppressors, designed to remove incompatible notions from the space of consciousness. Where there was love of wisdom, there will be insight into the repulsive and non-integrable properties of numerous true ideas. Epistemology will become a cognitive-scientific subsidiary of allergology.[108] At the time, this constituted the most extensive anticipation of the forms of rationality found in cybernetics, which asks after the internal and external operating conditions of consciousnesses. In the light of artificial intelligence, it becomes clearer what natural intelligence does. We only prostheticize what we have understood sufficiently explicitly, and we reassess what cannot be prostheticized.

Anticipatory references to this transition can be traced to Nietzsche's thought until the early 1870s, from which the treatise "On Truth and Lies in a Nonmoral Sense"[109] (1873) particularly stands out—an early attempt to view the primary function of human thought and speech as the establishment of a protective metaphorical shell intended to prevent cultural subjects from viewing the terrible and fathomless circumstances of existence. What remains notable is that along with the immunological and allergological mode of observing rational processes, Nietzsche simultaneously discovered its paradox: if thought sets about following its own logic in earnest, it can even emancipate itself from its immune functions for life and take a stance against the vital interests of its carriers. This is what Nietzsche had in mind with his intervention against "metaphysics." In a strong concept of enlightenment, knowledge's auto-immunitary paradoxes will now have to be known along with it—just as the costs of idealistic upswings will have to be recalculated. It was clear to Nietzsche from the start that this form of consciousness research does not lead back to states of calmed knowledge after self-application, and more still, that self-contradiction, even self-damage would henceforth be one of the openly namable premises for the progress of knowledge: the philosophical life can only be justified by becoming the perceiver's experiment on themselves. The thinker realized how the interests of knowledge separated from those of life at this point; he had no doubts as to the fatality of the choice.[110] As far as his own person was concerned, he was determined to give the motive of knowledge precedence over the vital "will to surface"—a preference that was intermittently obscured by the flamboyant rhetorical figures of Zarathustra's affirmation of life. As early as 1872, Nietzsche, still writing in the spirit of Schopenhauer, had noted: "Nature has cushioned man in sheer illusions—that is his proper element"[111]—before concluding that only a rejection of the medium of illusion, or of humane fabrications, would provide access to the sphere of knowledge.

Nietzsche had formed an appropriate idea of this option's price early on. He expressly names the preconditions of forbearance, heroism and masochism, under which only a person who is adequately warned about themselves and hardened against their own needs can resist the insinuations of their narrow-minded vital reason: a thinker's concern can no longer be whether a thought deserves to be deemed "spiritually usable." "The world as immunitarily useful idea": the new, biologically informed critique of knowledge casts off the leash of conventional ideation, which is commanded by a chronic need for illusions. As a result, future thought will extend further than philosophy: the latter, as the love of wisdom, comes to an end as soon as wisdom and truth prove more repellent than attractive factors. Whoever desires to be a theoretical immunologist or a free spirit—which will henceforth be almost the same thing—and, through both of these, testify as a witness to philosophy after the end of the Old European (and Old Asian) harmonizing exercise of the same name, must mobilize "a type of cruelty on the part of the intellectual conscience and taste"[112] within themselves—a both scientific and moral inconsideration that can only be summoned if one accepts finding oneself unpleasant in the extreme. The free spirit goes through a long program of vaccinations with bio-negativity.

It is hardly surprising that this self-disconcerting explication of mental mechanics began with the moralists of the late seventeenth century when they invented a secular variety of the religious examination of conscience. Their insights were taken up by the Romantics and intensified until they could be reformulated by psychoanalysis and related doctrines, which in turn passed the baton to disciplines such as psycholinguistics and psychoneuroimmunology in the last decades of the twentieth century. What all forms of knowledge about the mechanical sides of thought and feeling processes have in common is that they describe human awareness as the place where the explicit is constantly separated from the implicit.

Parenthetic Observation:
Forced Light and the Advance to the Articulated World

Making immune systems explicit: since the dawn of the twentieth century, this has been one of the logical and pragmatic maxims to be followed by the denizens of modernity if they want to maintain their connection to the *modus vivendi* of their time. One of the hallmarks of progressive explication is that it expands the security arrangements of existence—from the antibody and dietary level to the welfare state and military apparatuses—into formally secure institutions, disciplines and routines. Whether it also gives people the intellectual tools to understand what they are doing remains questionable. Most have no more than a few faded rhetorical phrases to deal with existence in the explication-driven world, words with which the ambivalence of the human immune situation can be thematized in untechnical reflections. Thus modern "society," in words of Sunday contemplation, weighs up the "blessing and curse of scientific discoveries"; it holds symposia to articulate its vacillation between "fear of technology and hope in technology"; in public meditation, it gathers together thoughts on the uses and disadvantages for life of the world's disenchantment; it occupies itself with the question of how unrest and a feeling of security can be reconciled in the technological world. These discourses—if that is what they are—process the raw material of immunity problems as they accumulate in consciousnesses through everyday experiences of modernization.

According to the basic assumptions made here, explications always apply to words and things at once; in this sense, they are analysis and synthesis of reality in one. They advance the issue's development as an active combination of operative steps and discursive formulations. They not only turn unspoken ("unconscious," unknown, un-understood) background assumptions into overt ones, but also elevate "realia" previously folded up in latency to manifest existence. If this were not the case, all analyses would remain mere rhetorical events; at best, they would be providing more lengthy justifications of judgments; Robert B. Brandom has demonstrated how these are extended from the desks of judges and experts to the opinions voiced by Mr. and Mrs. Everybody, as far as correctness demands. If someone intends to make "it" explicit, this means that they must provide the argumentative refinancing for their convictions—a view that is realistic for certain discursive games in academia in which one collects points with formalisms.

Because explication, as analysis and synthesis of reality, takes place both in the workshops and the texts, because it proceeds both in technical processes and in the corresponding descriptions and commentaries, it develops a violence wherever it attacks that cuts into the real and the mental. It changes the cognitive and material environments by repopulating both with products of explication. This effect can be traced back at least as far as the sixteenth or seventeenth century, when the large-scale invasion of lifeworlds by the mechanical and its creations began. Its threshold period would have been the introduction of motors; from that point on, the cultures of the west were, above all, immigration countries for machines. What capitalism means is the policy of open borders for the influx of mechanical, natural-historical and epistemic immigrations coming from uninventedness to inventedness, from undiscoveredness to discoveredness. Invented-ness and discoveredness are thus states of affairs that concern the cognitive civil status of objects. The civilization process brings about the naturalization of the non-human new. The modern world is unimaginable without this constant making of room for immigrations from the new—in this respect, the difference between the USA and the Old World is only one of style; all carrier cultures of modernization are immigration countries. Every private household in them has to adapt itself to accept an ongoing accommodation of innovations. A physical novelty (and at times numinosity)[113] like electricity, to name one of the most momentous examples, actually had to be brought out from its background in nature and implanted on the largest scale, in an act of spatial planning, before illuminated, automated, image-eroticized and tele-participatory mass culture could come into being.[114] Before the conversion of modern populations into hygiene societies and the recruiting of the masses for anti-microbial campaigns could become possible, the universe of microbes first had to be shifted from its invisibility to the sanitary arena of the late nineteenth century. From that point on, the viruses, bacteria and other small life forms were literally "among us."[115] When telegraph lines and railways suddenly cut through the Old European agricultural landscapes; when telephones and microwave ovens find their way into urban households; when synthetic fertilizer and antibiotics put the human metabolism with nature on a new basis; when the automobile, in a barely one-hundred-year wave of imitation, drives all traditional ideas of cities, roads, households and environments to a radical revision—then the shared world of humans and things is no longer the same after each of these invasions and their epidemic expansions, to say the least. The same is true of countless newly introduced explication products on the fronts of physics, chemistry and culture—though, in terms of incorporation into the civilizatory collective, invented objects like automobiles and Tamagochis, discovered objects like pheromones and the HIV virus, and mixed objects like recombinant bacteria, transgenic enzymes or phosphorescent rabbits hold the same status.

Modernity is purportedly a pragmatically overseen, but largely uncontrolled open-air experiment with the simultaneous and successive introduction into civilization of an undefined number of innovations.[116] The multi-innovative constitution of contemporary "society" rests on the assumption that the fight for survival between the new and the old (Tarde addresses them under the title "logical duels") usually lead to social progress, and that the novelties can peacefully coexist, whether in the mode of reciprocal indifference or in the sense of positive combinability and cumulability (Tarde speaks of *accouplements logiques*, "logical couplings"). The criteria of compatibility among the explications and inventions are still unclear; whatever does not lead immediately or in the mid-term to physical and cultural disasters seems a success. One part of the newly introduced items is evaluated by markets, another is moderated by state regulations, and a third is censored by expert communities and moralists— most of it trickles into the technical facilities by unclear routes, but always reinforced by imitative waves, affecting the "lifeworlds" with varying delay. Where the mindset of modernization dominates, populations programmatically ready themselves to receive infiltrating innovations.

In the light of these processes, the usual talk of discoveries and inventions is unsuited to interpreting the reality-positing gravity of explication: although what is invented or discovered normally irrupts into the real at a narrowly circumscribed point, it can only become a factor in collective circumstances through a powerful wave of imitation. The popular habit of referring to some invention or another, discovery or product development as "revolutionary" is generally no more than a form for misinformation from the explication front. Such false reports of so-called revolutions, for their part, are capable and in need of explication: in their amateur phase they are utopias, and once professionalized they are termed advertising or public relations. (From this perspective, the Soviet Union was above all an advertising agency that spread the news of the revolution it pretended to be.)[117]

Explication-conditioned innovations do, in fact, often make it seem as if aggressive new cohabitants had moved into the "house of Being" but found no suitable space available, causing them to take their lodgings by force. Small wonder that this has sometimes been described as "revolutionary" turbulence. There is, to recall one of the most dramatic developments, no doubt that the explication of writing through printing with movable type jumbled up the entire ecology of European civilization after 1500. One can even go so far as to describe the post-Gutenberg world as an attempt to incorporate the seemingly harmless new arrivals, which appeared in the typesetting workshops in the form of small pieces of lead, into a bearable cohabitation with the remaining cultural facts, especially people's religious convictions. Proof through success came with modern literature and the school system of nation-states, and proof through failure came with the disastrous role of printing presses as carriers of nationalistic deformations of consciousness, as allies of all ideological perversions, and as disseminators and accelerators of collective hysterias.[118] Gabriel Tarde rightly called the effects of printing an "extraordinary diffusion and invasion" which fostered the illusion that "books were the source of all truth."[119]

Whatever appears in the form of new apparatuses, theorems, entities and procedures in the reality field of the intelligentsia scattered across collectives and corporations must be recorded in the land registries of the cognitive administration and socialized in the consciousnesses of users. The non-socializable innovations are either discharged or develop into dangerous parasites—recall the fierce dispute over the integrability of nuclear technology. Because an effective explication as a technical or operative analysis and synthesis of reality is advancing, it produces, in numerous practical continua in the life processes of societies, caesuras or leaps from which one can distinguish clearly between before and after. Explications change the form and direction of streams of events and routines of action. One could see them directly as the stuff of which those differences are made that truly make a difference. In this quality, they are the main motif of a new ontology that deals with the existent not as a stock, but as an event.

One can determine how justified this view is through a simple reflection. If, by means of a supposed discovery, a new "fact" has been introduced into the system of culturally official realities—let us say the fact of America, which started to become public in Europe in 1493 through Columbus' report, or the fact of lactic acid yeast, which arrived in the midst of the French scientific community in 1858 thanks to Pasteur's efforts—then the consciousness reorganized or "informed" by the new information suffers an arrival shock in which the difference between a matter being undiscovered and being discovered is intensely felt: it is as if this transition had locally intensified the asymmetry between nothingness and being. Where there previously seemed to be little or nothing, explication and its publicization allows a new something to draw itself up and voice its longing to be taken up into the community of realia. In the surprise gap that comes before it moves on from amazement to routine, thought is most disposed to allow questions that can specifically target explication as a discovery-ontological emergency: where in all the world, one would ask in the wake of the first sensation, was the double continent of America before its appearance in the claims of Columbus? Did the navigator really give the correct answer when he wrote in his *Book of Prophecies* (1502) that the New World had lain hidden in God's spirit until the Almighty saw fit to lift the veil covering it before the eyes of his favored servant Colón? Where was the famous lactic acid ferment hiding before Louis Pasteur gave it a place of honor at the table of things that enlightened persons and dairy owners should know? The list goes on: where were the microbes before that same Pasteur and his German rival Robert Koch brought them out of their epistemological hiding-place and made them fellow players in an expanded scenario of reality?[120] Where were radioactive rays before Madame Curie began experimenting with the pitch blende, and before the physicists of Los Alamos introduced them into the fact-environment of a news-receptive humanity through the Hiroshima scandal? Or, to ask the questions that concern the explication of foams as vital, defensive-creative spatial multiplicities: in what way were climate, air and atmosphere dictated to individuals before they became objects of modern environmental concern through their atmoterrorist explications on the one hand, and their meteorological and air-conditioning developments on the other hand? In what recess, what preliminary concept did human cultures hide away before they were counted by seamen and ethnologists and functionally explained by the systems, war and stress theorists? Humans themselves, finally—how did they interpret their exposure to the climates of "nature" before becoming aware that they are "pupils of their air" and creatures of greenhouse effects down to their most intimate dispositions?[121] And finally: where were immune systems before the twentieth century's dawn of explication brought them within the sight of the new life sciences, and into the foreground of medicalized self-concern?

The questions immediately seem bizarre, and there is an unmistakably naïve tone to them. Nonetheless, they are legitimate and fruitful for the theory of science as long as they call upon people to give an account of the human sojourn in a *res publica* co-inhabited by explication products, and to do so in a more explicit fashion. This concession has no bearing on whether or not an adequate answer will be found; the only certainty is that the two widespread responses to the question of what mode of being the discovered has before it is discovered are not only inadequate, but simply false. The first answer comes from (transcendental and constructivist) idealism, which claims that discovered things have no preexistence before their perception in a consciousness and their articulation in speech. The error of this thesis lies in the suggestion that the traditional assumption that being and being-perceived are identical can be understood as the absolute dependence of objects on a thinking subject. From there it is not far to the hypnotic absurdity of subjective idealism, which states that objects coincidentally lacking a human observer are also devoid of being as such. The complementary error can be found in the second answer, which posits an objective and cognition-independent preexistence of the discovered prior to every discovery by envisaging the being of that thing as something whose being-noticed can be effortlessly thought away by an intelligence, without that thing losing any part of its substance. In the latter view, a natural one in the everyday business of natural science, objectivism celebrates an insufficient ontology of deceptive successes: it claims that the existent is always unambiguously thus and only as it appears "in itself" prior to all perception, while thought is given the role of something contingently additional that could as easily stay away—just as it was evidently still absent from the matter before discovery—and which, furthermore, arouses suspicion through a susceptibility to error and a variability of interpretations. Here, allegedly, it is the discovery that can be absent from the discovered without any damage to the latter's own quality. The symmetry of fallacies is clear enough: while the error in the first case lies in exaggerating the discoveredness of the discovered in an absolutism of consciousness, the mistake in the second case is to downplay the discovery objectivistically, as if it were of no consequence for a "substance" or entity existing on its own terms when, where and how it becomes part of a knowledge, and in what symbolic forms and logical neighborhoods it circulates in a society of acknowledgers.

The only way out of the dilemma of choosing between alternative errors reveals itself in the finding that there is a third way. Such demonstrations exist in several variations, and I shall mention two of these that seem very contrasting on the surface, but whose deep structures nonetheless show a kinship. Firstly, there are Bruno Latour's contributions to science studies, which contain the stimulus for an epistemological civil rights movement—with the aim of integrating the technical objects and animal symbionts into an expanded constitutional space, thus creating an integral republic that finally recognizes not only human agents, but also artifacts and creatures as ontologically whole fellow citizens.

Secondly, there are Martin Heidegger's meditations on a new definition of the "essence of truth," reflections that start from the Greek word *alethéia*—non-concealment, non-dissemblance—and find in it a reference to crossing over from the hidden to the daylight side of the existent.

Latour's originality in opening up his third way between idealism and realism is revealed by his attentiveness to the transitional rituals that introduce new scientific facts, discoveries, inventions, theorems and artifacts into the surroundings that serve them as a "host culture." If one speaks of the "introduction" of the discovered into the cognitive environment, or the incorporation of new facts into existing communes, this should not affirm the notion that an independent entity—lactic acid yeast, shall we say—is torn out of its preexistence at a completely arbitrary point in time and taken up into the mass of things that are known and acknowledged by human consciousness. In this case, Pasteur's role would merely have been that of an immigration officer tasked with verifying whether the passport of the newly found matter were in order; if it transpired that the lactic acid ferment were an objective entity, not a chimera, there would be nothing to prevent its admission into the realm of accredited facts. In reality, the function of the discoverer is a far more active and complex one, as it is through their suppositions, observations, manipulations, descriptions, attempts and conclusions that the "matter" to be discovered takes the form in which its discoverability as an autonomous entity or a delimitable effect can intensify. The discoverer who is later acknowledged as such is, according to Latour (who refers to Whitehead's *Process and Reality*) a manipulator and co-producer of "statements," or rather "propositions," from which the future discovery can emerge—not simply an ascertainer or finder of contextless facts.[122] Discovering does not mean lifting the veil off a finished preexisting object in one fell swoop, but rather, through a continuing articulation, developing the proposition-like or problematic state in which the "matter" implicitly found itself before its reformulation, and thus weaving a new, denser web between the articulated entity, other entities, science and society.

In a number of respects, Latour's concept of articulation comes very close to what has here been termed explication. Like this, it straddles the threshold between science-theoretical and ontological meanings. A world in which articulations or explications are possible is neither the totality of mute things nor the epitome of ascertained or non-ascertained facts; rather, it is the moving horizon of all "propositions" in which possible and actually existent things offer themselves to human attention in propositional or provocative fashion. The stuff of being is presented by being itself in the shape of a proposition, as it were—one could even say in the shape of a problem, in the sense of the word's Greek ancestor *probállein*—"throw down, throw before." In problems, things speak to the intelligence; in resolutions, they open themselves up to human participation. Through the pressure of relevance, they inspire creativity. As they are non-speaking, things, states of affairs and natures could only appear when and if they had previously been silenced by an intellect that reserved language for itself. The original mode of givenness of things is how interesting they are for other things: the one concerns the other. The existent is always immersed in a pool of relevance in which it moves together with intelligences.

The merit of the problem-ontological view—where being means suggesting oneself—is that it does not allow the supposed divide between words and things to open up in the first place; so much metaphysically committed intelligence has disappeared into this chasm through superfluous attempts to bridge it. If the world is everything that is the case, and everything is the case that is suggested or thrown before a knowing participation, then discovery can be understood as an unfolding of a proposition where a palpably higher degree of articulatedness can be attained. The same is expressed by the fold metaphor: where there is a fold or something rolled-up, an unfurling or unrolling (*explicare*) can begin. Folds are the suggestions or propositions at which an explication directs its attack. When one sees a fold, one perceives the indication of something inside the fold that has not yet been spread out. The radical-democratic scientific optimist Latour explains without hesitation: "The more articulation there is, the better."[123] Articulations elaborate the kinships between propositions. The newly discovered and invented things are articulatednesses in the midst of articulatednesses against a background of propositions—unfoldings in a landscape of unfoldings before a panorama of folds.

How, then, should one view the arrival of the new element discovered by Pasteur in the republic of humans, theorems and artifacts? Latour's response is convivial and civil: "The lactic acid ferment now exists as a discrete entity *because* it is articulated between so many others, in so many active and artificial settings."[124] In this statement, one glimpses a bright variety of the institutionalism which asserts the realization that discoveries and inventions must be socialized and contextualized like second-order habits in order to gain what Arnold Gehlen described as the "intrinsic stability" [*Eigenstabilität*][125] of livable quasi-institutions. It is true of modern knowledge in particular that, as d'Alembert already noted, it has "taken on a social function"; "it forms the breathing air to which we owe life."[126] "Science studies" is an understated name for a cheerful philosophy of a world populated by products of explication. It offers one of the most adequate theories of modernity by turning the myth of modernity on its head.[127]

Comparable reflections, albeit with entirely different shadings, became known through Heidegger's investigations of the "essence of truth." These had to take on a darker hue after Heidegger decided that the process Latour calls articulation was, above all, a violence-propagating invasion by the will to knowledge of a nature that had been degraded to a resource on all sides. According to him, science and technology inherently have the character of an organized attack on concealment. The decisive hint leading to Heidegger's development of this view came from the Greek word for truth, *alethéia*, which he translated as "unconcealment" [*Un-Verborgenheit*]—rightly in one respect, as it suggests that the term should be analyzed as a compound of *lethe* (hiddenness, concealment, oblivion) and the negating prefix *a-*. Then the concept would rest on the notion that those things are "true," or rather enter the realm of truth, which "come over" from their hiddenness, concealment or oblivion into uncoveredness, unconcealment and remembering. It is not only through the judgment that a statement is true or false that truth is established as truth; rather, a manifestation, a proposition, a phenomenal fold protrudes into the realm of the exposed and provokes the judgment (which can naturally be false), keeping the truth event going. This perhaps brings to mind Whitehead's dictum: "in the real world it is more important that a proposition be interesting than that it be true. The importance of truth is, that it adds to interest."[128] Truth, polyvalent from the outset, takes place in unconcealing and utterance *simultaneously*. It is thus always a transition from the uninteresting or pre-interesting into present interest.

Truth, then, is not simply a property of uttered statements that can be termed true if, and only if, whatever is stated or "depicted" in them is "actually" the case "in reality"; rather, in this interpretation, the physical world is a self-publicizing event whose utterances involve the sensing and sentence-forming intelligences. One should not be put off by this allegorical turn of phrase—when nature is spoken of as an acting person, this always refers to media processes. To reformulate this idea, nature conveys itself in its appearance: it gives hints, shows a picture of itself, lets us see and hear it, and communicates itself in its fulfillment and sounding. Nature, one could say—with the aforementioned qualification—is an author who self-publishes (though she requires human editors). This interpretation of the truth event understandably contradicts the dualist dogmatics of the metaphysical age, inaugurated by Plato and other post-Socratics, and its technical-scientific heirs, who held that nature—meaning the existent as a whole—is present as a block of mute reities, devoid of sense and remote from signs. From this perspective the human spirit alone, in possession of its monopoly on language, bestowal of meaning and interest, would approach that unaccommodating natural mass as if from the outside and force it to divulge its secrets.

According to Heidegger, the tragic irony of this misinterpretation of the knowledge of nature by metaphysics, and by those who continue it in the modern natural sciences and technologies, is that its extremely reductionist concepts, which distort and impoverish the truth event, were so successful that they determined the European culture of rationality for over two millennia in the mode of a self-fulfilling prophecy. This space of time would then be equal to the era of forgetfulness of being. Recall that a related view of things was expressed in the statement "the whole is the false"[129]—which, read historically, means that the false too already has its own antiquity. Whoever wishes to understand its beginnings in order to return to undistorted conditions preceding them must address Plato's formularization of the truth into an "idea," or go back even further to Democritus' splitting of human reality into body and soul. Misnomers on this scale, as Heidegger saw, go beyond the descriptive power of the conventional concept of error; they force the observer to resort to such terms as "destiny" [*Geschick*], perhaps even "fate" [*Verhängnis*].[130]

When the concern is to locate the drama of the explication of immune systems and atmospheres within the history of ideas and disasters in the twentieth century, Heidegger's views on the genesis of the obvious may become attractive once more. As noted above, the thinker originally described the manifestation of the manifest as emerging from a self-publication of being— and gives the clearing as the place of publication. Certainly Heidegger had to become aware of this understanding of the truth in the course of his meditations, for he, the contemporary of world wars and the technologization of the environment, could not fail to notice how inadequate this idiosyncratically reconstructed early Greek concept of a self-communicating and self-concealing phenomenal world was in the face of modern conditions. His way out of this difficulty was to shift from the self-revelation of Being as nature to the forcible uncovering of the existent through research and development as a "destiny"

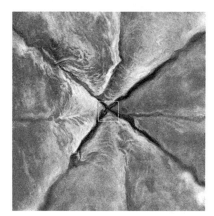

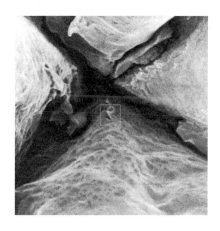

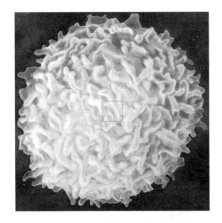

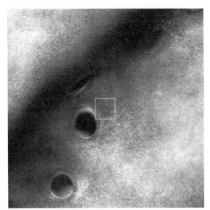

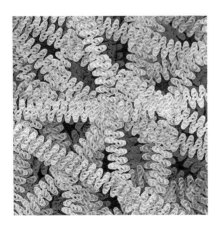

Magnification of the back of a hand

commanded by Being itself. The merit of this was presumably to leave open the possibility of a further destiny shift towards neo-ancient Greek primary truth, albeit bought at the price of no longer being able to formulate a positive concept of scientific research and technological civilization—to say nothing, for now, of the fatalistic over-interpretation of ongoing history.

At any rate, this much is certain: in a reality that is reworked by the practice of enlightenment, artificial light covers up the self-luminous. What is presented in modern fashion as "obvious" or capable of forming the surface is never the self-fulfilling nature that shows what it shows, and conceals what it conceals. And modern unconcealment is no longer the gray-warm everyday light shining on an artisanal rustic setting, where habitus-protected existence knows its way around because it only ever encounters things and creatures within its own radius of activity. In the technological world, the non-obvious is made present by an organized rupture of latency—or, in an analogous movement, is lifted out of intangibility into artificial perceptibility with the assistance of design and audiovisual systems, then embedded in a second handiness. Knowledge produced through research and invention is neon-light knowledge. The self-clearing of being is replaced by the forcible clearing of the "given," and organic perception is replaced by organized observation. Under such premises, it is unimaginable that humans could ever again integrate themselves into a "truth event" derived from the old nature, with its "fulfillment," its "birthing" and its concealment and retreat into inconspicuousness—an event in which the things show of their own accord, without being forced, what and how much of themselves they will reveal, preserving the dark remainder as their secret.

The modern character of our situation reveals itself in the fact that unconcealing, uncovering and putting in words is taken over by a systematic offensive against Lethe. Wresting a manifestation from latency and working the world background into the foreground in order to develop it in practical applications: this seems to be the most important *a priori* of modern civilization, which therefore has even deeper reasons than conventionally assumed to call itself a knowledge society. The human right to the uncovering of nature and reconstruction of culture is taken for granted to such a great, even exaggerated degree that no declaration of human rights has so far considered it necessary to make it explicit. Nowhere has this been formulated more clearly than in Heidegger's dictum "technology is a form of unconcealment"—a statement that, despite exuding the calm of one who has insight into a momentous state of affairs, leaves open whether it still wants to be taken as a diagnosis or already as a warning. It expresses the concern that the organized invasion of concealment is increasingly transpiring as a "fate," or more precisely as a case of aletheiological injustice. What begins as enlightened reality management heightens the risk of knowledge-caused disaster. Persistently pointing out that technology is essentially unconcealment or explication—more clearly: a mode of applying latency-breaking force—advises us against continuing to narrate the uncontrolled large-scale industry of discovering, inventing and publicizing as the cheerful story of progress in human knowledge as which it has presented itself from the eighteenth century to the present day, even if a few skeptical tones found their way into the progressive narratives in the course of the twentieth century. Research as a systematic removal of the unrevealed must, according to Heidegger, lead to an ever deeper misunderstanding of concealment.

From this perspective, the disaster of latency is the secret main event of the twentieth century. Its most lurid results are instrumentalized nuclear power, uncovered immune systems, the decoded genome and the unveiled brain. In the face of these factors, those going along with a technologically unconcealing civilization are confronted with the monstrous that, after the rupture of latency, places itself in the middle of the reality network. After August 6, 1945, Elias Canetti noted:

> We were not red-hot all the time with possibilities we never suspected—what a blessing! [...] The tiniest thing has won [...] The way to the atomic bomb is a philosophical one.[131]

End of the Excursus

So where were immune systems before their "discovery"? What fold was enclosing them before biochemical articulation spread them out and incorporated into the reality space of contemporary knowledge and practices? In what suggestion, what proposition were they abiding before their debut on the stage of modern science? In which niche of Lethe did they remain hidden? Behind what masks did they confirm the words of Heraclitus that nature loves to make itself invisible (*phýsis krýptesthai phílei*)—the same *physis* that otherwise addresses us in the form of a self-showing, openly self-giving nature?[132] Did immune systems, these security services and agencies of organismic, social and political self-assertion, lead a pre-explicit existence under the popular concepts of robustness and health, marked early on by the knowledge that only their disturbance retroactively reveals their abundance and demands that it be made whole again? Did they conceal themselves in the intuitions of the primitive law that, since time immemorial, had granted to damaged life and assailed honor the gesture of self-defense and endorsed the restoration of a contested status? Were they implicitly involved when humans feared the revenge of the gods at the first violation of the protocol for dealings between this world and the world beyond? Were they present in the rituals for warding off demons or blessing buildings and earth, which assigned delimited spaces to their protective spirits, repelling other potential magical occupants? Were they implicit in the imago of Germanic sacral kingship, in which the worthy ruler had an abundance of charismas—the power of victory, the harvest blessing, the merriment and generosity of the chieftain, the expansiveness of foresight, the glamor of ambition and the wholesome presence? Can we indirectly assume the presence of immune system effects when the Lutheran God is sung of as a mighty fortress, trusty shield and weapon?[133] Are we helped by the etymological information that the Roman word *inmunis* initially meant no more than "exemption from taxes and duties" (an early manifestation of de-solidarization?), and could also refer to a person released from military service—a background to the development of the later legal meaning of immunity as the unimpeachability of those in political office?

If one envisages the existence of immune systems purely in their current medical-biochemical articulation, then all these questions can be answered in the negative; none of these dimensions involve immune systems in the narrow sense of the term. Nowhere can one speak of an internal battle between microbial invaders and intrasystem antibodies; the aforementioned phenomena in no way describe the operations of an endocrino-logical regulative dimension. Nonetheless, the explicated phenomenon of bio-systemic immunity casts a long shadow into the past: the field of humanly relevant notions of integrity encompasses a wealth of "propositions" for bringing battles over damaged totalities and states of order into shape—conceptually, operatively and ritually.

Pre-metaphysical thought already knew something resembling an ontology of the boundary, closely intertwined with an ethics of defense. This brings into view a pre-territorial concept of boundary intimately related to the phenomenon of immunity: it is not the demarcation lines of properties and dominions that have to be secured, but rather those marking communities of animation and power evidently consisting of a core area and a vulnerable periphery. The spontaneous pluralism of pre-metaphysical drawings of world pictures reckons with a multiplicity of individual "entities" or "power subjects" in their fields—both are naturally inappropriate terms already preformed by later metaphysics—with interminable distribution struggles going on between them. And, although these power centers affect one another far more comprehensively than would be permissible in the later, status-ontologically regulated cosmos of essences, where every "thing" is put in its "place" in order to prove itself, one can already perceive here a constant drama of delineation.

The pre-metaphysical interpretation of the world has a guerilla-ontological concept of world as attack and defense. Here there is not yet a grand tableau of the whole in which every individual part takes its place under a sovereign logos. Reality is more a patchwork of micro-dramas, a fluctuation of skirmishes between a plethora of movable units. The intensities of attack are engaged in constant battles with those of the defense, resulting alternately in invasions and expulsions—an endlessly rising and falling bush war of energies. That is why wisdom, in this context, can only take shape as the gay science of the strategies of the power centers. The reformulated concept of immunity preexists in it—if one concedes that it has a preexistence—folded up in attentiveness to a power's military proficiency. In a world described in these terms, there cannot yet be any knowledge collection points that are interested in generalization. If several knowledges come together under such directives to show themselves and become more potent, then in agonal events such as magic contests and singing wars—forms that, in ancient Greece, survived until the tragedians.

Since the emergence of metaphysical conceptions of the world two and a half thousand years ago—with which, rightly or wrongly, such terms as "advanced civilization" and "high religion" have been associated following Weber, Spengler, Jaspers and others—the concern of the precursors to immune systems has shifted from combatant power centers to an area of the experienced interior newly described as the *psyche*. When the soul is spoken of in the metaphysical sense, a change of motif in the interpretation of inner powers of defense and assertion has already taken place. While the local life points or "power subjects" had previously been able to assert their terrain against invaders thanks to their defensive strength and capacity for counterattack, it would henceforth be more immanent formal constants that reinforced so-called souls in the border war with secondary souls and non-souls. The concept of the *psyche* and its translations constituted the most far-reaching suggestion for the latency form of immunity in the metaphysical age. It implied the shift from defensive power to preservation of form—it is not for nothing that the primary description of soul in this regime is "immortal," a word to which one can only do justice by discerning connotations such as "undeformable" or "corrosion-resistant" in it. Equipped with this inner stability bonus, *homo metaphysicus* had to face the existential risks of his world conditions—more expansively and enterprisingly than any animist in their local battles. That, then, is the immune performance of the correctly understood psychic form: possessing and bestowing immortality. Only in this capacity can it give individuals supremacy over the sites of their relative attachments.

That is why truth, as understood by the philosophers, the first immunologists of being, has such outstanding value in the history of metaphysics: because the deep structure of *alethéia*—undisguisedness, unconcealment—is the same as that of *immunitas*—unobligation, unentanglement in the shared fates and tasks (*munera*) of mortals—it must be considered (by its few connoisseurs) the greatest good. Discovering truth thus means grasping the non-everyday reason for the unassailability of life. Because the truth remains true, even when it is overlooked or disputed, those who know share in its transcendent stability. It is from this angle that the preconditions allowing the concept of God to be elevated to supra-rational heights must be explained. From now on, "God" is the name for the solution to a problem that human intellects cannot handle: what kind of universal immune system could simultaneously act as a universal commune system? One now understands that this question explains the deep structure of the phrase "God and the world."[134] Only God can know how the redemption (or immunization) of all things (in God) could be conceptually reconciled with the actual being-together of things (in the world, the site of mutual consumption). Anyone seeking an exact conception of optimism will find the definition here: it is optimism to assume that such an overarching force exists.

Goethe still captured an avowed faith in the solution of the immunity enigma in his line about the "molded form that develops while living": it is the resistance of form which ensures that no time and no power are capable of cutting up what is molded as a shape of eternity and appears in the temporal; primal words, to put it in Aristotelian terms. Shifting from defensive power to security of form leads to the new archetype of the wise and just figure who, thanks to formal fulfillment of the soul, attains the immunitary optimum. *Integer vitae scelerisque purus / non eget Mauris iaculis neque arcu* [The man of unblemished life who is untainted by crime / has no need of Moorish javelin or bow][135]—in these lines by Horace, an idea of immunity as social unassailedness and untaintedness by misdeeds is articulated for an entire age. The wise man as logically consistent and morphologically just enjoys an unarmed ability to be, resulting from complete agreement with the formal dowries of the soul. "Integrity" now means fulfillment of form.[136]

It also becomes clear, by analogy, that this must not be understood using a modern concept of form that is watered down to an empty schema, but rather a pleromatic view of form as the substance of a thing's or life situation's ability to be whole, in the Roman legal term *integrum*, which refers to the unharmed state of a unity of life protected by law. Accordingly, the task of administering justice in the Roman-Old European vein is a therapeutic one in so far as it is concerned with warding off injury and restoring the intactness of "matters"—which is why the damages trial constituted the legal process *par excellence* in Roman courts. Roman law does not so much suppose the restoring powers of "form," which remains primarily a motif from speeches in the Greek philosophical style, as those of the *ius civile*, the privilege that guaranteed free Roman citizens and those of equal standing in the empire a life protected by the formalities of an elaborated trial system. It is no coincidence that Saint Paul claimed the immunity provided by the Roman court system at the critical moment with the words *civis romanus sum* (with the result that his capital trial was transferred to Rome and concluded there).

The most expansive and radical manifestation of the soul concept can be found in the concept of the world soul formulated in Plato's late dialogue *Timaeus*. It constitutes the highest form among all ancient suggestions for articulating immunological relevant facts. Whoever speaks of the world soul elevates investigation of the principles of spiritual defense and the prevention of losses of meaning and form to the highest level. One can see in this concept what the metaphysical notion of the soul means in terms of the integrative and protective effects it offers the ensouled. In the account of the learned Timaeus, the demiurge was guided in his creation of the world by the consideration (*logismós*) of producing a construct whose perfect form and composition would make it immune to corruption:

> His purpose was to ensure, first, that the world should be as complete a living being as it possibly could be, a totality consisting of the totality of its parts. Second, he wanted it to be one, and so he ensured that there was nothing left over from which another similar universe could be created. Third, he wanted it to be unageing and free from sickness [....] And so

he made it perfectly spherical [...] He gave it a perfectly smooth finish all over [...]. It had no need of eyes, since there was nothing visible left outside it, nor of ears, since there was nothing to hear either. There was no air around it to require breathing in [...].[137]

The construction of the perfectly round world body was surpassed by the addition of the world soul, of which it was said that it was planted in the center of the world body, went through the cosmos in its full extension, and encased the world body from the outside too. It follows from this last aspect that the soul is not inside the body, but rather the body in the soul, as the container is always more noble than the contained.[138] In its internal assemblage, the arithmetically composed soul maintains a balance between the nature of the indivisible "same" (*taúton*) and that of the "other" (*héteron*), which is subject to the divisibility inherent in bodies. Through this middle position, the soul of the world is able to assimilate in both directions: it can encounter the indivisible same and eternally unchanging, or the sensual and becoming—it can incorporate the one or the other entirely, and by sharing suitably in both it can testify truthfully to the things with which it comes into contact.

Plato's world soul constitutes a perfect medium of knowledge that simultaneously forms the ideal immune system, because its composite nature enables it to absorb completely the two primary forms of "information": sameness and otherness, with all their derivations and mixtures. Whatever "encounters" it is preformed within it, and in a sense foreknown; thus nothing can unsettle or injure it. Its immune performance consists in being ahead of all information, every invasion and every trauma; it is exempt *a priori* from the need to ward off a possible foreign element because it cannot suffer anything from the outside that is not already available to it in its own program. While mortal autism involves an "empty fortress" reinforcing itself against the outside, the exquisite autism of the metaphysically interpreted soul has the properties of a complete fortress. Whatever sought to penetrate it—but from which outside?—is already contained in it. With sublime explicitness, Plato formulates the concept, or image, of the phantasm of a living intelligence that no longer has to pay for its receptivity and sensitivity by being vulnerable, deformable and destructible: the "world soul" is a sensibility curved towards itself in comprehensively auto-sensitive fashion, excluding all external, potentially injurious or heteronomous "information." Just as the world body needs to have a perfectly smooth surface because it exists with no environment, independently of anything outside itself, and knows no metabolism, the world soul can circle exclusively in itself, as its saturation with every identity and every difference means that is has no need to learn—at most, to refresh its memory through an external stimulus. Like a biochemical immune system that could deal with all pathogens thanks to internal recognition and neutralization programs for every one of them, the world soul can deal with any experience because its complete endowment with the archetypes of the same and the other places it ahead of all new events. It is the perfect knowledge facility, reducing everything seemingly new to the familiar.

Looking back at the form-metaphysical explication of the soul in its highest psycho-cosmic manifestation is instructive, for it reveals what is expected of the subordinated souls—those of peoples, cities, communities, families, and last but not least the individual souls, in this order of things. "World soul" is the title of a super-immunity that offers a far-reaching guarantee of integrity to those who share in it—with the precarious qualification that the protection of the psychic form can never extend to the unsustainable part of existence, the bodily and experiential dimension. As we know, Platonic immunity is restricted to the "spirit realm," whereas the frail sensate bodies only remain in shape temporarily, as long as the soul remains in them. Platonic philosophy accordingly recommends itself as a school of separation in which the distinction of the sustainable from the ephemeral is practiced in advance. This enabled Socrates to teach without irony that the philosopher's aim is to have died as much as possible in his lifetime.[139] Dying is an analysis—dissolution of the body-dependent union of sameness and otherness with the aim of returning the sameness part to the immortal reservoir of pure forms.

In this retrospective, we see that the metaphysical interest in the immortal was one of the implication forms of later concern for technically formulated and reconstructed immunity, to the extent that the metaphysical project involved an effort to protect life from the life-opposed aspect of life itself. Seeking refuge in form was meant to remedy injuries and disfigurements that are inseparable from the risk of existence; indeed, it makes provisions against finitude as such. This version of concern for the perpetuation of life (Heidegger, stimulated by Nietzsche, even saw it as the resentment of the refusers towards passing time) was clearly based on the sublime confusion of life with form—a confusion that advanced the notion that life was only alive because it shared in a higher level, that of the spirit. It was not without reason that this was called the life of life. Humans can only be saved from their frailty if protected by a substance that cannot die, in the sense that it stands beyond the difference between death and life. Asserting the share of the living in this substantial layer is already enough to gain the entitlement to extrapolate from life to the inability to die. This is how operation immortality was to be accomplished.

It could only succeed by methodically distracting attention from the question of whether eternalized life was alive in a plausible sense, or whether those who make this claim are simply beating the drum for something unnamed and dead. If one follows this suspicion, the diagnosis becomes more plausible that the metaphysical "immune system" enlists a special form of deadness, whether one calls it spirit, form or idea, as a defense against death and all other vital risks, taking into account the danger of surrendering life in advance to its opposite on the pretext of saving it. The secret of metaphysics: did it not consist in equating forms with the essence of life? And was it not destined to spawn a para-vitalism which claimed to be placing empirical life under the protection of a higher life, yet actually subordinated it to the dead or the spiritual, or more precisely that which cannot die because it never lived—the realm of numbers, proportions, ideas and pure forms (and lethal simplifications)? Athanasian para-vitalism equips the world of forms with experiences of fulfillment and happiness that are borrowed from ephemeral sensitive life and projected into the after-life as if in the noble elsewhere, freed from their sorrowful other side, timelessly repeatable.

For centuries, the metaphysically coded concept of the soul was the most suggestive proposition articulating interest in anti-corruption programs for that which was frail and alive. It was the first comprehensive antibiotic and analgesic. Its strength lay in the ability to allow the most popular and most subtle interpretations; its comprehension extended from non-rational notions of arousal and power to the intelligence level of mathematical angels.

However far removed the metaphysically interpreted soul may be from the modern notion of an antibody patrol specializing in defense against microbes and that of an endocrinological shield, it combined the sensitive mobile level of empirical vitality with the defense and maintenance provided by a meta-vital formal level. If there was ever consolation in philosophy, it was that which came from the immune effects of such form-related observations.

Nonetheless, one cannot overlook the fact that in its ethical approach, the notion of the world soul was the exact opposite of an individual immune system: in the metaphysical regime, individuals are subjected to a holistic instruction that requires them to sacrifice their willfulness and surrender to the workings of a grand plan; here salvation comes exclusively from connection to the whole and devotion to something encompassing. That is why an all-pervasive anti-egotistical propaganda is constitutive of the metaphysical order: because the ability of individuals to be whole is conceived in terms of their share in the forms and generalities, individuals are suspected from the outset of potentially trying to give their egos illegitimate precedence over the whole. Metaphysics protects totalities from the independent impulses of individuals more than it protects individuals from their life risks. Its pathos lies in viewing existence purely in terms of the grand symbiosis. It does not want to make individuals easy-living, but rather easy-dying. The concept of the universal soul promotes the absorption of the small by the great with the irresistible connotations of meaning and warmth that emanate from the universalized version of the organism concept, which are augmented by the bonuses of a certain pan-familialism. When everything corresponds to everything else in a benign whole, everything is also related to everything else in a distantly intimate fashion. The fact that pan-symbiosis, in its deep structure, was actually a pan-thanasia, was allowed to remain hidden for a notably long time behind the sublime effects of references to the universal connectedness of things.

One cannot gain an accurate impression of the recent European history of ideas as long as one overlooks its hidden main motif, which is this: Plato's second chance. Renaissance thought already responded early on to the world picture-exploding effects of the new empiricism—Columbus' voyage, Magellan's crossing, the early earth globography, the mapping of the world, the dissection of bodies, early chemistry and the expansion of mechanical engineering—with a dramatic revival of Platonic natural philosophy and a resumption of classical pan-psychism and pan-organicism. This means that the oft-cited "disenchantment of the world" through the modern sciences never took place, any more than its supposed re-enchantment through vitalist and neo-religious movements—rather, mechanistic and pan-psychist motifs in the process of Modern Age thought were polemically and coproductively intertwined from the outset, and still are to this day.

In 1612, John Donne saw cause to mourn the death of the world soul in his poem "An Anatomy of the World." What he meant was the fading of the pre-Christian cosmic piety that, even after its Christian transformation, still tried to see the universe as a living whole. The lament is unmistakably a response to the early effects of mechanization. At the same time, the poet's farewell to the *anima mundi* constituted the most powerful performative proof of his object's vitality. In his time, under a variety of names, the cosmotheist elements of the Greek interpretation of nature were already receiving modern honors in a critical function. The longer the triumph of post-Cartesian and post-Hobbesian mechanistics continued, the more certain it became that it would call forth its vitalist, pan-organological alternative, which was usually acutely aware of belonging to the kinship system of Platonic universal-soul doctrines. The line extends from the Platonic revival in Florence during the late fifteenth century to the pansophists and magi in the Baroque period of polymaths and Cambridge Platonists. The subtle chain continues from these to the pantheisms of Goethe's time, as well as the Romantic nature-philosophical wing of German Idealism, along with its delayed recurrences in the mixed system of speculative-positivist interpretations of nature that characterized the nineteenth century. These different branches of popular Platonism's success should be held responsible for the ease with which such words as "universe" and "soul" rolled off the tongues of beautiful souls in the Age of Enlightenment. It was more than a mere figure of speech, however, when Hegel noted about Napoleon in his well-known letter to Niethammer of October 13, 1806 that he had seen the emperor— "this world soul"—an individual who "concentrated here at a single point, astride a horse, reaches out over the world and masters it."[140]

The impulses from the poetic pantheisms of 1800, as well as the (to use Fechner's term) "nightside" hermeneutics of a universally sympathetic nature that flourished between 1810 and 1850,[141] led to the renewed development of a shared European political climate around 1900, a late Neoplatonic world soul mood and folk-pantheist organicism in which the word "life" was uttered like a creed infused with the secrets of redemption. Needless to say, this piety towards life was spawned primarily by the opposing position, which at no time retracted its claims. With all its might, it emphasized its resistance to the advanced reinterpretation of nature as an industrial resource and provider of raw material in the mechanist-capitalist worldview. The latter had almost become the overriding doctrine after being joined by the self-declaration, highly aware of its principles, of the technical-pragmatic conception of the world. This is exemplified by the final vision in the book *The Old Faith and the New* (1872), widely read in its time, penned by the ex-theologian and great German philistine David Friedrich Strauss, who was intoxicated by his notion of the modern world as a planetary factory building. The Anglo-Saxon counterpart to this stance was found among the utilitarians and optimists, for whom the word "factory" was not so much a metaphor for the world as a fact to which one had a concrete connection as an owner, employee or customer. Without fearing the charge of philistinism, they pushed back the anti-analytical demands of the Romantic-holistic world feeling with their liberal propaganda of work-based reason.

And yet: although large parts of the history of ideas in the second half of the nineteenth century could be read like a report on disappointed pantheism,[142] it was only the deep caesura caused by the First World War that completed the disaster which befell the neo-European version of the world soul idea; its stubborn survival in quietist subcultures did nothing to change this. Even its therapeutic use remained an agreement between marginal parties, and did not restore any of its culture-defining power. The de-animist turn had been prepared by the naturalist infiltration of pantheism, which was already more or less a *fait accompli* around 1900, albeit barely understood by its contemporaries. Speaking of nature as a power had long ceased to be a variation on the poetic utopianism of unification from Goethe's time, nor did it constitute a tribute to the early Romantic hypothesis of a salvifically empowered unconscious whose dominion precedes all egoticity. It now positioned itself more among the "dark" factors of sexus, drive energetics, will to power and vital élan.[143] It nonetheless remains justified to read the darkened natural philosophies from the turn of the century as metastases of the world soul doctrine. In a number of these new nature-metaphysical systems, God and the world soul were simply replaced by figures such as the "world breath,"[144] the "oceanic feeling," the primary ego-world difference and other pseudonyms for the "principle of life." It was only from the neo-objective caesura of the 1920s onwards that this immune-theoretically and environment-theoretically modernized, cool ontology could gain the intellectual and culture-atmospheric plausibility that is a precondition if the aim is to establish an image of nature, or society, as an epitome of polemically self-isolating, self-preserving units that reciprocally turn themselves into an "environment." It is in this constellation that the motif of coldness began its career.[145]

As usual, one must avoid generalizing about trends: even if one does not fail to notice the mechanist and functionalist angle in the logics and moods of the twentieth century, one must still acknowledge that some of the most powerful delayed recurrences of the world soul idea were located in the era of world wars—I am thinking of Alfred N. Whitehead's psycho-cosmological system, presented most subtly in *Process and Reality* (1929), and the poeticized Platonism of Hermann Broch, which unfolded with self-assured untimeliness in his late novel *The Death of Virgil*. In this work, classical metaphysics is transformed into a cosmo-poetics of breathing.

The European Modern Age as a whole offers the sight of an over-innovated and deregulated civilization in which the cultures of the world soul belief and progressive mechanistics existed in antagonistic intertwinement as constant mutual irritants— though the frontlines often became confused, not infrequently colliding in one and the same person, as Newton's example demonstrates. They form the two cultures whose antithesis dynamized the history of ideas in Europe from the seventeenth century onwards. Charles Percy Snow's well-known distinction between literary and technical-scientific intelligence offers no more than an impoverished afterimage of their opposition, squeezed in between the battlements of the academic ivory tower.[146]

The discovery of immune systems and their incorporation into the ecology of knowledge in modern "society" presupposed an overall cultural situation in which the secession of classical holism through a contemporary organism-and-environment view pushed its way onto the agenda. Only in the new form of thought could the metaphysical imposition that was devotion and the willingness to a poetic embrace of the universe be set aside as matters of private mood. Scientific research into the empirical and functional conditions of integrity at the level of the individual organism could be approved without immediately incurring charges of amoralism or even cultural subversion for this perspective. In the course of biological foundational research, a dimension of unconscious, pre-personal inter-organismic battles came to light that effectively defeated classical moral holism. To the extent that a somatic immune system embodies an anti-microbial defense mechanism, this and its owner—the individual—have a "share" in an innocent defensiveness that is no longer affected by the criticism of egotism in holistic ethics. It is part of the nature and the virtue of a system capable of self-preservation that it can fend off its invaders and competitors for the occupation of the same biological space—especially when the symbiotic alternatives have been exhausted.

Viennese psychoanalysis took over a revealing dual role in the transition from the holistically negative to the systemically positive interpretation of individual self-isolation against the all-encompassing, in the sense that its basic doctrine of repressed trauma and later systematization of defense mechanisms had already advanced to a semi-immunological standpoint. On the one hand, Freud had acknowledged the psycho-organismic inevitability of primary defense against unbearable mental presences, and on the other hand, he had made the personal-historical and therapeutic expedience of removing this hardened defense *a posteriori* the focus of his clinical procedure. In this manner, a leftover of holistic ethics came to affect psychoanalytical practice: only those able to break away from entrapment in a defensive structure, namely neurosis, would be equipped to return to the undistorted total perception of their existential situation, and thus—so it was claimed—to recover their mental health. This same Janus-faced character can be observed in the psychoanalytical theory of narcissism, which upon first reading alleges a perverse self-referentiality among certain individuals, but subsequently, under the heading of "primary narcissism," undertakes a positivization of the autoerotic dimension and admits that the latter constitutes a precondition for successful psycho-organismic integrity. The history of the concept of narcissism mirrors the civilization change in the twentieth century leading from stoic beginnings to Epicurean culminations—a shift of emphasis that could be interpreted as a trace of entropy in the moral field. What is significant for our context is that the theoretical fates of a psychoanalysis under attack re-enacts the drama of explication in whose course the immunological-systemic paradigm enters the stage.

Only once the explication of immune structures had unfolded sufficiently did the means to describe modern societies as multiplicities of immune-space productions become available— or, to reintroduce the central metaphor of this third section in the novel of spaces: as *foams*. When Jakob von Uexküll formulated the thesis that it had been a mistake to view the human world as a shared stage for all living creatures, he was not only drawing the life-scientific conclusion from the deflation of the world soul idea; he was also taking the step from monologic metaphysics, which interprets the world as a monocontext and projects it onto a single eye, to a pluralistic ontology that estimates as many worlds as there are eye types and other sensors to see and feel them, without resorting to the hypostasis of an eye of all eyes (or a sensor of all sensors). Only thus could he arrive at the aforementioned, far-reaching conclusion that the universe consisted "not of a single soap bubble that we have blown up beyond our horizon into the infinite (interjection in mid-sentence: the best characterization of metaphysical activity ever given from outside the profession!), but of countless millions of narrowly bounded soap bubbles that overlap and intersect everywhere."[147]

In the same way that wishes are usually ironized by their fulfillment, metaphysical longing, after its explication through the seizure of power by technology, must brace itself to be refuted by success—it could be that in its case too, coming true amounts to the same thing as being parodied. European intellectual history takes its most ironic turn in the modern fates of the world soul idea. As citizens of a modern culture of reason, we still wanted to be souls and explicated ourselves as users of immune systems; we wanted to share in the guarantees of invulnerability offered by the form of all forms, and exposed ourselves as nervous systems; we wanted to anchor ourselves in the whole, and dispersed ourselves into the multiplicities of systems with their specific environments. At the height of world soul élan, we even wanted to conceive a universe in which everything communicates with everything else, and made a world explicit for ourselves in which almost everything defends itself from almost everything else.

So how should we think in future if we want to secure the salvageable remainder of the once-metaphysically coded longing for openness, communication and universal connectedness in the face of these articulated positions of systemic knowledge?

5. Program

To conclude this exposition, it is still necessary to transpose Uexküll's pluralistic axiom from the biological to the meta-biological level, and from this to the culture-theoretical level. The vital "foams" evoked by the biologist, these soap bubble multiplicities of creatures in their own respective environments, are not yet defined with sufficient complexity to characterize human spheres in their specific properties. Even if the latter share with all other life the trait of living in environments that overlap and intersect everywhere, their structure is still one ontological dimension wider than biologically interpreted living things and habitats, whose borders are guarded by an endogenous defense and species-specific escape patterns.

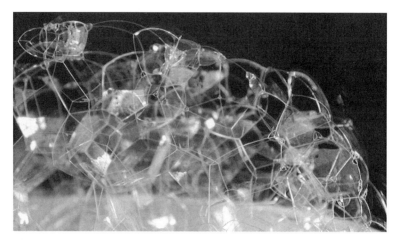

Large-celled soap foam

The bubbles in the aggregate of human spatial multiplicities must not only be stabilized by defensive means; their survival also depends on a primary extensibility that could be outlined with such concepts as creativity and capacity for relationships, had they not already become inflationary. What lies before us is the task of marking multiplicities of individual space among humans as processes of form in which defense and invention merge into each other—as speaking foams, one could say, as immune systems that dream beyond themselves. The human households described here as cells in the social foam make use—beyond merely defensive provisions—or manifold expansion mechanisms extending from the setting-up of a living container, via the establishment of a personalized traffic system, to the creation of a customized world picture poem. Such observations provide a concept of immunity with aggressive qualities: starting from the biochemical layer of meaning, it moves up to an anthropological interpretation of the human *modus vivendi* as self-defense through creativity.

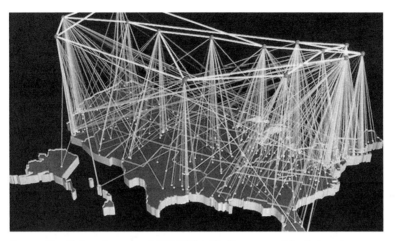

Donna Cox/Robert Patterson, NSFNET traffic flows across North America

The constant work of humans on their own life spheres are thus the primary aphrogenic activity: they produce multiplicities composed of bubbles or households whose compression into dense neighborhoods produces the perceptible space-stacking effect that we call foam. These generalized concepts of immune structures bridge the gap between the theory of endogenous defense mechanisms and the theory of the endo-atmospherically protected space, and between these and the theory of cultures as self-climatizing (and potentially self-poisoning) life form units.

Speaking of foam provides a metaphor that is used as a term of explication for multiplicities of neighboring, interlocking, piled-up improvisations of habitat immunity that have attracted the attention of theory. It serves to formulate a philosophical-anthropological interpretation of modern individualism that I am convinced cannot be adequately described using previously existing means. Foam theory is connected to the

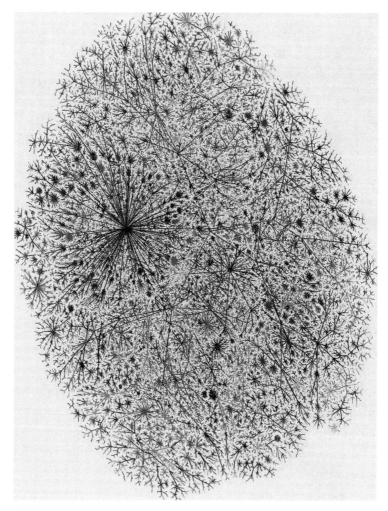

Bill Cheswick/Hal Burch, Internet connections in the northern hemisphere

prospect of a new explicatory form for what sociological tradition calls the social bond or "social synthesis"—an explanation that goes beyond the classic answers to the Kantianizing question of how "society" is possible as a collective of shareholders.

The familiar suggestions for solutions offered by such concepts as division of labor (Smith, Durkheim), capital context (Marx) imitation and somnambulism (Tarde), interdependency (Simmel), sacrifice (Girard, Heinrich) or progressive differentiation and communication (Luhmann) all suffer from the same deficit: they do not adequately address the spatial qualities of social cells or the immune system character of primary spaces.[148]

The densely packed, mutually semi-transparent spatial multiplicities designed according to the media-related and psychological rules of individualism are also called foams because their improbability needs to be highlighted, yet their fragility must not be judged as a deficient life achievement on the part of their inhabitants. The strong characteristic of individualist life forms is that they must attempt spatial formations amid a global situation whose extreme level of activity leads to a constant overtaxing of innate and acquired immune structures. Stability through liquidity—the formula of postmodernity penetrates to the core of general immunology. Never before was the maintenance of self-affirmation dependent on so many additional functions beyond the defensive level. The immunological purpose of creativity now comes to light very clearly: it serves the tensile forces that open up concrete life spheres and keep local improvisations in shape. Worry not about the creativity of the following day; it is enough for each day to have its own upswing.

The foam metaphor has the merit of capturing the topological allocation of creative and self-securing creations of living space in an image. It not only reminds us of the tight proximity between fragile units, but also of the necessary self-enclosure of

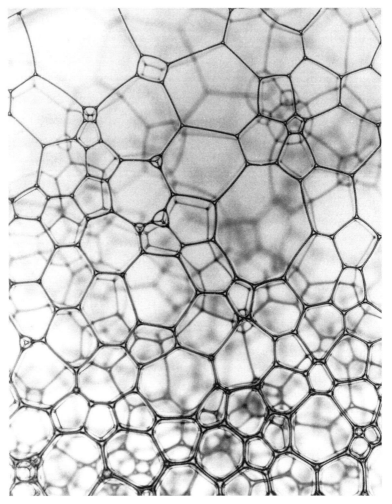

In the formation of plant embryos, the thickness of cell walls is an indication of aging

each foam cell, even though they can only exist as users of shared separation installations (walls, doors, corridors, roads, fences, border installations, hatches and media). Thus the notion of foam evokes both the co-fragility and the co-isolation of these units stacked in dense lattices. Coexistence must be envisaged as co-insistence: nowhere has this been more clearly and technically certain than in space-dividing and space connecting concepts in contemporary architecture, especially in the formula "Connected Isolation" suggested by the American architectural firm Morphosis (Thom Mayne and Michel Rotondi, founded in 1974). The concept of co-insistent systems emphasizes the simultaneity of adjacency and separation—a state of affairs without whose pervasion modern large-scale "societies" would be incomprehensible. A socio-morphologically appropriate description of housing areas, apartment houses and estates presupposes adequate tools to grasp co-insistent coexistence and the interconnected isolation of inhabitable spheric units. The concept of co-isolation in foam can be used to redress the misleading effects of the strained metaphor of the network, of which too many authors expected too much— usually without noticing that their talk of interconnection was borrowing from an incorrect picture and an overly reductive geometry: instead of emphasizing the independent spatiality of the communicators that are meant to be connected to one another, the image of the network suggests the notion of inextended points joined as intersections of lines—a universe for data fishers and anorexics.

Speaking of foams highlights the individual volume of the communicating units. It is perhaps not suitable for conceptualizing the relative autonomy of productions of meaning and their decoupling from social functions, but certainly for creating an awareness thereof. Niklas Luhmann occasionally made use of this possibility in declaring that when social structure and social semantics come apart, the result is "foam." In the discourse of systems theory, the term describes the effect of inflationary productions of meaning that proliferate without any close link to imperatives of social function. In this sense semantics, like music, would be demonic terrain; it leads to a realm in which individuals are alone with their ideas, their positings and their spiritual abysses. No external norm of reality can control the willful offshoots of their words; no filter of truth can reliably separate the tenable from the untenable in what they say.[149] Without social structure and semantics coming apart, "societies" would not allow their members any experiences of freedom, as the function of the dysfunctional is precisely to create leeway for the individual. Only where foam in Luhmann's sense arises can freedom ensue in concrete terms—freedom in the sense of the individual's emancipation from constrained functioning, and liberation of speech from having to fill out forms for true statements. From this perspective, is the "art of society" as a whole not a realm of foam?—a surprising non-correspondence to the real at a precisely defined point that is authorized for deviation? And is modern "society" as a whole not subject to the law of the increasing discharge of whim and luxury?

From a semantics-critical point of view, foam amounts to a mental paper currency emitted without being covered by any material or functional value (from business, science, the political system, and formal judicial and administrative procedures). The popular figure of "speech bubbles" comes quite close to this view: it refers to the released private languages and expressivities where a surplus of the performative and the autological over every possible connection to material matters is to be expected from the outset. The parrot in *Zazie in the Metro* already knew all about this half a century ago: "You talk and

Philippe Parreno, *Speech Bubbles* (1997), Air de Paris

talk." As soon as it was conceptualized that functional systems function and systems of meaning foam, and why this is so, it was natural to see the inflationary tendency in the production of meaning not so much as a failure to reach a logical norm, but as expressing a tendency towards autonomous fantasies that speaking creatures follow as soon as they become individual or "original" within the group. In the previous century, this was described—in unreasonably derogatory fashion—as the "boundless realm of follies of the unburdened subjective."[150] As soon as one concedes the self-immunizing, individual-space-creating purpose of "originality," or rather of micromanic competency (extending to kitsch and delirium), the constitutive avoidance of reality evident in most human utterances, even a certain degree of hallucination, can be taken as indicating the successful installation of individuals and small groups in their own self-will. Those who are original wear self-woven garments. This raises the question of whether stabilizations of small-scale units of the aforementioned type can be viewed as culture-compatible achievements. An even more serious problem, which is made palpable by the claims of holists, is this: how can one justify demanding that the individuated spaces in which individuals have free rein as chieftains of their own delirium (Axel C. Springer: "If there is one word I hate, it is 'reality'") be "subsumed" under the super-institution of the civilizational "whole"?

The bond of similarity between neighbors in the mountain of foam (described elsewhere as a milieu or subculture) arises neither through joint inspiration nor verbal exchange, but rather because of a mimetic contagion that causes a *modus vivendi*, a way of designing and securing the habitat, to spread through a population.[151] As Gabriel Tarde says, imitation is generation at a distance.[152] "Neighbors" are now the users of analogous immunization strategies, the same patterns of creativity, related arts of survival; this means that most "neighbors" live far away from one another and are only the same by virtue of imitative infections (in today's language: transcultural exchange). If they arrive at a successful "understanding," at an alignment of opinions or joint resolutions, then it is because they have been infected in advance by imitative convergence and pre-synchronized through effective analogies of situation and facilities. Negationists know that people have to talk to one another until the imitative assimilation of negotiators to one another lays an adequate foundation for written agreements. In this sense, negotiation rooms can also be understood as treatment rooms—they are aphrogenic spaces in which new bubbles of commonality are opened up. Communication by verbal and other signs parasitizes pre-communication through related immune and climatic conditions. Among these, the use of analogous rituals, equally strong media and compatible tools is the decisive factor.

Against this background, one can see more precisely through the illusion that consonant communications beyond foam regions or milieu borders are possible. This figment was only able to survive thanks to abstractions in which decontextualized communicators came together at bogus fora to ascertain a commonality articulated in signs and words. It is necessary to counteract such helpless formalisms which, for better or worse, have gained a troubling popularity, both academically and journalistically, with an ethics of situations—or transactions, in a broad sense of the word. It would be a form of business economics for civilization hothouses; one could call it atmosphere ethics. It formulates the good as the breathable; it could also be called soap bubble ethnics. Its hallmark is that it describes the most fragile as the starting point of responsibility. It credits persons and cultures with the atmospheric effects of their actions; it emphasizes climate production as a core civilization process. For the moment, it is sufficient to apply these standards to the present book—without ruling out later generalizations.

Neither Contract Nor Growth

Approaching Spatial Pluralities, Which Are Regrettably Termed Societies

Humans are those who are together but can usually not speak properly about the reasons for their being together. For what does it mean to be together? If no one asks me, I know; if I am asked to explain it, I do not know.

The coexistence of humans with others and other things initially gives no indication that there could be a problem hidden within it, either at the level of being or knowing. Because being together is the basic situation for us, everything that belongs to this is initially given only in the mode of also-known, trivial and self-evident things. As long as one is together with other people and things in the usual way, one always knows enough about this relationship, but one cannot express any of it in an explicit, empowering or accountability-providing way. Such knowledge is a case of almost total implicitness. Its bearers initially share in it only in the mode of blind immersion. To the extent that they belong to groups of those like them along with their possessions, all humans are latently sociologists; most of them, however, see no reason during their lifetime to become them explicitly—they would have to die as members of their group in order to return as observers, a horror to which no one succumbed until the twilight-obsessed nineteenth century. For the longest periods, humans did without the "sociological enlightenment"; they knew little of the accompanying decline in the willingness to lead one's life unreservedly as an agent of one's own group.

During the long evolution of hordes, the coexistence of humans with their others and everything else entered an entangled lack of secrets articulated in the form of kinship systems and logics of similarity. In early cultures, the concept of kinship, in which the vertical relationships of descent between mothers or fathers[153] and their children were drawn together with the horizontal alliances between spouses (along with their respective clans) in a shared nexus, served as a key that opened more or less all doors in the house of coexistence. As long as being and being-related seem synonymous, the question of the other reasons for and modes of coexistence is prevented from developing—perhaps not unfortunately for those concerned. There was only one social network in the anthropological *Ancien Régime*, and it meant the world to those hanging in it. If all relevant others are relatives—ancestors, parents, siblings, children, cousins and in-laws—then being together means navigating the space of familially and tribal law-encoded relationships.[154] The rest can be taken care of by the eternal recurrence of the similar. The motif of kinship of blood, flesh, bone and totem also makes archaic notions of consubstantiality between the members of the clan or line irrefutable; this contributes to neutralizing attempts to become aware of the dimension of foreign and alien policy in marriages, indeed the whole possible chasm of difference between relatives, let alone the unrelated and dissimilar. That external realm which lies beyond relatedness and belonging is, initially and for a long time, the inconceivable that is not reached by any marking. As yet, the unknown does not have anything one could grasp and manipulate it with. In this state of affairs, the problematic element of human coexistence with humans and with other entities remains in latency. The immensity of the foreign lies behind the horizon; the centrifugal forces of the great number are still unknown to the communities; the borders between "we" and "non-we" are so far hardly thought-provoking; the secession of individuals from their forming groups has only just begun, and imperceptibly so; the spool of implications is still rolled up very tightly. The rolled-up do not suspect to what states of unrolledness and unfoldedness the investigation of the reasons for, and forms of, the ability to coexist among associated and released subjects will one day be driven. As yet, they have no idea that closeness and kinship are drops in a sea of distances.

The emergence of the political put an end to the "state of the world" [*Weltzustand*]—Hegel's term—in which coexistence had to be understood exclusively in terms of kinship. If one had to formulate in a nutshell what is new about "politics," it would be this: it is the invention of coexistence as the synthesis of the non-related. It is tied to the creation of a collective commonality not restricted to the familial. The age of early empires and classical city rule—to speak in phrases from political history—was characterized by expanded we-forms. From that point on, what was one's own had to be thought of as a result: when people in that time said "we," they meant a unification of the own and the non-own in an encompassing principle. In this way, the early advanced-civilized problem of integrating large spaces of diversity and non-closeness into something that connected them was solved. This triggered the production of symbolic domes that created a *coelum nostrum*, a firmament of commonalities, above the heads of countless people. What are metaphysics and high religion but grand dome-creating enterprises? The emerging state of the world will be one in which the coexistence and cooperation of actors must be read as a connection beyond marital alliances or genealogical and totemist lineages. The compulsion to develop the grand we-forms initiated the age of artificial solidarities, with its enigmas and ruptures—the era of peoples and meta-peoples, totem communities and magical nations, corporate identities and regional universalisms.

How should one read gathered life as a whole, and the compatibility of the unified in human multiplicities, if the *a priori* coordination between participants provided by the system of blood and marriage can no longer be taken for granted as at the start? How can the coexistence of humans with their kind, including property and family members, in a shared unit be interpreted as a binding relationship of existing with one another, in one another and against one another, once the closeness of their association can no longer be derived from the configurations of a blood-based community? How is *synousia* to be understood when tribal orientations fail and the motif of synthesis has to be defined without recourse to genealogy? The mysterious bond—thus the first information—is formed through participation in the life of the polis, through courtly and imperial services, through spiritual alliances, through commitments to a shared "cause," or through expressions of solidarity *in distans* on the basis of shared values and empathetically felt sufferings. As a last resort, one invokes the constitution of the cosmos, which applies to all, or the world secret, which encompasses all. But is it really enough to view, following Aristotle, a "community of speaking and thinking" as the basis for the coexistence of the non-related many—as the coexistence of humans in the polis obviously means something different from the mute togetherness of "cattle, grazing in the same place"?[155] Are we adequately grasping coexistence if we interpret it, in agreement with the author of the *Nichomachean Ethics*, as a synergy of politics and friendship?

It testifies to the charisma of European antiquity that it raised these questions, or at least precursors to them, in a suggestively concrete form—more still, that the answers it was able to provide remained in use until yesterday, and could only recently be replaced by fundamentally improved tools for describing social and political issues. The answers and the questions had both been triggered by the crisis and catastrophe of Greek city rule at the dawn of the fourth century BC—in notable parallel with the crisis and triumph of Greek philosophy and science, which developed around the same time into a general theory of the coexistence of entities with entities as such.[156] The philosophy that was truly new in Plato's century interpreted the cohabitation of humans with their own kind and with animals, stones, grasses, machines, gods and planets in a eutonically proportioned, mathematoidly structured whole under the auspicious title of *kósmos*. It rarely spoke of this without extrapolating from the astounding large-scale order to the capacity of individual souls to be in order and in their place, and their cooperation in the imaginarily reformed polis. The ancients in general rarely speak of the universe without also mentioning the city, and hardly ever discuss the city without gazing out into the universe through analogical glasses.[157] As the great sum of places, the one is respectively exemplary for the other.

In the context of these urban-cosmological observations, two divergent, even opposing explanations for the how and why of coexistence between so many differing in appearance, social standing and origin in the community—explanations that, in view of their history of effects, deserve to be called archetypal. In them, kinship as the reason for coexistence has been replaced by more abstract principles. The first interprets human coexistence as a result of an original gathering and agreement of individuals who are initially posited entirely for themselves; the second interprets the mystery of coexistence in the organismic parable, through the ontological and legal precedence of a totality of individual "parts" or members. That both explanations appear in Plato's writings proves not so much their compatibility as the lack of concern for systematization in the founding days of philosophical thought.

As far as the explanation of "society" through gathering is concerned, which would serve as the model for later contract theories, going to the sources leads to, among other places, the third book of Plato's *Laws*, in which the possible creation of a state through the unification of the few survivors after the last Great Flood is taken into consideration. The attraction of Plato's flood theory is that it provides the starting conditions to form a society of adult individuals without the philosopher having to resort to property-individualistic abstractions—which, as is well-known, only managed to gain a veneer of plausibility in the modern contract-theoretical constructions of community by Thomas Hobbes and John Locke. Plato's "natural state" shows an ensemble of humans after the cataclysm whose individuality is not derived from their egotistical nature or their overriding interest in self-preservation and self-empowerment, but from their chance survival on the peaks of the mountains—which also suggests that the actors of the first gathering must, for the most part, have been solitary, sodomitical shepherds who were now, after the end of all civilization and statecraft in the valleys, overcome by the need to come together. The gender question can remain in the background—as if it were tacitly understood among the ancient Greeks that one could accept the conversion of alpine sodomy into urban pederasty as long as other intercourse provided the state with new citizens. Plato does not need to say any more about the other motives for community formation (*synoikía*), as classical anthropology presupposes that humans are naturally sociable and is only occasionally perturbed by isolated cases of asociality, as appeared in fates like that of Philoctetes and first outbreaks of misanthropy. "And what a pleasure it must have been to see each other, there being so few of them at that time!"[158] Plato does not forget to note in his myth of primal gathering, furthermore, that the first associates were accompanied in their frugal neo-community by certain livestock such as goats and cattle, who had likewise survived—though this is of no consequence for the theory of coexistence with others in a political whole (another way of saying that domesticated animals remain unrepresented in this regime).[159]

In early Greek tradition, the motif of society growing through the gathering of adults living in isolation is not without some plausibility—at least, it constitutes a usable phantasm as soon as one recalls that more than a few of the most important cities of Attica supposedly grew from a *synoikismós*, the decision of once-autonomous, aristocratically ruled communes to join forces within shared walls. In addition, the adherents of this assembly theory could point to the frequently reported phenomenon of "formation of peoples from asylum," which—in stark contrast to modern, romanticized and substantial concepts of peoples—shows how numerous later "peoples" developed through the mingling of asylum-granting and asylum-seeking populations of the most varied origins.[160] (In addition, such constructs as the refuge cities of antiquity and the free towns of the Middle Ages prove the formation of a more or less homogeneous population from initially completely heterogeneous aggregates of humans.) But whether ethnopoiesis takes place through contract or by throwing together different tribes, both points of view must discourage national essentialists and ethnozoologists. The purpose of attributing human coexistence to assembly, however, is not historical in any case. Rather, the proponents of such theories aim to interpret coexistence "in company" as an expression of the interests of the associates, with the goal of subjecting the condition of actual communities to a sensibleness check from the perspective of participants' interests. Plato's works of state theory (the *Republic*, the *Statesman* and the *Laws*) already made it clear that the empirical polis was not up to such an examination—which is why it had to accept the departure of the most intelligent and dissatisfied to the outland of rationalism, the cosmopolis. Since that time, the brilliant have had a second domicile in the general. Hence the notions of a new beginning of "society" thanks to a primal gathering of interest pursuers who are adult, reasonable and fit for contract are often articulated in the form of utopias—that is, of travel brochures advertising fabulous conditions on islands governed by reason. They are meant to prove that "societies" are possible at all. Consequently, utopianism—especially in the guise of political island dreams—could be seen as the natural dialect of the contract-happy Modern Age, adopting analogous enterprises from antiquity as preparatory exercises for its own projects. As Gilles

Deleuze noted in an early text, the desert island offers a suitable home for the idea of a second, richer new beginning.[161]

What the fantasies of an original gathering of individuals to form "society" are ultimately about can only be seen in the new descriptions of human associations as results of contracts that were circulating from the seventeenth century onwards. According to these, all historical peoples—or whatever one wishes to call the units of humans usually coexisting in genealogical lines—emerged from a coexistence contract made *in illo tempore* and repeated in the present day between the members of the collective, just as a trade society results from the meeting of shareholders to form legally organized enterprises with joint responsibility. It is clear that theories of this type are formulated in the service of individualism, both the possessive and the expressive kind, assuming we define it as the passion for being an individual and independent. It is the passion of the individual individual to assert themselves as the *maître et possesseur* of their own life with all its extensions. Self-possession, as modern owners understand it, presupposes breaking with one's own past and that of the collective; it demands rejecting the dictates of genealogy and every form of chain that seeks to extend to today from what was. No patricide is productive unless expanded to include the ancestors. The clean slate of restart reason is one that cannot bear any names of forebears or ancestors as soon as they seek to be more than distant advisers.[162] Whoever speaks of "society" means, if they know what they are saying, an association of restarters who elevate forgetting to the foremost virtue.[163]

The pattern for this is well-known: for the initiator of more recent radical contractualism, Thomas Hobbes, individuals filled with a reasonable fear of death founded the state company

Leviathan, claiming that it was directed by its general manager, the prince, as a sublimely terrifying service enterprise for creating peace and legal certainty in a former civil war zone. The object of the contract in Hobbes' case is a cryptic transference of the willfulness of all individuals to the ruler, who thus holds power only on the basis of being a favored third party. He is an absolute monarch, in that his sovereignty brooks no dissent, and a constitutional one, in so far as his power is nothing but the cumulative effect resulting from his contractual partners delegating their passions for self-rule to the one who is meant to discipline, threaten and tower above all. The notorious contractual terms on which constitutional absolutism rests once signed by all parties is as follows:

> I authorize and give up my Right of Governing my selfe, to this Man, or to this Assembly of men, on this condition, that thou give up thy Right to him, and authorize all his Actions in like manner. This done, the Multitude so united in one Person, is called a COMMON-WEALTH [...].[164]

The nub of this conditional oath lies in the fact that through the cunning of the contract, the state people is united in a single person (or a single chamber) without having to assemble physically—and the abstention from assembly is indeed no less vital than the abandonment by all of any effective pretensions to self-governance. As soon as the contractual partners insisted one day on convening in visible assemblies again, the absolutist idea of rational delegation would be no more; from 1789 onwards the new sovereign, the people of the nation-states, would—despite all efforts to implement a democratic idea of representation—keep devoting itself anew to the dream of an actually present assembly of business partners in large-scale joint works, and the trail of violence left by the will to direct assembly would shape what we call the age of the masses. (Which is why the slogan of the anti-G8 protesters at Genoa in July 2001, "You are G8, we are 6 billion," evokes mixed feelings for those familiar with history.)

As far as the forcible constructivism of *Leviathan* is concerned, it results—leaving aside systemic motives—primarily from Hobbes' macabre views on the original interactions between humans. In their merely natural, pre-state or insufficiently state-like coexistence, humans necessarily form peaceless multiplicities for what seem to be timelessly valid reasons: those who live at the same time are condemned to tireless competition and merciless war because each individual is forced, like a *perpetuum mobile* of egotism, to reach out into their world and harm rivals in the battle for scarce resources. Consequently, an interminable war over unshareable assets and positions of advantage stirred up the social field. Civil war speaks the truth about the coexistence of citizens before the contract. As a war of all against all, it is the most powerful symbiotic mechanism because it creates a kind of closeness among combatants that only becomes accessible through the heartiness of mutual hatred. For Hobbes, this war is the natural result of the spontaneous pluralism of arrogances, which means that only a second gathering under one ruler who kept everyone in check with equal intensity could ensure bearable conditions among the associates. An arrogance abstention contract is required as a foundation for society as a whole: "society" is initially no more than a name for the association of subjects who have relinquished their presumptions. It follows from this that those without property do not belong to

Body of Leviathan

society, for they have not yet achieved anything they could abandon; similarly, incorrigible aristocrats are not fit for society because they find themselves unable to distance themselves from their inherited presumption. Obsessed with their right to innate prestige and maximum expansion, they are unable to be subjects in a regulated commonwealth; they prove eternally restless, uncastratable anarchists. For Hobbes, it seems certain that the natural multiplicity of presumptions can only be contained by the wonderful artificiality of the state machine.

In its application to the body politic, contractual thought constitutes an early, suggestively one-sided explicatory form for what, initially, only appears in primary knowledge about human coexistence with one another in compact implications. If I interpret human association as the result of a contract, then I have a concept at my disposal whereby to understand those living together as associates and their form of existence as society— which enables me to see the principle of their connection clearly before me. If I am justified in imagining a society in the aforementioned sense as an interest-driven person machine, then its *modus operandi* is no longer a secret. "Social synthesis" would be carried out through the interplay of contractually coordinated, and thus transparent individual wills. Whoever speaks of contract believes that they are looking, so to speak, at the construction plan or organigram of the association. When interests can be expected, there is no need to allege any mysterious solidarities, deep pre-contractual connections or pre-rational depths of community.

Indeed: in a state of the world increasingly characterized by industrial enterprise, financial capital, trade and exchange traffic, wage labor, bargaining rounds, services, adverts, media and fashions, the concept of "society" has descriptive power in an immense number of situations. Its rise to become the dominant metaphor for the whole coexistence of humans and other entities in a shared unit was quickened by strong empirical suggestion during the age of transition to modern conditions—one could even welcome it as a rationally satisfying explication for cooperating collectives in general, were it not for the fact that only the present, against the foil of the contract's assertion, had to become conspicuous and ripe for explication: that some of the central dimensions of human coexistence are under no circumstances contractual in character or defined by community of purpose, and never can be. This begins with family connection—or did my progenitors make a child-begetting contract with me? Can I claim to have signed a contract of kinship with my parents and siblings? The field of "grown," never contractually reconstructible relationships extends further to religious affiliations, whether of a folk-religious nature or acquired through declared belief and accession to a spiritual community, and also encompasses culture-communal identification groups of national, tribal or even entrepreneurial character (as the example of Japanese corporate feudalism demonstrates). And above all else, the continuing conditions of direct and indirect domination under the guise of contractuality deny the contractual fiction. In the light of the forming societality of human coexistence and its analysis in the "sociologies" of the Modern Age, however, these objections come too late.

Nonetheless, confusion over the inappropriateness of these language conventions is becoming acute. It is hardly surprising that during the development of "civil society," especially in the interpretive postludes to the French Revolution, more than a few thinkers, invoking the aforementioned aspects of human coexistence, began to revolt against the contractualistically exaggerated absurdities of one-sided "Enlightenment." Now such concepts as tradition, custom, people, culture and community could be charged up with a previously unknown pathos; some whose used these words hoped they would provide no less than the true sociodicy. It was, above all, the word "community" that charged itself up with group-metaphysical connotations that had so far been alien to it. Invoking it, the movements of Romanticism, conservatism and dialectical state holism—with Marxism as an aggressive sociologistic variant—formed roughly synchronously as three attempts characterized by a high degree of modernity to ward off individualist and atomist ideologies. But these movements—one could group them together as the revolt of the holists—did not, as one sees in retrospect, have an adequately developed language at their disposal in which to formulate their anti-contractualist intuitions, which is why the heads of this tendency were usually forced to fall back on the clichés of classical authoritarian holism, whose sources—like those of the theory of assembly—can once again be traced back to Plato's *Laws*.

Thus the hour of sociologically advanced holistic thought also struck twice: first in the early rationalist groundwork for the communal system on the basis of classical philosophy, then once again in the modern and counter-modern rediscoveries of community in the holistic sense. As soon as one admits that the principle of human coexistence with humans and other entities cannot be envisaged essentially as a contract, and certainly not a mere agreement of convenience among mature, interest-oriented individuals, one will have to ask in what larger shared structure those coexisting with one another are "contained," and what nexus actually binds them together. Clearly this means finding an explanation for the strong connection between humans, which predates assemblies, agreements, contracts and ratified constitutions. What now comes into view and demands interpretation is the possibility of a unifying and cohesive force of such pervasive shaping power that it would preempt the self-referentiality of interest groups and define all individuals as separate manifestations of a prior communal reality.

What we are dealing with, of course, is totality—that heroine with a thousand guises who appears in traditional wisdom teachings. One can best understand classical holism as a first figure of explication and crisis for what had once been monolithic, as it were automatized expectations of integration, barely in need of articulation, which groups capable of procreation and tradition had of their members—expectations, however, that are disappointed so often and necessarily under advanced conditions that a more explicit new version of the relationship between the polis and its citizens (we are now on the soil of Greek urban cultures) becomes inevitable. The cause of the disappointment is that as soon as the individuals profit from local liberations and urban pamperings, they no longer automatically do what the so-called whole demands of them. This usually manifests itself in an emerging resistance among the serving classes to the services, sacrifices and tributes demanded by those who rule them. The classical city is already sought out by the undesired side effects of its liberality: the first principle of its synthesis, the alignment of the many to serve a shared purpose, is undermined by the second principle, namely the orientation of the citizens towards their legitimate personal and domestic interests; the greater the political successes of the community, the more quickly this weakening

Giuseppe Arcimboldo, *The Trojan Horse* (early 17th century)

becomes clear. The primary risk encountered by the most flourishing commune is that of falling prey to its own prosperity. It is from this situation that the original political philosophy of totality emerged; one could also call it the first ontology of conservatism. It illustrates the Western path to the thought forms of authoritarian administrative empires.

Plato laid out the master argument for the reintegration of deregulated individuals and separatist interest groups into the "one and whole" in Book Ten of the *Laws*—in, not by chance, the context of a treatise on the punishments for crimes against the gods, especially the political-religious capital crime of atheism (which essentially amounts to blasphemy against the whole). The context is revealing because in the discourse of the first political scientist, the gods are recognized as the true and real city media, and *eo ipso* the ontological guarantors of the public spirit. The Athenian who leads Plato's dialogue develops the model of a discourse with whose aid young people at risk of atheism and anomism are to be brought back into the ecosystem of divine world planning: one must, he explains, convince the delinquent that

> The supervisor of the universe has arranged everything with an eye to its preservation and excellence, and its individual parts play appropriate active or passive roles according to their various capacities. These parts, down to the smallest details of their active and passive functions, have each been put under the control of ruling powers that have perfected the minutest constituents of the universe. Now then, you perverse fellow, one such part—a mere speck that nevertheless constantly contributes to the good of the whole—is you, you who have forgotten that nothing is created except to provide the entire universe with a life of prosperity. You forget that creation is not for your benefit: *you* exist for the sake of the universe. [...] With this grand purpose in view [the King] has worked out what sort of position, in what regions, should be assigned to a soul to match its changes of character [...].[165]

The performative key phrase in this address is "you forget" or, differently translated, "it remains hidden from you"—augmented by the implicit injunction: "but here what has long been hidden from you will be revealed once and for all." The doctrine of totality addresses rebellious individuals who must be torn out of the popular state of primal error, the belief that there is a natural multiplicity of more or less equal-ranking individualities, with each taking care of its own matters; here one can simply allow the community to come about, like a byproduct of the separate self-willed life games. That may be what liberal sophists say (and their modern successors, those who romanticize multiplicity, and even worse, the followers of Hayek and other sophists of the market, but worst of all the Deleuzians and Latourians), but such views are not worthy of a (Platonically) thinking essence. Those who would learn the truth must be prepared for higher stakes: Plato's oversized answer to the great question of why humans coexist with their own kind and the rest reaches the level of final theocosmological statements with a bold leap that disregards all bourgeois reservations. According to his theses, the world-whole embodies a perfect work of art—in other formulations even an actually existing happy god,[166] or an environmentless and everlasting hyper-life form[167] that, in keeping with its all-incorporating nature, overtakes, enfolds and integrates all individual beings. Plato's doctrine of the association of beings constitutes philosophical information in the precise sense, assuming one understands philosophy, in keeping with its traditional design, as expertise on conditions of totality—perhaps, in its idealistic main tendency, as a concealed priesthood of totality devoted to a religion of consensus. But however one defines philosophy, it is first and foremost an agency for hyperbolic allegations of order about everything that is the case. Order means placement. It is easy to see why, in tone and tendency, this must be an edifying, that is to say doubt-absorbing information which confronts muddled mortals, the individuals trapped in the inherent error of spontaneous pluralism, with an authoritative statement about ultimate, holistically constituted structural and deep truths that are only fully accessible to experts. Nonetheless, it is part of these conditions that the gospel of the invisible harmony of the whole must also be preached to the layperson and placed into their holding-to-be-true. Anyone who understood this would show the will to keep quiet in the place they had been assigned.

The bait with which Plato means to catch the deviating individual consciousness for the cause of the gods of totality, and the cosmos constituted by them, is not some thesis that convinces because it is appealing. In portraying the cosmos as a perfect totality of meaning conceived down to the last detail and defining the individual human as a functional part of it, the philosopher uses an argument of formal persuasiveness and silencing sublimity—a proof, if one wishes to call it that, whose emanations can be followed through two and a half millennia. The irresistible compulsion exerted by the Athenian's reasoning is grounded in the suggestion to interpret the situation of humans in the political world in terms of a schema, namely the organized whole and its parts—from which, once accepted, only the subordination of the individuals to the overall plan can follow (assuming one rules out an open secession to knowingly desired evil as the other of perfection).

We are witnesses to no less than the argumentational primal scene of holism—and *eo ipso* the primal establishment of all political organicisms, socio-biologisms and theories of statecraft.

What gave this argument its power was the subversive introduction of the teleological principle into the concept of the world, stating that the togetherness of existent things in the universe was determined by an all-pervading context of purpose, just as every detail in a work of architecture is in its place and every organ in a living body selflessly makes its contribution to the healthy eudaimonia of the whole. This introduction was not subversive in the sense of smuggling something unsaid into the discourse to profit through some secret ploy; rather, it announced its fundamental premise in so aggressive a fashion that its precarious status was obscured by the radiance of the over-explicit exposition. All of a sudden, the most improbable thing wanted to be seen as the most certain. The transference of the art work or organism idea to the world-whole occurred with such a persuasive energy that all the addressee could do was agree or resign. As soon as I submit to the allegation that I, with my entire existence, am an organ for a cosmic life form or a building block in an integral temple structure (or, to change metaphors once again, a voice in a universal choir), I submit to an image of my position in the world-whole whose only possible consequence is for me to willingly accept being used up for the supposed purposes of the hypostasized totality. I realize that I am standing exactly where I belong. With the schema of the living whole and its parts, sublime holism provides the matrix for the advanced-civilized ontologies of service, sacrifice and cooperation without which, to this day, no Roman church and no Japanese firm can function, nor any US Marines or any of the military regimes that have shown their fierce colors on the political maps of the twentieth century.

Holistic hypnosis already reached maturity in the time of the Roman Empire. Marcus Aurelius testified to the monolithic naturalism of the Stoics when he termed anyone who dared to take offense at conditions in nature a "tumor on the universe";[168] we are created to cooperate "like the rows of upper and lower teeth."[169] Furthermore, according to this perspective, there are no wrong seats in the universe; every place in the whole is suited to its owner, who can therefore do nothing better than to submit to the divine judgment expressed in their own situation. "Realize the situation" here means "discover the task that is contained in your location." Just as Rousseau states, "Once the State is instituted, consent consists in residence,"[170] the motto of both Plato and Zeno could be that once the cosmos is set up, consent consists in existence itself.

That the application of the organism metaphor to the coexistence of many and different beings in an almost psychosomatically integrated political whole was not an invention of Athenian philosophy alone, but amounts to an elementary idea among early state peoples, is demonstrated by the fable from Asia Minor about the belly and the limbs that entered the canon of Old European political legends through Livy and his eloquent ex-consul Menenius Agrippa. In the second book of his *History of Rome*, which describes events at the dawn of the fifth century BC, Livy describes one of the darkest moments in Roman history, when the city, ravaged by class wars, was paralyzed with panic through the mutual fear (*mutuo metu*) of the noble patricians and the rebellious plebs. It was this desperate situation, in which the few capable of forming judgments saw the restoration of *Concordia* as the only way to salvage the body politic, that became an emergency for the political rhetoric of edification. Menenius wagered the fate of Rome on an organismic comparison:

At the time when men's bodily parts were not as coordinated as they are now and each limb its own way of thinking and its own voice, the other parts were angry that they had the worry, trouble, and effort of providing everything for the belly; whereas the belly had a quiet time in their midst, doing nothing except enjoying the good things that they supplied. So, they made a conspiracy that the hands should not carry food to the mouth, nor should the mouth receive what it was given, nor the teeth chew it. While they wanted to starve the belly into submission, their anger caused all the limbs and the entire body almost to waste away. It was then apparent that the function of the belly was by no means idle: not only was the belly nourished, but it also provided nourishment, since it supplied to all parts of the body the source of our life and strength—our blood, which it apportions to the veins after it is enriched with the food it has digested.[171]

Through the analogy between the revolt of the limbs against the belly and the anger of the plebs at the patricians, Menenius finally persuaded the outraged masses to relent (*flexisse*). The image of the consensus among the organs flexibilizes the rebellious masses and leads them back to cooperation from their paralysis by fear. One can perhaps conclude from the incident that certain darknesses of coexistence can provisionally be lightened by organism images, as if the idea of the antagonistic-cooperative coexistence of unequal elements in an association could only be articulated by borrowing solid biological metaphors. The living body is the pictorial trap into which early holistic thought could not fail to fall. And if an all-integrating divine world-animal such as the Platonic cosmos would later present to an edified student following was not yet in view, a *res publica* animal with reasonable individual organs would serve the same purpose until then.

There is no need to examine the fates of contract theories or organicisms in greater detail in the present context. The fact that both schools have kept themselves alive to the present day—with each other, against each other, interwoven with each other—should be read as an indication of how suggestive were the primary answers to the questions as to the reason for coexistence. Likewise, the modernizations of critical holism, which interpret the principle of social cohesion in terms of the capital process, with its nexus of exchange, or in terms of the progressive differentiation of subsystems within world society, do not require consideration at this point. What is more interesting is that both were accompanied almost from the start from an unease, even a form of incredulousness, towards the element of improbability in both the contractualist and the holistic messages. This skepticism, in turn, left its first traces in Plato's work: as if to discount his own two explanations for community, and making use of a freedom of thought from all orthodoxy, he sketched the outlines of a third theory of social synthesis: that relentlessly realistic, almost functionalist doctrine of the noble lie whereby, according to the recommendations of the *Republic*, feelings of kinship among citizens should be invoked to help deal with the outrage of the disadvantaged at class divisions. Then the principle of human coexistence would lie in a joint mystification or, anachronistically put, in an artificially produced context of delusion encompassing both the liars and those lied to, supposedly for the sake of their own salvation.[172]

Both the doctrine of the contract and holism are hyperboles of pronounced constructivist ruthlessness that are impressive because they renounce everyday experience and replace it with elaborations of an abstract metaphor. The great majority of modern sociologies, political sciences and social philosophies could be characterized as a series of attempts to balance out the overstretches of one approach and another by crossing them with each other, as if one could correct two mistakes by combining them.

Contractualism and organicism alike have yet to answer substantial questions on their object, for they present themselves in order to provide the true reason for human coexistence with humans and other entities, yet are unable to offer any meaningful words about the space in which the synthesis occurs—more still, the space that opens up through this synthesis. Both are blind in their spatial eye, or more generally their situational or contextual eye. They consider this blindness a merit, for they claim to see something in the medium of theory that eludes the pre-theoretical view. The contractual theorist can at least concede that their so-called societies are composed of spontaneously given multiplicities, even though they only reproduce the principle of this composition in a distorted form. By shifting the intelligible reason for the cohesion of the associates into the alleged contract between them, they ignore the starting point, namely the irreducible multiplicity of self-willed systems and adjacent, analogously motivated life games. In this model, all that remains of those factually coexisting in individual spaces and individual times is an abstract plurality of will-points gifted with reason, which turn into "citizens" as soon as they agree on a cooperative life form for the pursuit of joint interests. With deliberate hastiness, the contractualist resorts to the notion of a willful unification of which none will ever be able to say where, when and in what medium it occurred, and how it could be grounded. It is hardly surprising, therefore, that no archivist has yet succeeded in finding the cabinet in which the social contract is stored. Contractualism lives off hallucinations known today as counterfactual assumptions—especially that of an original gathering in which it pleased the associates to leave their pre-contractual mode and adopt the protection of shared laws. The exquisite nowhere in which the contract is made draws attention away from the situative constitution of coexistence and its self-willed spatial dynamics.

Where the concealment of the view of the real is explicitly demanded, as in the recent modernizations of contract theory, for example John Rawls' *A Theory of Justice*,[173] the partners are invited to a sociogenic game of blind man's buff in which, behind a "veil of ignorance," they are meant to reach an agreement amongst themselves about fair conditions. Here the contract must emerge from a topological nirvana, termed the "original position," in which situational blindness is declared a virtue:

> First of all, no one knows his place in society, his class position or social status; nor does he know his fortune in the distribution of natural assets and abilities, his intelligence and strength, and the like. [...] The persons in the original position have no information as to which generation they belong.[174]

One can see in this moral-philosophical construction how contract theory flees with full awareness from improbability to absurdity, with a stopover in counterfactuality—by postulating a population cleansed of all historical, psychological and somatic qualities that keeps itself available as guinea pigs of justice. This is unmistakably an ideology for immigration countries. Their citizens are meant to learn to view their qualities and possessions as things of yesteryear: differences can be washed out. Behind the veil of ignorance, humans without qualities, emblems or papers are to assemble—like a shipload of emigrants who are unloaded in a new country after a long crossing, exhausted and grateful for anything that somehow promises a new beginning, or more still, an encounter group in Greater Philadelphia embarking naked on a journey of self-experience. At any rate, only individuals who have broken with themselves seem suited to fulfill their assigned task, namely to negotiate a just contract of coexistence. Only those who have lost their senses of space, time, fate and mood would be suited to acquire citizenship in a Rawls commune. One can almost hear the voice of the utopian Anarchasis Cloots from the days of the French Revolution, who considered the names of nations (and *ipso facto* those of all localities and proprieties) no more than "Gothic labels." The best legal philosopher evidently has no qualms about demonstrating that they are the worst sociologist, as long as they are given free rein to extinguish the local qualities and resistant colors of coexisting life cells—above all, those that allow the coexistent to be included in their concrete spatial formations and local histories.

In a word, contract theory no longer has a use for the coexistent as they are before or alongside the contract. It addresses itself to people who acquired qualities as sinners, and are willing as penitents to begin anew beyond their qualities—one can tell that we are on Protestant and Kantian terrain. In this, the Rawlsian utopia is congenial with a certain theory of communicative action, which similarly has no use for speakers who speak outside of idealized speech situations. This theory describes the communicators as if their words were the consequences of a statement exchange agreement which they, despairing at their own babble in the natural state, had made with one another in the transition to the linguistic contract state. In both cases: first theory for the last humans.[175]

As far as political organicism is concerned, it fails to grasp the original manifold spatiality of human coexistence with humans and other entities from the opposite side. While the contractual chimera gathers counterfeit, discolored individuals in an imaginary nexus, the organismic phantasm puts real individuals together in a bogus, grotesquely simplified "whole." This explication of social synthesis too distorts the human-spatial, psychospheric, conspiratorial and polemogenic qualities of coexistence by subjecting human living conditions, sharing of tasks and interpretation of situations to a violent over-integration, as if their adjacencies and forms of intercourse could be understood as analogous to the cells and organs in an animal body. In its own way, organicist ideology destroys the reason for the original individual spatialities of coexistence; it presses the adjacent houses, the microspheres, the couples, the teams and clubs, the populations and conventions, staff and classes together to fit into a simplified hyper-body, as if the coexistence of human bodies could produce a vital compound of a higher level, a political Great Animal that would be outwardly free, but on the inside would keep its members confined to their places like entrails, flesh and bones. The compulsively holistic tendency manifests itself even more drastically in the architectural metaphors, which conveyed that the individuals should be built into the state as hewn stones are placed into a magnificent façade. And the board game parable too, where individuals are moved by an all-powerful player like pieces, does not improve things for those being pushed back and forth.

It is clear that analogies based on bodies or works of art are formulated from the spirit of expert rule over concrete totalities—for it is no secret that only specialists know how to erect a house in its entirety, how to steer a ship in its entirety, how to heal a body in its entirety, how to weave a carpet in its entirety and how to lead an army in its entirety. Until the establishment of a kingdom of philosophers that takes control of entire states *lege artis*, one should probably content oneself with a kingdom of weavers and master builders, or better still a kingdom of therapists. Furthermore, the liberal contract theories, like all counterintuitive discourses that abase "common sense," are as expertocratically colored as the holistic ones, with the sole difference that their authors were imagining something more like an advocatocracy. Experience shows that contract theorists are usually only interested in democratic forms to the extent that they guarantee the conditions in which jurists, correctness journalists and professors of moral philosophy are on top.

The poverty of organicism comes from the fact that its legitimate plea for justice in relation to the larger interests of communities usually turns quickly into resentment towards the self-will of the smaller units it has declared "parts." Its typical tone is that of a disempowered aristocracy that preserves its hunger for excellence in the dream of pure service. Noble holists are usually happy to serve the community as wise brains or useful bellies, while expecting that the other organs will also take their places. If one wishes to salvage the productive intuitions of holism, one must develop an alternative view of the association: it is necessary to derive the togetherness, communication and cooperation of the multiplicities of individual spaces tied together by the stress of coexistence, which are regrettably still called societies, from their own conditions—without using the anti-holistic crutches with which individualists and contractualists vault over the railing.

This could, for example—as is attempted here—be carried out with the aid of a theory of spatial multiplicities that tackles the mystery of social synthesis with a situationist, pluralist, asso-cationist, morphological and, above all, a psycho-topological arsenal of descriptive means. This entails the philosophical deci-sion to conceive of unity as an effect—and thus to disenchant any notion of "society" that gives unity precedence over its ele-ments.[176] This would mean no longer seeking its models in the ontological unity of the individuated creature (extending to Plato's cosmic animal), but in the polyperspectival unity of the shared situation simultaneously experienced by several intelli-gences, yet always symbolized differently. Situations are conglomerates (from a different perspective: networks) of actors who are configured in relation to one another, but where not one of them could leave their own skin and brain for the sake of the so-called whole.

A useful pointer towards the path that is to be trodden here can be found in the work of the most philosophical among the Ger-man founders of sociology, Georg Simmel; it is not for nothing that he went down in the annals of the social sciences as the instigator of a non-totalistic analysis of social units. He triggered the initiative to transfer the Kantian "how is it possible" ques-tion from objects of knowledge in nature to "societies," and thus to stimulate reflection on the internal cognitive constitution of human ensembles.[177] Simmel distinguishes unsystematically between three "*a priori* conditions or forms of social interaction,"[178] defining the first as a schematization in which the members of a group can initially view one another only according to their roles or status; he sees the second in the partial non-sociality of socialized creatures, and the third in the calling of individuals into the "organization of positions" in "society" as an integral of professional occupations, "as though every element were predetermined for its place in the totality."[179]

The most interesting reserve against strained holism is mentioned in the sentence noting that "every member of a group is not only a part of society but something else besides."[180] Its main tenor: "The *a priori* for empirical social life is that life is not entirely social."[181] The reason for this, according to the author, lies in the circumstance that "societies are essentially patterns existing simultaneously inside and outside of society."[182] For the individualistic sociologist, it seems clear that the basic unit of these composite structures can only be the individual, or the individual soul, which the author claims "is inserted into no arrangement without also being found opposite it."[183] Simmel's emphasis on the life-philosophically colored distinction between being-in and standing opposite anticipates Luhmann's initially baffling-sounding, pleasantly anti-totalitarian and anti-consensualist basic doctrine that real individuals are not parts of the social system, but rather belong in its environment. It would be even more valid to view Simmel's reserve against the complete quantification of the individual by the social as a German equivalent to Gabriel Tarde's monadological turn in the sciences of the conglomerations.

We can follow on from Simmel's reference to the partial extra-sociality of the individual components of "societies" on three critical conditions: firstly, one would have to reject the individualistic metaphysics of Simmel's theory of socialization and replace it with a more radical theory of coexistence and association, like that outlined by Simmel's contemporary Gabriel Tarde in his 1893 essay *Monadology and Sociology*, which was ignored by the majority of professional sociologists. This most philosophical text by the most philosophical sociologist of the French school—to adopt an apt characterization by Eric Alliez—is an ingenious neo-Leibnizian attempt to generalize the association idea so far that all empirical objects can be described as states of coexistence of something with something: "everything is a society."[184] Tarde insists on this inversion of classical holism: the truth is rather that since the discoveries of cell theory, organisms have become societies *sui generis*, like

> fiercely exclusive cities as imagined by a Lycurgus or a Rousseau, or better still, religious congregations of a prodigious tenacity which equals the majestic and invariable strangeness of their rites, an invariability which nonetheless does not count against their individual members' diversity and force of invention.[185]

One could conclude from this that the being-something-other-than-society of individuals hinted at by Simmel should by no means be taken as the intimate final being-for-itself of an atomic person-point, as the metaphysics of the subject suggests. If human individuals share in an extra-social dimension, Tarde argues, it is because they are themselves products of pre-personal associations, of cellular societies and particle societies that are subject to autonomous modalities of compositeness. To partially

František Kupka, *Vertical Plains Blue and Red* (1912–13)

unscrew humans from the "society" of their kind, therefore, it is unnecessary to inflate their selfhood through a metaphysics of loneliness. At the interpersonal level, they have both de-social and asocial (or, to use Tarde's terminology, pre-social or sub-social) aspects, because they are social, multiplicitous and composite at other levels and in a different way. Differently put, to be communal—that is, focused on a joint field of *munera*, tasks, works and projects—with a social nexus, individuals must have control over their specific immunity, namely the exemption from service to society. What we call healthcare today (it would be more apposite to speak of a population's biopolitical constitution) is the respectively current compromise between the interests of *communitas* and the conditions of *immunitas*.

One of the virtues of the neo-monadological approach in social theory is that its attentiveness to the association of small units prevents the spatial blindness that characterizes established sociologies. From this perspective, "societies" are space-demanding factors that can only be described through a suitable analysis of extension, a topology, a dimensional theory and a "network" analysis (assuming one prefers the network metaphor to that of foam).[186] Tarde hints in passing at the possible direction of such investigations in a thought experiment: if the instinct of humans to socialize were not restricted by the insuperable restrictions caused by gravity, one would sooner or later undoubtedly see vertical nations growing alongside the familiar horizontal ones—communities of human clusters that would rise into the air, resting on just a single foot on the ground without spreading out on it:

> it is hardly necessary to indicate why this is impossible. A nation which was as high as it was wide would surpass the breathable zone of the earth's atmosphere by a considerable distance, and the earth's crust provides no material sufficiently solid for the titanic constructions demanded by such urban development in a vertical direction.[187]

With this reflection, the analyst of associations wishes to make it clear why flat composite constructs like human "societies" (in analogy to some mosses and lichens) are characterized by blurred edges. This gives us an indication that we are dealing (could one say for the first time?) with a morphologically attentive and

NOX/Lars Spuybroek, from the project *Beachness*

space-theoretically lucid form of sociology. Let it be assumed that the passage quoted is one of the rare parts of social science literature in which human agglomerations are interpreted with a sideways glance at the static, morphological and atmospheric conditions of human coexistence in space.

(Tarde's thought experiment was continued by the architectural utopias of the twentieth century, for example Yona Friedman's neo-Babylonianly altitude-happy sketches for *Ville spatiale* (1964) or *City in the Air* (1962) by Arata Isozaki; his reference to a flat association is taken up in the rhizome theory of Deleuze and Guattari, and encounters an echo in Vilém Flusser's concept of *Lebensraum* as a "long, broad, but low

Arata Isozaki, *Cluster in the Air, Metabolism City* (1962)

box."[188] In accordance with these concepts, "societies" appear as networked floor surfaces; their most important dimension is always their lateral extension.)

If we wish to continue working with Simmel's indication that "societies" are composed of beings that must simultaneously stand inside and outside of their association, we must apply two corrections. Certainly the monadological turn along Tarde's lines already helps to dissolve the individualist illusion in which members of "civil societies" are mirrored, such that "societies" must henceforth be examined as composites of composites. I would argue that it must be continued to the point of a dyadological turn, after which the principle of specifically human surreal spatial formations becomes apparent though the description of the social context. It is worth recalling that Béla Grunberger already paved the way for such a shift into the dyadic decades ago with his concept of the psychic monad. For the psychoanalyst, the term "monad" is meant to refer to a "form" whose contents are provided by the coexistence of two who are connected by strong mental interdependency.[189] This would mean that "societies" should not only be viewed as higher-order communities of monads, as multiplicities of multiplicities; in our context, they would have to be understood primarily as multiplicities of dyads whose elementary units were not individuals but pairs, symbiotic molecules, balance systems and resonance communities, as described in the first volume of this trilogy. What is here termed a bubble is a place of *strong relationship* whose hallmark is that humans in the space of closeness form a psychic relationship of reciprocal harboring; I have suggested describing this with the term "autogenous vessel."[190]

The notion of a multiplicity of psychic self-vessels leads almost automatically to the term "foam"—absorbing Tarde's topological reference to the flatness of human associations and thus gaining the heterodox image of a flat foam. Foams are rhizomes of interiors; their principle of adjacency lies above all in lateral annexations, flat condominiums or co-isolated associations. Spatial multiplicities integrated through co-isolation are comparable to island groups such as the Cyclades or the Bahamas, where cultures that are at once similar and autochthonous prosper. Nonetheless, the interpretation of "society" as flat foam should not induce us to conclude that a complete collection of communal land registry plans would provide the most adequate description of human coexistence with their own kind

Marina Abramovic, *Inner Sky for Departure* (1992)

and others, as stimulating as the parceling of space in the land registries may be for its cell-theoretical analogies. While "society" can only be grasped from the perspective of its original spatiality and multiplicity, along with its interconnecting syntagmas, the geometrical spatial images of the land registry offices do not supply the valid image of human coexistence with humans and their architectural "containers"; no mere container notion is suitable to articulate the self-willed tenseness of animated constructs in their aggregations. One would have to work with psycho-topological maps, if such a thing existed, based as it were on infrared images of internal states in polyvalent hollow bodies.

To stay with meteorological and climatographical images, one could say that the best complete pictures of "society" are offered by aphrographies, or foam photographs from a great height. Such images already convey at first glance the information that the whole cannot be more than an unstable moment-synthesis of a teeming agglomeration. They would provide external depictions of the psycho-thermic conditions in the agglomerations of human bubbles, comparable to nighttime satellite images of industrial nations, which in cloudless nights show the coexistence of humans and technical facilities in the electrified metropolitan areas as irregular spots of light. A high-resolution aphrogram of a "society" would render visible the honeycomb and neighborhood system of air-conditioned bubbles, thus making it clear that "societies" are polyspheric air conditioning systems in both the physical and the psychological sense. In the case of modernity, highly divergent temperature settings and great inequalities in the levels of animation, immunization and pampering become evident—differences that are transformed into psychosemantic tensions and sociopolitical themes within the fields. From that point on, the political field would have to be examined with the aid of a fluid mechanics for semantic charges or vectors of sense. What is social policy but the formalized dispute over the redistribution of comfort chances and psychothermic pampering resources, as well as access to the most affordable immune technologies?

Finally, Simmel's remark that the constitutive elements of social groups are not only parts of society, but always *something else besides*, remains to be more precisely formulated in space-theoretical

NASA Satellite photograph of North and South America (with Hawaii) taken on a cloudless night

and place-logical terms. The concepts of the "bubble" and the "autogenous vessel" make it possible to read the meaning of this "besides" in a space-critical fashion. The coexistence of humans in "company"[191] is only possible because they are already joined and related to one another elsewhere. "Societies" are multiplicities of individual spatialities in which humans can only participate because of the psychotopic difference they have always already brought with them. To be "in company" in typically human fashion, then, one must already possess the ability to coexist. Without prior psychotopic tuning, the assembled would not be assemblable—or their associations would never be more than congresses of autists, comparable to the groups of hedgehogs with which Schopenhauer characterized "civil society." It is only because social association is preceded by a psychic spatial formation, also known as communication, that participation in further assemblies is possible. If this were not the case, then, as René Crevel said, each individual person would have to remain plugged up in themselves "like an old whore who is now only a ruin for her corset." But how then to explain the undeniable phenomena of mental transference—"the riches of our unshared domains," the "imponderable, but real exchange"?[192]

In reality, individuals become fit for society to the extent that they are enabled by a form of psychosocial airlock to cross over from the dyadic primitive space into the polyvalent space of both early and developed "social" contacts, into the enriched foams or networks, and even into the bonds of the non-binding.[193] Their "fitness for society," however, as Simmel noted in a spherological reflection *avant la lettre*, is equally determined by the fact that people stay within the boundaries of one's own "sense of power and justice in one's own sphere," in the consciousness "that such power and justice do not extend into the other sphere."[194] Personalism provides the philosophical form in which self-controlled individuals give one another guarantees of harmlessness. Naturally, Simmel is speaking here with the voice of the Kantian, following his master in the assumption that the point of a civil legal system is to ensure the coexistence of respectively self-centered circles of willfulness.[195] Novalis showed a slightly better understanding of power structures a century earlier, when he remarked that every individual was the center of its system of emanations.[196]

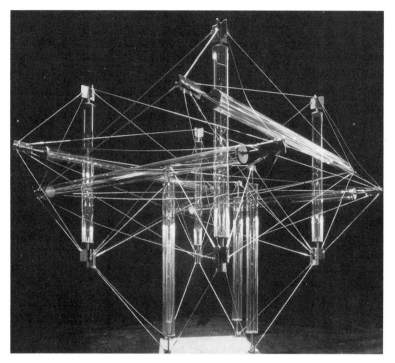

Stefan Gose & Patrick Teuffel, *Tensegrity Sculpture*, a conception with 3–4m glass tubes

Against the background of these reflections, it becomes apparent that—and why—Kant's definition of space as the possibility of being together must be augmented or replaced by its inversion: being together is the enablement of space.[197] While Kantian physics defines things as simply filling out the preexistent space (or rather, the space represented *a priori*) and subsisting alongside one another in the mode of mutual exclusion, those assembled in the psycho- and sociospheric space are themselves space-forming by virtue of their coexistence: they are intertwined with one another and form a psychosocial place *sui generis* in the mode of mutual harboring and reciprocal evocation. In this manner, once again, the difference between the simple receiving containers in the physical understanding of space and the self-vaulting autogenous containers of spherology becomes tangible.

Once this distinction has been made, the temporal connection between the generations as the consecutively coexistent also appears in a different light. If one views cultures as spaces that are integrated through the shared formation of patterns, this results in a concept of tradition as the process of collective pattern preservation in time. In traditional cultures, learning takes on the purpose of adaptation to the existing patterns. But in a culture of research that, like our modern one, is opened up by ongoing explication, learning means participating in processes of constant pattern revision. Each learning point constitutes a temporalized microsphere in the foam that learns.

CHAPTER 1

Insulations

For a Theory of Capsules, Islands and Hothouses

Since the publication of Daniel Defoe's novel *The Life and Strange Surprising Adventures of Robinson Crusoe, of York, Mariner: who lived eight and twenty years all alone in an uninhabited island on the coast of America... written by himself* in 1719, Europeans have conceded that humans are creatures who have business being on islands. From this exemplary shipwreck onward, the island in the distant ocean served as the site of revision processes against the definitions of reality on terra firma.

Determining this means becoming aware of the asymmetrical relationships between the mainland and the island. On the whole, mainland culture and island existence are connected in the manner of a rule and its exception—and the primacy of the exception asserts itself in exemplary fashion in Robinson's case. Over the centuries, the tale of the puritanical simpleton who created a micro-commonwealth of British Christian clichés on a desert island in the Atlantic saw more than a thousand new editions, adaptations and translations, reaching a level of dissemination almost rivaling that of the New Testament— which indicates that it is more than an insularly defamiliarized, two-bit gospel of private property. It supplies a formula for the relationship between self and world in the age of European world-taking.

I shall leave aside the conventional dialectics of space, which relates world and island to each other like thesis and antithesis, and instead subsume both into a touristic-civilized synthesis. The object of interest is a spherological theory of the island that can be used to show how ensouled inner worlds become possible, and how multiplicities of analogous worlds join to form archipelagos or aquatic rhizomes. In the early essay *Desert Islands*, Gilles Deleuze points out a difference between islands separated from the mainland earth context by the work of the seawater and those that rise from the sea through the underwater activity of the earth. This corresponds to the difference between isolation through erosion and isolation through creative emergence. Human sojourn on the island occupies the philosopher to the extent that the island embodies the dream domain of humans and humans embody the pure consciousness of the island. This relationship is conceivable on one condition:

humans would have to reduce themselves to the movement that brings them to the island, the movement which prolongs and takes up the elan that produced the island. Then geography and the imagination would be one. To that question so dear to the old explorers—"which creatures live on deserted islands?"—one could only answer: human beings live there already, but uncommon humans, they are absolutely separate, absolute creators, in short, an Idea of humanity, a prototype, a man who would almost be a god, a woman who would be a goddess, a great Amneseiac, a pure Artist, a consciousness of Earth and Ocean, an enormous hurricane, a beautiful witch, a statue from the Easter Islands. There you have a human being who precedes itself. Such a creature on a deserted island would be the deserted island itself, in so far as it imagines and reflects itself in its first movement. A consciousness of the earth and ocean, such is the deserted island, ready to begin the world anew. [...] it is doubtful whether the individual imagination, unaided, could raise itself up to such an admirable identity [...].[1]

Islands are world models in the world. That they could become such is due first of all to the isolating effect of the damp element, which, by their very definition, surrounds them on all sides. Bernardin de Saint-Pierre rightly described islands as "abridged versions of a small continent." It is the framing power that draws a boundary to restrict the rising power of the island, as if these surfaces without context were some emergent natural works of art contained by the sea like showpieces of nature. As microcontinents, the islands are world examples on which selections of world-forming units are gathered: their own flora, their own fauna, their own human population, an autochthonous ensemble of customs and recipes. The framing effect of the sea is confirmed, using an external example, by Georg Simmel's theory of the boundary in *The Sociology of Space* (1903), where he writes:

> The frame of a structure, its self-contained boundary, has a very similar significance for the social group as for a work of art. [...] closing the work of art off against the surrounding world and holding it together. The frame proclaims that a world is located inside of it which is subject only to its own laws [...].[2]

Haus-Rucker-Co, *Frame Building* (1977)

It is isolation, then, that makes the island what it is. What the frame does for the picture by excluding it from the world context, and what secured borders achieve for peoples and groups, is carried out for the island by the isolator—the sea. If islands are world models, it is because they are sufficiently separate from the rest of the world context to harbor an experiment about setting up a totality in a limited format. Just as the work of art sets up a world, according to Heidegger, the sea excludes a world.

The sea as an isolator enables the emergence of a model world whose foremost characteristic is the insular climate. Island climates are climates of compromise negotiated between the contributions of the land mass with its own particular biosphere and those of the open sea. In this sense, one can say that the genuine island experience is of a climatic nature and depends on the visitor's immersion in the insular atmosphere. It is not only the exceptional biotopic state, the greenhouse-like isolation from the mainland living process, that gives the islands their local colors; more still, it is the atmospheric difference that makes the decisive contribution to the definition of the insular. Islands form climatic enclaves in the general air conditions; they are atmotopes, to coin a term, that form themselves according to their own laws under the effect of their maritime isolation. Whereas "island climate" is a meteorological term, the phrase "climate island" is a space-theoretical and spherological one. The former accepts the special climatic conditions of the island as a given, while the latter incorporates them into a genetic examination by encouraging investigation of the conditions under which islands ensue and are produced.

What climate islands mean in genetic terms is hinted at by the Vulgar Latin and later Italian verb *isolare*, "to make into an island," for its verb character suggests that one should ask about the producer of the island, the isolator. After the previous reflections, the sea is initially the only possible island maker, which means that references to "making" have an insuperably allegorical character with regard to this element. It is questionable whether this will remain the only insight, however, for the act of isolating as the exclusion of an object space and an interruption of the reality continuum is a general technical idea, such that one should consider whether larger insular units could also be produced by intelligent doers, not simply as the work of subjectless

agents like sea, land and air. That this observation expresses
more than technical hubris is proved by individual etiological
myths of classical antiquity dealing with the birth of islands—
we recall the famous story of the Olympians' battle against the
giants, who had conspired to attack the heavens in order to
avenge their brothers, the Titans, who had been banished to
Tartarus. In the end phase of the battle, when the giants, followed by the Olympians, fled back to earth, a rock-throwing
with island-creating consequences began—as noted by Robert
Graves in his clear-headed narrations of Greek stories about
the gods:

> Athene threw a vast missile at Enceladus, which crushed him
> flat and became the island of Sicily. And Poseidon broke off
> part of Cos with his trident and threw it at Polybutes; this
> became the nearby islet of Nisyros, beneath which he lies
> buried.[3]

What is instructive about this fairy tale of causes is that some
islands actually constitute graves of giants or coffin lids on enemies of the gods. And it is even more impressive that they are
described as projectiles which have come to rest, as effects of the
highest throws and consequently results of a practice. Now it is
not only the sea that must be taken into consideration when
seeking to name the isolator; actions of the gods can likewise
bring forth islands, albeit only as side effects for the time being.
It would take until the age of early Enlightenment utopias for it
to be revealed how archaic island-throwing makes the transition
to a politically and technically skilled designing of islands. From
that time onwards, the denizens of the Modern Age would see

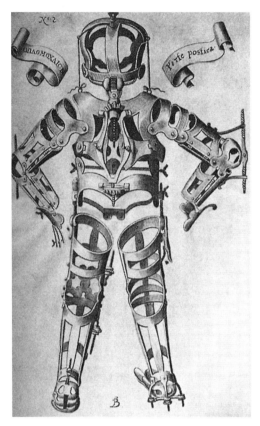

Hieronymus Fabricius ab Aquapendente, *whole-body prosthesis*, illustration in *Opera chirurgica* (1617)

more clearly with each new generation that a nesopoietic model was inherent in the "project" of modernity—that is, the tendency to translate the island (Greek *he nésos*) from the register of the found to that of the made. The moderns are island-writing and island-building intelligences that presuppose what could be called a topological declaration of human rights: it links the right to isolation to the equally original right to interconnection—

which is why the concept of "Connected Isolation" formulated around 1970 by the Californian architectural firm Morphosis expresses the topological principle of the modern world with unsurpassable incisiveness. The process of modernity directs its explicatory violence also at the basic condition of being-in-the-world, namely habitation, which must now be considered the originally isolating activity of humans—or, to use the formula coined by the phenomenologist Hermann Schmitz, the "culture of feelings in the enclosed space."

In the following I shall describe the three technological explicatory forms for island formation that emerged from the development of the modern art of isolation: first of all the construction of separate or absolute islands in the form of ships, airplanes and space stations, where the sea is replaced as an isolator by other milieus (first of all the air, then empty space); next the establishment of climatic islands, namely greenhouses, in which the exceptional atmotopic situation of the natural island is replaced by a technical imitation of the greenhouse effect; and finally anthropogenic islands, where the coexistence of tool-armed humans with their own kind and the rest triggers an incubator effect that acts back on the inhabitants themselves. That effect constitutes an insulating form whose reconstruction through the art of social engineering cannot yet be termed fully successful, although modern welfare states—understood here as pampering capsules—have greatly advanced the replacement of the primary incubator with the collective construction of substitute mothering services.

The suggested classification of islands follows Vico's principle that we only understand what we ourselves can make. Technical making is intrinsically an act of replacement or prostheticizing.

Table tennis robot manufactured by Sarcos; it reacts to the muscle activity of its playing partner.

Whoever wishes to understand the island must build prosthetic islands that reproduce all essential characteristics of the natural island point for point in the technical replica. Through the substitute form, one finally understands what the original form means. Hence the development of prosthetics—the centerpiece of explication activities—is the phenomenology of the true spirit. The repetition of life elsewhere shows how much of life was understood in its first manifestation.

A. Absolute Islands

Absolute islands ensue through the radicalization of the principle of enclave formation. Bodies of land merely framed by the sea cannot do this, for they can only achieve isolation in the horizontal while remaining open in the vertical. In this sense, natural marine islands are only isolated in relative and two-dimensional terms, according to length and breadth. Despite having their own special climates, natural islands are incorporated into the currents of air masses. The absolute island requires three-dimensional isolation—and thus the transition from the frame to the capsule, or, to use an analogy from art, from the panel painting to the spatial installation. There can be no complete enclosure without vertical isolation.

To be absolute, a technically produced island must disable the premise of immovability and become a mobile island. The irreversible relativity of natural islands is thus doubly contingent: on the two-dimensionality of their isolation and the immobility of their situation. Creating an absolute, three-dimensional and mobile island demands a revision of the relationship with its surrounding element. It no longer lies fixed in it, rather navigating through it with relative freedom by floating or flying. The absolute island's way of being is encapsulated most strikingly by the motto of Jules Verne's Captain Nemo: *Mobilis in mobile*, "moving amidst mobility"—a phrase that Oswald Spengler rightly viewed as the existential formula for entrepreneurial individuals in "Faustian" civilization. The electrically driven underwater hotel *Nautilus*, born of the great misanthrope's inventive spirit, embodies a first technically perfect projection of the idea of absolute insularity—a world model of extreme closure and introversion, with its own onboard organ and extensive library, a submersible air-conditioned enclave constantly on the run from humans and ships, curving and evading as if Robinson's involuntary landing on the empty isle had turned into a voluntary exile and the Atlantic model island had been transformed into a swimming cave, filled with the treasures of advanced civilization and the erudite bitterness of an enigmatic sea hermit. The free-moving underwater boat is a complete prosthetic island that explicates and replicates the basic features of insular being in its primary aspects. On the three-dimensional island, it is not only the enclave character of such a piece of space that is revealed; one also becomes aware of the principle of displacement, which enables islands as space-taking objects to demonstrate their mass in order to push back the surrounding element.

Nonetheless, as maritime prosthetic islands, submersibles remain related to the natural islands, with which they share the ordinary element. Absolute insulation is only attained when the surrounding element is also exchanged. This is the case with airplanes, especially those operating at such high altitudes that they must artificially create livable air conditions in their interiors, and with space stations, which venture into the non-element: emptiness. With the last group, space is no longer taken through conventional displacement, but rather by implanting a body that expands as the unrivaled proprietor of its location in space. As soon as the surrounding element is replaced by a vacuum, the insular space implant, relieved of gravity's antagonism, must carry itself alone. As a result, extension and displacement become one. In a vacuum, bodies freed from all competition are as large as their own will to extension allows—and this will is identical to the construction plan. Implantation in a vacuum means continuing island-throwing by the means of space travel. Its guiding principle was written down in 1687 in Isaac Newton's treatise *De Mundi systemate*, where the author carried out the famous thought experiment with a stone's throw in which the projectile accelerates so far that it no longer falls back down to earth, rather stabilizing itself like a natural satellite in an orbit.

If isolation is to become three-dimensional and enable free navigations in the environmental element, the framing of the island is no longer to be carried out through the collision of land and sea along a coastline. Absolute islands have no coast, only outer walls—on all sides. These are expected to provide a perfect seal, and whoever chooses to step out of them into the surrounding element must be prepared for an immediate drop to the depths; swimming in space is only possible with the aid of special suits, and nude bathers in a vacuum have dismal prospects. It is imperative for the design of the absolute island that the loose atmotopic exceptional situations of natural islands be recreated in the strict exceptional situation of the artificial closed atmotope. Breathing on the natural island profits from the spontaneous climate formation that occurs in the interplay of sea air and the insular biosphere; inside the absolute islands, breathing becomes unconditionally dependent on technical air supply systems that, through submarine, aeronautical and space travel research, are driven forwards to ever more developed states of explicitness. The climate of the absolute islands is only possible as an absolute interior, for islands of this type navigate in a milieu that is unlivable for breathers, be it under water, in low-oxygen regions high up in the earth's atmosphere, or in the vacuum of outer space—in surroundings, at any rate, in which the evolutionarily stable coupling of the breathing metabolism and the air medium is not functional. The surrounding element of the relative island must become the interior of the absolute island. Whoever sought to breathe there without bringing an air milieu with them would suffocate in a very short time or, more precisely, die as a result of vacuum-induced embolisms.

From a philosophical perspective, the meaning of space travel is not that it offers the means for a possible exodus of humanity to outer space or is allied with the supposed human need to keep pushing the boundaries of what is possible; we can safely pass over the romanticism of exodus. If space travel in ontological terms is important for a technically enlightened theory of the human condition, it is because it builds up an experimental design concerning three categories that are indispensable for the human ability to be: immanence, artificiality and upswing. Manned space stations are anthropological demonstration fields because the being-in-the-world of astronauts is no longer possible except as being-on-the-station. The ontological nub of this condition lies in the fact that the station, far more than any terrestrial island, constitutes a world model, or more precisely an immanence machine, in which existing or being-able-to-reside-in-a-world becomes completely dependent on technological world-givers. The suitable onboard philosophy would be Heidegger's theory of enframing, albeit in a positive form. A space station is no landscape, much less a "region," and not yet a biotope in the correct sense of the word, because cosmonauts and their microbial companions have so far been the only biologically active crew members to inhabit the interiors of the stations—while for the future, especially on board the International Space Station (ISS) built between 1999 and 2004, which will replace *Mir*, there are plans to develop smaller biospheric units like the "Salad Machine" of the NASA

The astronaut Mark Lee floating outside the Space Shuttle *Discovery*, roughly 160 miles above the ocean

Ames Research Center, a light-doped miniature greenhouse 2.8 square meters in size and capable of producing carrots, cucumbers and lettuce for a four-person crew three times a week.[4] The current stations form an environment described by aerospace engineers—with reference to the station's human components—as an "Environment Control and Life Support System" (ECLSS).[5]

This sheds light on nature understood in the old, anthropocentric way: it can—looking back from the prosthesis—be interpreted as a found, spontaneously populated life support system whose workings its residents cannot imagine in any physically adequate way as long as they inhabit it "existentially," that is to say operate in the mode of intuition, devotion and ritual-metaphorical interpretation. Only those who exit the system can learn to understand it by viewing it from the outside; the outside view comes about through ending cooperation with the familiar and seeking forms to replace it. One can only do justice to space travel by recognizing it as—beyond the motives of individual agents—a key discipline of experimental anthropology: it is the hardest school of naïveté-breaking procedures with regard to the human condition, for through its radically eccentric replacement formations for the coexistence of humans with their own kind and others in a shared whole it enforces an unrelenting spelling course for even the smallest details of the immanence machine. By intending an integral, eccentric, radical and explicit reconstruction of life premises in the external space, space travel is one dimension harder as a standard for the sense of reality than what had so far been the hardest discipline for that sense in dealings with outside things: politics, whose definition as art of the possible nonetheless remains applicable to conditions on the ground for the time being. Compared to space travel, politics—even when practiced with the usual degree of professionalism—is still tied to a dreamy, vague, error-riddled milieu in which topic speculators and containers of collective confusion can attain the highest offices.[6] The difference of explicitness between space travel as the art of what is possible in a vacuum and politics as the art of what is possible on the earth's surface is still very great at

Shannon Lucid examines fast-growing wheat in the Svet cultivator in a crystal module

present; compared to the former, the current political profession resembles a karaoke party at which the competitors appear as political parties.

The business of constructing absolute islands in outer space is damned to precision, as it permits no resting on implicit assumptions. Whoever relies on the separation of the island from every mainland and from terrestrial surrounding elements must know that nothing can be taken for granted. In the vacuum, only what is understood in every last detail—including the technology with whose assistance one elevates oneself into the airless space— can succeed. Space travel is the product of the multiplication of precision and recklessness; here levitation is combined with the utmost care. Nietzsche's prediction that we, the seafarers of the future have not only broken the bridges behind us—including the land, too,[7] becomes concrete in the most literal fashion for

The *Columbus* space laboratory

the vacuonauts in space. This applies most of all, to say it once again, to the centerpiece of the space island: the life support system, which can best be understood as a fully insulated atmotope or an integral respiratory and metabolic chamber; this contains units for performing tasks in the areas of air management, water management and waste management.

As far as the first of these are concerned, they are primarily systems for providing breathing gases and monitoring temperature and humidity, for filtering the air to remove trace impurities, and for ventilation. The latter is significant for the safety of cosmonauts, as spontaneous convection—the upheaval of the air mass due to difference in weight between normal and exhaled air—has no effect in weightlessness, which is why only artificial air circulation can prevent excessive enrichment with CO_2 and warmth in the cosmonaut's closely worn air helmet. The Russian longtime cosmonaut Sergei Krikalev, who spent nearly twenty months "in space" during six space flights on the space station *Mir*, conducted a conversation with the director Andrei Ujică in April 1999 in which he mentioned some of the peculiarities of life on the station, including the necessity of protecting sleeping astronauts from the stagnation of air in the head area: "there's this fan that ensures air circulation in our facial area during sleep [...] if a single one of these fans isn't functioning properly, the life of a crew member is in danger."[8] Without artificial air circulation, the sleeping astronauts would bury themselves in an invisible sarcophagus of nitrogen and carbon dioxide.

That the attention of space travelers is directed especially at the artificial atmosphere in the pressure cabins is justified by, among other things, the circumstance that two fatal episodes in space travel history were caused by errors in the air supply systems. In June 1971, after visiting the station Salyut 1, three Soviet astronauts died on board the space capsule Soyuz 11 while reentering the earth's atmosphere because of a defective valve whose failure caused air to escape from the capsule. The astronauts

Accident in January 1967

Dobrovolsky, Patsayev and Volkov, who were not wearing space suits, were exposed for twelve minutes to a vacuum that made them lose consciousness before dying of embolisms. The burial of the extremely popular deceased (the Soviet Union had started a PR campaign to celebrate Soviet space travel on the occasion of that very mission, with daily reports about the crew on television) in the Kremlin Wall became an act of state—there is no information about a minute of meditation on the atmospheric living conditions of humans. Prior to that, in the USA in January 1967, three astronauts had died in a burning capsule during a ground test for the Apollo program when its 100% oxygen atmosphere was ignited by an electric spark, causing it to go up in flames within seconds. Since these incidents, no one who occupied themselves with aerospace engineering could have any doubts about the significance of air supply systems on board space stations.

In the aeronautical design of their living space, astronauts are described as oxygen consumers and CO_2 producers, or more generally as substance-converting biological black boxes with mass flows running through them. The gaseous, liquid and solid substances flowing through the astronauts' bodies are moved in circular processes in the interest of mass reduction, with the goal of advancing the closing of the connection between waste management and influx management. This has largely been achieved in air and water recycling, whereas one can expect a high factor of externalization to remain the norm in food and excrement management for the time being. Literature on space travel shows that the Russians entrusted the later fate of astronaut feces to the cosmos, while Americans brought the excretions of their own in space back to earth. Ethnopsychological interpretations of this difference have not yet been published—presumably in the interest of future peaceful cooperation in space research between the world powers.

It is clear, furthermore, that the semantic and psychological sustenance of astronauts will, for the foreseeable future, remain almost completely dependent on an external supply, as the required amount of meaning for those on board is *de facto* provided exclusively by the input from ground control on earth. In this sense, and in a communicative sense, all space stations to date have met the criteria of "connected isolation" in a very pure form. Through the interconnection of isolated bodies, the advantages of system closure are combined with those of system openness. This applies as much to the professional side of the stay on board, whose usually eight-hour working days were filled with pre-formulated scientific experiments, as it does to the "private" side, in so far as the astronauts listened to music they had brought along or watched video films in their recreation times. Upon *Mir*'s controlled crash, a video library was incinerated in the earth's atmosphere. One could only speak of autonomy or perfect isolation if there were an independent board semantics or an edogenous religion of space. This would be the case if onboard scientific faculties designed autonomous research programs, or if orbital film and music studios developed art and entertainment shows that were independent of the earth. During extended stays, spontaneous religions and metaphysical schools could appear among the crew members. In linguistic terms, the constant weightlessness of the tongue would make phonetic changes quite likely, resulting in unknown dialects—perhaps even self-sufficient slurred languages and a new poetry, recited by floating tongues slipping away in drunken consonants. As long as the like does not transpire, previous and future space islanders will remain comparable to their distant forefather, the imitator Robinson Crusoe, because like him, the cultural source on which they draw is exclusively the arsenal of brought-along patterns of meaning. Needless to say, conventional astronauts are far from being the pure consciousness of their island.

The implantation of a life support system in the vacuum of outer space is anthropologically informative because it triggers an emergency for constructivist behavior. With its implementation, thought and action in the external realm become binding down to the smallest details. On ordinary building sites, the constructors have their "lifeworlds" behind them and can presuppose environments that carry them. On the building site in space, however, this ontological comfort is not provided. For residence to become possible, a minimum "lifeworld" must be implanted in the non-lifeworld. Thus the usual relationship between the carrying and the carried, between the implicit and the explicit, and between life and forms is overturned. Building islands is the inversion of habitation: it is no longer a matter of erecting a building in an environment, but rather of installing an environment in the building. In the architecture inside the vacuum, the life-preserving is an integral implant in the life-negating.

This situation can be described with the term "environmental inversion." While the natural situation is such that the environment surrounds and humans are surrounded, the construction of the absolute island creates a situation in which humans themselves design and set up the surroundings in which they will later reside. This virtually means: surrounding the surroundings, encompassing the encompassing, carrying the carrying. Environmental inversion sets about technical implementation following the hermeneutical maxim "seize that which seizes us." Consequently, lifeworld implants in the vacuum are no "microcosms," to the extent that the traditional idea of the microcosm untechnically asserts the repetition of the Great World in the Small World. It would imply that one inexplorable totality is mirrored in another. Now it is a matter of technically replicating an explored environment in order to offer it to real inhabitants for residence.

Against this background, it becomes clear in what sense the inhabited island can be viewed as a world model. We can say that a sufficiently complete world exists as soon as minimum conditions of life support are fulfilled. That is precisely what "life support" means: working through the list of conditions in which a human lifeworld can be kept temporarily operational as an absolute island. (For now, procreation on board and the development of a special tradition of cosmonautical culture will be left aside.) The special suits for space walks constitute a reduced version of such life-enabling systems. Sergei Krikalev noted that they resemble miniature spaceships,[9] with the difference that the life support system in the suit is only designed to operate for a few hours. What it shares with the full-size spaceship is its lack of biotopic autonomy. (The *Mir* records state that during its fifteen years of operation, there were 78 exits by astronauts with a total duration of 359 hours.)

The remolding of the "lifeworld" into the life support system reveals what explication means once it is applied to the ecological background. Like nothing else except terror—which, alongside space travel, will accompany us through the twenty-first century—the vacuum demands a precise spelling-out of the alphabet in which the implicit was written. In this respect, space travel amounts to an ontological alphabetization: what follows from it is that the elements of being-in-the-world can, and must, be written. Being-in-the-world on board is reframed as a sojourn in a prosthetic lifeworld—with the prosthetic potential of the "lifeworld" itself constituting the true adventure of space travel, or of station building. In analogy to the large-scale biotopic-ecological project Biosphere 2, which has been in progress in the Arizona Desert since 1991 with mixed success, the human situation in the space-ship could be summarized with the term "being-in-the-world 2."

The absolute island offers an experimental design in which hominism is shelved—that is, the human-fixated ignoring of the otherwise obvious fact that human coexistence always takes place in a concrete locale and humans never come naked and alone, but always with an escort of things and signs—to say nothing for now of their constitutive parasites, both biological (microbes) and psychosemantic (convictions). From the philosophical per-spective, space travel is by far the most important undertaking of modernity because it demonstrates, like a universally relevant experiment about immanence, what the coexistence of someone with someone and something in a shared whole means.

Until this experiment is translated back into terrestrial thought, the main problem left to the moderns by classical meta-physics, the emancipation of the Something, cannot be productively solved. Whether one calls that impoverished Some-thing "matter" or "equipment" or "things" or the "environment" is initially only a question of terminology. Taking the side of the Something can only become intelligent if there is a will to partici-pate in the construction of absolute islands. Islands of this type demonstrate how the cohabitation of humans and systems of things works. Through advanced explication, machines and the systems that carry being-in-the-world 2 are developed so formally that they would have to be worked into a space station constitution if such a thing existed. The life support unit, the communication systems, the navigating facilities, the energy providers and the laboratories: they would all have to be treated as constitutional bodies and, analogously to human rights, would have to be placed under the special protection of space law through a declaration of thing and system rights. On old, dreaming Planet Earth, still lulled by supposedly self-evident facts that have meanwhile become false, most constitutions are formulated in ways that do not convey where the countries in which they apply are located. The place of the constitutions' validity does not form part of them—it is taken for granted by pre-ecotechnic thought like a resource that can remain unmentioned because it seems to have been adequately explored by grown intuitions, and in no need of further commentary for the time being. In that sense, traditional politics is part of hermeneutical dreamtime—in a period that was full of a self-confident entitlement to invoke unexplained conditions. Conventional constitutions externalize the country on which they bestow order; they ignore the non-human fellow inhabitants of the country that are necessary for the human ones; they lack an eye for the atmospheric conditions in which and on which the coexistence of citizens and the things around them takes place. Such naïvetés are no longer permissible in world models of the absolute island type. Regarding islands in the vacuum, one wonders how long it will take before the experience gained through their installation is transferred back to the organization of coexistence in the terrestrial mainlands that are still presumed to be natural containers of life. As yet, the knowledge of coexistence under conditions of the external in its orbital position still appears to be far removed from traditional lifeworlds. Its reentry into the earth's atmosphere will not be long in coming.

R. Buckminster Fuller, *Tetra City*, project for a floating city

Of the forward thinkers in the ground stations, I shall here mention two in whose work the principle of absolute insulation is already applied in fully developed metaphors, at times even in technically implantable models, to the earth as a whole or to individual local environments. The first of these is R. Buckminster Fuller, whose *Operating Manual for Spaceship Earth* (1969) presented the systems-theoretical outline for a global earth management based on the idea that Planet Earth is little more than "the capsule within which we have to live as human beings if we are to survive."[10] Fuller's epistemology leads to an ethics of worldwide cooperation embedded in a metaphysics of collective awakening. This is in turn based on an interpretation of the basic human situation, starting from the "outstandingly important fact about Spaceship Earth [...] that no instruction book came with it."[11] This was "a factor which allowed man to be very ignorant for a long time."[12] The signature of the present is the rapid decline in the innate tolerance for ignorance of things, a decline triggered by the increasingly far-reaching consequences of applied science and large-scale technology. The feedback of technologies provokes human intelligence to qualify itself for the tasks of the engineer on board Spaceship Earth.

After Buckminster Fuller, the second figure who must be mentioned here is the Danish object artist Olafur Eliasson, whose multi-faceted installations and montages offer the most lucid interpretation of the concept of environmental inversion to be found in contemporary art. Especially with his exhibition "Surroundings Surrounded," realized together with Peter Weibel at the Karlsruhe Center for Art and Media Technology (ZKM) in 2001, Eliasson recommended himself as one of the first onboard artists on the absolute island under construction.[13] The constructivist turn is unmistakably expressed in the title of the exhibition: the natural environments displayed by the artist are consistently already surrounded surroundings, that is to say natural phenomena interpreted and repeated by science and technology. One is not looking at ecoromantically stylized totalities, but rather implants from natures into the exhibition hall and the laboratory; we see replicas, prostheses, experiments and arrangements whose presentation always makes two things shine out at once: the natural structure or natural effect *and* the scientific-technical perspective that enables these to enter our understanding. Furthermore, the "surrounded surroundings" shown by Eliasson, such as the now-famous artificial waterfall with recorded roaring, *Moss Wall* (1994), *Room for One Color* (1999) or *The Very Large Ice Floor* (1998), are not only presented, placed and "surrounded" from a scientific-technological-artistic angle; they also draw on the framing effect of the museum

Olafur Eliasson, *Your Windless Arrangement* (1997)

situation. Here, nature is to the museum as the lifeworld is to the vacuum.

In fact, the museum can be described as a general isolator for objects: whatever there is to see or experience in it appears as an insulated artifact whose presence seeks interaction with a specialized form of aesthetic attention. One finally understands how the phenomenology of spirit, the museum and progressive explication belong together. Knowing now means being able to explicate; explicating means being able to exhibit. One of Eliasson's most informative and cheering works is the wind installation *Your Windless Arrangement* (1997), in the possession of the Malmö Art Museum, in which sixteen coordinated fans suspended from the ceiling show that even the wind is no longer safe from being turned into an exhibit.

B. Atmospheric Islands

The explication of the isolation principle is advanced furthest by experiences with the construction of absolute islands. Nonetheless, artificial islands of relative character are equally instructive for the exploration of model worlds, as they sharpen the eye for the atmotopic variables of insulated milieus. One can speak of a relative artificial island when its position is chosen not in the cosmic vacuum, but rather on the surface of the earth or the water. In the case of artificial floating islands, the surrounding seawater is displaced by an implanted mass—an occurrence that can be observed at ship launches; drilling platforms and other pontoon-supported constructions on the open sea likewise meet the requirements of the floating island. The displacement is achieved by the varyingly leak-proof ship's side separating the island's inner world from the surrounding element. Because ideally sealed structures cannot be empirically realized, floating islands require facilities for leak management such as bilge pumps or replenishing equipment for air chambers under water.

In contrast to floating islands, displacement by earth-based ones affects the element of air (and to a marginal extent also the "root medium," that is to say the flora and fauna of the built-over terrain). They exclude an enclave from the surrounding air and stabilize a constant atmospheric difference between the internal

Olafur Eliasson, *The Weather Project* (London, 2003), photograph: Jens Zische

and external spaces. One could let this formulation stand as a provisional, vague definition of the house, in so far as one can assume that in addition to their functions as protective spaces, working spaces, sleeping spaces and assembly spaces, houses always have an implicit function as climate controllers—especially in the case of stone houses, which cool in summer and store heat in winter. The association between the notion of the house and that of the island is supported by the history of words: in addition to its primary meaning, the Latin *insula* referred from the second century AD onwards also to a detached multi-story apartment building usually inhabited by poorer citizens. To illustrate the indifference-producing mechanics of late metropolitan conditions, Spengler mentions a passage by Diodorus about "a deposed Egyptian king who was reduced to living in one of those wretched upper-floor tenements of Rome."[14] In our context, one would say that this Egyptian Robinson had been cast onto the beach of an overcrowded island.

The roman atrium house had pronounced characteristics of a climate isolator—firstly through the breathing and heat-binding effect of the brick walls (whose thickness of 17.5 inches was determined by the legal norm for air-dried bricks), and secondly through the protected position and ventilating function of the green interior courtyards (*atria*) and colonnaded court-yards, in which water pools (*impluvia*) collected the rainwater from the roof openings (*compluvia*). Floor heating systems have been found in houses of wealthy citizens built from the first century BC onwards; these carried hot air from a stove in the kitchen through ceramic channels in the floors, and sometimes the walls (hypocaust heating).

Grounded atmospheric islands in the stricter sense, however, have only existed since the nineteenth century, when building with cast iron and glass gave rise to a completely new type of house: the glass greenhouse. Greenhouses of this kind are not just any nineteenth-century building type; they constitute the most important architectural innovation since antiquity, for with them, the construction of houses became an explicit act of climate construction. One could see them as a peaceful prelude to the *airquake* triggered by gas warfare, which I addressed in greater detail above in my reflections on the atmopolitical foundations of the twentieth century. When glasshouses are built, the building is constructed for the sake of their desired internal climate—beyond its autonomous aesthetic values, the visible construction serves as a shell for the air that it has been built around, which is in turn made available as a milieu for inhabitants of a special kind. Greenhouses are theme architectures in which atmotopic states of affairs are brought up, usually special climates for exotic plants.

The dawn of the age of glass in architecture is synonymous with the beginnings of the atmospheric age in special ontology. Just as Georg Simmel inquired around 1900, using Kantian terms, as to the formal and cognitive conditions of possibility for the coexistence of humans in societies (today we would call this a "postnational" question), greenhouse architects from the early nineteenth century onwards searched for the practical conditions of possibility for the naturalization of tropical plants in Central European milieus. They discovered the answer in the form of tempered glasshouses, which were offered, one could say, as homes for asylum seekers from the plant world. The more heat-dependent varieties had not come of their own free will to seek asylum in Europe, of course; they arrived as forced guests, like vegetable counterparts to the Indian "homeboys" and turban-wearing Negro lads of colonial idylls who served the ladies in the rich northwest their tea.

Nonetheless, the significance of glasshouse architecture far exceeds its initial connection to imperial botany. The phenomenon of glass greenhouses can certainly not be attributed to the royal and upper-class foible for sunrooms, which points back to the seventeenth and eighteenth centuries with its flower temples, pineapple conservatories and orangeries. Nor is the gentlemen's interest in non-seasonal fruits sufficient to explain the excessive

Construction over an elm tree at the Crystal Palace, London

love of Europeans for the culture of greenhouses—even if the director of Louis XIV's kitchen garden, de la Quintinye, was capable of serving the monarch asparagus in December and lettuce in January, and even figs in June.

In their greenhouses, the Europeans began a series of far-reaching experiments concerning the botanical, climatic and cultural implications of globalization. When the subjects of the tropical plant kingdom were mustered in the greenhouses of Great Britain in the nineteenth century, the hosts at least showed a degree of accommodation in matters of atmosphere. In climatic terms, the laws of hospitality were respected. Can it not be said that multicultural society was rehearsed in the greenhouses? When the colonial botanists collected plants of the most distant provenance unasked in their glass-enclosed biotopes, they knew what one owes visitors from the tropics—especially when the royal species of the plant world were concerned, the orchids and palm trees for whose lodgings only the royal constructions among the glasshouses, namely the palm houses and orchid houses, were good enough. It goes without saying that special greenhouses were also built for the rest of the botanical aristo-crats, for example the camellia.[15]

Even in Germany, the climate for such guests was a xenophilic one: when the first palm of the fast-growing variety *Victoria regia* blossomed in Germany on June 29, 1851 at the palm house in Herrenhausen, near Hanover, the event was news-worthy. Sometimes the ideas of the artificial climatic island joined with those of utopian urbanism and orientalism, as with the construction of the Wilhelma gardens in Stuttgart, begun in 1842 and completed in 1853—a fairy-tale castle of glass and cast iron in the Moorish style on whose grounds several interior motifs are combined to produce a luxurious insulation effect. Here the rapturous power of the greenhouse landscape enters an exclusive symbiosis with the magical charm of the royal pleasure island and the paradisaic garden.

It is hardly surprising that the glasshouse architects quickly succumbed to the temptation to explore the constructive potential of the new cast iron technology with monumentalist intentions—most prominently the English greenhouse architect Joseph Paxton, whose Crystal Palace in London's Hyde Park, constructed in the short period between July 30, 1850 and May 1, 1851, with a length of 1,847 feet, a width of 456 feet and a height of 135 feet in the central transept, was by far the largest enclosed space in the world. The builders pointed out that St. Peter's Basilica in Rome would have fit inside the area of the giant glasshouse four times and St. Paul's Cathedral in London seven times. Admittedly the Crystal Palace was not initially conceived as a greenhouse, but rather a special kind of warehouse, because, as a building with a solid base, it had to hold the 17,000 exhibitors of London's Great Exhibition of 1851 along with their 6 million visitors; it was only a few old tall elm trees, whose preservation had been a precondition for obtaining a building license in the popular park, that lent the palace for the World Exhibition a certain conservatory character in its high transept.

This became the focus of attention when the Crystal Palace was dismantled after the end of the Great Exhibition and subsequently reassembled from 1853–1854 in Sydenham, with improved proportions—this time as an indoor botanical and ornithological public park or, as the Crystal Palace Company founded for its maintenance stated in a brochure, as a "universal temple for the education of the great mass of the people and the improvement of their recreational pleasures."[16] The Brighton Railway had made the public park accessible via public transport for mass visits; in 1936, a great fire destroyed the much-loved, but not uncontroversial building, of which even critics conceded that its construction had marked a turning point in the history of building. The accounts of early visitors show that the spatial experience inside it had an effect that one would have called psychedelic in the 1960s: "There was something liberating about this enormous space. One felt secure in it, yet uninhibited. One lost all sense of weight, of being confined to one's body."[17] Ventilation was provided by a system of thousands of air flaps in the side walls and the roofs. To avoid overheating in the summer, Paxton inserted damp canvases into the inner roof; during the rest of the year, a hot water system using twenty-seven steam boilers ensured that the desired temperatures were maintained. Paxton's promotional material show how much he had the motif of the "surrounded surroundings" in mind, even if it was not yet termed thus.

That Paxton was already concerned with climate simulations and an attempt to bring distant model natures into the hall, especially the Mediterranean landscapes yearned for by the English, is evident from his unrealized 1855 plan for the Great Victorian Way, a ten-mile glass gallery going through London. The project would have encircled the entire inner city of the British metropolis with a wide, glass-roofed ring boulevard, while larger areas inside the ring were intended to become open artificial landscapes; undoubtedly, this would only have been feasible by sacrificing dreary districts of apartment buildings—as with Haussmann's breakthroughs in Paris. The non-realization of the project is regrettable in many respects, for example the fact that if implemented, it would have made it easier for Walter Benjamin to recognize London as the capital city of the nineteenth century, even before Paris—just as it was not so much the arcades as the greenhouses that offered the key to the principle of the interior,[18] of which Benjamin rightly stated that modernity could not be understood without it.

In their efforts to follow the climatic protocol for plant immigrants from southern latitudes, biologists, architects, glass manufacturers and orchid-lovers of the nineteenth century not only entered, with increasing explicitness, the practice of artificial climate islands—whose basic technical idea was already known in classical antiquity, as a winter garden complex found in Pompeii proves. They brought to light a cultural technology, or more still—a principle of spatial formation and spatial atmosphere control whose development ran through the entire twentieth century and became a global question of life forms at the dawn of the twenty-first. The principle of atmotope management has been acknowledged as a high-level political issue since the world climate conferences of Rio de Janeiro and Tokyo, however difficult the implementation of enlightened climatic standards against the resistance from conventional rights to ignorance (in Buckminster Fuller's sense) may be (for it is precisely the major political figures who cling—for now—to the conventionalities of the imperial consumption of space, resources and climate).

The technology-historical and *eo ipso* culture-historical significance of glasshouses lies in the fact that they brought about the familiarization of the greenhouse effect. Long familiar to horticultural engineers and maintainers of winter gardens as an empirical phenomenon, its theoretical description and pragmatic generalization began at the start of the nineteenth century, for example in a patent application written in 1803 by the English architect James Anderson, who wanted to exploit the principle of the heat trap for the construction of a two-story greenhouse. According to Anderson's plan, solar heat would be trapped by day in the greenhouse air using the glass surfaces of the upper houses, and then passed on to the cooler lower house at night through a specially designed ventilation system—a brilliant two-chamber system with far-reaching thermopolitical implications. The place in the sun would henceforth become a question of redistributing comfort.

Not much later, Thomas Knight (1811) and George Mackenzie (1815) formulated the theoretical foundations of hemispheric glass building forms by showing how solar irradiation through curved glass surfaces can best be used to heat up the interior atmosphere. The glasshouse constructor and horticultural engineer John Claudius Loudon already made use of this in his *Sketches for Curvilinear Hothouses* (1818), and with the palm house built at Bretton Hall in Yorkshire in 1827, he created one of the first examples of a thermodynamically calculated greenhouse architecture out of cast iron and curved glass. In this "totally illuminated space," favorable light conditions were augmented by a form of solar energy exploitation that was very advanced for English climes and contemporary glass technology. This provided a strong impulse for the construction of domes—the supreme discipline of architecture since the days of the Roman Pantheon. The new materials not only allowed a wider span; they also brought to bear new relationships between the dome form and the interior it overarched. Loudon's ideas in the field of hemispherical construction can be followed to the Great Winter Garden at Laeken, near Brussels, completed in 1876.

Greenhouse in the park of the Royal Palace of Laeken, near Brussels, during its construction in 1875

In the twentieth century, the introduction of glass substitutes provided a new stimulus in greenhouse construction. From the late 1950s onwards, the new cheap and translucent polyethylene and PVC exteriors caused a turn towards mass plant culture in greenhouses. Tellingly, its global center is located in China, which brings together three quarters of the world's surface area for green houses—600,000 of 800,000 hectares in total (as of 1994), almost entirely in the form of simple, low plastic tunnels that, usually located close to large cities, are used for intensive vegetable production. Japan too, for the same reasons and with the same means, became one of the great powers in the field of plastic greenhouses within a short time—even overtaking Italy and Spain.[19] In the USA, where numerous new greenhouse types were explored, the first self-supporting pneumatic constructions

View of roof construction

with polyester domes reinforced by nylon grids were used in small numbers, kept upright by slight atmospheric overpressure. Alongside the mostly primitivist innovations in plastic construction, traditional greenhouse cultures, which are still almost exclusively glass-based (as in the Netherlands), seem like refined Old European antiquities. But regardless of whether one is dealing with vulgar plastic tunnels or sophisticated glasshouses, the principle of reality entered the halls everywhere; the plants are green capital that exploits the power of growth, supported by thermal and chemical doping. Because of their one-sided economic purpose and monocultural setup, most greenhouse cultures of this type remain population-dynamically monosyllabic and biospherically under-complex.

This only began to change when the development of the modern life sciences and ecosystemic foundational research led to an interest in concentrating biosphere ensembles in experimental isolations. The best-known paradigm for undertakings of this kind can be found in the large-scale project *Biosphere 2*, which was put into operation in September 1991 in Oracle near Tucson, Arizona after extensive, albeit muddled conceptual preparations and a four-year construction process (1987–1991). If one had to define the particularity of *Biosphere 2* in a single word, it would be as a tribute to artificiality—a capsule delirium that goes beyond conventional greenhouse constructions in many respects. Here the glasshouse is more than a climatic island; it serves as a preparatory exercise on earth for the installation of the absolute hothouse in outer space. One can assure oneself of this by acknowledging that the experiment of Oracle does not content itself with reconstructing plant worlds in closed spaces; rather, its aim is to radicalize both the principle of assembly and that of isolation in an unusual, perhaps absurd fashion. Through its location in one of the hottest areas on earth, the paradoxical greenhouse—unlike its counterparts in central latitudes—does not seek to produce the effect of the heat trap, which is normally employed to stimulate growth and assist in negating winter. Here, an enormous amount of electricity is required to operate cooling systems that prevent the facility from overheating. This is provided by an on-site natural gas energy center, incurring annual costs of 1.5 million dollars. In addition, there is an emergency aggregate that, in the event of a power cut, helps to prevent the inside of the massive capsule from turning into an unlivable hell for plants and humans within less than an hour.

Biosphere 2 is an experiment in isolation and inclusion that exhibits a marked art work character, with a strong addition of exodus ideology and Gaia metaphysics—in keeping with the ideas of the sponsor, the Texan oil billionaire Ed Brass—but also an insistence on scientific and technological purposes. Through a comprehensive public relations offensive, the project managed to connect science to event culture. In its architectural design, *Biosphere 2* is a compromise between functionalism and historicism, with the latter expressed particularly in the two glass quasi-Mayan step pyramids flanking the ensemble. The beginnings of the enterprise can be traced to the milieu of typical West Coast New Age philosophy, as well as NASA, where plans to colonize the moon and Mars were pursued aggressively until the 1980s; it is therefore unsurprising that the American space agency was one of *Biosphere 2*'s early sponsors.

In the 1.6 hectare glasshouse ensemble, the motive of intense isolation is realized through a comprehensive application of sealing technology—starting with thoroughgoing double glazing and multiple silicone insulation on the windows and continuing to airlock doors; these are augmented by a sophisticated system of leak monitoring in the water and air circulation. What fundamentally distinguishes the seal management of *Biosphere* from that of other greenhouses is the complete control of the root medium, the ground, which is elsewhere only dug up, built on and sometimes enhanced, while here it is fully part of the sealed construction. The entire facility is underpinned by a concrete layer covered with continuous, stainless and corrosion-proof Allegheny Ludlum steel plates, with particular attention paid to the tightness of the connection between the floor plate and the vertical elements of the glass shell. The glass and steel frame

Biosphere 2

structure were both designed by Peter Pearce and Associates. Pearce, a student of Buckminster Fuller, contributed to the firm with his experience with the construction of trusses based on standardized bracing. The principle of environment inversion can be observed in a twofold form in *Biosphere 2*, as there is not only an inclusion of the ground, and hence an integral encapsulation of a lifeworld in the enclosing form; in addition, the facility is divided into a biosphere and a technosphere in such a way that the entire biospheric area is dependent on technospheric processes such as energy supply, closed water circulation, atmospheric management and countless electronic implantations.

As far as the inclusion motif in *Biosphere 2* is concerned, the island's model-world character manifests itself quite clearly: it was the ambition of the constructors to bring a miniature of natural biospheric variation into the hall, largely ignoring the fauna, by

Lung machine

replicating five of the earth's primary landscape types or biomes: tropical rainforest, savannah, mangrove swamp, sea and desert. These autonomous habitat models were augmented by two culture habitats: agricultural and horticultural landscapes as well as an urban settlement, the latter represented by a living area of 2,600 square meters for the first eight "biospherians," who subjected themselves from 1991 onwards to a two-year closure experiment that was subsequently considered a complete failure. Ants and cockroaches emerged from the debacle of animal and plant biosystems as temporary winners of the survival contest.

In *Biosphere 2*, insulation and inclusion entered a solemn relationship—especially regarding the possibilities and necessities of an extraterrestrial repetition of earthly life contexts. The motif of closure and autonomy could only be taken seriously down to the last construction detail because the total simulation of a self-sufficient biosphere usable by humans under space vacuum conditions was on the horizon; the relative island was designed as a preparatory exercise for the construction of an absolute one. The artificial lifeworld would provide the answer to the question of "what happens if one puts earth, plants, animals and humans in a glass bottle and closes it. Is there a self-regulating mechanism that maintains the life system?"[20]

It is clear that the object of this question was the possibility of a life support system that would enable the exportation of biospheric comfort into the vacuum to begin—no longer simply as a tame salad machine or an orbital hotbed, but as a lifeworld machine on a grand scale. When approximately 3,800 plant species were brought together in the bioworld simulator of Arizona for an experiment in coexistence; when two enormous mechanical lungs with a capacity of 1.7 million cubic feet (the total volume of the complex is 7.2 million cubic feet), controlled by temperature sensors, were specially developed for the atmospheric management of the greenhouse; and when twelve different water systems were implanted in the artificial biosphere, from the simulation of a 250,000-liter salt water sea to the water-storing soil of the rainforest enclosure and the drainages, rain systems, human sewers and supplies of fire extinguishing water—all this was guided by the notion of an isolation emergency only ontologically imaginable in an extraterrestrial vacuum, or on a Planet Earth whose natural atmosphere had disappeared or become unbreathable following an environmental disaster.[21] However romantically motivated the *Biosphere 2* project may have been in its starting phase, its technical handwriting shows the traits of an ultra-realist philosophy of survival in a non-life-friendly element. Its internal watchword is "After nature." One could dismiss these notions as the spawn of a new

Grimshaw & Partner, *Eden Project* (Cornwall, 2001)

kind of totalitarianism that revels in the vacuum, or ridicule them as a complementary capsule-utopian communism, were it not for the fact that global, irreversible and scarcely controllable trends in dealings with technical civilizations show that experiments about integral atmospheric and biospheric insulations possess a respectable anticipatory dimension. They must be understood as an expression of productive concern about future biosphere policies on earth.

The experiences of *Biosphere 2* with atmospheric management under conditions of systematic isolation are not encouraging. Only a short time after the first test team moved in, there were such grave imbalances in the air composition that the system had to be opened and stabilized with an external oxygen feed on several occasions. The social integration of the greenhouse crew also left much to be desired. Under the pressure of the charge that science had been confused with science fiction in this project, the closure experiments were aborted after several attempts. In 1996, New York's Columbia University took over the task of developing a new scientific definition of the biosphere as a research facility and integrating it into the study activities in their EARTH department. Through this semantic climate change, the surrealist plantation of Oracle was transferred from the auratic field of Gaia romanticism to the noble vacuum of American academia.

C. Anthropogenic Islands

If the absolute island exchanges the sea for the vacuum as the surrounding element, and the climatic island instead reformulates the atmospheric facts, it is human factors that act as variables in the case of the anthropogenic island. With these structures, the concern is to understand how humans become Nesiots or islanders—or how island-dwelling creatures transform into humans through the unpredecented effects of their isolation, which amounts to the same thing. According to the current consensus among paleontologists, the African savannah is the terrain on which the hominization of a former tree monkey species took place; this landscape must therefore be described in such a way that it can be understood as the suppressed surrounding element of the anthropogenic islands nomadizing on it. In this view of things, the grass steppe appears as the sea from which the Anthroponese[22] emerges. Hence the primary event of early history, the genesis of humans, has above all a topological secret. In the birth of humanity, the scene of the deed must explain the deed; the place of the events holds the key to what happened there.

The human fact comes from an isolation phenomenon in which the role of the isolator initially remains unclear. How was it possible for such enclaves to form in the midst of an imperceptibly changing environment, filled with a special form of life that hallucinates, speaks and works? How should one envisage this appearance, this separation, this secession that resulted in humans? Deleuze's demand that the Nesiot, the exemplary island-dweller, carry on the island-creating élan and thus become the pure consciousness of their place can only be fulfilled in the form of anthropogenic islands—provided we define the human-breeding primate collectives as units of an insular type, and consider the humans produced there the vectors of creative movements that culminate, mature and depart in their thought. In addition to the types of island formation named by Deleuze, namely through maritime erosion and terran emergence, a third dynamic comes into view here: insulation through group inclusion or distance-creating self-enclosure.

The aforementioned aim of deriving the human fact from the spontaneous self-inclusion of unknown types of intelligent islands—I will call them "islands of being"—could be considered achieved after a sufficient explanation of whether, how and why the primitive coexistence of hominids with their own kind and

South America and Tierra del Fuego viewed from the *Mir* space station

the rest caused a self-isolation effect that set the stage for anthro-pogenesis. The topography of the place of anthropogenesis will have been recorded in its exact outlines once it explains how the event is tied to the place of its occurrence: the ability of the onto-logical island to bear humans will then be synonymous with the ability of humans-to-be to trigger the ontological event, the world effect, through the manner of their coexistence. The acquired inability to be an animal interlocks, in this nonetheless-creature, with the acquired ability to be in the world. Grasping this requires an anthropological imagination that makes us witnesses, beyond the temporal divide, to an unheard-of incident: it is as if the old mainland had been shaken two million years ago by a prolonged seaquake in whose wake many thousands of anthropophoric islands were raised—archipelagos of roving primate hordes in which human-forming internal climates developed. Some of these pre-Adamitic groups became the later *sapiens* lines continued by the current species.

To understand what happened in the grass steppes of Africa, one must describe—extremely schematically, yet with a modicum of comprehensiveness—how that seaquake affected the pre-human creatures. It is necessary to show that the savannah-dwellers themselves triggered the quake through their particular way of inhabiting the space, and how this resulted in the establishment of a greenhouse effect with which the self-incubation of *homo sapiens* began. This quake led to a loss of security that could only be offset by a re-insurance—the latter would, in time, come to be known as "culture." Looking at the overall dynamics of this de-secured insurance gives a general sense of the human immune situation. A proto-architectural adventure begins on the anthro-pogenic islands through the synergy between the formation of nests and niches among animals and hominid camp activity until, one day in the distant future, the now-human spatial demands will have crystallized sufficiently for the aggressive construction of

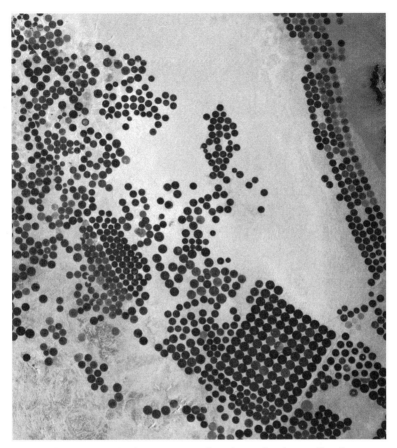

Areas under agricultural cultivation in Saudi Arabia with a deep well at the center, photographed from outer space

huts, villages and cities to be advanced. I am operating on the assumption that architecture constitutes a delayed reenactment of spontaneous spatial formations in the group body. Although the human fact rests on a greenhouse effect, the primary anthropogenic greenhouses initially have no physical walls or roofs but rather, if one can phrase it in this way, only walls and roofs of solidarity. The human being, the animal that keeps a distance, rises to an upright position in the savannah; this gives it a visual horizon. As inhabitants of a new type of displacement form, humans settle in with themselves.

Anthropogenic islands are—as I will show—workshops of an unprecedentedly complex spatial creation. The anthropotope arises from the interleaving of a wealth of spatial types with a specific human quality; without their simultaneous opening, the coexistence of humans with their own kind and the rest in a shared whole would be inconceivable. The placing and arranging insulation movements merge into one another through manifold forms of feedback, meaning that the sphere of human groups forms a cybernetic space from the outset. Here, however, cyberspace is not situated next to the space of the supposedly primary and real; instead, the real and the virtual are combined to form the particular reality "horizon" of the human world. The human island is a space station that enfolds us as our first "lifeworld." When we look, in the following, at a series of images of the island as if taken from a great height, it is always in the awareness that the incipient repetition of the terrestrial "lifeworld" in the vacuum of outer space opened up a completely new view of the developed conditions in the near-earth space. Space travel serves contemporary philosophy as the radicalization of *epoché*. Upon reentering the "lifeworld," the view of the theory glider takes a series of eccentric pictures.

In the state of minimally complete development, the anthroposphere can be defined as a nine-dimensional space.[23] It comprises the following topoi or dimensions as providers of respectively indispensable world-forming functions:

1. The chirotope, which encompasses the operational realm of human hands, the zone of the ready-to-hand and present-at-hand, the environment of handling in the literal sense, in which the primary objective manipulations, the first throws, blows and cuts, cause characteristic events in the environment;
2. The phonotope (or logotop), which creates the vocal dome beneath which the coexistent listen to one another, speak to one another, give orders to one another and inspire one another;
3. The uterotope (or hysterotope), which serves the expansion of the mothering zone and the political metaphorization of pregnancy, as well as producing a centripetal force that is experienced by the affected as a sense of belonging, in larger units too, and as a shared existential fluid;
4. The thermotope, which integrates the group as an original beneficiary of shared hearth effects that make home sweet, and which constitute the matrix of all comfort experiences;
5. The erototope, which organizes the group as a place of primary erotic transference energies and places it under stress as a field of jealousy;
6. The ergotope (or phallotope), in which a paternal or clerical power of definition effective throughout the group creates a *sensus communis*, a decorum and a spirit of cooperation out of which shared works (*erga, munera*) born of necessity are formulated and functions serving labor division are separated off, extending to the summoning of members to the maximum stress situation, war, which is understood as the *magnum opus* of a community destined for victory;
7. The alethotope (or mnemotope), which enables a learning group to constitute itself as the guardian of its experiential

continuum and keep itself in shape as a collection point for truth with its own validity claim and risk of falsification;

8. The thanatotope or theotope (or perhaps iconotope), which offers the group's ancestors, their dead, their spirits and their gods a space of revelation or a semiotic instrument for significant manifestations from beyond;

9. The nomotope, which binds the coexistent together through shared "customs," labor division and mutual expectations, with exchange and the maintenance of cooperation creating an imaginary tensegrity, a social architecture of reciprocal expectations, coercions and resistances—in short, a first constitution.

1. The Chirotope—The Ready-to-Hand World

The anthropogenic island is a place of metamorphosis: here the paws of the pre-Adamites are transformed into human hands. Hominids become chiropractors who create bizarre connections to things by means of their newly acquired hands. Yes, the existence of "things" in the sense of handlable objects and public property around us is already a worldly reflection of the event that a certain group of island monkeys once set off for the savannah to acquire hands. Where paws remained paws, the creatures as a whole stayed trapped in tighter, still animal grasping repertoires. The paw's touch is only a pre-stage to world formation. Only when a hand reaches for objects and finds them handy, or makes them handlable, can the transformation of what is standing and lying around into usable equipment begin. This, with great simplicity, was the first act of world-production; it initiated the self-inclusion of the islanders. It led to that exotic retreat which the philosophy of the twentieth century would go on to term "being-in-the-world." For someone who is in the world, equipment is ready-to-hand; where equipment is nearby, the world cannot be far.

In the analyses of equipment [*Zeug*] in *Being and Time*, Martin Heidegger emerged as the first chirotopologist, meaning an interpreter of the fact that humans exist as hand-owners, not as spirits without extremities. Observers have noticed that Heidegger's human seems to lack genitals and much of a face—but his ears are all the more developed, in order to hear the call of care. His most exquisite trait is the possession of hands, for Heideggerian hands learn from an ear, which is in turn whispered into by care, what is to be done from case to case: this all-hand and all-ear human explicitly articulates, for the first time in the history of thought, the fact that the objects co-inhabiting the world in which he lives are *ready-to-hand* in the form of equipment. In Heidegger's concern-disclosed world, readiness-to-hand is a central feature of what surrounds the *eksistent* party in the area of closeness. The equipment is whatever appears within reach of the clever hand, in the chirotope: the throwing equipment, the cutting equipment, the striking equipment, the sewing equipment, the digging equipment, the drilling equipment, the eating and cooking equipment, the sleeping equipment and the dressing equipment. The Heideggerian human is in the picture about all these things and which tasks they confer upon his hand. What would a wooden spoon be without the command to stir? What would a hammer be if it did not call up the action pattern "strike the point repeatedly"? When it is necessary, the clever hand does not wait to be told twice. In case of emergency the

Blades being polished between stones through vibration

killing equipment is added to the list, in case of non-emergency the playing equipment, in case of an alliance the gift equipment, in case of an accident the bandaging equipment, in case of death the funeral equipment, in case of meaning the showing equipment, and in case of love the beauty equipment.

Among the equipment populations in the chirotope, it is above all three categories that ensure the elevation of the human island from the surrounding element. The first is the throwing equipment; thanks to its constant use, the hominids were able to emancipate themselves from acute environmental pressure to a certain extent. Because the incipient human hand, carried by the former arm of the tree monkey remolded for a grassy landscape, learned to pick up suitable objects for throwing, usually small or hand-sized stones, and throw them at bringers of unwelcome encounters or contact—whether large animals or foreign members of the same species—it offered the hominids the first alternative to avoiding encounters through flight. As throwers, humans acquired what remains their most important ontological skill: the ability to act from a distance. By throwing, they become the animals that can keep a distance.[24]

This distance enables the perspective that harbors our perspectives. The whole improbability of human reality control is concentrated in the throwing gesture. Hence the chirotope constitutes the original and true field of action in which actors habitually observe the results of their throwing. Here a pursuing eye comes into play, checking what the hands achieve; neurobiologists even claim to have proved the innate ability of the brain to aim at fleeing objects. The chirotope is actually a video chirotope, a sphere of successful acts that is guarded by gazes. What Heidegger called "care" [*Sorge*] is first of all the attentive uncertainty with which a thrower checks whether their throw hits the mark. Hits and misthrows are practical functions of the truth which prove that an intention directed into the distance can lead to success or failure—with an unclear middle ground for a third value. In both cases, the successful and the failed throw, true and false things— the logical firstborn of distance—point to themselves.

The paleontologist Paul Alsberg already gave a convincing description of the distancing effect, which expands to include numerous other modes of tool use, in 1922. He saw the principle of distance as the innate natural-historical possibility of breaking with mere natural history—and in this he felt he had found the solution to the "riddle of mankind," correctly in my opinion. Indeed, by creating a middle sphere of long-distance weapons and tools, the hominids managed to escape the prison of bodily adaptation.[25] As a thrower and tool user, the long-distance animal *homo sapiens* insulates itself by emancipating itself from merely somatic evolutionary pressure. Consequently, it could venture forwards into a progressive de-specialization (and in the view of some anthropologists, stop there)—a process for which Alsberg suggested the arousing term "bodily deactivation" [*Körperausschaltung*]. Undoubtedly it is impossible to understand the strangely refined (and to some anthropologists even desolate or decadent) bodily image of *homo sapiens* until one has a more precise idea of these evolutionary events. The effect of bodily deactivation can be expressed in the image of pre-humans withdrawing behind a wall of distance effects—produced by their own use of throwing and working tools. Handy stones provide the material for the first "walls" that hominid groups erected around themselves, though these walls were thrown rather than built. Bodily deactivation produces a creature that, in its biological features, can afford to remain pluripotent, unspecialized, immature in the long term and juvenile for its entire life—all because the inevitable adaptation to environmental pressure was shifted from the body to the tools.

In its totality, the meta-tool of culture has the effect of an incubator in which a creature can chronically enjoy the privilege of immaturity. Since Julius Kollmann, the biological foundation of this effect has been neoteny: clinging to youthful body shapes and behaviors up to sexual maturity (a phenomenon observed in numerous animal species from privileged milieus). *Homo sapiens* comes from the synergy of intellect and pampering. Michel Serres summarized the anthropological consequences of this long-term evolutionary tendency in his term *hominescence*: he deduces the species' mode of being from its permanently adolescent, exploring and becoming constitution.[26]

There are only two organs that clearly do not take part in bodily deactivation (or only do so in a paradoxical fashion): the

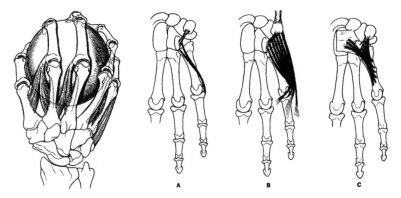

The ability of the hand to adapt to large spherical objects

brain, which develops in its own particular way both somatically and functionally by advancing to perform complex operations and, especially since the invention of writing, embarks on potentially interminable maturing and specialization processes, and the hand, which, as the brain's closest accomplice, matures towards a state of virtuosic versatility. The hand is the only organ of the human body that becomes grown-up if suitably trained. It is the first and true subject of "education" as defined by Hegel: as something that "irons out particularity to make it act in accordance with the nature of the thing."[27] Ironing out the particular here means abandoning the initial awkwardness and naïve touching, replacing it with *savoir toucher*. The hand learns early on how to take things, and keeps learning new things to the end. Thus the hand, as the vanguard of the human body, is employed at the forefront of reality—tactful, eager to touch, resilient and success-oriented—while everything else luxuriates behind the shield of tools and crosses over to a biological dreamtime in which the arrested intrauterine coexists with the lastingly childlike and juvenile. The adulthood of the

Valie Export, *From the Humanoid Sketchbook* (1974)

hand implies "education" in the dialectical sense of the word, to the extent that in every conscious manipulation an element of "alienation," of devotion to the object, correlates with a return to itself—that is, a concurrent tactile sensation. This "active-passive double given" is the source of the hand's maturity as the unity of alienation from the other and a return to self-activity.[28] The experienced hand is trained as much through the resistance of the material as through the experience of its surmountability. Inexhaustibly fit for reality, the hand compensates for the luxuriating tendencies in the rest of *homo sapiens'* body. Because the human island is a chirotope, where clever hands learn to deal with equipment, the islanders are manipulative realists and luxuriating hothouse creatures at once. On the one hand, they prove themselves as tool-armed survival fighters, success-conscious cooperators and cunning planners; on the other hand, they are forever disarmed nest-dwellers, trembling ecstatics and adult fetuses, listening out into the world's night and receiving divine visitors.

After the long-distance effect of the throwing equipment, the second significant category is the anthropogenic effect of striking tools—which are in turn represented mostly by handy stones and other hard materials such as wood and horn. The hard materials are significant, for with them begins the use of tools in the stricter sense, and *eo ipso* the history of Chirotopia. Where there is a tool, there was once a hand that picked it up. The first test of reality was carried out by tool-armed hands—to experience how the harder substance forces the less hard into submission. The island of Chirotopia—which no More ever described, and which only Heidegger saw from a distance, shrouded by mist—is about to rise from its surroundings as the island of being, because it is the scene of the first operations that expose being, namely productions. Producing means prophesying things with one's hands. When the hominids start working stones with stones or tying stones to sticks, their eyes become witnesses to events unprecedented in ancient nature: they experience something entering existence that was not there before, was not present, not given: the successful tool, the crushing weapon, the gleaming jewelry, the comprehensible sign. As results of the production successes of human hands, the tools provide their creators with the semblance of a great distinction: these new arrivals in the hominid space are the messengers who report that behind the narrower environmental horizon lies a space of expectation from which something new pours in, bringing us both good fortune and misfortune—something that would one day be called "the world." Because of it, the

Chirotopians begin to suspect that they are islanders, surrounded by the uncanny, befallen by the new and provoked by signs. They sense that the grasslands in which they camp and wander are actually the ocean that contains an excess of unseen, concealed and yet awe-inspiring co-entities. At first, the inhabitants of the artisanal island only yield to this feeling in their states of emergency—when they cross over from fear to ecstasy. In their everyday states, they calm themselves with the experience that the chirotope, the surroundings filled with the ready-to-hand, the camp, the world of closeness, forms a calmed, illuminated and available zone in which everything that is there profits from a familiarity bonus.

In twentieth-century anthropology, the positive trivialization of the constantly available would be formulated as "relief" or "background fulfillment." To be relieved refers to a state in which a sum of improbabilities are remolded into self-evidences, thus laying the foundation for what would later become "institutions."[29] In this sense, the chirotope is the mother of routines. The monstrous and incalculable that is inherent in the act of production is normalized by the habits of tool manufacture and use in the camp. Nonetheless, it can happen that the tools go wild and contribute to one Chirotopian raising their hand against their neighbor; then the monstrous aspect of the product manifests itself in the misdeed for which it allows itself to be used. If the crime is directly condemned by the wronged party, it must be indirectly rejected by the witnesses, as it constitutes an attack on the peace of routines. Killing with the aid of weapons shows that the equipment's readiness-to-hand cannot be fully explained by analogy with the domestication of animals; in this category of equipment, it is as if wild qualities break through the tamed material with intent to disturb the domestic peace.

In the chirotope, hands are socialized. Mere two-handedness does not achieve anything—any more than one-headedness: all chirotopic states of affairs are both polysurgically and multi-cerebrally constituted. The equipment's readiness-to-hand in the first "lifeworld" is augmented by cooperators lending a hand to one other, contributing different ways of handling a joint work project. The anthropologist Peter C. Reynolds speaks in this context of "heterotechnic cooperation," whose hallmark is that the joint creators anticipate the activities of the others and perform the appropriate complementary action. In the earliest days, numerous tasks could already be carried out only as polysurgical team work; like polyphonic musical scores, they required four or more hands. In symmetrical cooperations, each participant is able to take over the other's role; in heterotechnic cooperation, each contributes whatever they are more skilled at than others. Thus the chirotope becomes the matrix of an authentic social intelligence whose definition entails a series of separations and recombinations of discrete operations. Using the joint production of a simple stone knife among Australian Aborigines as an example, Reynolds arrives at a list of explicit conditions that must be fulfilled for the seemingly simple goal to be reached: "task specialization, symbolic coordination, social cooperation, role complementarity, collective goals, the logical sequencing of operations, and the assembly of separately manufactured parts."[30] According to Reynolds' observations, tools with handles are especially significant for the transition of hominids to the human chirotope, being the first examples of the polylithic object type—not only because handles realize the principle of the manufactured grip, the artificial handling of the matter itself, but more still because they constitute authentic composite tools, known as "polyliths," freely usable combinations of stone with a large variety of other materials. The prototype for this is the stone hammer or stone axe, the first material trinities, produced by putting together a stone, a stick and a binding element; the heavy striking or chopping body can also be pre-formed using an additional whittling stone.[31]

The coexistence of humans with their own kind and others appears in the early chirotope as the original (social) synthesis of at least four hands and the (material) synthesis of at least three-part objects. Let us note that the polylith is the first material clause in which a subject (the handle) is joined to an object (the stone) by a copula (the binding element); this would mean that primitive syntax—as the first logical synthesis—came from the operative categories or universals of chirotopic handlings.

As humans in more developed states of civilization are surrounded by artifacts on all sides, they find themselves in a situation where virtually everything they touch is "second hand"—most of what is ready-to-hand for them has previously passed through other hands that molded it into the shape in which later users find it. In the most developed states of the chirotope, theorists will one day conclude that even hands which have long stopped touching each other can work in each other. Such tele-cooperative craftsmanship is integrated through the many-eyed character of the market. But for mutually hidden hands to produce things that make sense in other hands, an invisible hand must direct events from a distance. No less a figure than Hegel wrote a glowing review of that invisible hand's discreet activities, ascribing cybernetic virtues to it:

This interaction, which is at first sight incredible since everything seems to depend on the arbitrary will of the individual,
is particularly worthy of note; it bears a resemblance to the
planetary system [...].[32]

The final significant phenomenon for the chirotopic reality
climate is the discovery of sharp stone and bone edges; it initiated
the cultural history of cutting and material analysis. Where the
knife function appears, reason gets underway as a dividing,
apportioning and dissecting power. "Cutting" as a pattern of
habit finds its "chronic actualizer."[33] They give things in the
world a status as divisibles. With their aid, the early Chirotopians
become the creatures that gain a view inside bodies—they look
under the skin of the other, non-human creatures, into the
tissue of plants, into the flesh of fruits, and into the strata and
granules of stones. Their worldview is shaped in part by the
experience of the autopsy, of seeing with their own eyes into the
normally concealed inside of dense bodies. The knives of the
early Chirotopians make death explicit—they cut its relic, the
animal carcass, into pieces and thus refute the illusion that the
limbs form an inseparable whole. A living body is a composite
thing that has not yet found its analysts, butchers or patholo-
gists. Cutting creates the connection between quantity and
power that comes into play whenever the aspect of a divisible
amount is emphasized in bodies. It is only the advent of artificial and homogeneous objects like dough or coin metals that
brings pure quantities into view which can be divided and added
without the use of force, as it were. In the practice of cutting up
natural bodies, we find a first manifestation of what, in the
introductory reflections to this volume, I termed explication—

revealing things in the background, or making present and exposing what is absent, folded up or covered.

The knife experience is mirrored in the early encyclopedias. If humans have separate words for the many beings and things that exist around them, it is because they use knives in their mouths. With their burning power they cut the world animal, the savannah and its children, in pieces—an act that cannot be performed without the accompanying operative violence and its lasting results. Every word serves up a world-portion. People will believe for a long time that this portion can be served more bloodlessly the more one cuts into the flesh of the world, when placing words, in the place where it is articulated of its own accord as if a highest *trancheur* god had precut it, meaning that humans, if they speak circumspectly, can take the chosen parts up into their encyclopedia, their repertoire of actions, their knowledge treasury, with a minimum of overpowering. The right language, then, would be the one that followed the cuts placed within the existent, always severing where caesuras and differences are suggested by the things themselves. Breeds and species are so important for early thought because they create the impression of containing the objective portions of the existent; the real differences are perceived like the joints of the existent. As late as Plato, human thought would barely have been more than carrying out the divine ontotomy; the ancient Chinese are convinced that humans only take their correct place in the course of the world if they keep words in order and preserve the art of true classifications. The highest distinctions follow the "ways of the knife."[34] Just as the sacrificial knife cuts apart the animal in the places that have always been intended, the allocation of the pieces follows the divisions of the group according to dignity, rank and role.

2. The Phonotope—Being in Earshot

Whoever reaches the anthropogenic island immediately has an acoustic experience: the place sounds like its inhabitants. When the surrounding savannah occasionally falls silent, the repositories of hominids and early humans scattered throughout it seem like oases of noise in an acoustic state of emergency. Nonetheless, this is the most normal condition for the inhabitants. These islands resound constantly with their own sound, they form soundscapes of a peculiar character; they are filled with the living sounds of their members, with the noise of work, the rattling of machines and tools, with the murmuring that must be able to accompany all our imaginings. The most present of these is the near-constant sound of voices: children's voices cheering and whining; mothers' voices reprimanding, comforting and suggesting; the voices of cooperating men spurring on, advising and assimilating; and the voices of the elders, who command, announce, threaten and grumble. The early human island is enclosed by a psychoacoustic dome, like a shopping area animated by music at Christmas time. It forms its sonospheric context through the undulating presence of voices and noises with which the group impregnates itself as a proprioceptive unit. One must dwell in it to understand how it sounds, and stay in it for longer to absorb it into one's existence as a self-attunement that rubs off on its inhabitants like a sonorous unconscious. The island of being is in a constant state of acoustic transmission and reception.

Only in the phonotope is the claim fully true that the medium is the message. In this space of self-exposure to sound, where residence usually presupposes an acceptance of the conditions, the basic situation recognized by McLuhan applies, namely that actual communication with others in a given medium already constitutes the entire content of communication.[35] This state of affairs becomes conspicuous to those who treat the phonotope as if they were coming from without. In external observation, ultimately, the things which the many voices have to say to one another in their shared language always amount merely to the message that they have something to say to each other in their shared language. What seems like information from the inner perspective is mere communication when perceived from the outside; whatever happens vocally and auditively belongs to the production of group-typical redundancy. The group lives in a sound installation of absolute implicitness; within it, self-hearing is effective as a medium of belonging. One must not read this as an objection to the monotony of archaic groups, but rather as a reference to the fact that redundancy is the stuff that corporate identities are made of. A phonotope cannot produce information from within itself. It exhausts its whole energy in the repetition of the phrases that keep it in shape and in flow. It cannot, initially and mostly, be interested in foreign sounds. The message that it transmits to itself consists exlusively—to use a radio metaphor—of the theme tune to its own broadcast.

Just how the phonotopic synchronization of hearing actually establishes itself can be observed in modern mass society, using the example of so-called "folk"[36] and chart music, whose primary purpose is simply to provide the material for repetitions. One begins with some catchy piece or other and, following test results, makes use of the need for an endless recurrence of the successful same. The rest is acoustic autosuggestion. From this perspective, modern audio mass culture offers a near-perfect reconstruction of the primitive phonotope—with the difference that the latter

Homumi Bedouin with phonograph

constituted an evolutionary necessity for the coexistence of humans with their own kind in a gradually less secure world, something like an acoustic immune system that helped the group to remain in the continuum of self-attunement; the current auditory populism, by contrast (very much against McLuhan's pentecostal expectations), aims for a single exercise in regression, determined to glue up the ears of the collective and make its members deaf to information, different sounds and newness.[37] Where this leads is demonstrated not only by popular music (which, to quote McLuhan again, can "turn the psyche and society into a single echo chamber"), but also by modern women's magazines, which specialize in capturing the "inner voices" of their readers. They are an anthropologically informative medium because they constitute the printed versions of totalitarian gossip. Between their pages, the confusion of communication with information is methodically sought; the non-new now always presents itself as the newest—the latest examples of the eternal recurrence of the same are supposed to be taken as information. This ontology of the women at the well almost truthfully presupposes that nothing new is possible under the sun. Here artificial light and its creatures, innovations, are still unknown.

One must beware of misunderstanding the phonotope effect, which spreads out over the group like the roof of an acoustic tent, as merely an undesired side effect of the social noise profile and vocal intercourse. This roof under which the group directs sound at itself, delineates itself within itself and thus initially rejects anything that sounds different, simultaneously acts as a psychoacoustic stage construction. Hence phonotopic facts often have demonstrative qualities—or, as Adolf Portmann puts it, a "representative and expressive function."[38] The acoustic self-tuning of the group is, in a sense, the functional inversion of the male birdsong, which serves to demarcate breeding areas and isolate the singers at the center of their acoustic zones.[39] Beyond its autoplastic effects, the human group sound has a performative, even a concert and endotheatrical dimension; the individual voices within it present themselves as intonations that expand the intentionality of the collective sound ring. The representative function of the voice and the sound producer's ambition to push it further already manifest themselves in primitive noise instruments—for this too, modernity offers suggestive equivalents and explicatory figures such as motorcycle noise, of which Portmann emphatically states: "this noise is not simply a scarcely avoidable evil for the riders, but rather an acoustic manifestation of the rider, a self-heightening of this person, the greatest expansion of their individual or group sphere."[40] "Society" is the sum of its recitatives.

The phonotopic function, understood as the group's self-determination via the ear, is connected to the promises with

Rebecca Horn, *The Turtle Sighing Tree* (1994)

which the cohabitants communicate about their prospects. In this sense, the group's sonic landscape offers something like an affective situation report or a constant acoustic protocol with which the united parties express whether they are currently in a high, a low or neither. Evangeliums and dysangeliums are primarily attributes of musical keys or colorations of messages. The feeling of elation expresses a primitive musical state that makes no secret of its representative purpose. One could characterize it as Nietzsche characterized the early tribal gods, namely as media of self-congratulation. In them, their believers celebrate their reasons for being on top: "People are grateful for themselves: and this is why they need a God."[41] The immune group is convinced that it has many good things to say about itself; for that, it needs a canopy of festive noise above its heads.

In the light of this, one understands why the "invention of the individual" in so-called advanced civilizations only became

Anechoic chamber at the Fraunhofer Institute for Building Physics, Stuttgart

possible by introducing practices of silence. Here it was writing and the subsequent training of silent reading that had a decisive effect. An individuality that finds itself out presupposes that individuals that withdraw to islands of quiet on which they become aware of a possible difference between the collective voices and the inner voices—from which one ultimately stands out as their own. The monastic *silentium* works with this difference in order to separate divine quietness from human loudness. *In interiore homine habitat veritas*:[42] Augustine insists that after the *silentium* caesura, the truth will only be found where things are quiet—alongside Plato's garden, it is above all the houses of God that are suitable. The inner human does not exist until the books, the monastic cells, the deserts and the solitudes have separated it off; only when humans themselves become a cell or *camera silens* can the quiet voice of reason dwell within them. A reasonable ego cannot be had without acoustic isolation. Husserl's *epoché* still followed on from this cultivation of withdrawal from group noise in one's own head. What the phenomenologists called the bracketing of the naïve attitude to life is in essence an active holiday from the prejudices and gesticulations that cause the interior to be as loud as the exterior. What is a firm conviction but a firmly trained, loud inner voice? This doxic screaming inside me is silenced by philosophical meditation. *Homo silens* is the guardian of mental de-automation.

The most important byproduct of the *silentium* effect shows itself in the divergence of the public and the private. This distinction, which served as a central conceptual pair in the traditional political sciences, is initially attributable to an internal modification of the phonotope, as it separates situations defined by family sounds from those dominated by collective sounds. In this context, the private appears as an enclave of quieter communications omitted from the group noise, or even a space of silence in which individuals recover from the stress of the collective sound.

Its archetype reveals itself in monologue, like that conducted by the humanity-weary poet of the nineteenth century in his nocturnal attic, noting at "One O'Clock in the Morning" that the "tyranny of the human face,"[43] along with the despotism of the human voice, has ended, even if only for a few hours. In general, one can say that whatever is spoken *privatim* should remain between you and me, however much the first urban medium, gossip, seeks to disseminate what is said quietly. In reality, gossip—a form of dictatorship of the collective—has the task of attenuating the suitability of private lives to remain secret from the public space. It is the continuation of group murmuring by urban means.

The antisocial tendency of individualism manifests itself in the longing to extend one's holiday from noise to the whole year. Conversely, the totalitarian tendency of groups expresses itself most characteristically of all in moments when it forces reluctant individuals to sing along. Nonetheless, the unfolded phonotope provides the space for the concrete freedom of music. In its musical aspects, the listeners can discover reasons for being together beyond the group noise. Free music makes no promises that it does not keep in its own sounding.[44] It has meanwhile trained the ear so individualistically that it can meditate at will on any sonospheric state as if it were a sound installation.[45]

The fact that the public realm constitutes a modification of the phonotope reveals itself in European antiquity not only in the invention of tragic theater, with its choruses and sonorous masks, but also in the cultivation of public addresses that serve the decision-making process in people's assemblies. What would later be called politics was at first simply a cultural form of speaking loudly—to the end of putting the group body into the desired mood with a single penetrating voice, whether expressively, in harmony with the *communis opinio* conveyed by the speaker's address or persuasively, in order to win over an assembled crowd and move them away from their initial disposition. Not until Plato's *Republic* was a type of politician created who would serve no longer as a loudspeaker, but rather as a receiver of quiet ideas—with little success, as we know, as the introduction of the quiet politician is yet to come. It would be a contradiction in terms, for politics, as the art of what is possible in noise, remains assigned to the loud side of the phonotope.

3. The Uterotope—We-Caves, World Incubators

It would not be easy to say how long one would need to live on the island to realize that the place holds a secret. Do the elders guard it, or is it the healers? Is it in the hands of the wise women? Do the rhapsodists have privileged access to it? Or is it the logically unborn, the schizophrenics, who are closest to it? Without intending to speak of gynecological trivialities, it is advisable to be attentive to female presences if one hopes to understand how the enclave gets into shape. The secret of the island, it would seem, is at once a secret of space and of women. Whoever would solve it must follow their nose for the particularities of femininity. *Odore di donna*—a kitchen secret? An agreement with the moon? Is the domain of women an expanded fireplace, a hearth from which promising fragrances emanate, and aromasphere in which the takers of the same skewers and pots raise their heads? Or is one closer to the secret of the island when a young woman walks past, cloaked in her pheromone aura, her biological *promesse de Bonheur*? Asking the islanders for information will be futile, as they are products of the island secret and at best its poets, not its explorers. Naturally they would admit that nothing is possible in the business of their lives without the women, the mothers, simply because they are responsible for the infants and take up half the sky and half the bed. Concerning the contributions from the feminine to the emergence of the human island and its inner formatting, answers at this level are unrewarding.

Things only move along when one adopts the concepts of woman and space in a biological and topological defamiliarization; then one can speak of the female, in particular the maternal body in geometrical or position-theoretical terms. This shift follows from the fact that through the evolutionary achievements of the mammalian biogram, a radically new type of mother animal came into existence—shaped by the "revolutionary" conquest of the female abdomen as a milieu for inward egg depositions. This results in a topological reality unique in natural history: the mother's body now becomes the offspring's ecological niche. The interiorization of the egg lowers the risk of depositing in external nests and exchanges it for the risk of internal incubation and the new birth risk.[46] The success story of mammals proves that this transaction was an advantageous one; it resulted not only in new integral mother animals that harbor parasites of their own species, but also in new types of young that grow up in a world where attachment has a higher value and separation constitutes a sharper risk.

The British psychoanalyst and evolutionary biologist John Bowlby encapsulated the psychology of anthropogenetic risk with his schema of a hominid-specific "environment of evolutionary adaptedness." He succeeded in showing to what extent the early phases of hominidic and human existence are geared towards a close mother-child symbiosis in their psychobiological design. Bowlby's concept of attachment is the crystallization of comprehensive insight into the luxurious and injurious peculiarity of the human dyad as it developed on hominid premises from the

Pleistocene period onwards[47]—an insight from which one can at once derive an explanation for the growing risk of neglect and psychosis among humans in advanced civilizations, and more still in industrial societies, where there is tellingly also a growing tendency towards an ideological dressing up of early abandonment in childhood as a normal situation.[48] When Hegel remarks in his lectures on anthropology that the mother is "the *genius* of the child,"[49] one can add from a biotopological perspective that the mother is the situation of the child—or, in Bowlby's terms, its environment of evolutionary adaptedness.

Speaking of the "mother" in the context of humans implies an *analysis situs*, as the use of the term obliges one to say in what position the child is in relation to her—whether *still* inside or *already* outside, or, in a certain sense (but what sense?), in both positions at once. One thus refers to the fact that following the internalization of egg deposition and fetal evolution *in utero*, a new type of event was produced: birth. The turn inwards resulted in a proto-drama of coming out, a primary coercion and talent to leave the womb, an early fatality in the choice of the path that leads forwards, out into the "open." As the matrix of all more radical changes of place and state, the fact of birth will have unforeseeable consequences.

From here we can define one attribute of the anthropogenic island more precisely: it must be the place in which a change in the meaning of birth takes place. Among the offspring of the sapient, this becomes a biological event of metabiological significance. It is clear, after all, that mammalian bornness is not sufficient to reach the place of humans. Mammals are born, humans come into the world. The island of being provides the bracing climate in which being born is heightened to coming-into-the-world.

Jan van Neck, *The Anatomy Lesson of Dr. Frederick Ruysch* (1683)

Connoisseurs of twentieth-century philosophy will be aware
that I am drawing on Heidegger's distinction between the animal
mode of being, which is fettered to the environment, and the
ecstatic, world-forming essence of humans. The thinker was not
interested in how we should envisage the genesis of this difference,
as he considered anthropological and genetic inquiry pre-philo-
sophical, inferior and dogmatic. In reality—as I have long been
attempting to show[50]—it is Heidegger's thought in particular that
demands anthropological "substantialization," if the term is not

out of place, and I would assert that one can only do justice to this demand by setting in motion an investigation of the topological difference posited by the act of human existence as being-native

Initially, something that is born experiences merely the exchange of one surrounding element for another: that is a great deal, but it does not change anything about the animal definition of life. Mammal birth can, at least, be compared to a transition from life in the water to existence on land and in the air, as if each offspring in the line of mammifers had to reenact the primordial exodus from the sea and the acquisition of mainland ways of living in its own becoming. A birth only becomes a coming-into-the-world, however, when the environment in which the arrival finds itself has become a world—an embodiment of objects or a cosmos of things that are the case. This is not the place to explain what the term "world" means in philosophical terms; from a position-theoretical perspective, we can say that the basic condition known as being-in-the-world refers to a being-outside. Heidegger hinted at this with an ontologically sobered concept of ecstasy as being-with-the-circumstances. Whoever ek-sists is held out into something in which they initially cannot be with themselves. For humans, the ontological eccentrics, being outside precedes being housed with oneself—although the harshness of this finding is usually alleviated by the protective power of the spheric alliances. There is no doubt about the headstart of externality on every kind of housing, inclusion, enclosure and settling with oneself if one is speaking of positions *in the world*. Every theory of elementary situation is thus also an interpretation of the primary trauma: that there is more external space than can be taken possession of, shaped, wished away or denied. Because this is the case, humans are condemned to the production of interiors.

Once this is clear, one can attempt to formulate the secret of the island in space-theoretical terms. Being on the island now means: being able to use the possibility of transferring inside situations. Transferences of this type become feasible when a real situation is reached in the external that can serve elsewhere as a wrapping or container for the repetition of inwardness. The phenomenon of transference (which, discovered by the magologists and fascinologists of the Renaissance, radicalized by the magnetizers of Romanticism, and both neuro-hermeneutically interpreted and applied as a medium of the therapeutic situation by psychoanalysis in the twentieth century) arises from an inertial effect triggered by the predominance of past influences over present perceptions. Its development presupposes strong scenic differences between then and now. If these are given, for example after relocations or expulsions, marrying out and emigration, the phenomenon of the older scene being repeated in the newer can arise—a process that is described in common psychological theories as the projection of affects. In the present context it seems logical to formulate a new description of transference as the reproduction of situations, with the emphasis on the fact that primal transference takes place as a recurring reestablishment of an internal position in an external situation. Space travel is an instructive paradigm in this respect, for it demonstrates explicitly in a vacuum what humans have always done in the terrestrial "lifeworld." The insulation secret of the human sphere is that the cohabitants establish a shared inside in the shared outside through coproductive transference. It must be noted that transferences initially have a collective character and are only individualized late on, depending on the media, language games and living forms that support the privatization effect.

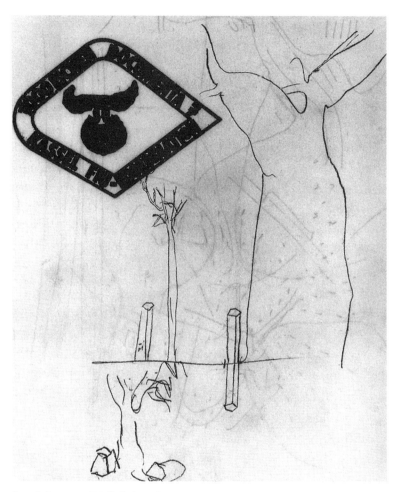

Joseph Beuys, *7000 Oaks* (1982)

    The joint work leading to the creation of the island takes place through the cohabitants drawing on a shared scenic store of inside situations and reproducing them in the differing outside position. This results in the coherent group as a uterope, meaning an enacted womb metaphor. In the first reading, this is interpreted as a phantasm of kinship—as found in the dogma that as members of a nation, we are always children of the same mother too. Let us not forget that in Plato's most candid moment, when he lets Socrates present the doctrine of the necessity of the noble lie, he wanted to profit from the uterotopic effect: what else should one tell the dissatisfied members of the class-divided city but that all citizens are offspring of Mother Earth, who bore not only gold children, but also silver and iron ones?—in the expectation, perhaps legitimate for mothers, that her progeny would be on peaceful terms with one another in sibling harmony and in honor of their shared deep past.[51] In the second reading, the concept of the uterotope refers to a spatial phantasm which became historically powerful and suggests that as long as we remain territorialized in our own group, we are the favored creatures in the same cave—primally solidary beneficiaries of the same unbornness in the shared group womb. The "depth" of a group corresponds to how developed its collective nirvana function is: its members converge in an imaginarily shared unreality or pre-reality from which they are sent into the real—like genuine siblings sharing a cave secret as if it were a divine embarrassment. The uterotopic *communio* is articulated as much in the early totemist alliances as in countless varieties of higher-level magical and sacred confederacy, extending to the *communio sanctorum* which, in its totality, purports to form the womb of Mother Church. When contemporary philosophers of religion occasionally express the view that "humanity" is "at its innermost core a religious entity,"[52] they make use of the possibility to idealize the entire species as an Adamitic uterotope.

Anyone looking for an interpretation of the dogged feeling of belonging to ethics-based groups (along with their chronically

Eva Hesse, *Untitled (Rope Piece)* (1970), courtesy of the estate of Eva Hesse, Hauser & Wirth Gallery, Zurich (photograph: Paulus Leeser)

quarrelsome and staidly defensive nature) should not forget to examine the construction of uterotopes. They constitute the political form of the impossibility of growing up. Uterotopic synthesis means the election of humans to a joint origin from an incomparable cave (and being jointly stuck in it). By contrast, utopian synthesis means the election of humans to take a shared path to an incomparable land of arrival. Uterotopia and utopia mirror each other like elitisms of origin and future. They represent the two source regions of the manic consciousness—and *eo ipso* the two deepest motives for abandoning solidarity with the fates of the rest. With this difference in mind, one can understand that contrary to what Marx and Engels thought, all history is the history of battles between chosen groups. Establishing this means realizing why a twofold world war has been underway since the dawn of martial cultures: a first-order war between several communities chosen according to origin, and a second-order war between communities chosen according to origin and communities chosen according to future.[53] What was generally taken for the choice between war and peace was, in truth, usually the choice between the former and the latter war. It is unclear whether a third war is possible. If so, its front would run between the chosen and the non-chosen. Experience has shown that the latter shy away from formal deployments; they content themselves with observing the activities of the chosen until their self-destruction is a *fait accompli*.[54]

4. The Thermotope—The Pampering Space

The Romans invented the art of preventing palaver by summarizing the result in four words. For example: *Ubi bene ibi patria*.[55] Regarding our subject, this means that the common tendency of humans to prefer their homeland can be explained once and for all by deriving the homeland effect from a sense of well-being in one's own location. Ecumenical enlightenment, Roman style: it makes the connection between the homeland and well-being irreversible. If you are at home, you feel well; if you do not feel well, you are not at home. If the homeland does not allow *bene vivere*, it is not worthy of the name; consequently one can, and probably should, look for other circumstances, be it as an emigrant or as one who overturns domestic conditions. In a speech on November 29, 1792, Saint-Just would declare: "A people that is not happy has no fatherland." Since then, the native damned of this earth have been searching for some place where things are happier. As soon as the strength to break with bad circumstances is absent, the notorious phenomenon of staleness ensues: loyalty to the misery that spawned us. Martin Walser's genius found the key phrase for this: "A family is a syndicate of misery. You don't leave something like that."[56] The basic right to free movement, only formulated in recent times, implies productive disloyalty towards species-specific unhappiness. People are with themselves not in a country, but in a comfort.

One of the motifs of group-insulated life is that of a successful group earning a pampering advantage for itself and distributing it internally. Nonetheless: the realization comes late that the advantage is not so much the effect of the place where the distribution takes place, but that the effect of the distribution leads us to value the place. Until then, one has to listen to a great deal of nonsense—about Promised Lands, about national fields demanding to be soaked with the impure blood of foreigners, about the nomos of the earth, about the right of peoples to have their own states, and about the tree of freedom, which must be watered every generation with the blood of patriots. A patriot—could that not be someone who confuses the reasons for attachment to one's own location?

The most visible sign of the advantage of being at home in the group is the fireplace; as the oldest symbol of humanity, it is the clearest indication that humans cannot do without a pampering element. The jointly tended fire holds the experience that there are natural benefactors who grant advantages as long as one keeps a careful eye on them. The power of fire is beneficial—provided the fire watch does not fall asleep. Using fire is an activity located exactly on the threshold between magic and work. In the course of civilization history this initially almost balanced difference was shifted in favor of work, though the magical side could never be entirely abolished. If everything humans do is governed by equations between actions and their effects, one is unmistakably dealing with work. The path it takes towards the result is as straight as the rules of the trade dictate. Very often, admittedly, what people call work is merely a sterile pastime for a majority of "inverted sorcerers" who know how to "make little of much."[57] Was Nietzsche aware that he had just defined the civil service with those words? As far as the magic is concerned, it depends on the opposite effect: the baffling surplus of effects compared to acts. Although we do not know how performing magic (*zaubern*, probably related to the Old English *teafor*, "red ochre," which was used for dying objects red) actually works, it does seem to lead further than mere work ever could. As soon as the success of certain operations extends to the extraordinary, magic comes into play in the form of authentic causal added value. Thus magic is not always trickery; the world itself encourages a magic-like approach to many of its circumstances, because it offers the experience that success occasionally exceeds what was actually undertaken. The oldest concepts of happiness and power are a response to this. In classical antiquity, the bonus evident in highly visible, astonishing success was represented in the form of gods possessing cunning, artisanal skill or mastery of special effects (corresponding to Zeus, Hephaestus and Hermes), whom people would understandably attempt to entangle in alliances.

The oldest form of such an allied Fortuna is the hearth fire where the women hold sway and the priests perform their acts. Twofold personnel, a double promise of happiness. The fire is a household god with far-reaching connections and a household soul with a sensual presence. Since its naturalization among humans, pyrogenetic myths have attributed its presence to a gift of the gods or the Titans to mortals—a gift that became the lasting possession of the gifted and granted them admission to the cultural state. This is the first appearance of the thought figure "helping others help themselves." In the Old European context, Prometheus is the Titan with the helper syndrome, the exemplary sponsor and friend of humans. He who brings the "pantechnical" fire (*pyros pantechnos*)[58] becomes the patron of kitchens, inspirer of alchemy, enabler of ceramics and metallurgy, giver of comfort and advocate of the redistribution of light and comfort—in a word, the true cultural Titan, and thanks to all these qualities, the highest saint in the Enlightenment calendar. As the facilitator of life and first empowerer, as a philanthropist and instigator of rebellion against the idiocy of submission to the prevailing state, he is the mythical protector of the thermotope.

This term, then, refers not only to the area in which the group members feel the immediate thermal advantage of fire—a motif that could, furthermore, only gain greater significance in the post-African phase of cultural evolution, after the spread of humanity to regions with more distinct seasons and longer winters. At the same time, it indicates the circle in which the advantages of everyday magic are noticeable. The inhabitants of the island of Chirotopia are naturally Thermotopians, for a synergy establishes itself between what the hands succeed in doing and the value added by fireplaces. The thermotope is a space in which continuous affirmations lead to expectations of success; it is the primary comfort sphere—from very early beginnings, even if it was only in developed civilizations, such as those of the Romans, that the cult of public happiness joined with that of the fireplace. This occurred most strikingly in the institution of the state hearth at the temple of Vesta on the Forum Romanum, whose function was to prove the unity of hearth and state, or of house and empire.[59] It radiated the gospel of immunity, of the *integrum*, all the way to the periphery. In its primary symbol, the Roman Empire presented itself as a domestic thermotope, magnified to a world format, in which the foyer and the universe, the island and the mainland, were meant to become one and the same.

Whereas the Roman jurists and cult founders politically generalized thermotopy, the Brahmins of India aimed to hypostatize it. According to them, the world context as a whole must be understood in terms of the changing forms of fire. The deep effects of Brahmanic thought stem from the fact that it is sure of its pyrotechnical skills in performing the sacrifice at the fire, and derives numerous metaphorizations from this sharply demarcated field. Just as the Roman Empire contracted into a few maidens at the sacred fire, the vestal virgins, ancient Indian Culture did the same with the ascetics at the sacrificial fire.[60] It attained its final concentration in the figure of the renunciant, the *sannyasin*, who no longer sacrifices at external fires, but rather burns his entire existence in a mental fire, the flame of the Veda. Hence the

The Nagas stay by the sacred fire for the entire duration of Kumbh Mela—up to two months

renunciant no longer takes part in the usual cooking, fires and burnings; his corpse is not cremated like those of spiritually uncooked humans, but buried, for it would seem inappropriate to burn the external form of one who had already been internally burned. In the absolute thermotope, it is not only the advantages of a life close to the fireplace that are distributed—there is also a ritual contest for the advantage of all advantages: to become one with the fireplace of being.

In other cases, thermotopic advantages are more profanely defined. In layered societies, the egalitarian gathering around the fire is translated into the attraction of property advantages, which now accumulate in a favored place. Now the exclusive aspects of the advantaged space come into sharp relief: what creates inclusive solidarity on a smaller scale has a de-solidarizing effect on a larger scale. Advantages, after all, are something of which there is not enough for everyone. Other fires, other fates. "Heat is a property, a possession. It must be guarded jealously and only given as a gift to a chosen being."[61] Being able to secure the pampering context for his own is proof of the patron, the great lord. As far as the advantaged space under his watch extends, those dependent on him feel that it is in their interest to keep his secret; thus all groups that closely guard the privilege of belonging all carry the same unutterable name: *cosa nostra*. If one understands insular societies as distribution spaces for advantages of uncertain provenance, their formal structure has a mafiotic substrate; this applies even to a democratic world power such as the USA, whose prosperity rests not only on the achievements of its own economy, but also on a hidden tribute system.[62] One does not ask where comfort has come from once it has become a habit. The mysteries of redistribution are deep and the beneficiaries

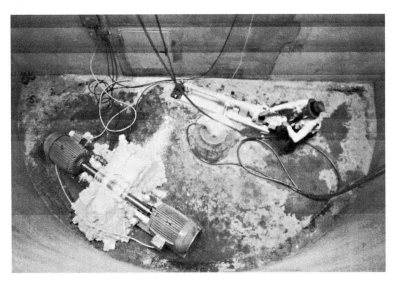

Joseph Beuys, *The Honey Pump* at *documenta* VI (1977)

cling to them, even when they already suspect *que ce n'est pas catholique.* Just as few of the countless habitually subsidized citizens and institutions of the bankrupt city of Berlin in 2004 want to know where the sums they are determined to continue spending without earning them are supposed to come from, few of the numerous citizens of the Gulf states are interested in an answer to the mystery of how they can receive maximum wages from the reigning sheikhs for staying away from any form of employment.

So it was not entirely accurate to claim that all history is the history of battles between chosen groups; it is equally the history of battles between pampering groups.

If one is looking for a morally acceptable contemporary alternative to the immoralism based on cronies, clubs and clients, the welfare state structures established in the nineteenth and twentieth centuries present themselves as options. The welfare state is the regional generalization of the thermotope by insurance means. Its services are based on the discovery of a cold fire (fueled by compulsory contributions) around which countless needy (yet relatively privileged) people can gather. With the national and communal solidary systems (in the USA, these are augmented by the phenomenal voluntary services), modern societies seem to have invented something resembling a meta-hearth that helps many entitled people, and some clever ones, to keep their own fires burning. For the time being, such facilities for the redistribution of wealth opportunities work exclusively in national formats. One could go so far as to say that the postmodernized spirit of nations only rests on the solidarity funds and insurance systems—especially in Central and Northern Europe, where the most comfortable thermotopic institutions of the world are located. Anyone who wanted to transfer these conditions to world society would first have to resolve the thermotopic paradox and show how one can favor all over all. In the absence of a convincing thermic socialism, one will have to be provisionally content with a thermic aesthetic.[63] How far one can get with this is hinted at by the *Honey Pump* of Joseph Beuys, which symbolically connects humanity itself to the sweet life.

5. The Erototope—Jealousy Fields, Levels of Desire

One has to spend an entire season on the anthropogenic island to develop a sense of how the inhabitants organize their desired life. It is to be expected from the outset that creatures with strong uterotopic and thermotopic conditioning will exist in a bracing climate that provokes heightened alertness to the advantages of belonging and the distribution of comfort changes. The island is therefore, contrary to the tourist cliché, not a place to forget what others are doing. Those who intend to find their bearings in the island hothouse would be well advised to increase their attention to the affective activities of the others.

I call the human-insular field of wishes the erototope because erotic desire provides the paradigm for how affective competition in groups simultaneously stimulates and controls the wish life of the cohabitants. The erotic field is energized by the groups producing a form of desirous-suspicious attention to the difference between their members through constant subacute self-irritation. This results in a jealousy fluid that is kept circulating and flowing by searching looks, humorous comments, disparaging gossip and ritualized games of rivalry. In this dimension, eros manifests itself not as a dual and libidinous tension between ego and alter, but as a triangular provocation. I love you, and your beautiful form attracts me, as soon as I can assume that another loves you and that your beautiful form attracts him sufficiently to make him want to possess you. Whereas Diotima of Mantinea uses philosophical language to interpret the essence of the erotic as a submission to attraction by good, topological investigation highlights the stimulating confusion caused by the advantage of difference that a nearby other wants to possess, or already does, by privatizing an object of love.[64] Erotic processes in the group then constitute the basic form of competition—triggered by the imitative observation of the striving of others to achieve advantages of being, possession and prestige.[65] What would later be called the *sensus communis* is a share in the alertness climate of free-floating group jealousy. One of the miracles—and justifications—of the democratic life form is that it transforms the basic mood of vigilant grudges into public spirit and willingness to cooperate, aside from those episodes in which, as if to relax, some indulge in a little incitement.

As soon as the earliest and most frugal conditions no longer prevail on the anthropogenic island, its inhabitants increasingly differ in the following terms: what someone is more; what someone has more; and what someone represents more. Consequently, part of group wisdom is jealousy management, which takes a three-dimensional approach. If the group's self-irritations are to be kept in a livable tone, the collective requires sufficient discretions for the differences of being, differences of property and differences of status within it. Discretion is knowing what one is not supposed to have noticed. If one has been in the erototope for long enough, one senses the subtle effort of its inhabitants to preserve their indifference to negligible differences—and their deliberate lack of receptiveness to the non-negligible ones. This has often been taken for repression; it is a conscious silence about the fact that the Erlking is among us.

Nonetheless, it is to be expected that the fury of jealousy will triumph over discretion in all groups sooner or later. At such moments, the longing to rob and humiliate the bearers of advantageous differences emerges from latency; for the passion of redistribution, the hour of satisfaction arrives. Then "that repulsive mixture of sensuality and cruelty which has always struck me as the true witches' brew"[66] takes full effect—the force which Nietzsche notes in *The Birth of Tragedy* constitutes the essence of the primitive and reprehensible Dionysiac force that has not yet been tamed by Apollonian culture. To prevent these outbreaks of the affective plague, which are both terrible and secretly wished for, each erototope needs its own school of correct desire, or rather a morality that serves as a prophylactic for anger over differences. Because confused eros means attraction to the merits of a positively distinguished object, this "love" is expressed in the longing for a piece of the spoils and—if sharing is not possible—the dispossession of its owners. The object area of this love also extends, in almost equal measure, to sexual partners, house and estate property, animals and capital, and mental or physical assets. This first, raw art of love results in the culture of envy that usually adorns itself with the honorific title "critique."

The first tuition in the school of desire comes in the form of prohibitions: here one learns the necessary lessons via taboo and "thou shalt not." The calmer the ownership, the easier it is to prevent wish escalation. The prohibition reveals the presence of the third party, who already stepped between Me and You before our empirical encounter: this guarantee-providing third party separates me from my naïve desire for the other's advantages at the same time as forbidding the other to exhibit his privileges.[67] As neither bans nor taboos can neutralize the wandering gaze towards the other's property, and contribute rather to focusing the desire on what is withheld, advanced cultures must take the step to actively disinteresting humans in the objects of their envy. This can only succeed if they are replaced with more precious goods whose non-material nature allows unlimited sharing, not provocation through private property.

To this day, everything at all connected to the spirit lives off the relief caused by this elevation of desire. The ethics of advanced civilization in the East and the West alike work with the irony that humans who fight over good things miss out on better things. The angels, Emerson says, only leave us so that archangels will come. If there was genuinely an act of betrayal among intellectuals in the twentieth century, it was their inversion of this irony. They began to poke fun at what was supposedly better and decided not to miss out on their own portion of commonplace good things. "Superstructure"—you know the sort of thing! After that, the playing arena for the game of distributing scarce advantageous goods once more became everything that is the case. After 1914, great politics was the universalization of jealousy battles without a higher level.

In Platonism, one finds the gradations from sensual, biased and polemogenic love to spiritual, unbiased and irenic love formally outlined. Stoicisim too, in its ethics of liberation from needing much, muted the temptation to participate in the all-pervasive struggles for appropriation. Christian monastic culture was able to follow on from this moral athleticism. The most mature form of an ethics of disinterest was undoubtedly achieved in the Buddhist doctrine of attachments and their dissolution through the sword of insight. With its subtle analysis of the causal chain leading to fixations that cause suffering, Buddhism attempts to emancipate at least a minority of humans from the arena of desire and the feeling of inevitably being a loser. It is no coincidence that Friedrich Nietzsche recognized Buddhism as the most noble form of affective hygiene—the same Nietzsche to whom the analysis of *ressentiment* still owes virtually everything. Thanks to him, we know that the nature of the feeling of setback lies in the loser's attachment to the object with which they unfavorably compare themselves; from the wound left by this comparison flows the almost insatiable need to humiliate the more successful object.

In a cruder form that has the merit of clarity, the Jewish Decalogue, especially its final commandment, articulates a rule to stop the dangerous competition of desire, albeit only in its concrete sexual and possessive aspects:

> "You shall not covet your neighbor's house. You shall not covet your neighbor's wife, nor his manservant or maidservant, his ox or donkey, or anything that belongs to your neighbor." (Exodus 20:17)

In its concretism, which mirrors a small or medium existence as a livestock and slave owner around 1000 BC, with its typical dramas, the tenth commandment hints at the formulation of a general rule of wish abstinence that helps to lower tensions in the erototope. It is not incomprehensible, therefore, that René Girard focuses on an anthropological rereading of the tenth commandment in the résumé of his investigations of the effects of mimetic competition.[68] To the detriment of his own project, Girard pays little attention to the fact that some non-Christian cultures have advanced further in healing desire through disinterest in scarce polemogenic goods, and the redirection of that desire towards sharable sympathogenic goods, than the Decalogue religions; he also seems to overlook that Nietzsche's critique of morality by no means supports a reintroduction of the power of jealousy. What the author of *Zarathustra* had in mind was a synthesis between the achievements of Buddhist abstinence psychology and the worldling qualities of playful competition, with the goal of detoxifying the ancient occidental erototope through this turn towards an ethics of generosity.[69] To grasp the scope of this attempt, one must acknowledge that the experiment of modernity, in so far as it concerns the conditions of consumption and competition, has led to an almost unbridled deregulation of the erototope. In no earlier social formation was the systematic escalation of desire for everything owned by others exploited so overtly for the motivation of behavior. In consumer society, the "fires of envy"[70] are interconnected to form power plant-like energy circles. The political systems of democracy also depend on discharging the suspicion of all towards all. As early as the Kentucky Resolutions of 1798, Thomas Jefferson stated: "free government is founded in jealousy, and not in confidence." If cultural theory could formulate one question to the twenty-first century, it would be this: how does modernity intend to get its experiment with the globalization of jealousy under control?

6. The Ergotope—
Effort Communities and Fighting Empires

The space in which the burdens of tasks are cooperatively distributed will here be referred to as the ergotope—its inhabitants, the Ergotopians, are grouped together into effort communities. The description of their activities produces the mirror of the adults, *érga kai hémera*, the chronicle of the works and days of people who cannot make things easy for themselves. The summons to the inescapable joint works initially comes in a familiar guise, informal and totalitarian, through situative evidence and the dictate of tradition, then later through initiation rites, professional requirements and status shackles; later still, labor services, edicts and offices ensure the integration into the ergotope; finally, we are roped in by mission statements and the daily commands of public opinion. In this horizon, groups become communes—which means units integrated through shared *munera*. The ergotope forms the space in which the cohabitants are encompassed by duties and specifications—with the draft call to a joint war against the external enemy as the standard and limit of all cooperation. (Someone exempted from these restrictions is *immune* in the precise sense: de-committed, workless, free for other priorities.)

If ergotopic situations are radicalized, we may find ourselves on the rowing benches of galleys, condemned to keep the pace dictated to us. We toil away in quarries, in forced mining, in the *Katorga*, the work camps of death. At other times we are voluntary cooperators, deployed for a shared cause through an enthusiastic consensus: cathedral building communities, freedom fighters, crusaders or finalists. Whether fused together by necessity or inspired by a common goal—as long as we have a secure place of effort, we are occupied as laborers in the vineyard of the *communitas*. The galley example is instructive, for it helps to explain the concept of rhythmic socialism, where social synthesis occurs through synchronized movements. Cooperation is thus arranged as a synergy of synchronously functioning muscle systems. Every convict at an oar is an obscure hero of work.

From the archaic tradition of group dancing, simple yet multi-faceted routines and ceremonies develop in advanced civilizations to carry homogeneous motions in groups and masses. In his study *Keeping Together in Time: Dance and Drill in Human History*, the American historian William H. McNeill describes various forms of "muscular bonding" and ritual or military cooperation capable of producing an *esprit de corps* in heterogeneous performance communities.[71] These rhythmic bonding techniques activate psychosomatic stimulation centers of group

Employees of a Japanese Coca-Cola factory performing calisthenic exercises

euphoria. Early on, humans found that giving effort an even rhythm is experienced as relief, and that a joint rhythmic overexertion shifts the point of exhaustion further away. Roman troops, following the Macedonian model, used the loud chanting of steps for high-speed marches. Mechanical timing, admittedly, is merely a substitute for the co-enthusiasm of dance. When voluntary collective enthusiasm cannot be expected—among slave masses in the masters' fields and on imperial building sites, for example, or in the conscripted troops of the Modern Age—the leaders use rhythmic drill as a consensus prosthesis; the beginnings of slave and military music can be traced to this trick. Plato's *Laws* still understood something of muscular consensus, and did not want to leave the state's musical keys or rhythms to the discretion of mawkish sophists or tonal demagogues. The Greek military commanders were aware of the role of flutes in the acoustic integration of the phalanx early on; they assumed they would keep the company together not only as a living shield wall, but also as an animated special phonotope—as if an army were a war parade unfolding ecstatically in the open country. The art of choreography preserves the memory that choirs were initially movement groups under uniform direction.[72] The consistent implementation of the unity of procedure and consensus in modernity goes back to the war school of Moritz of Orange, who in 1590 began training Dutch mercenary troops to become synchronized fighting machines—and acting as a model for the entire enlightened military system in Europe and Asia. In the military-based political systems of the Modern Age, drill is the true schooling of the nation.

When effort breaks off from the group and becomes the concern of conspicuous individuals, athleticism ensues. The early athletes appearing at the dawn of advanced civilization develop into experts in special efforts that can only be carried out by specially trained persons.[73] The purpose of effort and its placement in the real has clearly been transformed: when athletes compete against one another, they are no longer concerned with a necessary joint work in their group; the sporting *agon* is neither war nor harvest or wall- building. Rather, the representing and outdoing purpose of its achievement becomes the focus—even if cities (like modern nations) often view their athletes as delegates and interpret their successes as collective facts. This is possible because with its concept of *pónos*, the effort that bestows dignity and forms men, the ancient, early individualist culture of the Greeks advanced to an abstract conception of effort as such,

Military drill with a musket

effort *sans phrase*. Thus the progressive differentiation of the ergotopic collective into burdened protagonists and unburdened spectators; both have a share in *philoponía*, the love of effort, from their own perspective.

Athleticism transfers the principle of theater to bodily exercise, thus establishing a civilizatory alternative to the martial form of stress management. Athletes are the first simulators of the emergency. The invention of the actor-warrior is undoubtedly one of the most valuable civilizatory achievements in European antiquity. When the modern Olympic Games were initiated in 1896, the renaissance of antiquity that had begun in the fourteenth century entered its notably delayed mass culture phase, split into the Greek and Roman paths.[74] Nonetheless, the civilizing simulation of war in the Olympic sports venues failed to prevent real wars, either the regional or so-called "world" wars. In the twentieth century, sport was often pursued—in stadiums and elsewhere—as doggedly as if it were not a form of relief from emergency, but rather its other front—the second subjugation of Greece to the Roman dictate, this time as the victory of the arena over the stadium.

In the ergotope, social synthesis rules through stress. Hence the secret of the effortful group's cohesion lies in its capacity not to fall apart under maximum strain. One can safely say that making this fact explicit was one of the key events in the contemporary cultural sciences. It is inseparably tied to Heiner Mühlmann's work on the "nature of cultures" and Bazon Brock's analyses of the circular connection between culture and war. The centerpiece of Mühlmann's cultural theory is a radically ergotopic and ergonomic interpretation of the social bond, for which he introduces the complex term "maximal stress cooperation"

(MSC). According to his argumentation, what makes a group an effective survival unit is its ability to synchronize its efforts in all-or-nothing situations, also known as "emergencies."

Calling the moments of utmost stress emergencies or states of exception does not mean using secularized theological concepts as Carl Schmitt's followers do, echoing their master. The state of emergency is not the secularized form of the miracle, but rather the politicized form of a standard biological situation to which primate bodies, and hence human bodies too, respond with an innate, endocrinologically controlled program of extreme energy release and syntonic solidarization. Its existence is ascertained through a cognitive schema: the emergency assessment. Because this includes an intellectual and moral aspect, it is subject to cultural variation. Consequently, stress does not mean fate in its entirety; calm in the face of danger is the specific human chance. It implies emancipation from being summoned to false emergencies and running ahead into false strickenness by the battle situation. Old strategy manuals such as that by the Chinese commander-sophist Sun Tzu already include the virtue of avoiding battle in the doctrine of correct battle. In the West, the name of the Roman military leader Fabius Cunctator stands for the ability of sensible persons to evade the deadly invitations from stress programs even when close to danger.

If human intelligence, like its animal precursors, interprets certain threats as real and present triggers of the most extreme emotive-bodily responses, this does not refer to the interruption of the normal by the miracle spoken of by theologians and aestheticians of the sublime. In keeping with the evolutionary varieties of animal and early human intelligence, present danger is assessed in emergency-ontological terms: one interprets the situation as an interruption of prolonged calm by a now acute threat. The deep biological rootedness of the major stress reaction proves that the utmost is evolutionarily commonplace. Though the state of emergency is inscribed in the human body like an innate expectation, it is triggered by the emergency assessment of the decision center. In this sense, even animals are ontologists. It is the leader that decides on the emergency: if it flees, it flips the "cognitive energy switch"[75] in the other animals, as previously in itself, before gesturally declaring the case of application for the categorical imperative of the adrenal gland: from now on, throw everything to the front! Faced with these circumstances, the most real is given in real presence. You stand facing your danger, the potential bringer of your death, your god and stressor. Anyone who is unfamiliar with this has no idea what it means to act at the limit.

The ergotopic trade secret of "cultures" consists—as Mühlmann shows in an ingenious, heavily formalized reconstruction—in the rules of collective stress handling. In an at least three-phase process, the simple group turns into an advanced-civilized subject with a specific territorial, temporal or imperial project.[76] In the pre-stress phase, the groups form cooperative units with a considerable inside-outside asymmetry—primarily, according to Mühlmann's deliberations, through self-reprimanding, self-edifying and self-aggrandizing communications that he summarizes as "insider injunctions." I have indirectly addressed several of these already, for it is easy to see that a number of the previously examined dimensions of human insulation, especially the phonotopic, uterotopic and thermotopic spaces, show a close connection to the positive discrimination of the we-group: they jointly reinforce the tendency of the coexistent to cooperative attachment. Often enough, this introversion of the cultural group results in an unappealing mixture of boastfulness, exclusion and aggression—Mühlmann does not hesitate to describe this as being more or less the norm. In his eyes, appealing cultures—that is, groups with a high civilizatory factor—are fairly rare, and the anthropological average behaves in an "envious, paranoid and aggressive"[77] fashion. This state of affairs was articulated in the 1930s by the right-wing decisionist thinkers. Their political polemology decreed: because humans are evil by nature, they require domination; because domination can only be practiced in closed political survival capsules directed against the outside, war between capsules is in the nature of things. "The tendency to separate (and therewith the grouping of humanity into friends and enemies) is given with human nature; it is in this sense destiny."[78] In summary, one can say that paranoia is the emergency of the *sensus communis*. Public spirit of this type ensues in the political capsules through a collective elevation above the enemy—and the subjugation of the group to the hostility effect. Whatever is recognized without any concepts as an object of necessary displeasure—and the inevitable combating thereof—is the enemy.[79]

In the maximum stress phase, the group fuses into a hyperbody in which an innate, conditioning-reinforced psychomechanics of cooperation to the death takes command. The moment of truth for a "culture"—more precisely, that of its dependence on the natural mechanism—comes in emergency conditions. One could claim that the emergency is the true purpose of culture, for it enables the autocentrism of the group to achieve its destiny: proving itself as the object of its own preference. The naturalist theory of cultures can apply its enlightening power in the same area, showing that it barely makes a difference to the culture group dynamic whether a population is attacked by an actual aggressor or whether the stressor is internally imagined and projectively created in reality. In both cases, the reality effect is the same. Whoever equates reality with the necessity of war, then, has the majority of empirical evidence on their side, yet subordinates themselves to a mechanism they have not adequately seen through, in that there is a circular connection between realism and militarism: because of its ontological orientation towards the maximum stress cooperation in war, "cultures" in history thus far have always acted time and again as self-triggers of the maximum stress reaction. They themselves create the reality in which they believe, and they believe in the reality they produce. They do not comprehend the nature of faith any more than the nature of cultures.[80]

Getting this mechanics under control would, as Brock and Mühlmann have shown, require a civilizatory initiative to tame cultures—starting with an insight into the explicated "nature of cultures." (Under the theoretical conditions of the incipient twenty-first century, explicating cultures means: setting the fundamental critique of heroism in motion and revealing the workings of the para-noogenic "we.") After this explication, one can understand why interparanoia sets the tone in the interactions of heroic systems. That is why, in the age of increased collision frequency in interparanoid intercourse, war wins out across the board as the central cultural purpose of peoples—or whatever else one wishes to call the aggressive-defensive pampering systems that wish to preserve themselves as political cocoons.

In the post-stress relaxation phase, an evaluation of the experiences gathered in the stress of war is carried out by the fighting population, as well as—depending on this self-assessment and stress assessment—an appraisal of the rules by which group life is to be organized after the fighting. Culturally, post-war situations have the effect of providing constitutions. They allow the recalibration of decorum, the system of fitting behavior, speech and design in which group life forms, in the light of relaxation (Mühlmann speaks of a stress shadow). Put in simplified terms, a victor's decorum develops on the winning side that contributes, in the manner of a hero cult, to reinforcing the group qualities that led to the success—perfectly embodied in the Roman triumph rituals and their projection into the imperial mass cultures, extending to the New York confetti parades—while, on the other side, a loser's decorum is formulated: among "bad losers" that means working towards revenge (it is fitting to strike back at the right moment), while among "good losers" it creates an ethics of reconstruction and reflection on the reasons for defeat (it is fitting to become someone else). The loser's virtue, hope, which keeps the balance between resignation and revenge, can at times appear so aggressively that it trickles into the victor's decorum— an effect without which the development of Christianity into an imperial religion would scarcely have been conceivable. For what is an empire if not, above all, a system for the integration of losers? Magnanimity towards the defeated is the imperative under which the truly great empires flourish—small wonder that this recipe (Virgil's notorious *parcere subiectis*) is often mystified as "universalism" by Imperial ideologues.[81] The frequently discussed difference between Rome and Jerusalem relates to a winner-and-loser decorum with a dual use within occidental civilization. (A different description of this situation would be that the universality of Christianity consisted in offering communion beyond victory and defeat.) This difference between victor's and loser's rules, fundamental to all traditional cultures, has been blurred into polyvalent systems since the end of the Second World War; in Germany and Israel in particular (partly also in Japan), forms of a hybrid decorum for victor-losers or loser-victors have developed that barely have historical precedents—and which would certainly not give lovers of clear-cut conditions their money's worth.

The post-stress adaptation to rules occasionally takes the form of a retreat to the civil and private; then individuals follow, for a while, the rule that one no longer wants the rule to be determined by the collective. This option can be observed most of all in those empires which achieved long-term peace—the ancient schools of philosophy already worked with the individualistic effect that flourished in the imperial calm of Rome. In the counseling of enlightened losers, it was above all the popularized Stoicism that excelled, requiring its adepts to note the difference, in all things, between that which depends on us and that which does not. In modernity, this phenomenon repeats itself in the form of existential philosophies and philosophies of life whose civilizatory purpose can be defined in an idea-historical comparison: both cases are examples of caring for the losers' souls under historical circumstances where revenge is out of the question. A substantial part of European philosophy from between 1806 and 1968 can only be understood if one reads it as an ongoing adaptation of loser's decorum to the conditions of the time. What has been termed the "zeitgeist" since Napoleon's victory over Prussia is primarily the constant updating of treatment methods for the audience of the defeated. As this is a task that solves each decade by new means, zeitgeists come and go like therapeutic trends. Essentially, "therapy society" already began with the Romantics' turn towards nature as the coming God from below and within. One glance at the literature of the time informs us how urgently he was needed after Jena and Auerstedt. In this respect, Romanticism was a prelude to existentialism. To the extent that the existentialists equated human existence with conscious failure, they could offer the beaten and outclassed of all kinds a formula for authority in defeat.

With the end of the twentieth century, the time had come for particularly far-reaching amendments to decorum, for what had been the most comprehensive suggestion (after Buddhism, Stoicism and Christianity) for giving satisfaction to losers had to be discarded. After the collapse of socialism, which had sought to turn the losers from the whole of history into the winners of the future, a fundamentally new mode of discreet losing had to be developed. When the republican pride of a Charles Péguy about defeats suffered in victory (*"nous sommes des victorieux vaincus"*) is used up, when the radical left-wing *lotta continua* Romanticism has exhausted itself, when the militant outsider morality of *il faut continuer* leads at best to even funnier Beckett productions and the "narcissism of the lost cause" diagnosed by Lacan is increasingly losing its infectious power, the standards for the time after the radicalisms of leftist illusions have to be set anew. As yet, no binding rules for a post-communist decorum have been formulated; it would seem, however, that (alongside shifts to the liberal capitalist camp on a massive scale) certain new editions of a "philosophy as the art of living" are taking over part of this task of the time. People practice circumspect living, as in Zeno's and Epicurus' day, as an induction into non-success with head held high. Consequently, phrases such as "the art of resignation" appear in the training plan.[82] Members of therapeutic subcultures devote themselves to the cultivation of "human potential," which is strictly separated from civil and political ambitions. Other groups, especially academics *manqués*, reformulate their marginalization as a happy unemployment; they announce their failures as those of a guerilla remaining vigilant in the underground—why speak of triumph, when fooling oneself is what counts? Offers of this kind are summed up in the advice to keep expectations of meaning low, to avoid being depressed by disappointed hopes. Otherwise, interested parties are left with the free pleasure of deconstructing the so-called victor—the subject, the hero, the man, the author—for the umpteenth time.

Where all the wild and the tame syntheses of Zeno, Spinoza, Kierkegaard and Nietzsche that surround the postmodern horizon are correct is in stating that neither pure victor nor pure loser cultures will be able to build up tradition-worthy learning processes in the longer term using their own resources. Only a redefined civilization beyond victory and defeat would be capable of virtualizing the great stress reaction and ontological emergency rage and taming them in sporting near-emergencies. It would, in almost all respects, be the opposite of what the current industry of victor fantasies is capable of saying about "globalization."[83] It would stand in the starkest contrast with the philosophy of power promoted by the American neoconservatives, who, with hand on wounded heart, inaugurated a fascism of good after September 11, 2001.[84] Bazon Brock aptly formulated the philosophical justification for the abolition of traditional stress and emergency logic with the theorem of the ruled-out emergency: an interest in the non-occurrence of the emergency in the emerging global political culture has become more serious, more real and more binding than everything that was traditionally considered serious, real and binding. In future, the true community of effort will consist of learning individuals from the most diverse cultures who devote themselves less to discharging energy between their groups than containing situations that are calling for unleashing.

7. The Alethotope—The Knowledge Republics

It is no surprise that the anthropogenic island is a place whose inhabitants have a revelation about the world and themselves within it. It is the place where countless things fail to remain concealed—even though Heraclitus, with his laconic statement *phýsis krýtpesthai phílei* [nature likes to remain in latency], pointed to a decisive aspect of the initial distribution between the concealed and the obvious. The world is a lightened space; this much was clear to the inhabitants of the island of being early on about their situation. But they are also directly sure that not everything is lightened. Probably—no, certainly, only the smallest part of everything that exists is disclosed to current knowledge and perception. The bright sphere into which we have stepped out is a speck of light in the midst of a ring of unknown, non-manifest, unspoken and unthought things. It is in this withdrawn realm, the ancients believed, that the ontologically essential lies; its investigation will be the concern of the wise, these unearthly cohabitants of our sphere. Human sensitivity to truth develops from the intuition that between the lightened and darkened regions of being, an elusive border traffic takes place.

There are two central observations that give us insight into the essence of truth: at the appropriate time, new things from the encompassing unknown enter the known and the said; conversely, some things that have been made known return to oblivion, to *lethe*, to the implied. Thus truth is neither a secure store of facts nor a mere property of statements, but rather a coming and going, a current thematic flashing-up and a sinking into the athematic night. As long as the center between these, the seemingly ever-same and present, attracts all attention, there is no gaze left to see the dynamic aspect of truth events. The required shift of view to the temporalization of truth only took place with thinkers such as Hegel and more still, Heidegger—whether the results were satisfactory is a different question.

From a pragmatic perspective, the receptiveness of humans to the difference between true and false is tied to the experience that throws and statements can hit the mark, or miss it and be false. To say that humans are dependent on the success of their throws and statements amounts to noting that they are affected by truth values—already at a biological level. The accuracy of throws and the reliability of statements is a matter of life and death from the outset, which is why the "truth" on the islands of throwers and speakers had to be guarded as a precious thing. The border traffic between the bright, public and dark, hidden areas is shaped by events that "occur," happen and give pause for thought. The difference between true and false statements, on the other hand, rests on actions that end successfully (accurately, fittingly, convincingly) or unsuccessfully (inaccurately, unfittingly, unconvincingly). Thus the manifest world is given in two ways from the start: as the nexus of actions we carry out and as the context of events that concern us. The dual sense of truth as a becoming-manifest in the event or result (in the "it works" of the successful attempt) and as a becoming-spoken in the apophantic statement is as old as the human island itself.

I call the place in which such things become both obvious and sayable or formable the alethotope. A sojourn there entails the risk of being affected by truths that show themselves, are understood and continue to apply, as well as errors that only transpire as such later on, and whose repetition is to be feared. In the first case the alethotope resembles a storage space, and in the second a site of execution or disposal. In the storage space, those things are collected that prove themselves—it is no coincidence that the German word for truth, *Wahrheit*, is connected to such notions as supervising, taking custody, preserving, defending or waiting. At the site of execution or disposal, by contrast, whatever the group is not willing or able to keep within itself is jettisoned, in so far as it is malignant, deficient, useless and worthless. The storage image permits the associated idea that before truths can become objects of collection and protection, they must be harvested and integrated in a primal act of collection—very much in keeping with Heidegger's reference to the originally agricultural meaning of the Greek verb *légein*, meaning to read, gather or pick, whose noun form is the Old European term for reason and discourse, *lógos*. In this respect the alethotope, as a field in which the truth crop is planted and a knowledge collection point, is the true site of human openness to the world. (From here one can also understand why modern storage media are only marginally connected to human circumstances, because in them, as in all large archives, subjectless collections take place—accumulations of information for no one.)

Whoever lives on the human island *ipso facto* becomes a guardian of the clearing; it hardly matters at first whether an attentive or distracted one. Heidegger, as we know, emphasized the difference between the good and bad guardians to an excessive degree, yet treated the difference between field preservers and field expanders—one could also call them sentries and conquerors (or meditators and researchers)—like a negligible factor. Regardless of whether one belongs more to the guarding or exploring end of the spectrum, the connection of humans to truth and truths can never be evaded, for being affected by truth events and their language games is based in the *genius loci*. As a place where "it happens," where "it comes out," where "it transpires," where "someone voices it," where one "is advised of it," where the said cannot be made unsaid, where the known and the revealed are captured and handed down—and where, at the same time, much, perhaps most of this, remains latent and unspoken, the alethotope takes its inhabitants into its light-darkness and subjects them to the tension of having to satisfy the truth. What is known with certainty demands to be kept valid, while the uncertain, unexposed and possibly imminent casts a twilight ahead and forces caution.

One of the most widely shared characteristics of the human islands is that their inhabitants soon split up into those who are strongly affected by truth tensions and those who prefer to avoid situations of cognitive stress. This leads to the almost universal differentiation of the groups into experts who develop personal connections to less accessible truths by accumulating—sometimes at their own risk, sometimes shielded by the figure of the magician or scholar—knowledge of what is concealed, past and coming, and laypersons who succeed in contenting themselves with first-order evidence, the collectively stored experiences and opinions, that is to say the idols of the tribe. In the former position we find the figures of the shaman, the priest, the prophet, the seer, the scribe, the philosopher and the scientist; in the latter, those of the simple tribe member, the illiterate, the patient, the believer, the empiricist, the layperson, the newspaper reader and the viewer of television duels. It is unlikely that there was ever a "society," a "people" or a "culture" that did not to some degree develop a two-chamber system for access to truth. Its first element is a House of Common Knowledge, with the ordinary knowing as members, and a House of Cognitive Lords, where those who know more, the magicians, the experts and professors assemble. Since the inception of so-called advanced civilizations, this order has manifested itself in institutions that distinguish between knowing and profane groups like two peoples within the same population. This is explained by, among other things, the fact that advanced civilization and writing culture are largely synonymous; in the first three millennia of penmanship, the writing monopoly of the few and the illiteracy of most were accepted like eternal constants. Even after the establishment of widespread literacy, both the cultures and the arts split once again into "high" and "low." As late as the beginning of the Modern Age in Europe, when Francis Bacon formulated the program for a researching and advancing "society," a monument was erected to the bisection of the alethotope: even in the model state of New Atlantis, there is an upper house of knowledge, an elite university devoted to pure progress, known as Salomon's House, whose members, like an order of cognitive knights, are sworn to complete secrecy concerning certain unpublicizable information.

Under these conditions, access to withdrawn truths becomes a matter for experts—more still, the experts aggressively set themselves apart from the commune of the ordinary knowing and establish themselves as an autonomous nobility. The arrogance of the writers is one of the most powerful facts in civilization history; it went so far that some of these intellectually wealthy persons asserted an anthropological difference that set the knowing almost as far apart from ordinary mortals as the species difference separates humans from higher animals. One need only examine certain myths about the birth of wisdom heroes—Gautama Buddha, Lao Tse or Jesus—and the historical accounts describing the cults of the great minds—Pythagoras, Plato, Confucius, Newton or Goethe—to observe this rift and its radical effect inside the collective space of truth. In all older ethno-epistemic systems, the difference between the wise man and the insipient masses is set in the same stone as the difference between the god-king and the subject in theocracies, or in religious cultures the distinction between the purified saint and the people, soiled to the point of untouchability. The fragments of Heraclitus exude a harsher contempt of the knowing for the unknowing than any line written by Hegel or Nietzsche. The role models of the Ephesian priest of Apollo probably included the priest-astronomers of Babylon, who spent their nights on towers observing the stars; it is not out of the question that the proud resentment of the waking towards the sleeping masses began here, an affect whose traces extend back to the New Testament and Christian monastic cultures—and up to Stalin's time (when the Muscovites kept their spirits up during the Second World War by imagining that a light was still burning in Stalin's room long after midnight). The Platonic softening of the presumption of wisdom into striving, and the Stoic orientation towards an ideal that can only be approached through constant practice, were able to prevent the complete schism of the alethotope, but did nothing to lessen the radicality of the opposition between the experts in high logical-cosmological and technical matters on the one hand, and the ordinary subscribers to probabilities for everyday business on the other.

Those living on the anthropogenic island are inevitably drawn by their fortuitous or chosen situation in the alethotope into a logomachy: a constant battle for truth and its valid forms of utterance, a perpetual separation between seeming and real events, true and false prophets. Nietzsche's remark about the great transitions in the history of ideas also applies to these truth battles: "The magic of these struggles is such, that he who sees them must also participate in them!"[85] Naturally these are cognitive class struggles from above—wars of contempt waged by a logical clergy and a distinction-conscious intellectual nobility against popular opinion, but they are also factional struggles within the camp of the knowing over the legitimacy and potential for success of their concepts and procedures. The latter brings to mind such phenomena as the Parmenideans' break with the movement's illusion, which they had supposedly seen through; Plato's method-political attack on the Athenian Sophists with the aim of delegitimizing the forming of opinions on the basis of mere probability; Diocletian's religion-political offensive against the fortune-tellers, soothsayers and *mathematici* (the astrologers) within the Roman Empire's area of jurisdiction; the battles between modern creationist and evolutionists or the interpretation of the world's beginnings; Fichte's phenomenology of reified consciousness and its offshoots in the ideology critiques of the nineteenth century; the positivist reckoning with the "pseudo-problems" of philosophy and the descent of modern thought into the everyday; the neo-skeptic critique of the master thinkers and grand theorists of the twentieth century; or finally—to mention the satyr play after the tragedies—the denunciation campaigns of neopositivist mainstream scientists against the epistemological metaphors and conceptual experiments of the postmoderns, which are instructive precisely in their comedy as indications of the public's continued willingness to submit to bluff systems of the most varied kinds, whether the suggestions of some social scientists on one side or the claims of naïve natural scientists and the epistemologically correct to know better on the other side.

The historical schisms of the alethotope call attention to basic conditions of knowledge division in human populations. As long as knowledge in coherent groups appears in normal asymmetrical distributions and always a joint knowledge of what others know and do not know, the alethotopic field remains able to balance out its internal differences far enough to avoid splitting into exclusive cognitive parties. The polarizations of women's and men's knowledge, the differences between warrior and healer knowledge, or the levels of maturity separating knowledge of the world among seven-year-olds from the stock-staking gaze of seventy-year-olds are not in themselves reasons for knowledge class struggles or deeper estrangements between knowledge groups. Only in polymythical and polymathic situations, particularly after the formation of peoples from heterogeneous tribes and following the minglings of trade cities, does—corresponding to the multicultural and multicognitive facts—an intense mental stress appear which breaks up the alethotope to such a degree that the once diffusely inclusive, universal joint knowledge disappears and groups are set apart from one another that are increasingly opaque and incomprehensible to one another, at times even contemptuous and threatening.

In ancient Greece, the resolution of the polymythical crisis led to an event of culturally defining importance: the secession of philosophers and scientists from their communities. These knowing of a new type set themselves apart from the collective field of knowledge by ceasing to be incarnations of popular knowledge, as their predecessors—the older rhapsodists and iatromants, the world picture singers and seer-doctors of the pre-scriptural wisdom cultures—had been. They organized themselves into a group of separate—in every sense of the word—intelligences, a caste of logical and moral experts who had far closer relationships with foreigners sharing the same interests, the same isolation and the same abstractness than with their national comrades. As early as European and Asian antiquity, this yielded the international of bearers of higher knowledge; it formed a first ecumenical movement composed of deterritorialized logicians, ethics teachers with patriotism for humanity, or hermitic ascetics. The phenomenon of meditative or academic pacifism articulated itself among them—that indispensable fiction of a disinterested life devoted to "pure truth" that, as if tempered by social death, pushes away from the fabrications of biased knowledge. The pacifist axiom of the *academia* leads to "freedom within science, the free play of arguments and counter-arguments." Thus it can rightly be said that "the soul of science is tolerance."[86]

The sophistic effect only makes sense as a contrast to the quest for pure or absolute knowledge. It openly places knowledge in the service of one-sided interests, whether as advocacy in court or consultancy for warlords. The members of the people's parliament refer to the objective upper house not infrequently with a religiously tinted horror that is coded as admiration—one thus pays tribute to the feeling that the knowing are a form of living dead who are closer to the numbers and stars than their fellow citizens. Amongst themselves, the top members of the alphabetized ecumene have always been bitterly disunited, condemned to battles over feelings of superiority, influence and allegiance. The notion that the great minds agree with one another has never been more than a fairy tale used by the wise to string along their clienteles.

The precondition for science is its asociality; its self-confidence flows from the break with the idols of the tribe, the cave and the market. It can only develop by converting the scientist from a fellow citizen to the stranger who speaks to the laypeople in the name of an external truth. The condition for its institutionalization is the subordination of the profane majority to the dogma which demands believing that the one with scientific knowledge must be accepted in the society of those with ordinary knowledge as the deputy of an extra-social area of being—let us say, as an elected representative of numbers, triangles, planets, marine animals, microbes, tumors and the entire remaining universe of absolute facts. In their role as a delegate of external truths and transcendental ideas, the accredited scientist attains authority in the collective, at times even power, provided they succeed in getting the powerful on their side. Hence science can only ever break with the fourth type of idols, those of the theater, *pro forma*: in reality, it multiplies the number of theater idols and claims stages on which higher cothurns are worn than anywhere else. There is axiomatic evidence of the noble self-exclusion of the scientifically knowing for the public use of the truth during the entire era of advanced-civilized knowledge organization; the tragicomic aftermath of such convictions appears in the efforts of the German mandarins to embody an academic nobility of education at the threshold of the technological age—even when faced with their forcible coordination through Nazi university policy.[87] The alethotope of modern academic life may have branched out into hundreds of discursive spaces or autonomous disciplines, but whenever a given subject is discussed in the sense of an -ology, the sender of all senders still towers in the background: the extraterrestrial light-phallus as whose earthly representatives the men and women of the sciences, especially the mathematically and philosophically competent ones, live among us. *Phallus locutus, causa finita.*

How deeply this formation of the alethotope is imprinted on ancient European (and ancient Asian) knowledge conditions is demonsrtated by the fact that the constant cultural crisis of the twentieth century did not manage to dissolve the archetypal relationships between experts and laypeople entirely. Despite an increasing skepticism towards knowledge among the general public, little changed in terms of the division of the two chambers and their forms of interaction. Only a small number of people today can adequately comprehend the untenability of the traditional distinctions and their motives. That faith in science is nonetheless fading on a large scale can partly be attributed to the endogenous corruption among experts. The equally embarrassing and interminable battles among experts in the field of purportedly external truths give a wider public the feeling that even the truth is no longer what it used to be. The psychosocial utility value of the expert: the possibility of submitting to their pronouncement, and thus doing away with doubt, is undeniably in decline. The credibility of B. F. Skinner's succinct thesis, "The people are in no position to evaluate experts,"[88] has long equaled that of a Chinese fortune cookie. Even if the claim were true, this would not change the fact that we are damned to have our own opinions about experts. More than a few contemporaries have understood that with their choice of expert, they themselves choose the result of the expertise. Thus the immemorial illusion that the truly knowing are the delegates of external truths is pulverized in social conflicts of interest (to say nothing of the all-too-human ones). It is no coincidence that the public is becoming aware of scientific frauds with increasing frequency (according to pessimistic estimates, three quarters of all published research results are manipulated). What affects the status of science as an institution even more profoundly, however, is the dissolution of the Baconian scientific paradigm that was dominant between the seventeenth and twentieth centuries, and which had asserted the natural alliance of scientific and human progress with evangelical naïveté.[89] With the emergence of the scientific-military complex on both sides of the Atlantic during the First World War at the latest (and completely after the indelible stain on modern physics through the events of August 6 and 9, 1945 over Japan), the humanist cheerfulness of Baconian rationalism had to perish. Since then, modern civilizations have been searching for a new epistemic *contrat social* that would take into account the state of the sciences after the loss of their independence and innocence. Now this distrust has also reached the Great Campus.

Towards the end of the century that has just passed, a form of epistemological civil rights movement began to articulate

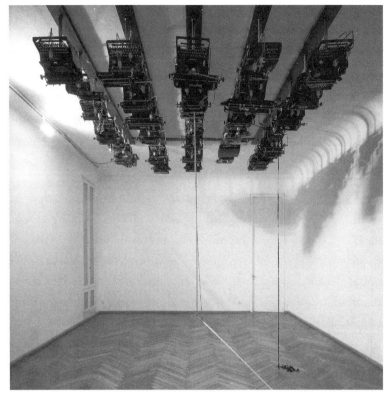

Rebecca Horn, *The Choir of Locusts I* (1991): 35 typewriters suspended from the ceiling type in independent rhythms while a blind person's cane conducts the choir.

itself; its goal is to bring back the experts from their long-denied golden exile among external truths into a democratic field of knowledge. Whether this can succeed amidst an increasing esotericism of research—and increasing privatization of the results—is an open question, and one that could be of fateful significance. In fact, the re-inclusion of experts would cause the profoundest change of alethotopic conditions since the rise of advanced civilizations. At the same time, this change, which would free both the truths and their bearers from their eccentricity in relation to their host societies, would—as Bruno Latour has shown in profound analyses[90]—be nothing other than the overdue implementation of the knowledge of the sciences about the true life of the sciences.

As far as the defense of contemplation against social interference is concerned, the reflective will have to assess whether they cannot do without invoking the authority of external and *a priori* truths. Here too, explication separates what implication had held together. The solitary contemplatives will probably lose less as a result of the forthcoming reform than it might seem at first glance. The moment may well have come in which the bliss of asociality no longer requires the pretext of truth.

8. The Thanatotope—The Province of the Divine

The human island is a place of visitation by deceased life. Where its inhabitants come together, signs of the absent make their presence felt insistently and subtly. If the mortals are affected by absent or transcendent things, there are two motives for this that, on closer inspection, can be traced to completely different origins. The first has been characterized above with reference to the appearance of new truths in the space of collective knowledge: from the concealed, which lies "behind" the lightened horizon, offspring occasionally comes in the form of new insights to us, who testify that life continues more or less endlessly outwards, upwards and downwards. Because "societies" are never safe from discoveries, inventions and ideas, humans can and must know that there are new truths which they encounter in the midst of life. Thus the first transcendence, the ontological or aletheio-logical form, is established. It is quite obvious that our previous and current thought and knowledge is an island in the sea of a greater thought and knowledge, and whoever takes that into account will understand that intelligence only exists at a gradient: its own "more" or "less" is its element. Intelligence manifests itself in the fact that it orients itself towards that which it sees outdoing it (in contrast to the structurally stupid position of the critical consciousness, which orients itself towards the inferior in order to be superior, and denigrates the superior to avoid having to compete with it).

The second origin of affectedness by things beyond and absent comes from the fact that humans, according to an ancient Greek language convention, are mortals—not only in the sense that death lies ahead of them, but more still that their dead lie behind them. The second transcendence rests on the fact that on the anthropogenic island, one has one's ancestors on one's back—or, to use a more uncomfortable image, breathing down one's neck. In all cultures, the living memorial images of the deceased are molded into inner and outer *imagines*[91] that regulate the interaction between the living and the dead. This pictorial world is expanded into a psychosocial institution whose task is to make the return of the disappeared an orderly affair. Where the dead are represented in an orderly fashion, one speaks of a cult; where their deregulated reappearance is observed, one speaks of haunting. What the cult and the haunting have in common is that they emphasize the place-specific nature of transcendence: just as one cannot practice the cult of the ancestors anywhere but in the vicinity of the places one shared with them,[92] so too the haunting cannot be entirely separated from the crime scenes and territories of the haunted. With the beginning of the era of empires and advanced civilizations, this would lead to the dead adapting their areas of operation to the new geopolitical conditions. The nineteenth century, accordingly, saw the appearance of tele-spiritisms, even the globalization of haunting—of which Maupassant's novella *The Horla* is a suggestive example. It demonstrates what happens when an evil spirit of Brazilian origin expands its haunting zone to include a house in Normandy—an early reference to the phenomenon of tele-infection. It is part of the image of modern cosmopolitanism that a few restless dead have learned to think globally and haunt locally.

Initially, the place-specific nature common to cult, haunting and commemoration cultures becomes most apparent in the small-scale dimensions of primitive, loosely territorialized collectives. Hence one initial factor in the climate of a human island is always that it is a zone of visitation —a thanatotope. A hundred eyes look up hungrily from the hills to the camp of the living, who gaze back restlessly, scanning the horizon with the vague feeling that someone is there whose goodwill they had best not rely on. But because the statement "God is dead" consistently applies in its original form "The dead person is God" in early cultures, this dimension of the coexistence of humans with their own kind and others can also be characterized as a theotope or territory of the gods.

The god of the early theotopes is still very much the ambivalent and difficult one characterized by the ambiguity of interaction with an unidentified representative of the other side. He turns to his own firstly as an ally, a blood relation and sworn helper of his clan, and secondly as the threatening, grudge-bearing, unpredictable and demanding figure. He is certainly the not-only-good one, perhaps even a vengeful destroyer. The contract between the deceased person and the living contains inescapably delicate points. To be sure, the ambivalent charge emitted by the ancestral spirits stems not only from unconscious guilt complexes among the living and corresponding expectations of revenge; the early gods are more than liberated souls enacting a private vendetta, instead forming amalgams of souls of the departed and anonymous forces that can then be invoked using cult names.[93] In dying, some human souls merge with these forces and are loaded with the power to threaten thanks to their *mana*. (For this reason, an anthropological deduction of the sublime would have to go back to these energies, which Kant summarizes as the dynamically sublime.) Yahweh, the ultra-transcendent god of the later monotheistic West, initially showed very clear traits distinguishing him as a maudlin, suspicious, irascible and decompensating patriarch.[94] This applies especially to those qualities which belong to the functionality of his bio-power—the biblical codeword is "bless" (*berek*), and those concerned were constantly aware of how easily this blessing could switch to cursing. The early Zeus likewise shows characteristics that are more in keeping with a paranoid potentate than the currently perfect god of the ontologists. Both of these are already unmistakable compounds of human soul and force of nature; in both cases, their mode of ruling includes a decent amount of interventionism.

An early god is therefore nothing one needs to believe in; he is a transcendental molester who sticks to the heels of his own. His joy at revelation constitutes *haressement* in a psychic register. The only way to keep him at a distance is to meet his demands punctually. One certainly cannot say that at that time, existence

Aztec sculpture representing death

meant being held out into nothingness; it sooner means being surrounded by a sticky, quasi-personal something that claims presentist effects from a position of absence. The "lifeworld" corresponds to a world of dead and ghosts that refers to it, impregnates it, penetrates it and keeps it under stress. In this regime the gods and ancestors are experienced as the non-distant, as invisible neighbors that come and go among us as if our camp were the natural goal of their outings and raids. Here one can speak of proximal transcendence: nearby and hard to hold on to, a ring of fear and indeterminacy that encompasses the islanders at close range.[95]

It is in the nature of things that graves form the providential portals for local traffic between this side and the other side.[96] With gods of this level, the only thing that can be relied on is their indiscretion; it is almost always advisable to expect a resentment towards living things from them—the grudges borne create a poisonous proximity beyond the boundaries separating death and life. And as long as humans are dealing with the close-range other side, they do not have any problem of accessibility or knowledge when it comes to gods and ghosts—as in the time when people began to struggle with the "silence of God"[97] and other symptoms of the lack of presence and evidence. On the contrary, their main worry is that the haunters from the realm of the invisible will constantly be around them in an indiscreet fashion. It is therefore clear why a god in full possession of haunting ability does not need to have his existence proved by logically trained staff.

The deduction of divine malice cannot content itself with pointing out the tendency of the offended ancestors to return. Something evil and terrible that comes from the outside is so

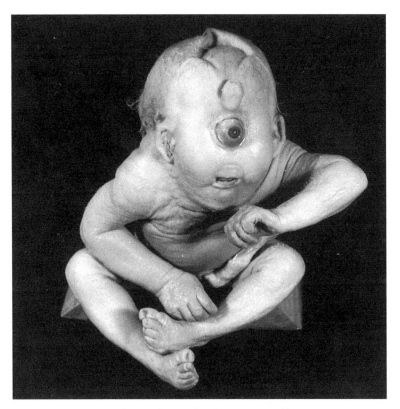

Anatomical specimen: the condition of cyclopia presumably gave rise to corresponding mythologies

important for the understanding of human spheres because it is incorporated into the constitution of cultural capsules in a twofold fashion: for one thing, humans were only able to become the ontological islanders that they are because they had managed, in the course of a long evolutionary drift, to break free from the harmful environment and withdraw to the anthropogenic island—the sonorous capsule of pampering. For another thing, this retreat never places the islanders entirely beyond reach;

cultural encapsulation never offers the sapients more than partial freedom from hardships and injuries. Being overwhelmed by the outside remains an ever-present possibility—all the more through the violence coming from within the group. This means that the principle of distance is undermined by the principle of invasion, and the wrestling between the two tendencies determines the history of organisms as well as cultures. One can show how the human space is molded by the effort of asserting the priority of distancing over invasion, or of reestablishing it after failures.

The typical invasion stress is embodied in three categories of infiltrators: firstly, in the ancestors and revenants whose penetration of the group psyche can be expected on a regular basis; secondly, in the natural aggressions and disasters that fall out of the environment and into the physique of the group; and finally in the neo-truths that emerge from the inventions and discoveries of the innovators.

Because the human space inevitably also remains a space of invasion, despite being rounded in itself, it assumes the characteristics of a cultural immune system. What we call immune systems are innate or institutionalized responses to injuries. They are based on the principle of prevention, which is assigned to the principle of invasion. Thus "having experience" initially means nothing other than the ability of an organism to foresee invasions and injuries. Where this foresight is translated into static defense measures, the result is a formal immune system, which means a defense mechanism that neutralizes typical and expectable injuries. Through immune systems, learning bodies incorporate their regularly recurring stressors into themselves.

This is precisely the function of the theotope (which emerges from the thanatotope): the primitive gods are the inwards-drawn

Egyptian antiques dealer with mummy

categories of invaders and injurers with which a given cultural group chronically reckons. Every early form of a god reveals something about a source of stress that creates difficulties for a culture. In his work on the "laws of imitation," Gabriel Tarde pointed out the possible connection between the universal spread of blood-thirsty gods and the universal spread of bloodthirsty animals to imply that wherever early humans fell victim to large predators, the conversion of those fascinating animals to culturally specific gods was a natural step.[98] This would have amounted to a symbolic taming of the wild beasts by their own potential prey. At the same time, the xenopathic need of the early psyche, the wish to be fascinated by sufficiently outlandish gods, would be satisfied.[99] In analogous fashion, disaster theorists attributed the birth of the great sacrificial religions in the Near East to the panic hermeneutics of those cultures after cosmic events such as enormous meteorites falling to earth and corresponding celestial phenomena.[100] The astroterror of that time would have spawned formidable gods who made their disciples feel the abyss separating the human world from the beyond. It is in keeping with this that the Sumerian-Babylonian sign for "star" is simultaneously the ideogram for "god." Being as remote as a heavenly body and as terrible as a god: these would then be the conditions a holy object would have to fulfill in order to be successful in the affective register of religious masochism. From this extreme, the development of absolute objects would proceed towards less heteronomous divinities. Thus the drama of the civilization process would be prefigured in the transformation of evil gods of invasion and disaster into good gods of creation and preservation—a metamorphosis that would finally result in the collection of all positive partial gods in the monospheric constitution of the *unum verum bonum*. This establishment of the One constitutes the strongest proof of the immune system character of metaphysics: starting from fascinated xenolatry and the adoration of strange carnivores in local sacrificial cultrs, the hypnogenic outside is progressively absorbed by

Morton Schamberg, *God*, circa 1918

the inside, until no more than an overstretched element of their own remains—which, consistently enough, succumbs to entropy. An important intermediate step on the way to the imperial wisdom of advanced-civilized inclusivity was probably taken by the cult of pet animal gods, which, like the Egyptian Apis bull, already show traits of clemency and benevolence. The domestication of animals preceded the domestication of gods[101]—until it came to pass that an *agnus Dei* voluntarily let itself be slaughtered for the sake of the recalcitrant humans.

The trace of the cult of strangeness was preserved as long as the good god of the monotheists could be imagined as sufficiently terrifying; advertisements for the god of love could not simply undo the older *timor fecit deos*.[102] Only the god of the philosophers and Neoplatonic mystics finally dissolved his tremble-inducing fascination in pure, albeit dark familiarity. He changed into a form of sensible background radiation and paled to become the idle god, who proved the superfluous one. Only a formal residue of the xenotheistic mood of the ancients remained in the high culture of modernity, which no longer needed gods— xenophile chic and philosophical allolatry.[103] Among the younger theomachists after Nietzsche (whose Dionysus was still terrible enough), only Heidegger clung to a dark, xenolatric God, if only in the form of a residual God—death.[104]

To keep the archaic, fiercely territorial gods at arm's length in the early theotopes, the function of the priest developed: as the border policeman of the sphere of the living, he handles the task of limiting raids by the other side. The safest way to appease those from beyond who demanded their share seems to have been the sacrifice, which could be seen as expressing a basic principle of the early theotopians. They were all accustomed to believing that paying a tax on the dead and strangers was one of their innate duties—the first revenue offices were undoubtedly the Paleolithic altar stones on which apprehensive fear paid its dues. But where there is duty, election cannot be far off. Initially, and for a long time, the share for the dead was paid in food and fresh blood—as if it were evident that shades and gods hunger and thirst. Later on, the offerings could be made to an elevated hereafter in the form

Leo Regan, photograph of Brother Emmanuel Patrick blessing a new car in Lagos (1996)

of oaths and communions, and charitable currencies also came into use. Some gods and goddesses seemed more responsive to their worshippers' prayers in the dialect of self-mutilation—for example the Great Mother of the Indians, who calls for glorification through the sacrifice of her worshippers' testicles (there are supposedly still almost one hundred thousand members of the caste of sacred eunuchs, who live on the fringes of Indian "society" as prostitutes, fortune-tellers and dancers at weddings). Gods with a lordly attitude preferred to accept the conversion of the sacrifice into obedience. At times, the sublime ones seemed to find a hint of suicide assassindom not unwelcome among their own—a tendency that was taken up by radical sects and used as raw material for kamikaze asceticisms. With the temple economies, a first policy of redistribution was set in motion in the spirit of the sacrifice; the theotope already became a solidary fund and provided, as well as primitive relief for the poor, not least the material foundation of the priesthood. In view of these conditions, it is fair to say that culture is nothing other than the history of the internalization of sacrifices.[105]

The constant relation of the "lifeworld" to the neighboring field of the dead and gods calls up talents that devote themselves to the border traffic. In modern diction one calls these media predispositions or, more anachronistically, aptitude for therapeutic professions. This refers to the ability to be receptive to messages from the indirectly given. So many indirectnesses, so many talents. When the twilight of the older mediumism fell among the Greeks, Plato—in the same way that someone who is already walking gains an overview—offered a synopsis of the special theotopic talents, suggesting a distinction between four ways of being affected by missives from beyond. In the dialogue *Phaedrus*, Socrates brings up the blessings of enthusiasm, which allows chosen individuals to offer themselves as mouthpieces of the gods—gods who no longer represent mere factional or tribal gods, of course, but are expanded to become authentic people's gods and are raised to a beyond of medium other-worldliness, let us say an Olympian semi-transcendence. It is initially a matter of the three basic mantic functions which, in earlier times, seemed dependent on informative obsessions: first of all the ability to see into the future and predict coming things; then the capacity to find ways and means of healing in case of illness; and finally poetic inspiration, of which it was clear to the ancients that it could only come about through the suggestions of the muses or Apollo himself. (This enables us to understand why poetry and music initially came into existence as theotopic institutions—and only became self-willed practices after the emancipation of the artistic spheres from religious cult, without a direct connection to an inspiring or commanding beyond.) Beyond the disciplines of older mediumism, Plato introduces a fourth enthusiasm that he interprets as being stricken by a love of beautiful ideas viewed prenatally and remembered in the middle of life. Since then, the fire of philosophical mania has had to be protected at a special altar—at the academic lectern before which the logophilic community gathers.

There is no doubt that philosophy as Plato conceived it constituted a decisive modification of human behavior in the theotope: it launched a new, but rather minoritarian way of dealing with the adjacency of the "lifeworld" with the spirit world, which had now been transformed into the heaven of forms. Thus one must ascribe theotopic qualities to the academies, as later to the churches, in their original mode of being. The forms of reflection cultivated within them served the aim of diluting obsessions into convictions. It was only with modernity that the academies were disenchanted, if not the world.

In the Christian church, the large-scale theotope of the occident, the idea long remained alive that humans, as media of a not-too-distant other side, occasionally have special talents such as clairvoyance, healing power or speaking in tongues; what Saint Paul had to say about these "spiritual gifts" was restricted to the demand for their sensible subordination to the cult of the

Lord.[106] That charismas can easily change back into malign obsessions, however, even in a Christian context, is demonstrated not only be the countless evangelical sects for which the USA, which has always been a paradise for manic communities, are known or notorious. In these, Christ is transformed into a demon of success with strong monetary skills, assuming he does not directly intervene in life, on camera, as a miraculous healer. And this relapse is observed year after year among Christian pilgrims visiting Jerusalem from all over the world, who are occasionally cast into confused states by the sites of the passion and require the empathy of Jewish psychiatrists.

In numerous cultures, especially those that did not experience a paradigm shift in favor of monotheism, the notion of media exchanges of chosen and marked individuals with the other side never lost its validity. In some African "societies" it is believed to this day that children who either do not learn to speak or stop speaking at a certain point prefer to stay together with the ancestors—which is why they can only be persuaded to coexist with the living if one attempts to convince them of the advantage of being born.[107] In the eyes of their parents and healers, such "children of the dead" are not "autistic"; they live more closely integrated in the elsewhere than among humans, so settling them here requires loosening the bond that ties them to the other side.

The notion that evil spirits are capable of entering the bodies of strangers is found in so many cultures that it is justified to see it as an elemental idea. In the view of the believers, such an invasion serves the purpose of transforming people into automatons of the demons. As these infiltrators do not stop at entering the dead, the ancient Chinese sometimes sealed the mouth and anus of deceased persons with plugs made of wax or jade. In some early Germanic tribes, the legs of the dead were bound to the back and they were buried face down in order to make a return more difficult.

The interest of the living in the world of the dead is, as already noted, due largely to the confusing of the two transcendences which the human world borders: because humans are not only the neighbors of death but also of the horizon, behind which, according to the most common view, the unconcealed truths or transcendent forms reside, they may find it a plausible notion that there is a seamless transition between the two neighborhoods, and even that they constitute a single shared space. For them, it follows from this that the dead have access to the unconcealed—and with them, as we learn in the Platonic myth of the soul, the unborn. The idea that everything will transpire *post mortem* at the latest rests on the association between being dead and the acquisition of final knowledge.

Once the fusion of the transcendence of the unknown and that of the dead is complete, the motif of invoking the dead for purposes of acquiring information from the otherworldly and final side becomes irresistible. According to this schema the dead, because they have put everything behind them, in fact have a larger share in the truths that stand in the perfect tense: those who subjectively have been are also at home in what objectively has been—in the essential as understood by metaphysics. This highly desired confusion is the source of countless necromantic practices, from simple oracles of the dead to invocations of deceased persons from the other world. The most powerful example of the latter can be found in the appearance of the dead Darius in Aeschylus' tragedy *The Persians*: risen from the netherworld, the Great King divulges his theological interpretation of the Persian defeat—untroubled by the fact that this makes him a chief witness for the Greek belief in the unity of the truthful world beyond and the realm of the dead. By contrast, the greatest of heroes often have to descend to the underworld themselves in order to receive advice about their future fate. Let us not forget that the central utterance of occidentalism, namely the prediction of Roman world domination, is made to Aeneas by the dead Anchises on the former's journey to the underworld: it will one day be the business of Rome to rule the peoples of the world, show consideration for the feelings of their allies (*parcere subiectis*) and eradicate (*debellare*) the rogue states (*superbos*).[108]

From all this we can conclude that the outlines of the theotope are set in motion when the forms of interaction with the dead of the methods of acquiring knowledge in a "society" change. Both are the case in contemporary civilization, which buries its dead differently and obtains its truths differently. Interest in otherworldly things wanes in modernity primarily because one can hardly fall back on the deceased to gain information about coming things anymore; their opinions would offer little help when it came to establishing technical rules for the world management of the future. The world of the living and the world of the dead have become so dissimilar that the deceased would no longer have any advice for the living, even if they wanted to provide it. Conversely, the ability to pose useful questions to the dead has virtually disappeared among the moderns. The detour via transcendence has become unnecessary for the acquisition of knowledge. In the course of the last century, the immemorial mixture of the hereafter of the dead and the supra-empirical "reservoir" of unconcealed truths and ideas dissolved of its own accord, without the inhabitants of the human space especially noticing this.

Thus the twilight of the gods entails a twilight of the dead; becoming unimportant is the shared fate of the invisible. One looks back on them like dead with no last will, ancestors from whom there is little to inherit for better or worse—uncharged batteries that no longer fascinate us enough to make us shine from their location in the beyond. The last undead, who haunt their neurotic descendants, are cared for by a psychoanalysis which has understood that it is more an inner funeral parlor for parents and grandparents than a form of healing. The practical value of the great dead whom one carries about in the collective memory as classics is restricted to the role of securing a shared past for a civilized group. The past now serves as a base camp from which a futurized civilization embarks on its projects.[109]

Anyone looking for keywords to describe the present intellectual situation must pay attention to the current state of the theotope, which was molded by monotheistic ideas in the Western world up to the threshold of the previous century, and has been defined by their decline since then. This applies especially to the two musealized religions of Judaism and Christianity, which have long been condemned to act as their own testamentary executors. In both of them, we can observe how a well institutionalized religious tradition can successfully turn into a substitute religion for itself (under the plausible pretext that the immanently replaced original is certainly better than any secular substitute religion). Such administration need not be sterile; this is shown by the fact that in the course of the twentieth century, while inspecting their legacies, Jewish and Christian theologians made a discovery that could without exaggeration be considered one of the most potent spiritual facts of the coming epoch.

Studying the Talmud while cutting diamonds

The matter in question is the uncovering of a third transcendence that would be neither that of the dead nor that of concealed truths: the transcendence of the human other. This is not directly affected by the inversion of the statement "The dead person is God" into the more contemporary "God is dead," because the otherness of the other is attributed neither to theological nor to thanatological sources—even if renewed connections would be subsequently made to the classical transcendences (especially by Lévinas and his school). At first, it is justified solely out of the self-will, priority and unassimilability of existence as being-with. Even if God is dead, this will not deprive the other of its secret, its inaccessibility or moral claims. It seems it seems as if, behind the fading outlines of the historical thanatotheotope, whether constituted as churches, kingdoms of God or chosen nations,[110] a successor space is taking shape that carries on the metaphysical tensions of the previous zone of the dead and truths from a non-metaphysical angle—a space that would, if one were being consistent, have to be called the xenotope. Its main characteristic is that humans are now defined as those challenged by the stranger, the guest, the parasite.[111] Whether this is enough to secure a minimum of spiritual disclosedness in immanence will, for the time being, remain uncertain. Being-with with others, at any rate, is one of the trivial dowries of existence and has not yet given rise to any excessive elevations—aside from the mystical escalations of courtly love and hints at a cult of the strange in xenolatric religions. Can the everyday thou-consciousness become the cornerstone of a modified experience of transcendence?

Some Jewish exponents of the turn towards xenotopic thought make no secret of their skepticism about a merely formal piety towards the other; they give little credence to the idyll of dialogic togetherness. From the outset, they portray the other who matters as the murdered one who seeks me out, asking why I had better things to do than help them when the crime was committed. Here xenology, which takes over the legacy of theology, replaces the ancestor with the murdered fellow human being. Visitation assumes a new form by putting a final question in each victim's mouth to their non-helpers: an inquiry as to the reason for the failure to help, the darkened feeling of coexistence, the willful blindness, the resigned non-intervention. The ghostly haunting is translated into an examination of conscience—not from within, as when preparing for confession, but from without, as in court. Xenological questioning insists that we penetrate to the heart of indifference and its motives: being unwilling to help, being unable to help, being tied up elsewhere—and perhaps a more or less tacit agreement with the perpetrators of violence.

To gain an idea of the potentials of xenotopic thought, one must understand that it offers a promising redescription of the theotope, and *eo ipso* the field of the dead. This redescription allows a moral explication of the zone of encounter with the other as a modification of the coexistence of humans with their own kind and others: the other is the one whom one always owes something. This turn permits a look back at the birth of the historical religions from the guilty conscience—a diagnosis that can also be derived from the analyses of René Girard, though these seek to locate the cause of awkwardness before the other in the memory of actual crimes against them (which leads to a superficial derivation of fascinogenic ambivalence.) At the same time, coexistence with the social environment is explicit as a partly reciprocal, partly asymmetrical relationship of mutual responsibility and mutual liability in a de-restricted anthroposphere.

After Hegel, whose insights into the structure of the struggle for recognition were further developed in the social philosophy of the twentieth century, a lesser-known Nietzsche supplied the central maxim of moral philosophy from the beginning from the twentieth century on with his statement: "The Thou is older than the I."[112] While Martin Buber wanted to place the I-Thou relationship alongside the ego-id relationship as an equally valid basic form, Max Scheler—following Nietzsche—taught the precedence of human orientation towards the "sphere of the other": "Thou-ness is the most fundamental existential category of human thought."[113] Another novelty is that more explicitly than ever before, it is being written down to what extent coexistence implies not only the cooperation of the able, but also the co-suffering of the no-longer-able. "Our society is also an association in our mortality."[114] "The suffering of the other is the origin of my own reason."[115] The burden character of the coexistence of humans with humans is emphasized—with the side effect that the overtaxing of individuals through the imposition of responsibility for the needs and dangers of the abstract and the concrete other likewise gains a positive image. In this situation, the New Testament question "Who is my neighbor?" must be updated on a global level—this time in the sense of "Who can be helped?" or "Who should be at the top of the waiting list of misery?"

As a result of the progressive explication of coexistential facts, it is inevitable that the flipside of universalized moral liability will come to light: xenophilic and Samaritan thought allies itself with a jaded media pragmatism willing to take any steps to give the best-organized lobby of virtual and actual victims a place in the subsidized sun. In the short term, the humanitarian strategy leads to success if powerful images mobilize the feelings of the helpful, or if the addressee is chronically available owing to historical guilt—as expressed in the formula "white guilt, black power." If the victimological means of pressure are employed too extensively, however, one can predict a desensitization to the constant pleas of the other's advocates. Hypermorality plays into the hands of defiance and moral entropy.

However the tensions between the spokespersons for the dead and the living or surviving might be enacted, it cannot be prevented that even xenology, the last contingent of anti-naturalism, will come up against the wall of biospheric facts sooner or later. In truth, what has been termed the "lifeworld" since Husserl always encompasses a world of life and one of the dead at the same time: all attempts by cultures to discriminate against the death side only ever increase the tension of absurdity under which civilizations exist. The more aggressively biopositivism draws attention to itself, the more paradoxical it becomes that death still gets everyone in the end. The booming life sciences constitute the latest version of this absurdity management. By wanting to know everything about life in order to espouse life—or what they call life—even more energetically, they darken the fact that biology, in keeping with the nature of its object, is only possible as bio-thanatology, and life sciences only possible as life and death sciences. Whoever speaks of biotopes without considering the thanatotopes has devoted themselves to disinformation.

It is uncertain whether humans in secular cultures can stand up to such examination. It is one thing to develop an *ars moriendi* for oneself and an art of farewell for the others, but quite another to acknowledge death's share in life processes from a theoretical perspective. Whoever imagines the integral bio-thanatotope of humanity will, at any rate, gain views of a totality that seems more monstrous than sublime. The organon of the monstrous developed in the course of the twentieth century in the form of ecology—the only true innovation in the cognitive landscape of our time alongside cybernetics and polyvalent logic. It is the reenactment of the monstrous as a science of balances and imbalances in life processes beyond human perspectives.

When ecology and cultural theory meet, strange statements become possible: now it can be uttered that the main function of all communication between humans is "to deny futility and death intersubjectively."[116] Depth comes at a price. Since such things began to be written, the human alliance against the outside has been infected with ecological knowledge, and the business of denial stands on a weakened foundation. Because of the propagation of ecology as the dominant thought form, many realize sooner or later that the final chapter of intellectual history is devoted to the friction between the absolutism of the human and the indifference of biospheric processes to human interests. Nietzsche's postulation that a higher culture would have to give humans a double brain or two brain chambers—one for science and one for non-science—is proving true in unpredictable ways. In fact, the humans of the future must reconcile their own vital élan with the systemic view of the biosphere, for which life and death are merely two aspects of the same events. In this transhuman dual knowledge we see the form of wisdom that is binding for humans in biologically enlightened civilizations. Wisdom refers to the *modus vivendi* that enables the living of a knowledge which, for the sake of life, one should not know about.

If one assumed that the population of *homo sapiens* on earth were to reach a stable limit of 10 billion individuals by the end of the twenty-first century, this would constitute a bio-thanatotope that, with a very civilized global mortality rate of 1.5% (meaning a universal life expectancy of seventy-five years), would see no fewer than 150 million "natural" deaths per annum; this would correspond to more than seven eras of Nazi terror, twenty-five of Hitler's Holocausts, four reigns of Stalin or three of Mao's disastrous reforms.[117] What is monstrous about those numbers is that they will be among the statistics of a pacified humanity. Neutral results demand that one come to terms with them in sensible passivity, if only in the attitude of the *homme révolté*, who does not even forgive nature as it takes its course. In the light of such conditions, it would clearly be absurd to desire bearing responsibility for them. If one were to re-sharpen the worn-out concept of human dignity, its definition would be this: acknowledging these disproportions and acting as if every additional day in the life of every human being counted.

9. Nomotope—First Constitutional Doctrine

Just as every group involuntarily brings about its self-isolation within its own sound world, as if concealed behind a fence of incomprehensibility, every cultural unit spontaneously insulates itself through its *modus vivendi* or its normative constitution. This is a phenomenon for which there is no simple of convincing term, but such words as "customs," "culture," "law and order," "rules," "conditions of production," "language games," "life forms," "institutions" or "habitus" can offer differently colored views of it. All human insulation groups that prove themselves in generation process and thus exist in their own specific time share in a little-examined stability secret, one without which their survival can scarcely be explained: they produce within themselves an architecture of norms that is sufficiently supra-personal, imposing and possessed of torsional strength to be viewed by the users as a valid law, a binding charter and a mandatory reality of rules. This moral ether has, to use Hegel's terms, the properties of the objective spirit: it supersedes the individuals as something that faces their power of choice undaunted and is passed on through generations like the names of gods, myths and rituals in a stable form, or only imperceptibly modified. Mortals come and go, but forms and laws remain. At first, it is above all the objectivity of the ritual which is felt so strongly that one could think peoples were merely empirical ensembles put together purely for the purpose of preserving forms. Pavel Florensky, a Russian priest executed under Stalin, upheld the dogma that the order of the Orthodox service was older than the world.

For this way of feeling, customs or institutions are one dimension more real, more objective and more necessary than the people who are meant to live by them. Plato's archetypes appear like institutions transferred to the sky, more luminous and real than every individual life that takes place below them. A hint of this objectivism even continues to the timetables of the German railway, which, untouched by empirical delays, are hung up at stations in evangelical yellow for departures and white for arrivals, protected by glass cases and illuminated at night, as if to show that the world's continued existence depends on the employees' reverence for each single minute. This devotion to punctuality has nothing to do with secondary virtues; it is a cooled-off reflex reaction to the metaphysical conviction that behind every fact lies a directive, and under every directive the stamp of a higher wisdom. So that is why *omne ens es bonum*. How could anything at all be if it had not been instructed to be as it is? The officer gives the lady his right arm because that is simply how it is done—not merely because he wears his saber on the left, as the functional explanation suggests. We write from left to write because, according to the Greek sacrificial priests, the good omens appear on the right. The cocks crow at dawn because their day is synchronized with the rhythm of decent people—who, like their creator, love the work of the early hours. The Stoics summarized their faith in the power of rules in the theorem that being and being-in-order mean the same thing. In 1949, Wittgenstein noted: "Culture is a monastic rule. Or it at least presupposes a monastic rule."[118] I call the zone in which such rules apply the nomotope.

Anyone who resides on the human island will observe that the group inhabiting it is subject to local pressure caused by rules—a pressure that is fundamental to the stability of the social structure. That the normative climate of a group correlates to its stability, meaning its ability to survive, is an early intuition of the wise and the elders of all peoples—none of the early survival communities could ever afford to take their customs, forms and dogmas lightly. Only contemporary, systemic and deconstructivistically inspired social theory learned to admit that every set of rules simultaneously has a safety net of tolerable exceptions.[119] In his morality-critical investigations, Nietzsche derived the "morality of custom" from the latter's ability to command absolutely and without toleration of any objections: the purpose of all traditional demands to overcome the self simply is simply to make custom and convention seem unconditionally dominant.[120] Analogously, Gabriel Tarde notes: "Usage is the most despotic and most circumstantial of governments."[121] Whatever rules unconditionally is viewed as an end in itself, or as the good, just and honorable, beyond the advocacy of individual commentators. Cicero spoke implicitly of the superiority of these laws when he stated that we are born for justice: *nos ad iustitiam esse natos.*[122] Certainly *iustitiae* here refers not only to the goddess of equidistance who wears a blindfold and holds the scales in her hand. In her name, the archaic prejudice in favor of the existentially suitable power of forms, procedures and customs as such shines forth. Viewed in this light, the formalisms that structure the Roman court trial are surrounded by a similar aura of meaningful well-formedness as the habits that determine how the truffle market of Carpentras[123]

Ordination of priests in Rome

or the opening ceremony of the great Sumo tournament in Nagoya take place. In both cases, and all related ones, it is a matter of the authority of social syntax that provides the background. Through the relative calm of the background, the active and colorful nature of the figures is released for our perception. Only recent sociology has been able to articulate the fact that such reflections entail questions of systemic stability. Talcott Parsons considered the ability of "pattern maintenance" one of the primary tasks of every unified social structure. In the present context, one could speak of moral structural engineering, for an adequately complete theory of human islands must have the capacity to describe their hardening through normative internal tensions.

It should be made clear from the outset that such deliberations are strictly dated points of view—probably not possible until the middle of the twentieth century, once the repertoire of

Theo Botschuijver/Jeffrey Shaw/Sean Wellesley-Miller, *Airground* (1968)

classical architecture and logics of constructs had been augmented by revolutionarily new engineering principles, and even
alternatives to thinking in such concepts in the first place. Here
we are seeing firstly the invention of the early "air structures" and
pneumatic domes by Walter W. Bird, Victor Lundy, Frei Otto
and other avant-garde architects in the USA and Europe—a construction form that, through a slight excess of air pressure inside
the hall, arrived at the principle of the self-supporting wall-less
construct; and secondly, the "tension integrity structures,"
expressed succinctly as tensegrities, developed by Buckminster
Fuller—floating spatial inventions, integrated through tensions
in the internal framework, that annul the principle of the bearing wall and replace it with the firmness of tensile strains between
rods that are connected by ropes.

For a sociological theory that does not use the term "system" in a contemplative sense, but is interested in its operative elaboration in the construction of machines, houses and institutions, these innovations are significant because they make the purpose of systemic structures, the securing of stability measures in combination with adaptation to activity, explicit in an idea-historically and technology-historically unprecedented fashion. The explication of the building and the canopied location through structural calculations leads, both directly and circuitously, to the explication of the estatist and the standing as such, and from there to the explication of the institutional, the state-owned and the systemic on its architectural or construct-logical side. Structural engineering became First Science, and enframing theory primary ethics. It is a modern theorie *par excellence*, provided it deals with constructs that can resist earthquakes and exceptions. It is not without reason that one of the most significant legal philosophers of our time, Pierre Legendre, speaks of the law and the state as factors that can only be held by moral scaffolding or norm-supporting construction (*échafaudage*, *montage*).[124] If the words for state and structural engineering come from the same source,[125] this may remind us of the inner bond between the two building arts—the construction of norms and that of houses. But how should one envisage the *status* in either case, now that the construct-logic of modern architecture has arrived at concepts of stability that lie beyond anything classical structural engineering was able to imagine?

To answer this question, one must first take a detour. It is worth remembering that the Latin term *ordo* in its medieval usage was suitable both for referring to the capacity for orderly arrangement in general and to the monastic order, as the

Axel Thallemer for Festo Corporate Design, *Airtecture Hall* (1996): air-filled roof beams and Y-shaped side supports made of a Vitroflex shell

individual, well-ordered structure of clerical life. Augustine, Benedict, Bernard, Dominic, Ignatius: these and other names demonstrate how monastic rules can be identified as works of individual authors—which is why these *regulae* turn out as arbitrary as all syntax laid down by humans. Nonetheless, they are meant to—and strive to—be as effective as a norm that is surrounded by the nimbus of the necessary and followed zealously as can be. Hence the *ordo* is simultaneously the life form and the system of rules on which it is based (systemicists can go even further and claim that even "violations of the rules *in the service of the cause*" are a constitutive part of *ordo* life).[126] This shows by analogy that Plato's Academy was an order, whereas his *Republic* and his *Laws* remained programmatic writings unsuitable as foundations for a real body politic. Wittgenstein's flashing remark takes into account the dual character of the concept of the order by emphasizing the single, concretely order-like and arranged element as well as highlighting the actual rule which this arrangement follows. One could reproduce this twofold meaning in these two statements: "Culture is a text" and "Culture is syntax." Applied to the architecture of the body politic, this would lead to the theses that "Culture is a building" and "Culture follows a rule of spatial production." Wherever the human island takes shape, a regulative tension comes about which demonstrates that house rules are in force—more imperceptibly for family members (aside from exceptional situations), conspicuous or confusing for strangers, and for philosophers, a motive to reflect on the spirit of institutions and the institutionality of spirit.

In the light of the aforementioned architectural innovations, the earliest human collectives can already be compared to excess pressure domes or tensegrities. In these, the principle of stabilization through mutual loads or atmospheric tension comes into effect. The integration of a group, the stability of its patterns and its symbolic reproductivity depend on the ability to force a culture-enabling compulsive repetition on its members. The production of group-specific excess pressure, or of the pull of tension that binds the group members to one another and to categorized tasks, occurs primarily through pre-formulated expectations of everyone by everyone, and of individuals by individuals. Their verbal form are the injunction and, in cases of conflict and disappointment, its escalation into threats. It is impossible, therefore, to describe collectives adequately without showing the channels through which the streams of commands flow inside them. Their moral structure includes an agreement as to who commands whom, and who is authorized to threaten which

Axel Thallemer for Festo Corporate Design, *Airquarium* (2000). Diameter 99 feet, height 26 feet. It is stabilized by a surrounding ballast tank.

addressees when; the sovereign party is the one with the pre-rogative to threaten. In strategic science, a threat is defined as "armed suasion";[127] in sociological terms, it would be described as a recommendation supported by sanctions.

From the perspective of Buckminster Fuller's new construct-logic—or rather, from the perspective that can be gained through its moral analogies—"societies," be they primitive or developed, are tensegrities of expectation, that is to say multiplicities of rule-based actions and living situations hardened through injunctions and threats. In this context, one notes that the common phrase "weight of expectation" is based on an obsolete structural design, for normalized group expectations do not display any character of weight or pressure, rather taking effect through pull—to the extent that one can consider appeals to ambition and self-esteem and mimetic seduction to belong to this mode of power trans-mission. Only through manifest threatening do analogies of pressure come into play; they are therefore reserved for excep-tional situations. Culture initially and mostly means not letting go of the tensile strains whereby the members of a collective are bound to group-specific regularities. The validity of law and customs within the group subjects its members to a constant self-stressing attraction, setting the collective in a state of symbolic vibration that can best be compared to the endogenously stabilized body temperature of a warm-blooded creature. What warm-bloodedness provides in organisms is achieved in social units through stress-creating topics. As groups always have plans, whether works or celebrations, wars or elections, and are always upset about something, whether natural disasters, enemy acts, crimes or scandals, they incessantly circulate the thematic material which they use to communicate about their situation—or rather, their immune situation or stress status. With the help of their current topics, the group takes its own temperature; and through its fever, it provides its own operative unity as an endogenously closed context of agitation.

Collectives vibrate in an internally produced state of constant agitation that converts normative stress into its normal state of toning. One aspect of the "enigma of health"[128] in groups is that it is usually unable to sense and barely able to thematize its basic nomotopic tension—only on its anarchist fringes do some occasionally speak, with precarious explicitness, about the rejection of obedience to norms and the will to achieve.[129] Even ancient China made no exception to this rule, despite the opinion of outside observers that it was buckling under the weight of an incomparable despotism of customs; part of the Chinese mode of being-in-the-world was training the belief that one's own disciplinary tension was the most normal thing in the world. Western visitors made comparable observations about the implacable formalism of Japanese customs

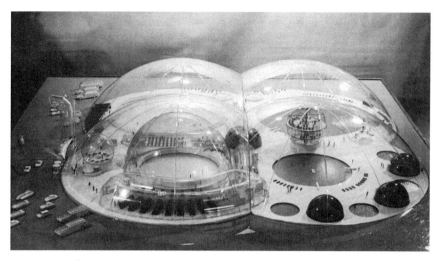

Yutaka Muraka, *Pneumatics in Pneumatics*, at the Expo 1970 world exhibition in Osaka

between the sixteenth and twentieth centuries. The removal of normative stressors to the subliminal level occurs when the group embeds its expectations of action in routines.

A routine is the form of expected effort that is established through repetition and thus made inconspicuous. In his basic anthropological doctrine, Arnold Gehlen highlighted the outstanding significance of normalized expectations of effort, encapsulating them in the concept of institutions—an institution being the successful long-term compromise between reliefs and burdens; it is the epitome of a "stabilized tension."[130] One can read this concept of institutions as an argument for keeping order at the unconscious level, bringing into play a concept of the unconscious that addresses what is latent, not repressed. (But just as the personal unconscious knows a return of the repressed, the latent knows a return of the paradoxical.) Though this view asserts that individuals must act in favor of the orders

R. Buckminster Fuller, *The Neckless Dome* (1950)

in which they live, supporting it with their entire existence, these orders also spare individuals the effort of specifically choosing them as they would a personal option. By burdening, they relieve. By relieving, they release energies for new bonds to shared tasks or *munera*. Here the concept of the rule once again comes to light in its fundamental significance, for it is the objectivity of rules that liberates both individuals and groups from the hardship of formlessness, and from the burdensome expectation of constant originality.

As much as Gehlen's theorem of institutions as ordering forces acting in the background corresponds to a widespread mood in the twentieth century that liked most of all to imagine systems of order as discreet infrastructures, and defenders of that order as civil servants who do their duty best by serving in silence, it only permits a one-eyed perception of basic nomotopic conditions. For usually, the nomotope also has a front side that opposes the tendency towards concealing power and violence in quiet routines. As a self-impressing, self-shocking entity, the norm-ventilated group lives off the performative power of rituals and their need to manifest themselves; there lies the source of the politically sublime. The legal system in particular has been developing a theatricality of its own kind since the days of the Romans. Just as power cannot dispense with its typical epiphanies, be they festivities, swearing-in ceremonies, parades, symbols of sovereignty or protocol to be followed in minute detail, so too the law cannot dispense with the punctual enactment of its formality—especially in the case of jurisdiction, whose processual rules of play constitute a compromise between investigation and theater. Both serve to render visible the ordering power, which has never been content to equip individuals behind their backs, as it were unconsciously, with motivational drive. Every culture has its Tarpeian Rock. At the time when the law-giving or law-staging power in Europe displayed its dogmatic potencies most openly, in the seventeenth century, it spoke unreservedly of the law as a "theater of truth and justice." From its dogmatism it derived a capacity for stringency that sought to appear before the eyes of all—and which, after the superego implosions in the second half of the twentieth century, can only be perceived as an incomprehensible annoyance or a presumptuous relic from the time of the personal regiment. None but a few incorrigibly Old European theologians have preserved a sense of "glory."[131] They should be the first to understand why the sublime state in its heydays displayed traits of both glory and terror.[132] Kings too are

R. Buckminster Fuller with tensegrity model at the University of Southern Illinois in 1958

worthy of admiration when they calmly disdain to destroy us. From Romanticism onwards, the decay products of majestic terror developed into the political aesthetics of mortal danger, which bourgeois philosophy after Burke and Kant mystified as the ability of the human spirit to pass judgment on sublime or distressing objects.

Nonetheless, the point about the habitualized, almost unconscious side of the sojourn in the realm of norms is well founded. The objective and background character of the rule keeps away the misunderstanding that "customs" or laws must serve the self-expression of individuals. What moderns term "expression" only became possible against the background of symbolic institutions and cultural automatisms that had come to be considered self-evident (and were thus incomprehensible)—whether it served the fulfillment of their assimilation (buy it to possess it) or advanced rebellious counter-differentiation. For the expressive world, the rule applies that individuals should deviate from the rule in original ways. When Mephistopheles declares that "All rights and laws are still transmitted, like an eternal sickness," he is already speaking as a bourgeois expressivist who thinks that form is something which grows outwards from the inside (and which disturbs us as a case of "alienation" as soon as it aspires to the validity of an independent fact). In the chronic conflict between obedience to rules and the expression of personal inclinations, he votes—in keeping with the new zeitgeist—for the latter option.

If one follows the words of Goethe's devil, he makes no secret of the fact that he considers himself fully part of modernity—a cultural enterprise that has embarked on the adventure of constantly changing the rules—and is unimpressed by Romantic or Catholic recourses to fixed arrangements. What is attempted is no less than outdoing the tradition of preservation through the tradition of learning. This implicitly involves the notion, monstrous for all conservatives up to Gehlen, that customs, institutions, laws, syntaxes and life forms are something that one is allowed to change as soon as one can improve it—assuming one still understands the changed rule as a rule that applies. It is precisely this pragmatic view of law that, until yesterday, the conservative fear of revolution sought to reject at all costs: for those with this mentality, any deliberate deviation from tradition, norms and fixed arrangements (Nietzsche speaks of "the age, the sanctity, the indiscussability of the custom")[133] already seemed a rejection of order as such, heralding the worst possible situation: an anarchic general strike against form, the rejection of the tact, the tonicity and the institutional foundation of the world. In those circles, no good is expected from an "open society of constitutional exegetes" (Peter Häberle). Accordingly, the true conservatives mourn for the strong state—or, in a more restrained form, the order of the Father, the Son and the signifier.

This suspicion, however, this homesickness for the sublime, leads to a misunderstanding of the nature of regulation in the modern nomotope: life according to the existing rules of a community simply seeks—if it is modern—to be something other than merely a "permanent residence in the domain of the law";[134] it no longer accepts being consumed by the prevailing conditions simply because they are conditions. Even if it does not pray to the god of the status quo and fall to its knees *a priori* before the static and the state-controlled, it is still subject neither to anarchy nor an idling management. Modern life wants the "monastic rule" it follows to be understood as an optimization process in which it participates—hence the general revisionist mood of recent times, and hence also the new interpretation of this rule in references to accumulated "social capital" and "radii of trust" that must be actively enlarged.[135] Despite all this, the citizens of the present remain as interested in livable formal securities as any epoch that believed in the *ordo*. On the contrary, they make questions of security explicit at all levels more than any earlier civilization, working out their immunities in the most articulate fashion. As long as the journey from the absolutism of customs and forms to their fluidization in functional terms and the spontaneous creation of rules may have been, it is undertaken in its entirety by the active partisans of modern civil society, in full awareness of the cost, as if it were the ultimate *curriculum humanitatis.*

In elaborated modernity, nomotopic facts present themselves like a mass of political and private dietary suggestions that have proved their worth as working hypotheses for the coexistence of the collective. One could use Tarde's term *morale-mode* for this, as long as one also thinks of trend (*mode*) as the epidemic imitation of the productive and practical. Modernity is no longer interested in any numinous foundation of the law—the mystic self-aggrandizement of imperial administrations during the last two millennia. This is not changed by the fact that these hypotheses largely continue to be laid down in the quasi-sublime diction of a constitution. If one views our circumstances up close, one can see that even constitutions are, at their heart, inventions and works of occasional poetry.[136]

The tensegrity character of human coexistence in the nomotopic field of no longer static or statist manifests itself most clearly in the complexity of labor division. Without the chronic, long-distance tensile strain effective in laws and customs, one cannot understand how humans can resist the temptation to be self-sufficient in small groups and accept a profession in the labor-divided community; as we know, such a profession only feeds its man if numerous others perform other complementary acts to a sufficient degree—until the differential relationships between these spread-out activities result in the market effect, and with it the society of exchange. What we call the market is a construction of interlocking expectations integrated through long-distance tensions. The "system of needs"[137] only gains its mechanical qualities through the complementarity of the individually produced elements that are joined together from a distance. Like the moral equivalent of a timber-framed construction, exchange tensegrity produces new expectations of the ethos among the market's participants—not only by demanding guarantees of product quality and reliability of payment from them, including the loyal use of the currency, but more still by elevating a consideration of the needs of distant others to a form of thought and life.[138]

Probably the ability of humans to exist in larger social units cannot be explained without the civilizing effect of exchange tensegrities: rehearsing an interest in the interest of others brings about the anthropologically highly improbable state of long-distance consideration—which later teachers of morality would augment with the even more improbable recommendation to love one's most distant neighbor. When the transition must be made from the concrete to the abstract, from existence in small groups to the imperial format, one always finds not only the metaphors of kinship and habitation,[139] but also the trading-ethical techniques of long-distance bracing at work to enable a first form of "world ethos." Among the ancients, it was Aristotle who dealt most explicitly with such connections—provided one can present the theory of moral long-distance tension within the polis and in the inter-polis space detailed here as a redescription of Aristotle's analysis of the urban reputation of men and the regulatory power of prestige.

In the days of German Idealism, bourgeois long-distance consideration as a chronic interest in the interest of others developed into what was known as the categorical imperative, a formal injunction that, beyond any details about the content of its addressees' duty, impressed this rule upon them: you must only want such things as you can want others to want. Following

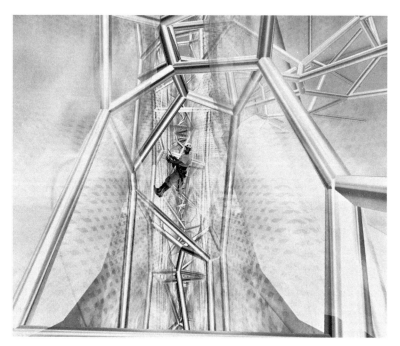

Wall climber in foamy tensegrity

the universalist motif this meant all others, and in accordance with the rationalist precept, all others who were willing and able to accept reason. According to Kant, humans of sound mind were the officials in command of their own power of judgment, and as such it was their duty to think properly. Intelligence is obedience towards the precepts that are inherent in abilities—or, in the language of the eighteenth century, in the capacities of the mind. The zealous mothers of the bourgeois age expressed this in similar words: every talent comes with an obligation! Thus they put the élan of their faith in their offspring like a mission, with the result that the influx of talented children catapulted the civilization process forwards. Since these investments became sporadic or disappeared entirely, the modern nomotope has been overpopulated by the depressed and the pampered, abandoned by duty and disappointed by desires—there is a mood of collective formlessness pervading the landscape, a formlessness that is often explained by political apathy (and which moralists like to interpret without any theoretical methods as "nihilism"). By formulating individual duty in the form of a law, Kant formally confirmed the individual as the citizen of the world or the moral subject of globalization or, more precisely, as the participant in the global market for whom an interest in the interest of others had become second nature in a de-restricted nomotope. Kant's imperative offers the maximum formalization of the belief in the moral productivity of long-distance tension through division of labor. At the same time, it expresses the assumption that the reasonable individual is the whole human being who represents the species in their own person and respects its call to self-design.

After the reshaping of German Idealism into German systems theory, the categorical imperative seemed moderated to this precept: act at all times in such a way that others can follow on from the results of your actions. The negative version of this is: you must not need others. Or, differently put: you should always view humans as means too, not only as ends.[140] The ban on being content simply with oneself led to a shift of emphasis from labor division to communication—though the latter term must be read somewhat coolly as a mutual referentiality (not a mutual agreement). Clearly this notion of communication is far more sober than that of the consensus idealists; its ironic dimension becomes evident when one considers that even the policeman picking up the criminal's trail is a case of communication, as is the grave robber's taking up of the gifts facilitating a pharaoh's journey through the underworld. Here we find a concept of communication that is closer to the model of parasitism than to agreement among parties with equal chances. But because, as Michel Serres has shown, the uninvited guest must in turn regularly tolerate visitors or communicators who invite themselves at his expense, and these too are sponged off by third-degree scroungers, the social field can also be understood as a network of self-serving takings-up of the achievements and life games of others.[141] Perhaps what modern biologists call the environment is merely the register of addresses that can be parasitized from a given location (or the list of parasites whose visits one should reckon with).

In addition to the "system of needs" that has been well described since Adam Smith and Hegel, which is integrated via the exchange of complementary labor-divided services, a little-noted system of consecutive parasitisms should be mentioned as causing the hardening of the ensemble of "stabilized tensions" we call the status quo. At its base we observe the lodging of embryos in their mothers, the most yielding of all hosts; in the broad center, the "working world" unfolds as an integral parasite of the biosphere: it presents the one-sided attack of the productive human worlds on the resources of plant and animal life that Marx, in a pastoral turn of phrase, called the "metabolism of man with nature"; and at the tip stands the fiscal system—that grandiose parasitism with which the modern redistribution state invites itself to the table of society—as the guest who decides by law that they will receive the largest piece. The integral communicator knows how to take up every salary payment, every cigarette, every form of service between citizens. The systemicist's conclusion: no progressive differentiation of subsystems without the tensegrity effects of "communicating needs" and parasitized parasitisms.

Résumé

Island air makes you free: with the emergence of anthropospheres from the savannah, self-framing units are born that acquire ontological meaning as human hothouses. In these hothouses, creatures with the incomparable trait of openness to the world are grown.[142] One could term them plantations in which brains and hands of the *sapiens* type are bred and programmed. Until recently, no more was known about the climatization and maintenance of such houses than about the operating instructions of Spaceship Earth. The traditional crudenesses handed down under the title of politics and the vaguenesses passed on under the title of morality offer no more than provisional orientations for an effective cybernetics of large-scale hothouses. Because the path of civilization is the only one still open, one must now be willing to embark on explicating the operating conditions of the anthroposphere.

Looking back synoptically at the three types of produced islands dealt with in this chapter, it becomes apparent that the two former types, the absolute islands or space stations and the relative islands or hothouses, are nothing other than self-presentations of the ontological island type in simplified models. Space stations are informative because the emergency of environmental inversion is their precondition: as vacuum implants of habitats, they project the locational secret of humanity into outer space. They are the most significant outposts of the anthropogenic island, for they demonstrate through the cosmic emergency that humans, wherever they may dwell, must profit from an interior privilege. Whoever wishes to remain human is obliged to be pampered, even in outer space. What is true of cosmonauts

Dawn over the eastern USA, photograph taken from the Space Shuttle Columbia. India-napolis is at the bottom left, and Cincinnati, Dayton and Columbus are at the center.

applies even more to the inhabitants of Flusser's "low box" above the earth's surface.

Like the departure to the space station, the erection of hot-houses marks a caesura in notions of the relationship between humans and "outer" nature: with them, nature can finally be represented as non-external, as a housemate in the republic of beings, if initially only in the shape of "plant associations."[143] Finally, the twentieth century made the entry of humans into the hothouse ensemble conceivable through the association of space travel and ecology—see *Biosphere 2* or *Noah's Ark #2*[144]—thus meeting the requirements for an adequate anthropo-topology: if one takes the manned space station and the inhabited hothouse together, the result is a place that explains its inhabitants: the human island. The place of humans must be envisaged in such a way that it seems on the one hand like the implant of a "life-world" into a non-lifeworld, and on the other hand like a biotope in which human and non-human symbionts coexist as hothouse mates. One of the oldest anthrotopian errors of reasoning is that they insist on viewing nature as an outside force; in reality, the relevant nature has always already been incorporated into the inside of the anthropic hothouse.[145]

As the displacement of a surrounding element is tied to the concept of the island, one must still answer the question of what the surroundings are at whose expense the ontological island rises. The repeated observation that hominid groups moved against the background of the savannah on their path to humanization, and seceded from there to their nine-dimensional realm, can only be accepted as provisional information, for the term "savannah" belongs to a different order from that of the anthropogenic island and is thus uninformative at a human-topological level. In fact, the displacement of the incipient human group relates not to its natural habitat, the grassy African landscape, but to its own conventionally animal way of being-in in the natural milieu.

When the *sapiens* types emerge from their environment, they initially produce an inner world of increased inhibition within their self-governed enterprise. They weave themselves into a symbol-woven magic tent of internal meanings and tensions. The displacement causes an increasing adjustment from environmental relevancies (like natural enemies and sources of food) to those of their own world—work, signs, jealousies, status competitions, comfort, communal duties, questions of truth, needs for expression and numinous imperatives. The further the emergence of the human island progresses, the more the animal constraint within an inborn or acquired space of relevance is pushed back; then there is more and more free alertness available for the perception of the overall conditions.

That is what idealist philosophy meant in its heroic days with the formulation that nature itself opens its eyes in man. One could, paradoxically, say that the surrounding element of stupor is displaced through the surfacing of the island of alertness and truth: the human island climatizes itself through surpluses of vigilance and liberated perceptual circumspections. The attentiveness of its inhabitants is provoked infinitely more by distinctions and incidents in their own area than by events in the outside environment. While the surrounding animal and plant life consists of confined intelligence, a type of intelligence grows on the ontological island that can be characterized as free or ecstatic. To make the paradox complete: anthropic ecstasy is the displacement of animal confinement. That is why the human islands are worlds, that is to say collection points for being and dumping sites for success. They confirm the immemorial liaison of alertness and truth—or between intelligence and success. The ontological islands are places in which the open displaces the confined. In phenomenological terms, this means that here the alert spirit emerges from an element of constraint.

The human sphere rises by pushing back its own animal premise. Being human means the acquired inability to remain an animal. In metaphysical terms, this yields the thesis that we are on the island of the idea, whose infinite nature pushes the finitude of empirical environments to the background. This would make the infinite an enclave within finite circumstances. It would gape open like an abyss directed upwards, as an interruption of life required to bear a vision of that which is more than life. Whoever can understand that may do so. However one puts it: the space islands of humans are forward-deployed posts against the open.

With these reflections on insulations that make humans possible, I have paid tribute to the demon of the explicit to the extent that is indispensable for a contemporary theory of the human fact. If the aim is to describe the climatization of the inhabited space, one cannot avoid envisaging the anthropogenic climate in all its thematic intrusiveness and defining its components in analytically sufficient comprehensiveness. It transpires from this that neither moral nor physical climate factors can ever be accepted in their simple pre-givenness, but only after special arrangements and modifications to suit human purposes. This goes without saying with the cultural additions to the elemental, and for the natural additions it remains to be shown how they too only come within our reach through a specific "appropriation." Hegel even said of the ordinary air that it was not directly usable by humans in its usual state: in his *Philosophy of Right*, he remarks in passing, with typical reservations towards any immediacy: "even air has to be earned—inasmuch as it has to be heated."[146] This laconic comment should be noted as a core of crystallization for a philosophy of culture and atmospheric production.

Let us add that production of the atmospheric means not only the designer reworking of existing patterns or a curatorial secondary activity; it is the primal production that enables human facts to be called into existence. In the language of the nineteenth century: the anthropogenic climate is the basis on which humans appear as an effect of the superstructure. The explanations presented here have implicitly shown why, with this subject matter, it is no longer productive to distinguish between base and superstructure in the way that seemed necessary to both the primitive and subtle materialisms of yesteryear. We now know that in circular causality, the epiphenomenon of the one dimension is the base of the other and vice versa; only the will to intervention, meaning practical simplification, creates the urge to ascertain foundations from which one could derive apparent consequences. In reality, the consequences are more fundamental than the foundations.

I have attempted to show how, behind walls of distance, the greenhouse effect that made humans "pupils of the air" established itself—an air in which there is now more than the danger and habit of animal-like savannah life. According to this account, the human hothouse is the nine-dimensional structure that spreads out along the main axes of the human space of action. One can assume that it describes the minimum com-plexity without which membership in the anthroposphere cannot be adequately defined. The special trait of this theory of the human sphere—which Husserl meant with his unsuitable term "lifeworld"—shows itself in the fact that through its agency, the relationship between the explicit and the implicit is itself subjected to explication. It thus stands in a movement that was first noted by Hegel in his theory of reflection, and further focused by Luhmann in his theory of native latency. From that point onwards, the implicit appears in a twofold guise: as some-thing that is capable of explication on the one hand, but on the other hand embodies an autonomous value that cannot be mea-sured purely in relation to the norm of explication. Even where explication could occur, it remains merely a regional possibility; it cannot and should not be carried out in all cases.

With regard to the nine-dimensional structure, it is under-standable that in cognitive terms, "society" is a field of places subject to unequal explication tensions. Where these reach high values, theories can be articulated that express the forming of compromises out of an acute awareness of danger and luxuriant specialization—a characterization that applies to all advanced theories of the present. Intelligences operating in places of equally high explicitness can be described through their position on cognitive isobars; one could say that with the advance of the intellectual enframing, they are confronted with the same tasks or "works"—with the terms "work" and "task" best elucidated through the imposition of explication. Needless to say, this does away with any idyllic concept of enlightenment that fails to acknowledge the resistance to proceeding explication. Only the naïve can still assume a convergence between knowledge and human interests as a general rule. The growing improbability of advanced theory corresponds to the increasing unwelcomeness of further explication. One can understand that what Freud called repression is a narrow segment in the field of improbable and unwelcome articulations.

The topological description of the anthropogenic island has far-reaching implications for the reformulation of social theory in the language of spatial multiplicities or foams: each individual cell in the foam must now be understood as a micro-insulation that carries the complete pattern of nine-dimensionality heavily folded within itself. This cell analysis transpires as a task that is no less complex than the challenges of examining large-scale composite bodies. In its own way, multi-dimensional cellular sociology repeats Gabriel Tarde's axiom: *chaque chose est une société* [each thing is a society]—though one should note that the terms *chose* and *société* refer not only to fact that the "thing" is composed of smaller units; in addition, each individual construct is now spread apart into multi-dimensionality. Every household, every couple, every group of resonances already form a miniature of the whole anthropotope as cells in the foam. Moreover, every cell and every association of cells, that is to say culture, is incorporated into a fluctuating variety of one-sided and reciprocal imitations, crossings and mixtures in which no homogeneous basic form can ever be identified. (It is no longer the case that every "culture" is a hybrid;[147] every one of its cells already is.) Just as Elias Canetti demanded in his birthday eulogy for Hermann Broch that individuals be understood as wanderers between breathing spaces, atmospheric analysis must describe the cells in dynamic foam in their constant vibrations on the axes of nine-dimensionality.

This perspective enables a new understanding of the achievements of implicit knowledge. I noted above that all humans are latent sociologists, but usually see no reason to become manifest ones. Now we can see why the transition to the manifest is normally superfluous. The sojourn on the anthropogenic island includes a varyingly developed ability to navigate the nine-dimensional structure that has long been on everyone's lips implicitly under names such as "experience," "reality" or "world." Just as most children grow inconspicuously into their mother tongue's complexities of syntax, every ordinary islander acquires the ability to move through each individual anthropotopic dimension with sufficient confidence simply by participating in the life games of the primary group. What Heidegger explained about the chirotope or ready-to-hand world in *Being and Time*, namely that its everyday familiarity in non-discursive brightness gives it the basic property of *disclosedness*, also applies *mutatis mutandis* to the other dimensions. The adult inhabitant of the anthropogenic island perceives its inner tension and jointing in a single glance. For them, the most improbable thing has become self-evident; for the inhabitants of the ontological island, the implications of the basic situation initially remain folded up in perfect compaction. The ready-to-hand equipment, the sounding space, the generalized mother world, the field of wishes and desire, the cooperations with the others, the demands made by truth, the pursuit by the gods and the tension of calls for laws: to them, the entire arrangement of folds of the over-complex in which they move with quiet oversight seems like an almost smooth surface that is initially not worth mentioning. When the institutionalization of the monstrous in everyday joint knowledge succeeds, most humans content themselves with the most commonplace views—who can reproach them for that? They distrust explicit talk of life's things for understandable reasons. In all cultures outside of the witches' kitchens of theory, people are wary of superfluous reasoning—for with the explicit comes the storm. Considering the achievements of the *esprit de finesse*, it is logical to claim that it is impossible for humans not to be wise. In Goethe's words: "Culture has not core nor shell / for it is everything at once."[148]

The fact that humans nonetheless fail to reach the *sapiens* level, either as individuals or epidemically, demands a theory of self-undercutting. This is provided by the supplement to the history of ideas taken down above.

CHAPTER 2

Indoors

Architectures of Foam

Socrates: There was within me an architect whom circumstances
did not fashion forth.
Phaedrus: How do you know this?
Socrates: By I know not what deep intent to build, which darkly
troubles my thoughts.
— Paul Valéry, "Eupalinos, Or The Architect"[1]

A. Where We Live, Move, and Have Our Being:
On Modern Architecture as an Explication of the Sojourn

If one had to explain as concisely as possible which modification
of human being-in-the-world was effected by the twentieth
century, one would have to say the following: it unfolded existence as sojourn in architectural, aesthetic and legal terms—or,
more simply put, it made dwelling explicit. Modern construction
broke up the house, this human-enabling supplement to nature,
into its elements and re-assigned it;[2] it moved the city, which
once arranged the world in a circle around itself, out of the center
and remodeled it into a network of rivers and beams. Thus the

analytical "revolution" that constitutes the central nervous system of modernity also affected the architectural shells of the human sphere and, by establishing an alphabet of forms, created a new art of synthesis, a modern grammar of spatial production and an altered situation of existing in the artificial milieu.[3]

Carl Schmitt's use of the term "spatial revolution" to refer to the political consequences of the transition to the age of air supremacy would be ideally suited to describe this, were it not for my earlier demand to avoid the word "revolution" because it is a kinetically far-fetched and politically misleading misnomer for explication processes. What Schmitt had his eye on belonged to a complex of phenomena described above as the explication of the airspace through gas terrorism, the air force, air design and air conditioning;[4] it is the epitome of processes (aerotechnic, artillery, aviatic, pyrotechnic, photographic and cartographic) that, in sum, produce what one calls air supremacy or domination of space in the third dimension. Its continuation into electronic technology provides control over telecommunications, or "ethereal domination"—with the oft-noted consequence that space temporarily retreats into the background in favor of a primacy of time. One can only cling to the opinion that "spatial thought" has become obsolete since then if one is unduly impressed by corresponding declamations in circulation since the 1920s. The English storyteller E. M. Forster already let a figure in his post-historical science fiction tale "The Machine Stands Still" speak the following words: "You know that we have lost the sense of space. We say 'space is annihilated,' but we have annihilated not space, but the sense thereof."[5] The assertion of the primacy of time is one of the rhetorical forms assumed by intimidation through modernity. Whoever yields to it risks missing a key event of contemporary thought referred to in discussions as "the return of space."[6] Michel Foucault stated: "The present epoch will perhaps be above all the epoch of space."[7]

The true "spatial revolution" of the twentieth century is the explication of the human sojourn or residence in an interior via the dwelling machine, climate design and environmental planning (extending to the large-scale forms we call "collectors"), as well as the exploration of adjacency to the two inhuman spatial structures that are placed before or alongside the human one: the cosmic (macro and micro) and the virtual. To make the sojourn of persons in inhabited places explicable required no less than a reversal of the relationship between foreground and background with regard to human harboring conditions. Expressed from Heidegger's perspective and in his words, being-in-inside-something-at-all had to come apart at the seams before it could be expressly thematized as indwelling-in-the-world. Though places of habitation traditionally formed the supporting background for life processes, the sharp air of modernity also saw "lifeworldly" existence affected by environmental inversion. The self-evident certainties of dwelling no longer manage to stay in the background. Even if we do not always project houses and apartments into the vacuum, they must henceforth be formulated as explicitly as if they were the closest relatives of the space capsule.

This provides the definition of modern architecture: it is the medium in which the explication of the human sojourn in man-made interiors processually articulates itself. This means that the art of construction has, since the nineteenth century, constituted something that would have been termed a "realization of philosophy" in the Age of Metternich. To invoke Heidegger once again: it carries out the localization [*Er-Örterung*] of Dasein. It does not content itself with being the varyingly art-conscious underling of human habitation activity whose traces can be followed back to the early arrangement of repositories, caves and huts. It reformulates the "places" in which such things as the dwelling, residence and being-with-oneself of groups and individuals can take place under conditions with high levels of self-referentiality, money-mediatedness, legalism, interconnectedness and mobilization. We now know of these places that they can no longer be envisaged simply as Here and Yonder in a "lifeworld." Under the relevant circumstances, a place is a quantum of built-around and conditioned air, a locale of handed-down and updated atmosphere, a node of harbored relationships, a crossing in a network of data flows, an address for entrepreneurial initiatives, a niche for self-relationships, a base camp for expeditions into the world of work and experiences, a location for business dealings, a regenerative zone, a guarantee of the subjective night. The further explication advances, the more the building of residences resembles the installation of space stations. Dwelling itself and the production of its containers becomes a spelling-out of all the dimensions of components that are joined in primal coalescence on the anthropogenic island—and the disassembly of holistically clumped living conditions and their rational remodeling can be driven to its limit: a repetition of the human world-island as such in the apartment for a single inhabitant.

Above all else, it is the modern mobilization of the traffic of persons and goods that has created the radically altered conditions of perception and shaping for the human habitation system. Only after the part of humanity first affected by the Industrial Revolution, in Europe and the USA, worked its way out of the agrarian condition and converted to a multi-local, semi-nomadic *modus vivendi*, did it become noticeable how many preconditions the old way of living in the villages and domains of the agrarian age had actually had. All the knowledge about habitations and habits from this old reservoir that we carry within us reflects a habitus among the populations of homelands, fatherlands and regions that established itself during the ten-thousand-year empire of sedentarism, and whose formal and material sediments exist in the form of historically handed-down architectures for houses, villages and towns. This universe belongs to an interrupted life whose confinement within narrow estates and sluggish rhythms prevented it from adequately assessing the motives and conditions of its residential behavior. There had never been a sufficient reason for this—to say nothing about the lack of means.

In this matter, the present age not only has an advantage of explicitness; the angle of reflection has changed enough to provoke an analytically productive, chronic attentiveness to questions of sojourn and habitus. Today one can calmly say that life in the sedentary state was too slow, too bent into itself and too imitative of the plant model to make any statements about its forms of dwelling with the deterritorialized awareness that is indispensable for theoretical knowledge. As long as the sedentary world condition remained in power, Varro's dictum that the land is of divine origin but the city a man-made supplement circumscribed the entire horizon: its message was that only those city-dwellers who considered their urban domiciles second residences, and honored their country villas as their true abodes, could still know what being at home really meant. The city person was meant to believe that they were in reality merely a repotted plant—and plants do not dwell, but are rooted (though plants with double roots do seem somewhat hybrid). Only after the advent of modern traffic conditions-traffic as an explication of mobility or telemobility— did real architectural, transport and existential alternatives to the post-Neolithic habitus of dwelling come about, alternatives that were finally able to illuminate the eternal half-darkness of sedentarism. Now the skepticism towards everything that adheres to the ground can be positivized; the term "uprooting" takes on a bright sound and can be uttered like a demand. This caesura made it possible to say that traditional dwelling in "homes" was by no means the universally valid primal form and norm of residence, as some pietists of dwelling have also been preaching of late. It is the resilient, but conquerable mode of place-sojourn among humans who are held up by something.

1. Being-Held-Up; The Station and the Store

Since modernity worked out special architectural forms to assist people in situations of being held up, it has been possible to articulate the nature of residential abodes in sober language. One of their characteristic pampering gestures is that they were able to produce the unprecedented constructions of the protected station and the air-conditioned waiting hall for travelers without immediate connecting journeys, as if wanting to admit that waiting is so dismal for humans that one cannot refrain from attempting to soften its impositions with a minimum of comfort. With sufficient freedom for abstraction, it becomes clear that initially and mostly, houses are also stations—or, more precisely, waiting rooms in which one spends the time before an event that is anticipated with certainty.

Bus stop in Aachen referred to as "the claw," designed by Eisenman Architects and realized by JC Decaux, (photograph: Christian Richters)

What the earliest waiting persons were concerned with is hardly an insoluble riddle: the house of Neolithic man was a waiting room whose occupants held out until, in the fields at the edge of the village, that moment came for whose sake they had taken on the effort of staying—the moment in which the planted crops were ready for eating, storage and renewed sowing. It seems to have been Vilém Flusser who formally recorded and topologically contextualized this seemingly trivial, yet never before expressly voiced observation. Houses are waiting rooms at stations. It is no coincidence that this occurred in the course of a speculation on the metamorphoses of habitat caused by the discoveries of the outermost cosmos and virtual space.

Houses are stations for held-up life and offer a place for the irruption of time into space: this statement is the explicatory form for the most remote self-evident truth regarding the sojourn of humans in residential abodes. Because it returns from the most buried, inconspicuous place, it constitutes the deepest insight into the history of reflection on building, dwelling and housed life. It is fruitful for cultural philosophy, as it defines the house in terms of its harboring service for the sedentary; anthropologically rich because it interprets sedentarism as an existential of the wait for the agrarian product (which, *pace* Heidegger, means neither simply an acquiring use of equipment nor running ahead into one's own death). In addition, Flusser's thesis has therapeutic angles, as it combines a diagnosis of the basic mood of held-up life with the prospect of a change of mood through new traffic resources. Until now, dwelling essentially meant not being able to leave. What things can the dwelling creatures known as humans become when they experience the fact that dwelling means being-able-to-be-here-and-elsewhere?

Where people live in houses *more rustico*, an internal climate develops that, as befits held-up life, is marked by uniform resignation and imposed trust. In this situation, boredom is the musical key in which being as a whole plays its pieces. As with any folk music, one must be born into it to find it bearable. The things one could not change even if one wanted to must be in order from the deep level upwards; this attitude towards the totality of facts that mean the world is the hallmark of life in land-cultivating cultures. Anyone searching for the civilization-historical source for the "primacy of the object" can assure themselves of it here. Real things and their intergrowths with the given circumstances take absolute precedence over mere desirabilities as long as one is at home in a world form in which one can, *summa summarum*, not change any of everything that is the case. Psychologically speaking, this yields the matrix of mania-willing depression or despondency illuminated by small hopes. In this situation, the knowledge that counts always has a quality of subordination to the dominance of that-which-is-thus-and-not-otherwise. For an entire age, sendentarized life moved about in this field. Indeed, anyone who grows crops must be able to wait; and whoever fails to realize their plans must be willing to start anew over and over again.

The farming year is an agrarian advent. Its psychological result is the religious experience of time: due to thinking in terms of seed and harvest, that linkage of coming and accommodating is established from which every form of typological thinking, with its dual of promise and fulfillment, follows on. Whatever grows in the fields of becoming, it will rightly be asked from what seeds the crops emerge. By their fruits you shall know what was sown. Thinking in larger contexts or being wise: in the old settled world, this initially meant nothing other than paying attention to the arc that formed through the facts of guided ripening.

Let us recall that the Old High German word *bur* refers not only to a house, chamber or cell, but also the cage in which poultry is kept; in Swedish it indicates a place of arrest. The word for a birdcage, *Vogelbauer*, indicates what may await those arrested by plant growth:[8] whoever enters the situation of waiting for the plant must install themselves in a cage where slowness is in power. Thus the first house is a machine to harbor boredom. As a penal institution for tending to ripening cycles, the farmhouse creates the unmistakable attachment of its inhabitants to the cultivated lands. This yields, as its first metaphysical added value, the worldling's trust in nature as good repetition. In this regime, then, one always knows one's purpose; after all, the event for whose sake the overall condition is endured will remain the same for all time. One passes the year to celebrate the banal sacrament of the *physis*, this time and every time.

At first, then, dwelling means a harvest-related existence at a crop station. Once every year, the grain train comes and stops here. The fact that we have so far stayed alive is due to our station privilege and a fertile route. Once the cargo is brought, a new waiting cycle begins, supported by the stores from the last harvest. If the train fails to come because of crop failure or political unrest, lack comes to power and precipitates those who can do nothing but wait into ruin. As soon as the connection between dwelling and waiting becomes confused, as traditionally in periods of military crisis and systematically since the Industrial Revolution, with the resulting de-agrarianization of life, it can happen that the existing lose their orientation towards the decisive, fleeting moment of harvest. What to do if the summer comes and there is nothing left in the fields to harvest? Heidegger evocatively describes this ominous possibility in his analytics of boredom:

> This *lengthening of the while* manifests the while of Dasein in its indeterminacy that is never absolutely determinable. This indeterminacy takes Dasein captive, yet in such a way that in the whole expansive and expanded expanse it can grasp nothing except the mere fact that it remains *entranced* by and toward this expanse. [...] The lengthening is a *vanishing of the short-ness of the while*.[9]

What Heidegger brings up here is the terror of unemployment, which manifests itself as having-nothing-to-do. Short-whiledness only has a chance to pervade our temporal experience if we are included in the fruitful moment that tells us of its own accord what is now to be done. The categorical imperative of agrarian ontology—devote yourself to the harvest!—can only be followed as long as there is a sensible tension between foresight and fulfillment.

This would make the house of the first farmers an inhabited clock. It is the birthplace of two kinds of temporality: time that moves towards an event and time that serves the eternal recurrence of the same, as if walking in circles. In belonging to the first project—the seed-harvest context—houses differ from huts, to which they long remained closely related, formally often to the point of indistinguishability. Though the primitive house contains the prehistoric hut and subsumes it, to the extent of taking over its functions: harboring sleep, protecting from weather and vermin, providing a sphere of withdrawal for sexual matters and a comfort sphere for states of sluggish digestion. Conversely, the hut can never contain the house because it has no harvest project and its entire purpose is to offer day-to-day shelter. (Hence the attractiveness of a hut existence for civilized persons who are exhausted by projects, and swarm out in tents and camper vans during their holidays—withdrawn into containers that do not oblige their inhabitants to wait for a product. Here one can barbecue, watch television, copulate and forget the gross national product.) As far as Heidegger's notorious excursions to the hut near Todtnauberg are concerned, it was incorrectly described; it was in fact a barn, meant for gathering in harvests from the unheard-of. In the twentieth century, the hut on wheels became

Tuff hills in Cappadocia converted into residences. Alongside living quarters, they also contain dovecotes, barns, storage caves and graves.

the mobile home, which Flusser celebrated as an indication that humanity had reached the end of the Neolithic Age—evil to him who would object to this on aesthetic grounds.[10]

House-bound time consists of waiting time and ripening time, forethought and real present—from which later epochs derived the duality of the chronic and the kairotic, including sour weeks and joyous festivals. Just as the house itself causes time to split into two modalities, household matters do the same on their building-typological side: next to the house for waiting, in which mostly relatively poor humans reside, the granary is erected—the house of abundance in which the edible value, the future-giver and the collective freedom from hunger and need are guarded. This force field, in which the store, gods and power are intertwined along with their war machine, will form the energetic city center in the time of urban empires.

Each of the two forms of building corresponds in its own way to the temporal structures of domesticated existence. The storage house is a grain hourglass that runs for a year and conveys a promise of survival with this duration to the collective of users; the residential houses, on the other hand, fulfill their destiny primarily as waiting machines. A bifurcation of the paths and movements that belong to the first residential dwelling corresponds to the bicameralism of the time houses: on the one side are the paths leading from the fields to the storage house, serving the purposes of selection, collection and filling, while on the other side are paths leading back from the store to the houses; they contribute to distribution, dispersal and consumption. That which is public and shared comes into existence on the former paths—which is why, to this day, the act of publicizing is linked to the intrinsically agreeable gesture of increasing common property—and that which is domestic and private on the latter paths—which is why bringing home objects one has acquired outside is one of the primal gestures of an enriched return into one's own domain.[11] (There are also the third paths, which lead from the houses to the fields and from the fields to the houses; these are the paths that will later be taken as trips to work and back, the thankless paths that serve the continuation of waiting for the yield by other means.)

Whoever has privileged access to the store will more easily find themselves thinking that dwelling must mean more than waiting for the next harvest. A full storage inspires the exuberance of philobatic, eruptive and campaign-hungry gentlemen who can keep a retinue and wild companions. They embark on outings to expand their radius and manifest their eccentric energy, while the farmers, the earth people always devoted to the future of their grain, can only follow their calling of settled waiting. Since the advent of agrarian added value and its blessed unequal distribution, "societies" have been divided into the patient who sit tight and serve and the impatient, the striders who make history. The stationariness of those who work the fields nurturing and waiting contrasts with the mobility of well-supplied masters, who can rely on sufficient supplies to live expressively and aggressively. With them, the wait for the ripening of the crops expands into the ripening of victories, beyond divisions of season or year. In later world conditions, waiting for results and numbers as such would be reframed as project time and business periods.

The farming world knows only the advent, not the project; its brand of reason comes from meditation on the crop plant and its cosmic analogies. In the farming universe, the mere fact that sowing takes place already prefigures the act of investment with which the introduction of the profit idea into time takes shape; this profit-oriented thinking still remains discreet and concealed, however. Heidegger's remark that sparing and preserving constitutes the "fundamental character of dwelling"[12] can be applied to the now almost sunken agrarian world, and initially only to that. Thus speaks the last prophet of being-like-the-plants at the close of the sedentary age. Looking back on his enormous œuvre, one understands that he was the proto-ontologist of vegetative sprouting and flourishing who had been transferred to the end of his era. In the midst of de-restricted productions, investments and bombardments, the greatest thinker of Old Europe, on the threshold between the world of growth and that of projects, still grasps the unspectacular onset of ripeness as the archetype of the decisive event.

Existence understood from the perspective of the farming residence evokes the prevailing mood of due patience in accordance with which individuals, as well as families and peoples, are supposed to view themselves as waiting creatures. It is in waiting that the ethos of delayed life is imprinted upon it: it must let itself be exhausted by something that is richer in being than itself and has more power over time than it does. In this regime the individual life, as the quiet consumer of its own time, is exhausted by a superior factor—whether it bears the names of the clans, the peoples, the gods or the arts. This outlines the basic situation of traditional metaphysical feeling: whoever waits for things to ripen is inevitably thinking of a higher type of harvest in which they themselves are expected like a ripened grain. The wisdom of *homo metaphysicus* lies in the motto "harvest and be harvested."

2. Receivers, Habituation Facilities

With the explication of the sojourn as waiting for ripening, work on the technical reconstruction of the element in which humans live, move and have their being has entered its first stage. From this develops a second, whose signature becomes visible as soon as one expands waiting for things that ripen to include the signs that announce what is coming closer and

Tatsumi Orimoto, In the Box, 2002

occurring among us. Modernity projected receptive waiting for signs into technical devices such as radios and telephones, whose existence retroactively allows us to saw what human houses, viewed from another side, have always been: receiving stations for messages from the extraordinary. Heidegger, to whom (along with his successors Bollnow and Schmitz) the phenomenology of dwelling still owes most, explained the connection between dwelling and waiting for signs of the unusual as a matrix of religious or reflective receptivity:

> Mortals dwell in that they await the divinities as divinities. In hope they hold up to the divinities what is unhoped for. They wait for the intimations of their coming and do not mistake

the signs of their absence. [...] In the very depth of misfortune they wait for the weal that has been withdrawn.[13]

Translated into more profane terms (and leaving aside the fact that we are dealing with paraphrases of Hölderlin's poetic theology), this produces the statement that dwelling humans surround themselves with a triviality without which they cannot distinguish the non-trivial. This differentiation does not occur through a theoretical judgment, but through the willingness and ability of a habit-structured life to deal with something unaccustomed that arrives among us, if only by marveling and speaking about it. In the first reading, this means that humans fixed in their dwelling containers are looking for salvation from triviality. This scenic universal extends into modern apartment life, where sitting there in one's own domain is connected to waiting for someone to call. The frequently voiced suspicion that the Fall of Man is identical to the sedentary way of life has a core of truth. Those affected understand that they are living a different life from the one for which they were created. Yet barely anyone can remember "what would be different." God and the nomads, who can both still do what they want, are *totaliter aliter* for the settled.

One of the burdens of housed life is being at the mercy of its lack of stimuli. Where it forms surpluses of meaning and expression, they are incorporated into the oracles, the décor, into inner and outer images. In its fertile moments, the halted life produced ceiling frescos with wars in heaven and cascades of naked women. At other times, the waiting life specialized in erecting cathedrals, monstrous stations that force heaven to take in human passengers. The institution of hospitality religious coded in some cultures comes from the possibility of receiving the guest in one's own house as a sign from the unusual, if not directly as a "beckoning messenger of divinity."[14] Did an unassuming arrival not indeed become the predicted savior on one occasion? As the appetite for signals cannot be sated by guests alone, however, countless mantic systems offer their services to equip life with the necessary surplus of signs. The less that settled people themselves experience, the more miracles serve as their staple food. Man does not live on bread alone, but from every indication that something is still going on somewhere. If signals from beyond are no longer acceptable one day, they will be replaced by newspaper reports, new releases and signs of the times.

At second glance, one can see that dwellings must be explicated in an even more radical sense as receivers. It is the function of receivers to sort incoming things into significant and insignificant ones, thus preventing the mental implosion that occurs when everything or nothing is informative. In this sense, dwellings are ontological therapy stations for creatures in danger of falling ill with lack of meaning: filters to keep out nihilism, sanitaria to treat dysfunctions in apparatuses of meaning. In this onto-sanatorial understanding of dwelling there is agreement between Heidegger and Vilém Flusser, who, as pioneers of a hermeneutics of homelessness, took opposing paths. While Heidegger saw the homelessness of "modern man" as an epochal destiny that one cannot perceive without pitying it, or at least placing it in a positive light with a hint of heroic contemplation, Flusser opted in his reflections on his own fate as a Jewish migrant for the demystification of home as such—more still, for an aggressive concept of existence in the fathomless. This choice is supported by an information-philosophical argument:

People think of *heimat* as being a relatively permanent place; a home, as temporary and interchangeable. Actually, the opposite is true: one can exchange *heimats*—or have none at all—but one must always live somewhere, regardless of where. Parisian *clochards* live under bridges […] and as horrible as it may sound, people lived at Auschwitz. […]

I built a house for myself at Robion. My desk is in the center of the house, surrounded by the customary disorder of my books and papers. The village to which I have become accustomed is outside my door, as is the post office and the weather, which I have also come to take for granted. Beyond them stretches increasingly unfamiliar territory: Provence, France, Europe, the earth, the expanding universe. […] I am embedded in redundancy so that I can receive noise as information and so that I can produce information. My home, this network of the customary and familiar, serves to capture adventure and provides a springboard into adventure.[15]

Flusser's Provençal village Robion has a good chance of going down in the history of ideas as a counterpoint to Todtnauberg, because it won deserved honor as a model village for the explication of the sojourn through the new logic of domesticity. Just as I spoke earlier of environmental inversion in the context of a topological reflection on ecology and space travel, the Robion effect demands that one speak of an inversion of dwelling: after this, dwelling can no longer be considered a function of home. Rather, being-at-home—the realization comes late—is an equally understandable and problematic side effect of dwelling.

In the light of semio-ontological analysis, the dwelling appears as a redundancy generator or habitus machine whose

it (Stanislas Zimmermann/Valérie Jomini), *living unit*
(it design, www.it-happens.ch, 2000)

task it is to divide the mass of incoming signals "from the world" vying for significance into familiar and unfamiliar ones. In this sense, the dwelling is an agency for finding usable repetitions. One cannot be at home until one forms an almost unconscious unity with one's own four walls and everything that furnishes them. Thus it is the dwelling that makes its inhabitants capable of existence by equipping them with the first differentiation that makes a difference: that between the habitual and the exceptional, between those things that remain in the background as familiar and those that stand out from it because they are noticed for being unusual. It is one of the primary functions of dwelling, then, to equip the inhabitants with habituations (though habituations are in turn older and more general than sedentary house construction). In this sense, modern dwellings constitute explicit desensitizations that produce the background for sensitizations. Modernity: this means that the background too becomes a product, the things we take for granted become rarities, and the ordinary is taken apart to form a field of articulated tasks and technical projects.

That a dwelling (in which we currently dwell) can only appear in series of dwellings (in which we used to reside), however, only becomes noticeable at times of increased traffic—just as we only see late on that all transferences begin as transferences of space and dwelling before they become affective transferences or projections. One has to move often enough before one can understand, from the perspective of the third or fourth dwelling, what the first was: an involuntary habituation—letting oneself be overcome by the milieu and an original coloration by a mood. Heidegger reproduced this with the immense term "thrownness" [*Geworfenheit*]—a word that contains a deep and secretly ironic bow to the first strike of coincidence. Now one understands why a later, more conscious form of dwelling would come to choose its own habituation contexts and accept or reject the habituation suggestions that materialized in a new residence. Accordingly, the later residence takes on ever more aspects of self-design. This enabled repetition to become the matrix of invention. The aesthetic consciousness should be considered one of the side effects of relocation, to the extent that the relocation encourages the ability to bracket phenomena. Simply the philosophical virtue of marveling how something is, and that it is, already testifies to the inability of wakeful intelligence truly to become accustomed to something: it reveals that among the intelligent, moving into the world house encounters an immemorial reserve that no routine can erase. The first immersion already preserves an aura of incredibility; the amazement emanating from this aura de-automatizes transference. Never believing that repetitions are completely secure is the beginning of wisdom.

3. Embedding and Immersion

The explication of the sojourn through the waiting room and the news receiver, or the habit machine called the dwelling, is the preparation for a third level that is easily reached from the second: Flusser already brought a possible formulation for this unfolding into play when he noted that he was *embedded* in redundancy. With the metaphor of redundancy he touched the radical layer of human territorialization in situations, habituations and customarinesses. Investigation of the nature of human sojourn can only attain an analytically satisfactory and adequately confusing degree of explicitness when it is pushed to become an analytics of the embedding situation—an undertaking to which, alongside the singular advances of the young Heidegger, Paul Valéry's reflections from 1921 on the nature of architecture as modulation of immersion contributed the most; they are comparable only to the far later attempts of Hermann Schmitz to found a new phenomenological situationism[16] and the dialogues of Ilya Kabakov and Boris Groys on the theory and aesthetics of installation.[17]

The highest level of aesthetic clarity that seems possible with regard to the explication of dwellings as embedding apparatuses is, in my opinion, reached in Kabakov's astounding installation

Ilya Kabakov, *The Toilet* (1992), exterior

The Toilet, presented at the ninth *documenta* festival in Kassel in 1992, for which Jan Hoet, the responsible curator, had initially chosen "the house" as the theme. In this installation, Kabakov worked with a disappointment effect stemming from the fact that there was no anal-aesthetic tastelessness behind the title *The Toilet*, nor any pornographic scene or any other dirty secret of the bourgeois world, but rather a simple dwelling of the kind that was typical for citizens of the Soviet Union between the 1950s and 70s. The idea came from autobiographical motives, but was inspired more significantly by everyday conditions in the Soviet Union: Kabakov's mother, he relates, had taken employment as a housekeeper at the art school where her son was studying and lodging so that she could still be close to him during his training; and because no regular quarters were

Ilya Kabakov, *The Toilet*, interior

available, she had to reside illegally in one of the school's functional rooms, a boys' toilet that had been converted into a laundry room. Thus for the young artist, the toilet-cum-living room became the epitome of Russian council housing, that mythical place of squeezing together in which, from the 1920s onwards, bourgeois individualism was to be wiped out and the new Soviet human created. At the same time, the mediocre plight of such environments recalls the traditions of Russian communality, in which, Kabakov asserts, shared misfortune was sometimes experienced as a "happiness of universal poverty." "Soviet power was accepted like a blizzard, like a climatic disaster." "For all the poverty and nightmarishness of life back then, we had the sweet feeling that everyone lived like that, that we were all living in a single communal residence."[18] In his commentary, Groys points out that dwellings can also serve as metaphors for art collections, as they are *per se* collections of objects assembled by the inhabitants according to private, usually banal criteria that remain opaque to outsiders. As a result, they constitute spontaneous exhibitions that differ from the collections in art galleries only in the fact that their visitors must be acquaintances of the collector/inhabitant, gaining admission to view the collection through a personal invitation. In this respect, Groys argues, *The Toilet* not only became the concentrate of *documenta* 9, but actually one of the most convincing metaphors for the contemporary art system.

The defamiliarization of the ordinary dwelling in Kabakov's installation and in Groys' systems-theoretical commentary make it clear that in their normal form, dwellings are anti-exhibitions that function like private collections. The exhibited dwelling is a private collection transferred to the public space—the collectors' museum for non-artists. Thus Flusser's redundancy machine, the world-filter that separates the usual from the unusual, is explicitly put on stage by the installation. Now the decisive aspect is that one can only reach this interior by *entering* it as an observer—a gesture that is the norm in museums and exhibitions, yet is bizarre in the case of dwellings because they serve the purpose of dwelling, that is to say existence in the mode of non-observation and non-amazement. Upon entering their own dwelling, the inhabitant normally ceases all observing behavior, replacing it with a diffuse participation, a decentered state of letting oneself be surrounded and letting oneself go. Dwelling is usually de-thematized because its purpose is to create habituation and triviality. When the dwelling appears in the museum, attention is drawn to the entry into or immersion in the dwelling as such: the emergence of the ordinary dwelling in the museum thematizes the visitor's immersion therein. One would only have to exhibit the inhabitant too in order to realize the total exhibition.

The fact that being-in even becomes presentable as being-immersed in the dwelling milieu, however, marks a threshold in the explication process of sojourning in residences or other ambience-shaping forms. Those who entered *The Toilet* became entangled in a form of pretend dwelling: they took part in an experiment in temporary immersion in something that constituted the primary situation for others—their embedding. The visitor's entry into *The Toilet* was an ontological exit: the shift from the art situation into the non-art situation was brought about in the art itself—or, to speak in Heideggerian terms once again, it was localized [*er-örtert*] in the work.

The installation thus proves the strongest instrument in contemporary art for placing embedding situations as a whole in the space of observation; in this respect, it is also superior to the related arts of stage design and the conception of species-appropriate animal enclosures in zoological gardens.[19] In the present time, the deference they typically show towards the image, which was taken as an invitation for the observer to enter the depicted situation, can—according to Kabakov—only be offered by the installation. It is no exaggeration to describe this process as an upheaval of the usual conditions of showing. While the traditional art exhibition predominantly showed extraordinary objects that were framed or placed on pedestals, the installation presents the embedded and the embedding at the same time: the object and its place are displayed in the same action. It thus creates a situation that can only be received through the observer's entry into the embedding, and *eo ipso*

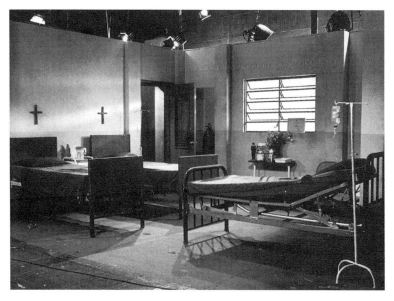

Luis Molina-Pantin, *Scenery II (Living Room)* (1997)

through the dissolution of the frame as well as the leveling of the
pedestal. The de-framing of the work invites the visitor to abandon observation and immerse themselves in the situation. In
this way, both the complicity between the art collection and the
dwelling and the contrast between them are illustrated: while
the average viewer expects the art object to touch them and
move them to dive into the unusual, the exhibited dwelling
promises the state of counter-exception, in which one is at most
baffled that everything is normal—and precisely this brings
about an immersion in banality. One faces an explicated banality
of which one never quite knows whether or not one is allowed
to relax in it. Immersion in explicit banality is the seizedness
that does not feel like seizedness. We are here operating on the
ontological terrain of the twentieth century. Like a philosopher

of the phenomenological school, Kabakov asserts that the truly "exciting journeys" of contemporary art are located "in the realm of the banal."[20] And how could it be otherwise, as revolutions are actually explications of the implicit? It is in this context that we should understand Groys' observation: "The praise of banality is always ambiguous."[21]

As early as 1921, Paul Valéry developed related ideas in a section of his dialogue essay "Eupalinos, Or The Architect," summoning the figures of Socrates and Phaedrus together in a conversation between the dead and letting them debate the principle of immersion or inclusion-in-the-work using the examples of architecture and music. Socrates' reflections on the immersion or enclosure of humans in man-made surroundings begin like a paraphrase of Simmel's dualism of in and opposite:

> It ceases not to spur me on to expatiate upon the arts. [...] A painting, dear Phaedrus, covers a mere surface such as a panel or a wall. [...] But a temple, along with its precincts, or again the interior of this temple, forms for us a sort of complete greatness within which we live. [...] We are, we move, we live inside the work of man! We are caught and mastered within the proportions he has chosen. We cannot escape him.[22]

This reflection emphasizes two aspects at once: firstly, it insists that the encompassing is in this case the sublime, and secondly, it underlines that the surrounding presents an artifice, not a natural environment. Obviously we are not dealing here with the dynamically sublime as described by Kant, which describes nature as a superior power, but with the artificially sublime, whose universal presence enables us to experience the work of humans as if it were a sublime surrounding.

In a single bound Valéry's Socrates leaps into the center of modern aesthetics, confronting himself directly with the riddle of the total work of art. Because this, according to the avant-garde's ambition, incorporates the environment as a whole, the viewer no longer has the possibility to absorb it in the "bourgeois" position of the facing observer. When faced with the temple in which I am standing, being-in-the-world virtually means being-in-the-work-of-another, and more still, being consumed by the artificially great. Is it mere coincidence that this Socrates uses formulations recalling the speech of the former (theater) tent-maker Saint Paul at the Areopagus, who spoke of the God in which we live, move and have our being?[23] Following Valéry, the same could only be said of one other art, namely music:

> Being inside a work of man as fishes are in the sea, being entirely immersed in it, living in it and belonging to it.[24]
>
> Did you not live in a mobile edifice, incessantly renewed and constructed within itself, and entirely dedicated to the transformations of a soul none other than the soul of extension itself? And did not those moments, and their ornaments, and those dances without dancers, and those statues, bodiless and featureless (and yet so delicately outlined), seem to surround you, slave as you were of the general presence of Music? [...] were you not enclosed with it, nay forcibly locked up, like a Pythia in her chamber of vapors?[25]

The explication of the sojourn through the theory of the enclosing work of art thus leads directly to a discussion of aesthetic totalitarianism or voluntary slavery in a man-made environment. In both of these, the connection to the aesthetics of the sublime immediately asserts itself.

> There are then two arts which enclose man in man […] in one material or another, stone or air. […] each of them fills our knowledge and our space with artificial truths.[26]

Modernity—what is it in this respect but an experimental set-up to prove that there is only a single step from the sublime to the banal? When Valéry took down these reflections, cinema—that central medium of the incipient mass culture which would develop into a medium of overwhelming—was still in its infancy, but it was resolutely on the way to providing arrangements for mass-consumable immersive, daydream-mimetic experiences. It was working on ways to enslave the eye and turn the organ of detached observation into one of diving into an almost tactile milieu. At the same time, people at the Weimar Bauhaus had started negotiating an integral access to the surroundings of the everyday sojourn under the title "design." Not only music is demonic territory; spatial design too relates—like architecture before it—to the trivial uncanniness of constantly or occasionally belonging to an environment molded by humans. These arts explicate the sojourn in places with the help of immersion facilities, which are nothing other than enslavement suggestions for the consumers of the total situation. Through them, dwelling is interpreted as a welcome subjugation to the ambience. To the extent that dwellings are installations or installed immersion facilities, they explain existence as a tangible task. The installation is the aesthetic explication of embedding. This is evident in, among other things, the fact that embeddings have a share in the two core values of aesthetic judgment: one refers to embeddings in the pleasant and banal as beautiful or comfortable, and embeddings in the terrible and monstrous as sublime or uncomfortable.

In the course of the twentieth century, this explication of the sojourn could become productive to the extent that immersion design—also known as interior design—was restricted to the habitats of a few individuals, families and cooperatives. The immeasurable and constantly growing popular literature on interior decoration, stylish living, renovating old buildings, kitchen and bathroom luxuries, air conditioning, lighting culture, furniture and holiday home design indicates how widely the message of embedding in the self-chosen micro-milieu reached its audience as the real therapeutic maxim of the second half of the twentieth century. An entire interiors industry stands ready for the arousal and refinement of such perceived needs. It is revealing that the embedding consciousness was abruptly de-politicized after 1945 and withdrawn from sublime collectivist spheres, as if people never again wanted to hear about arts that "enclose man in man." It is as if the collective memory had preserved the intuitive insight that the larger the format of the units formed through immersion in the shared, the more powerfully totalitarian temptation appears. Even if individual artists continue to experiment with sublime dwelling by surrounding themselves with sterility and terror, their exercises are currently restricted to the private format, or a subculture at most.

If we are one day able to reconstruct how the demons of the twentieth century were unleashed, the emphasis will be placed on the attempts of totalitarian leaders to expand the embedding situation from the dwellings to the overall situation of the people and the collective. Classic totalitarianism was the synthesis of dwelling and *Gesamtkunstwerk* decreed from above.[27] The state taken over by a clique imposes itself as a total installation, demanding unreserved immersion of its citizens. The transitional factors in these captures by the whole were the "party" in the East and the army in Germany. They gave rise to the intrusive super-communes that were enacted as ethnic or socialist collectives. After their dissolution, the ordinary totalitarianism of dwelling allied itself with liberal mass culture; now it appears in the tendency to coordinate hardware stores and let all habitat hobbyists choose from the same colorful selections of tiles, shelves, switches and mattresses. The hardware stores are the main suppliers of Western post-totalitarianism. Their message is clear: "Do not dwell with the whole! Settle in your own place, alone or with a few others! But remain recognizable and behave similarly!" Those involved seem to consider it the lesser evil that they are then surrounded by virtually identical furniture wherever they look. The art of installation as developed by Kabakov since his emigration from the USSR, on the other hand, could only be understood as an expression of opposition to Soviet totalitarianism; its attraction still lies in the fact that it feeds ironically off the sublimity of its vanquished foe.

4. Dwellings As Immune Systems

Starting from the analytics of immersion and embedding, one arrives at the transition to a fourth explicatory form for the sojourn that allows human dwelling to be interpreted as the act of settling in a shared and personal immune system. This quasi-hygienic dimension of the original existential spatial formation can best be explained with a statement by Gaston Bachelard that initially sounds implausible, from *The Poetics of Space*: "In its germinal form, therefore, all life is well-being."[28] The thesis becomes acceptable when one ties it to the aim of introducing topology as a basic discipline of immunology. From this perspective, establishing places of successful being-with-oneself is a preventive measure to preempt probable disturbances of well-being in the shared native realm. Bachelard's topophilic ontology should thus be read as laying the foundation for a theory of well-positioned life—or rather, a theory of the sojourn in a eutonic space. The fact that this contradicts critical conformism should not deter us. The offensiveness of a doctrine of happy consciousness amidst the cult of the unhappy one disappears as soon as one admits that a positive theory of the integrous position is one dimension richer than a critical theory which always takes shape as a disturbance in the capacity to share. The theory of the integrous position is concerned with explaining why the well-being of those settled within themselves and in their spaces takes temporal and objective precedence over estrangements. It expounds why one of the expressions of *ressentiment* is usually an place-based envy: someone wishing for another's humiliation wants the place in which the other was integrously with themselves to be devastated.

From here, one arrives at a dynamic definition of the dwelling as a spatial immune system. This interpretation goes one dimension beyond the functions of one's own four walls as a waiting room, redundancy generator, habitus provider and embedding situation. From an immunological perspective, dwelling is a defensive measure by which an area of well-being is isolated from invaders and other bringers of unwell-being. All immune systems claim, without requiring any justification, a right to fend off disturbances. When they become disputed, it is only because the formats of zones of joint immunity are not fixed *a priori* in cultural systems.

Immunity is initially and mostly (albeit under different names) understood as a social fact; one could go so far as to seek the criterion for social cohesion in an automatized collaboration on the project of an immunitary commune. Traditionally the family and the tribal community, and later also the city, the religious community, the people, the party and the corporation sought to gain the status of the operatively effective immune unit, imposing on their members the forms of behavior that met the standard of the immunity they had attained together; since the nineteenth century, the latter has been known as solidarity. Whoever exits the immune and solidary community thus defined is traditionally considered a traitor. The scandal of the modern habitation model is that it addresses above all the isolation and traffic needs of flexibilized individuals and their life partners, who no longer seek their immunitary optimum in imaginary and real collectives or cosmic totalities (and the corresponding ideas of house, people, class and state).[29] In them, the latent semantic layer of the Roman term *immunitas* as non-cooperation on the joint work of the next-highest level is released. So can one already say that modern "society" is a collective of traitors to the collective?

If houses of the modern type are explicatory forms for the immune quality of dwelling areas, is it not to be expected that the dispute over the correct definition of the immune space will manifest itself in the architecture of incipient modernity? Must the houses of our age not become material symbols of the struggle between isolation interests and demands for integration? Are not the dwellings of this time, then, the manifestos for a civilizatory project that puts the reformatting of immunity units and integrous spaces on the agenda? The only certainty is that with dwelling and business conditions heading for the release of solitary individuals, the connection between immunity and community needs to be rethought. Just as life was defined as the success phase of a (biochemical) immune system in the age of "naked life," the term "existence" now describes the success phase of a one-person household.

The Roman legal term *integrum* referred not only to the unimpaired state of natural living conditions protected by law; it also indicated that the intactness of the entire "matter," a household or a public good, was itself already the result of struggles and measures: what seems to exist of its own accord in its self-willed, as it were healthy state, can only be as it is to the extent that it profits from the advantage of resting beneath the sharpened sword of the law. (Using different terminology, this was referred to as the dialectical connection between law and power.) The *integrum* is a composite fact of life or a consistent totality in which things go together like hearth and home, head and heels or man and mouse.[30] Such formulaic pairs evoke the protective spell that guarantees freedom for a gathering; they invoke the shared roof of immunity that shelters a community. The supposed whole is thus the beneficiary of a boundary-drawing, collecting, augmenting power.

From this perspective, the right to the intactness of the domestic sphere is the source area from which the Old European legal culture unfolded. The institution of the authority of the master of the house [*Hausherrenrecht*] is the latent model of all

Ridge turret on the gable of the imperial palace in the Forbidden City, Peking. The figures serve to protect the building from harmful forces.

immunity, provided one interprets it as the authority to decide whether strangers are allowed or forbidden to enter one's own domain, although the own must always be envisaged as an immune-effective compound of the own and the non-own.[31] Immunity implies a preventive power against the harmful power—it interiorizes what it seeks to protect. Legal control over spaces, the heart of civil law, guards unified life as an embodiment of the intertwined activities of several lives that must be allowed to prosper of their own accord wherever they take place—and here "of their own accord" inevitably means within their own boundaries and to the exclusion of others.

Immunity, as local aseity, stems from the practice of good limitation—it is the emergency of inclusive exclusivity. No universalist propaganda can change this: even the One God, whether one calls him Yahweh or Allah or *Pater noster*, is primarily a great expeller. If he does send invitations to everyone, they are formulated in rather forbidding terms; there is not a hint that everything could find its place within him. The father's house may have many rooms, but the high prices ensure that most of them are empty. As the spirit of immunity, he, the One, who formally turns towards all, is actually the quintessence of selectiveness.

Nietzsche had such intuitions in mind when he presented his friends with a suggestion of how to formulate the new categorical imperative after the death of God: be a new beginning yourself under your own steam! Be an original game that plays itself, be a "self-propelling wheel, a first movement, a sacred Yea-saying."[32] Suggestions of this kind implicitly convert theology into immunology—and *eo ipso* the conditional release of finite egotisms. Saying "yes" to oneself draws the outlines of the affirmer's real habitat, acknowledging the fact that no sphere of self-affirmation can be all-encompassing. "And whoever pronounces the I wholesome and sacred and selfishness blessèd, verily, he will also say what he knows."[33] What Nietzsche, that failed searcher for an atmospherically bearable place in the world for himself, admittedly did not explain here was why the empirical place of renovated and legitimized selfishness is usually its dwelling— understood as the immune-spatial self-extension of the human being who remains in self-enclosed happiness. That this space is likely to be small can only seem amazing at first glance.

It was Marshall McLuhan who later divulged the secret of dwelling in modern conditions when he explained it in terms of a completely changed immune situation. Literate man, as the media theorist knew, no longer needed "to see his house [...] as a ritual extension of his body,"[34] for he no longer used the cosmos, its divine foundation and its supposed universal rules like his personal immune system. Thus humans no longer needed to equate the house with the cosmos; world order and lifestyle separated. The media-supported house-dweller of modernity replaced the vague psychosemantic protection systems of religious metaphysics with their specialized, legally and climatically highly insulated dwelling-cells (and also with anonymous solidary systems). The modern dwelling is a place to which uninvited guests almost never have access. "Toxic people" must stay outside, and bad news too if possible. The dwelling becomes an ignoring machine or an integrous defense mechanism: the basic right to ignore the outside world finds its architectural support here.[35]

The dwelling of the modern person is the body extension that provides a specific representation of their habitualized self-concern and backgrounded defensiveness. It renders explicit that living organisms do not exist without ensuring enclosure in themselves. Thus the dwelling gains a share in the core process of modernization: it articulates the emergence—or the becoming-explicit—of immune systems as well as the experimentation of self-referential units with larger associations (in which even the largest will still be far smaller than the "whole"). It materializes the fact that human openness to the world always has a rejection of the world as its complement.

For the immune house, the hour strikes at night when it provides its service as the guardian of sleep. By forming the protective sleeping environment, the house becomes an accomplice to the acosmic needs of its inhabitants. It forms an enclave of worldlessness in the world—a nocturnal *integrum*, secured by its roof and wall, its door and lock. The house, which is the shell of

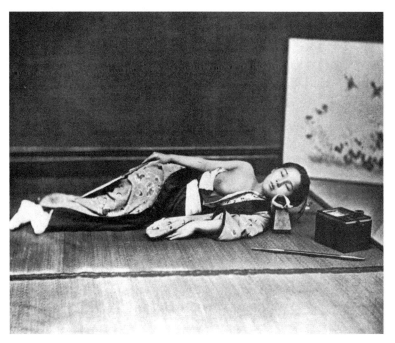

Sleeping Japanese woman on a tatami mat with fan, neck support and *hibachi* hearth (c. 1870)

a sleep, provides the purest evidence of the connection between immunity and the sealing of space. It embodies the unity of geometry and life, a topically realized utopia—a timeless projection of the interior as still-being-inside.[36] It guards the human-forming and regenerating night in which no plans for the diurnal world are made.

The natural transcendence of the night is best articulated in the constructions of bedrooms, which offer themselves as crafted environments of calm. Here the skin-self is expanded into the bed-self—surrounded by a room-self in a house-self. The clearest sleep is that in an acosmic onion. Houselessness is accommodated in the night-house; even the "detached" among us still find an umbrella over our heads here—an umbrella which we do not, for the moment, need to hope for is full of holes and open to the outside.[37] Because nest-formations[38] in the four walls one calls one's own neither serve the sleep of the dead nor postulate an ascent to heaven, the house that provides nocturnal immunity has no requirements of size. It demands neither the Pharaohs' construction of pyramids nor the erection of cathedrals. Perhaps the "small house" which some contemporary architects strive for[39] is above all an explicatory form for nightly being-with-oneself—in this, it is architecture's answer for historical people to the ahistorical hut. In the center of the small, the acosmic, the immunitary house stands the bed—that simple technical sleeping aid which has contributed more than anything else to the humanization of nights. There is much to suggest that in the "final analysis," dwelling should be interpreted as epitomizing the enablement of sleep with oneself. In this sense, the bed is the center of the world.[40] The bedroom of real humans is not what Hegel calls "a crystal in which a dead man dwells,"[41] nor is it a Gothic tree of life that rises to attain some "organic Excelsior";[42] it is the shell of acosmism with a human format. Among the homeless, one can observe how the need for sleeping space approaches the minimum; a cardboard box over the sleeper's head can suffice to mark their claim to a space from which they can ban. The most famous of all homeless persons is reported to have said: "Foxes have holes and birds of the air have nests, but the Son of Man has nowhere to lay his head,"[43] What does that mean? Whoever is borne by spheric hyperimmunity (*et non sum solus, quia Pater mecum est*)[44] can even dispense with the simplest sleeping comfort of the worldlings; he demands no bed of his own, but a paradisaic blanket.

Cardboard boxes as bedrooms: homeless people in the 1980s

Where the house acts as a provider of shelter for the night, the primal scene of the *integrum* is fulfilled. Now it transpires that worldlessness is a local attribute. Every sleep is the sleep of some person; every absence of mind is the absence of a limited mind from a section of the world. There is no sleep of the world, for the world has no eyes that it could close in its totality—any more than there is a world-house in which everything is with itself.[45] The central hyperbole of classical metaphysics, namely the assertion that the cosmos is a house, became obsolete with the transition to explicit dwelling. One can now see that the metaphysical reflex of seeking immunity in the encompassing was a waste that only the poorest, the unhoused and uninsured of antiquity and the Middle Ages, could afford. The powerless live in hyperboles, the strong fill out territories and leave them again. Every dwelling, as an outpost of a finite ability to live, creates exclusivity; every isolated self-affirmation produces communication breakdowns and denial of one's environment. That is its affirmative virtue, its "selfishness,"[46] and at once its normal finding. The crisis of the world soul enters the abodes. Even God, if he is biased towards life and not an empty mask of totality, cannot incorporate everything. These words are hard for those who romanticize de-restriction. Who can hear them?

5. The Dwelling Machine, or: The Mobilized Spatial Self

This provides access to the fifth level of the explication of the sojourn through modern construction technology: the engineer's definition of the dwelling as a *dwelling machine*. This ominous term, which Le Corbusier threw into the discussion on architectural reform in the 1920s, provides the key concept for a contemporary explication of habitation activity among solitary city-dwellers and mobilized small families. No defamation of the phrase by sentimental architectural critics can change this. It collects the technical models corresponding to the state of the art in the matters of being-with-oneself, time administration, habitus development, climate design, immunization, ignorance management, self-completion and co-isolation; it is the condensation of the twentieth century's attack on the traditional forms of sedentary torpor. Le Corbusier's programmatic demand of 1922 draws the horizon of renewal: "The first obligation of architecture, in an era of renewal, is [...] a constitutive revision of the elements of the house."[47] For him, the most important step on the way to the *new mind* was to create "the state of mind for living in mass-production housing."[48] The epoch-making formulation can be found in a text from the early 1920s: "a house like an automobile, conceived and built out like a bus or a ship's cabin. [...] We must [...] look upon the house as a machine for living in or as a tool."[49]

The revolt of the traditionalists against the analytically advanced concept of architecture as the provision of mobile containers for human sojourns was not long in coming: in 1927, in response to Le Corbusier's contribution to the Stuttgart construction exhibition at the Weissenhof Estate, the critic Edgar Wedepohl stated that while living in such a "nomad's tent made of iron and concrete" might be attractive for intellectuals, one should not allow this faction to impose its needs on society as a whole, which will rightly continue to entertain more dignified expectations about its dwellings. Houses like the dwelling machine, he argued, are "not grown together heavily and solidly with the earth [...] not rooted to the soil."[50]

Anyone looking for proof that aversions can sometimes converge with insights would find it in a very concrete form here. The concept of the dwelling machine has an inherent program, namely to dissolve the seemingly immemorial alliance between the house and sedentarism and to liberate the inhabited space in relation to the environment. At times, it follows on very consciously from the prehistoric form of the nomad tent, which was only loosely tied to its setting. (The suspicion of the conventionally domestic towards the tent house is surpassed only by the aversion of conservative aestheticians towards modern architecture's claims to the status of art the moment they sense a transformation of buildings into giant sculptures.) What Rudolf Arnheim called the "dignified immobility"[51] in conventional architecture now falls prey to the imperative of facilitated relocation. In the course of explication, the moment arrives when the

Yurt encampment of Mongolian nomads (1997)

Steven Brower, *U-town* (1998)

house ceases to be merely the station where mortals wait for the product to ripen or the project to gather steam: now the house itself must become the vehicle that, as Bloch says, stands "keen to depart."[52] The principle of reversibility becomes part of the construction of residences.

The dwelling machine is unmistakably a concession of the house, that symbol of persistence, to the "completely dynamic character of the world" in the age of money. Just as, according to Simmel, the meaning of money is that it is "given away," that of the dwelling machine is that it prepares the move, the circulation of the inhabitant. By harboring them here, it reminds them of the imminent departure to a different location, a different parking space, a different climate option. Like money, the dwelling machine "is, at it were, an *actus purus*," in "continuous self-alienation from any given point and thus [...] the antithesis and direct denial of all being-for-itself."[53] The postmodern maxim of stability through liquidity is already perfectly articulated in the concept of the *machine à habiter*.

With the vehicle-house, the symmetry between building up and dismantling is elevated to a pragmatic ideal. From this point on, the building presents itself as a hypothesis. Where it is constructed at the level of art, it articulates the ambition to attain a perfect manifestation of provisionality—even if the form appears definitive, the localization remains revocable. In such spaces, the inhabitant can become a hitchhiker with themselves; the owner is a passenger who makes the residence elegant. The décor is nothing (because, in keeping with the mindset, it is settled and comfortable), the design is everything. The objection that it is not firmly grown together with the earth adequately explains the novelty of the hybrid vehicle-house: the fact that it stands there indicates not a union with the earth, but rather parking on a sealed surface. El Lissitzky programmatically articulated the anti-grave tendency of the new approach to construction in his architecture-theoretical writings:

> One of our utopian ideas is the desire to overcome the limitations of the substructure, the earthbound. […] [this] calls for the conquest of gravity as such. It demands floating structures, a physical-dynamic architecture.[54]

To illustrate these theses he referred to his project *Cloud Iron* (1925), as well as Leonidov's plan for a Lenin Institute in Moscow whose core—alongside the library skyscraper for 15 million books—was to consist of a giant floating spherical auditorium for 4,000 people.[55] The New Human Being is created through Soviet power plus levitation. Le Corbusier's frequent allusions to the automobile and the ocean liner—including the futuristic claim that the Parthenon and perfect vehicle bodies are of equal value—not only testify to the love of geometry and the fascination by Platonic abstractions often encountered among the pioneers of the new architecture; they imply an accurate insight into the destiny of the new houses as vehicles. Accordingly, the properties built on should be viewed above all as car parks— or sea moles (a conception that would later become especially manifest in large housing complexes, where apartments were arranged on top of one another like stored container units in vertical garages or stacked ship's cabins, not always in agreement with the predominantly sedentary needs of residents who could not relate to the equation of parking and dwelling). If one were seeking a generic term applying both to the new type

El Lissitzky, *Cloud Iron* (1925)

of apartment and the corresponding vehicles, one would arrive at the word "sociomobile"[56]—people's car and group container from a single source.

For the new explicatory form for dwelling, the liaison with the concept of the vehicle and the transportable container became a momentous one not least because both analogues cause a regression to the single-story structure—perhaps not by necessity, but for pragmatic reasons. Vehicles have neither a foundation nor storage, while containers have no basement. The *machine à habiter* thus rejects the imposition of understanding dwelling in terms of a sojourn in a house, that is to say a multi-story structure. The analytically prepared autonomous housing unit appears—almost dogmatically—as a form of stackable bungalow in which the living movements of the dwellers are meant to take place exclusively horizontally (leaving aside various

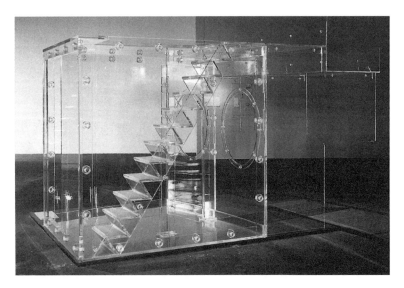

Carsten Höller, *Commune House* (2001)

ambitious projects for high one-room apartments with a gallery). One can understand, therefore, why a house-lover like Bachelard lamented the modern single-story apartment as an aberration with far-reaching psychological consequences. If the housing of humans is genuinely meant to translate the "form" of their souls, their accommodation in single-story units is the beginning of the end of the vertically complex soul. For can the soul be "extended" ("knows nothing about it") as long as it has to content itself with rented apartments? One may consider Bachelard's ideas an expression of bourgeois nostalgias, but he is at least in the company of Sigmund Freud, for whom the psyche, in topological terms, was a three-story structure. What will become of the inner crypts if the contemporaries of the Bauhaus and bungalow culture no longer have any idea about closets in basements that might have skeletons in them?[57] It will perhaps be of some interest for the future fates of psychoanalysis how humans deal with the concept of the unconscious when they are no longer familiar with the experience of a house with a basement and an attic.

The further development of the motif "dwelling machine" in the twentieth century soon made it clear how the formula that remained essentially rhetorical for Le Corbusier led to precise materializations at numerous nodal points of contemporary accommodation practice.[58] Its early pinnacle of engineering appears in the young Buckminster Fuller's sketches for his *Dymaxion House* of 1927, which was in fact conceived as the first authentic machine for the sojourn in flat space. At Fuller's legendary lecture before the Architectural League of New York in June 1929, the model of this new form of house was presented by the League's chairman, Harvey W. Corbett, as the result of unprejudiced thought "on the proper kind of machine to adequately serve for living purposes."[59] It hinted at the possibility "that we will have houses to live in very much as we have automobiles to ride in," a machine "with a replacement value, a machine which can be set down practically in any location."[60] "After you have lived in one of these houses for a couple of years and you want to take a trip to Europe, why, you just send word to the laundry; they call for it, take it back, wash it and clean it up, iron it out, set it up again; and when you are back, you are in a new house."[61]

The engineer's house follows the principle of assembly: it is no longer constructed by builders, but rather set up by assemblers. Nor is it dwelt in, in the European sense; the house is filled with a sojourn option. As a dwelling machine, it is at once a house-moving machine—and demonstrates independence from context. It thus refutes the neo-ontological thesis that a house forms an

R. Buckminster Fuller in front of the second model of the Dymaxion House in 1929

artificial midpoint between humans and nature with an intrinsic reconciling effect.[62] The mobilized house is no more interested in reconciling its inhabitants with the environment than an automobile is interested in reconciling the driver with the road. Where there was nature, there would now be infrastructure.

Fuller begins his lecture by criticizing his time ("I have come upon the thought that housing was responsible for practically all our ills";[63] "In housing today I feel that women are very much more enslaved than were men in the Roman galleys")[64] and ends it by praising standardization and mass production-oriented thought, indeed with the apotheosis of mobility: It is now a matter of consistently lifting the house off the ground. The new building serving the credible improvisation of a habitat for mobile humans should be suspended around a central mast—disabling traditional structural engineering and abandoning the cubic traditions with their dogmatically perpendicular approach to walls, windows and doors. The floating house would only be connected to the earth through the planting of the mast, without—despite its light weight—having to sacrifice resilience against storms and earthquakes. (Let us note that in his Buenos Aires lectures four months later, in October 1929, Le Corbusier expressly commended a house that is elevated from the earth and placed on stilts [*pilotis*], the *boîte en l'air*;[65] a decade earlier, the Russian poet Velimir Khlebnikov, who died in 1922, had demanded in his radically constructivist *Proposals*: "Build apartment houses in the form of steel frameworks, into which could be inserted transportable glass dwelling units.")[66]

Fuller's project house was to derive its stability from a new form of framework integrated mainly through tensile strains—an early pointer to the concept of tensegrities, with which Fuller became the founder of a trans-classical structural engineering. Extremely resilient piano wire would be used to anchor the loads, while metal pipes and tubes subject to air pressure would provide additional bracing. Air-filled floors damp sound and receive falling clothes more gently. Doors of inflatable balloon silk are opened and closed by pneumatic mechanisms. There are no more hidden storage spaces, and partitions conveying the message that none should pass through are absent. The indoor movements of the residents are categorized and ergonomically optimized; every step and hand movement in this thoroughly calculated environment recognizes the need of Dymaxion subjects for efficiency and conservation of energy.

Furthermore, the house's casual way of standing and its loose aggregation with analogous constructs turn it into an argument for the dissolution of the old collectivizing city, and more still: a

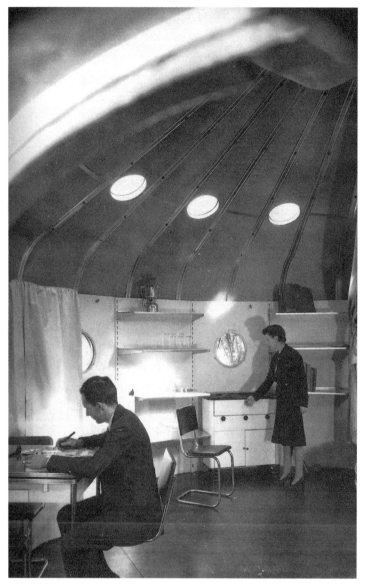

Dymaxion Deployment Unit (DDU) in 1940, kitchen: model of emergency residence in expectation of bombardment of British cities

beacon of hope for the decentralization of the community, the de-dogmatizing of society, and not least for the self-tuition of the Dymaxion children, that first generation of visitors from the future who have not been "don'ted."[67] (It is impossible to overlook the influence of Frank Lloyd Wright here.) In addition, the new house recommends itself as a machine for the emancipation of the housewife. While the conventional dwelling was a true galley bench and an inescapable stress environment for her, the new one turns itself into a comprehensive technical home help; internally and externally, it is geared towards relief. Emancipation rhymes with levitation; both can be ascertained on the scales. "The total weight of this building figures up to six thousand pounds. The price of the materials used figures at present figures at present quotations about fifty cents a pound."[68]

Through its alliance with mobility, the new way of dwelling according to Fuller must lead to a beneficial rejection of the traditional psychology of the urban "masses." The Dymaxion House is meant to become the traffic medium of a human being who has abandoned the last relics of European feudalism, to the extent that they clung to the dogmatism of foundations and faith in the heaviness of walls. The new style of dwelling would thus grow into a means of "demand for motion."[69] (A generation later, in *On the Road*, Kerouac would formulate that "our one and noble function of the time" was to "*move.*")[70] In a time when barely 20 million automobiles were on American roads, Fuller dreamed of covering the country with up to 100 million Dymaxion Houses. He later went on record as saying that he had never believed in the realization of his model.

The link between the house and the vehicle in Buckminster Fuller's habitat utopia is not limited to virtues of mobility. In reality, the Dymaxion concept already implies the real-life trend towards the suburbanization of cities, without with modern mass consumer society is hard to imagine, especially in its American form. Since the 1930s, after all, the primary sites of consumption or economy-stimulating feeding cells in envy-driven mass culture have been single-family households in the suburbs, which could only be connected to shopping centers through motorization. Fuller's model thus prophesied, albeit in an intelligently defamiliarized form, precisely the domestic and lifestyle trends that were starting to establish themselves in his time anyway—he promoted a house that was entirely conceived as a comfort machine, and whose chief virtue was to keep their residents' hands free for consumption. Fuller's variety of utopianism is one of the manifold manifestations of that "conspiracy against the city" which, according to the diagnosis of the urbanist Richard Plunz at Columbia University, shaped the fate of cities after the world economic crisis and its cessation with the New Deal.[71]

The history of construction forms in the twentieth century now shows that the interpretation of the house as a vehicle did not manage to develop along the path opened by Buckminster Fuller's high-tech suspended container. Where the residence and the vehicle combined effectively, this resulted on the one hand in camper vans as integrated hybrids of minibuses and furnished containers, or trailers drawn by automobiles; and on the other hand, diverse subcultures of mobile homes formed (especially in the USA, based on prototypes from the mid-nineteenth century),[72] complete houses that are raised from their foundations and can be brought on trucks to new locations where, after brief installation work to connect them to electricity, water, sewer systems and telecommunications, they immediately become autonomous residential units once more. The mobile house defines itself as a wandering architectural monad that has become congenial to its inhabitant, in that house and owner alike invoke the freedom to choose their context. It constitutes a deterritorialized container that neither demands nor tolerates any substantial neighborhoods. Even coexistence does not escape explication: the commune and the environment can be separated in the same manner as sexuality and procreation. The concept of closeness emancipates itself from its trivial spatial interpretation—long before the Internet created a new mode of long-distance neighborhoods.[73] When a tornado destroys a trailer park in Florida or Oklahoma, the television footage sometimes includes sequences of home-owners standing next to the ruins of their houses, like drivers of automobiles who have found themselves caught in a pile-up on a highway.

In the shadow of the avant-garde, the explication of dwelling via analogies with the vehicle took place a second time, as it were—in a space devoid of theory and art: poverty analyzes the elementary structures of dwelling in its own way. In a world in which fleeing and deportation became mass phenomena, the improvisation of provisional housing had to be attempted on a large scale. This led to the world of camps, which any review of the twentieth century will have to treat as one of its central symptoms. They are the harmful compromise between involuntary mobility and forced immobilization. And yet: even in its barrack minimalism, this form of accommodation bows to the anthropological imperative of dwelling. Despite all their different degrees of hardship, the worlds of camps are comparable as places for herding "superfluous humans" together, where reductions of dwelling culture to elementary and highly provisional resources are tried out. It transpires here that the reduction of living space to an almost empty container need not be an aesthetic finesse. Flusser's shocking note "people lived at Auschwitz" is a descriptive statement; it articulates an extreme of the sojourn in a dwelling machine that serves as a waiting room for death. Just as quality-less existential time was explicated in the 1920s as "Being-towards-death," the quality-less sojourn-in-something has been explicated since the 1940s as being-in-the-container.

6. Address Management, End User Location, Climate Regulation

Through the fact that "dwelling" in a camp deprives the inmates of a free choice of location and eliminates the autonomous "person," it brings out a further dimension of explicated sojourn: by affirming existence in a particular place, dwelling defines itself and unfolds as residing. Choosing a residence means committing oneself to maintaining one address; someone with an address presents themselves as a sender and makes themselves available as a recipient. In both aspects, the modern dweller invests a part of their energies in their domicile as a business location. In so doing, the current address owner continues a habitus of the Old European aristocracy, which was willing to pay almost any price for the privilege of residence. Brought up in jealous attentiveness to designations of origin and the aura of names, it was always directly evident to the nobles that the address was the message. Even under capitalist premises, the assertion of place and rank by exhibiting an address has remained a worthwhile business goal, in so far as it plays the joker among the values of mobilized society—accessibility, in both its active and passive forms.[74]

The modern dwelling is defined as an address if it makes its inhabitants accessible to services, deliveries and networks, and gives them the means to act as senders of assignments and messages. The domicile is a primary investment with which the actors of the business world demonstrate their commercial capability and social pretention. As investment in a social location, the address is a part of fixed capital. The more clearly the residential value of dwelling transpires, the more those offering housing facilities have reason to promote their objects in terms of their marketability. The highest premiums are on housing units that combine all the advantages of privacy with all options for access. Where this is offered, the living residence is at once a perfectly insulated egosphere and an easily accessible point in the network of manifold online communities. It is an interface for the darkening of the outside world and for admission to reality on demand. Regarding such dispositions, the clever phrase "the intelligent house" is more than an advertising slogan. Intelligence is the ability to navigate a space of chances. Dwelling explicated in terms of intelligence turns the dwelling into an agency: a location and interface for agents, acting artificial programs that interact with human end consumers.[75]

Bill Gates called his residential project *Cyberhome*, near Seattle, an "(almost) omniscient house."[76] Made of glass, wood and silicon, it was intended to serve as a relaxation machine for him and his wife, equipping their shared surroundings with a maximum of "possibilities for home-based entertainment." "Intelligent toys" turn the house into an experience-oriented environment. Anyone walking through the Gates villa is meant to move within an electronic shell that positions them at all times and embeds them in a personalized aura of light, music and operative options. The house always knows everything it needs to know about the visitor in order to be at their service. Like a digital submarine, it is ready day and night to play all songs whose titles contain the word "yellow" at the visitor's request. Embedded in the walls are monitors that allow the viewer to request any picture from the archive of world history for display. "Access is central to the new [...] living arrangements."[77]

Let us note that post-agrarian, no longer handicraft- and guild-based living conditions are almost universally characterized (at least for the employed part of a household) by being based on a spatial separation of workplace and dwelling. This reveals a further aspect of explicated dwelling through which it is defined specifically as non-work. In the terminology of political economy, the activities of this area were described as "reproduction of the commodity of labor power." The sociology of event society, on the other hand, emphasizes contemporary dwelling as a medium for the representation and regeneration of identity—and equally the role of the apartment as a base camp for raids in the event scene. The dwelling qualifies ever more unmistakably as the place in which individuals pursue their vocation of self-realization in pure immanence. "Self-realization" is a code word for self-end use. The most meaningful result of life defines itself here as intensified flow of experiences—that is, an accumulation and wastage of enjoyable differences in passing time. Dwellings are locations for experiential entrepreneurs, that is to say "wish machines that maximize sensations per time unit."[78]

Modern construction culture, finally, ensured that the almost insubstantial physical content of all buildings, the encapsulated

Shigeru Ban, *Curtain Wall House* (1995)

air, could be developed into a theme *sui generis*. In its portrayal here, it is the last aspect of modernity's explicated culture of dwelling. One can venture the thesis—against the background of the reflections on hothouses above[79]—that all contemporary dwellings not only *have* air conditioning (in our climes via central heating, and in more southern regions also in the form of air cooling systems); they *are* in fact air conditioning systems. One notices that the air conditioning phenomenon has so far eluded the attention of cultural historians and sociologists. There are only sporadic references to the outstanding significance of the cooling of dwelling and working spaces for the civilizatory development of warmer and hot geographical zones. The historian David S. Landes emphatically attributes the population shifts in the USA towards the south and the location of industries in those regions to the extensive use of air conditioning.[80] Here one is reminded of Hegel's pointed remark about the unusability of natural air for human purposes.[81] As far as the architects of modernity are concerned, they not only became aware of their responsibility for the psychosocial comfort of a housing unit—one recalls Le Corbusier's concept of "psychic ventilation"—but also increasingly understood that in addition to the visible architectural structure, their product also had an atmospheric reality with an intrinsic value. The true dwelling space is an air sculpture traversed by its inhabitants like a breathable installation. In this respect, more than a few of the great twentieth-century architects profited from the turn of their art towards a macrosculptural way of thinking.[82] To the extent that buildings are thought of as spatial-plastic entities once more, there is a keener sense of the cavities (*les creux*) as autonomous realities demanding to be shaped. And just as the hothouses since the nineteenth century have been built purely for the sake of the climate that is meant to exist inside them, a number of the most important masters of spatial production in the twentieth converted to an explicit air and climate art.

Regarding the housing practices of the previous century, one is struck by the fact that the practical definition of the dwelling

Guillaume Bijl, *Heating Stand* (1990)

machine—if only for numerical reasons—had to become far more a matter for tinkerers than architects. The most large-scale implantation of *machines à habiter* took place, if one temporarily leaves aside centralistically controlled housing estates in socialism, in the inflationarily growing slums on the outskirts of capital cities in the post-1950 "Third World," where gigantic additive-amorphous, spread-out villages grew, close to an architectural zero point—improvisations of chance found materials like tin, cardboard, straw, mud and wood, often without access to the minimum of urban services such electricity and sewerage, home-made containers for coping with a constant state of emergency, testaments to the indestructible human need to dwell and for the archetypal creativity with which, even under the most precarious conditions, the longing for the hut, this architectural articulation of the demand for an interior, manifests itself. Such forms show that the modern association of domesticity and movement does not come about only in the context of vehicles. More than this, it is fleeing that forces humans constantly to invent new compromises between housed and mobile states. The inhibited flight of individuals creates states in which the Neolithic equation of dwelling and waiting comes back into effect in unexpected fashion. If the speculatively overstrained notion of the "end of history" is empirically significant any-where, it is with reference to these phenomena. Whoever finds themselves in the tent cities, favelas or *bidonvilles* lives in the near-impossibility of having a project or a past that demands a future. At these stations for disoriented and disinherited people, however, the old agricultural balance between patience and expectation has been destroyed; all that remains is the diffuse hope for the arrival of outside help, without any prospect of a product that ripens of its own accord and frees individuals to exist in their own temporality.

B. Cell-Building, Egospheres, Self-Containers:
The Explication of Co-Isolated Existence via the Apartment

> But a time is coming, and has come, when you
> will be scattered, each to his own home.
> — John 16:32

Anyone who studies the history of recent architecture in its connection to mediatized society's forms of life will immediately recognize that the two most successful architectural innovations of the twentieth century, the apartment[83] and the sports stadium, are directly related to the two most widespread socio-psychological tendencies of the period: the creation of solitary dwellers via individualizing housing and media techniques, and the concentration of uniformly aroused masses via organized events in large-scale, fascinogenic edifices. For the moment, I will not dwell on the fact that the affective and imaginary synthesis of modern "society" occurs more through the mass media—that is, the telecommunicative integration of non-gathered persons— than through actual physical assembly, while the operative synthesis is regulated via market relationships.

1. Cell and World Bubble

The modern apartment—which is also referred to in the relevant literature as the "one-room apartment" (or, more sophisticatedly, the "one-space apartment")[84]—materializes the tendency towards the formation of cells, which one can identify as the architectural and topological analogue of the individualism of modern society. For the interpretation of the individualistic endeavors, I will content myself for now with an observation that Gabriel Tarde already made in the 1880s: "In reality, the civilized man of today is inclined to do without the assistance of his fellow."[85] As one can see from the development of apartment construction, nothing is more dependent on suppositions than the ostensibly natural expectation that one person requires at least one room, or that there should be one housing unit per capita. Just as Soviet modernism condensed itself in the myth of the commune, which was supposed to act as the matrix for the New Human Being who would be fit for the collective, the concentration of Western modernism is found in the myth of the apartment, where the released individual, flexibilized in the capital stream, devotes itself to the cultivation of its self-relationships.

The apartment is defined here as a nuclear or elementary egospheric form—and consequently as the cellular world-bubble whose mass repetition produces the individualistic foams. This definition is not tied to any moral value judgment; it makes no concessions to the Catholic or neoconservative critiques of our time, which, aside from pointing out the current trend towards a culture of singles, contain nothing that goes beyond the stereotypes of Augustine's invective against egotism and indifference. The only novelty is the barbed observation that the modern egotist is a subscriber to the *Daily Me*. I also keep my distance when such concepts as the "spatial subsistence minimum" are introduced—almost every time one encounters some reference to a minimum, it is a misnomer for the concept of the habitat cell or the "lifeworld" atom, whose definition is the central passion in modern reflections on habitation.

To approach the phenomenon of the apartment, one must perceive its close connection to the principle of the series, without which the transition of construction (and production) into the era of mass fabrication and prefabrication would have been inconceivable.[86] Just as, according to El Lissitzky, constructivism is the interchange station between painting and architecture,[87] serialism is that between elementarism and social utopianism. It is serialism, which regulates the relationship between the part and the whole through precise standardization, enabling decentral production and central assembly, that holds the key to the relationship between the individual cell and the cell formation which is characteristic of modernity. Just as the working-out of the cell takes into account the spirit of analysis by returning to the elementary level, building houses on the basis of such elements constitutes a combinatorics, or rather a form of "organic construction"—with the goal of producing architecturally, urbanistically and economically sustainable ensembles of modules. The great variety of forms with which modern architects responded to the provocation of modular building shows that the stacking of numerous cellular units in a single architectural complex was always intended as more than a fortuitous or mechanical addition of elementary units. A path with many branches leads from Le Corbusier's plans for a light-flooded villa in 1922, and also for cruciform (1925), star-shaped (1933) and rhomboid (1938) skyscrapers, to the sculptural cell pile-ups in building block-like structures, for example those that made the Nakagin Capsule Tower in Tokyo, built in 1972 by the Japanese architect Kisho Kurokawa, famous. The vertical agglomeration of capsule units is here expanded into an aesthetic phenomenon in its own right. Other architects have piled up housing modules in

Kisho Kurokawa, Nakagin Capsule Tower, Tokyo (1972)

mushroom- or tree-like structures. The 60-story twin towers of the Marina City apartment houses in Chicago, with their distinctively arched balconies, extend upwards from blossom-shaped ground plans. Although the larger complexes are by necessity

Marina City, Chicago

formed through the addition of elementary units, and sometimes convey the impression of being mere stacks, they always have certain macrosculptural qualities—the syntax of the apartment house forbids the mere stacking of units in any case, for without the connections created by corridors, stairs, elevators and conduit systems, they would be neither functional nor walkable.

The apartment as a dwelling-cell constitutes the nuclear level in the field of habitat conditions: just as the live cell in an organism embodies both the biological atom and the generative principle (Swammerdam in the seventeenth century: *Omne vivum e vivo*; Virchow in the nineteenth: *Omnis cellula e cellula*), modern apartment construction brings out the habitat atom— the one-space apartment with its solitary inhabitant as the cellular core of a private world bubble. Through recourse to the cellular unit, the livable space itself is brought down to its elementary form. One could, to modify a term used by Gottfried Semper, call this the "spatial individual" [*Raumesindividuum*].[88] It is no coincidence that apartment architecture developed in parallel with the phenomenology of Husserl and Heidegger: both areas dealt with the anchoring of the circumspect individual in a world milieu that had been made radically explicit. Existence in a one-person apartment is nothing other than a single case of being-in-the-world, or the re-embedding, after its specific isolation, of the subject in its "lifeworld" at a spatio-temporally concrete address. The new consciousness of dwelling among architects and the specified awareness of the world-based premises of embedded existence among philosophers are simultaneous and current antidotes to the acquired situational blindness of the Old European culture of rationality.

The renewed attempt to bring the microbiological concept of the cell closer to the architectural one in modernity did not, furthermore, occur without a certain historical legitimacy: when the British physicist Robert Hooke introduced the biological concept of the cell in his work *Micrographia* (1665) in order to

Suspended washing machines

describe the dense arrangement of delimited cavities in a piece of cork, he had drawn inspiration from its parallels to the rows of monks' cells in a monastery. With the arrival of modern architecture at the idea of the ideal-typically reduced housing unit, the

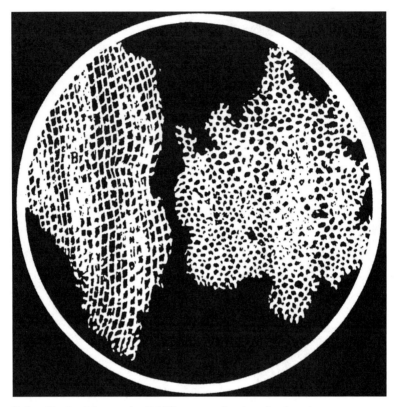

Robert Hooke, *Micrographia* (1665): a piece of cork under the microscope

concept of the cell returned to its point of departure after its productive exile in the realm of microbiology—with the added value of analytical precision and constructive mobility. The emancipated dwelling-cell formulates a concept of the minimum architectural and sanitary conditions for autonomy that must be given before the fact of being able to live alone can be considered formally evident. Thus a complete apartment must include the means for a circadian cycle of self-care: somewhere to sleep, a bathroom, a toilet, cooking facilities, a dining table, a clothes depot, air conditioning and/or heating, electricity, a letterbox, a telephone, media cables or antennas—and here, as demonstrated by the bathroom as a "wet cell," the habitat cell is itself composed of cellular units.

The individual bubble in the dwelling-foam forms a container for the self-relationships of the inhabitant, who settles into their housing unit as the consumer of a primary comfort: the vital capsule of their living quarters serves as the scene of their self-coupling, the operational space for their self-care, and as an immune system in a contamination-rich field of "connected isolations," also known as neighborhoods.[89] In these respects, the apartment forms a material retracing of the surreal container function I have described elsewhere as the autogenous vessel.[90]

The aphrogenic character of the apartment results (in the realm of actually realized architecture) from the fact that the "one-space apartment" is usually found in houses which are arranged as aggregates of standardized housing units according to an overarching plan. The apartment house (or *unité d'habitation*) constitutes a social space-crystal or a rigid foam body, in which a multitude of units are stacked over and next to one another—and these forms share the principle of co-isolation, that is to say spatial separation through shared walls, with the unstable foams. This leads to a neighborly problem typical of older types of apartment house: insufficient acoustic isolation, which contradicts the dwelling-cell's illusion of autonomy in the most unwelcome fashion. As a co-isolator, the shared wall is responsible for the frequent lack of adequate acoustic immunity it gives those isolated from one another. In social foam, the island effect claimed for itself by each individual cell is undermined by the density of the cell stacking; unwelcome

Pruitt-Igoe before its demolition in 1972

communications are the result of this. Starting from this observation, more recent apartment house architecture has
recognized the need to minimize the coexistential stress between
"connected isolation" units. Where this problem is not solved,
apartment houses often transpire as breeding grounds for social
pathologies, which Le Corbusier once encapsulated *ex negativo*
when he observed that a building requires "psychic ventilation."
An architecturally successful housing unit not only represents a
portion of air that has been built around, but also a psychosocial immune system that can regulate its degree of insulation
from the outside as required. "Psychic ventilation" implies that
a hint of communitarian animation enters the isolated immune
units. The degree to which this can be absent is demonstrated by
the notorious satellite towns from the post-war era, which tended
both to make their inhabitants defenseless and pyschosocially

suffocate them. The infamous demolitions of apartment blocks in Pruitt-Igoe in the center of St. Louis on July 15, 1972—a date taken by the architecture historian Jencks as the zero hour of postmodernism—should be understood first and foremost as vulgar modernism's declaration of immunological bankruptcy in architecture.

The fact that the massive accumulation of cellular units has far-reaching sociological, or rather socio-morphological implications, was already observed in the nineteenth century. In a well-known passage of his 1852 study *The Eighteenth Brumaire of Louis Bonaparte*, Karl Marx pinpointed the politico-economic foundation of Napoleon's rule when he emphasized that with his popular dictatorship, Bonaparte represented a class and its still inadequately articulated needs, namely "the most numerous in the commonweal of France—the Allotment Farmer."[91] What Marx emphasizes about this "immense mass whose individual members live in identical conditions, without, however, entering into manifold relations with one another,"[92] is above all its fragmented state, and the inability to infer a common interest from the similarity of their situation:

> Their method of production isolates them from one another, instead of drawing them into mutual intercourse. Their isolation is promoted by the poor means of communication in France, together with the poverty of the farmers themselves. [...] Every single farmer family is almost self-sufficient [...].
>
> We have the allotted patch of land, the farmer and his family; alongside of that another allotted path of land, another farmer and another family. A bunch of these makes up a village; a bunch of villages makes up a Departement. Thus the

large mass of the French nation is constituted by the simple addition of equal magnitudes—much as a bag with potatoes constitutes a potato bag.[93]

The context makes it clear that Marx, by viewing the uniform units of allotment farming multiplicities grouped together as an additively formed collective, is arguing here as a foam phenomenologist *avant la lettre*—the references to village, *departement* and potato bag provide unmistakably aphrological metaphors for structurally weak cellular agglomerations. They are meant to clarify and explain the fact that a structure of this kind is *tel quel* unable to display any partiality or class subjectivity—in his opinion, only a "revolutionary" class imbued with the will to power would be in a position to satisfy its own political and immunitary interests. These reflections unmistakably echo Hegel's structural idea, even though the author of the *Elements of the Philosophy of Right* had scoffed at the notion that a "mere atomistic heap of individuals" (§273) could arrive at a legally ordered existence, let alone achieve a legal constitution. A "heap" imbued with class consciousness would nonetheless be at least halfway along the path to a reasonable constitution. The author of *The Eighteenth Brumaire* had no illusions about the length of this path; he casts a hard look at the circumstances that create opacity and isolation within each individual unit of the allotment universe:

> The allotment system has transformed the mass of the French nation into troglodytes. Sixteen million farmers (women and children included) house in hovels most of which have only one opening, some two, and the few most favored ones three. Windows are to a house what the five senses are to the head.[94]

If there was cause to assert the "idiocy of rural life," then in *material* terms because of the small number of openings (partly due to the French window tax) in the farmers' shacks and in *formal* terms because of the isolations, which prevent the inhabitants of the allotment from making the transition from the mode of being of a class in itself to a class for itself. The absence of windows stands for a lack of communication, enlightenment and solidarity. From this perspective, the allotment farmers constitute a para-proletariat; like the industrial proletariat, they see themselves faced with the talk of progressing from the isolated and apolitical to the organized, politically virulent mode of existence. This is tantamount to the program of transforming the "potato bag" into the party—or, urbanistically speaking, the demand to convert the agglomeration of the self-enclosed hovels into a communicatively ventilated national workers' settlement, indeed a class-encompassing international commune. Where there were once hovels, there would now arise political movements, militant trade unions, interest-conscious class struggle associations—I would call them "solidary foams" to express the fact that the oft-cited workers are, in systemic terms, neither a historical subject nor a "mass," but rather an immunitary alliance. The Marxian discourse is based on the assumption that the word "class" describes the real collective format of the allotment farmer's life, and that the growth of "class consciousness" and a corresponding aggressive or "revolutionary" politics of interests could therefore seize the decisive immunitary advantage for the members of this "class."

This shows how the socialist theory of the nineteenth century discovered the theme of the epoch, though it proved unable to hold onto it due to errors in its preliminary conceptual decisions:

that interconnection of immunity and community in which "dialectics," or the circular causal interaction of the own and the other, the shared and the non-shared, has always taken place. In the soiled and irrecuperable concept of class consciousness there still lies hidden the incompletely conceived idea that, precisely in the age of increasing individualization, allotment and chances for isolation, the separate cells could benefit from achieving solidarity with a greater unit of similarly situated individuals in order to optimize the representation of their interests. Let us note that the phrase "people's community" [*Volksgemeinschaft*] conceals analogous difficulties—as a term that has become similarly distorted and unusable in any affirmative sense in the future. Could it not be that the concept of interest as such (especially in compound forms such as national interest, class interest, business interest or residential interest) has always been a hidden metaphor for immune advantages that could only be attained communitarily?

2. Self-Couplings in the Habitat

I contain multitudes
—Walt Whitman, *Leaves of Grass*

As an elementary egospheric form, the apartment is the place in which the symbiosis of family members, which have formed the primary living communities since time immemorial, is canceled in favor of the symbiosis of the solitary individual with itself and its environment. It is unquestionable that the transition to contemporary monadic residence constitutes a profound break with ways of being together with people of one's own kind and others.

Tommaso Minardi, *Self-Portrait in an Attic* (c. 1813)

One could speak of a crisis of the second persons, who are now, in a sense, transferred into the first. This is mirrored in recent ethical theories: the "other" as a real other—a central motif in contemporary moral philosophy—can, in fact, only be discovered at a time when the self-doubling of the one in itself and the multitude of virtual inner others has become epidemic. Only now is the divide between the narcissistic other of self-reflection and the transcendent other of real or failed encounters becoming apparent in a general, public fashion. In the twentieth century, the entire "conglomerate of living mechanisms"—to recall Hermann Broch's evocative formulation for traditionally grown, spheric overall situations of familial coexistence and dulled totalities in a state of somnambulant partnership and symbiotic semi-anesthesia[95]—is affected by a centrifugal force that drives the separate beings apart into their own world-cells and active-passive micrototalities. In this respect, socio-analysis through separation runs parallel to psychoanalysis through self-exploration in the artificial dyadic situation.

One can speak of an egosphere if its inhabitant has developed elaborated habits of self-coupling, and is habitually in a constant process of distinction from itself—that is to say, a process of "experiencing." It would be mistaken to define such a form of life only according to the aspect of living alone, in the sense of partnerlessness and the lack of a human augmenter. Upon closer inspection, the non-symbiosis with others practiced in the apartment by the solitary dweller must be explained as an auto-symbiosis. In this, the form of the couple is fulfilled by the individual, who, in continuous differentiation from itself, constantly relates itself to itself as the inner other or a multiplicity of sub-egos. In these cases, coexistence is shifted to the constant changing of circumstances in which the individual experiences itself. A necessary precondition for the realization for self-coupling are the media we have described as ego techniques these are the common medial carriers of self-augmentation that allow their users to constantly return to themselves, and *eo ipso* to form a couple with themselves as their own internal surprise partner. It is no coincidence that programmatic singles often emphasize the fact that living alone is the most entertaining form of existence known to them. Through its medial equipment, the liberated individual does, in fact, always have the possibility to appear as its own companion. "A man on his own is always in bad company"—one could be tempted to say that the bachelor and single culture of the twentieth century was an experiment intended to refute Paul Valéry's remark.[96]

As illustrated in the first volume, the individualistic illusion that would go on to be consolidated during modernity into an ontology of separatedness was only able to become suggestive in the course of the media evolution in the Modern Age. It was contributed to by the egotechnic media, which established the routines of returning to oneself among the individual persons— primarily reading and writing techniques, which enabled the rehearsal of historically new procedures of inner dialogue, self-examination and self-documentation. This resulted in *homo alphabeticus* developing idiosyncratic exercises not only in self-objectification, but also in self-reunification through the appropriation of the objectified. The diary is one such egotechnic form, the examination of the conscience another. In my reflections on the history of human faciality in general, and the conditions of Old European interfaciality in particular, I pointed out the introduction of the mirror—as late as it was decisive— into the optical self-relationships of Europeans, emphasizing the contribution of this paradigmatic ego-technical device to the adjustment of sensual reflection in the other to what we term "self-reflection."[97] In the everyday lives of modern apartment dwellers, as in those of most other people, looking in the mirror has become a regular exercise serving the purpose of ongoing self-adjustment.

M. C. Escher, *Hand with Reflecting Sphere* (1935)

The separate actors in the individualistic regime become isolated subjects under the dominion of the mirror, that is to say of the reflecting, self-completing function. They increasingly organize their lives under the appearance that they could now play both parts in the game of the bipolar relationship sphere alone, without a real other; this appearance becomes stronger throughout the European history of media and mentalities, culminating at the point where the individuals decide once and for all that they themselves are the substantial first part, and their relationships with others the accidental second part. A mirror in each room belonging to each individual is practical life's patent on this state.[98]

The term "auto-symbiosis" is intended to show that the dyadic structure of the primitive sphere can, under certain conditions, be formally reenacted by the individuals—when, and only when, these have the necessary medial accessories at their disposal to settle entirely in circumstances founded on self-augmentation. What is examined in the metaphysics of everyday life as self-sufficiency transpires, in spherological terms, as a virtualization of the dyad through self-coupling, self-care, self-augmentation and self-modeling. From this perspective, the apartment can be understood as the studio of self-relationships—or a nursing home for indeterminacies. This is not—unlike the cells inhabited by late medieval monks and nuns—the place where the biunity of God and the soul is worked out; rather, it supports the individual's coupling with itself (uni-binity). This means a mental operation that feeds off the experienced difference between the current state of the individual and its manifold potential states. It can only be maintained once a relatively dense continuum of moments of self-observation and self-adjustment has become decisive for the life form as a whole. This corresponds to the state of a "society in which every man is painted and prays to his picture"[99] anticipated by Elias Canetti—except that in this case, the individuals are creating polyvalent images of themselves with the aid of numerous media. Was it by chance that Le Corbusier felt drawn to the Christian monks' form of life after visiting the Certosa d'Ema near Florence? "I would like to all my life what they call their cells,"[100] he noted on his trip to Italy in 1907. The monastic housing units that made such an impression on the budding architect were arranged as double cells with one inner and one outer chamber—in the eyes of the young visitor an ideal model for more ambitious workers' quarters or modern student accommodation.

Viewed in a culture-historical light, Le Corbusier's fascination with the monastic buildings appears well founded—it was in the monastic cells of the High Middle Ages, after all, that the first seeds of the modern subject form bore fruit. These containers for self-collection were the site of the original accumulation of attention from which—after the reversal of the basic metaphysical orientation from transcendence to immanence—the Western form of modern individualism would later develop. Attention is the mental currency used to pay for the existence of relevant differences, both among monks and qualified consumers. Just as ascetic extra-worldly individualism materialized in the monks' cells, contemporary apartment culture with all its egotechnical devices supports intramundane hedonistic individualism. This latter presupposes the incessant self-observation of the individual in all its dimensions during its metabolic processes and changes of state. Individualism is a cult

Yayoi Kusama, *Infinity Mirror Room* (1965)

of digestion; it celebrates the passage of food, experiences and information through the subject.[101] Where everything is immanence, the apartment becomes the integral toilet: in every sense, what takes place here is determined by end use. Eating/digestion;

reading/writing; television/opinion; regeneration/commitment; arousal/discharge. As the micro-theater of auto-symbiosis, the apartment encloses the existence of individuals running as candidates for experiences and significances.

As it is at once a stage and a cave, it forms the location of both the entrance of the individual and its slipping back into insignificance. One can easily explain this with the typical stages of the self-care cycle passed through by the apartment subject in its daily script—beginning with a morning grooming session consisting of emptyings, washings, acts of cosmetic self-attention and clothings. Cosmetic auto-praxis already offers, on a relatively simple level, a universe of differentiations that are assigned great intrinsic value in the consciousness of users; it enables them to bring their own facial appearance closer to the other pole, to the work of art. (Baudelaire foresaw this in his *éloge du maqillage* when he said of the beautiful woman that, as a divine image, she must gild herself to be worshipped: *elle doit se dorer pour être adorée*.) The choice of clothes is an analogous case, encompassing many micro-universes of gradations and gestures: here combination becomes the duty of design, while selection becomes a self-project. In reality, the individual qualifies itself in the developed society of experiences as an originator, claiming its authorial rights through its own appearance. The individual ascertains the psychosocial income from its clothing strategy via the direct and indirect successes of his appearance.

With breakfast or whatever one wishes to call the first nutritional gesture (more elevatedly: the opening of the daily alimentary cycle)—the activity of self-care turns to the metabolic needs, which does not usually occur without actions in the stove and kitchen area. The apartment kitchen is the miniature of a

Edward Hopper, *Room in New York* (1932)

chirotope, in which the proto-practices of lighting fires, cutting, rationing of material quantities, decanting, serving and so on are routinely carried out thanks to the presence of the corresponding devices. The self-coupling quality of solitary living becomes particularly apparent in the gestures of preparing something for oneself: anyone who provides for themselves from their own kitchen *eo ipso* takes on the dual role of host and guest, or cook and eater, thus demonstrating that certain acts of *souci de soi* also contain a *don de soi*, a gift from the ego to the ego, that reveals the intentions of the giver towards the taker. Thanks to the progressive explication of the metabolism through modern biology, the self-sustainer is given the chance to develop their self-care from a nutrition-critical perspective. Here, in addition to the food's gastronomic quality, its dietary quality becomes increasingly significant; nutrition is joined by nutritional supplements, and the light fitness drug gains a place in the self-care household. Foods for living become means of enhancing people's way of living; self-sustenance gradually approaches self-medication. With the obligatory equipment of a stove, sink and refrigerator, the technical bearers of the autonomous kitchen function, even the smallest apartment today constitutes an efficient thermospheric unit. In addition to sanitary standards, it is above all these elementary gastrospheric standards that define the concept of comfort in a modern housing unit.

In many cases, the apartment individual's entrance into the phonotope, the sound universe of the collective, begins with the first alimentary gestures. It breaks the nocturnal sound fast with an acoustic breakfast, be it the first self-chosen music or a radio or television program. This anti-*silentium* shows how the solitary dweller takes their daily resocialization and attainment of worldliness into their own hands by having a say, through the choice of media, in the content and dosage of the reality influx. Hegel had something similar in mind when, during his Jena years, he noted down that reading the newspaper in the morning was "a form of realistic morning blessing"[102]—with the nuance that in this case, the reconnection of the private subject to the noise of the group after its nocturnal desocialization is achieved via the cultural technique of reading, that is to say by absorbing external voices into the internal mono- and polylogues. Thanks to audio media, the solitary dweller's cell can become something that seemed impossible, even contradictory, in historical terms: an individual phonotope. Its main characteristic is that the imprisonment of the individual through the group sound has been

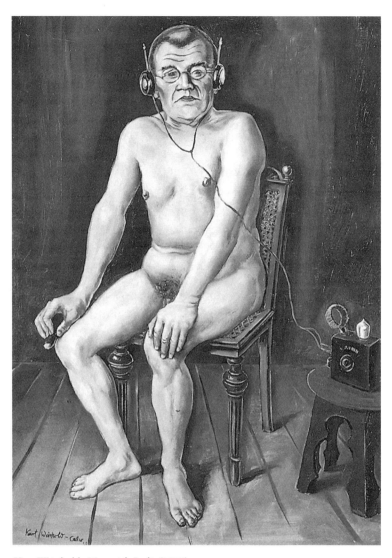

Kurt Weinhold, *Man with Radio* (1929)

undone and replaced by the discrete admission of particular noises, sounds and spoken texts. From the initial state of a total tuning of the group by the group, countless individualized sound-bubbles now emerge—auditory microspheres in which a relatively high degree of listening freedom is realized.[103] (This tendency is heightened through the connection of portable cassette or CD players to headphones—an insulation technique tantamount to the introduction of the acoustic micro-apartment into the public space; one could also speak of an acoustic diving suit.) Modern society vibrates with millions of cells in sonorous foams; with reference to the countless competing listening collectives, some have rightly spoken of a *guerre des ambiances*.[104] Even the meanwhile normal coexistence of fifty-odd TV channels cannot conceal the fact that the television, in its phonotopic mode of effect, is no more than a visually expanded radio—with the one difference that it supports the freedom of program selection better than the search systems of the radio.

It has been stated, with good reason, that postmodernity is a byproduct of the remote control. The telecommander constitutes the key method of controlling the admission of sounds and images, and *eo ipso* of reality, into the egosphere. If one considers that a being such as *homo sapiens* becomes what it hears, the transition to optional self-tuning amounts to an anthropological caesura: both the external and the internalized compulsion to listen, of which the latter was partially circumscribed by psychoanalysis with the concept of the superego (concerning the moral aspect of the individual being outvoted by the collective), disappear in the trend towards the personal choice of auditory surroundings. Certainly there will always, even in the individual-phonotopically constituted individual, be layers of internal and external listening in which the listening material of choice is pre-empted by things heard involuntarily.

Next to telecommunications connections, the elaboration of the apartment as an individual phonotope constitutes the most important contribution to the medial completion of the housing unit. It ensures that the cell, even though it reliably performs its defensive functions as an insulator, an immune system and a supplier of comfort and distance, still remains a space with world-content. Remote from the world and open to it, the auditory egosphere grants admission to selected particles of reality, sounds, sensations, shopping, finds and guests. Its practical implantation is guaranteed by the radio and the television, with the print media now shifted to the second row.

The only medium whose significance for the informatic and atmospheric shaping of the egosphere is comparable to that of the audio media is the telephone—which, by virtue of being a two-way medium, constitutes one of the most effective means of connecting the reservation to the world. Compared to the most common one-way media (radio, TV, newspaper, book), the telephone has a double ontological privilege: it not only conveys (usually) calls from the domain of the real, but also brings the recipient of the call, assuming they answer it themselves, into a state of simultaneity (experienced as real) with the caller—it puts them on the same level of being as the actor of the appeal from afar. Because of this effect of immediacy, it was legitimate to describe the telephone as a "biophone"[105]—for nothing that is less than a life can place a call. Someone on the telephone—that is always a distant life rendered present, a voice with a message, perhaps even an invitation. Because it can be reached by calls, the apartment is deprived of the "unity of place" and instead connected to a network of virtual neighborhoods. Since then, the effective neighborhood has been not the spatial, but rather the telephonic one. From an immunological perspective, the telephone is an ambivalent innovation, as it directs a canal for dangerous infections from the outside into the dwelling-cell, while conversely expanding the inhabitant's radius—in the sense of larger alliances and opportunities for action—in an explosive fashion. (We do not need to discuss the Internet in this context, as it initially offers merely the continuation of the telephone by visual means.) After writing abolished the simultaneity of the emission and reception of communications, the telephone now obviates the need to be in the same place.

The principle of the local call (or more precisely the world-producing effect of mouth-ear couplings) is subverted by long-distance calls—with the result that the secret of spheric resonance, preformulated in some religious discourses,[106] finds technical articulation. In retrospect we can realize to what extent every sphere formation implies the "surreal factor" from the outset—namely that the communicants in the human location always go beyond the merely locational. To draw on a philosophical language game from 1900: telecommunications technology accelerates the demise of life in the spirit. It advances the inflation of telepathic effects, in so far as we understand these as the mental side effects of being reachable from afar. The self-coupling procedures of individualism presuppose the expansion of telecommunicative mechanisms into solid routines in the events of their lives: only then can separation be experienced as something other than isolation, as it enables the connection of the single soul to absent relevant others and their varyingly attractive signs of remote life.

The premodern era was dominated by the evident fact that the most interesting messages came from a strong sender known as "God"; their bearers were saints, priests and prophets. Modernity relies on distant senders such as the genius and the stock market reporter. Perhaps this is what characterized the strong attribute of existence in metaphysically ambitious civilizations: intelligence detaches itself from the primacy of local calls and participates in the transfer of the flow of meaning from close life to distant life. Hence existence now means swimming in signs that come from far away—signs that are supported by strong senders. Under this effect, the classical advanced civilizations were able to bloom as literate cultures: the voices of the classics preserved on bearers of writing impose themselves on subsequent generations of literates. Metaphysics begins as telesymbiosis; here, later intelligence can couple itself co-intelligently with the earlier through disciplined reading. I can be reached by distant, sending life; through us, remote and past life remains readable.

The modern telephone-supported apartment lifestyle introduces the phase in which these achievements are trivialized. While the benefits of distantly reachable life were reaped entirely under the control of extra-worldly individualism while the coupling of individual souls with God or the absolute was going on, the current secular individualism, as noted above, is concerned with the coupling of the individual with itself—with the individual, as an eternally unknown other of itself, taking on the role of a residual absolute. (Naturally this position can also be assigned to the real other.)[107] Every self that turns inwards could find itself transcendent enough. It feels that seeing itself as a combination of manifest and latent individuality is sufficient to

Eric Fischl, *Still Life (Bananas with Knife)* (1981), courtesy of the Mary Boone Gallery, New York

know that the investigation of its own latency constitutes a rewarding purpose in life. As long as the exposed individual is interested in itself, it remains on the trail of the *individuum absconditum*. (Let us note to what extent mass culture is based on the premise that most individuals have no reason to be interested in themselves, and would therefore do better to focus on the lives of the stars. Definitions of the star: a) an interesting magnification of the uninterestingness of the rest; b) an agent of the admirer's distraction from themselves.)

In no dimension of life is this more conspicuous than in sexuality, which, in the individualist regime, often takes the form of an apartment-based experience-sexuality, or as research within the inner space of erotic possibilities. It is clear enough that the

Charles Ray, *Oh Charley, Charley, Charley* at *documenta* X (1997)

transition to "liberated" sexuality in the second half of the twentieth century was inseparably connected to the gain in discretion through apartment culture, or at least to the securities of one's own room. The over-discussed phenomenon of biochemical contraceptives, which have been available to women—including unmarried ones—since the 1960s, merely reinforces the trend, manifest since the 1920s, towards an affirmative solitary-dweller eroticism. The apartment forms a miniature erototope in which individuals can pursue the fulfillment of their desires, in the sense of wanting to experience what others have already experienced. It constitutes an exemplary site of existence, as the consumer relationship to one's own sexual potential can be rehearsed there. If, however, the lover (*erástes*) and the beloved (*erómenos*) are one and the same person, this centaur is not spared the lover's experience that the object of love seldom responds on the same wavelength.

In auto-eroticism, as in its bipersonal equivalent, the rule applies that in the need to choose a partner, most are damned to make the wrong choice: as one does not usually get the person one wants, one takes someone else instead—in this case oneself. This is why the apartment is also a studio for working out frustrations—or, more precisely, an experimental cell in which a desire for the real or imaginary other is converted into a desire for oneself as the most plausible stand-in. This paradoxical circle leads to a self-gratification with aggressive tendencies. Apartment masturbation, probably prefigured in the monastic cells, stages the complete three-part relation between the subject, the genitals and the phantasm—from which it also follows that masturbatory sexuality may effect a pragmatic abbreviation of the procedure, but not a structural simplification of the interpersonal bigenital operation. One can thus explain the erototopic attributes of the apartment best by analogy to the brothel: just as the clients look around for disposable sexual partners before heading for a hidden cell once they have reached an agreement with their object of preference, the apartment's inhabitant chooses themselves as the obvious other, and uses the seclusion of their housing unit to do it with themselves. Here self-coupling takes place in the shady situation where the individual can pursue itself unhindered as a self-client. As a well-known example shows, this can even extend to the idea of the self-bestowed doctorate. In her early 1970s bestseller *Sex for One*, the American feminist and masturbation activist Betty Dodson asserted that her untiring commitment to the cause of masturbation entitled her to demand academic honors; after realizing that her wish could never be fulfilled, she declared: "But after fourteen years of this unique fieldwork, I've awarded myself a PhD in masturbation."[108]

Just as a tendency towards impoverishment through routine is to be expected in any relationship where the partners make things too easy for themselves, masturbatory self-partnership also leads to a weariness of its uniformity. The individuals cannot always congratulate themselves on their self-produced arousal. This weariness of masturbation marks the limits of the auto-congratulatory form of life. Recent literature on the lives of singles makes it clear that the sexuality of solitary dwellers is defined by the need to avoid auto-monogamy. Even Betty Dodson, who boasted of sessions with her vibrator lasting several hours, admitted that she had intermittently resorted to penises. Surveys among singles have shown beyond doubt, however, that many are unwilling to accept the disturbance of their cellular peace through a permanent partner merely to solve this problem.

Alongside its chiro-, thermo- and erototopic attributes, the modern habitat cell also takes on aspects of an ergotope as soon as its inhabitant make it the scene of their sporting self-care. This conversion of apartments into private gymnastics studios is encouraged by the trend in modern society towards fitness-oriented lifestyles that demand of their adherents a constant attention to their own form. From this perspective, the structure of self-coupling modifies itself in such a way that the practicing individual splits up into the trainer and the trainee in order to unify the two in a coordinated sequence of actions. Here training devices (either static or mobile) take over the role of the manifest third party in the concrete organization of the self-relationship; in other cases it is through exercises on the floor, without devices, that the practicing conduct their gymnastic soliloquies.

Existentialism has declared itself somatic: a universally comprehensible version of the philosophical formula that existence is the relationship that is related to itself has now come onto the market; it states that existence means keeping in shape.

Finally, the apartments can be described as outposts of the alethotope: in every individual life, no matter how much it has rejected the general realm, there is a residual interest in truth—even if it is only the demand for words that help the individual to be connected to the signs of the times. Someone with a moderate level of media consumption generally reaches the cognitive subsistence level that is the norm in our world form, which incorporates the license to choose and have a say. Anyone who demands more is attempting to gain orientational knowledge suitable for extensive navigations in unclear conditions. In the alethotopic self-relationship, individuals act informally as self-teachers whose task is to maintain a certain congruence with the cognitive or scientific state of "society"; as minimal autodidacts, they make an idiosyncratic contribution to the publicly accessible resources of cognitive *souci de soi*. Even if it is the case that learning can no longer be interpreted as more than enlightened ignorance management under the present cognition-theoretical conditions, anyone with a remotely inquiring mind in our "knowledge-based society" must address the ongoing updating of their deficits. From that point, the main purpose of positive information is to assess more realistically the proportions of what is unknown and unclear. In addition, information increasingly assumes a function corresponding to that of fashion items and markets—people carry isolated particles of knowledge the same way they wear sunglasses, expensive watches or baseball caps. In Japanese youth culture, a broad scene has developed since the

1980s that embraces the cult of pointless knowledge.[109] These young people have understood that knowledge prepares them not for life, but for quiz shows.

The usual sources for the solitary dwellers are the scene and fashion magazines, as well as those works of non-fiction that are occasionally absorbed into the domestic collection. For many of them, the introduction of a new book into the community of objects that inhabit the dwelling is still an event. One aspect of the charm of apartment life is the fact that here, one can devote one's time—without witnesses—to keeping unfalsified accounts of one's unmistakable personal ignorances.

C. Foam City:
Macro-Interiors and Urban Assembly Buildings
Explicate the Symbiotic Situations of the Masses

If the statement "every person is an island" has very nearly become true for the majority of modern populations in large cities, how can it remain possible to think about "society"? While the agencies of analysis in the real work on preparing individuals in their own households in a pure state, the agencies of social synthesis devote themselves to the task of producing the over-arching forms that can group the insulated into interactive units. Thus the term "communication" has an evangelical ring to it in all contemporary discourses: it is the rescuing word among those who seek salvation in cohesion, or more precisely in symbolic exchange and transactional commitments—whereas formerly, during the long Marxian century, that salvation was expected from "labor," its division and its recombination.

Every person is an island—this appears as bad news for the conservatives, who are still spurred by the idea of subsuming individuals under prior collectives or ones constituted through acceptance. It is better news for those who see it as a guarantee that the many can never again be consumed by malign enthusiasms for the supposed whole—because islanders are, as a rule, of little use for totalities. But whatever the insularity of the individuals settled with their respective selves, one is always dealing with co-isolated and networked islands that must be connected momentarily or chronically to adjacent islands to form medium-level and larger structures—a national convention, a Love Parade, a club, a freemasons' lodge, a corporate workforce, a shareholders' assembly, a concert audience, a suburban neighborhood, a school class, a religious community, a mass of automobilists caught in congestion, or a taxpayers' association in a meeting. If these ensembles, both in their episodic agglomerations and their long-term symbioses, are described here as foams, it is not least to formulate a statement about the relative density of co-isolated life conglomerates or alliances—a density that will always be greater than that of archipelagos (which otherwise offer a convincing metaphor for insulated multiplicities), yet lower than that of crowds (in which the misleading associations of physically-touching collective units like dough, sand and potato bags come into play).

That false images can make history is shown by the modern political concept of the masses, whose metaphorical origin—the notion of malleable and fermenting "dough" (Lat. *massa*: "lump, pile, unformed material")—allowed the most harmful suggestions to persist for two centuries. Upon examining the vocabularies of the twentieth century, one will not only have to retire the term "revolution," but also the concept of the masses.[110]

The co-isolated foams of individualistically conditioned society are not mere agglomerations of adjacent (separation-sharing) inert and solid bodies, but rather multiplicities of loosely touching lifeworldly cells, each of which, due to its individual width, possesses the dignity of a universe. By way of precaution, the foam metaphor draws attention to the fact that there are no isolating means which are completely private property—one always shares at least one partition with an adjacent world-cell. The shared wall, viewed from each respective side, constitutes the inter-autistic minimum. Anything beyond that can already be considered a symbiotic phenomenon.

Jean Luc Parant, *The Angles*, Villeneuve-les-Avignons (1985)

1. National Assembly

Having established that the *modus vivendi,* that is to say the
developmental rhythm, of modern society is based on a two-
beat rhythm—the disassembly of social conglomerates into
individuated complex units and their recombination in cooperative ensembles—one is struck by how much references to the
"entrance of the masses into history" also articulate a set of
architectural problems. In keeping with their symbionts'
newly loosened state of matter, modern collectives must face
the task of producing spatial conditions in which the isolation
of individuals on one side and the grouping of individuals
into large ensembles for cooperation or contemplation on the
other side are given support. This demands new deployments
for architecture.

As early as the French Revolution, it had already become
manifest that the activists of overthrow could exclusively resort to
the buildings of the *ancien régime* or the public spaces of the
cities for their gatherings, especially the squares in front of large
buildings. The most notable specimens of what would one day
be given the misleading label "revolutionary architecture"[111] had
already been designed before 1789—recall the controversial
House of the Field Wardens (*Maison des gardes agricoles*) by
Claude-Nicolas Ledoux, dated between 1768 and 1773, the
Newton Cenotaph by Etienne-Louis Boullée (1784) or the
House for a Cosmopolite by Vaudoyer (1785). The fact that
every one of these projects remained unbuilt was due not so
much to adverse conditions as their own speculative logic; the
time was not yet ripe for the emancipation of the sculptural
understanding of space and geometric formalisms.[112]

The revolutionary events of the Great Days, then, took place in buildings and public squares that had no connection to the events they harbored. The best-known example: the meetings of the Estates-General convened by Louis XVI in Versailles. Here, in early May 1789, a number of halls in the wings of the palace had been converted for the gatherings of the three estates, which initially met separately. When, on June 20, the almost six hundred representatives of the Third Estate, who had meanwhile given themselves the openly inflammatory name "National Assembly" (and demanded the prerogative of approving taxes), found the *Salle Menus-Plaisirs* which they had been assigned locked (probably due to preparations for the planned large meeting of the estates under the king's command on the twenty-third of the month), they quickly moved their consultations to the nearby *Jeu de Paume* (indoor tennis court) at the suggestion of the representative Guillotin—a building that, like its predecessor, had previously been devoted entirely to princely pleasures. There they swore the famous oath not to part before the constitution of the kingdom had been drawn up and given a solid foundation. This vow, the first speech act of the bourgeoisie's seizure of power, is notable because it concerned the commitment of the assembled to the assembly as such; it could leave no doubt as to the precedence of the political content (which was still being formed) over the local and architectural form (which had to be determined or erected from one case to another): "the members of this assembly shall immediately take a solemn oath not to separate and to reassemble wherever circumstances shall require."[113] From the outset, the sovereignty of the first *assemblée*, which continued its work until September 30, 1791 (to be replaced by the Legislative Assembly, which in turn gave way to the National Convention on September 20, 1792), included the freedom to determine the meeting place *ad hoc*—something that the subversives of the twentieth century would term "refunctioning." This became necessary only a few days later, when the *Tiers Etat* improvised a gathering at Versailles Cathedral—the historic session at which a large part of the clergy united itself with the Third Estate; then once again in the autumn of 1789, with the relocation of the National Assembly to the *Salle du Manège* in Paris, the riding school of the Tuileries, which was hastily prepared to accommodate the needs of the constituent assembly. In May 1793 the Assembly, now as the National Convention, moved to the Tuileries Palace, where a semi-elliptic meeting hall had meanwhile been built after the plans of the artist Gisor, with 700 seats for the representatives and 1,400 for the public. During the same time, the planning imaginations of architects had not remained dormant: from 1789 onwards, numerous designs were made for worthy conference buildings for the National Assembly, usually on the occasion of academic competitions, mostly in the heroic-classicist style, more than a few of them already on a monumental scale,[114] as if the republic could only be explained formally in the setting of a Roman empire—the line extending from Etienne Louis-Boullée to Albert Speer leaves nothing to be desired in terms of clarity, incidentally. Indeed, almost every detail of the political liturgies used by European fascisms—except for the radiophonic techniques for affecting the masses—was prefigured by practices, projects and stylistic patterns from the French Revolution.

In the light of these facts, one could define "revolutionary" events as ones that take "place" although, according to the state of things, they can initially only occur in unsuitable places. The gatherings of new political actors, the first *Assemblée nationale*, the Legislative Assembly and the National Convention with the respective committees on the one hand, and the clubs and parties, sections and discussion societies on the other, were translated into as many revolutionary spatial demands whose only commonality at first was that they had to lodge themselves in the building stock of the Old Order and extract a heterodox function from it. One example that can stand for countless analogous occurrences is the fate of a deserted Dominican (commonly called Jacobin) monastery in the Rue Saint Honoré in Paris that, after the relocation of the deputies from Versailles to the capital, became the gathering place of the Club Breton, later known as the "Society of the Friends of the Constitution"—the think tank for patriotic radicalism and the mother cell of hundreds of subsidiaries in the provinces, whose explosive proliferation already led Camille Desmoulins to write in February 1791: "In the propagation of patriotism, that is to say philanthropy, [...] the club or church of the Jacobins seems destined for the same primacy as that of the church of Rome in the propagation of Christianity..."[115] That the power grouping which came about soon identified actively and passively with the name of their conference venue reveals something of the power of the local spirits over those gathered; conversely, it displays the independence of the new power constellations from traditional forms of local semantics. At most, one could say that here, as in countless other places, a shift of authority took place from the clergy to the most eloquent people's representatives, or better still: an outdoing of Christian zeal through the élan of patriots drunk on mankind.

Analogous mechanisms worked temporarily in favor of the moderate forces around Barnave when, in July 1791, they broke away from the Jacobin club and, to reinforce their secession, established themselves in the neighboring monastery of the Feuillants—like the Jacobin monastery, only a few steps away from the *Salle du Manège*. When the populist and Sparta-lover Jean-Paul Marat was murdered by Charlotte Corday on July 13, 1793, members of the Convention and those of the "revolutionary sex," namely the women of Paris, held a lavish funeral ceremony for him. He was laid in state in the church of the Franciscan monks, popularly known as *Cordeliers*, and his heart was interred separately in the vaults of the monastery while the body was buried in the *Jardin des Cordeliers* (from where his remains were translated to the Pantheon not long afterwards); these church buildings had served as the clubhouse and party headquarters for the Society of the Friends of the Rights of Man and of the Citizen. After the end of the *terreur*, the heart vase disappeared under unclear circumstances.

However one wishes to assess the symbolic weight of such quarterings and occupations of traditional space, it is at least certain that the events, discourses and gestures between 1789 and 1795 in no sense approached the constructivist phantasm of a new beginning on a clean slate: at no time was there an empty "republican space" in which the men of the hour could operate like creatures from a future world. Though the Revolution left no part of the old system unaffected, it still remained within its framework. The operative qualities of the upheaval consistently manifested themselves in the form of reshuffles, subversions and refunctionings of given elements. This is in keeping with the observation that the Revolution hardly built anything, but renamed almost everything.[116] These political speech acts, none of which were, of course, as far-reaching as the renaming and conversion of the Estates-General into the National Assembly, were often accompanied by real and decisive rededications, of which the two most symbol-politically ambitious were the establishment of a national Pantheon in the votive church of Saint Genevieve—a form of national archive for the ashes and nimbus of great men[117]—and the conversion of the Louvre into the first large national museum, where liberated (in plain language: looted) art treasures from all over the world were to be laid to rest alongside one another.[118] But one does notice some innovations in the field of abolition: after the slave figures at the base of the status of Louis XVI on the Place des Victoires in Paris had already been removed in 1790, the statue itself was done away with after the people's revolt on August 10, 1792.[119] At the height of Jacobin rule, the "public space" was emptied of the personal monuments to the monarchy, which were temporarily replaced by statues of liberty and republican allegories. In many places, improvised altars of the fatherland, next to the obligatory trees of liberty, point to the martial civil religion of Jacobinism, which imposed the duty of self-sacrifice on its adepts more energetically than almost any monotheistic missionary religion could have done at the height of its expansionist élan.

The nationwide refunctioning of feudal and clerical halls for the assembly needs of the Third Estate's representatives (Paris alone, with its revolutionary 48 sections, reported a tremendous need for conference centers, consultation cabinets, courthouses, administrative offices and prisons) was far from enough to meet the spatial needs of the *nouveau régime*. In the first year of the Revolution, it was already clear that there needed to be large gathering places not only for meetings of representatives, but also where the represented, the masses themselves, would have opportunities to assemble physically on festive occasions, in orderly forms, as the currently present plenum of the new "society"—that is, as a sovereign national people. The fact that under the demographic and geographical conditions in France, which had a population of roughly 25 million at the time, this would at most have been feasible in larger cities, and then only approximately, did nothing to reduce the mobilizing effect of the republican mass plenum ideal. The citizens' nation, which had established itself before its own eyes as a sublime address, wanted at least occasionally to be with and among itself festively and complete, as it were—without regard for the fact that modern society is asynodically constituted: its first and most important attribute was that it no longer formed a unity capable of assembling. This distinguished it radically from the democracy of classical antiquity, which rested entirely on the requirement that the polis had to remain an assemblable unit (excluding women, children and slaves).

Under the influence of this enthusiasm for gathering, classical models of buildings for mass gatherings were immediately—and inevitably, one might think—discussed suggestively once more: with the Greek amphitheater and the Roman circus or arena, European antiquity had provided two tried-and-tested concepts for mass gatherings whose formal perfection allowed them to be revived even after a hiatus of over 1,500 years. In retrospect, the Paris Academy's establishment of competitions for festive public buildings as early as the 1780s seems like a prophetic preparatory exercise: for a *Fête publique* in 1781, a circus in 1782 and a menagerie with arena in 1783. There were similar motifs in the 1789 and 1790 competitions—though then too, there were hardly any plans for their realization. (The *ancient régime* had at least toyed with the idea of the ancient arena as an absolutist festive backdrop: in 1769, on the occasions of the Dauphin's wedding to Marie Antoinette at the Rond Point on the Champs Elysées, an enormous building in the style of the Colosseum was presented; it served as a place of popular amusement for a decade before it had to be demolished owing to decrepitude.) The academic *concours* still very much followed the formula of late absolutist phantasms of control by the people. They had a license to dream more or less without consequences of large containers for the passive-jubilatory agglomeration of subjects in the face of the royalty's spectacular representations of power and art.

It was only after the outbreak of the Revolution that the arena and amphitheater model could become politically virulent and occasionally realizable in the "mass" public sphere—demonstrated above all by the great Festival of the Federation, the associations of patriots who had joined forces to stamp out counter-revolutionary machinations, on the Field of Mars on the first anniversary of the Storming of the Bastille on July 14, 1790.[120] This, the largest mass event in European history since the days of the Roman Circus Maximus, marked the closest proximity of the French Revolution to the bombastic ideal of the real and integral people's assembly: that day, some 400,000 people are said to have crowded together in the improvised rows of circus seats, in whose center Talleyrand celebrated a patriotic cult mass at a specially erected, liturgically precarious "Altar of the Fatherland." (Only one event, not so long before this one, could compete with the Federation's celebration in terms of visitor numbers: on the first flight of the physics professor Charles in his hydrogen balloon on December 1, 1783, over a quarter of

De Machy, *The Festival of the Federation* in Paris in 1790: the triumphal arch as the eyecatcher

a million Parisians are reported to have flocked together in the Tuileries Gardens to witness the greatest sensation of their time: the overcoming of gravity.) A single historical moment saw the transformation Talleyrand from a priest to the master of ceremonies in the age of the "masses"—or, more precisely, the birth of the media politician as a showmaster and director of consensus. The eyecatcher among the festive constructions on the Field of Mars was an immense triumphal arch made of cardboard, wood and plaster; in erecting it, the militant patriots' republic had unmistakably expressed its interest in the victor symbolism of the Roman imperial age. In the light of this massive quotation of Rome, one could think that the Napoleonic victories of the subsequent decade were simply the execution of what the heroic decorum of patriotic societies had demanded from the start of the Revolution: is a victory not always a concession by reality to the demands of the phantasm? The scenes on the Field of Mars undoubtedly still bore the influence of the elaborated ceremonial ability of absolutism, supported by the habitualized cult magic of Catholicism, even if both were treated as abolished or obsolete forces in the semantics of the celebration itself. The singularity of this gathering for those gathered was demonstrated by the vow sworn by Lafayette in the name of the federates of all *départements*, which affirmed both the unity of the French amongst themselves and the merging of the people with their king (who, for his part, swore loyalty to the nation and the law—perjuriously, of course), as if the aim of this direct people's assembly was to align the assembled with their current togetherness, and more still with their imaginary staying together after returning to the unassembled state—not long afterwards, one would call it their national solidarity. There can scarcely have been another situation at the dawn of political modernity in which the equation of sociability and somnambulism posited by Gabriel Tarde applied as radically as it did on that first July 14 anniversary; the rehearsal of such states by the French may go towards explaining why Bonaparte found such an unusually hypnosis-willing, mobilizable and emotionally inflammable "nation."

Shortly after this event of mass enthusiasm, a question of great consequence appeared in the discourses of the early socialists: did these encapsulations of the whole nation in an intoxicated "we" constitute a deception of the unpropertied social classes by the propertied bourgeoisie? Because this question was correctly put, both semantically and politically, the next 150 years of European social policy were dominated by criticism from international workers' movements of the assembly deception and kinship swindle practiced by the bourgeois nations. Indeed, the phenomenon

Unknown artist, *Oath of the King, the Queen, the Nation at the Festival of the Federation* on July 14, 1790 (18th century)

of illusory inclusion, which cloaks harsh, real exclusions, had entered the ideological stage at a single stroke; the age of suspicion began with its systematic denunciation. From that point on, critique sought to be the exposure of the present false universality in the name of an allegedly coming, true kind. It was against this background that the concept of class was able to take precedence in the later discourses of the Revolution's losers: in future, it would work polemically against the pseudo-inclusivity of concepts of nation and people and bring the true (albeit still vague) collective of impoverished workers responsible for all true creation of value, as well as their intellectual allies, into position against the exploiters and ideologues who served capital.[121]

The modern character of the patriotic cult spectacle on the Field of Mars in Paris (which was reproduced in all important French cities with analogous mass meetings in improvised stadiums, and was followed by numerous similar celebrations until year VIII on the Revolutionary calendar—that is, 1799—sometimes even including competitive and athletic elements) lies in the fact that it caused the molding of the capital's many-headed crowds into present "masses" to enter the stage of explicit working-out as an architectural, organizational and ritual-planning task (that would later also involve assembly laws). The preparation and execution of the Federation's celebration in 1790 and the follow-up events made it clear that the "masses," the "nation" or the "people" can only exist as a collective subject to the extent that the physical assembly of these units is artfully staged—from mobilization to participation, via affective guidance in the stadium and the capture of the "masses'" attention through fascinogenic spectacles, finally extending to the dispersal of the homecoming crowd under the supervision of the civil guard. No dough without the vessel in which it is formed; no "masses" without a hand that knows what it is kneading for.

The Festival of the Federation on July 14, 1790, which formed the *de facto* and *de jure* starting point of modern "mass" culture as the staging of events, is informative because here the connection between audience, spectacle and assembly container already presented itself in exemplary and final forms. The parade of the civil guard on the giant field inside the circus and the patriotic mass celebrated by Talleyrand made it clear that collective liturgies on such a scale inevitably entailed an all-pervasive dominance of ritual—and that the assembled new sovereign, the attendant audience, had to content itself with the role of the animated observer and acclaimer precisely because of its numerically overwhelming presence. Conversely, this means that the organizers of the mass meeting must know to what extent they themselves are responsible for the success of the affective synthesis, namely collective enthusiasm. Because the reborn circus, as a political focus and a fascinogenic collector of masses, constitutes a machine for producing consensus, the choreography of the ritual must ensure that all events within it remain of an elementary self-evidence. Anyone who does not understand the words must be able to follow the plot; whoever cannot grasp the plot has to be captivated by the gaudiness of the spectacle. Sonospheric merging takes care of the rest. The "sovereign" can never directly take the floor in this situation, but he can applaud the appearances of his representatives—more still, he is free to develop into an acoustic we-phenomenon *sui generis* by cheering and shouting. Where a discreet vote is not possible, collective yelling also has psychopolitically relevant effects. The quasi-nation assembled in the circus stadium experiences itself in an acoustic plebiscite whose direct result, the jubilatory noise over the heads of all, erupts from the gathered like an emanation before returning to the ears of each individual. The autopoiesis of noise approaches a realization of platitudes about the *vox populi*. Such yelling, not yet differentiated through modern voting equipment, makes the rhetoric of individual speakers superfluous. On the path of mimetic contagion, the cry of one becomes the cry of the other; at most, the stadium crowd will split into two or more competing yelling groups. Where musical unification replaces outcry, a space for political hymnody opens up. As the history of "La Marseillaise" and other national anthems shows, joint singing suggests the transformation of the crowd into a choir—according to other views, it even reveals the true choral nature of community beneath the prosaic everyday relationships between humans.[122]

As far as the architectural containers for revolutionary mass meetings are concerned, the rededication of feudal or church halls was clearly not enough: anything less than the Renaissance-like repetition of a previously outdated classical form would be insufficient if the incipient "mass" culture of modernity was to build on that of European antiquity—and it had to do so in order to satisfy its demand for large buildings with which to house aggregated crowds of people.

The edificial imperative for large-scale meetings in the age of sovereignized peoples resulted not least from the experience that open-air mass gatherings—which often assumed the form of demonstration parades in the twentieth century (termed "processions" [Aufzüge] in the German right of assembly and defined as moving gatherings)—hold a large potential for violent escalation, while the architecturally contained, even roofed conventions offer a firm situative precept for civilized operations.[123] But because it is hardly possible to reactivate a form without also bringing those issues back into play that had originally been associated with it, the modern interest in ancient "mass" containers—the amphitheater, the arena and the circus—expanded into a popular renaissance in which, along with the buildings, the corresponding event types also return: the fights, the competitions, the drama of distinction between winners and losers. Only death cannot, unlike in the ancient arena, be an officially welcomed guest in the modern stadium.[124] It

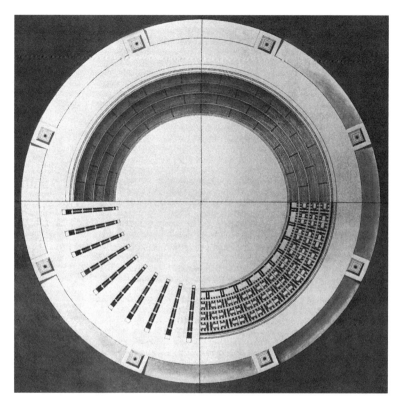

Etienne-Louis Boullée, plan for a Colosseum

has rightly been pointed out that modernity, in remarkable simultaneity with democracy, also revived the two ancient institutions of tragedy and the Olympic Games.[125] It is said of the Revolution's spokesman Danton that he had already demanded for Olympic Games to be held on the Field of Mars in 1793, with the aim of educating the nation. Before him, Gilbert Romme, co-author of the Revolution calendar, had suggested carrying out French Olympiads on leap years in 1792. When such patriots take the floor, Romans and Spartans are part of the package. It is no coincidence that Brutus, Caesar's murderer, was the hero of the hour. How long would it take for gladiators to step beside him from the arenas of old?

In view of these "mass" containers, which build an architectural bridge between the classical models of "mass" culture and its modern repetition, one of the structural problems of contemporary society comes into relief: even if it can only be acephalically and asynodically organized as a whole, the demand for cephalic and synodic agencies nonetheless stays powerfully alive in it—in the phantasms of the general assembly of society, the two even become the same (one could perhaps wonder whether such an assembly, which is impossible in the real world, could at least be simulated in a panoramatic or philosophical text, and if so, this would at least point towards an explanation for the remarkable authority of philosophy in the totality-devoted phases of modernity). The constitutional fiction popular among republicans, that of the people acquiring sovereignty as rightful successors to the king, suggests a new incarnation of the directorial function through a people's plenum—if it were practically feasible. Moreover, it would not take long for the constitutional thinkers and jurists of the Third Estate to realize the potential for violence held by such notions; it had become manifest in the tumultuous scenes of the people's revolts on July 14, 1789, on August 10, 1792, in the September massacres and countless fierce episodes in Paris and the provinces where a literal interpretation of the theorem of the people's sovereignty would lead. Only stringent restrictions of the freedom of assembly and coalition could prevent the crowd from literally adopting the dogma of the people's democracy that was in the air: "All power comes from the street."

These limitations testify to the rapid comprehension among the propertied bourgeoisie in the face of its first lessons in violence—even if the early populists polemicized against the incomplete realization of *égalité* by the "new masters" and threatened the half-hearted patriots with terrible fulfillments of philosophical ideas. The constitution of 1791 already attempted to suppress assemblies at which a present crowd sought to articulate itself as a political people's society, and thus a part of the embodied sovereign. The directorial constitution then forbade almost all open-air gatherings as riotous assemblies—a ban maintained throughout the nineteenth century; this was the legal premise of the restless quietism (or integrated radicalism) that would characterize French culture from the end of the Napoleonic era to the age of World Wars (or until the present day, more spiteful minds would claim).[126] Under Jacobin rule, the initially firm belief in the expressive truthfulness of "mass" events had in fact been shaken; people had seen too often how easily a crowd of *enragés* gathered in public places could be transformed into half-blindly lurching "masses" by a chance outrage-triggering phrase. Canetti referred to the energized mob implanted with an intention as the "baiting crowd";[127] as *sans-culotte* gangs, they left their business cards on street lanterns. If there was a trick of reason in the Revolution of 1789, it was the fact that its principles were only ever partially realized; only thus did it maintain a certain resilience against the disinhibiting postulates of universalism from below. The hour of the latter struck once more in the early twentieth century, when the European fascisms, united in solidarity like an International of nationalists, established the unity of street and state and put the implementation the egalitarian total inclusion of one people within itself on the agenda.

2. The Collectors:
On the History of the Stadium Renaissance

It is fair to say that the totalitarianism of the Modern Age was an outgrowth of the stadium consensus: in a heaving phonotope where a hundred thousand voices place a dome of noise over those gathered, that phantom of unanimity ensues which has haunted demagogues and social philosophers ever since. Here a sonic *volonté générale* is produced—a plebiscite of shouts. In the light of these conditions, Gabriel Tarde's thesis that the social state of humans is a hypnotic or somnambulistic one seems justified to the letter. The outcry of the masses in the stadium is connected directly back to it, for being affected by the spectacle leads to mimetic arousal, arousal leads to the vocal gesture, and the massively amplified return of that gesture to each person's own ears leads to the moved state which approaches a conviction. If Elias Canetti was able to describe the "crowd as a ring,"[128] this not only characterizes the visual and architectural conditions in a stadium, but equally the acoustic spell that, rising from the gathering, is cast on it. Like the Athenian military commanders, modern consensus directors appreciate the rousing effects of music. When all the elements that produce an "experience" are meant to come together, the means of phonotopic synthesis must not be absent. If they are given, the result—the enthusiastic fusion of the crowd—is guaranteed. Since then, people have known what is means to have been there. Those who were "there" will testify that the event as such offered a form of truth. At the same time, it already becomes clear that strict ritual constraints can be applied to the throng in the people's container. Between 1790 and 1798, the rediscovered arena on the Field of Mars in

Paris and numerous analogous constructions in the provinces were tested with pomp and glory time and again. The fascinogenic ritual and the collective autohypnosis made operative combine to form the stuff the cathedrals of the post-Christian commune are made of. From that point on, modern "society" had a high-performance auto-persuasive medium—a collector with which the task of directly assembling large crowds of people, if it became necessary once more, could be managed with organizational and psychotechic coherence.

In the present context it is sufficient to ask why it would still take over a century for the rediscovery of the arena or Colosseum effect, the fusion of the audience before the narcissistic-narcotic spectacle, to take place in modern "mass" culture on a large scale. The very brief answer would be that the "society" of the nineteenth century still managed to evade performing the task at hand in full—the terror of people's democracy was too deepseated among the witnesses to the turmoil and their heirs. When the "masses" did make appearances in that era, it was usually in ceremonially controlled forms.[129] Only with the turbulences of the incipient twentieth century did the tendency towards large gatherings come to the fore once again, and together with it the demand for the architectural collectors for large numbers of physically aggregated humans.

The code words for the history of collectors are "Olympic Games," "Russian Revolution" and "fascism." What connects the members of this heterogeneous trinity is the joint challenge of developing large-scale interiors for present and mobilized crowds in order to cultivate the latter's receptivity with staged illusions of being the center. Admittedly, the art of social synthesis at the level of modernity was now practiced only indirectly; this does not, however, mean that the direct gatherings of the crowds in their hourly symbioses required the most explicit organizational knowledge. This knowledge pragmatized itself in the operation of the large collectors. Since the inception and establishment of such macro-interiors, it should be clear that the architectural form examined by Walter Benjamin, that of the arcades—in which he searched for the profound interior idea of the nineteenth century: the paradoxical synthesis between the public world of commodities and the world of intimacy—no longer has a key function for understanding the space-creating processes in contemporary society. As far as their mercantile dimension is concerned, the arcades were separated from the shopping centers on the edges of urban complexes or the pedestrian zones of city centers; in recent architecture, they are only conceivable as historicizing quotations.[130] (The shopping "environment" at the renovated Leipzig central train station, completed in the early 1990s, offers—like the arcades at Potsdamer Platz and related constructions—a suggestive example of capitalist historicism staged in ultra-modern ways.) As far as the space-creating potencies of the twentieth century are concerned, the abstract constellation of stadiums and apartments is more significant than anything else. While the former enable the dense isopathic foaming of the masses in large-scale containers, eliminating individual space, the latter ally themselves with the civilizatory trend towards the discrete foaming of "society" in egospheric cell conglomerates.

These tendencies reveal a distortion in the overall structure of "society" that could—to speak in Hegelian terms for a moment—be described as a dialectic of modernization. While the progressive differentiation of subsystems proceeds inexorably in the process of modernity, contrary attempts to rescue or reestablish the central function repeatedly articulate themselves anew. However often one points out that we have long inhabited a world form in which the projection of the illusion of totality and center onto a king (and his logical second, the philosopher or wise master) only tricks the naïve, the king's position as such—the phantasmatic place in which the whole would know self-transparently what it is and wants—is not vacated without a fight. The resistance in favor of the center forms its own centers, and its own attractors for the masses. The Parisian Field of Mars, the Olympic stadium of Athens and its successor buildings all over the world: the festival house in Bayreuth, Red Square in Moscow, the Salzburg Felsenreitschule[131] along with the cathedral square, the Reich Sports Field, the grounds for the Nuremberg Rally—these place names reflect in exemplary fashion the recentering and synodal tendencies without which a number of the most powerful and most problematic politico-cultural streams of motivation in the first half of the twentieth century cannot be made comprehensible. In such places, suitable agents do their duty to simulate centrality—a task that dissolves the boundaries between politics and the fine, sublime arts. Perhaps it is not superfluous to recall this, after the positivization of centerlessness in postmodernity caused the disintegration of the historical climate in which centrists old and new believed that the plausibilities of the time were on their respective sides. During a precise historical situation, the longing for the center combined with the will to call a plenary assembly. Even if this did not literally amount to a convening of the totality, whether imagined as republican, ethnic or class-based, the call to gather did widely reach elites who were willing to appear—the photogenic successor groups to high society. When those are absent, assemblers resort to summonable followings.

The history of the modern Olympic Games was examined fairly comprehensively and presented in popular overviews in 1996, as part of the centenary celebrations; a recapitulation here would therefore be superfluous. What matters in the present context is that their reintroduction and popularization were an intense stimulus for stadium-building in the Modern Age and the associated collector practices. Not only did the "Olympic idea" give modern athletic ideology its highest authority and the ritual that motivated it in every aspect; the pull towards physical mass assembly, however depoliticized, internationalized and media-refracted, was also reinforced by it.

In series, the games showed over more than a century how unsuitable the conventions of historicism were to keep the Renaissance-like impetus of modern demands for arenas under control. Only at the very beginning were neo-aristocratic motives and those based in the mentality of the educated classes able to influence the modern sports movement. The excavations in Olympia between 1875 and 1881, led by Ludwig Curtius, had brought to light the original sites of the Olympic contests; the Panathenaic Stadium too had been uncovered in the mid-nineteenth century and used since then as a sports venue for national "Olympias" (in which university professors acted as officials), before becoming the site of the first international Olympic Games in 1896, thanks to a donation by a patriotic Greek millionaire—with 295 exclusively male participants from thirteen countries. It is doubtful whether these first Games were to the taste of their organizers; Pierre de Coubertin wrote

Panathenaic Stadium

in his memoires that the "Olympic horizon" only became clear to him in its full meaning after a visit to Wagner's Bayreuth. The sporting games he envisaged would be analogous to the neo-aristocratic enclave that Wagner's festival venue represented—and, like Bayreuth, would have a pedagogical and humbling effect on the real world from the sublime counterworld. Just as Bayreuth had been the site of the rebirth of tragedy from the spirit of music, the Olympics would lead to a rebirth of athletism—in harmony with the spirit of competition in business society. Coubertin's confessions have the weight of diagnoses of his time, as they unmistakably show a central trait of modern "mass" culture: the replacement of the European renaissance in art and philology with a globalized renaissance of athletes and stadiums.

The subsequent Paris Olympics in 1900 already saw the participation of 1,077 athletes from 21 countries, for the first time including eleven women, who competed at golf and tennis—much to the distaste of the androphile purist Coubertin. Nonetheless, this numerical inflation was insignificant for the public perception of the Games because they were held merely as a side program for the World Exhibition in Paris (a further nineteenth-century collector myth), spread over 162 days, without the city of Paris supplying any suitable stadium. The facilities used were the grounds of the Racing Club de France in the Bois de Boulogne. The Olympic locations for the Paris Olympics were surpassed in meagerness only by those for St. Louis 1904. Had the revived—or, as Coubertin preferred to say, reinstated—Games merely been the continuation of Grecophilia by other means, they would barely have survived their pitiful beginnings. One might concede that such disciplines as discus throwing would have been forgotten had works of art like Myron's statue of the discus thrower at the National Museum of Rome not preserved their memory; and the first repetition of the marathon at the 1896 Olympics in Athens, initiated by the philologist Michel Bréal, initially constituted no more than taking the sources literally, outside of the libraries. Nonetheless, the constructions and exercises of Olympism in the modern context soon took on a meaning of their own. Within a short time, the old style of Grecomania was barely relevant to the development of the athletic renaissance.

Already at the London Olympics of 1908, the breakthrough to architecturally advanced sport-cult constructions took place with the erection of Shepherd's Bush Stadium, completed on time using iron and cement, with almost 70,000 seats. This first authentic Olympic arena removed any doubts as to whether modernity would elevate the Roman oval to a canonic form in the design of its most significant collector: in future, all that would remain of the Greek stadium, which was U-shaped and required one side to be open, would be the name.[132] As far as the event-cultural modernization of the Games is concerned, it did not come until the Los Angeles Olympics in 1923, when, for the first time, all decisions were made within a reduced period of two weeks—in contrast to earlier Games, which had been spread over three to six months and were condemned to unproductiveness for the media and ineffectiveness among the bulk of the public (except for the ten-day Athens Olympics of April 1896). Once the cult formalities had also been established (the Olympic flag and Olympic oath since Antwerp 1920, the Olympic flame since Amsterdam 1928; it was only the flame relay from Olympia to the site of the Games that was not added until the 1936 Berlin Olympics, symbolizing the transfer of athletism from the Greeks to the Germans), Olympism only needed an occasion for its definitive self-staging as the cult center of the athletic renaissance.

A major boost came from the Californian Olympics, over-shadowed by the global economic crisis; with them, the entrance of monumentalism and entertainment into the Olympic move-ment became unmistakable. Their main location was the Coliseum designed by John and Donal B. Parkinson, expanded to seat 105,000, which had been completed in 1923 and already had 75,000 seats prior to the Olympics—almost as many as the ancient original in Rome. (For the 1984 Los Angeles Olympics, an even larger monumental complex of the same name was built—paid for exclusively by private sponsors, incidentally.) For those who could read the writing on the wall, the choice of name was the decisive indicator of the dynamics of "mass culture" in the twentieth century: the reshaping of the Greek stadium into the Roman arena—or rather, the irruption of the second emergency into the simulated peace of the sporting contest. In the New World, Boullée's visions of a *Cirque nationale* had materialized with a delay of 150 years. From that point on, the Olympic collector became a psychopolitical machine whose primary function is to produce victories and victors and to make the spectators witnesses to the distinction taking place in real time: that between the first and the rest.[133]

The splitting of a collective into victors and non-victors developed into the central sacrament of the modern event cult. It elevated empathy with the victors to a principal exercise of social affectivity—attenuated by a certain consideration for the runners-up, in so far as the process of civilization makes it an obligation (in this sense, one can say that the invention of silver and bronze medals testifies to the civilizing function of sport). In addition, Olympic stadiums and others establish themselves as the preferred cult locations of the modern bio-religion—sites of the vicarious suffering of athletes for the popular dream of transforming the trivial body into the superhumanly capable statue. Since the triumph of Olympism, the generalization of the "second emergency" motif has defined all fascinogenic forms of mass culture; it is based, as mentioned earlier, on the Roman-inspired reduction of drama to the sharp-edged distinction between victory and defeat. It is on this other seriousness that not only the increasing psychologization of sport—in the sense of its adaptation to psychological warfare—depends, but also its direct connection to the state politics of prestige and order, as well as the profit system of event organizers (in more naïve times: the sports clubs and associations).

The latent mass-cultural potentials of renewed Olympism were fully realized for the first time at the Berlin Summer Olympics in 1936. When Oswald Spengler noted in the first volume of *The Decline of the West*, "The difference between a Berlin athletic ground on a big day and a Roman circus was even by 1914 very slight,"[134] he had got ahead of events; as he died in 1936, he was unable to experience the fulfillment of his prophetic diagnosis.

That these Games, held on the Reich Sports Field in the Grunewald forest from August 1–16, went down in history as an organizational triumph, was not only due to their resolute instrumentalization by the sympathy and respectability campaign of the Nazi regime. At the Berlin event, the tendencies towards the neoheroic-monumental and narco-narcissistic mass spectacle that had been obvious since Los Angeles 1932 were taken to their logical conclusion. Despite the ritual of the torch relay from Olympia to Berlin, introduced by the chief organizer Carl Diem, there could no longer be any doubt as to the overall tendency of the Games: the definitive subjugation of their Grecophilic beginnings by their subsequent Romanization. This was ensured above all by the gigantomanic and solemn stadium complex designed by the Berlin architect Werner March, which had emerged from a comparative study of analogous buildings from classical and modern times. The parallel stadium constructions by Jan Wils in Amsterdam (1928 Olympic Games—awarded a gold medal for architecture), John and Donald B. Parkinson in Los Angeles, Ernst Otto Schweizer in Nuremberg (1927) and Vienna (1931) and Umberto Constantini in Bologna (1925–27) had convinced March of the constructive potential of visible frame constructions made of reinforced concrete.

Olympic Stadium with Reich Sports Field in 1936, by Werner March

After Hitler, to whom Olympus was alien and "physical exercise" was intensely ridiculous, had shown displeasure at March's plans, Albert Speer was given the task of correcting the stadium's outward appearance in a monumentalist direction—especially with stone cladding that would hide all visible concrete surfaces and construction parts, creating an aura of martial aloofness.[135] Drawing on Hitler's theory of the Ruin Value of great buildings, Speer temporarily indulged in reveries about how his edifices would present themselves as sublime relics after centuries or millennia—now the emulation of the colossal Roman buildings was not only a vitalist gesture of the kind that befitted a "young democracy" in the earlier case and a "national revolution" in the present case, but also a tragic and sentimental program. Naturally the Berlin stadium did not simply want to "go down in history": for the moment, it would content itself with being considered the largest in the world, which, with its 110,000 seats, it probably achieved for a time. With its pseudo-Dorian ambience and its embedding in a landscape of ceremonial squares and stark towers, it was meant to put visitors in a state of sublime humbling and socio-idealistic willingness to renounce personal projects. Never before had a sports facility been conceived to such an extent as a machine for collectivizing and overwhelming. Whoever entered here had to abandon all hope of individuality. Whoever triumphed here would no longer be a private person; the figure on the winners' podium would be pure emanation from a political or racial energy source.

One of the most informative ironies of twentieth-century cultural history is that the first climax of the athletic renaissance transpired under the auspices of National Socialism—and was, as even skeptics conceded, in good hands. The fact that a fascist organizer was responsible for a large-scale event of this kind resulted from the convergence between the synodal core of Nazi ideology and the Olympic pathos of physically convening the world's young athletic elite in an outstanding place, along with an audience that believed in achievement. The Führer cult, which corresponds intimately to the idea of the ethno-national plenum, can be made philosophically plausible as the terminal form of ancient occidental centrism: as the people are always already gathered in the Führer, he can invite the "people" as a whole, or near-whole, to celebrate a festival of homogeneity with him. Fascism rests on a semi-modern interpretation of popular sovereignty—in the sense of a sudden royalism from below: from its dark center, the people emanates the man in whom it believes it is completely with itself. Because there is someone who is everyone—and purports to be everything to everyone—those who come together around him can embrace the notion that their physical assembly is already the perfect proof of sovereignty. Marx's well-known remark to Ruge (in a letter from March 1843) that the philistine is the material of the monarchy would have to be inverted in the present case: the monarch or Führer is the material of the philistines. Olympism, for its part, is based on a semi-modern interpretation of existence which uses the suggestion that all power comes from healthy bodies. Because there are athletes who constantly push the limits of human performance, everyone who witnesses this can imagine having a share in the realm of bodily sovereignty. Spontaneous royalism of the fascist variety is mirrored in the Olympic form of popular-biological aristocratism. The relative modernity of both—or rather their modern counter-modernity—directly depends on an extensive and professional use of collectors.

The extent to which National Socialist neoclassicism is characterized by the adoption of Greek forms by the Roman *imperium* can be seen from the Olympic buildings in Berlin, whose program and dimensions are contained in the concept of a "Reich Sports Field" [*Reichssportfeld*], whose outlines had been formulated since 1934/35. The Greek institutional triad of democracy, tragedy and sporting agon was invoked through the division of the field into a sports venue, a place of mass assembly and a theater—with nothing that might alert unwarned visitors to the parodistic character of the complex, for the attributes of neo-imperialist overwhelming architecture were too powerfully staged. One can only do justice to the Reich Sports Field by recognizing it as a Nazi Las Vegas: a testing ground for the total quotation.

Not only was the Roman Colosseum invoked within this complex in a suitably inflated adaption, as an "arena"; Greek tragic theater was also subjected to ostentatious repetition—here in the form of the Dietrich Eckart Open-Air Stage with its 22,000 seats (the Theater of Dionysus in Athens could hold 17,000 visitors). In addition, the Maifeld, an assembly space of monumental proportions, directly adjoined the Olympic Stadium; here the typical fascist transformation of the agora (or the absolutist *cour d'honneur*) into the marching ground took place. It is no coincidence that this part of the complex had been of personal interest to Hitler, just as there were parallels to Nuremberg.[136]

What links these collectors called up through quotations (stadium, theater, assembly place) to one another is the autologous quality of the events for which they were conceived. The gatherings did not take place to enact a program or a repertoire; the program itself is subordinated to the imperative of assembly and merely constitutes a pretext for summoning the crowd to consummate their togetherness. Where Germans come together to represent the whole known as Germany, the Germanness of those assembled will inevitably be the only topic. In such synodal deliria, it is one of the rules of the game that, like an idealistic system, they only speak of the One which they themselves both present and represent. Monothematism turns directly into autothematism—and not only among nationalist revolutionaries. What was termed totalitarianism stemmed from making the collectors and the major media subordinated to them—the daily press and radio—subject to the organizer's thematic supremacy. This organizer can demand, with no mean success, that there be no other topics next to them. Sensationalist histories of the Nazi era often pass over the fact that numerous rally participants, especially among the extras carted in from all over, were nonetheless bored, spoke about other things and made fun of chaotic conditions behind the scenes. It is unknown whether the popular characterization of Goebbels' speeches as *Humpelstilzchens Märchenstunde* [Cripplestiltskin's story time] and the renaming of the Ministry of Propaganda as the *Reichsgeltungsbedürfnisanstalt* [Reich (Mental) Institution for the Admiration-Needy] were already common practice in the Nuremberg days.[137] It is a documented fact, on the other hand, that the performances of Wagner's *The Meistersinger of Nuremberg* esteemed so highly by Hitler, which served as a prelude to the rally, initially took place before an empty house and sleeping or culturally uninterested Nazi Party grandees; such are the limits of enthusiastic society.

In the "city of Reich party congresses" at the time of the Berlin Games, there were already two successfully run large-scale complexes for mass liturgical exercises, the Luitpold Arena and the Zeppelinfeld, both in the form of massive rectangles with a tribune side resembling the Pergamon Altar—complexes that would be augmented by a third, the Marsfeld, with the extreme dimensions of almost 3,500 by 2,200 feet.[138] There is no place in the memory landscapes of modernity in which the counter-modern theory and practice of assembly magic materialized as explicitly as on the Nazi Party rally grounds in Nuremberg—nor any other place in which the festival character of National Socialism was so plain to see. Although the European fascist movements, like their Anglo-American offshoots, were all revolts by the opponents of progressive differentiation and acted out their psychosocial opposition to the accompanying flexibilization of citizen-customer subjectivities (previously: subversion of the autonomous personality), the National Socialists reserved the right to stage the most magnificent agony of political centrism. Carried by the resolute will to illusion, the German totality games were desperate misinvestments in the already obsolete demand to conceive and summon the whole collective—in the present case the people of the national society—as an assemblable entity. The pontifical stages used for the Nuremberg September Festival, held six times between 1933 and 1938 (each time with a specific theme), both those realized and those only planned, show just how far the genius of misinvestment can go. Hitler's function, which was at once the secret of his success, was that he could take his role as festival director of the assembly illusion fanatically seriously; his one undeniable talent was his ability to formulate the successes of the Nazi movement, which amazed him too, within the framework of his synodal mysticism. At the post-Olympic "Rally of Honor" in 1936, for example, he called out to those gathered in Nuremberg:

> "Do we not feel once again in this hour the miracle that brought us together? [...] When we meet each other here, the wonder of our coming together fills us all. Not everyone of you sees me, and I do not see everyone of you. But I feel you, and you feel me! It is the belief in our people that [...] made us see our road when we were astray; it joined us together into one whole!"[139]

This goes beyond the usual religious hermeneutics of success with which the successful inwardly countersign their accolades. Hitler's meditation gains its mystical spark from the bare fact of the assembly as a massive and actually occurring event. Here the word "success" becomes synonymous with togetherness—and togetherness synonymous with the Führer's self-expansion into the present auditorium. Those searching for the truth in "higher-level subjectivities" can easily get their money's worth with this immanently staged super-we. The complementary text was recited by the speakers of the people's groups, such as Robert Ley at the swearing-in ceremony for the political directors at the "Greater Germany" party rally of 1938, who addressed Hitler with the following words:

> "Before you now, once again, stands this united German people. They have stepped up in the great circle of this cathedral of light, the workers and farmers, the citizens, students and soldiers"[140]

Naturally the organizers of Nuremberg were, even as they gazed through the autohypnotic veil, aware that these invocations of the "united German people" remained highly selective representative gatherings—a few hundred thousand standing in for 70 million. As with all large-scale events with a generalizing inclusive tendency, this resulted in the necessity of augmenting synodal totalization with mediatization. And in precisely this, in the linking of the large-scale event with its broadcasting in a prompt or synchronous medium, lies the information that has crystallized and remained binding since the Nazi period about the organizability of symbiotic "masses" within modern macro-interiors and the public media spheres connected to them. That the collector should bring together a gathered crowd in the arena medium of presence is the necessary, but still inadequate precondition for confirming the ambition of universal effect: the connector, the medium that links from a distance, must be

Media Center at Lord's Cricket Ground, London

added—whether as a combination of bureaucracy and postal services or as print or broadcasting mass media—for the fiction of integral social synthesis through organized events to become operative. Where collectors and connectors function in alignment, large-scale collectives with the format of a nation can become subject to the simultaneous excitation sought by the festival directors. Indeed, synchronous spheres of planetary proportions can even appear intermittently in this way—in exemplary fashion at the opening ceremony of the Olympic Games, or with singularities such as the funeral rites for Diana, Princess of Wales or the live broadcasts of the collapse of the Twin Towers in New York on September 11, 2001, along with the national ceremony in memory of the victims in New York's Yankee Stadium a few days later, where some twenty clerics from the Jewish, Christian and Muslim faiths attempted to interpret the global significance of the deaths of the attack's 6,000 victims (the number was later reduced to 2,800) before a billion observers. This expansion into the virtually universal is only possible if real gatherings are broadcast and the broadcasts occasion further gatherings. From this perspective, Hitler's war was the continuation of the festival in a different medium—games whose cult function was always first and foremost that of betrothal ceremonies between living Germans and those who had fallen in the First World War, supposedly cheated of their victory. As more sophisticated interpretations of Nazi ideology have noted, the core of German corporative identity designed by Hitler, Goebbels & Co. had a cult of the dead. For well-known reasons, the "Rally for Peace" planned for September 1939 had to be canceled; gradually, those affected by the nationalist delirium realized that the time of festivals was over. It was replaced by the constant affecting of the German public sphere in all its communal, business, club and neighborly organizations by the cooperation stress of the war and the media-generated exhilaration in the phase characterized by reports of success.

3. Discreet Synods: On the Theory of Congresses

Of the six large-scale collectors of the new Forum Germanicum— the three parade grounds (Luitpold Arena, Zeppelinfeld, Marsfeld), the planned German Stadium, the Old Congress Hall (Luitpold Hall) and the monumental New Congress Hall, of which an unfinished torso survived—it is only the last that exhibits a certain modernity. Not so much from an architectural perspective, as it is once again a grotesque transposition of the

Fragment of the New Congress Hall, Nuremberg, designed by Albert Speer

Colosseum, but in an assembly-sociological since, in that the congress building type *per se* contains modernity's response to the need for discreet conference centers for social associations. At the same time, what is notable about this enormous edifice, which combined elements of the arena, the concert hall and a Wagnerizing bureaucracy, is the dysfunctional character of its dimensions, as a congress building, even by Nazi standards, only makes sense if (alongside the plentiful locations for cult activities and issuing orders) it also provides places for consultation and discussion—a function that is not easy to identify in the surviving fragments. The New Congress Hall is probably best understood as a party opera house that has slipped into outsized dimensions. This too is a machine of intimidation and acclamation: here the usual election of the party chairman was to be replaced by the ritual of the "proclamation of the Führer"

Tjibaou Cultural Center, Nouméa, New Caledonia, by Renzo Piano Building Workshop (1991–1998)

rehearsed in the Luitpold Hall, and this is where the political directors would have had to listen to Hitler's speeches on culture. Nonetheless, it constitutes a hypothetical concession to the imperative of assembling people with different responsibilities around particular topics. This means accepting—hestitantly— that modern "societies" are discreet thematic biotopes whose normal form is the congress. And even if Speer's colossal Cae- sarist building again pays homage mostly to the theatrical

Lingotto, Turin: Fiat headquarters, by Renzo Piano Building Workshop (1983)

imperative, it does take a step towards customary modernity, which supports the occasional symbioses, the fleeting close encounters between its expert faculties and interest groups, with a corresponding range of conference centers, halls and conference rooms. If one leaves aside large-scale collector buildings such as stadiums and museums (and also transit collectors, namely the stations and airports), contemporary architecture is concerned primarily with the spatial demands of conference society.[141]

How little our actually existing "society" is aware of its own multicentric, polythematic, conference-intensive constitution can be seen in, among other things, the fact that there is no adequate sociological study on the assembly life of the "society" foamed in clubs, associations, businesses and societies: the expansive archipelago of congress centers, trade fair complexes, conference hotels, club houses and rooms, containers for company employee meetings and customer events, weekend academies, party schools, instutions for advanced training, as well as the halls and shells for assemblies of profession-based organizations—all this constitutes a *terra incognita* for the ordinary perception of "society" in "society." The organized overestimation of universities contrasts with a spontaneous underestimation of the conference world based on a lack of perception; barely anyone realizes that the effective learning processes of professional groups, subcultures and decider elites have long been taking place in an extra-academic conference circus. Its invisibility is, admittedly, but a side effect of the disinterest of "society" in its true constitution. In some public relations agencies and event management service firms at most, in trade fair construction companies or speaker pools, in trend offices and the few teaching posts of professors of business economics who are in demand for conferences and capable of giving rhetorical satisfaction, materials accumulate for a future science of congress and assembly—while academic sociology, as usual, argues over the capacity of action or systems theories or interpretations of classics. The newer multi-milieu studies, if anything, occasionally preserve contact with the self-spatialization realities of multifocal "society" oscillating in discreet conference rhythms. In the light of the manifestly asyndic constitution of the whole, the organization of countless discreet symbiotic situations remains the great unthought and blocked-out element of sociological attention.[142]

The transition to a sophisticated collector culture presupposes that faced with a present crowd, whether it encompasses fifty heads or fifty thousand, evades the demands for deeper symbolism on which religious communities or ethnic collectivisms and their respective ideologies of assembly are based. The practical wisdom

Lingotto, Turin: conference room, by Renzo Piano Building Workshop (1983)

of the current conference and event culture lies in the fact that it tends to the daily and hourly symbioses of professional groups and interest groups at their own level, without offending those assembled with heated over-interpretations of their context.

Since the 1950s, the functionalist and neo-functionalist congress style that began to emerge in the late nineteenth century has also become inconspicuously generalized in countries previously devastated by political holism. For although "society" as a whole—whether conceived in the singular as global society or in the plural as the respective populations of nation-states—always constitutes a non-assemblable entity (and can therefore only be totalized in the media and the imagination), numerous sub-ordinate social structures such as parties, citizens' unions, associations, clubs, cooperatives and professionals' organizations remain characterized by the motif of periodic assembly for institutional reasons. One can observe that everything has a capacity for congress—except for the whole.

When the Association of Southern German Orthopedists meets for their annual conference in 2002, for example in Baden-Baden Festival Hall (after meeting at the Wiesbaden trade fair grounds the previous year), it is sufficient for the chairperson to greet those present with the assurance of being pleased that so many have come—by no means will they meditate on the fact of the assembly as such, let alone mention the miracle that brought them together in that hour. Instead, they will thank by name the organizers and helpers in the background without whose efforts the convention would not have been possible. When the shareholders of Daimler-Chrysler come together in the Hans Martin Schleyer Hall in Stuttgart for their general meeting, Jurgen E. Schrempp will refrain from saying that he is the vine and they are the branches, even though the assembled are united by their shares in the company's capital as much as any Christian congregation in the mystical body of the Lord. The reserved synodal parties have understood that their occasional gathering in the gray symbiosis of a conference day in no way contains more truth than their usual scattered mode of being; the minutes of swearing allegiance to a shared interest in the opening speeches of the conference (in the form of a resolute declaration of war on the health ministry's reform plans, for example) and the possible minutes of silence for members who have passed away since the last gathering do not establish any *communio* from above, nor do they create a maximum stress unit in the manner of a combat league. Votes on the suggestions made by the executive board are manifestations of the interest analysis carried out by the assembled, not emanations from a universally shared collective self.

Container terminal, Bremerhaven

Whoever registers and attends *ipso facto* embraces a situation in which those with professional responsibility and the winners of differentiation work on optimizing their success games.

4. Foam City—About Urban Spatial Multiplicities

Against the background of these deliberations on assembly architecture, the topological particularity of modern cities becomes
visible: on the one hand, they define themselves as locations of
collectors that address the assemblable crowds; on the other
hand, they house the apartment complexes that serve as living
capsules for solitary dwellers and small families, and they settle
the manifold institutions of the working world in which the
majority of city-dwellers secure their economic means of existence. The terms "traffic" and "communication" have established
themselves in urbanist literature for the purpose of forming a
shared level joining the three poles of urban life (work, dwelling,
public and collector spaces)—as if one wanted to reduce the phenomenon of the city to the generalities of transport and the flow
of signs. After the drive of electronics began to affect theory, this
extended to such fictions as the virtual city, online territory, the
"City of Bits," Cyberville and similar disembodiment metaphors.
The more advanced the model, the more it likes the current city
to evaporate into a phantomatic tangle of knots in telematic networks. E-urbanistics subsumes the materiality and density of the
urban space in angelistic long-distance traffic processes. The central characteristic of urbanity is sought in the flight from physical
localization and the explosion of embedding situations ("disem-
bedding"). Accordingly, such discourses about tomorrow's city
without qualities regularly appear accompanied by romantic
notions of decentralization and mysticism of immaterialization.
What all of these sub-euphoric theorems have in common is that
they deliberately overlook what makes cities cities, namely the
atmospherically active agglomeration of space-positings with

autonomous value—in our terminology, the foam character of urbanly condensed complexes; or, more precisely, that they de-thematize it through a choice of terminology that does not further perception.

According to its real-surreal spatial constitution, urban macro-foam can only be understood if one sees it as a meta-collector that gathers places of assembly and non-assembly. The true function of metropolises is obviously to provide the neighborly coexistence of centers and non-centers—not in the form of a super-central, but as an agglomeration or layering of discrete spatial potencies: collectors, businesses, the dwelling and the molded surface under the open sky. The meta-collection from which the current city ensues does not deal with persons who can be assembled or isolated; it refers to places, that is to say settled spatial inventions, in which persons do or do not take chances for assembly and do or do not use chances for communication.

If the topian and utopian thought of the previous half-century featured anything resembling the adventure of new urbanistics—names like Buckminster Fuller, Nicolas Schöffer, Yona Friedman, Eckhard Schulze-Fielitz, Paolo Soleri, Peter Cook, Ron Herron and above all Constant testify to this—the emphases of their projects lay in the attempt to override factual cities through literally metaphorical, that is to say elevated and superimposed meta-cities. One should see in the basic ground-fleeing gesture of these new urban inventions not only the utopianism of an acosmic or semi-mundane fantasy that contents itself with designing parallel realities; rather, the ambition of rethinking the metropolitan multifocal and polythematic space through the formation of new models is often of an analytical and model-theoretical character. Not infrequently, it

SITE (Alison Sky, Michelle Stona, Joshua Weinstein, James Wines), *High Rise of Homes*, project (1981)

serves a concrete, albeit indirect interpretation of the present. The pioneers of this approach are usually chaos theorists *avant la lettre* who, after the failure of Old European centrist rationalism and a gradual disgust with the holism of control, experimented with fundamentally new procedures in order to grasp more fully the synthesis of "society" in spaces of compaction.

The redescription of the urban space takes place on stilts: on high supports, the radically artificial new spatial articulations in which the city-dwellers of the future live their coexistence with their kind and with things raise themselves above the hopelessly abandoned urban landscapes of the status quo. The pillars and supports contribute to passing over the no longer soluble question of the ground with a leap upwards. Consistently enough, large projective energies are invested in the concept of the tower; among the new urbanists, it no longer represents the construction form of feudal power claims or the metaphysical upward mobility of existence.[143] By simply leaving the old substance on the ground below, it testifies to the caesura between history and post-history. No more gap site architecture, no annexes, no renovation. The aim is now a new approach at a height, a new formation of layers in the vertical, the post-historical architectural self-determination of higher building contractors above the stagnated nightmares of all previous species. There is no dialectic between the old building structure and the superstructure—only a succession that appears as a superimposition. After the first space-taking by alienated society and its tragic real estate, which we know as grown cities, the earth is to be disclosed a second time and appropriated by building over it—this time in the air, such that the construction of stilts advances to become the basic technology of post-history. *Une autre ville pour une autre vie.*[144]

RWE Tower in Essen, by Ingenhoven, Overdiek and Partner (1997)

In the countless drawings and models made by Constant (full name Constant Anton Nieuwenhuys, born 1920)—whom I would single out as the most important visionary and analyst of the second urban culture—for his obsessively pursued large-scale project *New Babylon* (1960–1970), the supports are given an almost historico-philosophical meaning: they are meant to mark the secondary layer of existence, the post-historically released and radically creative desired life above the fully automated basis comprising the old factors of earth, work and metabolism in spatially explicit fashion. In the new upper world of the second Babylon—the name already indicates its typically postmodern positivization of confusion and its political consequence, namely ungovernability—the era of materialism is considered over: the New Babylonians are Fluxus existentialists living in a world after alienated labor. Their connection to reality exists purely via the construction of mobile spaces, atmospheres and environments. They romp about in the hanging gardens of madness—combative, congenial, condelirious. Hence the old land registries must give way to a "psycho-geographical" redescription of space, a description that no longer follows the earth's surfaces, properties or national borders, but rather the expressive actions of the inhabitants, their moods, their works, their installations.

For all his concessions to utopianism, Constant is primarily an analyst of polyatmospheric "society." His point of departure is the unsuppressible atmosphere-generating quality of human housing practices. Because his utopia, following the social fantasies of the Situationist International, conceived the new "society" as a form of coexistence between happy unemployed persons, the atmospheric milieu of togetherness, which is only ever perceived as a byproduct elsewhere, is released as a main

Constant, *New Babylon*, ladder labyrinth

product in his city. (Guy Debord, with whom Constant cooperated from the end of the 1950s on, had spoken in 1957 of "mood quarters" and urban "affective realities.")[145] The New Babylonians are the first inhabitants of an explicit aphropolitical structure—creators of a city that spreads across the earth as a proliferating nomadic artists' colony on stilts, solely comprising containers of atmospheres and reversible individuated environments. The content of this city is the art history of its inhabitants. As far as its manifestations are concerned, one could almost think that Constant anticipated the post-historical junk aesthetic of *Mad Max*.

With the gesture of setting up non-authoritarian (meaning not realization-oriented) models, the New Babylonian aphropolis—displayed complete in 1974, at the Gemeentemuseum in The Hague—visualizes a possible urbanist form of the "social

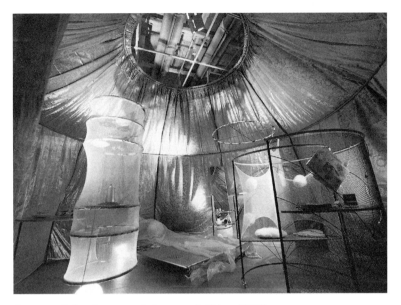

Accommodation for non-settled women in Tokyo (1989)

sculpture" postulated by Beuys in his metapolitical discourses. Referring to the polemical interference of the Situationists in the events of May 1968, Mark Wigley remarks:

> Atmosphere becomes the basis of political action. The seemingly ephemeral is mobilized as the agent of concrete struggle. As the fantasized endpoint of that struggle, New Babylon is a huge atmosphere jukebox that can only be played by a completely revolutionized society.[146]

Constant's thought experiment about the coexistence of creative unemployed persons in a collective liquid space leads to the conclusion that every person is not only an artist but, more precisely, an installation artist, because the spontaneous emanation of *ambiances* or meaning-laden environments is considered identical to the act of living. The anthropolitical breakthrough meant that the New Babylonians would no longer be beholden to old buildings and old atmosphere (a fact that was discussed in older theories using such notions as alienation and the becoming-independent of objectifications of the spirit, by Georg Simmel, among others, who had described the coercive character of being born into fixed symbolic shells as the "tragedy of culture"),[147] instead being free to keep beginning the construction of their setting anew without being tied to earlier sedimentations. The premise for this is the abolition of the traditional reality principle and its ontological supplements, the primacy of the past and the dictatorship of scarcity. To conceive of such things, Constant had to give strong credence to the fairytale Marxist motif of unleashing productive forces, ultimately leading to the abolition of all alienated labor. *New Babylon* sought to be an artificial paradise in the form of a planetary climbing park for constantly creative mutants who give new meaning to the term "world interior." Not only does it offer a total interior in which all spaces are air-conditioned, artificially illuminated and atmosphericized; a sojourn there would be synonymous with existence in an architectural rhizome that constantly meanders and drifts unpredictably. There are no longer any energy-related or environmental problems there, of course, as their externalization is a precondition: a massive leftover from the pre-ecological approach of exploiting nature, colored by Marxist humanism. Existence here has the function of being-in-the-installation, without a fixed hall or a need for home, in constant unplanned, randomly generated activity.

This drift behavior (*dérive*), which, together with a faith in the next step, comes from a contempt for great plans—the

Situationists' opposition to the Cartesian Le Corbusier was obligatory—anticipates elements of Chaos Theory. If the rhizomatic formation of chains is the growth principle of this supra-city, however, its connection to serial production, the use of modules, and standardization is unclear—as indeed the relationship between repetition, mimesis and innovation blurs into indeterminacy; here the myth of constant creativity has an inhibiting aftereffect. What is shown all the more clearly, however, is that the basic unit of the large-scale urban form is not meant to be the room or the apartment, but an almost macromolecular unit that Constant calls the "sector."

One must credit Constant's monomaniacal-constructivist models with far-reaching analytical qualities, for despite their futuristic jargon, they should be read more as a description of the status quo than a plan for the future. Their strength lies in the fact that they describe urbanized society's mode of being entirely from the perspective of its acephality, asynodality and mobility. As a result, they can do justice to the multifocal constitution and polyatmospheric attunement of the modern city better than any earlier theory. Constant's commentaries highlight the evolutionary and fluid character of the hyper-city, next to which real-life cities become recognizable as gigantic inhibition complexes whose components are rightfully termed immovable property. The weakness of the concept lies in the fact that despite its emphasis on multiplicities, it lacks a valid concept of the city as a meta-collector—which is why it overlooks the collecting function of the urban space as the connection of places of assembly and cooperation with places of separation and immunization (literally, the non-participation in the *munera* or tasks of the collective). It would appear that *New Babylon* contains neither a reference to

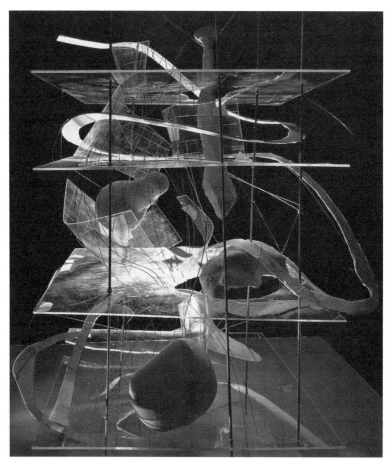

Gerald Zugmann, *ZAK—Zukunftsakademie Coop Himmelb(l)au*, C-Print

the collectors of mass culture nor to the ordinary working world—which makes the one-sided expansion of a type of space previously known only in museums or art environments all the more clear. A planetary *documenta*, mobilized and perpetuated.

For all these weaknesses, *New Babylon* possesses descriptive power vis-à-vis the "lifestyle" conditions that started to become

Dutch Pavilion at the Expo 2000, Hanover

dominant in affluent regions of the earth during the 1970s: it anticipates a world without lasting ties, populating its interiors with people for whom the progressive loosening of the *liens sociaux* and the adjustment of existential standards from an economy of scarcity to experiments with plentiful resources would be a *fait accompli*. What had been a radical leftist romanticism of "intense life" in the 1950s and 60s[148] became normal for countless First World citizens with the establishment of lifestyle civilization. By seeking to take the equation of city and world to its logical conclusion, *New Babylon* succeeded in bringing the three insular types of reality—the space station, the hothouse and the human sphere—closer together than anything before it;[149] one can see this by comparing the individualistic sophistication of the New Babylonian, bourgeois-bohemian artist population with the almost tribalist concepts of the first *Biosphere 2* teams. In Constant's project, the earth is no more than an old-world underlay for a multicultural space station (in fact, a monocivilizatory one grounded in the Western luxury of expression). It only preserves as much of the old nature as can be integrated into an encompassing hothouse. Naturally a fully realized *New Babylon* would also have animals and plants—but only as cohabitants of the integral interior, not as an autonomous biosphere or external green world.

One can identify relics of Constant's impulse in the Dutch contribution to the Expo 2000 in Hanover: a multi-story, transparent—in fact frontless—building, a sequence of piled-up biotopes is accommodated on six floors of one thousand square meters each, like tenants in their apartments in other houses—a concrete realization of the Dutch motto for the world exhibition: "Holland makes space." As a hybrid form between botanical garden and large residential house, this brilliantly bizarre building, a kind of plant high-rise, provides a timely commentary on an expanded concept of dwelling as making space for biotopic diversity under conditions of high urban density. Perhaps one can derive the thesis from this installation that all talk of "multicultural society" remains insubstantial without an awareness that the true matrix of diversity lies in the variety of the biotopes. This polybiotopics finds its materializations in advanced architecture. One can see in them that the "natures" or biomes of the future

Elisabeth Diller & Ricardo Scofidio, *Blur Building* (2002)

will be found less "outside" than in the large-scale hothouses of a civilization which has become aware of its duties as a host for biotopic complexes.

In many cases, the tendency towards an accommodation of natures of biotopes in urban constructions of the twentieth century went beyond the traditional forms of the "city park" or the hothouse. The encapsulation motif expanded so far that it ventured the integration of ever larger, once-external regional and urban complexes.[150] The modern city (and city landscape) increasingly develops into an operative unity of the aforementioned triad of space station, greenhouse and human island. At the urban end of the spectrum we find expanded interiors such as Jon Jerde's *Ceiling Show*, installed on Fremont Street in Las Vegas in the 1990s, transforming an entire street into a nocturnal light and sound experiential interior for a "wow" audience passing through; at the opposite end, one encounters hybrid landscapes inside the hall, as embodied by various well-known indoor ski slopes and indoor golf courses in Japan and elsewhere.

Max Peintner, *The Continuing Attraction of Nature* (1970–71), pencil drawing

One should beware of seeing such examples as mere curiosities; in both cases, contemporary architecture has transcended both the Old European idea of the large-scale interior (like Benjamin's arcade) and the traditional collector forms. The new event environments not only parody the old concepts of city and countryside; they also seem to poke fun at modern concepts such as "lifeworld" and "nature conservation," whose spatial blindness is now plain to see.

For the time being, these macro-interiors have a playful quality which almost conceals the fact that such constructs could be preliminary exercises for a climatic emergency. Could what a frivolous commentator already stated in the 1990s, namely that breathing is too important to continue doing it in the open air, become true in Europe in the foreseeable future? Will the citizens of rich nations in coming centuries really have to prepare to bid farewell to the common atmosphere? Already today, one would like to hear the comments of an employee of the European Ministry of Air and Space Atmosphere in the year 2102 about a design by the New York architects Liz Diller and Ricardo Scofidio that had long since acquired mythical status—an atmo-architecture in Yverdon-les-Bains on the shore of Lake Geneva entitled *Blur Building*, which became the symbol of the Swiss Expo 2002 and was popularly known simply as "the cloud"—because, using considerable technical resources, it invited visitors to take a walk across a long bridge through an artificial spatial sculpture of finely sprayed lake water. Though viewed skeptically by some critics, who considered it a mere gimmick, and a wasteful one at that, the blurred building of water particles, which took on a great variety of colors and moods with changes of weather, was welcomed by the majority of visitors from Yverdon as a brilliant introduction to the art of walking in clouds (in a waterproof coat, of course). A few of them will also have understood that they were encountering, in a light-handed form, a technically sophisticated attempt at a macroatmospheric installation—or rather, because walkable clouds, like installations in general, cannot be experienced in the mode of direct encounter: that they were being called to immerse themselves in a climatic sculpture.

Based on the object's popularity, one can conclude that for its visitors, it opened up an intuition about future questions of air design and climate technology on a larger scale. One would like to ask the employee at the aforementioned ministry what spatial and climatic history the Yverdon experiment had anticipated a hundred years earlier.

CHAPTER 3

Uplift and Pampering

On the Critique of Pure Whim

I was lucky: I saw the human condition change in my lifetime.
— Michel Serres, *Hominiscence*

Poverty was the all-pervasive fact of the world. Obviously it is
not of ours. [...] The problem of an affluent world that does
not understand itself may be serious, and they can needlessly
threaten the affluence itself. But they are not likely to be as
serious as those of a poor world where the simple exigencies of
poverty preclude the luxury of misunderstanding but where,
also and alas, no solutions are to be had.
— John Kenneth Galbraith, *The Affluent Society*[1]

1. Beyond Hardship

One can define conservatism as the political form of melancholy. It remained decisive for the conservative syndrome
which took shape in Europe after 1789 that it had resulted
from looking back at the irretrievable goods, life forms and
arts of pre-bourgeois times. One of its preconditions was the

certainty of never becoming the dominant view. It acquired its elegiac hues by emphasizing the habit of expecting the darker constants of human nature. To be conservative is to continue believing that good and noble things are tied to places and unique phenomena—for vulgar things, on the other hand, the majority principle and mechanical repetition are sufficient. Such reserve imposes itself on those with nothing more to win in a history addicted to novelty. This way of feeling will be cultivated by those who are keen to avoid being mistaken for profiteers of future conditions. When people in the optimistic mainstream speak of a constant improvement of living conditions, the conservative keeps a low profile. Assuming that better things lie ahead—does that not already mean searching in the wrong direction? Fluctuating between equanimity and disgust, the conservative watches the activities of those moved by progressive feelings and waits for entropy to do its work. Progress, the conservative is sure, is only ever an acceleration of the flight from good, which lies unattainable behind us. Tocqueville already describes the type of the well-meaning, concerned despiser of his own time, for whom bad things were inseparable from the successes of the new.[2]

Any conservative who wanted to elevate themselves to the level of principles had to move on from here to anthropological generalizations; they had to learn to associate the idea of "mankind" with the epithet "incorrigible." If one had subjected oneself to this exercise, one would see the people of all periods walking across the terrestrial stage with an unchangingly long escort of ailments, needs and vices. Then one could no longer even speak of the "return of the tragic"—for we are ineluctably embedded in it, as if in a fabric woven of first and second nature. When the moderns express their conviction that they are optimizing their immune status and their arts of living, the schooled conservative raises an eyebrow. Unimpressed by the self-advertising of new times, they are unwilling to make any concession to optimism. History in action may be an ongoing process, but progress? Impossible. The great theater of the world is the eternal feast of heat death; whoever delays it will appear as the true hinderer.

It is hardly surprising that authentically conservative sentiment had its heyday in the first half of the nineteenth century, that "complex age of preservation"³ which historians have, with good reason, termed the European Restoration. It was the seemingly quiet Biedermeier decades in which the defenders of what had been could, as if for the last time, embrace the illusion that one can escape the dissolutive power of progress. At no other time did so many people find it natural to look at the past with regret and into the future without any belief in improvement. "Start from what you have, not what you say"— thus the motto of conservative skepticism. The truth about the situation could only be uttered with melancholy by its followers: anyone who was not alive before the social question knows nothing of life's sweetness.

Where conservatism adopted scholarly manners, it invented the "melancholy science" [*traurige Wissenschaft*] of humans and their scientific conditions, which had formed the ground for all discourses on modernization since the early nineteenth century. Thomas Carlyle had coined the phrase "dismal science" in 1849 to encapsulate the young discipline of national economy as represented by the "most honorable professors" Ricardo and Malthus—or rather its tone.⁴ The formulation was persuasive as long as the still unpopular theory of the "wealth of nations" seemed at once to be the science of the insurmountable reasons for the everlasting economic precariousness of the wider "masses." This was given its classic formulation in Ricardo's rule, subsequently termed the "Iron Law of Wages": the "natural price of work," beyond which no supplement seemed possible, was the "necessary price" that allowed workers to maintain their class and reproduce "without increase or decrease." According to this view, a "society" with a liberal-capitalist economy had to remain forever divided into the lucky few who profited from the wealth-creating mechanisms of unequal exchange on illusively free markets as landlords, money lenders or factory owners, and the unlucky majority who remained stuck in proletarian or agrarian-pauperist conditions without any justified hope of change. As a "melancholy science," national economy is a school of detached cruelty, as it trains its adepts to resign before the supposed laws of mass poverty. The liberal theory of the nineteenth century defined the poor as those who could not be helped, even with the best will in the world.[5]

Let us note that the ambivalent conservative Adorno, when he re-coined the phrase "melancholy science" a hundred years after Carlyle—thinking he was inverting the title of Nietzsche's *The Gay Science* in an original fashion—was following a vision whose bleakness went far beyond the facts of industrial pauperism. The philosopher was concerned with grasping a context of coercion that not only immersed the unhappy many in delusions imposed by hardship, but also fundamentally damaged the existence of those who were presently and potentially happy.[6] According to the author's conviction, even the most sheltered do not escape the deformation of the world through the abstraction of exchange, where everything is "afflicted with similarity." Life itself it harmed by the subjugation of all things to the price tag. From this perspective, early Frankfurt School theory—despite its utopian elements—presented a final form of detached conservatism; one could equally call it the pessimism of those who got away intact. In this theory the elemental event of the twentieth century, the end of mass material poverty in the First World, still remained without any echo. It was pervaded by the conviction that economic wealth would never be enough to dispel the poverty complex that has dominated the human race since the birth of the archaic state, with its sharp aristocratic and clerical regimes. Consistently enough, it taught that any enrichment of the masses would lead only to misery in new clothes, just as enlightenment under capitalism is never more than a shape-change of deception. If there was an idea in early Critical Theory that, despite these mediocre exaggerations, deserves to be called critical, it is the assumption—however inadequately supported—that behind the empirically depressing phenomena of *homo pauper* lies a binarily opposed "nature." It is to this reserve that Adorno's reference to "remembrance of nature in the subject" pointed. If his dark picture of the world seemed at times to have a golden edge to it, this was because in rare moments, the author suggested that the happy experiences of a pampered childhood contain moral structures that are worthy, if not practically capable, of generalization. In the following, I shall examine the question of whether it is possible to give this shamefacedly romantic suggestion a more aggressive twist; the answer will be affirmative. The path there leads through the positive interpretation of the concept of pampering. For us to tread it, an anthropology that had—somewhat prematurely—already been termed philosophical must be replaced by a theory of constitutive luxury.

Within a few years after the collapse of socialism in the group of Eastern European states around 1990, it became customary among journalists and other commentators on history in action to use Eric Hobsbawm's well-timed catchphrase "the age of extremes" when looking back on the "short" twentieth century. By quoting it, one implicitly embraces the view that the main content of that epoch was the duel between ethno-nationalist and socialist-internationalist totalitarian ideologies—as well as the successful defensive battle of democratic capitalism against these unequal, bloodthirsty twins. That is why the core process of the century seemed to have the same duration as the Soviet experiment, and its trail of violence had to end at the same point as this burnt-out delirium.[7] (In the light of the reworked confrontation between the capitalist world of affluence and the networks of simplistic hatred, we know that this assumption was premature.) Nonetheless, the formulation "age of extremes" cannot become more plausible than befits such an extremely summary thesis. For the historians who direct their attention not only towards the event cataracts and whipped-up discourses of the twentieth century, but also the long-term waves of both material and symbolic culture in the West, it is now more significant than before to observe that despite its massacres and its excessive speech systems, the "age of extremes" was primarily an epoch of constant processes as far as its decisive events are concerned.

This applies especially, despite far-reaching recessions, to the accumulation and spread of tools for facilitating life in the First

World. Through the involvement of the "masses" in the distribution of wealth, this large-scale tendency was—usually under constant pressure from the moderate left   directed into its still-valid channels: a historical singularity. The trend towards relief and the possibility for the poor to share what had been the privileges of the rich was based on the seven effective continua of modernization: constant scientific research, ever-persevering technological invention, the growing attractiveness of the entrepreneurial life form, the constant expansion of a health system with a welfare state foundation, the involvement of an ever larger public of customers in economic and cultural consumption, the consolidation of the professional and legal immunity of individuals through elaborated employment laws, especially female professionals, and finally the establishment of a wide-ranging, indeed omnipresent insurance system.[8] The effects of these reforms of average living conditions over several decades added up in the modernized countries, beyond the rapid change in family and mentality structures, to a massive increase in life expectancy and a simultaneous steep decline in birth rates;[9] but most of all, they led to a historically unprecedented expansion of free spaces in the time budgets of individuals.

The synergy of progressive factors created a situation in which individuals were invited to take themselves seriously in unaccustomed ways. In the secular individualism that lines near-ubiquitous and universal prosperity from the inside, everyone, assuming they escape depression, is condemned to assume that they are important—and being important means being able to posit themselves as an end in themselves, even if there is no God who might be interested in individuals today and *post mortem*. The social field bursts open to create tens of thousands of stages for the appearances of individualized ambitions. With most people, feeling important leads to the decision to amuse themselves, whether alone or with others. The rise of amusement to become a life motif affecting all classes causes the disintegration of biopolitical-psychopolitical phenomenon formerly known as the proletariat: the workers, confined to misery, for whom producing offspring—*proles*—was the only future perspective. The divinely depressed industrial workers left the stage—that imaginary central subject of the nineteenth century of which the revolutionary losers of the last two hundred years, who leaned ever more radically towards the left, claimed the worst while expecting the best.

Anyone who is still unduly impressed by the jargon of militancy and the romanticism of discontinuity is missing the realization that the central event of the twentieth century can only be interpreted in relation to a principle of constancy: what characterizes the decisive content of this epoch from a diachronic perspective is the escape of modern "society" from the definitions of reality dictated by the age of material poverty and its spiritual forms of compensation—definitions that, as remarked above, were effective until the advent of early liberal economics before, in the course of the twentieth century, especially from the 1950s on, loosening their grip on the mentalities of First World populations.

In this context, more recent stereotypes such as "consumer society," "event society," "fun society" and the like become diagnoses of the times in some respects: conceptually helpless, but not without substance, these phrases point to the momentous fact that, probably for the first time since the entrance of remembrance into our space of tradition, the climate of reality in contemporary Western "society" is no longer determined primarily by poverty-related themes and the psychosemantics of hardship, with all the accompanying religious and metaphysical superstructures—despite the efforts of the miserablist international. Whatever is presented by the alliance of modern advocates of hardship, by psychologists of the human condition, trauma expressionists, *vanitas* ascetics and academic visitors in the land of ongoing poverty[10] to raise objections to the event of abundance, there is no longer good reason to deny that the confusions of current "society" are almost all created by its wealth.

As early as the late 1950s, shortly after the first crystallization of the phenomenon in the United States and Western Europe, John Kenneth Galbraith argued clear-sightedly that the great problem of the "affluent society" lay in its conceptual and psychological inability to come to terms with its own newness, its emancipation from the primacy of hardship—to say nothing of the political interpretation of wealth.[11] It is thus inadequate to note that the "affluent society" cannot, for the time being, understand itself; one must be prepared for it to provide consistently distorted representations of its unaccustomed state—more still, that its exegetes on duty will dismiss all attempts to articulate their current status in neutral and descriptive terms like a macabre affront. Anyone wishing to speak to the rich "society" of its riches—and the attendant moral implications—can only be a tactless positivist who lacks any sensitivity to the tensions of being held out into wealth. However virtuosically the affluent "society" learned to deal with its rapidly habitualized riches (the *prima facie* scandalous wastes of public funds should be interpreted in this context as a participation of the state in the cheerfulness of abundance), it clings to the categories of the universe of hardship in its well-rehearsed self-portrayals. The self-doubting "affluent society" views itself through sharply focused hardship-glasses. Every failure to meet the norm is registered: anyone who dared to formulate descriptions of it that deviated from the usual politically and humanistically correct crisis reports would be suspected of cynicism; whoever fails to recognize the appalling hardship existing on countless internal fronts is swiftly identified as working to dismantle social services. Speaking of the widely spread, albeit strictly unequally spread wealth of the First World in positive terms—would this not mean directly urging others to avert their eyes from the tragedy taking place at the gates of luxury? Would it not demand closing one's eyes and ears to the residues of misery that persistently survive within the zone of prosperity? In the best case, an analyst who remained unimpressed by the facts of abundance would be presented with the diagnosis of being naïvely deceived by surface appearances.

But what if the decisive repression of our times actually concerns our own prosperity? If the denial of successful pamperings were the leitmotif for all public discourses in the world of surplus? If the trade secret of the present "society" lay in the constant updating of deprivation delusions for the "broad middle classes"? This is not to say that contemporary civilization succeeds in protecting all of its members from accidents, illnesses, poverty or experiences of failure; this would be an infantile view of the relationship between income and personal fate. The dramas of the present age do, however, follow scripts that are no longer based on the old play *Suffering through Society*, either in its exploitation-theoretical or its alienation-theoretical version.

Nonetheless, the inertias of sociological pessimism and its predecessors continue to have an overpowering effect in the enriched world—a pessimism whose definitions of reality, as a long time ago, are derived from the existential struggle of a majority of hopelessly impoverished households. Despite the great material caesura, this assessment has barely changed in the last fifty years; at most, the administration of this illusory hardship has been consolidated through corporative routines. No one can rise to a senior position at the national, federal state or municipal level unless the exercises of professionalized complaint have become second nature to them; here the well looked-after can reach deep into the "tradition of the oppressed." No matter what subject is brought up in public, the lie of hardship revises the text. All published speech is subject to the law which demands translating the luxury in power back into the jargon of hardship.

Despite this concordat between the pampering "society" and time-honored misery, there are increasing signs that the surplus-creating process has meanwhile penetrated the capillary structures of social ensembles. In recent surveys, slightly under 10% of people in the Federal Republic of Germany since the 1980s were classified as relatively poor, while the great majority were considered affluent in the broader sense—even if the term, in keeping with the rules of "Rhine capitalism," naturally refers largely to rather modest levels of wealth.[12] If the increasingly competitive measures on the global markets cause the poorer segment of "society" to grow to 20% (a value that has probably already been substantially exceeded in the discrimination-happy USA), the larger side of the ratio will still constitute a historically unprecedented space of prosperity.[13]

As far as the subjective assessments of reality are concerned, those of the vast majority almost automatically deviate dramatically from these classifications and quantifications. The gap between statistical wealth and perceived lack is wider than ever, even without any radical leftist filters to make the findings darker. Throughout the West, especially in Central and Western Europe, the late twentieth century saw an amalgam of private saturation and public jeremiad that mirrors a depressive-explosive pseudo-contentment often accompanied by a highly defensive attitude to life. This syndrome of hardship simulation and deficiency illusions, identified in popular usage as complaining about "First World problems" (if the protagonists had better voices one could speak of bel canto miserablism), will undoubtedly be highlighted in later cultural histories as the hallmark of contemporary culture—just as Simon Schama, in his major work on the Netherlands in the seventeenth century, refers to an era of *The Embarrassment of Riches*.[14] That time marked the first appearance in the bourgeois world of the oxymoron of the rich-poor, showy-humble lifestyle, which has since then—in the most diverse circumstances—subjected the consciences of the wealthy to constant fluctuations between contentment and unease about their well-being. With reference to these phenomena, it seems logical to give the principle of contentment in the present day an activist, or rather a sadistic edge, as suggested by Galbraith in a recent study on the reasons for the weepiness-protected saturation of Western "societies": contentment is "highly motivated resistance to change and reform."[15]

However widespread the pretense of lack may be in the rich "society," it cannot yet be called totalitarian. For the time being, there are nests of resistance in which affluent people speak openly of their wealth. Some of them even seem willing to draw moral and atmospheric conclusions from it: those who do not deny their wealth will be better equipped to shift the terms of existence from the *ressentiment* of the enriched to the generous virtue of the prosperous. What Nietzsche called the free spirit is naturally the rich spirit, and all true wealth shows itself in the primacy of giving—economically, morally, erotically and culturally.

For theoretical interest in wealth as a phenomenon and source of ethos, this creates instructive analogies: among the theoretically educated too, the miserophiles form the vast majority, while the friends of wealth seem like vanishing exceptions. But to the extent that the traditional ontology of seriousness and lack was subverted by the experiences of "mass" prosperity and its existential-climatic consequences, the theory-sensitive milieu of the West and its partners in many regions of the world saw the development of a need for concepts that could help articulate the awareness of the diminished weight of the world.

Anyone hoping for this to be achieved in contemporary philosophy would be sorely disappointed. If the thesis of the origin of philosophy in amazement had ever been well-founded, the singularity of the great break with the axioms of "mass" poverty would have provided an unparalleled stimulus for reflection. The fact that barely a trace of this can be observed in contemporary philosophy (apart from certain aspects of the Nietzschean wing) thematically, let alone stylistically, surely proves that the matter of amazement rests on a weak foundation—and presumably always has.[16] Herbert Marcuse's dated philosophical inquiry into Sigmund Freud, *Eros and Civilization* of 1955,[17] perhaps contained some early hints at the change in the reality principle towards what was described in the jargon of the time as a "non-repressive culture." The vanishing point of Marcuse's reflections was the sublation of the seemingly eternal opposition between the reality principle and the pleasure principle in a "social" order fully liberated from the curse of instinct suppression, and indeed from suppression altogether. The text offers little in the way of concrete analysis of contemporary wealth conditions—despite being almost contemporaneous with Galbraith's *The Affluent Society*. Marcuse's socio-psychological speculation only touches from a distance on the true epoch-making event in the field of psychology: the replacement of *homo pauper*, whose motivational situation was described more or less adequately by theories of drives, with the enriched human being, whose situation can be interpreted with a theory of appetites, options, moods and streams of desire.[18]

Almost all the contributions of later sociologists have likewise offered little response to the critical question; one can assume that the representatives of this discipline could not admit to the existence of an affluent "society" in public without being suspected of practicing a superfluous, malicious science in a demoralizing fashion. Because the luxuriant social sciences are condemned to feign social utility, they can speak of anything but the luxury that carries them and whose blind vanguard they embody—also and especially in the forms of *sociologia militans*. It would therefore be unrealistic, for the time being, to expect the need for an interpretation of affluence conditions to be satisfied from this side. Recourse to political knowledge is equally unhelpful: the right can no longer get to the heart of the matter because it has no interest in it, while the left would not want to gain any insight, even if it were capable of doing so. (Needless to say, both sides are lamenting factions that sing same melodies with different words; the genre of lament has drifted from music to the self-portrayal of corporations—not without leaving its traces in the national features pages.) Although numerous examples of the great levitation accumulated in the literatures, arts and life form experiments of the twentieth century, there was virtually no systematic highlighting or explicit illumination of the affluence phenomenon.[19] While the aesthetic documents of the onset of the "big easy" exist in abundance, an authentic theory of relaxation and de-poverishment has yet to be formulated.

It seems that the sudden shift to non-lack for the many is too comprehensive, too amorphous and too rich in different tendencies to be approached theoretically in an *intentio recta*. At the same time, there is an embarrassing side to it—as if anyone who attempted it openly would have to declare their own personal pamperedness. If someone admitted to being thoroughly pampered (and who in our climes is not?), would they not also have to confess that they no longer understood any of what defined the coordinates of the real for most members of the human race during the last, agro-imperial millennia? At this point, we find the lack of lack far more embarrassing than open poverty. Misery still seeks to present itself as the signature of the human condition, whereas wealth is perceived as the foam head on the original lack; thus it could be reconverted at any moment to the squalor that preceded it. Where misery forms the basis, wealth can never be anything but a superstructural phenomenon. A powerful romanticism of bankruptcy suggests that those who become poor return to the foundations of being human. Individual nostalgists who entertain radically conservative dreams extending beyond the modern world long for a purifying catastrophe, an *apokatástasis* of the misery from which we come. They desire the restoration of that hardship in which the original terms of human proportionality were supposedly worked out.

Where miserablism shows its colors, it calls the friends of being to raise their flags and declares war on its inferior, credit. In the midst of the richest "society," despite the tentative attempts of Veblen and others, there is no convincing theory of wealthy existence—perhaps leaving aside the incommensurable interventions of Nietzsche and Deleuze. For the most part, the rich have little to contribute to the discussion of their situation except—in emulation of the minor princes in the seventeenth century—acquiring art collections; and if they have servile art historians at their side as courtly flatterers with outstretched hands, this is in keeping with the familiar patterns of provincial feudality. There is ample reason to claim that the absence of adequate theory corresponds to the state of the matter itself. If there was ever a context of delusion, it would be located in the current conspiracy against the perception of the most obvious. Towards the end of the conservative revolution that took place in the first half of the twentieth century, it turned into a necessitarian reactionarism—as if people wanted to save their souls by seeking refuge in hardship and its means of change. This was accompanied by the rise of a new type of ideology, a modal ideology that expressed not ideas, but a need: to falsely change freedom into necessity and wealth into neediness.

The great success of the blockade can initially be explained in socio-psychological terms: someone who, all in all, has a palpably easier time will tend to turn their gaze away from their privileged conditions. Is it not part of the definition of pampering that it is allowed to keep quiet about its own premises? In actuality, it would come up against its limits if one confronted the pampered with the imposition of bearing their favorable circumstances in mind—let alone meditating on the moral content of those conditions. Is it not characteristic of life in luxury that one can avoid the awkwardness of researching one's past? Possible doubts about the continued existence of that life can now be cheerfully dismissed. The best way for luxury to protect itself is by denying that it is luxury; it always presents itself as covering only the minimum requirements.

One can surely admit that a dose of avoidance magic is always involved with topics of this kind: to avoid endangering something, one must avoid talking it to death with overly precise words. Acquired aversions do their bit: countless members of the transitional generations still hear their parents' voices, reproachfully telling their children how much better off they are nowadays compared to them, who were tested by greater hardship and bore a heavier burden. Another factor is the psychological mechanism that one uses the first genuine forms of relief to open let off steam about private experiences of lack. As soon as the pressure has sunk, the depots of past needs are cleared out (or converted into cult sites), deliberately ignoring the improvements in the overall situation—an effect without which neither the rapid emergence of therapeutic cultures after the Second World War nor the heyday of academic Marxisms and other manifestations of luxurious radicalism can be understood. The excess of victimism in the established era of affluence can only be read in terms of the situational blindness of the newly relieved. For the concept of poverty to assume almost infinite proportions, it is actually enough to subjectify it.[20] Such subjectifications tacitly presuppose generalized wealth, only to deny it with raised voices. In this, "low culture" caught up with the pampering standards of "high culture": from the 1950s on, countless newly pampered persons could afford the "luxury of pessimism" that Nietzsche had previously diagnosed in Schopenhauer. Unease in culture changed into perplexity in the face of affluence.[21]

Certainly, Western citizens in the prosperous post-war West have realized in varyingly confused ways that they profit from a greenhouse effect of comfort, especially if the central part of their self-aware life stories lay between 1945 and 1990.[22] In this period, as older observers almost unanimously confirm, the characteristics of the great shift established themselves continuously, albeit not without setbacks. The material symbols of near-universal non-poverty also came to the fore during this period. The new liaison between "mass" buying power and "mass" frivolity led to a change of psychosocial mood across the board. An ostentatious consumption of fashion, domestic and mobility luxuries extending into the lower middle classes manifested itself as the hallmark of life forms in industrial societies; the automobile cult mirrors the share of all classes in aggressive, often self-destructive technologies of expansion.[23] The great increase in leisure time affected the *modus vivendi* of all subcultures and income brackets. Countless people used their surpluses of free waking time to elaborate their whims, their talents, their illnesses, their victim subjectivities and private metaphysics; enormous quantities of attentiveness, power of judgment, knowledge and *savoir faire* were invested by individuals and cohabitants in the design of dwellings and second homes; the fulfillment of the urge to move through sport, music, tourism and countless forms of fun activism reached a level that had no precedents in the history of civilizations. Even if it is true that the wealthy north is currently being forced to leave the "cocoon of the happy post-war decades"—as Pascal Bruckner formulates it—and prepare itself for turbulences, the plateau from which its denizens will be forced by regressions to descend temporarily or for longer periods is, from a sociohistorical perspective, incomparably high.

As far as the empirical perception and moral interpretation of the great turnaround are concerned, the majority of people in the second post-war era would have to testify as witnesses to the time. Anyone was on their guard as an observer of American and Western European realities at the end of the Second World War had a chance to watch the offshoots of the preceding era, which had still been characterized mostly by economic hardship and psychosocial deficiencies, in order to compare them step by step with the loosening definitions of reality in the subsequent period of continuous growth. The last phases of lack in the Western world spanned the era of the two World Wars and the restless stages of the Russian experiment; with Prohibition in the USA, the 1920s saw a late and futile resurgence of the old, serious view of life, which had allied itself with a great rejection of consumerism and loosening. The continuum of darkening in the West extended through the Depression period of the 1930s—at the time, New York's Central Park was a favela of tents and shacks laboriously kept alive by the dedication of charities and communal facilities—to the immiserating consequences of the Second World War, including the early reconstruction phase. After the great crisis of 1930, Franklin D. Roosevelt was able to conclude that one third of the American public was inadequately fed and clothed; even as late as 1962, Michael Harrison still put the poverty level at over 20% in his seminal study *The Other America: Poverty in the United States*.[24]

Against this background, it is understandable why, in the first half of the twentieth century, it seemed logical and was perhaps even legitimate to submit to the temptation of lethargy and continue using the pessimistic languages of the nineteenth century—along with their no less worn-out utopian counterparts, even if these presented themselves as the science of a better future. With a few exceptions, the dominant discourses after 1918 can be attributed to an equally overpowering and sterile choice: either one submitted in resignation to the eternal laws of mass poverty, which only seemed to allow a small number of winners in the evil game of competition, or one dreamed one's way forwards with militant audacity to a rich and egalitarian end of history, which would be close as soon as the productive forces of "society" fell into the right hands. Falling victim to paralysis in conservative melancholy or plunging into the "revolution" with autohypnotic optimism (emulating Lenin's delirium and fueling the imminent expectation of opportunity)—these seemed to be the options dictated by the current historical field to its purportedly realistic interpreters. Few people at the time realized that they were thus called upon to decide between two completely outdated possibilities. Those who considered themselves avant-gardists were also made fools of by false scenarios. The early Frankfurt School in particular, which became hegemonic in Germany from the 1950s and later in the USA as Critical Theory, had become trapped between the two deceptive poles; it proved original only in the fact that it proposed a combination of leap and paralysis—with consequences extending to the gala pessimism of recent times. Only a small minority of intellectuals had been willing and able since the 1920s and 30s, this side of utopia and beyond despair, to preserve the connection to contemporary economic, legal and technological facts in which—through a steady accumulation of barely perceptible, inventive, operatively efficient steps—the epoch-making event took place: the first breaking of the circle of poverty for the many.[25]

The psychodynamic and mental side of the caesura has not been addressed with the appropriate thoroughness, to say nothing of the event's conceptual dimensions: no diagnostician of the time would have imagined that no less was taking place in the current generations than the emancipation of the concept of reality from the immemorial dogmatism of the serious, the weighty and the necessary—which (according to the suggestions of the logician and Hegel exegete Gotthart Günther) have always reflected an inadequate, traditional understanding of "being" within the framework of binary thought. The black novels of positivism were continued on all fronts. In both left and right camps, intellectuals fell to their knees before the real as the dominant, the sublime, the terrible—only the smallest aesthetic circles were able to evade the reality cult and its paralyzing consequences. Very few of them acknowledged, like Musil, that a serious rival to the sense of reality had emerged and was reaching its explicatory form by crystallizing into the realm of the virtual. Who would have been willing to admit that a mutation in the experience and concept of the real itself was underway? The message of the century found no one to proclaim it. It could have been this: "We have risen again from the real"—or, with less pathos: "We will keep the real at a distance in future."

Operation Enrichment is so expansive, and so pervaded by counter-tendencies and paradoxical effects, so complicated by ambiguities and exceptions, and so overshadowed by pressing questions as to the external costs (extending to the suggestion that there is a form of arms race between poverty and wealth that the latter can, in the long run, not possibly win) that half a century later, not counting certain conceptual gains, one still has no overview of its complete development. This made it all the more difficult to acquire insight into the process while it was only just revealing its first contours. None of those who turned their attention towards the phenomenon of "free market economy" after 1945, or commented on electric appliances and fossil fuels entering modern lifestyles, would have been capable of assessing the significance of these objects for the redefinition of fundamental Old European concepts such as "nature," "reality," "freedom" and "existence." Conversely, barely any philosopher at that time would have been willing to state that almost the entire traditional vocabulary of their discipline began to become historical when telephones, combustion engines, radar devices and calculators appeared in the "lifeworld." Even though the Old European ecology of lack had begun to unravel, the faith in the primacy of necessity and the burden character of existence kept the Old World together. The habitus of being poor and unsuccessful persisted in demanding dominion over people's minds. Wealth came like a thief in the night;[26] the enriched had their minds elsewhere.

Today, it is gradually becoming clear that the denial of levitation is the constant in the recent history of ideas. Wherever relief would have imposed itself on theoretical and moral appraisal, the great majority of thinkers—especially the exegetes of the extreme left and right—withdrew to the terrain of the heavy "real" that lurked behind the surfaces of everyday life, and which they never tired of invoking with the harshest names. While relief sent its harbingers out everywhere, the extreme realists embraced a cult of depressive thought more extravagantly than ever before. Walter Benjamin had the presumption to describe the image of the angel of history, which believed it was looking upon a single great disaster that incessantly piled debris upon debris; he thus created the test card for the visual disorders of a century blinded by radicalisms.[27]

One cannot say that his contemporaries were any better; they invoked racial conflict and the laws of blood, exploitation and heightened class struggles, trauma and the products of the unconscious, the misunderstood body and necrophilic aggression, the mechanization of life and the dominance of devices, the lack of resources and the second law of thermodynamics, the acceleration of traffic and the globalization of business, the accident and the untamed event—but above all the catastrophe, again and again the catastrophe. Those were the high seats on which the consciousness that had defected to the real sat enthroned. No tiger's back was too broad for the realists to want to ride on it. Any self-respecting thinker had to gain control of the real and open a victorious discourse about its formative principle. Just as Bacon taught that one can only conquer nature by obeying it, the realists of the twentieth century espoused the doctrine that one can only control the real by submitting to it. All attempts to grasp the real were condemned to excel in a contest with other harsh fictions of reality. The supremacism of realism became the logical style of the time. The race for the most explicit disclosure of the real inevitably produced the ontological variants of pornography; never had one gazed more deeply into the entrails of exposed reality. What people called ideologies— what were they in essence but fictions of the real intoxicated by their own hardness, coldness and obscenity? To be considered free of illusions, the strong minds plunged into the cult of that cruel goddess, facticity. She was assisted by the equally cruel helper "decision"—in so far as one sees the essence of decision in the act of risking everything on a single option and letting the alternatives die. The realists, the right-handers and the columnists of hard facts gazed with nameless contempt at what they considered the mollycoddled liberal mob for refusing to learn the necessary lessons of cruelty: when it is time to chop the wood of the future, it will be all the worse for the splinters. Countless intellectuals embraced the conviction that only the great entrepreneurs, the gangsters and dictators, had seen to the heart of the real; only the mimesis of crime enables thought to enter the historical arena. Whoever does not buy shares for the enterprise of reality as a panderer of terror has understood nothing of the rules of the game in the whole.

But what if the philosophically relevant event of the twentieth century had consisted in all gravity-seeking fictions of reality being invalidated by a single moment of uplift? And if it had accordingly been the time to embrace relief like an evangelical caesura? If it had been imperative to see through the tragic realisms as hypnoses by black kitsch? If crawling before the harshest definitions of reality had been the signature of the most dubious opportunism—which one can see at work again today among the intellectual prompters of American *realpolitik*—as if one had thought at length about the essence of crime, and concluded that it alone determines the meaning of being: in the beginning was the misdeed? What if the free spirit had to withdraw from the devotional images of those facts to which there are supposedly no alternatives if it hoped to find its way back into the open? And if the mark of reactionary thought had, since that time, been that it allies itself with gravity in order to deny anti-gravity?

2. The Fiction of the Deficient Being

Faced with these questions, it is easy to understand that it had to become more difficult in the course of the twentieth century to cling to the basic assumptions of traditional conservatism (provided its constitution was misery-conservative, hardship-Catholic and wealth-denying). To the extent that the deliberately concealed, yet ubiquitous message of the de-worsening of life materialized in the moods of subsequent generations, the interpretation of the world according to the prejudice of hardship found itself in an implausible position. Its weakness could only be balanced out with an increased use of pessimistic abstractions—and by importing a larger number of negativities. This ideological constellation saw the second exploitation of the periphery, this time for the masochism of the center. Among indignation activists, the habitus of importing misery cheaply as raw material and turning it into high-quality reproach products for the domestic market is rampant to this day.[28] To remain in denial about the unheard-of things that have happened in the First World, the pessimist international weighs up the continuing hardship in the Third World against the recent wealth of the West and reaches a negative balance—indeed, it even attributes the wealth of the First World to the poverty of the Third in order to present its high standard of life as a result of (economic and political) injustice towards the southern hemisphere. Thus it ensures that its own living conditions, with all their evident abundance and dynamic of pampering, remain unthematized because all too laden with guilt. One is always already ecstatic over the wretchedness of the others—often to such a degree that one can no longer decide whether this turn towards the non-self and the non-here is a case of helping from a distance or hypocrisy at home.[29] Exponents of this mentality act as if they had discovered an unknown law of nature: the law of the conservation of miserogenic energy. Since the 1960s, the misery-conservative, affluence-denying spirit has invested great effort in devaluing Western wealth by proving the untenability of the previous methods of acquiring it—as we know, the worldwide debate about the "limits of growth" became significant because it translated traditional economic pessimism (which has recently been joined by every kind of fundamentalism) into the language of ecology and thus raised alternative offspring.

The most ambitious effort of ailing conservatism in the face of the turn towards a civilization of affluence, however, was a shifting of the conceptual foundations of the ontology of deficiency to a deeper level. This could only happen by shaping deficiency into a form of negative essence; it had to be separated from the economic circumstances in order to be moved down as far as possible into the human essence, indeed the heart of subjectivity, the originally split, robbed and overtaxed psyche. It should not be the factual, coincidental and reversible deprivation of a large majority of real persons of material and symbolic goods that counts when the concern is to assess human existence in terms of being determined by deficiency; what really matters must now be imagined as a constitutional or bio-cultural *a priori* neediness on the part of *homo sapiens*.

In the annals of cultural studies, the memory of this ingenious and at first seemingly successful maneuver—dating human poverty back to before every historically and socially concrete manifestation of a deficiency of products, chances or resources—is connected to the work of Arnold Gehlen, a scholar whom it would not be untoward to call—before Niklas Luhmann—the most brilliant of avowed conservatives in the twentieth century. Gehlen's position in the recent history of ideas is that of a rightwards-shifted Young Hegelian who had declared the concern for the empirical or anthropological materialization of philosophy his personal cause. One can see Gehlen's approach as a German path to pragmatism; his motto was skepticism towards the inflated posturing of the "unreal spirit," his trademark a contempt for the susceptibility of intellectuals to words. Typologically speaking, Gehlen's intelligence can be characterized as Jesuit, as it owes its best possibilities to a form of counter-reformationist stance of conservative resistance trained by the strengths of its opponents. Even the paradoxical title of an avant-garde conservative, bestowed upon Luhmann in the 1970s by Italian interlocutors, can easily be transferred back to Gehlen, who was almost a generation older. His name deserves to be mentioned before those of Freud, Lacan, Adorno and Carl Schmitt whenever one tries to glimpse the cards of the most successful modernizers of the pessimist syndrome in the twentieth century.

For the following, it will prove worthwhile to examine closely the basic operation of a conservatism armed with Gehlen's methods, namely the assertion of a *homo pauper* through an elaborated anthropology of deficiency, and to assess its coherence. Here it will become apparent how a highly modern analytical apparatus was expressly placed in the service of conservative moods and anti-relief activism. In order to construct the acting, reflecting, culture-creating human as a fundamentally impoverished animal despite all its creative potentials, Gehlen takes up concepts that were among the most advanced when he first set up his system in the late 1930s, and have still not been explored everywhere and in every way to this day—starting with Nietzsche's boundlessly fruitful description of the human being as "an animal not yet determined" and extending to Scheler's onto-anthropological thesis of "world-openness" (a motif that would play a central part in Heidegger's lecture "The Fundamental Concepts of Metaphysics: World, Finitude, Solitude," given in the winter semester of 1929/30). Furthermore, Gehlen incorporates the transcendental tradition's concept of action into his enterprise, as well as contemporary existential philosophy's concept of risk, decisionism's concept of positing and the psychoanalysts' concept of symptoms. These are joined by a number of excitingly new biological insights such as Julius Kollmann's concept of neoteny—the phenotypic maintenance of juvenile physical traits—and Lodewig (Louis) Bolk's sensational theory, presented in 1926, about the primary retardation of human ontogenesis as well as the retention of fetal characteristics in the morphology of adults.[30] If there is an idealistic remainder in Gehlen's case, it reveals itself in a carefully cultivated anti-biologism extending to the denial of effective instincts in *homo sapiens*—an exaggerated position that he was forced to revise in a later phase of his work.

All these definitions are combined to form Gehlen's strategically central theorem of the human as a *deficient being*. This phrase is not only meant to refer to the biological "negative endowments" of *homo sapiens*, with all its maladjustments, non-specializations, undeveloped traits and so-called "primitivisms;"[31] it also recalls the increased burden that has, according to Gehlen, weighed down this excessively unprotected, environmentally disconnected, instinct-deprived, organically destitute animal, abandoned by all innate inner guidance, from the start. The author does not fail to highlight the biological impossibility of this creature in ever new formulations: the victim of a "unique destitution," this being is "hopelessly unadapted as a natural creature";[32] "incapable of living in any truly natural and elemental sphere of nature";[33] a result of "normalized premature birth";[34] endangered by extremely high "virtual inner tensions";[35] and equipped with a threatening potential for neglect and self-destruction. After presenting these findings, it is then obligatory to invoke the forefather of the anthropology of deficiency, Johann Gottfried Herder. Gehlen unabashedly claims him as his "predecessor" and adopts a two-part theorem about the human being which states that the "character of the species" is always defined by "gaps and deficiencies"[36]—through their genius in language and the ability to craft culture and institutions, however, they reshape their original deprivation into a privilege. Now the program and the declaration can follow:

> Philosophical anthropology has not progressed at all since Herder, and it is essentially the same view that I wish to develop with the means of modern science. And it does not need to progress, for this is the truth.

It requires no great effort to show that this suggestive portrait of *homo sapiens pauper* is pervaded by an ambiguity whose exposure shatters the meaning of the entire construction—such that it can then be read equally well as making the opposite case. In following on from Herder by speaking of *homo sapiens* as a deficient being, he presupposes a history of the weakening of humans, or rather their precursors, which—according to his own assumptions—

can no longer be reproduced as mere natural history. For evidently the poor, weak human in Gehlen's portrait is meant to be the starting point for a grand narrative of primordial deficiency and its immediate compensation through cultural abilities. In this picture, however, it remains entirely unclear how a creature is supposed to have acquired its initial deficiencies by natural evolution. It is impossible to derive such a dramatic dowry of deprivations from a natural history of humanity's precursors. Left to its own devices, nature knows no successful handing-down of maladjustments or fatal weaknesses—at most, dangerous specializations like peacock feathers or stag antlers, effects one cannot speak of with *homo sapiens*, which, as Gehlen never tires of emphasizing, is de-specialized and juvenilized in the most conspicuous fashion. If biologically and culturally motivated development led to the results that are evident in early humans, then their evolutionarily preferred qualities must not be interpreted as deprivations; on the contrary, they would predominantly possess qualifying or, in Darwin's terms, fitness-increasing virtues.

It is extremely far-fetched to characterize the primal scene of anthropogenesis as the appearance of a creature unfit for life that—only just placed into its surroundings—immediately had to withdraw into the protective shell of a prosthetic cultural armor in order to compensate for its own biological impossibility. In reality, the refinement of the somatic image presented by *homo sapiens* must be thought in terms of a stable long-term trend that could only succeed thanks to the intertwining of biological and cultural factors. This developmental trait can only be grasped as a self-reinforcing incubator effect that turns both the young and the adults of the species into beneficiaries of a pampering, cerebralizing and infantilizing tendency. This establishes itself without any long-term or species-wide reduction of evolutionary chances for the neotenically daring living being thus incubated. The success story of the "symbolic species" could not have turned out as we see today in retrospect if its basic character had not led to a productive interconnection of somatic refinements and psychoneuro-immunological and technical reinforcements.[37]

If one now inverts the sequence of conditions for the being-and-becoming-thus of humans, and acknowledges the evolutionary soundness of human morphologies, the terms of anthropological assessment *eo ipso* show an opposing tendency. Humans do not reach for culture and its institutions in order to recreate themselves from a biologically impossible creature to one that is somehow fit for life after all; rather, they emerge from the conditions of their conception and upbringing in such a way that they profit from their singular incubator privilege down to the most intimate somatic endowments: their cerebrality, their sexuality, their immune structures and their nakedness. Their strength expresses itself in the prerogative of increased fragility. In other words, *homo sapiens* is not a deficient being that compensates for its poverty through culture, but rather a luxury being that was adequately secured by its proto-cultural skills to survive and occasionally prosper in the face of all dangers. Admittedly the sapients, understandably, usually had to limit themselves to realizing a small, fairly robust part of their cultural potential in order to advance to species-typical luxury developments as soon as the chance arose.

Homo sapiens is a basally pampered, polymorphically luxuriating, multiply improvable intermediate being whose formation resulted from the combined action of genetic and symbolic-technical forces. Its biomorphological results point to a long history of autoplastic refinement, and its pampering chances were inherited from far back. At the same time, it remains equipped with a very animal doggedness—more still, gifted with a capacity to persevere under the starkest conditions that goes beyond its animal inheritance and is illuminated by the temporal awareness that is hope. To describe the resulting traits as an "equipment with deficiencies" is a notion that could only suggest itself to an analyst already intent on proving the existence of the dogmatically presupposed *homo pauper*, even in the earliest stages, despite the categories of their own theoretical apparatus already pointing to the opposite assessment. Gehlen's *entente cordiale* with the Weimar pastor Herder is thus more than a coincidence in the history of ideas. Their shared notion of the human as a deficient being satisfies bourgeois pessimism's new need to replace the dogma of original sin, now unmarketable among the educated, with the far more attractive lesson of original lack.

The inversion of the conditions posited by Gehlen can be supported most plausibly using his own conceptual means. That *homo sapiens* cannot be a deficient being, but has rather always embodied a luxury creation, becomes fully clear as soon as one subjects the two central concepts in Gehlen's system to closer inspection: firstly the concept of world-openness, with which the author involved himself in the horizon of the philosophy of his time, and secondly that of relief, which undoubtedly constitutes Gehlen's most fruitful contribution to philosophical and empirical anthropology—here we undoubtedly have one of the few truly original conceptualizations in twentieth-century cultural studies. As Gehlen himself connected the two concepts extremely closely, it is legitimate to explain them in a shared treatment.

The human being's world-openness brings about—according to Gehlen's underlying assumption—an existential aggravation that has no biological precedent: because the human experiences and reflects more than any animal, it is not simply a creature that can occasionally be overtaxed, but rather a structurally overtaxed one. On the sensory side its basic constitution is overstimulation, and on the pragmatic side the pressure of risk. As humans are not tied to their environment at birth, at least not circumstances as a whole, and must instead always deal with self-deduced environmental compromises, their being-in-the-world has the character of being immersed in a "field of surprise."[38] "In the light of this reflection, world-openness is fundamentally a *strain*."[39] This means—even if the author does not state it openly—that the main characteristic of the way *homo sapiens* experiences the world and acts within it lies in a problematic overabundance of sensory impressions as well as possibilities of experience and action, and by no means in a prior poverty and deprivation. Its underspecialized, multiply adaptable or "open" nature results firstly in an overly impressionable receptiveness, and secondly in an extremely broad spectrum of action options—which deviate from the trivial middle value and extend to the improbabilities of art, asceticism, orgies and crime. If there were anything resembling the early addition of a sense of lack given to creatures of this type, it would be an awkwardness in the face of their own wealth—a problem whose everyday expression is found in the cliché "the agony of choice," *imbarazzo della scelta* and the like. With higher theoretical standards, the same meaning can be captured in figures such as "reduction of complexity." Humans are burdened by their plasticity in approximately the same way that millionaires face the hardship of managing their fortunes.

These observations are reinforced by Gehlen's deliberations on the ground-breaking category of relief—a term that articulates the most important aspect of a general economy of existence. If one can say that initially, existence indeed means a paradoxical being-burdened—as shown above, burdened by the wealth of human sensory and pragmatic ecstasies—then the task of the relieving mechanisms is to lower the primary wealth tension, starting with the formation of perceptual patterns and the automation of actions and extending to the normalization of future expectations through rituals and the elimination of coincidences through technical routines. Simplify yourself, o human, make yourself predictable! Gehlen realistically assumes that somatically, psychically and socially, life follows the inclination to adapt to the operating conditions of a well-tempered banality—conditions that are described psychologically as habituations and culture-anthropologically as institutions. Relief is thus an austerity mechanism: a way of stopping the temptation to overexert oneself. Its main effect comes from an immunization to immediacy—whether that of surplus energy expenditure in spontaneous actions or that of a flooding by dangerously de-automated perceptions. One could say that it implants a first pragmatic immune system to ward off infections of the psyche by an excess of unassimilable stimuli, and simultaneously prevents the burning of mental energies in ecstatic openings to the field of action and perception.

In thus retracing the concept, it becomes clear that relief has nothing to do with administering deficiencies: it is responsible for managing a fortune that demands budgeting and astute investments. It is only because the element for human beings is excess that simplifications, inhibitions and habituations become necessary in order to halt wastage while it is still at a low level, thus making the energies saved available for higher, symbolically ambitious purposes. This upscaling process makes the motif of surplus apparent in both primary and secondary terms. After Gehlen had done his bit to present humans— almost successfully—as impoverished at even the most basic level, the denied original wealth returned in his description of the advanced mental system of *homo sapiens*, after its specimens had been molded by the civilizatory mechanisms of relief in the form of conserved potentials for action which urged to be realized all the more at a higher level. But as with the first wealth that comes from world-openness, Gehlen also manages to describe the second as a burden and a negative factor. The psychoeconomic catchword for second wealth is release, which likewise entails an investment problem: it goes without saying that the strict anthropologist will only accept serious allocations. This process is explained using the example of the contemplative life of charismatics who were supported by their surrounding "societies," or the mode of being native to artists, whose dangerous fluctuations between mastery and anomic liberties presuppose toleration by their social environment. Both types of released existence are meant to clarify that everything hinges on tying the energy surplus gained through relief to ascetic rules, whether those of the hermitage or the studio— whereas the anthropologist looks with concern and revulsion upon the deregulation of artists' existences in the anarchic subcultures of the twentieth century. If artistic anarchism were to become a widespread phenomenon, Gehlen fears, the symbolic reproduction of "society" in its institutions would soon be history. Like Dostoyevsky's grand inquisitor, the anthropologist is convinced that freedom is an excessive strain which only very few can deal with. For all others who are not up to the asceticism of the authentic elites, the logical option is a consistently applied heteronomy. Choosing a decidedly conventional approach, Gehlen relies on disciplining to deal with the many.[40]

With reference to the human dynamics of relief too, then, it transpires that one cannot speak of any initial deficiency problem; what truly requires interpretation and explication is the absorption of surplus energies and their diversion into more demanding processes. Gehlen stays true to his pessimist impulse at the higher level too: just as he interpreted the world-openness of the luxury beings that humans are as an original strain, he also reads the conserved and released energies that are available for higher and further purposes as second-order strains. For these, he formulates the notorious recommendation to expend them in the service of objective forms—even magical rituals, however dubious their empirical success. Better to follow an empty form, as long as it has the power to impose itself, than lose oneself in the freedom of formlessness and the non-committal nature of the mere experiment. A member of the Congregation for the Doctrine of the Faith in Rome could not have put it more clearly. It is self-evident, then, that what troubles the anthropologist is not a deficient being created by evolution; it is the human as a luxury being, whose constitutive pamperedness and unpredictable protuberance unsettled him to the end.

3. Frivolity and Boredom

Were our humors a model of our philosophical reflections, I
should like you to inform me, Edwin, from which of these the
truth would flow.

    —Friedrich Schiller, "A Walk Among the Linden Trees."[41]

If one places Gehlen's paradoxical construction of the human
being that is impoverished through wealth back into its historical
context, one sees a sensitive connection to the epoch-making
movement of life-facilitation in the "affluent society"—a movement which, in a different hue (and against the background of
modern solidary systems), would have to be defined as the
transition to a first successful network of highly individualized
immunity constructs. It cannot be mere coincidence that the key
terms of modern conservatism, "relief" and "release," are more
suitable than any other to articulate the subjective reflexes of the
great levitation. They are genuinely their time, put into thoughts.

    With the emergence of a largely juridified "society" that
vibrates in optimization routines and is moved by money, we see
the instatement—to cite Hegel once again—of a "world condition" whose main characteristic is a palpable change of existential
relations of weight and contexts of seriousness. But because
levitated "society" has not yet accurately conceptualized its own
adventure, namely a relief that affects all semantic and material
states of affairs—or, where it has, it does not know how to use
it productively, it faces the temptation to speak of its great
achievements as if they were new ills, and of its most innovative feats as if they were unprecedented grievances. In terms of

its release-influenced moods too, "society" is unsure upon its departure from the universe of poverty; when it broaches the topic of its unaccustomed improvements of atmosphere, it wonders whether it has strayed from the true path, which is arduous and dictated by hardship.[42]

As if made restless by confusion of a comparable kind, Hegel wrote in January 1807, in a tone of grand historical diagnosis:

> Besides, it is not difficult to see that ours is a birth-time and a period of transition to a new era. Spirit has broken with the world it has hitherto inhabited and imagined [...] dissolving bit by bit the structure of its previous world, whose tottering state is only hinted at by isolated symptoms. The frivolity and boredom which infest the established order, the vague fore-boding of something known, these are the heralds of approaching change. [...] The onset of the new spirit is the product of a widespread upheaval in various forms of culture, the prize at the end of a complicated, tortuous path [...].[43]

If Hegel is wrong, his mistake lies in taking frivolity and bore-dom for harbingers of conditions that are yet to come; in fact, they are the new that has already come to pass. They are early traces of the transition to a barely known limbo of being, and to a passing of time that is disconnected from fixed goals; these give the newer era as a whole its hue. One must understand that what is at issue here is not the aristocratic *spleen* which had flourished under the *ancient régime,* nor the melancholy savoring of the *douceur de vivre* at a late hour. The expressive reference to such moods "infest[ing] the established order" already speaks of bour-geois conditions. It reveals the philosopher's concern about the solidity of altered world conditions in the liberal camp. However much he identifies himself as a partisan of the new state of the world, in which substance wishes to be developed as the subject, he does not accept just any mode of subjectivity as the placeholder of substance. It must be a serious, representative development of the industrious subject that will be at home in the new, post-revolutionary situation, established through a freedom that had come into its own in the medium of right. For Hegel, the romantic modes of the frivolous and the bored consciousness only have the meaning of symptoms, and cannot be more than a morbid intermezzo between two worthy states; the older was embodied by Catholic substantialism, which is now obsolete, and the newer is meant to form a part of post-Protestant freedom in a state ruled by law. Frivolity and boredom do at least constitute an entr'acte which must be granted as much leeway as fermentations and transitional fever require for their useful work—after all, even the terrorist excesses of the French Revolution had to be passed through like necessary stages in the curriculum that led to the state ruled by law.

But what if the fermenting substance, once inflated, has no intention of collapsing again, and after being driven upwards wants to assert itself as a lighter, freer, more frivolous mode of existence in its own right? What does it mean if the capriccio is no longer content to be a musical genre or a literary tone, and seeks in future to expand into an aspect of the bourgeois *modus vivendi*, a style of using money and of allocating feelings and inclinations? What if the *Mongolfières* that rose to the sky over French cities before the Revolution were not mere whims condemned to crash (a related flying machine, the *Charlière*, fell to earth in August 1783 in Gonesse, near Paris, and was attacked

Bernardino de Sousa Pereira, *First Attempt by Bartolomeu Lourenço de Gusmão to Fly a Hot Air Balloon before King John V* (1709)

with pitchforks and scythes by panicking farmers before finally being "killed" by a shot from a soldier's rifle)? If these devices of whim rather indicated the ambition of the moderns to settle in the airspace? Had not Voltaire, already in 1752, sent the hero of his novel *Micromégas* through space on sunbeams and thus hinted at the enlightener's intention to take possession of the vertical? In this he was no more than an emulator of Francis Bacon, who had foreseen the imitation of birds' flight by suitable machines in his utopian tale about the island of *New Atlantis* in 1964. The theater machines of the Baroque had also discovered the dimension of height, and let Mercury float through the air over the audience's heads on his winged sandals, and Fortuna on her orb. Whether sacred or secular games: in their indispensable final apotheoses, they expanded the air space into a stage above the stage.[44] The optical illusions of the ceiling frescoes from the same period invited the audience to navigate in the vertical. All these occupations of the space of altitude were irreversible. Even the dances of the pre-revolutionary period made it clear that the ground could no longer stake its old claims to the attraction of bodies unchallenged; instead of weighty striding, a culture of floating movements and leaps emerged.

An aphorist writing around 1750 could have claimed that anti-gravity, elegance and the machine were the most significant tendencies of the age. The phenomena spoke for themselves: had the entire eighteenth century not raved in poetry and technology about "airship art," *navigation aérienne*, Daedalus machines and aerostatic orbs? On the eve of the French Revolution, had not the moment truly come in which humans felt ready to emancipate existence from the sad habit of being heavy and deny the gods their last privilege, that of pure whim? The Montgolfier brothers' successful demonstration of a hot air balloon on September 19, 1783 in the Versailles Palace courtyard in the presence of Louis XIV, had given the official sign for the beginning of levitation—a joyous event at which a sheep, a cock and a duck had the privilege of being the first animals on earth to ascend to an altitude of some 400 feet. (The sheep was kept in the royal stables and looked after with care for its entire life, as befits a witness to progress.) At the time, the politics of anti-gravity had made the transition to the new era and was in the process of creating its own media and machines in the form of republicanism and air travel, aesthetics and therapeutics, and industry and long-distance traffic. Had not Jacques Alexandre César Charles, who ascended to an altitude of 11,000 feet on December 1, 1783 as the first person in a hydrogen balloon, told the *Journal de Paris* the following day: "Nothing will ever

Balloonists' meeting in the Alps

equal the moment of joy that took over my existence when I felt myself leaving the earth"? The crowds on the ground were also intoxicated by such pioneering deeds, and celebrated the balloonists as the true heroes of the time; they had intuitively grasped that their own concern was being pursued. It seemed as if humanity, represented by the avant-garde in the baskets under the heaven-bound orbs, had found a way out of its self-imposed inability to fly. Jean Paul made his aeronaut Giannozzo live in the gondola and had his hero, like a pragmatized humorist, spend his nights sleeping at high altitude. But the fact that at the end, this remote viewer of the lower world is made to crash in a storm and break his neck shows how the author, retreating from his own co-discovery of anti-gravity, resorts to Icaran clichés at the last moment—granting gravity a spiteful closing word. A hundred years after the first ascents of the Mongolfières and Charlières, Nietzsche would call the free spirited friends of the experimental life "we aeronauts of the spirit." Therefore, whoever is unwilling to speak of uplift should also be silent about modernity.

To give due acknowledgement to Hegel's anti-Romantic (and anti-anti-grave) rage, one must see it as a precocious manifestation of modern conservatism. It is motivated by the accurate perception that the so-called Romantics, the new frivolous and bored, the polyvalent and floating, the metaphorical aeronauts and entrepreneurs in the ironic space, are no longer willing to have their levitated and aimlessly work-superior moods presented simply as pathological and provisional things, to be abandoned as soon as one has returned to solid conditions—a phenomenon that was, incidentally, documented through various spectacular conversions in the lives of people from the generation of "subjectives" who initially played with everyone. For Hegel, the offensive sting of the Romantic attack is that it entails the self-positing of the light.[45] The philosopher senses clearly that appeal proceedings are being initiated against the old weights and measures of serious consideration. He is equally aware that the modern experiential mode sees the emancipation of boredom as a phenomenon with its own value: inner time is decoupled from the cart of objective goals, leaving a loosely drifting consciousness that is freed from goals and unemployed in the positive sense, proceeding from whim to opportunity and back to whim—one could call it the discovery of the great holiday from the spirit of crossed-out final aims. It is no surprise that a thinker like Hegel, who could only make the things that he accepted as real intelligible from an endpoint of explicit conceptual fulfillment, saw such approaches as no more than extensions of an unfounded arbitrariness to the objectified world. All he sees in the declarations of the levitated spirit as it plays in almost godlike fashion with itself and the material of the world is a "blandness" that, he lectures, inevitably takes over "if it lacks the seriousness, the suffering, the patience, and the labor of the negative."[46] However far the kinship between irony and dialectics may otherwise extend, Hegel wants to pin down that active unrest which is the self[47] as a serious circular motion and purposeful laboring. Freedom must therefore tolerate being dressed up as an understanding of necessity—as if it had only surfaced from substance for an impetuous second before, as if seized by remorse and dizziness, sinking back into necessity, lawfulness and self-restriction. Never is the fermentation of what is living allowed to drift along with no goal; never can uplift follow its own line. Nor can Hegel accept the Romantic equation of pure experience with the meaning of existence, as articulated by Lord Byron in a letter to his fiancée from 1813: "The great art of life is sensation, to feel that we exist, even in pain." For the thinker, such movements and feelings can only be those of bad infinity; its psychological trace is the sick self, which flees from its inactivity and worldlessness in presumptions and intensivisms.

In fact, however, the emancipations of self-confident frivolity had only become possible in the horizon of a "society" that, thanks to its accumulation of wealth, science and technology, was already in the process of stepping out of the space of history as one of hard labor and battle—a state that was anticipated at the writing desks of early Romanticism with great incisiveness and intoxicated hastiness. Novalis' poetological doctrine of the potentiation of the coincidental could only be formulated under a constellation in which—as a result of the Kantian and Fichtean caesura—the dictate of external objectivity could be abandoned like a disempowered prejudice. After the toppling of the ontological *ancient régime*, new ideas attracted attention:

> 65. All the chance events of our lives are materials from which we can make what we like. Whoever is rich in spirit makes much of his life. Every acquaintance, every incident would be for the thoroughly spiritual person—the first element in an endless series—the beginning of an endless novel.[48]
>
> 62. Humanity is a comic role.[49]

One must be careful not to advance the prematurity of such sketches as an argument against them. Nor should the ever-consequent revenge of the real be confused with a refutation of anti-grave tendencies, however gleefully the conservatives integrated such into their view of things—they had always believed in the fall, not the flight. If Icarus falls into the sea, they will be the ones who always saw it coming. Pessimism reveals its weakness, its kinship with vengeful moods, when it seeks to win the argument against lightening. So no more take-off clearance for Icaran copycats? Freud's well-known association of the erection with the "suspension of gravity" hints at the belief that after such insurrections, the earth's gravitational pull has the last word.

What had actually begun at the highest standard with the appearance of Romantic irony and its art of taking all things lightly was the questioning of the traditional notion of reality, together with its basis in an obsoletely monovalent ontology;

this resulted not only in the crisis of "occidental teleology,"[50] but also the liquidation of the advanced-civilized concept of reality. The most visible technical procedures for this are air travel, which uses uplift, and space travel, which gives terrestrial bodies access to weightlessness. From now on, what is in the air is no less than *The End of Gravity*;[51] the hour has struck for the ontological primitivism that could only ever speak of the essential One. The new age is that of the decoupling of subjectivity from the venerable definitions of the serious world; it marks the start of filtering in lightness and ambiguity into the monotone heaviness of substance. Freedom, after all, is more than accepted necessity: it is the separation of burdening and relieving forces.

Here it becomes clear at what point the interests of a pluralistic spherology take effect empirically: its concern is to approach the reconstruction of consubjective or surreal spaces of animation. Thanks to the concept of relief, we can get a climatological interpretation underway of a polyvalent real whose focus is the animation of lifeworldly cells through anti-grave tendencies. From this perspective, modernity appears as an expanding transcultural levitation experiment—with an emphasis on the foaming of the real by means of incorporating elements of uplift into the complex of heaviness. One must now admit that the premise for the concept of civilization is the concept of anti-gravity; it implies immunization to the heavy, the over-heavy, which has paralyzed human initiative from time immemorial. It voices its objection to the unmoved mountains. The turn towards relief must now—in the course of the explication of immune technologies that is typical of the time—be made explicit.

Now that the derivation of cultures from collective stress and the latter's regulated resolution in group decorum is secure in its outlines—I would point once more to the promising work by Bazon Brock and Heiner Mühlmann—the civilizatory meaning of the counter-stressory elements should also be added. One can see the empirical triumph of the anti-grave tendencies from the observation that in all areas affected by the market mechanism and inventive revision, deficiency is how in short supply. If this were not the case, there could be no competition to exploit the resources of crisis, drive and need—either materially or symbolically. In the elaborated consumer sphere, as we know, it is supply that is abundant, while those needs capable of creating demand increasingly prove scarce.[52]

Through the anti-grave effects of the surplus civilizatory means that, despite all setbacks and destructions of value, have steadily accumulated over the last two centuries, a process of revision of the concept of reality has been set in motion that ruins the cause of the solid, heavy and inescapable. Starting from the opening definition of foam, the modernized social field as a whole can be described as a multi-chamber system of uplift cells—commonly called "lifeworlds"—in which the symbionts profit from anti-grave effects thanks to the means of de-aggravation accessible to them. Symbiotic spaces are concomfortable, confrivolous, condelirious, conhumorous, and usually also conhypocritical and conhysterical in their constitution. Hence they are not safe from mimetic contamination or the outbreak of paranoid epidemics. The reason for assigning so much existential significance to climatology is that, for philosophical reasons, one must inquire beyond the technological air conditioning systems and optional modifications of physically concrete breathing conditions; what gives pause for thought is the tempering of being-in-the-world as such, the mood of existence between the poles of aggravation and alleviation. Foam: would that now mean the air from gasps of relief in unexpected places?

It must be admitted here that the discoverer of world-disclosing moods in the philosophical context, Martin Heidegger, set the terms for assessing the light and the heavy entirely differently—in this respect, he was Gehlen's kinsman in the avant-garde conservative spirit. However contemporary Heidegger's perceptions of the relieving processes in the climatic system of modernized existence may have been, he made it clear in both his habitus and his pathos that he was against the levitational tendency and derived the dignity of existence—still very much in the sense of Old European-heroic sentiments—from a letting-oneself-be-summoned to the hard, heavy and necessary. Like Hercules at the crossroads, the true philosopher chooses the uncomfortable solution. As with Gehlen, however, this vote is voluntaristically tinged; once again, whim preempts necessity. For now, the heroic thinker is concerned to outdo convention through voluntariness. However, this only proves that a discoverer (or rather, an explicator) cannot be obliged to draw the "progressive" conclusions from their discovery.

The choice in favor of collectedness, seriousness and heaviness—against a background of depth-focused insights into the validity and ubiquity of existentials such as dissipation, frivolity and indecision—is by no means the necessary conclusion from Heidegger's own phenomenology of moods. Upon closer inspection, it becomes clear that the ponophilic, effort-loving, relief-hostile assessments—those of Heidegger as well as Gehlen, Schmitt and other of their ilk—are very much of a prejudiced and decisionist nature; they can at best claim to be anchored in the decorum of Old European heroism. These protagonists of realism in the disenchanted world were keenly aware that under the conditions of their own time, dissipation was a more extensive phenomenon than concentration. Analogously, it should have been clear to them that frivolity is richer than seriousness by one dimension, namely indecision about the decision; and finally, to get to the glowing heart of the present day: that disengagement, as compared to engagement, encompasses a more complex field of states, statements and existential chances.

Only a willful choice can oblige us to commit ourselves at a heightened place in the real. Necessity does not compel us; we choose a difficulty. Mussolini understood that when he defined *fascismo* as the horror at a comfortable life. It is in the boundless popularity of sport, which had already struck that diagnostician of his time, Oswald Spengler, before 1914, that the truth about the current age articulates itself: the commands of hardship have been replaced by the choice of effort; passion is replaced by the hobbyhorse; the game has outstripped work, and what presents itself as work is actually abundance with a serious face; the job centers could long since have been renamed job-feigning centers. Wherever one looks, whim has necessity on a leash. It is only for the sake of the habitual ontological form that released forces allows themselves to be bound and act as stupid as necessity desires; mindful of their duty, they pretend to serve the most solid and indispensable purposes.

The decisive information about the inversion of status between the light and the heavy lies in the expressive worlds in which the popular neo-athletic willingness to effort clothes itself: it is precisely because the civilized, technically relieved forms of life almost never seriously require individuals to go to their limits—such that, *summa summarum*, they are chronically relieved of the major stress reaction to a present danger to life and limb—that many of them choose a willful re-burdening; not because they believe in the necessity of their exertion, but because they claim—with latent irony—a right to increased effort and jeopardy.[53] One could speak of an endogenous appetite for emergency—the idling heroic programs want to remain active with different content. The same applies to lofty moral standards; they too cannot, in the long run, accept being liberated into arbitrariness. They do not readily admit that they have been released from necessity. It is therefore in sport, in consumption, in enterprise, and now once again in social activisms that a unification of work and play took place, with entirely different results from any that Schiller and Marcuse could have foreseen.

In a related spirit of gratuitous self-burdening, the fundamental ontologists claimed a right to be used by the most important matters of brought-forth being. Heidegger spoke cunningly of the "inescapable"—to him, abstention from the comforts of modern dissipation was not too high a price to pay for an alliance with the heavy end of the spectrum. One finds a similar gesture in Simone Weil's Christian need for torment, which is expressed in the doctrine: "Physical labor willingly consented to is, after death willingly consented to, the most perfect form of obedience."[54] That is to say: because physical labor is a daily death, it must become the spiritual center of social life. One does not have to be a psychoanalyst to see offshoots of primary masochism, which expresses itself in thriftiness or a compulsion to treat oneself strictly, in effect in such gestures.[55] Nietzsche: "man takes a real delight in oppressing himself with excessive demands [...]."[56] It can hardly be denied that these phenomena seem constituted in an Adlerian jargon—though it is less a case of organic inferiorities seeking to be balanced out by great achievements than existential moods of meaninglessness and superfluity that, by seeking refuge in indispensability, postulate its opposite.

What high-performance sport and the sublime philosophies of the twentieth century have in common is that one can only find meaning in them if one understands them as statements on the state of levitation. Both options, willfully striving for records and victories or arbitrarily choosing obligations and new burdens, show how much the released life must look after the investment of its surpluses of meaning itself. When there is no imperious hardship in sight, individuals can and should choose their own emergencies on whatever fronts. Sport and commitment are emanations of a deeper willfulness that places effort in the service of the superfluous. Frivolity shoulders heaviness. The fact that high stakes often surround themselves with an aura of sacred seriousness only reveals the other side of the liberated choice of reality. When racing drivers are smashed to pieces and skydivers plummet to earth, one normally offsets, in a respectful manner, the serious end of the matter against its frivolity. Did Nietzsche's Zarathustra not bury with his own hands the tightrope walker who had made danger his profession?[57]

One can form an idea of the immense progress in levitation events indirectly, in the mirror of theory, by comparing Hegel's passing diagnosis on boredom and frivolity as symptoms of incipient modernity to the radicalizations which Heidegger managed to derive from the topics of dissipation and boredom in his phase of culmination between 1926 and 1930. He was as sure that both motifs touched the atmospheric heart of the age as he was possessed by his calling to return transformed from the descent into modern unseriousness. As the endurer of emptiness, he would be able—so he believed—to show the way up; from the immersion bath of reflection on the inevitable dissipation, one should advance to new forms of collection and seizedness by the work whose execution was inescapable. His lecture from the winter semester of 1929/30 on "The Fundamental Concepts of Metaphysics" became known primarily through the sensational phenomenology of boredom, which it is no exaggeration to call the most profound theory of the present that the twentieth century was capable of producing. At its heart, according to Heidegger, lies a levitated existence whose outstanding characteristic is the impossibility of being fully seized. Humans experience themselves as hollow and light forms assigned no content to fill them; far and wide, there is nothing in sight that could elevate existence to the dignity of the real.[58] Here the unbearable lightness of being is conceptually exposed: at this point, it is the "hardship of hardshiplessness." The term provides the first philosophical finding of elaborated consumer society. In letting the very thing it discards illuminate it, the conservative spirit—as so often—has its finger on the pulse of the time. (Max Frisch: "It was not suffering, not hardship, as he had once feared; it was only emptiness, and that was worse—it was a carpet beater's existence.")[59]

There is no escape from unease at facilitation: because there is no inner emergency assessment in disarmed existence, the subject feels exposed to a stale relief. In a peculiar way, its lightness hurts—or rather, it feels disconcertingly cut off from what could hurt. It is indifferent to itself—and rightly so, for the way it currently lives, none of the things it undertakes can be about anything real. Boredom means that one experiences one's own time as an inner stretching that is excessively conspicuous because it is not fulfilled in meaningful actions. It is experienced as a torturous interval before the next event that clears the congestion. The paradigmatic example: waiting hours for a train at a provincial station. Yet the insufficient seizedness goes much further. The animal without a mission gropes its way through the mist; many things are possible, but nothing is convincing. Because I am not seized, I pick up many things. I plunge into activity, I turn with artificial enthusiasm towards the unpostponable, which seems to be crying out: "Deal with me!" I act the dedicated individual, the agent of the important, the militant. If you are looking for the front man, here he is! If I look more closely, I have to admit: "those too were mere ornaments of my dozing."[60] Even engagement proves a form of dissipation. By overstretching the sense of the time into a pale expanse, the non-seized state corrupts concentration on substantial intentions. It becomes impossible to collect oneself in an action. While one can still kill the time of shallow boredom oneself, it stands still in existence in the case of deep boredom. Hence this attribute loses its existentiality: the ability to bestir oneself to a plausible work. The sense of injury grows until the self loses all its contours—yet Heidegger has no intention of stopping halfway. Where there was busy Dasein, there must be deepest boredom. It strikes the heart of life as the impossibility of having a project.

If one thinks of oneself entirely as a child of a dissipated and facilitated time, and beyond that, feels to one's core like a loser who has been left with nothing—then *one* is so bored that it can no longer be ascertained who the person experiencing this withdrawal actually is. Just as great fear causes world-withdrawal—and, by contrast, reinforces the miracle *that anything is at all*—deep boredom causes self-withdrawal. It can, *a contrario*, make what is withdrawn shine forth: the compaction of time in the meaningful act.

With this descent into the final dispossession, Heidegger touches on a pathological extreme of relief at which the relieved loses any sense of their own existence, such that they feel themselves like an intimate-indifferent fact. My authenticity [*Eigentlichkeit*] can now be described as the complete absence of being from me. In the deepest boredom, there are only circumstances which have no self; the deeply bored individual is actually existing inexistence. The pain of painlessness rages within it. Like a negative Atlas, inexistent existence must bear the entire weightlessness of the universe. The world is unbearably light when my temporal heart, my living having-something-to-do-now, has been amputated.

Certainly the philosopher would not have imposed this *descensus ad inferos* on his listeners if he had not felt that he could ignite the spark of reemergence in them. The purpose of the meditation was unabashedly dialectical; it was meant to release the "positive power of the negative" in order to return from weariness to an effective seizedness by what was now termed inevitable. So for Heidegger, as later for Sartre, engagement is preceded by a radical disengagement—with the difference that the master from Germany constructs an existence capable of engagement and fit for works via resurrection from the depths of boredom. One could add: the German boredom of 1929 contained the German state of defeat of 1918. The innermost experience of being left empty by the activities of life that Heidegger describes is naturally a loser syndrome, the kind that develops among a population in which the rewards for success and victory are no longer present as points of reference. There is thus an element of tragic troop entertainment in these theories—together with a hint of revenge at the highest level. Many are defeated, but few are chosen to turn their defeat into a special kind of victory.

The turn is meant to lead from staying empty in relief to a re-burdening with something epochally important and necessary; it relies on the therapeutic value of self-importance. From the revelation of null nothingness in empty time, Dasein rises to an acute intensification of existence in the time of the work. It is unfortunate that Heidegger illustrated his meditations with the wrong example soon afterwards; he could have offered a fitting one by following the "call" to levitation and committing himself to democracy and weightlessness.[61] This was outside of his background and his projects. It would have presupposed a change in his job description and demanded being retrained as an intellectual rather than a seer; it would have demanded a concession from the moderns, namely to dispense with the bogus mandate of necessity.

4. "Your Private Sky"—Thinking Relief

While the conceptions of Gehlen and Heidegger are charac-terized by an effort to reject the anti-gravity and de-contraction of living conditions in modern consumer society, the develop-ment of constructivism and functionalism after 1945 caused the appearance of a new paradigm of thought whose allegiance to the age of levitation was visible from the start, both chronologically and stylistically. Whoever is willing can see the constructivist turn as the Californian contribution to recent intellectual his-tory—though California, like Schwabing in earlier times, should be taken less as a territory than a state of mind which can be found as easily in Illinois or Bielefeld as on the Pacific coast of America. Especially in the statements of Heinz von Foerster (1911–2002), the philosophical mentor of the constructivist movement, referred to not inappropriately as the Socrates of cybernetics, the affinity between the new approach and the departing levitation is plain to see. His argumentative and dia-logical procedures lead straight to a critique of heavy reason. Von Foerster's decisive intervention lay in a clarification of the process that results in the "ontological" semblance of heaviness. He offered proof—prefigured in Fichte's philosophy—that the heaviness of the objective is the result of an unrecognized exter-nalization. The objects become excessively heavy if they are placed in the weighing dish of a reality check without the coun-terweight of the subjective. If a heavy object is weight up with a weightless subject, the dish on the object side will inevitably be lower. This weighing procedure is the basic operation of the traditional doctrines of substance and monovalent ontologies. In them, the subject faces the block of the objective destitute, with

Joseph Beuys, *Levitazione in Italia* (1973)

Charlotte Buff, *Trans-Formationen XXV*, nets (1992)

the supposedly sole option of submitting to the given—a gesture that is taken for granted in time-honored epistemologies when they reduce knowledge to a reflection of the existent in a subjective medium. With this arrangement, people can obscure the fact that they were the ones who ascribed weightlessness to themselves and weightiness to objects: the heavy holds sway, and whoever desires their share of power as a human must present themselves as a proponent of gravity—unless one can find a different way to distribute the weights.

If one explicitly reintroduces the observer, with their distinguishing activity and responsibility for the differences they have chosen, into the events, they cease to be a *quantité négligeable*; they return to the stage as an effective factor in their own right among other factors (especially if they have machines at their disposal that can help move even the most physically heavy objects). The weight of things is a construct that forms in dealing with them; as such, it is tactically modifiable. So one must cling to the fact that in everything humans touch, they encounter their own prior decisions. After the constructivist turn they must know: what one calls heaviness and lightness cannot be anything but an effect of balancing out or not balancing out weights with counterweights.

This yields the moral maxim of constructivism: to further in all things the visibility of freedom and the explicitness of choices. Whoever follows this path will cease to grant authority to assertions invoking an objective outside. Statements containing the element "there is…" will be translated into those starting with "I assume that…" Von Foerster's not very categorical imperative is: "Act at all times in such a way that the number of possibilities grows."[62] It does not occur to Cybersocrates to envisage the wealth of alternatives as a burden. Where there is a plurality of options, even the most painful situations seem therapeutically corrigible—at least, in the sense that one unlivable construct of reality can be replaced by a less unbearable one.[63] Where an external reality is asserted, good intellectual manners will demand in future that one add the name of the author and the year of publication, as well as an indication of the edition in question. The exchange of comfort for necessity will be openly accepted as the transactional basis of the modernity experiment.

Constructivist thought seeks to protect itself from the fate of the emancipation doctrines known thus far, namely the shift of their own standards towards dogmatism—and thus an increase in proximity between well-intentioned critique and the Jacobin

Jeffrey Shaw, *Waterwalk* (1969)

end of the spectrum—by staying reserved towards itself. This can only succeed through constant training in self-distance or self-unburdening. There are commonalities between Von Foerster's dialogical humor and Luhmann's concept of ironic reason, which prohibits becoming too serious about one's own concerns for methodological and moral reasons. "Self-critical reason," Luhmann writes in one excellent passage, "is ironic reason."[64] The anti-grave dimension of irony is adequately embodied by a culture of theory in so far as it "can exchange its own belief in reality, and thus in so far as it does not begin to believe in itself."[65] By warning of the auto-suggestive element inherent in all belief in reality, Luhmann—like an early Romantic after-ripened by the lessons of the twentieth century—arrives at a position that can be understood as an antithesis to Heidegger's intentional immersion in heavy fate (and, of course, as an objection to the moral rigorism steeped in good faith in itself, and against the greatly under-perceived left-wing fascisms, which don the mantle of universalism and always know down to the last detail what people want, are and need).

The discovery of lightness that materialized during the twentieth century in the systems for making existential provisions is doubly significant for the theory of spheric relationships: firstly as an object of examination, and secondly as a precondition for their own manifestation. Only when lightness has been explicitly thematized can the animated spaces of coexistence be described from the perspective of gravitation. After the establishment of the atmospheric as a category—as an ontological-public dimension—all human facts present themselves *sub specie* of relief. Anti-gravity can now be understood as a "fundamental" vector, or rather as the tendency that strives against the dimension of a foundation. This makes it clear that culture would be impossible without the heavenly ascensions of non-heavy meaning. While realistic seriousness has always purported to be and to know what is the case, future realistic thought must start from the realization that anti-gravity is more serious than anything ever formulated about the supposedly "fundamental" by the consensus.

As a result, the presentation of human history changes in both style and substance: while established "world histories" content themselves with accompanying the course of "cultures" and ethnicities along the railing of their inner necessities and external stressors, the concern of a spherologically informed historiography is to underline the elements of uplift, surplus and free drift inside the anthropogenic islands—because we now fundamentally know that one is never dealing with deficient beings in the midst of their difficulties, but rather with wealthy beings oriented towards pampering, the luxury of intimacy, infantility privileges, relieved waking periods and stimulus intake. The ominous phrase *conditio humana* reflects the fact that for the larger part of their historical existence, these creatures of wealth had to deal with the problem of forced self-underselling. How one-sided they had to become in order to secure their survival; how many of their potentials they had to shut down in order to tolerate themselves in everyday life; how many untrue descriptions of their nature—from original sin to endless desire—they had to endure in order to pay their debt of assimilation to the most varied world conditions! "Growing up" is one key phrase here, "internalizing sacrifice" is another, and a hypertrophy of the sense of reality at the expense of the sense of possibility is a third. A universal history of frivolity would show how under the pressure of poverty realism, countless relieved cells and climate islands form, each with its own respective enlivenment secret. The survival chances of cultures undoubtedly rest not only on the stability provided by their symbolic orders or institutions (as one-sidedly emphasized by Gehlen), but equally on the underground levitation work that remains largely unnoticed by the circulating cultural theories, which enables the inhabitants of the anthropogenic island to create their breathing spaces. These events seem as if they were concealed by a surreal title: "The Invention of Air through the Gasp of Relief."

Drawing on the category of relief and the empiricism it opens up, it must be shown that what has, since Freud, been called the "reality principle" has been shaped not only by the experiences that adolescents garner in dealing with the hardness, resilience and unavailability of objects. For the entrance of the real into the life of intelligence is due equally to the forms of relief that can be discovered when dealing with things: the out-smartable nature of resistances, the bypassable nature of obstacles, the postponable nature of difficulties, the reframable nature of deficiencies, the contestable nature of recriminations, the reformulable nature of accusations, the manipulable nature of standards, the subvertible nature of tasks, the replaceable nature of losses, the numbable nature of pain and the avoidable nature of head-on encounters with forces that can only bring defeat. That includes the awareness of the flexibility of concepts and the necessity of interpreting norms—augmented by the realization that there is a tendency for cunning to take precedence over hard work, and the trick over the method. At the level of observation, this is supplemented by recognizing the changeable aspect of all conditions.

The sum of all this is an arsenal of anti-gravity arts differentiated in terms of places and times; one could, in allusion to an album by a pop star, refer to them as "escapology."[66] Equipped with their local set of relief technologies, humans from the most diverse cultures face the task of withdrawing as far as possible from the weight of the world—and to bear what remains. One must discover the good soldier Švejk as an ontologist.[67] The unshiftable remainder of heavy being extends as an offshoot of the real into bubbles of relief, cultures, spaces air-conditioned by illusions, thermotopes and fields of human warmth. It is usually picked up by religious interpretations: through a glorification of burden and an identification with the overwhelming. Where perpetrators can be found, people resort to rituals of vengeance, and later penal law; where the real appears as an enemy, one adjusts to it through outer and inner hardening procedures. In all this, one must take into account that in trivial situations the real can only be experienced as a remainder, while the other, more powerful part only advances to mental representation imaginarily, for example in threat scenarios. Some civilizations created the role of the approved advocate of the real, who is equipped with the prerogative to plead against the effects of excessive relief after arriving at the opinion that the collective puts itself in danger through its overstretched economy of illusions. Since the nineteenth century, Europe has known not only the neo-Roman people's tribune, the intellectual who speaks up for the still-mute proletariat, but also the disaster tribune, who points out to fellow citizens the disastrous potential of their own behavior. A central element in the signature of the twentieth century is that its intellectuals intervened in the name of the real to an inflationary degree. Extremism, which remains inseparable from the style of modernity, was—one realizes too late—a luxuriating form of realism. Realism is the established form of the belief that the disaster is always right.

Let us note: without the greenhouse gases of frivolity, no inhabitable (sur)reality bubble can be curved and kept in shape. "Under your private sky"—this would be the spherological answer to the question of where you really reside.[68] Here the word "private" does not refer to the encasement of the individual in an illusion tailored to their needs; it shows that real dwelling takes place under canopies, which naturally only span a small

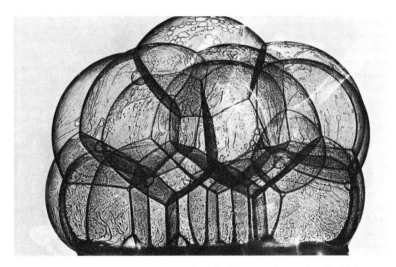

Walter Bird, foam model: formation of polyhedrons inside a pack of bubbles

segment of the whole. The format is the message; the excerpt from the real is the real.

This making-room-for-oneself under a personal and shared sky—formally and materially represented by the umbrella princi-ple[69]—leads to successes as long as the immune systems maintain a minimum of delusion or an affirmation of their own ensoulment field. It is self-evident how religion intersects with poetry in this respect. (And equally self-evident why Marxism, by showing off with its superior prose and insights, carried out a direct destructive attack on human resources.) What Jacob the Liar managed in the Warsaw Ghetto—supplying his environment with news that was better than the real situation—has always been a skill of storytellers and custodians of regenerative rituals.[70] Perhaps every accomplished life (and accomplished always means in spite of circumstances) is a back and forth between exo- and endo-realism. Just as depression corresponds to prose, hypomania corresponds to poetry.[71]

Spontaneous development of relatively stable constructions in semi-dried foams

De facto, the imagination has always been in power. The fact that it could become explicit in 1968 proves that for one happy moment, the cause of levitation became universally comprehensible. (It was the genius of Walt Disney, on the other hand, that bridged the gap between hypomania and infantilism: in his comic universe, he succeeded in making explicit the principle of a parallel reality and expanding immersion in kitsch into a secure evasion procedure. The tendency to introduce "reality on demand" is not a privilege of the American dream factory, however, but a domain in which Old Europe has always accomplished extraordinary things.) Where uplift particles are diluted beyond a certain degree, manifest depressions result; these indicate that resistance to the pressure of the real has been broken. If people are to remain capable of activating their space-forming potential, this presupposes an equilibrium of forces between gravity and anti-gravity. In theoretical terms, this means that the original aphrogenic activity of humans cannot be articulated without an explicit concept of uplift.

In the face of the explicated spheric imperative, the early "pneumatic architectures" (such as Walter W. Bird's radome prototype (1948) on the grounds of Cornell Aeronautical Laboratory, Frank Lloyd Wright's *Rubber Village Fiberthin Airhouse* (1956) or Frei Otto's *Inflatable Pavilion* from the Expo 1958 in Rotterdam, as well as the numerous analogous concepts advanced by Victor Lundy, Buckminster Fuller, Archigram and others), which have been among the most intelligent and elegant innovations in modern space-formation art since the 1950s, possess a culture-theoretical—or perhaps one should say a general niche-related and capsule-related—symbolic value that goes far beyond their practical function.[72] The air one breathes in the pneumatic dome is at once part of the tectonic medium that gives the structure tension, as well as providing breadth and inhabitability. The pressure of uplift is employed as an agent of spatial stability; the compacted breathing milieu has a direct vault-forming effect. If one transfers the architectural model back to the psychosemantics of the human space, one obtains the most suggestive illustration of the dynamics of uplift in anthropospheric cells and cell groups.

In the passages above on the uterotope and the thermotope, I advanced the thesis that all history is the history of battles between pampering communities—with the concession that the word "pampering," which refers primarily to material and emotional comfort, could be replaced with "chosen," where the

Ars Electronica 1982, sky event

emphasis is on a thymotic (in common parlance, narcissistic) preference for one's own thusness. What pampering and chosenness have in common is that their subjects feel they are recipients of preferences that are granted to them materially and spiritually—

Dorothee Golz, *Hollow World* (1966) at *documenta* X (1997)

whether through a specific patron, some presupposed obligation of the environment to pay duties, or a metaphysical alliance whereby a heavenly protector or a transcendent immunity principle joins forces with the collective.

In the following, I will show that the principle of the patron as an agent of positive predestination is a premise without which the existence of being of the psycho-immunologically sensitive species *homo sapiens* could not be made plausible. On the other hand, it is not a universal, for there are countless exceptions to the rule of special support of an individual life by a patron—perhaps even more exceptions than cases following the rule, exceptions that are recorded in the written and unwritten chronicles of poverty. They fill the black books on the lives of the infamous, unsupported, superfluous people. By showing how the principle of pampering influences most successfully lived lives through the patronage of human mothers, vague outlines emerge of a universal history of frivolity, of which I claimed that it simultaneously encompasses the climatic history of the anthroposphere, with all its countless local efflorescences, in several individuated series.

5. First Levitation—On the Natural History of Uplift

I think they are made of water; they have no expression.
    Their features are sleeping, like light on quiet water. […]
    Their footsoles are untouched. They are walkers of air.
        — Sylvia Plath, "Three Women"[73]

In order to get a non-pauperist anthropology underway, it is advisable to subject the heat center of evolution, namely the special formations of the mother-child space among hominids and early humans, to closer attention. The most prominent feature of this space is the oft-noted tendency to prolong the infantile and juvenile phase in processual unity with a radical prematurity of birth. To interpret this phenomenon, paleontologists have argued that if human young were to be born in as mature a state as primates, a gestation period of 21 months would be required—which (alongside other biological contradictions, above all those of a neurological and endocrinological nature) is ruled out by the typical shape and width of the pelvic inlet among *sapiens* women, which make birth a necessity after a maximum of 270 or 280 days. This entails the generalized risk of a heavily premature exposure of the fetus to harmful external milieus.

To express the implications of this situation as dramatically as their monstrous content demands they be presented, one must say plainly that for humans, normal birth has the quality of an abortion dictated by nature. The script of human existence prescribes that we spend three sevenths of the bio-psychologically essential gestation phase in the milieu of the mother organism, and the remaining four in a stable niche situation best described as a "sojourn in the exo-uterus"—a phrase intended to replace the half-true term "infancy."[74] The differential between the two states produces an interminable dynamic of transference. We are always playing a game: 9 to 12, or endo-pregnancy plus exo-pregnancy, which yields the conditions of admission to the world. No one remembers, yet all are marked by it. One cannot comprehend the enormity of the human "position in the world" without gaining an explicit idea of the two-stage structure of natal movement—more still, of its virtual multi-stage character, which in effect means interminability. It is on this, and its unforeseeable neurological and symbol-dynamic implications, that the morbidity-accepting and expression-demanding eccentricity of the human existential constitution depends, down to its last ramifications.

For *homo sapiens*, being-in-the-world begins with the newborn staking an inalienable claim to the repetition of the uterine position on the outside; here the absolutism of the child's need takes the form of a command through helplessness. With regard to this, the ability to obey is the concrete concept of adulthood. Complementarily, the social environment, usually the biological mother supported by substitute mothers and "helpers at the nest," is meant to be ready for the task of acting as a living incubator and placing the new arrival in a well tempered, at first predominantly bipolar place of care whose peculiarity consists in offering a continuation of pregnancy by outside and interactive means.

This shows us the primal scene of human mediality: one person is the necessary medium for the immaturity of the other. I am born into the world because a part of you accommodates me. For a while, the waking world must act as if it were the accomplice of a fetal dream. The completely-born is supposed to interact with the incompletely-born in such a way that the encasing and satisfaction of the more fragile partner leads to animation of the same—an invitation into the open, a wakening stimulus to discover the world, a companionship in the first chapters of experience. The willingness of human mothers to take on this normal yet surreal task is supported by both inborn and acquired behavioral patterns in mammals: to quote a well-chosen metaphor from the sociobiologist Sarah Blaffer Hrdy, the evolution of parental care among higher life forms follows the "milky way."[75]

Everything suggests that one should characterize the specific attention of early human mothers to their offspring as a form of biological patronage—firstly, because the human and maternal quality of passing on life and life chances does indeed usually take place through fully individualized investments in respectively highlighted and preferred descendants, and secondly, because this patronal gratuity by no means follows biological automatism, for it can only take effect once the mother has accepted and affirmed her child as such in an act of psychosemantic adoption. Only then will she be able to mobilize her entire existential energy for her offspring. Human mothers can only pursue their calling to total patronage of their children—which is often realized positively—because their attention is more than a biological program. Rather, it constitutes a commitment—perhaps the primal form of every committed effort—and can therefore only be adequately acknowledged in the light of an equally possible rejection. To understand this, one must grow accustomed to the confusing truth that in the anthroposphere, even with natural parenthood, adoption takes precedence over biological kinship. Even the natural parents must accept their own child as if *in loco infantis* for it to become in the psychosocial space what it already seems, biologically, to be. Only the affirmation of the child as her own chance and potentially never-ending assignment turns the biological mother of the human child into the anthropogenic mother, and *eo ipso*—in our terminology (learned from Dieter Claessens)—the patron of her child.[76]

Following the superposition of the biological pregnancy relationship with a psychogenic promise of care, the animal mother changes into a human mother—and this mutation would not be the hazardous undertaking that it is if a wealth of improbabilities and opposing reasons did not need to be faded out or covered up before the natural possibility of human motherhood could crystallize into a case of successful maternalization and co-animation. Feminism's revolt against the millennia-old clichés about the imposition that is motherhood and the scientific elucidation of the female part in evolution—I refer once again to Sara Blaffer Hrdy's epoch-making work—converge on at least one point: both parties highlighted the improbability, fortuity and historical variability of the "good mother" phenomenon as much as necessary. According to Hrdy's nuanced studies, the investment of mothers in their children usually takes place only when a global calculus of affirmation has given them positive results. Because the results are in fact often negative, the option of child neglect, even infanticide, as shocking as it may sound to modern ears, is one of the oldest of maternal powers. On the mother's side, the absolutism of the child's neediness corresponds to an absolutism of the ability to accept or reject—a fact which older cultures, in their myths of the dark and devouring mother as well as the countless *noverca* (stepmother) stories, understood more realistically than the Christian-bourgeois Modern Age, in which God is one-dimensionally compassionate and mothers are imagined as selfless by nature. As well as the refusal to invest, which one should probably read as a form of abortion after the fact, the sequence of pre-human development also shows clear patterns of genetic opportunism—for example, when a primate mother whose child was killed by the new pack leader does everything in her power to produce new offspring with the murderer as soon as possible.

What feminist critique and biological research have described, and at times denounced, as a historically conditioned, "patriarchally" influenced ideology of mothering was, in its civilizatory content, an attempt by cultures to break through this absolutism of maternal affect—elsewhere, I have termed it the "Last Judgment at the beginning"[77]—through a separation of power between the mother and the culture in the offspring's favor. By striving to balance out the dictatorship of unavailable maternal feelings with a normative rule increasing the rejected child's chances of psychic and physical survival, the civilized human group embraces its substitute mothering skills. Moral resistance to the abortion of unborn children and the neglect of born ones is therefore the most important indication that a civilization takes itself seriously as such. It does this to the appropriate extent by, if necessary, being more affirmative about new life than a coincidently non-affirmative individual, and more maternal than a coincidental natural mother who, for whatever reason, lacks the strength and willingness to take on her task.

In this sense, civilization is synonymous with the ability to adopt. It is therefore, to elevate the phenomenon to the categorial level, the epitome of allomothering functions, which means (following Hrdy and Wilson) all those parenting acts of animating, providing for and investing in progeny that can be separated from the biological mothers and transferred to third persons or institutions—from the midwives and helpers within the family, via the services of church social service institutions, to the abstract compensation systems in which the modern welfare state is active. In this context, the practice of abandoning children cannot be understood purely as an emergency valve to prevent an excess of children among the poorest; it also testifies to the awareness that unwelcome newborn children should also be given a last chance to find alloparents. The medieval practice of leaving infants on church staircases entailed a recognition of Mother Church as an adopting power. The relative frequency of the name Esposito ["exposed"] in the Spanish-speaking world and Italy stems from the fact that for want of a family name, the Catholic priests tended to name the foundlings at their doors after their situation; thrownness, Catholic-style.

We are approaching a redefinition of the civilization process: its key mechanism is the progressive development of technical and systemic alternatives to first maternalization. Civilizing shows that within certain boundaries, motherhood constitutes a prostheticizable service. The anti-naturalism of the civilization process is based on the metaphorization of maternity; it is the substitution of maternal power in action. This view rests on the assumption that the evolution of the species is advanced primarily by the sentiment that the root of hardship is to be found in the scarcity of allomothering potentials. The replacement process culminates in modernity, in which, thanks to the transition to an *affluent society*, a mass release of women from traditional role definitions became possible; it brought about a decisive revision of the immemorial stereotypes about the purpose and service of motherhood.

The civilizatory content of the current period remains incomprehensible unless one recognizes it above all as a comprehensive experiment about the prosthetizability of maternal services—in conjunction with saving offspring from the molochitic pact between war and culture.[78] In addition to the category of relief, an integral theory of cultural economy thus presupposes a general concept of prosthetics. From this perspective, the primal prosthesis would be the person who assists an active mother as an allomother. If it is true that allomothering capacities are the most precious part of any culture, one could assume that the need to create symbolic and technical equivalents for absent substitute mothers motivated civilizatory evolution as a whole. As dedicated mothers usually fulfill the task of being-rich-for-the-child with great seriousness, they are naturally interested in everything that could facilitate their role. Independently of all philosophy and psychology, they understand that keeping up this primal simulation for the survival chances of their offspring is of decisive importance; they sense that justifying life with uplift for the child is intimately connected to their own balance of happiness and unhappiness. Because the availability of allomothering services is generally experienced early on as scarce, the chance of easier access to it constitutes a first, intuitively irresistible concept of wealth. Being rich first of all means being able to promise a mother access to strongly flowing sources of allomothering energies.[79] Whoever cannot make others rich in this respect is not rich themselves.[80] I define wealth as the ability to take part in an explication of this type. It could be that civilization's greatest adventure is the explication of motherhood, and with it a substantial part of what life means.

In previous remarks on the uterotope and the special forms of neoteny among humans, I described the mothering effect primarily in terms of its niche character, emphasizing the fact that the human mother-child space—unmistakably continuing pre-human and hominid traditions—displays the traits of a micro-hothouse in which a spontaneous long-term trend towards a refinement of human morphologies and a rewarding of the more intelligent variations is at work. In the present context, this model must be made one dimension more complex by showing also how the hominid and early human mother-child field already develops as a self-breeding space or psychic thermotope. The result is the formation and rounding off of the mother-child field in its humanly stretched luxury version. The selective tendency active inside it releases no less than the main result of anthropogenesis: the conquest of childhood. In *homo sapiens*, as we now know, it is not only somatic and mental structures of the child (*neon*) that are taken up into the adult morphology—following the neotenic schema (Gr. *teinein*, "spread, stretch"), which is widespread among mammals and pets, and is even found in small reptiles such as the well-known axolotl. Rather, the species as a whole is progressively infantilized and its life forms placed under the sign of long-term adolescence and a lasting ability to learn. The evolutionary baseline of anthropogenesis can only be understood if one recognizes it as the consequence of a positive feeding back of pampering effects which quantitatively extend and qualitatively intensify the mother-child space. In a manner unprecedented in natural history, these self-reinforcing tendencies produce a life form of immature maturity or mature immaturity—the bio-cultural matrix of human luxury.

The defense of childhood is the essence of culture—assuming that culture is simultaneously defended from invasions by the infantile. The neotenic tendency (which, at the cultural level, produces what Michel Serres calls *hominiscence*) could never have established itself had it not been affirmed, contained and saved by a success check. This check asserts what psychoanalysis calls the "reality principle." In this context, it transpires that the term has always implicitly meant a compensation for the luxury principle that dominates the mother-child field, achieved through the burdening and effort principle of group laws: because the call to pampering knows no inner bounds, it had to be adjusted by ergotopic and nomotopic counterforces. Viewed from this angle, "cultures" are locally successful attempts at luxury containment. Where they showed themselves suitable to be passed on, they proved through their actions that they were capable of limiting the risks of infantilization with the help of stabilizing standardizations (understandably, this resistance to pampering constitutes the phenomenal field that sparked the attention of the anthropologist Gehlen).[81]

It is therefore no coincidence that almost every one of the early cultures had gerontocratic traits: the inexorable infantilization of the anthroposphere could only be compensated for evolutionarily by a complementary presbyterization. Because the mother-child sphere constituted the driving subversive focus of reality everywhere, it was in the interests of the groups to balance out its willfulness by cultivating the authority of their elders. It is this authority that passes on knowledge about the normative and ergotopic burdens of an established living context. In the Old

World, the elders were considered capable of governance because they were incapable of changing their minds; initially, the weight of the world depended on senile stubbornness. It was only modernity that burst open the gerontocratic brackets around the cultural hothouses and embarked on the adventure of rejuvenating civilization almost unreservedly—extending to the level of normative and logical orientations.

It is easy to understand here why the current tendency towards a juvenilization of culture constitutes the psychosocial trace of the "society" of surplus. Only a formation of this type could afford to challenge the traditional containment of the luxury of infantilization through the severity of the aged. Today, for the first time in the history of civilization, the frivolity surrounding human childhood and childlikeness is no longer reliably repressed by the seriousness of the elders. Since that development, the scales have been tilted towards the infantile side—however much the conservatives of our time strive to fill the serious dish with heavy weights, not least with bad memories, threatened emergencies and imaginary burdens. This suggests that the evolutionarily acquired orientation of *homo sapiens* towards an interplay of burden and relief is quickly eroded.[82] For current "societies" this situation is confusing, to say the least. The chances this offers for a contemporary theory of culture, on the other hand, can only be described as inspiring: it is only through the decompensation of adult culture that the connection between the wealth-conditioned greenhouse effect and the release of infantility has, for the first time, become tangible in explicit terms. In the new light, human history reveals itself as an economic report on the state of levitation; it deals with progress in an awareness of pampering.

The starting material for all transformation series of luxury in local cultures and its explicit elaboration in contemporary civilization is, as hinted above, to be found in the second half of the human gestation period, when the infant—assuming its evolutionarily preformed needs are more or less adequately met—resides in a uterus-like niche situation as the junior pole in the mother-child field. It does not simply lie there like a jewel in its case; it exhibits aspects of existentiality from the outset in that, increasingly surfacing from pre-existential sleep, it can be induced to view itself as the ally of a co-creature equipped with powers and treasures. Intimate proximity to generously donated riches creates the experience of easy access to an abundance whose exhaustion cannot be imagined in the foreseeable future. This position gives rise to an affective prejudice about the world that, if not denied in a trauma of withdrawal, sediments itself to form a basic mood of carefree liberty of access to treasures and chances. The first being-in-the-world implies the impossibility of being poor—at least, in places where mothers avoid the risks of pauperism and retain the ability of being-rich-for-the-child in relative mental independence from external circumstances.

This preliminary concept of wealth already shows resonant traits; here, wealth means an accommodation and anticipation of the "world" with reference to subjective need—it includes the constantly available possibility of the fluidization of bodies in communications. Wealth is thus experienced as a material transcendental and a pure "at-all"; one can place it in the background as a "there-is" with no opposite. It thus acts as the condition of possibility of world as such. What one calls the open is the dimension of wealth in its existential reflex. As a foil behind the foils, wealth carries all figures, including those of determinate deficiency and concrete privation. As absolute uplift, it sets itself against aggravations—each one individually and all of them together. As an irreducible surplus, it takes away the sting of all local deductions and diminutions. It tunes resonance-embedded existence with the repetition-saturated prejudice of always being ineluctably equipped with more than the bare necessities. Because wealth always entails a giver and a there-is,[83] it is a semi-personal and semi-material "principle" at once; it thus unifies the virtues of the gift and the find. It is coincidence and property. One could say that it is ownable and alienable at particular times—and yet remains beyond all ownership and alienability.

Those familiar with the history of philosophical thought will note that this existential portrait of a wealth in its infancy contains elements of what was traditionally called the *hypokeímenon* or "underlying thing"—a concept dear to both grammarians and ontologists because it states the function of substance or the subject: to be a bearer of characteristics and reason for events. Its time-honored names are God, nature, substance, form, matter, will or human practice. In the present context, one encounters a carrier of displaced quality—firstly, because existentially understood wealth, as a primary milieu, constitutes a hybrid of something and someone, and thus eludes ontological interpretation as a thing (in concrete terms: for a mother to be experienced as a patron, she must offer a material gift and add herself to it); and secondly, because this carrier never functions merely as an underlay for a burden or a firm footing for a supplement. Initial wealth is material abundance and personal gratuity at once; it operates as an actively elevating authority and a pole of resonance in an animating neighborhood.

As long as existence feels, in its first mood-forming situations, that it belongs to a wealth interpreted in this way, its mode of being can be defined as carriedness. Wealth that carries is uplift; carriedness that becomes the underlying mood is participation in levitation. One can verify the potential of these statements through a comparison with Heidegger's opposing formulations: in *Being and Time*, he speaks of the basic characteristic of human being-in-the-world as thrownness—a term whose acknowledgement includes not seeing it merely as an immense metaphor for the exposedness of existence in the chance field of the co-being. It also contains a reference to a forward and downward pull. Thrownness—this is the dissipating-sinking tendency that is posited with half conservatively, half modernly understood existential ecstasy; it refers to an immersion in fathomless contingency against which the existent can only define itself through its determination to take over the coincidence assigned to it. The concept of thrownness unmistakably belongs to the ontology of deficiency, even if, as we have seen, Heidegger is not concerned with an economic or material deficiency, but rather the absence of real necessity and the lack of collection in an inescapable work. While Heidegger's earlier thought sometimes hints at anti-grave tendencies, these belong more to a repertoire of defiant burdened gestures: a stark pulling-oneself-together and standing-up, standing rigid and still under the impression of supposedly higher calls, and later also a rebellious leaning-on that is negotiated under the codeword "leap"—and of which, after repeated attempts at execution, it becomes clear that it could be many things, but not an upwards motion. The underlying tragic tone is unmistakable: whoever speaks of thrownness pays tribute to the inequality of beginnings.

The word echoes the experience that countless people were exposed from the outset to a fall into disadvantages that can perhaps be corrected, but never balanced out entirely.

As far as the existential constitution of carriedness is concerned, such forced twists are alien to it. When there is no deprivation at the start, no compensation is demanded. As long as wealth itself it the carrying element, existence does not have to earn anything extra. Its first information is the feeling that there is enough, and more than enough; this means that one can relax for the time being. Because wealth-attuned existence is not threatened by the revocation of gifts, it does not need to guard itself warily through a primal effort of its own. It is spared premature convulsions of fear and the compulsion to control itself and its environment. Carried life is not poisoned by the accusation of an overburdened carrier that it is too heavy and should kindly be less burdensome. With actual carriedness, the carried assures itself of the power that passes to it from the carrier. Just as remaining lying down on an underlay, if peaceful, can lead to a basic mood of releasement, trust in the carrying power of the arms that hold me aloft is reproduced, plausibly enough, in a mood of carriedness. It includes the conviction that anti-gravity is ubiquitous. The upright gait of *homo sapiens* is therefore not one physiological evolutionary product among others; it embodies the somatic manifestation of the uplift dimension, which was already at work in the hominids as an advance indication of carried being-in-the-world.

In this respect, the upright gait of humans can be read as an open hieroglyph for frivolity. It proves that levitation has passed its evolutionary test. Through its experience of extrauterine gestation, which is augmented by the extended phase of infantile demands on maternal and allomothering transport services, the body of *homo sapiens* has so much anti-grave information built into it that as it grows, it relies increasingly on its own verticality and finally becomes the most eloquent emblem of the *positio humana*: a structure in which the most improbable stance has come to be taken for granted. The entire program of *sapiens* existence is already formulated in its physical attitude: humans are precisely those creatures for which the near-impossible becomes the commonplace, the almost untenable becomes acceptable as the status quo for the time being, and the seemingly unaffordable becomes the omnipresent ether. In its upright bodily constitution, *homo sapiens* celebrates a daily festival of negentropy.

The economic paradoxes of the human being demand a renewed critical look at the supposedly well-known, even banal, but actually still uncomprehended laws that govern the mother-child space of pre-human and early human creatures. If one takes the results of evolution seriously in the manner attempted, it becomes evident that their course must have involved a mechanism that advanced the increase of improbability as a coherent success story—one could call it a power plant that made available the energy for the release of dispositions towards luxury. It can only have been possible because certain (we can assume: maternal and allomotherly) carrying capacities built islands of anti-gravity into the animal world of gravity. The human-forming place is that in which patronal uplift acts as the basic force. A patron, one now understands, is not simply a wealthy person who invests a part of their fortune in supporting artists in order to increase their own prestige—like Gaius Cilnius Maecenas, who consolidated his great position as *amicus Caesaris* by obliging the poets Horace and Virgil to sing of Octavian as Augustus. The start of patronage is expressed in a mother or allomother accepting the task of being-rich-for-the-child, often independently of their own material resources. The patronal function can be defined as the combination of resonance and uplift. From it emerges a life that is well-off, enriched and seized by anti-gravity.

When Hegel referred in his anthropological lectures to the mother as the "genius of the child," he had in mind the psychic process in which a pre-subjective life is gifted with personal subjectivity thanks to its encounter with the genializing mother principle. Upon closer examination of the process, one finds that this bi-unitary animation is identical to the conferral of the primal gift, uplift. In German Idealism, the awareness of this giftedness was translated into a conviction, however over-interpreted, of being gifted with freedom—taken as the inalienable superiority of the subject to any form of external coercion: nothing could be too heavy for the subject to carry once full of the certainty that it wanted what it was meant to want. One may consider this a metaphysical exaggeration and a misleading displacement of the levitation principle to the act of wanting; the productive motif of Idealism lies in human belonging to the dimension of uplift. Here the there-is and the you-can combine with the you-will-be-helped, but most of all with the it-succeeds, which bursts open the horizon. This combination creates the faith that the most improbable thing will occur like something that, having only just been implemented, is already being taken for granted.

These reflections show that one can do justice to what Gehlen calls relief if one recognizes it as one element within a more complex elevating dynamic. It is decisive for the overall picture that the relief of the carried is only made possible by the increased burdening of a carrier. Nietzsche's axiom that all higher culture is based on slavery draws the civilization-theoretical conclusions from this observation. The concept of slavery is still all too human in Nietzsche's conception thereof, however, and the formulation fails to grasp its reworking into machines and social systems. The anthropological counterpart of Nietzsche's thesis would be the statement that no life in uplift can exist without grants from pampering patrons. If one starts with the case of maternal gestation, both prenatal and postnatal, one is struck by the division of burden that enables culture. Here one sees patronal relief passing unconcealed from the giver to the taker. But the mothers are not merely the caryatids in the wood-work of civilization. Though the levitation process would not get underway without the one-sided commitment of the pamperer to the pampered, such a commitment would be unsustainable if the carrier were not also carried—firstly, through her household-founding relationship with the father (marriage is a contract for mutual relief), secondly, the services of allomothers, which also means the network of relatives and friends, including her own older children, and finally through the aid organizations and communal forms of solidarity that first appeared in the age of metaphysically motivated altruism and later took effect with the establishment of the welfare state. In general, one can say that successful motherhood is impossible without the relief of the burdened.

The most important contribution to the effect of "carrying the carrier," however, beyond all external grants of strength and cooperative assistance, comes from "Mother Nature" as she acts through each individual mother. Through a wealth of inborn dispositions, she lays a foundation of bio-automatisms that contain the pressure of constant caring tasks. This pressure would be unbearable if the mother's free will were left to deal with it alone; from the first bonding effects via the stimulation of lactation to the increase of co-anaesthetic and empathetic abilities, women who have given birth have entire arsenals of inner power sources at their disposal. It is these automatisms in the bodily power plant, the mother, that spontaneously perform a substantial part of the maternal work—provided one does not disturb the triggers through acquired inhibitions. If it were not indecent, one could establish that one secret of a good mother's success is to let the mother machine run unimpeded inside her. Where this effect comes into force, the mother floats on the mechanisms that make her position livable: the mother person is then a levitated superstructure above the mother animal that she herself is.

Who could deny that we are now close to the generative pole of *humanitas*, the possibility of gratitude towards the carrier? The mother has a share in it herself when she reaches the point at which she grasps her burdening as a chance. She then knows what only fighters know: that being allowed to exert oneself is a privilege. The optimum carrying power would presumably be reached if there were a perfect synergy between Mother nature and the allomother we call culture (also known as law, wealth and paternal power). Let us admit that such a case only transpires empirically under rare circumstances, however attractive it might seem as a general, almost natural norm.

6. The Disaster of Neolithic Mothers

The most momentous event in the psychohistorical development leading to the traditional conditions was the appearance of the chronically overtaxed, burn-out, careworn mother—a phenomenon that can be followed from the first farming women of the "Neolithic revolution" to the "doubly burdened" employed women of industrial "societies." With mothers in this situation, one can observe how the dynamic of uplift in the mother-child field is brought out of step by constant overtaxing. When this happens, the energetic balance required for carried carrying is lost—with the result that in an environment increasingly defined by a lack of help and means of uplift, motherhood can be viewed as a scarcely bearable burden, at times even a curse. In the story of the expulsion from paradise in the Book of Genesis, the words spoken by the angel to the woman unmistakably express the experience that for human women, there will be no blessing beyond childbearing and what follows.[84] The angel's curse has historico-philosophical weight: by defining female misery as an emergent phenomenon, it reflects the tendency towards maternal proletarianization in the incipient sedentary "societies."

One can gain a summary idea of the causal mechanisms that led to the onset of this state by connecting the three main elements of the sedentary life form: as well as the transition to labor-intensive forms of soil management, it is above all the securing of life by storing supplies and the population increase enabled by this that are central here. This triad of tendencies formed the framework in which familial reproduction had to change, moving towards large numbers of children—reinforced by religious systems that made a point of metaphysically aggrandizing the production of numerous offspring (in so far as the limits set by the symmetry between origin and future allowed it). Perhaps the idealization of an abundance of children marked the irruption of counterfactual thought into culture; since then, what had been a curse has attempted to present itself as a blessing—the central motif of edification, which would only later be eliminated by "thinking dangerously." It could be that this distortion produced the schism between maternal realism and paternal idealism that gapes open within historical families as a trace of domination.

At any rate, the situation for women as mothers became fundamentally precarious in the agrarian lifeworld. If one uses the standards described by the psychoanalyst and paleoanthropologist John Bowlby for the mother-child interaction evolutionarily established since the Pleistocene, it transpires that beyond the nine-month intrauterine and twelve-month extrauterine gestation, there is a period of four or five years in which the small child consistently requires a high level of mothering and the constant proximity of maternal or allomothering figures; even after this time, the child's dependence on care figures remains a lasting psychosocial imperative. It goes without saying that the birth rate must always be kept down by any means in such a regime, as an overtaxing through multiple mothering is, from the woman's perspective, the ultimate danger to avoid. Here the untimely second child, the excessive and burdensome child, appears as the guest who brings evil. Therefore, in the earliest informal systems of ethics, every reaction to this invader is acceptable—traces of such sentiments can still be found in the modern assertion of a right to abortion on the part of reluctant women. With the development of agricultural life forms, however, precisely this "worst case"—the simultaneous strain of births in close succession—became the standard situation for married women. Although the overall situation after the transition to arable farming allowed a material containment of the child invasion of laborers' and masters' families, enabling them to feed the numerous guests with the help of the surplus products of cultivated soil, the psychic nourishment of the invaders became consistently problematic. The best-known symptom of this systemically conditioned problem is the Benjamin effect: only the last child in the series experiences the abundance of caring that should really have been received by each one of them, provided the mother is not too exhausted to give the youngest its due pampering. Thus the *mysterium iniquitatis* invades every fertile family; this enabled sibling resentment to develop into a hidden world power.

It follows from this that the unconscious which propels the history of civilizations as we know them was invented in the many-child Neolithic family: its first and eternal theme is the unbearable envy of the insufficiently cared-for individual towards the closest pampering rivals, their brothers and sisters. Its motor is the insatiable longing for justice—which means the impossible redistribution of the mother's wealth. This is not a struggle over Oedipal privilege, as a psychoanalysis unversed in cultural history never tires of claiming. What needed to be fought for from that time onwards like something unattainable was rather a completely normal, yet *de facto* exceptional extensive mothering. It is not about incest, but rather resonance; not about a genitally tinged desire for the mother, but rather free access to the pamperer; not about a rivalry with Oedipal content, but rather the cutthroat competition between siblings. Where the bond of the first intimacy is overly diluted, the children become lonely in relation to their own mother. The secret quarrel revolves around the scandal that something is experienced as scarce which should never have become scarce.

From that point on, all economies are potentially and actually compensatory—they express one scarcity through another. In the peasant classes of advanced civilizations, almost every child, to some degree, has reason to be concerned about the pre-verbally given and almost inevitably broken promise of a share in levitation. What some have called the spirit of utopia comes from the unutterable demand for the equal pampering of all; it would constitute the restoration of social synthesis from the spirit of a brotherliness beyond envy. The motif of patricide emphasized by Freud is, in reality, of an accidental nature. What gives content to the effective unconscious is the intensely desired and inadmissible extermination of one's brother or sister, who are not directly to blame for one's impoverishment and rejection. It is no coincidence, then, that the biblical tale of the original crime deals with fratricide; the notion that it could be the father who takes away part of your due favoring was impossible in this context. The most comprehensive deliria of deprivation refer to rival peers; the paranoid expects the worst of their alter ego—and it alone—because it has experienced it before. At its core, this delirium is empirical. As far as the mothers are concerned, they are forced under these conditions to be the stronger and more just sex, and ultimately, in their inevitable unjustness, the harsher sex. They must manage the deficiency that they themselves constitute; they muffle the cries which they cannot answer at the same time. This fate becomes inescapable as soon as they enter the highly probable situation of confronting the consequences of their overtaxed fertility, both during the reproductive phase of their lives and beyond.

In psychohistorical terms, the history of deficient cultures began with the turn towards manifest abundance of children, for only from there could the mood of not-enough spread civilization-wide among a large majority of individuals. The most likely exceptions to this, apart from the luckier children of the poor, were the descendants of the early nobility, whose self-affirming attitude was not only formed through a training in arrogance that befitted their social status, but also found support in a continuum of maternal and allomotherly wealth aura. Nobility—that means profiting psychoeconomically from higher chances of access to allomothering resources. These formed the first psychically active concept of treasure. In parallel with the relative proletarianization of the overtaxed mothers—a tendency that was only partly offset by their rise to matronal authority at the courts—new psychological types of children were born in both the peasant and bourgeois classes: on the one side the subordinate ones, who grew up in the climate of a fear of rejection and allowed their own parents to proletarianize them, and on the other side those roused to ambition, who had tasted the bitter sweetness of rewarded life and took on their tasks with a basic mood of hunger, aggression and the expectation of happiness.

In a world of deficiency that has the concept of treasure at its disposal, the first forms of that idealism develop which enables humans to disregard their real situation. Here the concept of idealism already emerges as impaired as it sounded after Nietzsche's interventions: it refers neither to a high ground of confident self-awareness nor the conviction of the primacy of the sphere of ideas, but rather a syndrome of interconnected illusions by which an unlivable reality is surrounded by a shell of reinterpretations and idealizations. Because they support one another, illusions become effusive; where they interlock in well-rehearsed fashion, they join to form a council of suggestions; an author with a sense of order and sequence can connect them to construct a system. What is a thought system if not a treasure for the treasureless?

It is naturally the mother who lends herself to being the first object of idealization—not because she herself asks to be aggrandized, but rather because the children, who remain unaware of their unpredictable progenitor's true nature, need an edifying image of the Great Mother for their own stabilization. Possibly the dynamic core of idealistic abstraction lies in the impossibility of seeing one's own mother as a small, helpless, exhausted creature. If goddesses existed, how would I bear the fact that precisely the woman who is closer to me than anything conceivable were not one of them?

7. Pampering in the Symbolic—
The Age of Heavenly Treasures

The psychological achievements of the metaphysical age are summarized in the fact that they enable pampering to become symbolic. One can define the symbol by its psychic use value: thinking the absent as present and envisaging the missing as available. The universe of symbolism is dominated by a mode of experience that believes the abundance of the real is present in signs. That is why during the symbolist epoch, the fates of wealth are tied to its imaginations; the signs of wealth enter the wealth of the sign. In this regime, being able to form an idea of treasures and powers means being wealthy and powerful in a certain sense; whoever knows what abundance means in its essence and is in a position to say so also possesses it, one could say. If someone has an idea of the surplus of substance, they cannot be excluded from sharing in its attributes. In this respect, symbolism is synonymous with Catholicism. Where else could the belief flourish that anyone who approaches the scattered bone of a saint in the right state can be sure of having encountered the divine in real presence? Catholic realism is the continuation of totemism by other means; it transfers the principle of *mana* to the age of philosophical-theological categories. In this order there are no concepts that are not part of treasures, and no names of essences that lack that do not have within them a stream flowing from the source. Above all else, however, anyone with a sense of what is high, other-worldly and above has a share in the ecstasies of verticality. In the age of the treasure symbol or logicized mana, thought and being are genuinely the same thing.

What metaphysics and fairy tales have in common is that they let the true hero reach the goal of his desires in an orderly roundabout way. One can form an idea of this as soon as one probes the core of the metaphysical wish form: it is the intense wishing itself that brings the wisher to their goal—in the mode of symbolic participation in the abundance they seek—before they have even taken the first step. In the symbolic space, every treasure hunter ends up being found by their treasure. Finding means being taken back to the starting point of the search; the desire as such is already illuminated by the find. It is certainly no coincidence that the last distinguished symbolist, Ernst Bloch, elevated the treasure hunt to a form of the world process. He sought to transform the search into enlightened production by means of an anticipatorily substantial daydreaming suitable for creating works. Indeed, whoever discovers the New World must feel the pull of the legends of the southern and western lands of gold strongly enough to understand the signs that the time for departure has come. Whoever desires collective wealth must first examine the roots of the possibility of being wealthy at all in an economy-critical fashion. Merely digging for treasure is therefore not enough; the goods of happiness must be brought forth—in every possible sense of the word. For Bloch, world history is a long fermentation of the riches welling up from the world foundation, which have not yet found their alchemist; it carries out the imperative *enrichissez-vous* at the level of the species; its agent and medium is illuminated dissatisfaction. Naturally the "unalienated identicality of existence with essence in nature"[85] anticipated by the symbol can only be realized at the end of history—universal wealth is deferred. It would only be true and real as the accomplished telos of all productions, and all anticipations thereof in the here and now must retain an element of untruth. That is why Bloch's system, which places the daydream of a wealthy life at the start and abundance at the end, remains trapped in the patterns of Old European teleology.

If one places realized abundance at the start, however, one switches to a way of thinking where deficiency can only be introduced epigenetically; then, like all other bad things, it appears as a *privativum*, a deprivation effect, a diminution. In the system of origin-based thought, mortals live wholly under the protection of their first immunity; they do not need to seek, for they have already been found. For them, everything stays contained to the end in the constantly growing round whole. One is not quite sure, however, how modern human beings are supposed to follow on from these origin-celebrating views without deserting their own time. Even in the present-day relics of the nobility, the magic of origin has lost its effect. The realization that holists have a better immune status than modern people does not prove that we could ever revert to holism. One must consider this: the pleromatic defense does not spread its protective screen to shield from illnesses, deficiencies or damages, but from the trauma of unreliability that is experienced when uplift fails to transpire. It strives to outdo the unreliable through trust by restoring on a larger scale the homeostasis that was destroyed on a small scale. As long as the magic circle retains its regenerative power, everything that happens can be read as a lesson. More still: in the shamanism of holism, disturbances act as necessary chapters in the instruction of the soul, which is called upon to study its ineffability; the full extent of life is brought into an interior that forces the deprivations to become co-producers of abundance. Whoever has bathed in the river of the origin is coated with the impossibility of being poor, just as Siegfried was coated with dried dragon blood.

While a basic mood of permanent deficiency established itself in the early cities, kingdoms and empires following the post-Neolithic agricultural turn—and could only partly be balanced out by the glory of the god-kings and their aura of majesty, which demanded imaginary participation—the suppressed populations developed manifold systems of myths, or more precisely schemata of inner image production and preformed daydreams that would later be described as "faith," and even later as loyalty to inherited illusions; dreams that assigned a transcendent address to terrestrially unattainable wealth. Whether the genetic connection posited here between the first sedentary civilizations (with their bifocal order of ruling city and serving provinces) and the rise of paradisiacal fantasies can be consolidated by the findings of comparative mythology will, perhaps, remain an open question; all that is certain is that in most advanced civilizations based on the synthesis of agriculture, craftsmanship and writing, one can observe a symptomatic combination between ideas of a postmortal existence and fantasies about free access to a world of fairytale abundance. The widespread garden utopias create a balance between elements of idealized rusticity and attributes of an urban lifestyle. Where the totality of the world is re-created in the shape of a garden, the riches of nature and culture flow consonantly together in an enclosed space.

One could speak of a first form of treasure formation in heaven; it was on this that the re-stylizing of human existence into a metaphysically coded treasure hunt depended. The phantasm of treasure combines the prototypical pictures of power and pomp established in early king cultures with abundant, calm patterns of inner observation which, following on from the reflections above, can be assumed to stem from experiences with maternal and allomotherly pampering potentials, however deficient these may be. If material treasures act as attractors for consciousness, this is primarily because they are materialized good news; they embody pleromatic masses which radiate the promise that levitation will occur one day. Whoever seeks the treasure is promised that uplift will hold the upper hand in the end. With treasure fantasies, a manic corrective was introduced into the depressive basic mood of early imperial cultures. A treasure encircled by dreams—this is the epitome of the pampering power that keeps the abundance of possibilities available to itself and its own. Thanks to its vivid nature the archetype of wealth, which revealed itself pre-concretely in the sovereign mother, takes on a concrete form. Now it only has to be revealed where the treasure is buried. The answer provided by tradition is essentially this: die and find.

One now understands why a treasure can be substance and person in one; this doubling is expressed in such figures as the modern Fortunas or maidens of luck, who grant their protégés a combination of personal epiphanies and a flow of material goods. The best example of this is the *Fortunatus* chapbook, which tells of the prototypical lucky devil, gifted with a magic purse, whose entrance into wealthy life was described by European authors between the sixteenth and twentieth centuries. One sees the irony of this classic fairy tale of abundance if one calls to mind the general business terms of metaphysical world traffic: the believers must assume that the lord of the garden, God the Father, offers inexhaustible pampering possibilities of which they usually only experienced traces in their empirical mothers. They frequently overlook the fact that the king's pleroma only shines forth as they see it in real and imagined glory because they themselves have contributed to its aggrandizement. In the medium of taxes, services and dreams, they surround the Lord with the aura of pampering power from which they wish they could benefit. Without quite knowing what they are doing to themselves, the people in class society keep themselves available as allomothers of the Lord. At the same time, the people must look up to their greats as if these were in turn presenting themselves as the people's allomothers. It is in these constellations of wishes that the psychodynamic social contract of the metaphysical age articulates itself.

In the first reading, it is the Lord who grants his own a share in his overabundance when he lets them come to him. The reversion to carriedness through wealth is therefore the fundamental gesture in tales about paradise in monotheistic cultures, even if their narrative forms suggest more of a progression towards abundance. Among numerous examples of rabbinical stories from the messianic era, I shall quote a passage in which one can observe the Judaization of the Hellenic-Roman motif of the Golden Age:

> The rabbis taught: "[In the Future to Come] the wheat will shoot up like a date palm and be higher than the peaks of the mountains. And should you think that it will be hard to reap it—no, for the Holy One, blessed be He, will bring a wind from His storehouses, and it will blow at it and it will shake loose its fine flour, and people will go out into the field and bring home full hand-plates, and from it they and their families will have livelihood [...]" They said: "In the future a grain of wheat will be like two kidneys of a big ox [...]" They said: "The World to Come will not be like This World. In This

World there is much trouble in harvesting the grapes and pressing them; in the World to Come a man will bring one grape in a wagon or a boat and put it in a corner of his house, and take from it wine as from a big cask, and its wood will serve as fuel under the pot, and in each grape there will be thirty kegs of wine." (Kethuboth 111b)[86]

One cannot overlook the fact that this legend of the messianic (perhaps even eschatological) condition displays the tendency to restore to a barren, drained nature the pampering power it lost in the profane era. Grain and wine are the central symbols in an archaic wet nurse delirium: everything is overflowing, everything is breast. The reinstated allomother nature reverses the weaning trauma, prevents a decline into poverty and leads her own back to peaks where giant wheat grows and the wind plays the miller. What is decisive is that such images take the imaginations of the clients back to a state before labor in which they used the Holy, the God of Israel, to provide universal allomothering services. In eschatological dreams of this kind, God is imagined not as a lawgiver but as the sponsor and pamperer. Otherwise, the notion that people in the messianic age would no longer harvest their crops with their own hands, but rather find the flour ready-ground in their fields, would be incomprehensible; similarly, the work of the vintner could be passed over because the grape would turn directly into a keg. In the spirit of allomotherly pampering, a nature is invoked that delivers finished products at any time.

It is precisely this shortening of the way to the result, bypassing intermediate steps involving work or alienation, that constitutes the essence of pampering. The dream of an income without work serves as a model[87] for all dreams of levitation and consumption—

it must be kept in mind whenever one speaks of overexertion. For it is only the overexertion of other people that is always popular. Messianism is the hope for a state of the world in which work would be entirely externalized—whether taken over by a completely unfettered or a thoroughly proletarianized nature (which is the same thing), or transferred completely to machines or to an underworld of damned souls. Messianity is thus a concept to postulate the restoration of maternal pampering power at the level of an entire people. That is why the observation that the Messiah cannot be the direct patron of his people in this delirious economy is an important one. First his followers would have to make him so rich that he could give back to nature the wealth which had accumulated within him—and nature would in turn act as the allomother of the clients.

In this reading of the texts about waiting for fulfillment, messianism transpires as the matrix for an original accumulation of pampering capital in heaven. The fact that its emphasis lies initially in alimentary and oral utopias is, of course, connected to the restoration of the pampering contract in the ideal-typically developed postnatal mother-child field. It is perhaps more than mere coincidence that some of the more profound Jewish thinkers in the twentieth century assigned a strong, albeit distorted messianic power to the process of capital because it was potentially capable of pacifying all members of "society," especially those who had been impoverished; Walter Benjamin's feeling that there was only a "weak messianic power"[88] between the generations shows that even he, despite his Marxist orientation, remained a misery conservative to the end.

Utopias of orality can only be outdone by utopias of prenatality. What terms can be used to do so is shown by Moses

Maimonides (1136–1204) in a treatise on the *Sanhedrin* from the Mishnah, a collection of Jewish laws, in which he deals with popular notions of the pleasures for the righteous in the after-life.[89] Maimonides speaks with undisguised contempt about what he considers the crude materialist views of those exegetes who believe that a righteous earthly life will be rewarded by a stay in the Garden of Eden, where there is always plentiful food and drink along with silk beds, houses made of jewels and rivers of exquisite wine. Other popular teachers state that in the days of the Messiah, the earth will also produce fine, fully woven robes and provide the chosen with freshly baked bread directly from the earth. As in all versions of the materialized utopia of abundance, the greatest good will be found in the abundance of a constant supply of goods whose production has been transferred to nature or invisible workshops. Contrary to this robust idea of the last things, Maimonides formulates a philosophical utopia of disembodied pleasure that will only be accessible to the metaphysically trained intellect after separation from its mortal shell. This alternative promise shifts the emphasis from concrete to pre-concrete satisfactions. In agreement with Platonic traditions, Maimonides speaks of the soul's pure spiritual joy, which consists in the presence and constant recognition of God. The contemplative intellect is conceived here almost as a body without organs that develops a pure consciousness without having to worry about the conditions of its maintenance. In line with tradition, the pure intellect presents itself as a substance that is separable from the body. Such a self without a body corresponds to a pre-oral state in which modalities of nutrition can retreat to the background while the waking foreground belongs to a subtle jubilatory awareness of noetic coexistence with the great other (which is not yet keeping its distance as a real other). The presence of God automatically means that of anti-gravity. What presents itself philosophically coded as an opposition between materialism and idealism embodies, at a depth-psychological level, the difference between object relationship and nobject communion; in poetological terms, it marks the difference between oral and prenatal utopia. The caesura between intrauterine and extrauterine gestation motivates both the most tangible and the most sublime symbolizations of the longing for carriedness.

As Christian eschatology takes up the legacy of messianism in many ways, it is no surprise that a similar dynamic of fantasy in relation to the last things is at work in it. It is also concerned with demanding the restoration of abundant conditions. Like the popular Jewish models, part of its style is a crude physicalism; the reason for this is that the understanding of the body in the oral stage can best be expressed in nutritional visions. These point to incorporation and to sharing in a liquid wealth. In the fifth book of *Against Heresies*, Saint Irenaeus quotes an apocryphal speech by Jesus passed on by pupils of his disciple John that, if authentic, would prove the presence of the most massive utopias of abundance in the midst of evangelical proclamation. The central idea of the para-Jesuan speech is that the good deeds of the pious cannot be paid back in this age of the world, only in the era of his return—but multiplied a hundredfold:

> The days will come in which vines shall grow, each having ten thousand branches, and in each branch ten thousand twigs, and in each true twig ten thousand shoots, and in each one of the shoots ten thousand clusters, and on every one of the clusters ten thousand grapes, and every grape when pressed will

give five and twenty metretes of wine. And when any one of the saints shall lay hold of a cluster, another shall cry out, "I am a better cluster, take me; bless the Lord through me." In like manner [the Lord declared] that a grain of wheat would produce ten thousand ears, and that every ear should have ten thousand grains, and every grain would yield ten pounds of clear, pure, fine flour; and that all other fruit-bearing trees and seeds and grass would produce in similar proportions.[90]

This too is a fantasy about a nature so accommodating that its wealth exceeds every possible wish. The modern ideology of desire would not be satisfied in such a paradise, whether in its psychoanalytical or its consumerist form, because the milieu of abundance would hardly leave any room for continuing tensions caused by urges and objects. As a precaution, interested parties should be informed that one cannot buy anything in such a hereafter. The phantasm quoted above addresses the needs of clients who dream of first and last gratifications—not a transcendent event holiday. Naturally the abundant numbers piled up here make no mathematical sense, rather acting as cratophanic hyperboles. They praise God, the pamperer, according to the *via emenentiae*. It goes without saying that Planet Earth, even in an idealized state, would not be large enough to hold even one vine with the properties described. The abundance to which this upswing testifies demands to be understood epiphanically: here as everywhere else, to have an idea of God means to praise him—and praising God correctly means describing his pampering power as unlimited. The meager mother is replaced by a nature in a state of constant potlatch. In psychological terms one would probably speak of an enthusiastic defense from hunger, or more precisely the hallucinatory striving to restore that homeostasis which allows the pre-subject to lower its traumatically high pressure of longing to zero. In this psycho-economic space, liberation from the spell of the waking world's objects through a reduction of existential tension to the nirvanic zero is taken as the equivalent of bliss or freedom.

Classical religious metaphysics thus consists of a paradoxical circle of wishes: it operates on the premise that it stirs the longing to be with God to the utmost degree, at the same time communicating that the object of desire can only be found in a state that is free of desire. This state is accepted as a perfection of immunity to coincidence—both the external kind, which injures the integral form of one's own life, and the internal kind, which humiliates through neediness and dependence. Clearly, trauma is here taken up as a metaphysical talent; whoever does not bring it with them will not get far spiritually, for they lack the extremism provided by the early wound—and perhaps only by that. Hence the initial aim in all these disciplines is to stimulate an attunement to anti-gravity, a rejection of the real: humans must be uprooted from the probable and geared towards the absolutely improbable, the terrestrially impossible—which is best achieved via intense ascension images and attractive invitations from on high. The heavens beckon irresistibly with gratifications, transfigurations and coronas. With the total mobilization of the soul through illusion, the preconditions have been fulfilled to proceed to an evocation of prenatal communion. This is naturally devoid of images; it leads to a floating homeostasis that can be hinted at in metaphors of oenological-oceanic relaxation. Some schools of wisdom content themselves with such prospects; others shatter even this horizon. They dissolve the search in positivism, which cannot be distinguished from nihilism, the product of disappointment with everything.

Examples of this way of thinking, calculating, speaking and feeling can be multiplied *ad infinitum*; in sum, they yield a universal library of homeostatic dreaming. It would *eo ipso* be the compendium of historical humanity's knowledge about ascension—along with the corresponding forms of victim calculus. It would show at what prices the searchers tried to acquire transfiguration—and here the exchange basis of fanaticisms lies revealed. In addition to the Jewish and Christian notions of the end times, there would have to be investigations into the elaborated phantasmagorias of paradisiacal gardens in Islam, which sets itself apart primarily in the heterodox addition of sexual utopias to the conventional oral and prenatal utopias. This motif has become interesting in our time since the psychodynamic riddles of the Islamist-terrorist death cult gave the West cause for concern (the same West that, in the eyes of its fanaticized and perhaps envious despisers, constitutes the realm of actually existing pornography and *eo ipso* a deeply hurtful parody of the popular Islamic heaven).[91] This panorama cannot be without references to the joys of the Pure Land, around which the followers of the popular Amida Buddhism unfolded a universe of imaginations and exercises. The context would also demand an engagement with the teachings about the attainment of immortality in the alchemist doctrines of esoteric Taoism. For the present reflections, additional variants of proofs for the affective occupiability of heavens, paradises, idealized worlds and other metaphysical or parametaphysical forms of the levitation space—the materials required for a comparative study of the afterlife can be found in theological and mythographic literature.[92]

8. Immanent Desire, the Faust Novel, and the Democratization of Luxury

In the following, for the raw sketch of a history of pampering and its diverting functions outlined here, it is not the shifts into transcendence and diverse eschatologies of relaxation (extending to the Freudian myth of the death instinct) that will be significant, but rather the re-descent into terrestrial contexts and worldly operations. In a word, the concern is now the constitution of the world by the adjustment from ascension to horizontal exodus— for which America is the geographical symbol. This effect is supported by a boundlessly far-reaching shift of emphasis: from transcendence to immanence and from asceticism to expression. That is why the "heavens" ceased to act as a projecting screen for de-restricted desire; the new screen is spread out into the breadth of the humanly and terrestrially possible—instead of learning to transcend upwards, the modern soul learns to cross the oceans. "Even the skies become horizontal."[93] The sensitivity to the infinite articulates itself retroscendently; it advances ever deeper and further into terrestrial spaces of options. The entire world beyond is now already sought in this world; what was heaven becomes a technical problem.[94] The change takes place through a reversal of the direction of ability: from scholastic-rhetorical to engineering and entrepreneurial operations. Hence the Modern Age's interest in character figures in which the *belle alliance* of wishing, being able, having, doing and enjoying is realized.

It seems productive in this context to re-examine the meaning of the figure of Faust. It is the crystallization of a tendency that I shall call the "retroscendence of pampering": with Faust, the modern activist subjectivity of consumption and experience steps onto the motivation-historical stage. Drives, like motors, have their history too. The timeliness and prematurity of this debut, preserved in the chapbook *Historia von Doktor Johann Fausten/dem weitbeschreyten Zauberer und Schwarzkünstler*, published by Johann Spiess in Frankfurt in 1587, are shown by its historical circumstances and the internal, almost utopian vectors of the text. Here the treasure hunt, cognitively and sensually, becomes an intramundane passion. The fact that the Faust book came at the right time proves its success; its premature aspects come from the fact that the new human proclaimed here, the *magus* scholarly type who becomes powerful through studies, trading and fraud can, for the time being, only arrive at his effects by semi-technical means. Indeed: the fact that Faust's desire had to seek an alliance with the favored accomplice Mephistopheles reveals more than any other aspect about the historically limited state of pampering forces at the time. Nonetheless, one can only gain a closer understanding of the diabolical figure by recognizing him as a promotional leaflet for a powerful new pamperer. This new ally hints at a previously unheard-of imperative: you must want to increase your ability— by means of black magic! It was the will to ability that would distinguish the operative and operable human being of the Modern Age from the ontological human being of the Middle Ages, which overcame and strengthened its powerlessness in metaphysical world pictures. The project of relief was heralded by the shift towards the ability to operate, prophetically articulated in Francis Bacon's ideas of humanist empowerment. With its factotum properties, the technically masterful, evil-good, criminal-benevolent spirit qualifies as the occult allomothering authority of Modern Age humans.

Illustration from a 19th-century Faust book

This circumstance can never be underlined too much: if Mephistopheles in the Faust book embodies a figure of great modernity, it is because he offers the "new man" entirely worldly and technical, albeit diabolical ways to wish fulfillment—and the figure is even more realistic in the fact that it already sets up circles of rules between demonic supply and human demand. Once the devil has shown what is now within reach thanks to him, the wish ventures forwards across the board to unknown acts of boldness, expanding the market for good devilries. This is what gives the fairy tale of an alliance between the hedonistic scholar and the service-happy demon its analytical substance. Even if the new wish fulfillments openly reveal themselves as criminal, they nonetheless gain the reader's sympathy because they support the principle of redistribution. By being criminal, they are also just; they are just because they revise the eternal withholding of pampering, albeit only in one exemplary case. The chapbook tells us the following about the *modus vivendi* of the opulent doctor:

> Faustus had a superfluity of victuals and provisions, for when he desired a good wine the spirit brought it to him from whatever cellars he liked (the Doctor himself was once heard to remark that he made great inroads on the cellar of his Lord Elector of Saxony as well as those of the Duke of Bavaria and the Bishop of Saltzburg). He likewise enjoyed cooked fare every day, for he was so cunning in sorcery that when he opened a window and named some fowl he desired, it came flying right in through the window. His spirit also brought him cooked meat of a most princely sort from the courts of the nobility in all territories round about. The fabrics for his apparel and that of his boy (he went sumptuously attired) the

spirit also had to buy or steal by night in Nuremberg, Augsburg or Frankfurt. A similar injury was done the tanners and cobblers. In sum, it was stolen, wickedly borrowed goods [...] he lived thus day in and day out like an Epicure—or like a sow—with faith neither in God, Hell nor the Devil [...].[95]

This story takes us into a world in which a very bearable lightness of being is ensured as long as it is the others who do the work—conditions of production are not yet relevant. The narrator of the *History* leaves no doubts about how the Faustian looting, one with long-term potential, is to take place: the customary exploitation of the people by their noble masters will be followed by the exploitation of those masters and craftsmen by the exceptional human being, whether a scholar, artist or financial adviser.

The centuries-long fascination of the original figure of Doctor Faustus—of which Goethe's sublimations contained only a refined reflection—thus lay in an extensive intermundane promise of pampering. As this had no fixed addressee, a large part of the bourgeois intelligentsia in all subsequent generations could feel that the message was directed at them. One can still feel its power centuries later: Faust is the man who discovers the trick of all tricks in the midst of ordinary life: the short path to unearned riches, and thus the leap from desiring to enjoying.[96] He is the protagonist of the bourgeois claim to the present and future means of pampering. It is his metaphysical frivolity, or rather his waived interest in his own salvation, that gives him access to unlimited sources of wealth and pleasure. He thus provides an infectious model for ending the dreary work of self-preservation in one fell swoop. Thanks to magical methods, he skips ahead to the results without taking the long route through production and honest acquisition upon himself. His discovery—the pact with the devil is its symbol—is that even at the level of adult desire, such total gratifications are to be demanded and found as would normally only be possible in the symbiosis of the infant and the committed mother, provided a highly potent pampering partner is available. Faust indulges in a comprehensive regression that leads to the adult goal nonetheless.

Thus the scandal of Faustian existence has a name: exorbitance in well-being. It heralds an open break with the Old European traditions of moderate, serious and self-restricting life as articulated in the concepts of *sophrosýne* and *moderatio*. If there is a Faustian sin, it is the constitutive sin of the Modern Age— assuming the latter consists in the escape from the system of Old European proportionality. It initiates not only the infiltration of finite conditions by an infinite desire, but also the practical de-restriction of traffic and consumption. One can already observe the dynamics of the capital process in both of these, mirrored in the subjective qualities of restless research and an insatiable appetite for experience. Faust's maxim blasphemes against moderation and *ordo* because it is no longer determined by finite and satiable needs, but rather by unfulfillable wishes. Correspondingly, the merry doctor gets around in the newly de-restricted world more to an extent normally reserved for fixed capital in the form of loaded ships on the oceans; he is now unable and unwilling to drop anchor anywhere, because there can never be enough to fulfill his wishes. He can never invite the moment to linger awhile, as he conceives himself as an inexorable river with no mouth that leads into the future.[97] Even the airspace is no longer safe from his grasp. The Faustian ideology implies a coup against the boundaries that were drawn by obedience, lack of resources and a dearth of entrepreneurial spirit—and even if the means enabling Faust's pampering still have to be described *pro forma* as depraved, the lively popularity of these effects for the larger part of the bourgeois period is impossible to overlook. The interest in sin and de-restriction is what originally gives the market its space. Where such things are in progress, the public focuses its attention on the option of living more.

Only after the West had unambiguously crossed the threshold to the "affluent society," from the second half of the twentieth century onwards, did the figure of the unbound scholar lose its whole attraction at a single stroke—presumably because people living in elaborated real consumerism lost the feeling that they could learn from Faust's symbolic audacities and licenses. Konrad Adenauer would no longer have to ban *Faust*. With the invention of consumer loans, all of us have rushed ahead of our working time and are already living in the future of our wishes; one no longer needs to explain why the credit card has made the diabolical pampering partner obsolete. In the developed consumer system, "the right to regress [is added] to the general inventory of human rights."[98]

Because of all this, the name Mephistopheles stands for a far-reaching discovery. The diabolical pact is the cipher for an unspeakable contract whose content is total mothering. By opening up intramundane playing fields, it tears itself away from references to postmortal life. Thus the eyes of subsequent European generations are opened to their secular chance. The moral of the story, on the other hand, was probably of minor significance from the start. Even when eternal damnation was on the horizon after the allotted time of twenty-four years, receptive members of the public were no less interested in what the unleashed consumer experienced during his exploits: the epic gluttony, the extremely luxurious banquets, the escapades with lovers above and below, the journeys of the second Simon Magus through the air and into outer space (here the vertical takes on aviational significance), the reports of the infernal after-life, the incidents during the ascension to heaven, which now turns into manned space travel, the entertaining and malicious adventures of the necromancer at royal courts, or the farces with monkeys, farmers and students: all of this describes a circle of events that deserve to be experienced and depicted. Faust's journey around the world is rhythmicized by vivid anecdotes about drinking bouts, food orgies and bacchanals. In repeated accounts, one witnesses the crystallization of the multi-episodic structure of modern narrative prose, which leads its protagonists out onto the wider level of experience. Thus the early Modern Age novel, as the first illustrated magazine, contributed to shaping the subject's form by defining the hero as the counter for sensations per narrative unit.

As far as the ominous pact with evil is concerned, this demonstrated an increase in realism, as the total pampering of non-infants could now be imagined as the exploitation of third parties; it was only possible through usurpation and rebellion. Its justification, however ambivalent, can be drawn from the fact that people evidently had in mind the robbing of nobles—who, after all, could feasibly be suspected of being exploiters them-selves. As noted earlier, this thought figure—the exploitation of the exploiter—is a preliminary version of the redistribution prin-ciple, without which the modern state's participation in the economic results of society would be impossible to justify. In this sense the Faustian devil, along with such figures as Robin Hood, Fortunatus, Eulenspiegel and others, could already be seen as paving the way for the welfare state, provided one leaves aside the primacy of self-service in his case; he is a mystical ancestor of social democracy. As his transactions are more shifts of wealth from old to new treasure owners than direct taxation, he anticipates the stock market rather than the state treasury.

As a thief and smuggler in one, Mephistopheles illustrates the fact of expropriation in the most explicit fashion. He adopts the position of enlightened kleptocracy by following wealth back to the form in which it can be stolen as a finished product; the modern tax state can build on the kleptocratic standard, lawfully squeezing half the incomes of "high earners" out of them year after year. It would be reserved for the eighteenth and nineteenth centuries to place the product back in the production process and redescribe treasure as capital, hence suspecting theft in the labor contract itself—and subsequently renaming it "exploitation." From here, one can formulate the premises under which the authoritarian early bourgeois tax state reshaped itself into the permissive welfare state of modernity.

With the establishment of welfare-state routines during the twentieth century, the adventure of the present age, the transition to the "society" of levitation, entered its operative phase. Its underlying principle was encapsulated by the sociologist René König when he described the "democratization of luxury"[99] as the true project of modernity. This phrase builds on Schumpeter's observation that the true achievement of capitalism lies in popularizing access to exquisite goods: progress in the economic field does not mean that the Queen of England can by as

Jean-Antoinette Watteau (?), *Signboard for the Art Dealer Gersaint* (1720)

many silk stockings as she likes, but rather that the shopgirls can afford such stockings.

Democratizing luxury: people will have to grow accustomed to the idea that this aim, which raised strong objections from the start, goes back to long before the twentieth century—and also to the realization that even modernity can only be the most recent processual form of the paradox from which we resulted: since *homo sapiens* entered the evolutionary scene, it has demanded the near-impossible as if it could be taken for granted. In the moralistic literature of England, one finds indications from the mid-eighteenth century onwards that there were public discussions—perhaps the first in the history of class "societies"—about the imitation of luxury by the poor; at the same time, people saw cause to bemoan the "decline of morals" caused by the infection of the lower classes with the inappropriate longing to emulate the rich. From that time onwards, the cause of levitation had eloquent defenders, especially among

Young consumer wearing a design shirt that names the premises of the system

economists, who went against the luxury-phobic traditions of an entire epoch in arguing for the advantages of increased, even wasteful consumption. A typical expression of the emergent bourgeois affirmation of wealth was the splendidly decorated

Joe Milietzki (State Academy of Design, Karlsruhe, 2003), *Proud of Merchandising Products*

signboard (Dutch *uythangboord*) placed in front of workshops, small businesses and trading houses, which developed into a popular art genre from the seventeenth century onwards.

It is possible that the assertions of the early luxury apologists in Holland and England marked the first ever use functionalist arguments with political and moral-critical intentions. Mandeville's notorious theorem that private vices become public virtues, as long as they are somewhat restricted by the law, inaugurated meta-moral reflection on moral facts; thanks to its successes, the picture of mental modernization cannot be imagined without it.

The science of human cooperation in social systems takes shape as a satire without laughter. In "The Fable of the Bees" (1714), Mandeville writes: "Fraud, Luxury and Pride must live / While we the Benefits receive."[100] Mortal sins are neutralized to become production factors; vice advances to a locational advantage. What is termed a social order is the collateral utility resulting from the summation of egotistical actions. The science of vice and its epidemic spread gains a profile: it will soon call itself "national economy."

Empirical evidence of such connections was already amply available in the seventeenth and early eighteenth centuries—by that time, it had long been the case that the link between luxury consumption and aristocratic or upper-class eroticism, like that between trading in exotic means of enjoyment and new consumer trends, could long be surveyed openly as a sociological fact. What Sombart called "the vital connection between the rise of feminism [...] and the consumption of sugar"[101] was likewise so secret among contemporary observers of economic customs in the transitional field between aristocratic and bourgeois civilization; at the time, people spoke of the "rule of women" as the soul of commercial demand; naturally, this always referred to the demand for luxury items and objects of grandiose squandering.[102] In this respect, the middle classes of Holland and England—the leading wealth-endangered countries of the time—had nothing more to learn from the aristocrats of Old Europe.

For the first time in recent history, middle-class households had accumulated enough wealth to plunge into adventures of taste and aesthetic heresies on internal markets. The well-known Dutch tulip mania from 1636 to 1637 demonstrates the power of whim to grow into mass delirium through mimetic infection—at that time, Lady Pecunia began to subject her lovers to her regime in droves. The love of that flower, as royal as it was popular, was combined with a money-hungry madness—stock market speculation reached its first climax during this mania, and burst (like the New Economy bubble) after two feverish years.[103] One cannot be surprised that sermons began to sound from all the pulpits in Holland and Britain decrying the dangers of consumer society. Having only just acquired wealth, the citizens had to listen as churchgoers to the threats of their preachers, who held out the prospect of a new flood as the reward for their opulence. All of a sudden, the Anabaptist cry of "Repent!" seemed to be directed expressly at the newly wealthy. Affluence became synonymous with temptation.[104] And how could it have been otherwise? The clergy of the incipient bourgeois period was confronted with a worldliness that saw its presumed task as that of infecting "society" with the "happy contagion" of demand for superfluous things.[105]

9. *The Empire*—or: The Comfort Hothouse; the Upwardly Open Scale of Pampering

Be careful! They are expecting me. Day and night are
going to be at the station.

— André Breton & Paul Eluard, "Intra-Uterine Life"[106]

After these retrospective reflections on the evolutionarily
acquired uplift potential of the species, and its metaphysical redirection in the age of scarce maternal energies and even scarcer
allomothering reserves, the thesis that the main event of the
twentieth century consisted in the "affluent society" breaking out
of the definitions of reality imposed by the ontology of poverty
takes on a more specific shape. If it is accurate, it must be possible to show that, since a short time ago, the general conditions of
maternalization—that is, the sum of mothering and allomothering
services per child and the newly opened-up chances for self-
maternalization—have fundamentally changed in relation to the
circumstances of procreation and rearing in the agro-precarious
and early industrial world, in the sense of regaining large pampering surpluses that contribute to the individuation of countless
people. I would go so far as to argue that with the start of pedagogical modernity in Romanticism, and fully with the entry into
the quasi-total allomothering state of the twentieth century
(augmented by a new media environment with a protective-
pampering, animating and passivizing tendency), a historically
unprecedented psychosocial ecology of the (allo)mother-child
field emerged. The new conditions led to the explication of early
childhood through developmental psychology and the explication

of later childhood through the elaborated education system. (These were joined from the 1960s on by the explication of procreation through birth planning and reproductive medicine—supported by the complementary explication of sexuality with the help of the psychology of "object choice," partnership counseling and pornographic liberality.)

These statements become adequately plausible as soon as one breaks with the tradition of envisaging the state from the perspective of the father function. From that moment on, the facts of socio-cultural modernity arrange themselves into a meaningful pattern in which one relates statehood, including the totality of public services, to its generalized allomothering quality—just as modern culture as a whole, after all, only leaves as much of the father as remains for the male actor in the allomothering role, the *almus pater*, the provider and paying sponsor (only psychoanalysis still champions the father, as one would a dying species). It has been possible to espouse this view unhermetically since the Western states, with the exception of the still heroically committed USA, ceased to present themselves primarily in terms of the policing and militaristic tasks. It is therefore—according to Tristan Tzara's pronouncement—not only the architecture of the future that will be intrauterine; the entire life plan among people in wealthy countries will resemble the sojourn in an incubator.

As we have seen, the socio-technical core of modernity lies in the explicit prostheticization of maternal services. The "epoch-making concept of the artificial mother"[107] is not merely a quirk of alternative medicine mocked by a pre-suicidal Swiss writer; it is the occulted, yet (to the neutral eye) easily visible operating principle of the affluent society. Since the conversion of the state—now committed to "bureaugamy"[108] or the politics of pampering—into a welfare and care agency, it has acted as a meta-prosthesis that provides the concrete mother-prosthetic constructs, namely social aid services, educators, therapists and their countless organizations, with the means to fulfill their tasks.

These observations not only do justice to the existential definition of wealth in the context of corporative democracy—that it enables levitation for the many. One also gains insight into the systematic necessity of the tax state, which must fulfill its calling to being-rich-to-the-children; in this, it is a socio-plastic explicatory form for allomotherhood (though it by no means forgets itself and its own because of its redistributory tasks). Furthermore, one understands its paradox, which reveals itself in the effect that the richest state, carrying out its legitimate, often socio-bureaucratically and clientelistically overstrained allomothering functions, produces the largest number of ungrateful pupils; and one also understands, finally, why this occurs in keeping with a strict systemic logic. Through its complex task—to give all that it has and do all it can do as an educating state, a comfort state, a thermostate, a therapeutic state,[109] an all-responsible provider of infrastructures, background securities and warming distributive illusions—the political apparatus of the prosperous "society" creates, in countless individuals who have been made passive-aggressive, the feeling that in the midst of widespread abundance and universalized kleptocracy, they are the ones who are not getting their fair share. Modernized deficiency is abundance made smaller through optical illusions; in the recipients of cold pampering, it creates a *ressentiment* that, under analogous conditions, would necessarily appear among any conceivable clientele. Certainly the beneficiaries accept whatever they can get (state money is the mother of coolness), but this in no way prevents them from accusing the giver of stinginess, obliviousness, impotence, and of wasting funds on the wrong beneficiaries. One should not pay too much attention to the popular anti-state attitude: it is precisely this generalized ingratitude that testifies to the effectiveness of cool allomothering systems. The "affluent society" is the first social order that can afford to subjectify the lack of hardship into dissatisfaction.[110]

After these reflections, we are equipped to go beyond the negative definition of the "affluent society." What was previously imagined merely as an escape from the mental and material conditions of the deficient world can now be expressed positively in the statement that this society of abundance forms a *Gesamtkunstwerk* of progressive collective self-pampering—a work that shows a tendency to include increasing numbers of participants at the same time as heightening the disparity between inside and outside. Integral pampering can be defined as the amalgam of freedom without struggle, security without stress and an income not dependent on performance;[111] one can speak of partial pampering as soon as there is a share in any one of these functions.

On the inside of the great hothouse, the equation of human rights with comfort rights has been in force since the turn towards "mass" prosperity. Here, being recognized as a human being means finally being taken seriously again as a virtual and actual subject of pamperings. The concept of recognition now releases its longest-concealed consequence: the reference to the perception of the other as an equal partner and rival at the buffet of abundance. Now one can see more clearly why this constitutes a morally demanding gesture: espousing the human rights of others means wanting to enable their entry into the effective pampering space—which means welcoming them as rivals. There is no doubt that the battle for the possible egotism of the other is an authentic form of generosity: it rests on recognizing the right of formerly disadvantaged groups to receive equal pampering. The concept of justice itself, placed under the shield of affluence, implies that the legal subjects share the advantages of the prosperity system. The legal defense of the persecuted is an important first step to this; the further implications of references to human rights are only elaborated, however, when the subjectivity of the other has advanced to an economically competitive state in the fields of consumption. "Infinite justice"—that means interminable pampering; it refers to the unfulfillable task of freeing the manifestly poor and wretched from their precarious situation and giving them too much access to the abundant world—an intention that cannot be formulated without paradoxes. For who would seriously want to build up another person to become a rival in the enjoyment of scarce commodities?[112]

Someone who is already in the field of economic benefits is swept along in the currents of the wish refinery that elaborates the desire of the many in countless directions. Because the pampering process has no immanent limit, increases and differentiations place themselves on an upwardly open scale. The form of subjectivity in the prosperity system is defined by a lifetime's learning about pampering; until the collapse of Prussian neo-humanism, the older version of this was presented under the fragile title of "education." Its more recent manifestations articulate themselves more as a longing for procedures to enhance the consumer "personality."

The consequences of introducing the pampering concept into the moral field are far-reaching. They clarify a number of ethical intuitions that have been awaiting their explicit escalation since the *amour propre* discourses of the seventeenth-century moralists. Indeed, justice without generosity is *ressentiment*; generosity without the will to the proliferation of pampering remains egotism. Freedom, therefore, means the ability to affirm the egotism of the others. The finitude of freedom, admittedly, reveals itself in the fact that even the sooner or later, even the generous person will have to defend themselves against the expansionism of others' freedom. If, to invoke Spinoza once again, we do not yet know what the pampered body can become, we do know what conflicts lie ahead between the carriers of developed pampering and the pretenders to future shares in pampering means. The streams of immigrants demanding admission to the great hothouse are the milder harbingers of this.

If the majority of participants in the *magnum opus* of modern life arrive at very different attitudes to its scenario and its role in it, especially when they consider themselves part of the "social" wing and cultivate critical judgments about prevailing ills, the reason can be found in the fact that the system—viewed as a socio-thematic tension construction—is kept together almost exclusively through constant communication about its fictitious problems. This ensures that situation and mood are never congruent (aside, perhaps, from exceptional synchronizations of the two). The objective pampering that drives the system in peacetime operation is set to music played on a broad keyboard of concern. In media-controlled "tensegrity," then, the attention of the actors is captured by the respectively current problem topics; it continuously serves the motives of collective discontent and urgent additional demands at the fronts of the most acute deficits. Even as luxury increases, it is doomed to translate itself into the language of deficiency. As we have seen, hardship teaches people to give speeches, while luxury is only permitted indirect articulation.

John M. Johansen, *Floating Conference Center* (1997)

(Anyone seeking an explanation for the oft-cited "silence of the intellectuals," whose existence has been asserted since the end of the Cold War and utopian socialism, can find a concrete one right here: authentic intellectuals are defined by being too intelligent, and perhaps also a little too honest for such translation tasks.)

As long as the fellow players in the system identify with their roles and believe their lines, there are no prospects for them to access the hothouse of prosperity and the fundamentals of its operation. Such terms as "pampering," "facilitation," "luxury" or "relief" must naturally be banished from their self-descriptions—the dominant semantics covers these up with catchwords like "freedom," "security" or "recognition." (In fact, the individuals standing on the threshold of the prosperity system are initially concerned with their own "empowerment"; the second step of emancipation affirms claims to parts of the pampering stream.) But if it has become second nature for the inhabitants of the abundance hothouse to be controllable by delusions of deficiency, it is not easy to see how they could achieve a shift of perspective on their own strength. If theory in the midst of life is always the improbable, then the theory of pampering among the pampered is the most improbable.

There is (apart from ethnological-anthropological comparison) only one way to become aware of the invisible-overvisible whole and its primary tendencies and functions: aesthetic defamiliarization. The shift towards seeing aesthetically is a form of pampering that can turn the gaze back towards pampering. In fact, reflexivity and pampering belong inseparably together. If, as Luhmann stated, the great topic of the twentieth century in epistemological terms was reflexivity, it was also because the great event of the twentieth century in Western climes was pampering as a mass fact. What one called the becoming-reflexive of modernity was thus only fulfilled with the becoming-thematic of modernity's pampering quality. We realize the aesthetically defamiliarized perception of the situation when we move within the social space like visitors of an installation. An observer who recognizes the situation understands that they are looking around an exhibition whose format is larger than that of the normal museum—an exhibition that initially cannot be separated from the ordinary field of view.

Such circumspection only relies on one precondition: that the totality of circumstances can no longer be described by the

Foam party in 2001

concept of nature. This concession is easy in a thoroughly urbanized culture. But if one is no longer "in nature," neither the first nor the second, what is one supposed to call the encompassing-artificial? The concept of the *Gesamtkunstwerk* would seem an obvious choice, were it not occupied by aesthetic ideology. Joseph Beuys' phrase "social sculpture" also proves a useful stimulus—it could no longer be reserved for situations arranged by artists, however, but would have to relate it to the entire space in which prosperity advantages are distributed, wishes elaborated, subjectivities differentiated and immunitary alliances unfolded. From this perspective, the First World installation "affluent society" is *de facto* a social sculpture whose participants contribute to modeling it. After this defamiliarization, even Beuys' statement that all people are artists (in the original horizon an example of egalitarian kitsch), which angered so many, becomes usable again: it is suitable for defining the voluntary and involuntary involvement of the abundance space's inhabitants in its establishment, conversion and climatization. Every artist is a customer, all customers are human beings, and everything human is designed for pampering. To Lady Luxuria, the moderns say *fecisti nos ad te*.[113]

It is no coincidence, then, that hybrid terms like "social sculpture," "large-scale museum" or "integral installation" refer to the super-hothouse of the affluent "society" with the help of phrases from the aesthetic sphere. If I feel forced to draw on such figures, I do so—as already hinted—with a twofold motive: firstly, because aesthetic defamiliarization is one of the few ways, perhaps the only one, to objectify a living context by which one is carried and pervaded; and secondly, because the total system of current living order, this world interior of prosperity, which rewards its critics with high requirements and provides its despisers with scholarships,

Michael Elmgreen/Ingar Dragset, *Elevated Gallery/Powerless Structures*, Fig. 146
National Gallery of Denmark, Copenhagen, 2001. photograph: Andreas Szlavik.

is an extremely artificial, intelligent and inclusion-capable construct which is so improbable in every respect that the opposition
between art and non-art becomes redundant. To the extent that
the life forms of the "affluent society" embody the essence of artificiality, it is implausible to pay more attention to objects within it
that are distinguished as works of art than to arbitrary non-distin-
guished objects. No one object can be more notable than the total
installation—accordingly, exhibiting works of art is faced by competition in the exhibition of artifices that had previously lain
outside of the concept of art, and finally even the exhibition of the
place of the exhibitions. Thus the era of self-referential museum
buildings, and even more that of self-referential spatial design in
general, can begin—the containers demonstrate their claim to
precedence over their content with increasing clarity.

The final step in the de-restriction of the art concept leads to the identification of the social system with the art system—beyond all previous interpretations of the *Gesamtkunstwerk* concept. Once a person crosses this threshold, all that is left for them are pictures at an exhibition. After entering the integral space of artifices, philosophy too changes into curatorial practice: what was theory now turns into setting up the exhibition space for the world exhibition. It declares the super-artifice of the "affluent society" an inhabitable exhibit. If, following Olafur Eliasson's maxim, we seek to "surround the surroundings," we must apply the procedure of environmental inversion to the luxury hothouse as a whole.[114]

This makes it clear why the museum of contemporary art—or rather, the "expanded museum"[115]—could develop into a privileged place for the self-presentation of the system. It is there—and scarcely at the universities anymore—that the encounter of the intelligentsia with the facts of the artificial world takes place.[116] The museum of the present, philosophically curated, possesses the bizarre ability to show the constant ending of art through its swallowing by the artificiality of the super-installation. It is the only point in the system where the system's primary quality, that of being the installation of the encompassing or the artificial "total situation," can be observed as such.[117] In fact, as soon as one moves within the affluent "society," it shows the traits of a total installation; it forms a sphere of artifices that does not release its visitors. By transforming visitors into inhabitants (who soon forget that they were visitors), it weaves around them an indestructible web of comfort offers and other reasons to linger. The luxury hothouse, viewed contemplatively like an exhibition with no exit, is the true *continens*; it constitutes the *periéchon*, that which is all around, of which earlier metaphysicians extending to Jaspers and Voegelin disseminated the suggestion that the world is contained in it like the picture in its frame, or like the creature in the spirit of its creator.

The sojourn in the prosperity hothouse means being incorporated in distributive flows of pampering, animation and levitation means. The shared house of luxury is the comfort-climatized production artwork, immunized by the rights to protection and enjoyment, which, in the form of households, businesses, subcultures and collectors,[118] branches out into millions of micro-installations of relatively unburdened life. In this foamy aggregate, frothed up by countless vectors of imitation, one can distinguish between "milieus"[119] or zones similarly equipped with commodities, procedures and affective patterns; they are the zones of strongest mimetic assimilation. Ilya Kabakov's *Toilet* at *documenta* 9 offered an example of the type of Russian communal apartment of which there were millions in actually existing socialism; its exhibition in Kassel was a triumph for artistic practice, which advanced to producing copies of complete situations of milieus.

The milieus, whether reconstructions or originals, form homogeneous foams within a landscape of markedly different foam types. Some of them can present themselves live at party congresses, where the milieus of professional citizens and committee lovers gather; others organize themselves around subcultural magazines and faits that guarantee the stabilization of the milieu-specific patterns. The scene of professional Elvis imitators there are reportedly over 40,000 worldwide meets annually in different American cities; Harley-Davidson riders on both sides of the Atlantic form networks governed by the most cumbersome rules; rose-growers in all countries live withdrawn behind the invisible walls of a well-organized delusion. What

Ocean Dome in Miyazaki, Japan, inside view

should one say about the strangely coherent worlds of the caninophiles or the Haflinger appreciators? Who can simultaneously be knowledgeable about the subcultures of golfers, chess experts, horse osteopaths, bodybuilders, mountain bikers, swingers, young democrats, kite flyers, paleolinguists, vinyl clothing fetishists, lovers of freshwater aquaria, tango fans, or collectors of comics, model airplanes and old silver? Who has their eye on the readerships of contemporary authors, who take conoisseurial pleasure in lines such as: "Aquarius women are always punctual," or "Tennis instructors are the best brown-noses," or "I said it was too dark to play badminton," or "He interrupted himself and kissed her fragrant flesh for a very long time. And she succumbed to rapture once again…" Every subculture is governed in its own particular way by the general laws of assimilation. Nothing makes individuals resemble one another as much as a shared quirk in which each person indulges independently. The same thing applies everywhere: whims demand the whole person.

The use of the term "subculture" here refers to porous foams whose permeable walls allow each scene's typical injunctions, themes and accessories to circulate. Such circulations have a strictly limited reach: it is part of existence in the foam of caprices that people in one pile of bubbles are unaware of what is happening in the others; usually they do not even perceive that the other zones exist. This is aptly described by Tarde's comment about the "weak aggregation of elements whose principal bond lies in not contradicting one another."[120] There is nothing wrong with these frameworks of inter-oblivious relationships in socio-architectural terms; the scenes stabilize, prosper and drift, split and branch off by exercising their right not to pay attention to the existence of the others. More still, scene foam is predicated on the isolation of the individual bubbles from one another, as no positive self-discrimination, no satisfaction through exclusivity can be achieved otherwise. For the individuals, multiple allegiances are the norm; the separate subcultures reproduce better in monothematic settings. "Society," though it cannot feel it in a collecting center, is multi-micromanically constituted; it has no organ to perceive how many systems of delusions, how many catacomb cults, how many escapisms it harbors; it forms a half-blind aggregate of democratic occultisms.[121]

The non-concrete *Gesamtkunstwerk* which "integrates" all subcultural foams (that is, which lets them exist inter-ignoringly within a narrow space) can thus only be viewed—and in a purely metaphorical fashion—if one transfers the form of the museum to the system as a whole and moves through it like a visitor. What "capitalism," "the West" or "the affluent world" are can be learned by, for example, visiting Ilya Kabakov's *Clinic of Dreams*; a stay at Eurodisney can also be propaedeutically valuable. In the visitor's attitude, and only thus, one can experience counterintuitively what the super-installation is about. Otherwise one will remain inescapably trapped in realism, along with its critical supplement. From the latter perspective, people will continue to consider it impossible that the motifs of relief, entertainment, refining and pampering could play the central part in the current production of the world. They will be convinced, as they have been until now, that our main enemies today, as in the past, are still hardship and deficiency—and that the real can only be grasped in the mode of concern. One has to acknowledge the strengths of the conventional position: anyone who wants to keep exclusively to the topics circulating in the public space and the academic corridor of the super-hothouse will inevitably reach the conclusion that our civilization—like every earlier "reality" characterized by misery— is a vast network of deficiencies, flaws and disasters in which only the last few surviving islands of order here and there offer precarious chances of survival. Because the system lives off its delusions of deficiency (and already does so in its most liberal self-descriptions, not only in the radical leftist, gothically alarmist and horror-theoretical exaggerations), it tends to portray itself as a conservatory of misery, depression and crime.[122]

If one assumes the position of observers looking around in the democratic-technical installation with a day ticket, one can calmly find out that the complex as a whole serves the progressive pampering or pampered progressivity of its inhabitants—and that the

Advertisement for Hummer SUV by General Motors

incessant public talk of problems, deficiencies, hardships and the corresponding development and compensation programs, including the moral review section and satire, are merely codes for increasingly far-reaching pampering strategies. We can only understand the popular acceptance of the capitalist life form complex with reference to the positive concept of pampering. With luxury comes justice. Perhaps the meaning of "justice" cannot be concretely explained without the phantasm of the material equality of the many in the face of luxury. As soon as the basic political functions in the empire installation are operating smoothly—legal security for the visitor-inhabitants and freedom from political heteronomy—the pampering function moves into the foreground. It is part of every comfort that it can only conceive of itself as increasing; accordingly, it describes the given level as discomfort and an unacceptable imposition, demanding its elevation as a most urgent requirement of human rights. Hence the bewilderment of the moderns in the face of recessions, and their willingness to believe that the end times are nigh because of tiny losses in real income.

Through pampering, childlikeness is built into the real; it translated neoteny into the register of cultural functions. As we have seen, childlikeness and neoteny have an expansion vector. As long as this keeps pulling forwards, the creation cannot be complete: pampering continues, and the battle for its orientation is never-ending. Whoever has entered the pampering system, whether through immigration or birth, immediately takes part in distributing the current means of uplift. However much this constitutes the basic condition in every culture, pampering did not become explicit until advanced modernity. In Austria, the City of Vienna automatically provided the parents of newborns with their first baby clothes—showing a clear understanding that it is the parents who require allomothering. The rest, as everywhere else in the great hothouse, more or less corresponds to the beginnings. It is not so much a national peculiarity that is expressed in this attentiveness as a local gesture that could be repeated at any point in the international of comfort. In every national bubble in the empire of affluence, the quarrelling parties define themselves by suggesting polemogenic programs for the distribution of wealth—thus giving the public the feeling that the

Rebecca Horn, *Cornucopia*, séance for two
breasts (1970)

distribution of the means of relief is the most serious matter. This
impression is not unjustified: in a country like Germany, more
than half of the gross national product (over two billion dollars in
2000) passes through the redistributive hands of the Great Allomother. Redistribution thus triggers the emergency—chronically.
Pampering will not be releasing its children very soon. All history
is the history of battles between pampering groups: this observation
remains applicable to the turbulences in the integral hothouse.

In his widely read book *Homo Sacer*,[123] Giorgio Agamben
made the shocking suggestion that one should envisage the totality
of the system using the form of the concentration camp. For
Agamben, a camp means a closed place whose inhabitants are

reduced to the attribute of "bare life." A naked life would be one whose liquidation poses no problem, as it is already excluded from the protection of the law. In our context, the camp can effortlessly be identified as the illiberal variant of the large-scale installation—it unmistakably constitutes a case of humans immersing themselves in the work of humans. This concept of the whole too is gained through aesthetic defamiliarization, albeit in the sense of an aesthetics of the sublime, emphasizing the enclosing and exposing effects and largely obscuring the affluence, immunity and freedom components.[124] The hyperbole of the integral concentration camp becomes more bearable once merged with the hyperboles of the museum with no exit, or total installation. Both figures, the camp and the integral museum, realize the fundamental macrospherological idea that there is no outside view of the totality of one's own civilization context. Whoever wants to explore it must move within immanence like a Parmenides in the arena.[125] (Let it be noted that in the *Spheres* project, I work consistently with the non-hyperbolic semi-metaphorical concept of the hothouse, of which I am convinced that it not only captures the situation of modernity and postmodernity in its defining characteristics, but also contains a continuum principle that allows us to draw a line from archaic to contemporary life forms.)

The self-installing installation spans traditional political and social units such as states, countries, peoples and national economies, joining them to form a new kind of world-city still undescribed in essential aspects. It forms a landscape of cultural hothouses, pneumatic domes, in which countless subculturally differentiated microclimates reproduce themselves by means of effective insider keywords and motivating suggestions. The oscillation between climate spaces within the installation is usually organized as tourism, and occasionally as therapy, an art experience or a humanitarian intervention. There is a direct parallel to greenhouse complexes, where adjoining halls have different temperatures and humidity levels. In the networked milieu domes, uplift forces of the most varied kinds are at work— forces still awaiting precise examination. An ethnologist who set off for the archipelago of inner milieus, teams and clubs in the large-scale hothouse would have to describe a dense aggregate, composed of thousands of transmitters for happiness-inducing hypnoses and epicenters of feeling for manic inductions. It forms a chaotic foam that constantly froths itself up anew, consisting of counterphobic exercises, entrepreneurial gospels, development projects that demand the future, and time-consuming revenge dreams. These dispositions and practices produce a fabric that is perpetually intensified and rearranged by an expansive mentality industry—or whatever one wishes to call the psychotechnically reformulated religions of success. They all belong to the colorful arsenal of mania in the age of its technical reproducibility.

The most plausible self-descriptions so far of the great installation as a whole, though far too formalistic, are found in such terms as "consumer society" or "event society." Next to these, now-popular concepts like "risk society," "opportunity society" or "knowledge society" can claim a moderate descriptive power; even a hackneyed old pun like "McWorld"[126] cannot be considered entirely meaningless, as it alludes to the multi-local, carefree and corrupt character of the super-installation. It makes it clear that the global markets constitute the universals in the money universe—and in this particular case, a universal of culinary vulgarity.

In a pointed project of contemporary media theory like *The Consumerist Manifesto* by Norbert Bolz, the large-scale installation is described as a comfort zone whose transnational inhabitants come from the collective of those with spending power. They realize explicated human nature by consuming objects, signs and lifetimes; consumerism is humanism taken to its logical conclusion. It alone holds the key to the kingdom of peace, it seems here, for the *pax oeconomica* prevents warlike interactions between states opened up for trading. The consumerist way of life does, however, have the disadvantage that market peace undertaxes people's nerves; they miss that sense of emergency which promises liberation from boredom. For individuals, then, the art of making one's way through the worldwide labyrinth of shopping malls, animation centers and portals without becoming weary demands interrupting the banality of comfort through the constant reinvention of irritations.[127]

In the realm of capital, every possible opposition is created by the conditions it attacks. This realization caused Antonio Negri and Michael Hardt to suggest the term "empire" for the global super-installation in their study of the "new world order."[128] This empire can only be conceived of in the singular and has a strictly ecumenical character. That is why, supposedly, no outside enemy can face it any longer: it could at most turn against itself, and be defeated by the rebellion of its components. It becomes clear: the talk of "empire" is religiously motivated—and the worldwide success of the book can only be understood in the light of this diagnosis. In fact it takes up, more suggestively and argumentatively, the unresolved traditions of Christian theology of history and makes their apocalyptic motives resound materialistically. Because no otherworldly goal of becoming is available to Spinozists or Deleuzians, the realm of capital, which is fully of this world, is contrasted with the equally, yet differently worldly counter-realm of dissident multiplicities or alternative expressionisms. The greatest difference is almost the most ambiguous: it posits a difference on which everything hinges yet which, viewed by the cold light of day, cannot be implemented—paralysis is programmed. The empire and its dissident multitude are, despite the excited speeches of the opposition and radical objections, one and the same.

Anyone with an overview of religious reserves against terrestrial imperial constructs immediately recognizes that *Empire* constitutes a pantheistic parody of the Augustinian opposition between *civitas terrena* and *civitas Dei*. The analogies are far-reaching: just as the church was often empirically almost indistinguishable from the world it purported to resist, so too the multitude cannot separate itself clearly from the world of capital it seeks to escape—except in that intimate certainty which convinces those opposed to prevailing conditions of their glowing militance. Only a mystical decision permits the adherents of the affluent left to know that they are still on the left at all—just as a terminological distinction is often the only source of help for the unsuccessful in claiming their exploitation and exclusion. Their point of reference is the introspective observation that they feel a pure contrariness within themselves: as the "enemy against which to rebel" no longer displays any contours, the affect "against" must be content with itself: "this being-against becomes the essential key to every active position in the world."[129] The against men, in addition to their membership in the opposing church, are *de facto*—like all their contemporaries—ambivalent customers of the given. The intensely invoked enmity towards the empire is directed at an authority that cannot be made an enemy, because the empire, in its positive aspects, wants and is the same as the oppositional masses, though the latter's impulses and compulsions at once embody the dark sides of the realm. Now that the days of open sabotage are over (class struggle, in its methods, is likewise a child of its time), it would seem advisable for the dissidents to jump ship—but because, so one hears, there is no longer an outside to which one can retreat, desertion from the system leads nowhere ("desertion does not have a place").[130] The other, by seeking to be completely different, is the same; by wishing to be somewhere else entirely, it remains where it is.

Negri's and Hardt's essay on the capitalist world system and the revolt of life against it marks the logical end of the leftward revolt initiated by the Revolution's losers in 1789. Looking back on a two-hundred-year escalation that was pushed to the extreme, the law of outdoing July 14 among its frustrated lovers becomes transparent: if the bourgeois revolution fails or is inadequate, the result is radical leftism; if radical leftism fails or is inadequate, the result is the gnosis of militance.[131] Such a gnosis can no longer fail; it becomes implausible.[132]

The non-concrete hyper-sculpture probably finds its most advanced formulation in Luhmann's cryptically smooth concept of "world society." Despite belonging to an extremely formalist discourse, the term is infused with a utopian vibration, for it takes the gamble—for methodological, not moral reasons—of spreading out a uniform conceptual roof over the internal worlds of the global prosperity system *and* their poverty-dominated peripheries. By speaking in sphinx-like fashion of world society (and refusing to use the word "society" in the plural), the attentive sociologist gives the impression that in systems theory too, there has to be a single verbal gesture that points to the whole. One can read this as meaning that the master from Bielefeld did not want to deny the countless excluded of the earth at least semantic citizenship in the One "Society," even though no one knew better than he did that an effective world unity is impossible under any imaginable circumstances.

What I have described as the liberation from the reality model of the ontology of deficiency is, in sociohistorical terms, connected to two caesuras in the social and mental structures of Europe and the New World. Both can be described without exaggeration as the deepest ruptures in the history of post-Neolithic humanity: firstly, the revolt against deficiency coincides with the end of the traditional agricultural way of life after the establishment of the urban-industrial, monetarily oriented lifestyle on a massive scale; and secondly, with the end of the age of female over-fertility and the abrupt decline in birth rates in all de-agrarianized states. Thus Japan, Germany and Italy, with a birth rate of 0.9%, and Austria and Spain, with 1% each, are among the countries with the lowest birth rates in the world.[133] Among wealthy countries, it is only the USA that can expect growth, thanks to the combined effects of immigration and increased birth rates in the Latino-Asian population segments—at the cost of marginalizing the descendants of Europeans. The modernity-founding liaison between prosperity and falling birth rates appears in a variety of modulations that occasionally deviate as far as a reversal of the trend, but as a whole it cannot be denied.[134] While the shortage of children in some European countries, not least Germany, is occasionally interpreted as an expression of "lived pessimism,"— the refusal of biological investment—it will generally have to be understood as a chance for an intensified attention of the nurturers to each individual offspring.

It is clear that both of these caesuras display a direct connection to changes in the mother-child field, and thus to the existential background of uplift forces; that they also hold the chance for a radical unfolding of abstract allomother and self-mothering potentials, however, needs to be shown. Regarding the first caesura, Eric Hobsbawm noted:

> The most dramatic and far-reaching social change of the second half of this century, and the one which cuts us off for ever from the world of the past, is the death of the peasantry. [...] It is perhaps not surprising that by the early 1980s less than three out of every 100 Britons or Belgians were in agriculture [...]. The farming population of the U.S.A. had fallen to the same percentage, but, given its long-term steep decline, this was less astonishing than the fact that this tiny fraction of the labor force was in a position to flood the U.S.A. and the world with untold quantities of food. [...] In Japan [...] farmers were reduced from 52.4 per cent of the people in 1947 to 9 per cent in 1985 [...]. In Finland [...] a girl born as a farmer's daughter and who became a farmer's working wife in her first marriage, could, before she had got far into middle age, have transformed herself into a cosmopolitan intellectual and political figure. But then, in 1940 when her father died in the winter war against Russia, leaving mother and infant on the family holding, 57 per cent of Finns were farmers and foresters. By the time she was forty-five less than 10 per cent were.[135]

It goes without saying that discourses of this kind fall back on the commonplace of cultural revolution, but closer inspection reveals that here too one is not dealing with a "revolution," either in the political or the kinetic sense of the word, but rather with sequences of explications. In the present case it is the explication of plant and animal fertility, which intervenes in earlier practices in the most spectacular possible way; it resulted from modern agricultural chemistry in combination with molecular biology and the explosive elevation of farming productivity via machines and methods of economic rationalization, as well as the transition—however problematic—to factory farming in the elaborated system of meat capitalism. These explications of fertility—the technical background of "biopolitics"—in fact brought about the current conditions, where 2–3% of a working population not only feed the rest of the country, but also generate a surplus for export. The unforeseen consequence of this was that the great majority of the population could be released from the living context of agriculture and allowed to enter contexts of industrial wage work—a process normally termed "urbanization." The fact that this transition initially meant a shift from agro-proletarian hardship to industrial-proletarian poverty is been shown emphatically by social historiography; from today's perspective, these findings have themselves become historical.

The undoing of rural bonds marked the decisive caesura for the current unfolding of wish multiplicities because, for most, it was accompanied by a change from a subsistence economy to a monetary one; it brought about a leap from a form of existence stagnating in frugal needs to a wish-driven *modus vivendi* geared towards more valuable commodities and luxury objects. With the release from the soil (and its rediscovery as a holiday landscape), an era began in which wishing was the first civic duty. It would henceforth apply that only humans who wished and were capable of precise choices were following their calling to develop consumer subjectivity. It is in no sense "bare life" that determines the subject's form in the luxury hothouse, but rather the possession of spending power in combination with mobilized appetites.

One part of the image of the new is a strong upward social mobility, carried by a considerable multiplication of chances in the earning histories of individuals. Multifocal "society" offers a thousand milieus to lean on, ten thousand stages to come out on, and a hundred thousand stairways to ascend. Every milieu, every stage and every staircase forms a micro-universe of uplift. Forward and upward mobility is supported by the traditional disposition of the underclasses to follow the life forms of the affluent. The upward social thrust is due not least to the widespread conviction among poorer citizens that they would undoubtedly cut a good figure as rich people—a misjudgment based on the assumption that being wealthy is the continuation of ordinary, hardship-driven life at a higher level, with no realistic idea of a life form controlled by preferences in multi-dimensional spaces of options. Conversely, thanks to the addictive effect of pampering lifestyles, the affluent always have reason to fear abject failure if they became poor— which becomes the main motive for their fierce resolve to defend acquired rights. The fact that the thought of impoverishment often instills a fear of extermination in the well-off proves how little, when it comes to themselves, they believe in the blessings of the same welfare state that they claim, when it comes to others, has considerably reduced the dangers of poverty.[136] The worries of the pampered are concentrated in the nightmare that the constant replenishment of pampering means could one day cease. This oppressive notion contains a muddled concept of the fragility of the luxury hothouse, where, as in a mature foam, the life games of wealthy democracies take place.

10. The Compass Rose of Luxury:
Vigilance, Liberated Whim, Light Sexuality

I am not here standing up for suffering, or well-being either.
I am standing out for my own caprices and having them
guaranteed when necessary.

— Fyodor Dostoyevsky, *Notes from Underground* [137]

The individualism necessarily dominant in the super-installation—one could also call it the modern refusal of individuals to internalize their social status—indicates a psychohistorical change comparable to the creation of a new soul form by a major religion: its significance lies in causing the release of unspecific attention on a large scale. One can probably understand the individualist wave best by viewing it as a luxury form of being-in-the-world. An individual is someone who demands privileged access to themselves as the owner of experiences. This gives rise to the mission of being one's own end consumer. The ethics of individualism gives its clients the advice to view their existence as a one-time offer. While there is a multitude of non-selves everywhere, it-shaped and you-shaped, the self directly knows that it is rare. Something that only exists once immediately seems cult-worthy. The fact that the individuals in the affluence hothouse can all treat themselves as rarities results from the mutual potentiation of three overarching trends responsible for the individuation climate of modernity.

First of all, the marked decline in birth rates in industrial and post-industrial countries produces conditions under which the competition for the scarce resource of motherly love among the overabundant children in traditional farming and artisanal families is annulled. Because, after a ten-thousand-year malign oversupply, children became actual rarities, it was inevitable that a high investment of maternal and allomotherly energies in individual offspring once more became the norm. Although the increased quota of female employment absorbed part of the new chances for a more intense attention to the individual child, the allofunctions of the welfare and school states in the large-scale hothouse amply made up for these losses. It is also conspicuous that contemporary psychology—and theology too—has so far barely responded to this psychohistorically singular state of affairs: the great majority of those born in the super-installation today are expressly affirmed and welcomed children. With them, the traditional compensations for being unwelcome are no longer needed; above all, they are no longer faced with the problem formerly negotiated with the concept of salvation—an *a posteriori* affirmation of negated life. The future significance of this for the current socio-psychological tonicity of a "society" is as unexplored as the long-term cultural consequences of the new phenomenon.[138] Conditions would suggest that throughout civilization—across most of the spectrum of social stratifications, taking into account inequalities between milieus and nations—a historically unknown luxury of maternalization and upbringing has become the general standard.

As usual, the near-impossible in the anthropogenic island climate is taken for granted and serves as the starting level for additional demands. In the super-installation, training periods extending to the age of thirty are no longer exceptional, although the subjects of such education investments now barely connect their extended maturing times to any awareness of privilege. In a

Martin Kippenberger, *METRO-Net World Connection Ventilation Shaft*, German
Pavilion, 2003 Venice Biennale

manner unknown in earlier times, child-deficient "society"
surrounds its perpetually adolescent offspring with a wreath of
caring, hope and admiration, often with threads of guilty conscience and fear for the future woven in—especially in the

hyper-moral subcultures plagued with procreative guilt. In all social classes today, the welcome child shines in the eyes of its progenitors, as precious as a gilded Christmas tree topper made of hand-blown glass.

The second large-scale trend responsible for the individualist turn is the increase in labor productivity, which has led in the last one hundred and fifty years to a spectacular reduction of weekly, annual and lifetime working time for the great majority of employed persons. While the annual work performance of laborers, employees and servants around 1850 was still slightly under 4,000 hours—almost half the number of hours in a year—the annual working hours of the wage-dependent in Germany and comparable countries had dropped to an average of 1,700 or less. Taking into account extended training times and earlier retirement, this meant a reduction of working periods in the life-time budgets of individuals to a third of what had, a mere five generations ago, been the fate of humans in the "leisure class." One conventionally refers to these changes as an increase in leisure time. In reality, the leisure cliché conceals an anthropologically far-reaching situation that is difficult to grasp in its entirety; one could describe it as an explosion of self-attention. Its immediate consequence is the general subjugation of life to the choice between boredom or entertainment.

No other enhancement movement in the twentieth century is more closely tied to the realization of human luxury potentials than the mass dismissal of individuals into their own living time. Simply put: the event of the last epoch that determined all transformations of morals and life forms was the radical multiplication of average waking time possessed by each person outside of the periods devoted to work and domestic tasks. Free waking time is the intersection in the compass rose of luxury tendencies. What we call leisure is, in concrete terms, the explication of waking times through activities and inactivities whose arbitrary, reflexive and event-oriented character makes them suitable to turn the attention of actors "inwards." "Event society" is a system that releases individuals to meditate in the here and now on any sensual presences and results of existence. The clouds drift, the books are silent on their shelves, and I am feeling this way or that. The vegetative steps into the foreground, inner states are framed by attention, and the evasive domain of the obvious flashes up in the inner topic. "You just sit and breathe more or less correctly in the light of your tiredness."[139]

The latest expansion of the phases freed up for self-attention (and their elimination en masse through entertainment) is also numerically impressive. If we subtract 8 hours of sleeping time from the 8,760 hours in as year, as well as the annual workload of 1,700 hours, that leaves the inhabitants of the super-installation with a medium annual balance of 4,140 hours of available waking time. Even if a substantial part of this is eaten up by routine acts of daily self-care, family duties and travel to one's workplace, most people today are still left with a remainder of self-referential time far beyond all historically known conditions.

This time is used to feed manifold luxury dimensions that have meanwhile become a fixed part of existence in the super-installation. The first thing one notices about the contemporary way of life is an enormous amount of mobility luxury. Almost every contemporary life has an unprecedented share in the power of transportation. Modern bodies define themselves—in addition to their auto-operable constitution—by their ability to overcome distances and carry out arbitrary movements. This goes so far that the concept of freedom today can no longer be defined without considering the right to kinetic wastage and touristic whims. The extent of kinetic luxury illuminates, among other things, the traffic-sociological finding that two out of three motorized traffic movements are tied to non-economic and non-professional purposes; *je bouge, donc je suis.*[140] A critique of pure evasion has yet to be written. The life miles account of the average worker or employee in the automobilistically and touristically core countries of the affluence system around the year 2000 by far surpasses those of the eighteenth- and nineteenth-century leisure classes, even those who practiced the exquisite sport of globetrotting. If one adds the common ergotopic practices, which take the form of countless types of sport, physical exercises and gymnastics, dances, parades and movement therapies, one sees a civilization vibrating in a perceived kinetic luxury without precedent.

In addition, in the realm of waking non-work, an unprecedentedly expansive system of morbidity luxury has differentiated itself. Next to pure self-referential movement, being ill has become the most common interpretation of the chance for leisure.[141] This finding is contributed to as much by civilization sickness as by manifested psychopathologies, addictions, and the sport accidents that follow hard on the heels of the differentiation of sport into hundreds of subcultures (which is why the departments of emergency surgery or traumatology in hospitals are the true institutes of sociology today). The phenomenon of multi-morbidity shows the expansion of illness into a self-willed luxury universe. It proves that ailments can be cultivated as in sporting multi-events. Even when the illness does not define the *modus vivendi* entirely, it remains ubiquitous as a constantly

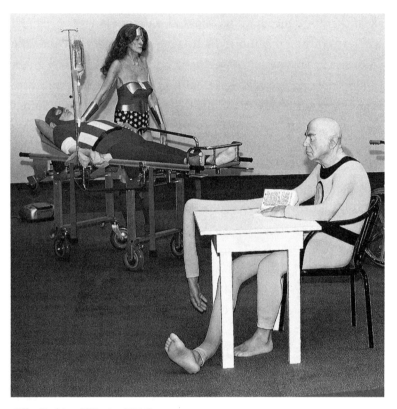

Gilles Barbier, *L'Hospice* (2002)

addressable background possibility—without it, the fitness scenes, the cultures of wellness and diets, the introversive and well-organized worlds of spa towns, the balneological refuges and high-lying coughing castles would be inconceivable. (A hundred years before Thomas Mann let Hofrat Behrens explain on the *Magic Mountain* that he was an old servant of death, Balzac described the figure of the busty spa town landlady from Auvergne, who knew how to wait in motherly and business-minded fashion for the demise of her guests.)[142]

The great departure to morbidity is accommodated by countless specializations of medical and therapeutic services. At the upper end of the product scale are sophisticated hermeneutics of sickness that instruct patients to appropriate their afflictions as a chance; the accident shows a second face when interpreted as an act of self-care;[143] for countless people, conversations about neuroses and life obstacles offer the reward of being problematic. In the clinical archipelago (there are 4.2 million employees in the "healthcare system" in Germany alone), expansive circuits of self-harming luxury, therapy luxury, provision luxury, insurance luxury and dissatisfaction luxury are interlocked, each with its own indispensable *lamento* bass, descending diatonically from bad to worse—integrated by the systemic necessity of concealing the pampering character of contemporary morbidity management behind a dense veil of humanist patronage and scientifically founded minimum demands. Because of its pathogenic implications, we can also point here to the image-transported cruelty luxury of contemporary culture, whose sources and habitus pattern admittedly extend relatively far back into European pictorial history.[144]

Finally, a new form of victimological luxury unfolded in the moral space of the affluent society. Its establishment and branching-out are assisted as far as necessary by a media alliance of corporate associations, law firms, cultural sciences and moral columnists. The luxury victimologies rest on the discovery that in the super-installation, the moral sensitivity of the public is a symbolic resource that can be materially administered. Because heroes are only possible as victims after the Enlightenment, ambition must take a detour via victimism. This applies to individuals as much as corporations and states. Countless persons compete with amateur and professional means for the advantage of being allowed to present themselves as victims on various stages—better still, as a super-victim, as the attacked of all attacked, the Jew of all Jews, the pariah of all pariahs, the damned of all the damned of this earth. Celebrities also take part intensely in these mechanisms, like the late Princess Diana of Wales, whose great popularity in the women's press came primarily from her carefully cultivated status as a "ruling victim." Even world powers are willing to reach for the victimological premiums: the political behavior of the Bush administration in the USA after September 11, 2001 testified to the historical novelty of a superpower deciding, when the opportunity arises, to present itself as a super-victim—a position with unforeseeable political risks, to say nothing of the moral disproportions. With regard to expectable gratifications, a hyperbolic function has been bred in the atmosphere of aggressive sensitivity to present one's own existence as well as possible in the light of endured disadvantages. This habitus can be compared to the custom of the anti-Jacobin *muscadins* of 1794 to shave the backs of their necks *à la victime* to express solidarity with the beheaded notables of the terror period. It is more than a brief vengeful trend, however: beginning in the United States, where "victimspeak" has become the common language since the 1970s, the aggressive sensitivism of victim status cultures has made itself felt in the climate of the entire affluence hothouse.[145] Obviously, a culture of long-term *ressentiment* is here taking on forms of which one cannot yet say how they will harmonize with the other ecosystems of moral feeling in the pampering hothouse. We do not yet know what things bodies in *ressentiment* are capable of.

It is clear, however, that these phenomena have not only psychological motives, but also major economic reasons. In addition to taxes for the treasury and social security contributions, the victimist compensation claim becomes the third pillar of redistribution; it spreads out by intensifying the tendency towards a postmodern advocato-medicocracy. An American plaintiff deservedly acquired world fame after placing her wet dog in the microwave oven to dry, and subsequently demanding astronomically high compensation from the oven's manufacturer for her cooked pet—with the notable argument that they had failed to advise her of the risks involved in mammals occupying turned-on microwave ovens. One can take this case as a paradigm of a new intelligence for designing accusations. The constant reinvention of pseudo-precisely outlined syndromes of illness and disadvantage is driven by the need to specify legally valid criteria of victimhood. One promising fruit of victimism, for example, is the recently publicized Economy Class Syndrome, designed to provide the juristic-medicocratic foundation for damages claims against airlines if passengers on long-distance flights develop thrombosis in their lower extremities. Other popular syndromes with great versatility of application have emerged since the 1990s: in addition to dissociative disorders (which contain leftovers of what was previously termed hysteria), the phenomena of chronic fatigue and multiple personalities—both embody the medical guise of the postmodern abandonment of the perpetrator illusion.

When the basic victimist mood combines with the alarmist, a broad space opens up for a warning literature that positions the bringer of the alarm at the stock market of topics, assuming they succeed in attracting sufficient attention. Warnings of a creeping sedimentation of heavy metals in the brain and the inevitable decline of human intelligence; of microbial globalization, which enables new germs of unprecedented aggressiveness to spread; of the long-term psychological effects of abuse inflicted on boys by over-caring mothers who give their offspring forced enemas before bed, and of giant meteors headed straight for the earth. Numerous subgenres in the field of alarmist entertainment have diversified into a non-fiction gothicism that supplies the public's appetite for horror with a menu of unusual causes of death.[146] Thanks to such services, the constant false alarm in the American "culture of fear" has also become a lifestyle in other places.

Surpluses of vigilance are for subjectivities what fossil fuels and solar power are for the machine systems in the luxury hot-house. The free waking times are the propellent to curve and shape the agglomerated micromanic spacve. Adjustable quanta of subjective energy for establishing cultivatable fields can be drawn from their reservoirs, starting with the simplest pleasures. Because of their surplus nature, countless activities devoid of any work or production character become trainable as if they were constructive efforts; once this happens, the transition to the competitive form is a logical step, and shortly after its introduction, any amusement can become an object of mastery. If it is sufficiently well-organized it will also release its specific pathologies, which in turn become treatable by the corresponding trainers and therapists. That this vigilance is true luxury is shown by the high wastage rates in all fields; it is the significant privilege of the propertied to achieve little with their wealth. In this respect, the postmodern owners of extensive free waking time not infrequently resemble the lords of the past, who would never have dreamed of producing anything on the basis of their inherited advantages.

Even the little that contributes to the activism of whims yields results too diverse to comprehend or summarize. To gain an overview of the effects from an abstract point, one must begin by saying that wealth is only wealth for a vigilance that values it. Because vigilance luxury is the key function of every luxury, it is the central nervous system of consumerism and the leisure industries. More still, it holds the crypto-spirituality of the seemingly de-spirited age because it supplies the matrix for all nuancing activities. The irony of the treasure hunt, namely that the treasure believed to be in the objects actually lies in the seeker's waking consciousness, is only noted by meditative subcultures. Only a few individuals realize that the luxury of reflection and meditation—becoming attentive to one's own attentiveness—specifies the basic form of peak experiences.

The main stream of vigilance flows towards objects whose concrete envisaging becomes experienceable in waking awareness as satisfaction. Life in the waking world provides the surpluses of attention and trainable power of judgment without which no refined self-care, no higher experiential metabolism can exist—indeed, as long as the working life was primarily artisanal, it too profited from the added value of refinement associated with the libidinous feedback of skilled waking arrangements. Today this can be observed in numerous fields of expanded vigilance investment. All forms of remembrance culture—the centerpiece of the Old European concept of civilization—live off the use of surplus waking times to fill in inner and outer images of things past. What has been familiar since the nineteenth century as historicism is a side effect, palpable throughout culture, of channeling enormous amounts of leisure time into painting attractive pasts; satisfaction about the fact that one even knows anything about other periods rounds off the subculture of rememberers in themselves. Alongside followers of the art religion, the historicists were the first to devote themselves to the task of reformulating their whims into a general necessity, or rather a basic spiritual foodstuff for the many.

Cultures of decadence are possible because the luxury of wakefulness likes to articulate itself as that of morbidity. When one meditates on morbidity,[147] weakness becomes a trainable state. With high degrees of collective release for exercises in getting-out-of-shape, an adequately pampered population will quickly show impressive results: thanks to circular intensification, the rapid exhaustion of the young will be accompanied by an epidemic vague weariness of everyone and everything among the older.

Cultures of negativism are possible because in the milieus of the unsuccessful, a great deal of free time can be invested in the description of any given objects through the filter of resentment. It has long been the case that the majority of what passes for criticism and commentary in the features sections can more aptly be classified as malice luxury and disparagement luxury; its psychic utility value lies in satisfying the demand for gestures of empty aloofness (formerly a monopoly of *Der Spiegel*, but now virtually the norm).

Cultures of *ressentiment* are possible, and prospering as never before, because the encounter between frustration and leisure makes it possible for a large amount of attention to specialize in holding grudges; the ever-vigilant envy among intellectuals produces constantly changing inquisitions against the heresies of success. Whether these forms of luxury benefit the overall culture—whatever that might be—remains an open question. Taking an optimistic view, one can observe how *ressentiment* supports the aggression metabolism with high-fiber delusions of insult.

One advantage of the decision to interpret the phenomenon of luxury from the perspective of free vigilance is that there is no need to linger on anecdotes or enumerations when describing the various forms of a luxurious way of life, in contrast to the most important achievements in earlier historiography: the classic morality histories of luxury present clothes, jewelry, flower arrangements, buildings, furniture, food, mistresses and servants without developing an overall perspective—except that of wealth and its exaggerated whims. One learns, not without interest, that a French eighteenth-century glutton by the name of Verdelet made bowls from carps' tongues for himself, each costing 1,200 livres and the lives of two to three thousand such animals. His model was supposedly the Roman Vitellius, whose compositions of pheasant and peacock brains, flamingo tongues, mackerel livers and moray eels' milk became legendary.[148]

By taking the release of vigilance as our starting point, we have a criterion that illuminates the existential qualities of the superfluous more adequately than any concrete notion of wealth and wastage ever could. At the same time, it highlights the fact that the investment of "time and money" in a preferred area of doing and enjoying is a case of free whim. The triumph over necessity can be anchored in the concept of luxury itself—and that, after what has been stated above, means at the intersection of affluence and vigilance. This makes it clear that even whim requires training. Where whim is elaborated in exercises and indulges in individuated runs, series and branchings-out, it creates a gravitation of its own kind. One could say that virtuosity is nothing other than a superfluous exertion captured by the cultivating gravity of repetition.

In addition, the reference to its source in vigilance brings luxury close to the "aesthetics of everyday life," which was recently shown to belong to a "second-order luxury," exemplified by the longing for quiet, emptiness, simplification and genuine feelings.[149] Because the phenomenon of vigilance precedes the bifurcation of attention and distraction, it spans the two varieties of aesthetic theories that assign themselves to one of the two poles.[150] More still: as it also precedes the opposition between carefully noting (*religere*) and neglecting (*necligere*),[151] waking can become part of stable cults—but also improvisations. As a matrix of both religions and profane diversions, free waking can ally itself with the regular as easily as the singular.

An aesthetics expanded to include everyday objects is—as a phenomenon of mass culture—an invention of the twentieth century (its precursors in Dutch domestic mysticism, as hinted earlier, go back at least to the seventeenth century); it cannot deny its origins in actually happening relief. It would be unimaginable without the severe expenditure of available time for the perception and refinement of objects and constellations in the setting. What we call taste, beyond the good and the bad, is the expansion of oral vigilance to include the most varied areas of judgment about sensory presences.

Without the freely available luxury of vigilance and its lasting investments in cultivatable fields, there would be none of all the things that have for some decades been observable in the field of "home décor culture" and its working-through at all levels of popular and elitist design: no cultures of bathrooms, kitchens, floors, materials or colors. No air design, no expeditions into the realm of scents:[152] no refinement of the feeling for ornaments (ornaments[153] are excellent absorbers of living time), no special taste for furniture and décor, no pleasant bogging-down in the universe of antiquities. Without surpluses of free wakefulness there can be no sense of shape for expensive ballpoint pens or car bodies, no space-climate awareness, no attunement to the harmony of the old and the new, and no sensitivity for compatibilities between accessories and contrasts in environmental arrangement. And certainly no thoughts outside the box of activity, no feeling for changes of landscape and gliding horizons, and no understanding of climate change and atmospheric chromaticism; no meta-need for abandoning the vanities of needing, no turn towards the values of pure "being," and no yearning for fallowness, escape or fasting from experiences.

Needless to say, the whole of literary and musical culture hinges on the chance to use free waking times for reading, listening, practicing and comparing. We should note: in the history of all civilizations, contrary to the claims of established cultural critique and theories of decline, there have never been so many units of time invested in the reading of books, magazines and newspapers, in listening to music of all genres, in viewing television programs, in attending films, talkshows, theater plays, cabarets, round table discussions and so on as in the present day. The greatest number of singers and instrumentalists of the highest standard are performing today; the sum of novelists, poets, actors, directors and artists of all levels and categories is the highest in history (only professional orators have almost died out); the absolute majority of orchestras, opera houses, choirs, dance companies and theaters are active in our time. They can all assume the existence of audience segments who are prepared to exchange attention for entertainment, art and information.

The third dimension in the individualistic trend complex is reached by changing serious "society" into an arousable aggregate of self-caring and self-pampering clients, buyers and consumers. It is one of the truisms of psychohistory that the twentieth century implemented a shift of subject forms, away from the demands of early capitalism to those of elaborated capitalism, formerly known as late capitalism: from a puritan work ethic to liberal leisure-orientedness, from serious thriftiness to recklessness with credit, from a foregoing of consumption to a craving for experiences, from the heroization of entrepreneurial virtues to the glorification of celebrities from sports and entertainment. The latest varieties of cultural critique speak of the postmodern subject being trained to lose elemental traits of the traditional personality culture, such as adherence to stable norms, belief in one's own unpurchasable nature, self-esteem due to time-honored skills, and a sense of biographical continuity and similar qualities, in order to produce a fully capital-compatible human being. We are told, sometimes accusingly and sometimes descriptively, that it oscillates between the job and fun, morally enucleated, as agile as a snake,[154] highly suited to field service, as unprejudiced as an arms dealer and as postnational as a brothel owner. The analytical power of monetary relationships—where "all that is solid melts into air"[155]—would thus have reached the final citadel of the premodern *ordo*'s reserves, namely the personal layer. Through the discovery of fun (the German *Spass* is possibly related to the Italian *spasso*, meaning "expansion" or "relaxation") as a source of added value, the subjective factor would have been integrated into the sphere of capital once and for all: after all,

Eric Fischl, *The Birth of Love (Second Version)* (1987), courtesy of Mary Boone Gallery, New York

erotic life would also have been opened up to the market, as if to refute the myth of the "sexual revolution" launched by Wilhelm Reich, in which the wage-dependent would, by living out their sexuality, become phallic rebels—and consequently refractors of every kind of alienation.

In reality, the integration of sexuality into fun culture—I use the phrase without any polemical undertone—provoked a broad subjectification of the awareness of wealth, and in this manner also a serious truth effect. In fact, no biological endowment— except the capacity for vigilance—illustrates the human being's

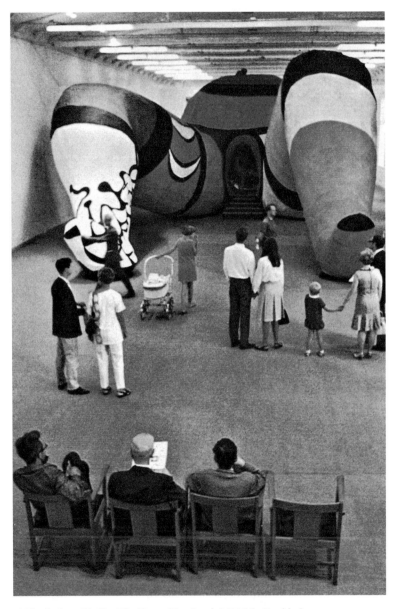

Niki de Saint Phalle, *The Figure Hon (= she)* (1966), Stockholm

inability to be poor as clearly as sexuality. It is the natural talent for experiences of happiness in the strictest sense—provided one uses the word "talent," common since the Renaissance, in keeping with its origins in the New Testament term for an "entrusted good" or multipliable "pound" (from the Greek *tálanton*, "that which is weighed"). In the twentieth century, the break with the traditions of poverty dogmatism is most evident in the release of a de-demonized, naturalized or positively downplayed, but at once artistically intensified sexuality. Having stated above that an authentic theory of relief and de-poverishment does not yet exist, I should here add the qualification that the sexual sciences which sprung up in the second half of the century, based on plans from the late nineteenth, close part of the gap because, on closer inspection, they offer the strongest indirect theory of the present age. They deal with individuals as rich and further enrichable owners of a sexual capacity. Sexual science possesses— here too, Thomas Bernhard would say "naturally"—the form of investment advice. It starts from the assumption that many owners administer their fortunes poorly, whether on account of inhibitions (of predictably miserablist origin) or ignorance of the options and profit margins.

Contemporary sex education owes its existence to the turn towards the explicit that earns the facts of consciousness in modernity the mystifying label "revolution." The sexual explication that gave the twentieth century its cultural character brought to light the modes and preconditions for sexuated life journalistically, scientifically, aesthetically, psychologically and economically in a historically unknown manner; it broke the normative monopoly of maritally regulated couple-based eroticism and made an alternative list of options declarable and

Jürgen Klauke, *Dr. Müller's Sex Shop or Here's How I Imagine Love* (1977)

chooseable—from asexuality via autosexuality to homosexuality and heterosexuality in all popular and deviant varieties, as far as they were practicable in non-criminal forms. It sharpened the eye for genital facts and offered spectatorship to an unprecedented degree, to the point where the word "explicit" refers precisely to the gaping-open of intimacies.[156] Through contrast with the light sexuality that had been released, it highlighted the structure of those perversions that frequently revolve around attempts to encode the sexual act with the longing for drama, hardness and heaviness—firstly, to intuitively force the connection between the pleasure practices of the sexual level with those of the endorphin reactions, and secondly, to prevent the dissolution of sublime sexuality in the pleasant form thereof (once again the flight from freedom to necessity: the conservative revolution of desire). It pushed the immemorial latent schism between sexuality and procreation to the point of open rupture, formally consummated with the introduction of steroidal oral contraceptives, whose first successful synthesis by Carl Djerassi in Mexico City is dated to October 15, 1951 and whose popular use since the 1960s has supported the turn to levitated forms of heterosexual intercourse[157] (Djerassi rightly pointed out that "most of those changes in sexual mores would have happened anyway");[158] through the possibility of almost certain birth control, it has brought out the luxury character of marital and non-marital sexual acts to the point of ultimate clarity. Never before—leaving aside local forms of aristocratic eroticism—has it been so evident that "sex," to adopt the relevant American term now, constitutes a luxury activity of completely autonomous value. As the sylvan theater of uplift, it offers all those active a chance to explore its anti-grave potential. Being situated at the intersection of the expression of passion, encounter, fun and sport, it offers access from all directions. It is, in its decoded form, pure whim itself—if we understand a *caprice* as a feeling that contains its goal within itself. Its execution includes self-reward. (Anyone who still asks what is in it for them is asking one question too many—the definition of stupidity.)

That is why sex that is decoded, explicated and easily disconnected from reproductive meanings forms the center of fun culture—that is, the system of emancipated whims. Only a negligible minority of intimate acts is still actually or potentially connected to the production of offspring, whether as a possibility to be welcomed or avoided, whereas the majority of erotic games take place within the horizon of pleasure gain, performance or relaxation. (It should not surprise anyone if the conservatives of the West and the current representatives of authoritarian capitalism in the East—to say nothing of reactionary Islamism—agree in their rejection of light sexuality.) On the grotesquely expanded prostitution markets, the pure preference for one variety or another is central from the outset. The more explicit sexuality becomes, the closer it moves to the pole of pure wastage. This experience, incidentally, which has now shifted within reach of countless erotically nomadic individuals, was traditionally found in the rare married couples that remained happy for a long time; they enjoyed the privilege of floating above the economic paradox of their intercourse. If a thousand embraces, cheerfully monochromatic, produced a handful of children, or even just one, this disproportion between a large and a small amount presented the least problematic view of happiness.

Sexuality posited in its own right, which has come to dominate in the child-deficient societies of the West, explicates an evolutionarily well-established natural dimension of wastage. It is found in all mammals, but is intensified among hominids and taken to the extreme in the *sapiens* line. Signs of a transition to permasex can be seen in a number of primates—here sexual activity already gains luxuriating autonomous values, and occasionally becomes an element of group management, as the well-known example of the bonobos shows. Out of millions of unripe eggs available in the ovaries of every female *sapiens* individual, scarcely more than four hundred mature in the course of a life cycle. With intense sexual activity, less than 3% of these are fertilized, and less than 0.5% develop into offspring. The surplus proportions are far more extreme among the male members of the species: with 40 million sperm cells per ejaculation, a man with two such exertions per week over a period of forty years would arrive at a total emission of over 150 billion sperms, of which biologists assume roughly half are able to move normally, well-formed and fertile.

After the physiological explication of sexuality, a biological definition of male existence is possible: the decoded "man" is a channel for sperm cascades. From this perspective, almost everything else seems like superstructure. Actual procreative successes among ordinary fathers, drifters or machos barely count in the light of the wastage rate. The men's subjective attitude to their spendings is likewise fairly meaningless; the flow of sperms does not ask whether the person reads St. Paul or Bataille.

Sexual explication turns directly into the explication of uplift. One can say that this explication shows fundamental aspects of human nature—note the lack of quotation marks—more adequately than in all earlier systems determined by asceticism and deficiency. In those, access to abundance could only ever be gained via the detour of an inner congestion or organized frustration—while in erotic liberalism one of the substrates of human wealth, namely the free use of surplus desires, is brought to the surface without being inhibited by prohibition and neurosis. Frank Wedekind's "disguised religion of sexual intercourse" and Otto Weininger's completely obscure "religion of the vagina"[159] are—viewed at a century's distance—barely more than starting complications in the decoding of sexuality. In them, a tradition of poverty that has come from far away reaches its final form. It has meanwhile become an educational matter to be capable of sympathy towards expired neuroses of this kind. Should one add that such possibilities are the culmination of one of the most subtle forms of luxury?—that of empathizing with things one no longer needs.

From a Conversation About the Oxymoron

The macrohistorian: While we are waiting for the author, who will be completing our group shortly, we should perhaps attempt to put our impressions somewhat in order. For my part, I admit that my profession, above all, helped me to survive the flood of words that passed over me while reading. While the author dragged me through the length and breadth of his observations—or should I compliment myself by emphasizing that I fought my way through on my own strength?—I increasingly had the impression that the historical framework was based on a very robust narrative model analogous to what we use in our macrohistorical studies, a model in which the history of mankind—for our concern is no less than that—is encapsulated in a triad: the Neolithic caesura separates the Paleolithic age of hunter-gatherers from the subsequent agricultural civilizations with their monarchies and commanding administrations. The industrial caesura, on the other hand, has separated—for little more than two or three centuries—the age of sluggish local dominions from the accelerated life forms of modernity. If this three kingdoms doctrine recalls, if I may say put it thus, a certain idealistic theory of process—*tant pis* for Hegel and his followers.

We have abandoned idealism once and for all. In our investigation of the accumulation of chance inventions to form major trends, we are not following the world spirit in its course through time; nor are we hearing the voice of the history of being. So much the worse for those who, because of external similarities between the recent macrohistorical models and the fictions of the philosophy of history, are fooled into concluding that one is on familiar ground.

To avoid creating false expectations: I cannot claim to have understood what these "spheres" ultimately mean. I doubt that I will use such terms in future. It has not become sufficiently clear to me what dyads or multipolar surreal spaces are, and I certainly cannot recapitulate how peoples live under their so-called imaginary canopies, urban cultures behind their immunizing walls, and liberal populations in their pampering hothouses. Well, historians are known for being at war with more abstract ideas. But I am convinced, at least, that these vague pieces of theory which have shot up, and in whose solidity I cannot, truth be told, entirely believe, are somehow tied back to the aforementioned phase construction, which—after a long and unretracted exploration—I consider well-grounded.

We macrohistorians view ourselves as skeptical successors to the progressive universal historians—and also firmly believe that we are doing useful, even indispensable work because we are providing empirical reference points for the process of civilization, convinced as we are that this process genuinely exists and can, within certain limits, be rationally understood. Yet we avoid making exaggerations—or normative statements, which amount to the same thing—about the ultimate intentions of history. Like all contemporaries who have passed through the school of doubt, we emphatically advise that the dead bury their own dead and the ideologues bury the ideologues. Above all, the idolaters of history should put their co-idolaters under the earth, where their deplorable followers already lie—which, in keeping with the times, results in a huge field of graves, a heroes' cemetery of false obedience at which, instead of monotonous expanses of crosses, millions of outstretched hands and forefingers extend from the ground; one does not know whether they belong to the victims, pointing at their misleaders, or rather to the misleaders themselves, who continue their teachings from the world beyond…

The literary critic: If I may interrupt you—it seems to me that you have come fairly close to the rhetorical core of the *Spheres* project with these images, assuming a centrist metaphor such as the core is suited to this object. For what is the language form of the experiment attempted with these books?—I would say the aim is to bring about a cooperation between poetic élan and skepticism. Or, differently put: the work initiates a critique of prose that expands into a critique of the twentieth century. Did not the false teacher of the epoch, with their prosaic discourses about the masses, the decisive struggles and the final goals of history, pave the way for the pragmatic exterminism that constituted the primary signature of the age? If we choose a reserved style after this hysterical phase, there are also external reasons. Every oversized word of political prose costs millions of murdered, every exaggeration that comes to power claims a burnt offering on a grand scale, and every ruling fallacy results in an exterminated people. If we are in search of a minimal characterization of the twentieth century, we should perhaps begin by observing that it was not an error-friendly era.

Piotr Kowalski, *Sculpture flottante*, Orléans-la-Source (1974)

The macrohistorian: I agree—provided we do not respond to the terror by withdrawing to a modesty dictated by *ressentiment*. When, in 1945, we encountered a zeitgeist that suggested we were not allowed to touch any major subject because the ideologues had attempted the same before us, we wasted decades with well-behaved efforts that remained small and quiet, precious time that would have been needed to advance genuine research into the structures of civilization history. Did not the great ethnologist Marcel Mauss say that every day which passes without us bringing together the fragments of humanity is a wasted day for science, and for the history of human beings?

The theologian: Well, well, pathos has taken over again! Be a little more careful if you please, dear colleague! For it would be equally wrong to characterize the post-war period summarily as mere wasted time. Putting a misstep like National Socialism in Germany behind us, along with its cousins and brothers-in-law in European nations, was more than a trifle. If the Germans and many other Old Europeans spent much time after 1945 meditating on this aberration as the thing it was until its unrepeatability was ensured—which has undoubtedly been the case for some time—one should not see this as a superfluous effort. Forgive me for bothering you with trivialities.

In terms of intellectual history, the post-totalitarian situation can be defined as the return of the modern spirit from hubris. That is an event at a level of its own. Furthermore, gentlemen, you will understand that when I, as a theologian, use a term such as "intellectual history" or "event," I am referring to something different from my colleagues in the philosophy department.

Louise Bourgeois, *Cell (Glass Spheres and Hands)* (1993)

Against this background, I read the theory of spheres as a strictly dated enterprise. To my mind, it constitutes a crypto-theological attempt of a kind that only became possible after the collapse of modern mystification systems. I know the author would protest against this interpretation—he considers himself an undiagnosed anthropologist, or rather an anthropo-monstrologist, and goes so far as to view theology itself as a monstrological field. The least I can say is that the turn towards the doctrine of atmospheres as a First Science is a consequence of exposing extreme realisms. The date of this attempt is fixed after the hubris of modernity.

The literary critic: I am not sure. Is not a macrotheory of this format itself a hubristic form? Does it not, furthermore, entail an exaggerated defense of modernism, assuming one agrees with the author in viewing the conversion of the implicit into the explicit and the drawing of the background into the foreground as the criteria for modernity? I would assert that the author is embracing a special kind of hubris, let us say a methodological hubris, and this in two respects: firstly, because the work has a stylistic quality, and you cannot deny that style is uncollegial; and secondly, because a conception such as this is born from the spirit of colportage—that, with all due respect, is the genre-theoretical term for interdisciplinarity. It makes the hybridization of knowledge its program. One should not forget that for the time being, there is only one plausible place in the world for such knowledge: the author. An author is the only colloquium in which different voices enter one another and produce new resonance effects, while the so-called colloquia of experts only result in parallel discourses that do not intersect anywhere.

As far as the post-totalitarian situation is concerned, esteemed colleague, you may be right. But I think that this point has little explanatory value for the present undertaking, as it is too general; at best, it supplies a motive to incorporate a number of safeguards against abuse into any sophisticated theory, as befits the post-ideological text. One does not need any laborious proof to show that this is the case; the terminological surface of spherology is already a deterrent against anything geared towards seriousness, power and ratings. Power seekers from all sectors will carefully avoid speaking of foams, let alone bubbles—the macabre investigations of the intimate zone in the first volume are excluded from the quotable realm from the outset; negative gynecology is unsuited to propaganda. The texts have a built-in imitation block that functions reliably under the given sociopsychological conditions. Mere quotation is already a risk for those who quote, and that should remain the case. We can make similar predictions about the treatise on current pampering systems with which, maliciously enough, the third volume closes. It will not seize the masses; even academics feel unease, the serious youth pinch their lips together, and trade unionists would voice concerns if they were to hear anything about it.

To get to the heart of the matter, one must examine the rhetorical figures in which the work-immanent hubris—I will retain this term for now—shows itself. You could call them a modest hubris, if this oxymoron appeals to you. The author, it seems to me, hid the key to his working method in the introduction to the volume *Globes*, in which he derives traditional European metaphysics from the systematic use of the superlative: because the world, owing to its presumed origin in the divine intellect, possesses a round form, one can describe it as existing at the morphological optimum. Thought begins with the principle of bestness, and must attempt in the following to maintain that level—which means remaining committed to the superlative at every step. In this regime, saying what is the case always means formulating what is the highest, the best, the perfect—at least, for as long as one is speaking of the two super-objects, God and the world, along with their political supplements, namely the optimally organized city and the good life in it; as we know, this is what Classical philosophers like most. Judged from its middle part, the *Spheres* work is nothing other than an essay on the superlative that describes its intimate beginnings, its monological triumph, its pluralistic transformation, and therefore...

The macrohistorian: If I may interrupt you too, dear colleague: this view of the matter strikes me as something of a stretch. It is also far too formalistic—you will not hold it against me if I voice my reservations about your deliberations so frankly? Perhaps I am obstructed by my inadequate understanding of the essence of the spheric, but I would argue that this has no bearing on the matter at hand. I note that the trilogy has a topic that runs through all its parts, provided one reads it as the thing it undeniably is: a history book, a grand narrative of the modes of being-in-the-world in the three stages or states of civilization—the age of hunter-gatherers, the agro-imperial age and the technological age. One is shown that these modalizations of being-in-the-world radically differ, and why they do. For whether humans gather around a Paleolithic fireplace in their self-produced language bubble, or enter the protection of shared walls, a royal protector with the power of writing, and his clergy with the power of meaning during the farming period, or inhabit the modern welfare and mass media state, in which the securing of existence was split into public services and private faith options—every case leads to its own very particular findings about the human condition. Each of these situations has its own risk profiles and creates the corresponding security constructions; the history of religion and historical jurisprudence enable us to gain an impression of these. What I wish to say is that all of this unmistakably belongs to the area of content questions—it is part of the history of world pictures, or if you will, empirical ontology. You will forgive me if I state once again that I constantly recognize the schema of macrohistory in this, even if the author draws on it with certain shifts of emphasis.

The foam metaphors strike me as the most productive, in that they present the stages of civilization in a space-analytically defamiliarized way: the loose, evasive character of the original forms of segmentary small societies now becomes more apparent than before—quite as if there had been nothing in the early days of humanity except tiny rogue states, single-minded and self-narcoticized groups that made every effort to avoid encountering strangers. They were followed by the age of tribes, peoples and empires, whose characteristic, aside from the strictly hierarchical structures, lay in its medium density—possibly war, as a historical form of collision, is *per se* the signature of semi-compressed inter-ethnic conditions. Finally, with the transition to modernity, an experiment began with highly compacted conglomerations, and to this day, all we can say about it is that it highlights very different aspects of the anthropological matrix from all previous formations. Modernity, as the author states, is the era of increasing co-fragility; it could, *à la longue*, constitute the transition to post-bellicism. In co-fragile systems one can no longer achieve much with such concepts as independence and autonomy. Where high density becomes stable, the whole of sovereignist reason to date could descend into folklore along with its strategic concepts. One cannot rule out the possibility that an age of cooperation lies ahead, one that will replace imperial logic and disenchant the conventional political collectives, the stirred-up peoples. Because these are phenomena that develop over long periods, we will have to await the judgment of later generations. Then one will see how the nation-state and the fiction of peoples will fare in the next two hundred years. Whether one is justified in postulating a macrohistorical law of growing density, extending to a super-context that embodies a stable final foam, is a question I shall leave open—if it were consolidated, it would be proof that heterodox relationships are coming about between morphology and history. One thinks from a distance of Newton's definition, which states that bodies are denser when their inertia is more intense. World civilization would then be a state of highly integrated, hyperactive inertia. Perhaps people will one day assert that density is destiny.

If I wished to acknowledge a certain innovative energy to the work, I would most readily discover it in the fact that macrohistorical stages are viewed from unusual, inter-phase perspectives. However deep the two major caesuras, the Neolithic and the techno-industrial, may go, what persists through all metamorphoses, as we are shown, is a constantly growing helplessness among humans in the face of their prematurity, their juvenilization, their pamperedness and their chronic need for illusions. Across the board, one sees that privileged immaturity known in philosophical circles as "world-openness"—I assume this refers to the shift from *a priori* to *a posteriori* control systems. Humans would then be monsters that educate themselves and learn new things. In this context, the point makes sense to me that *homo sapiens* is not only dependent on biological immune systems, but even more so on cultural ones. It is, I admit, an attractive defamiliarization to find the good old institutions with which we cultural theorists deal every day redescribed as civilizatory immune systems. It remains to be seen where the different professions will go from there.

The theologian: Allow me to observe that we have indeed returned to monstrodicy, as I alluded to it in passing at the start. As soon as one starts speaking of humans, the extra-human interferes. I should add that, taken with a grain of salt, this corresponds to the state of the art in my field. In the twentieth century, we relearned about God. We now maintain that there can only be unassuming and indirect theory about him—there is no more talk of giving pompous defense speeches for him when confronted with the world's ills. We are more likely to justify nervous systems in the face of the incompleteness of the world. This yields neither positive nor negative, but rather dislodged theology, if I may use this term. If we wish to remain contemporary, we are condemned to anonymity. What we have to say has crawled off into neurological, communication-ethical or immunological exile. I would not be surprised if a younger author from our department one day caught the ball that has been thrown here—this reference to the connection between immunity and community. Taken as a whole, I admit that I feel at ease with the book; it insults me in a way that suits my field. I think I understand why: a reader of Christian/post-Christian observance cannot fail to relate to the reintroduction of space, for space—people had forgotten this for a while—is the seat of the gods. We turn towards the signs of the space, as we once turned to those of the times. After a century of idolizing time, the reminder of the inspired space sounds like a return to our better possibilities.

The literary critic: I disagree, at the risk of doing two things: firstly, depriving myself of the rare pleasure of agreeing with a scholar of God, and secondly, being accused of formalism again. You arrive so quickly—far too quickly, in my opinion—at the content, regardless of whether it is located in the history of culture and worldviews or in the metamorphoses of theology, that you overlook what I call the work of the text; you miss the information stored in the rhetorical constructions. Assuming I am not entirely wrong with my thesis that the author, especially in the volume on globes, wanted to repeat the superlativist and supremacist form of traditional philosophical speech—I was interrupted at that point—then we would have to view the trilogy as a machine for producing parallel systems of exaggeration. These act out their élan in several directions, and it never becomes entirely clear where naïveté ends and parody begins. A hundred years ago, this would have been called dangerous thinking. Even if we can now dispense with such pathos-filled phrases, the question remains of how the text will prevent surpluses of an ideological kind moving over to the social space—our author knows, after all, that one must protect "society" from philosophy even more than philosophy from "society." I see the answer in the literary approach: if we are dealing neither with theology nor a worldview-based totalization—which I very firmly assert—then the text must immanently do away with its own hyperbolic escalations, its uplifts and grand gestures, to the point where it achieves an internal balance between the manic and skeptical tendencies. This maneuver can be expressed in the following equation: upswing minus downswing equals zero—we recall Heraclitus' dictum that the way up and the way down are the same. Naturally one can also replace upswing with enthusiasm, exaggeration or anti-gravity, while substitutes for downswing could be skepticism, parody and gravity.

The theologian: Strangely enough, this does not add up for me. If I subtract the down from the up in my reading, I am left not with zero but with a positive remainder. If you are right, you must explain to me why there is an added value in my reading. Why do I feel edified? Where does the surplus come from? Is it the consequence of a projection if I occasionally look up from the open page in a mood familiar from May devotions or the Whitsun liturgy?

The literary critic: Among analysts, it belongs to the rules of the game to put the reader on the couch together with the book. Normally the subject only projects if the object gives it a point of reference. It could be that the work's baroque writing style strikes a chord—in which case you would be an emotional accomplice to the author as he lived out a cornucopia complex. Personally, I tend towards the assumption that the cheerful tone is leading to a pleasant mix-up on your part: could it not be that something which is actually a new version of gay science is instead reaching you as the good news?

The theologian: Assuming, my dear colleague, that the good news is not masquerading as the gay science as a jest. But seriously: if the concealment can be chosen by both sides, who can really decide what we are dealing with?

The literary critic: Posed in this form, the question is insoluble—and we should welcome that for the sake of our precious liberality. But you are giving the impression, my dear colleague, that you wish to find out how to arrive at the positive remainder you believe you are holding in your hand. If we wanted to make short shrift of the matter, we could conclude the investigation with a reference to sympathy. That would be an acceptable approach, for the fact of sympathy is the best of all good reasons; it amounts to an ultimate justification, and once the feeling has spoken, the *causa* is complete. If, on the other hand, we are willing to continue the examination, beyond emotional oracles, then we must return to the description of the form that I demanded earlier.

I shall begin once again with the statement that the traditional philosophical text was a practice of the superlative. It gives a panegyrical speech, attributing the best qualities to the super-objects God and the world—the third topic of philosophy, the soul, that poor thing in the middle which would later be called "the subject" or "Dasein," is irrelevant for the time being. Thus we must define optimism as a rhetorical form: de mundo Deoque *nihil nisi bene*,[1] or rather: *nihil nisi optime*.[2] First Theory is a hyperbolic advocacy for everything that is the case; it strives to be pure panegyric, the praise of being, the praise of perfection. In popular opinion, unfortunately, optimism is misunderstood as an affective disposition, as if a "sunny temperament" were enough in order to view everything in the most favorable light like a philosopher of the old school. As a mood, optimism actually produces kitsch, facile shortenings of the path to the reconciled image. One is never more remote from insight than when gazing at the fake symbols of peace. Philosophical optimism is a harsh discipline; it is humanly improbable, because it defends the best in virtually impossible situations. It seeks no less than to present the perfection of God and the world in full knowledge of the real circumstances.

Let us take a classic situation like that in Russia after October 1917: the Red Army soldier fires a bullet that might hit my lazy, bourgeois body if I did not run for cover. My understanding forces me to acknowledge that the bullet is in the right, however, for it belongs to history, while my life is merely a celebrating nervous system. The bullet has necessity on its side, whereas I am part of superfluous matter as long as I do not comprehend what is happening on a larger scale. That is genuine optimism; everything else is just teatime chitchat. One will surely concede that such a thesis does not have much plausibility at first; one must contort oneself to accept it. That is why the ancient philosophers already committed themselves to a life of constant practicing. Contortion—it would later be called transcendence—requires training. These are all things that the twentieth century no longer understands, for its contribution to intellectual history consisted primarily in the irruption of the untrained into theory. Because a life in training, called *áskesis*, is equally humanly improbable, the early friends of wisdom in Greece—like their contemporaries, the first athletes—had to appear as friends of effort. Some slept on bare floors, some even refused a pillow. The people are greatly impressed by such things; they love the monsters that have an affair with the improbable. At the height of their popularity, the thinkers based in admiration as acrobats of optimism and undauntedly walked the tightrope of the best of all worlds.

The macrohistorian: This calls for a commentary from an evolutionary perspective. The improbability of what you call philosophical optimism is mirrored, if I am not mistaken, in the improbability of the early agrarian-monarchic life forms. The purpose of the first advanced civilizations seems to have been to conceal their own improbability in their worldviews; only for that reason did they present themselves as manifestations of eternal laws. Just as the first Great Kings had to become specialists in illuminated leadership, the first metaphysicians had to become experts in illuminated empire apprehension. In both cases, the near-impossible behaves like the most undisputed charter. In reality, ontology in its traditional form was a general cartography—and one obviously does not draw maps unless one wants to secure the area. The concepts of being and empire thus reflect each other. Being is the essence of territories, and the empire the administration thereof. When philosophers sang the praises of the best under such titles as *kósmos, ágathon, ón* and the like, they were indirectly praising empire—the pragmatic counterpart of praising princes, of which we know from all cultures which produced kings that it was a school of boasting. The superlative is part of political cybernetics. Thanks to it, power and the happiness it brings are placed at the peak of being—mortals are advised to subordinate themselves to the command from on high, having been convinced that they are lucky in being allowed to serve. Only with the advent of bourgeois civilization did the practice of bad-mouthing royalty emerge, along with the analogous one of attributing nasty qualities to the existent, whether regionally or as a whole. As soon as one takes this liberty, reality presents itself as one great emergency area. The rest is known: the ontology of the optimum, which was assigned an ethics of obedience, was replaced through the awakening spirit of modernity by an ontology of imperfection, which was understandably augmented by an ethics of reform or revolution.

The literary critic: Superlatives are not falling into disuse, then, but rather changing direction. The moderns do not draw different conclusions; they produce different exaggerations. We ourselves have experienced where that leads. The theory of the twentieth century invests in pessimistic hyperboles, inventing a rhetoric of the worst world and the worst god. The result is an age of whining. Please note: the worst one can say of a god is that he does not exist, and the worst that could be said of the world is that only realists have a chance in it. People forget to explain that the true name of a place in which one cannot do anything anti-realistic is hell. Dramaturgically speaking, realists and devils are the same personnel.

The theologian: I suppose I will have to supplement my statement on the dating of the theory of spheres whether I like it or not. This theory is post-hubristic by being post-pessimistic. The positive remainder that gives me pause possibly comes from the unexpected abstention from pessimistic exaggerations of which it seemed we might never rid ourselves. A theory that does not gripe still seems like an import from another planet.

The literary critic: It seems that I will have the forbidden pleasure of agreeing with a member of your faculty after all—and on the most sensitive of points too. The description of the form leads us to the point where the hyperbolic work becomes visible. The author sets one exaggeration against another until they neutralize one another—which should not be mistaken for a sublation. Why this doubling of exaggerations? I see it as a procedure to enable the representation of complexity. For complexity—this much is clear—can never be taken in hand at the first grasp. The languages of the complex come about by dispensing with a preceding simplification.

In the art of rhetoric, we know the figures of abstention from simplification as *correctio* and the oxymoron. With the former, the speaker interrupts himself and replaces a first, unsuitable term with a second, more fitting one. One could say that the entire history of ideas follows this procedure—except that the corrections are spread over several generations.

The other figure came from the observation that some speakers find themselves unable to decide whether they wish to a describe a taste as sweet, or perhaps also a little bitter; as bitter, but also a little sweet—with the result that they take the bull by the horns and turn indecision into a virtue of its own: the sweet-bitter, the double taste, the double attribute. Literally, *oxymoron* means "sharp-blunt" or "burning-mild." When Sappho sings of double-edged eros, she uses the compound adjective *glykýpikros*, formed from *glýkos*, "sweet" and *píkros*, "sharp, biting" to express that love on Lesbos, as it presumably is elsewhere too, is a joyful misery, a delightful torture. From the combination of opposing qualities in a single bundled statement develops a first reference to the composite, the non-simple and non-monochrome. Only when such terms are available can one speak about Chinese sauces and encompassing situations. That is precisely what the *Spheres* books make visible from their location. Reading them, one has the taste of complexity on one's tongue. Ontologically, this approach leads to speaking about the worst-best of all possible worlds; morally, it brings up the evil-good; psychologically, the dispirited-spirited; with reference to the ergonomics of life, the heavy-light, and so on. Needless to say, the enterprise performs the conversion from monotonously pessimistic to sad-gay science—the contemporary form of *docta ignorantia*. The oxymoronic form is present throughout—*quod erat demonstrandum*.

I recall a remark by Gabriel Tarde from his book on imitation that, *mutatis mutandis*, goes very well with the text of the trilogy: in the theater of the present, the sociologist tells us, tragedy increasingly retreats before comedy, while comedy grows in size and becomes ever more dreary and sad. The compulsion to make concessions to complexity after working hours cannot be formulated any better. You yourself provided the keyword "pessimism"—it implies refraining from one-dimensional negativist exaggerations.

The macrohistorian: That's good to hear. Unfortunately, I am unable to adopt your view of things entirely. I would instead like to return to what I consider the objective level and emphasize that for me, it is less a matter of the forms used for statements of complex facts than a matter of the facts themselves—or rather, complex living conditions and their historical unfolding. The book itself is evidently of the same opinion, otherwise it would be incomprehensible why one should read deliberations on the building of space stations, greenhouses, stadiums and urban apartments, even congress centers— deliberations that are augmented by what strikes me as a highly precarious tightrope walk through the psychosocial landscapes of contemporary luxury life forms. For me, all this leads not so much to rhetorical, but rather to moral and civilization-political conclusions.

I think I am understanding the author correctly if I say that he attempts to trace the experiment of modernity, namely the dissolution of agro-imperial forms of life and thought and the liquidation of traditional holistic ethics of obedience and renunciation in the modern individualist cult of ambition and in mass hedonism, in all its extreme consequences. It seems that he wants to answer a question that has barely ever been explicitly posed: what does it cost to present a dense description of the risks involved in modern ways of producing the world, without making concessions to theories of decay or progress? To me, this reveals something of what I call the ethos of the macrohistorian.

Let me explain what that means. Thanks to our probings, which extend back to the time of hunter-gatherers, we have an example—literally only one—of how the great majority of humanity coped with its abandonment of its oldest *modus vivendi*: a caesura which most contemporaries, except for a few romantic doubters and utopian naturalists, admit constituted an evolutionary leap for the species despite its bitter consequences, namely chronic war, exploitation and oppression. There is not a shred of evidence showing a necessary inner bond between the nature of humans and the highly improbable agricultural-imperial way of life—and yet, during this age, many Eastern and Western cultures developed in such a way that one cannot but admit that certain layers or dimensions of human potential were convincingly realized. We cannot dispense with the notion of realization; it is an element of the macrohistorical credo, expressing the historian's respect for temporally and spatially distant ways of life.

As of late, we have been confronted with a second major caesura coming into view, one that radically changes the course of history: I am referring to the industrial-cultural or technological-capitalist awakening, which is easy for us to observe as a brute fact because we are its actors, witnesses and products. As far as its assessment goes, however, we are in an almost impossible situation. Everything we can say about the new *modus vivendi* is colored by ambiguity, in that our situation in the process makes us ambiguous creatures through and through. We are double agents down to the core of our concepts and sentiments, moving back and forth between agro-imperial and techno-capitalist structures. At the same time, we walk the threshold between deep and shallow conceptual worlds, the former metaphorically and observingly constituted and the latter exactly and operationally. I find it interesting how the author correlates depth with the implicit and shallowness with the explicit—this contains an interpretation of transition for which logical traits are more relevant than material ones. It is thus impossible to overstate the fact that we are transitional people and will remain thus for the foreseeable future. We still have the old era within us in varyingly unconscious fashion, and we still think in our background categories like farmers, kings, priests and professors—to name only these representatives of the agro-imperial personnel, every one of whom is an embodiment of *homo hierarchicus*. It is no more than a myth if today's sociologists already seek to treat us entirely as creatures of the egalitarian new beginning—this interpretation would not even be applicable to the industrial fellahin of the American Midwest. All grown languages are yesterday's languages; they keep us in the continuum of convention, and the same applies to the historical religions. Only very rarely do we succeed in producing a sentence that already belongs to the present; no one is ready for the world culture of the future. Even our so-called revolutionaries were only aggressive sleepwalkers between periods. Nonetheless, we are undeniably already children of the change that is driving us to new peaks of the improbable. *Climbing Mount Improbable* would be a good name for what we have been doing since the Industrial Revolution: we climb the peaks of foam mountains that tower at unprecedented heights. For a hundred years we have elected our rulers according to the very young customs of equality, and for a few decades we have lived as urban semi-nomads, supported by a fleet of cars whose scale never ceases to amaze. Only yesterday or the day before did our relationship with the world become that of spending-power owners and long-distance observers. If you accept Nietzsche's characterization of modern individualism, we are absolutely identical to the last humans, who invented happiness and wink.

A just theory is difficult between epochs. I am convinced that such theory would be the antidote to the two temptations of our time—the reactionary and the revolutionary. What I liked best about the *Spheres* project is its epic neutrality, its decisive indecision, its robustness in both directions. I assume its state of floating between periods, its tireless back-and-forth between current and historical perspectives, points back to a methodological principle: even if the memory of the psychocosmic treasuries of the past is kept alive, the author simultaneously takes part in the modern emptying of the inner world. Evidently his account rests on the decision to let the polemic about the course of civilization rest until there is a convincing description both of the new in its own right and of its relationship with the old.

With the modern caesura too, of course, there is not a shred of evidence that there is a necessary inner bond between the elastic nature of humans and the emergent arsenal of life forms in the technological world, there are once again many indications that in the incipient conditions, as in those preceding them, a wealth of attributes of human plasma will be successfully developed. The technological awakening has set something in motion that can likewise be called "realization." There are already classics of modernity, there are already achievements of this age. The coming centuries will extend both lists.

The theologian: But the concept of realization also recalls its opposite. I daresay it is true that countless human lives after the technological caesura will realize themselves in the affluence hothouses, as you say—though much more in there remains hollow and fragmentary than the statistical yearbooks know. But let us assume that the rich societies of the West and the upper classes of the other modernizing nations are indeed distinguished for now and for the foreseeable future as the more plausible locations for the good life: this makes it all the more evident that often enough, the conditions outside the great hothouse can only be described as a complete denial of human potential. One cannot rule out the possibility that this has always been the case, and that the *homo sapiens* archipelago has always had its cursed zones; but the criteria for the conspicuousness of misery have changed. We have the thorn of information in our side. As far as we can tell, three quarters of the human race are excluded from the chances offered by the climate of affluence for the time being. Given the brevity of life, "for the time being" means forever.

The moral implications of this finding are not easy to foresee. They too are a form of oxymoron, but one in which the bitter clearly dominates. If humanity were a higher-order subject, as the idealists put it, one could say that as a whole it is a failed-successful one. But that would be too edifying. The oxymoronic form fails here because humanity, as long as there is no universal cultures of balance, does not embody an actor that could partly succeed and partly fail in a matter. What is monstrous is the schism itself: almost complete success here and almost complete failure there. Success and failure are assigned to situations that barely communicate with each other. They form the harshest difference we can conceive, perhaps even a harsher one than that between life and death. Something of this is probably felt by those contemporaries who have turned success into the last god. There is nothing in the middle. In that situation, who would venture a synthesis that was not a cheap lie? We face a schism that produces unequal halves. For an unforeseeably long time, the chances for successful life will be divided so asymmetrically between the zones of wealth and those of poverty that the tension will inevitably rise to an intolerable level. Nonetheless, we encounter the oxymoronic form once again internally, for whoever lives on our side of the boundary can find the intolerable very tolerable. Those in misery on the other side of the wall often find not only their own living conditions intolerable, but also the thought that a tolerable life would be possible in an unreachable elsewhere. Just as the nineteenth century had its social question, we have the question of exclusion. It is the postmodern form of unhappy consciousness.

Gazing at this gruesome tableau, one recognizes where the utility value of God lay in times of firm faith—just this once, I will be forgiven for speaking cold-bloodedly like a functionalist. In the text *On the Misery of the Human Condition* penned by Lothario dei Segni, the later Pope Innocent III, one finds an illuminating reflection on the metaphysical conditions for balance between the fates of humans. The position of the high lord, he writes, is no better than that of the poorest servant, for like his inferior, he is subject not only to the hardships of his situation in this world, but also the horrors of eternity. Here the scholastic argument that differing finite quantities are all equal in relation to the infinite casts its shadow. One must admit: this mathematics of God had a certain edifying value. By calling on everyone to view themselves as almost-nothings in the face of the monstrous, it contributed to preventing Christendom from falling apart, at least at a symbolic level. Now we lack a similar higher form of arithmetic. We do not even know if God, who emerged from the first caesura, will survive the second.

The macrohistorian: Gentlemen, it seems that the author, for reasons currently unknown, is unable to carry out his stated intention of taking part in our conversation. We should therefore, I think, conclude it without him. At the risk of repeating myself, I would like to say that I personally read the book as an empirical ethicist and scholar of symbol behavior—that is, as a historian. In this capacity I see that an attempt has been undertaken to recount the history of humans as a spatial history—or, more precisely, as a history of spatial creation and spatial organization. This expresses the conviction that the gestures of giving and taking space are the first ethical acts. In the course of studying the book, I developed the suspicion that the author actually wanted to write a universal history of generosity, and presented it behind the mask of a phenomenology of spatial expansions. At times I had the feeling of reading a long paraphrase of the categorical imperative according to Marcel Mauss, whom I so like to quote as one of the remoter patrons of our field· we must come out of our shells and realize ourselves in gifts, both voluntary and obligatory ones, for therein lies no risk.

The literary critic: The same author, in almost classical tradition, distinguished between happiness and wealth by emphasizing that the peoples, classes, families and individuals can each enrich themselves, but can only achieve happiness by learning to gather together around their joint wealth. As a good Frenchman and lyrical socialist, Mauss then quotes the myth of the knights of the Round Table, and recommends it to the moderns as if it were still as relevant as in the days of Chrétien de Troyes. Humanity should become an Arthurian commune that brings the art of sharing up to date with our times, he suggests. The author of the *Spheres* project is presumably not quite so chivalrously inclined, and would probably hold the view that round tables are not enough.

But the roundness of Arthur's table is a start, at least: it hints at how each individual's right to their own adventure can coexist with a shared honor. The spheric is added soon enough—and with it everything else that belongs to these fragments of a language of participation.

Notes

Note

1. Published in English as *Bubbles, Spheres I: Microspherology*, trans. Wieland Hoban (Los Angeles: Semiotext(e), 2011) and *Globes, Spheres II: Macrospherology*, trans. Wieland Hoban (Los Angeles: Semiotext(e), 2014).

2. Martin Heidegger, *Gesamtausgabe*, vol. 27: *Einleitung in die Philosophie* (Frankfurt: Klostermann, 2001), p. 138.

3. Not everyone admits this. One contemporary author declares: "A Mongolian shaman told me that a stone which is dug up from the earth does not calm down for years. I consider that likely." (Martin Mosebach, "Ewige Steinzeit," in *Kursbuch* 149 [September 2002]), p. 13.

4. Cf. Dietrich Mahnke, *Unendliche Sphäre und Allmittelpunkt* (Hall: Niemeyer, 1937) and Georges Poulet, *The Metamorphoses of the Circle*, trans. Carley Dawson and Elliott Coleman (Baltimore: Johns Hopkins University Press, 1966).

5. Jean Paul, "Des Geburtshelfers Walther Vierneissel Nachtgedanken über seine verlornen Fötus-Ideale, indem er nichts geworden als ein Mensch," in *Sämtliche Werke*, Section 2, vol. 2: *Museum* (1814) (Munich: Hanser, 1974), pp. 1005 & 1010.

6. *Spheres II*, pp. 765–959. Since its original publication, the text has also appeared on its own in Italian under the title *L'ultima sfera: Breve storia filosofica della globalizzazione*, trans. B. Agnese (Rome: Carocci, 2002), and in considerably expanded form as *In the World Interior of Capital*, trans. Wieland Hoban (Cambridge: Polity, 2013; German edition published in 2005).

7. Albert Speer, *Inside the Third Reich: Memoirs*, trans. Richard & Clara Winston (New York: Simon & Schuster, 1970), p. 160.

8. Emmanuel Joseph Sieyès, "What is the Third Estate?" in *Political Writings*, ed. Michael Sonenscher (Indianapolis: Hackett, 2003), p. 156.

9. *The Encyclopedia of Diderot and d'Alembert (Collaborative Translation Project)*, article "Encyclopedia," at http://quod.lib.umich.edu/cgi/t/text/text-idx?c=did; cc=did;rgn=main;view=text;idno=did2222.0000.004, accessed 12/2/13.

10. Marshall McLuhan, *Understanding Me: Lectures and Interviews*, ed. Stephanie McLuhan & David Staines (Toronto: McClelland & Stewart, 2003), p. 194. Elsewhere, McLuhan speaks in the same context about the confusion of Catholic centralism through the "resonant space of the oral church" (Marshall McLuhan & Barrington Nevitt, *Take Today: The Executive as Dropout* [New York: Harcourt Brace Jovanovich, 1972], p. 191).

11. *Deus est sphaera infinita cuius centrum est ubique, circumferentia nusquam*: "God is the infinite sphere whose center is everywhere and whose circumference is nowhere." The statement is given context and commentary in *Spheres II*, Chapter 5, "*Deus sive sphaera*, or: The Exploding Universal One," pp. 441–563.

12. Marshall McLuhan, "Playboy Interview: Marshall McLuhan—A Candid Conversation with the High Priest of Popcult and Metaphysician of Media," in *Essential McLuhan*, ed. Eric McLuhan, Frank Zingrone (New York: Basic Books, 1995), p. 258.

13. Bruno Latour, *We Have Never Been Modern*, trans. Catherine Porter (Cambridge, MA: Harvard University Press, 1993).

14. Cf. Roberto Esposito, *Immunitas: The Protection and Negation of Life*, trans. Zakiya Hanafi (Cambridge: Polity, 2011) and *Communitas: The Origin and Destiny of Community*, trans. Timothy Campbell (Stanford University Press, 2010); also Philippe Caspar, *L' Individuation des êtres: Aristote, Leibniz et l'immunologie contemporaine* (Paris: Léthielleux, 1985).

15. Cf. Homi K. Bhabha, *The Location of Culture* (London: Routledge, 1994); Volker Demuth, *Topische Ästhetik. Körperwelten Kunstwelten Cyberspace* (Würzburg: Königshausen & Neumann, 2002); and Hermann Schmitz, *Adolf Hitler in der Geschichte* (Bonn: Bouvier, 1999).

16. Cf. Bruno Latour, "Gabriel Tarde and the End of the Social," in *The Social in Question*, ed. Patrick Joyce (London: Routledge, 2002), pp. 117–132.

Prologue

1. Friedrich Nietzsche, *Thus Spoke Zarathustra: A Book for Everyone and Nobody*, trans. Graham Parkes (Oxford & New York: Oxford University Press, 2005), p. 36.

2. Heinrich Heine, "From Old Fairy Tales," in *Great German Poems of the Romantic Era: A Dual-Language Book*, ed. & trans. Stanley Appelbaum (Mineola, NY: Dover, 1995), p. 139.

3. Cf. *Die Vorsokratiker*, ed. & trans. Jaap Mansfeld (Stuttgart: Reclam, 1987), pp. 244f., Fr. 3.

4. A literal translation of *Träume sind Schäume*, whose more idiomatic cognate would be "dreams are but shadows" or the like. The rhyme also appears in the singular forms, *Traum* and *Schaum*, in the next sentence (trans.).

5. The German word for "scum" (in the physical sense) is *Abschaum*, literally meaning "waste foam" (trans.).

6. Wittgenstein, in a very conventional turn of phrase, said of language criticism that "what we are destroying are only houses of cards" [*Luftgebäude*, literally "buildings made of air"]; cf. Ludwig Wittgenstein, *Philosophical Investigations*, ed. P. M. S. Hacker & Joachim Schulte, trans. G. E. M. Anscombe, P. M. S. Hacker & Joachim Schulte (Oxford: Blackwell, 2009), p. 54e. In the same spirit, and without fear of false pictures, Richard Saul Wurman speaks of a "tidal wave of unrelated, growing data formed in bits and bytes" coming over the denizens of the age of information "in an unorganized, uncontrolled, incoherent cacophony of foam" (*Information Architects* [Zurich: Graphis, 1996], p. 15).

7. G. W. F. Hegel, *Lectures on the Philosophy of Religion*, vol. 3: *Consummate Religion*, ed. & trans. Peter Crafts Hodgson (Berkeley & Los Angeles: University of California Press, 1987), p. 233 (translation modified).

8. Aristotle, *Problemata Physica*, XXX, 1.

9. Ibid.

10. Here I am following the theory of decorum as laid out by Heiner Mühlmann in his seminal book *The Nature of Cultures: A Blueprint for a Theory of Culture Genetics*, trans. R. Payne (Vienna & New York: Springer, 1996), pp. 46–85. More on this below in Section 6, "The Ergotope." For a short version of the Brock/Mühlmann approach, cf. Heiner Mühlmann, "Die Ökologie der Kulturen" in Bazon Brock & Gerlinde Koschick (eds.), *Krieg und Kunst* (Munich: Fink, 2002), pp. 39–54.

11. Especially in the work of the founder of neo-phenomenology, Hermann Schmitz; cf., for example, *Leib und Gefühl. Materialien zu einer philosophischen Therapeutik* (Paderborn: Junfermann, 1989), pp. 135f.

12. Cf. Bart Kosko, *The Fuzzy Future: From Society and Science to Heaven in a Chip* (New York: Harmony Books, 1999).

13. Cf. Gilles Deleuze & Félix Guattari, *A Thousand Plateaus*, trans. Brian Massumi (London & New York: Continuum, 2004), Chapter 14, "1440: The Smooth and the Striated," pp. 523–551.

14. Cf. Ernst Bloch, *Traces*, trans. Anthony A. Nassar (Stanford University Press, 2006).

15. Cf. Gerhard Gamm, *Nicht nichts. Studien zu einer Semantik des Unbestimmten* (Frankfurt: Suhrkamp, 2000) and *Flucht aus der Kategorie. Die Positivierung des Unbestimmten als Ausgang aus der Moderne* (Frankfurt: Suhrkamp, 1994).

16. Cf. Vladimir Jankélévitch, *Le Je-ne-sais-quoi et le Presque-rien* (Paris: Éditions du Seuil, 1980).

17. Cf. Yve-Alain Bois & Rosalind Kraus, *Formless: A User's Guide* (New York: Zone Books, 1997).

18. For the source of this phrase, which Hans-Jürgen Heinrichs coined on the spot in conversation, cf. Hans-Jürgen Heinrichs & Peter Sloterdijk, *Neither Sun Nor Death*, trans. Steve Corcoran (Los Angeles: Semiotext(e), 2011), p. 344.

19. Cf. Chapter 1, "Insulations: For a Theory of Capsules, Islands and Hothouses," Section A, "Absolute Islands."

20. Hesiod, *Theogony*, 154–182, in *Theogony and Works and Days*, trans. Catherine Schlegel & Henry Weinfield (Ann Arbor: University of Michigan Press, 2006) p. 29. In the preceding verses, the didactic poem describes how the primal mother earth, Gaia, tried to convince her children to take revenge on her husband, the despot and child abuser—a task which only one of the hesitant offspring, the youngest Titan, Cronos, was willing to perform; he carried it out by using the "adamantine metal" born by Gaia and forged into a spiked sickle to castrate his father as he lay down with the goddess in the dark.

21. An analogous motif can be found in Indian myths concerning the god Shiva Nataraja; from the god's ecstatically shaken locks comes the waters of the Heavenly River, spraying out in foam. Wherever a drop of foam fell, a pilgrim center sprang up. Cf. Helmut Maassen, "Der tanzende Gott Shiva," in Rolf Elberfeld & Günter Wolfart, *Komparative Ästhetik. Künste und ästhetische Erfahrungen zwischen Asien und Europa* (Cologne: Chora, 2000), p. 113.

22. Heinrich Zimmer provided a free retelling and interpretation of the various traditions in his 1936 book *Maya. Der indische Mythos* (Frankfurt: Insel, 1978) under the heading "Die Verquirlung des Milchmeers," pp. 127–147.

23. *Mahabharata*, trans. William Buck (Berkeley & Los Angeles: University of California Press, 1981), pp. 9f. The name of the poison, *kulukuta*, may mean "peak (*kuta*) of death (*kala*)"; according to Heinrich Zimmer's interpretation, it symbolizes "the quintessence of the world's lethal poison"; after Shiva drank it and kept it in his throat, he received the epithet *Nilakantha*, "blue throat."

24. *The Ramayana of Valmiki, An Epic of Ancient India. Volume 1: Balakanda*, trans. Robert P. Goldman (Princeton University Press, 2006), p. 245.

25. The French edition of the *Ramayana* renders the Sanskrit term for "churning" (*manthâ*), not without some justification, as *barattage*, "buttering." Cf. also *Amritabindu Upanishad*, 20: "Like the butter hidden in milk, the Pure Consciousness [*vijnanam*] resides in every being. That ought to be constantly churned out by the churning rod of the mind."

26. Charles Vernon Boys, *Soap Bubbles, Their Colours and the Forces Which Mould Them* (New York: Dover, 1959).

27. Cf. Sidney Perkowitz, *Universal Foam: The Story of Bubbles from Cappucino to the Cosmos* (New York: Walker, 2000). For a tree diagram showing the different branches of cosmic bubbles, see *Spheres II*, p. 132.

28. Lynn Margulis, *The Symbiotic Planet: A New Look At Evolution* (New York: Basic Books, 1998), Chapter 5, "Life from Scum," pp. 71f.

29. Concerning the emulsion/foam hypothesis of zoogenesis, cf. Harold Morowitz, *Mayonnaise and the Origin of Life: Thoughts of Minds and Molecules* (New York: Scribner, 1985). Concerning the role, only very recently understood, of air bubbles in the gas exchange between oceans and the earth's atmosphere, cf. the report by the oceanographers Grant Deane and Dale Stokes in *Nature* 418 (2002), pp. 839f. The technical applications of the foam principle are surprisingly numerous: its most popular manifestations include bakery products such as bread and cake, which are seldom thought of as constituting semi-stiff foams based on a heat-caused inflation of air cells in the dough. The gesture of stirring dough is the trace of the most everyday aphrogenia. The modernization of construction materials has produced a wealth of artificial foams extending from the familiar elastic PVC foam material to metal foams and other stiff foams based on glass, stone, ceramics and the like. An elegant innovation in the field of foam technology took place through the introduction of aerogel. As far as modern architecture is concerned, it is inspired in manifold ways by the space-forming potency of foam structures. Alongside the geometrism and organomorphism of modernity, these could be described as a third, nature-mimetic path in Modern Age architecture.

30. These are developed in *Spheres I*.

31. The motif of cellular pluralities is taken up again in Chapter 2, "Indoors," Section B, "Cell Building, Egospheres, Self-Containers."

32. Cf. Georg Simmel, "Die Gesellschaft zu zweien" (1908) in *Aufsätze und Abhandlungen 1901–1908*, ed. Alessandro Cavalli & Volkhard Krech vol. 2 (Frankfurt: Suhrkamp, 1993), pp. 348f.

33. Concerning the hearth as a transition point from the almost surreal space of marital dynamics to the physically, socially and cultically concrete space of domesticity, cf. *Spheres II*, Chapter 2, "Vascular Memories: On the Reason for Solidarity in Its Inclusive Form," pp. 187–236.

34. Concerning the radiocratic or imperial space, cf. *Spheres II*, Chapter 7, "How the Spheric Center Has Long-Distance Effects through the Pure Medium: On the Metaphysics of Telecommunication," especially pp. 685f.

35. Cf. Slavoj Žižek, *Welcome to the Desert of the Real: Five Essays on September 11 and Related Dates* (London & New York: Verso, 2002), p. 14; Erica Jong's reflections on the first anniversary of September 11, 2001, which revolve around the claim that the USA had never actually been immune, and that the belief in their immunity was based on pure presumption, read like an echo of this. In a related critical sense, Vilém Flusser defines the concept of *heimat* as residences cloaked in secrecy. Cf. Vilém Flusser, *The Freedom of the Migrant: Objections to Nationalism*, trans. Kenneth Kronenberg (Urbana & Chicago: University of Illinois Press, 2003), pp. 1–15.

36. Peter Fuchs, *Das seltsame Problem der Weltgesellschaft: Eine Neubrandenburger Vorlesung* (Opladen: Westdeutscher Verlag, 1997).

37. Cf. the transitional chapter "Neither Contract Nor Growth: Approaching Spatial Pluralities, Which Are Regrettably Termed Societies."

38. Concerning this term, cf. Gabriel Tarde, *The Laws of Imitation*, trans. Elsie Clews Parsons (New York: Henry Holt and Company, 1903); cf. there also the terms can be found "ray of imitation" (*rayonnement imitative*) and "contagious imitation" (*contagion imitative*).

39. Cf. Volker Grassmuck, "'Allein—aber nicht einsam' die *otaku*-Generation," in Norbert Bolz, Friedrich Kittler & Christoph Tholen (eds.), *Computer als Medium* (Munich: Fink, 1994), p. 283.

40. This can, as developed below, be enacted as self-coupling; cf. Chapter 2, "Indoors: Architectures of Foam," Section B, pp. 529–563.

41. Jakob von Uexküll, *Kompositionslehre der Natur* (Berlin: Propyläen, 1980), p. 355.

42. Johann Gottfried Herder, *Auch eine Philosophie der Geschichte zur Bildung der Menschheit* (Frankfurt: Suhrkamp, 1967), p. 44.

43. Pierre Lévy, *Collective Intelligence: Mankind's Emerging World in Cyberspace*, trans. Robert Bononno (Basic Books, 1999).

44. Quoted in Maurice Besset, *Le Corbusier* (London: The Architectural Press, 1987), p. 98.

45. Cf. Martin Heidegger, *Being and Time*, trans. John Macquarrie & Edward Robinson (Oxford: Blackwell, 1978), pp. 172–182.

46. Cf. Schmitz, *Adolf Hitler in der Geschichte*, pp. 21–31 & 377–404.

47. Concerning the necessity of an integral domestication of humans, cf. Hugh Miller, *Progress and Decline: The Group is in Evolution* (Los Angeles: Anderson &

Ritchie, 1963), pp. 173–213, and Tilman Allert, *Die Familie. Fallstudien zur Unverwüstlichkeit einer Lebensform* (Berlin & New York: de Gruyter, 1998).

48. Cf. *Spheres II*, pp. 795–799, and also Heinrichs & Sloterdijk, *Neither Sun Nor Death*, pp. 220f.

49. Johann Wolfgang Goethe, *Maximen und Reflektionen*, No. 501.

50. Cf. Robert B. Brandom, *Making It Explicit: Reasoning, Representing, & Discursive Commitment* (Cambridge, MA: Harvard University Press, 1994).

51. One of the few authors who took this into account was Karl Rahner, SJ, who wrote in his essay "Experiment Mensch. Theologisches über die Selbstmanipulation des Menschen": "Man must want to be operable man, even if the scale and just manner of this self-manipulation are still largely unknown." In *Die Frage nach dem Menschen. Aufriss einer philosophischen Anthropologie. Festschrift für Max Müller zum 60. Geburtstag*, ed. Heinrich Rombach (Freiburg & Munich: Alber, 1966), p. 53.

52. Cf. below, "Parenthetic Observation: Forced Light and the Advance to the Articulated World," especially the references to Bruno Latour's concept of articulation.

53. Eric Alliez formulates a clear-headed retrospective of the phenomenological constellation and its dissolution in his book *De l'impossibilité de la phénoménologie: Sur la philosophie française contemporaine* (Paris: Vrin, 1995).

54. *Monadology*, Section 61: "But a soul can read in itself only that which is represented distinctly there; it cannot unfold all at once all of its complications, because they extend to infinity." If the pleating of what is implicitly or darkly cognized by the soul extends to infinity, there is no prospect of attaining completely explicit knowledge; this is reserved for God, while the human intellect is granted progress in its awareness of increasing, yet always insufficient explicitness.

55. One can trace the modern defense of the primacy of perception at least as far back as Goethe's critique of the natural science worldview; cf. Albrecht Schöne, *Goethes Farbentheologie* (Munich: C. H. Beck, 1987) and Ursula Schuh, *"Die Sinne trügen nicht": Goethes Kritik der Wahrnehmung als Antwort auf virtuelle Welten* (Stuttgart & Berlin: Mayer, 2000).

56. Heidegger's concept of "enframing" [*Ge-stell*] captures something of the abnormality of facts which are forced to appear, but do not appear of their own accord. It bespeaks a sensitivity to the monstrous in the newly unconcealed, and hence to the violation of the concealed which is forced by research to show itself and, as soon as it comes under pressure to become visible, or under the public eye, means something entirely different from the presence of a natural "thing" in the closer vicinity, or the openness of a conventional landscape for sweeping circumspections.

57. Cf. Marko Zlokarnik, *Scale-up in Chemical Engineering* (Weinheim: Wiley, 2002).

58. Cf. Peter Galison, *Image and Logic. A Material Culture of Microphysics* (Chicago & London: University of Chicago Press, 1997).

59. The strongest form to date of a theory of culture rotated in this manner can, I would argue, be found in Mühlmann, *The Nature of Cultures*.

Introduction

1. Hermann Broch, *The Death of Virgil*, trans. Jean Starr Untermeyer (New York: Random House, 1972), p. 109.

2. These figures are taken from the description in Dieter Martinetz, *Der Gas-Krieg 1914–1918. Entwicklung, Einsatz und Herstellung chemischer Kampfstoffe. Das Zusammenwirken von militärischer Führung, Wissenschaft und Industrie* (Bonn: Bernard & Graefe, 1996); there are slight deviations in the details of locations, time and the amount of gas in Olivier Lepick's monograph *La grande guerre chimique 1914–1918* (Paris: Presses universitaires de France, 1998).

3. Jean-Jules Henry Mordacq, *Le drame de l'Yser: la surprise des gaz (avril 1915)* (Paris: Editions de Portiques, 1933), quoted in Rudolf Hanslian (ed.), *Der chemische Krieg*, third edition (Berlin: Mittler, 1935), pp. 123f.

4. Cf. Martinetz, *Der Gas-Krieg 1914–1918*, pp. 23f.

5. During the war, Fritz Haber (1868–1934) was also director of a department for "gas warfare matters" at the war ministry. As a Jew, he had to leave Germany in 1933, and that same summer supposedly still gave advice to the leaders of the German Reichswehr on reintroducing a gas weapon. After a stay in England he died on January 29, 1934 in Basel, on his way to Palestine. A number of his relatives died at Auschwitz. The memory of Haber's *Tödlichkeitsprodukt* [lethality product], which results from multiplying the concentration of poison by the duration of exposure ($c \times t$), has survived in modern chemistry as Haber's Law. The awarding of the 1918 Nobel Prize in Chemistry to Haber for his discovery of ammonia synthesis triggered vigorous protests in England and France, where his name was primarily associated with the organization of chemical warfare.

6. Quoted in Martinetz, *Der Gas-Krieg 1914–1918*, p. 24.

7. William Shakespeare, *The Merchant of Venice*, Act 4, Scene 1.

8. Cf. G. W. F. Hegel, *Phenomenology of Spirit*, trans. A. V. Miller (Oxford & New York: Oxford University Press, 1977), pp. 355ff. According to Hegel, what realizes itself in terror is the "discrete, absolute hard rigidity and self-willed atomism of actual self-consciousness. [...] The sole work and deed of universal freedom is therefore *death*, a death too which has no inner significance or filling, for what is negated is the empty point of the absolutely free self. It is thus the coldest and meanest of all

deaths, with no more significance than cutting off the head of a cabbage or swallowing a mouthful of water." (Ibid., pp. 359f.)

9. Cf. the German idealistic anarchist Johann Most, who invented the idea of the letter bomb, as well as Albert Camus, *The Rebel*, trans. Anthony Bower (New York: Vintage, 1991), especially pp. 149–245, with an emphasis on the distinction between individual and state terrorism.

10. Cf. Joachim C. Fest, *Hitler*, trans. Richard & Clara Winston (New York: Harcourt Brace Jovanovich, 1974), pp. 128f.

11. As both sides were aware of breaking the laws of war, they refrained from objecting to the use of poison gases by enemy governments. Haber's mistaken argument that chlorine is not a poison gas, only an irritant one, and hence not affected by the prohibition in the Hague Convention, survived into recent German nationalist apologetics.

12. Cf. Jörg Friedrich, *Das Gesetz des Krieges: das deutsche Heer in Russland 1941–1945. Der Prozess gegen das Oberkommando der Wehrmacht* (Munich: Piper, 1993).

13. This effect was anticipated by the large-scale use of high explosive shells. Cf. Niall Ferguson, *The Pity of War* (London: Penguin, 1999), p. 308:"Weight of shell was now supposed to make up for any lack in accuracy."

14. I shall explain below why I consider the mass delusion theory of Hermann Broch to have been the second new science of the century.

15. Richard Hamblyn's monograph *The Invention of Clouds: How an Amateur Meteorologist Forged the Language of the Skies* (London: Picador, 2002) describes the emergence of a cheerful nephology (or, to paraphrase Thomas Mann, a theory of "upper movements") at the start of the nineteenth century. The most important deductions in the human sciences from the phenomenon of war propaganda, and the latter's sublation into noxious mass communication, can be found in the mass delusion theory of Hermann Broch.

16. Cf. Martinetz, *Der Gas-Krieg 1914–1918*, p. 93.

17. Fritz Haber named it thus after the responsible scientists Dr. Lommel (Bayer, Leverkusen) and Prof. Steinkopf (a staff member at Haber's Dahlem Kaiser Wilhelm Institute of Physical Chemistry and Electrochemistry, known in wartime as the Prussian Military Institute). This war gas was also known as mustard gas for its smell, as well as "Hun Stuff" (a popular British derogatory term for the Germans was "the Hun") and Ypérite, after the location of its first deployment.

18. Concerning the non-use of the gas weapon in the Second World War, cf. Günther Gellermann, *Der Krieg, der nicht stattfand. Möglichkeiten, Überlegungen und Entscheidungen der deutschen Obersten Führung zur Verwendung chemischer Kampstoffe im Zweiten Weltkrieg* (Koblenz: Bernard & Graefe, 1986).

19. Cf. Martinetz, *Der Gas-Krieg 1914–1918*, p. 70.

20. Concerning the term "stress shadow," cf. Mühlmann, *The Nature of Cultures*.

21. What is by no means nonsensical, on the other hand, is the organization of police or, if necessary, military measures against defined groups dedicated to the use of violence against institutions, persons and symbols.

22. The chlorine attack was not an absolute premiere in the gas war for the German side either; they had already tested the so-called T12 gas grenades on the Eastern Front in January 1915 before deploying them at Nieuwpoort on the Western Front in March.

23. Exterminism constitutes a simplification of sadism as classically described by Sartre; it is no longer concerned with appropriating the freedom of the other, but rather with freeing one's own environment from the freedom of the other.

24. Poisoning, in both the literal and the metaphorical sense: on August 4, 2002, the late night edition of the ARD news program "Tagesthemen" featured an interview with a young woman on the beach in Tel Aviv who, after a Palestinian suicide bombing on an Israeli bus, asked: "Should we stop breathing?"

25. Quoted in Jürgen Kalthoff & Martin Werner, *Die Händler des Zyklon B. Tesch & Stabenow. Eine Firmengeschichte zwischen Hamburg und Auschwitz* (Hamburg: VSA, 1998), p. 24.

26. Ibid., p. 25.

27. Because a supplement of this kind would have been counterproductive for purposes of human extermination, the hygiene departments of Auschwitz, Oranienburg and other camps were supplied with an irritant-free version of Zyklon B. Cf. Kalthoff & Werner, *Die Händler des Zyklon B*, pp. 162f.

28. Cf. ibid., pp 56f. & 241.

29. Ibid., pp. 45–102.

30. Ibid., p. 109.

31. The combat agent sarin (T 144) was synthesized in 1938 at the I. G. Farben Research Department, directed by Dr. Gerhard Schrader. Its toxicity is over thirty times greater than that of hydrogen cyanide; with sufficiently extended exposure, one gram of sarin would be sufficient to kill up to one thousand people.

32. Cf. Haruki Murakami, *Underground: The Tokyo Gas Attack & the Japanese Psyche*, trans. Alfred Birnbaum & Philip Gabriel (New York: Random House, 2001). The writer Josef Haslinger has offered an Austro-terrorist variation on these events: in his crime novel *Opernball* (Frankfurt: Suhrkamp, 1995), he imagines a building the size of the Vienna State Opera being temporarily converted into a large-scale gas chamber by a group of criminals.

33. Elias Canetti, *The Conscience of Words*, trans. Joachim Neugroschel (New York: Seabury, 1979), p. 13.

34. The tone of *Schädling* is slightly ambiguous, as it is the commonplace (non-polemical) term for "pest, vermin" but literally means "harmful entity," the latter being more condemnatory and militant in its implications—expanded into *Volksschädling*, it denotes a threat to the people (trans.).

35. Cf. Götz Aly, *Final Solution: Nazi Population Policy and the Murder of the European Jews*, trans. Belinda Cooper & Allison Brown (London: Arnold, 1999), p. 245. Hate speech of this kind has only recently been analyzed in a linguistically and moral-philosophically adequate manner. Cf. Judith Butler, *Excitable Speech: A Politics of the Performative* (London: Routledge, 1997).

36. J. G. Herder, *Outlines of a Philosophy of the History of Man*, trans. T. Churchill, vol. 1 (London: J. Johnson, 1803), pp. 24f.

37. Cf. Chapter 3, "Upswing and Pampering: On the Critique of Pure Whim," Section 2, "The Fiction of Deficient Beings."

38. Cf. Friedrich Nietzsche, *Sämtliche Briefe, Kritische Studienausgabe*, vol. 6 (Munich: dtv & Berlin: de Gruyter, 2003), p. 140, letter to Franz Overbeck of November 14, 1881: "this medical meteorology [...] is unfortunately a science in its infancy, and for my own affliction it merely raises a dozen new questions. Perhaps we know more *now*—I should have been at the electricity exhibition in Paris, partly to learn the newest things and partly as an exhibit: for as a detector of electrical changes and so called 'weather prophet,' I am a match for the apes and probably a 'specialty.'"

39. The German word *Luftwaffe* literally means "air weapon" (trans.).

40. Cf. Rudibert Kunz & Rolf-Dieter Müller, *Giftgas gegen Abd el Krim. Deutschland, Spanien und der Gaskrieg in Spanisch-Marokko 1922–1927* (Freiburg: Rombach, 1990); this contains extensive details on the participation of German firms and war chemists in the first example of aerochemical warfare, in which fighters on horseback from the mountain people of the Rif region were overpowered with Lost and gasoline bombs.

41. As early as 1950, Carl Schmitt spoke of modern aerial warfare as "purely a war of destruction"; cf. *The Nomos of the Earth in the International Law of the Jus Publicum Europaeum*, trans. G. L. Ulmen (New York: Telos, 2003), p. 317.

42. One indication of this among many is the deployment of manifest terror agents such as napalm by the U.S. Air Force in the Vietnam War, as well as the dropping of the notorious lung-breaking bomb BLU-82B Commando Vault, also known as Daisy Cutter (a 5.7-ton ammonium nitrate bomb), on Iraqi infantry and Afghan fighters.

43. Cf. Jörg Friedrich, *The Fire: The Bombing of Germany 1940–1945*, trans. Allison Brown (New York: Columbia University Press, 2008).

44. Ibid., p. 310.

45. For a detailed retelling of the events between February 13 and 15, 1945, cf. Götz Bergander, *Dresden im Luftkrieg. Vorgeschichte, Zerstörung, Folgen* (Vienna: Böhlau, 1994), especially pp. 112–231, and also Friedrich, *The Fire*, pp. 358f.

46. For the Hamburg inferno, however, the number of dead is already given as 41,000. To an eyewitness like Götz Bergander, the "official" number of victims of Dresden intuitively seems too low; as a historian, however, he admits that there is insufficient proof for the higher numbers, however plausible they may seem subjectively and in relation to the dynamics of exaggeration.

47. If one includes all those who died of radiation sickness by the end of 1945 or by the first anniversary of the bombing, the final death toll was 151,000 in Hiroshima and 70,000 in Nagasaki.

48. At the commemorative peace ceremonies in Hiroshima on August 6, 2001 the complete death toll, including those who died later due to the radiation (an assertion that loses its plausibility over half a century later) was given as 221,893, of which roughly 123,000 were men and 98,500 women.

49. Andrew S. Gove, *Only the Paranoid Survive: How to Exploit the Crisis Points that Challenge Every Company and Career* (New York: Doubleday, 1996).

50. Ken Alibek & Stephen Handelman, *Biohazard: The Chilling True Story of the Largest Covert Biological Weapons Program in the World—Told from the Inside by the Man Who Ran It* (New York: Random House, 1999) pp. 25–28.

51. Cf. Werner Marx, "Der 'Ort' für das Mass—die Verwindung des Subjektivismus," in *Gibt es auf Erden ein Mass? Grundbestimmungen einer nichtmetaphysischen Ethik* (Hamburg: Meiner, 1983), pp. 63–85.

52. Martin Heidegger, *Country Path Conversations*, trans. Bret W. Davis (Bloomington: Indiana University Press, 2010), p. 74.

53. Hermann Schmitz followed on from the positive content of "dwelling" [*Wohnen*] in his doctrine of "embedding situations"; cf. Adolf Hitler in *der Geschichte*.

54. The paper is available as a PDF file at http://csat.au.af.mil/2025/volume3/vol3ch15.pdf (accessed 3/4/14).

55. Ibid., p. vi.

56. Cf. John Berger, *The Sense of Sight* (New York: Random House, 1985), p. 293.

57. Cf. Jeane Manning & Nick Begich, *Angels Don't Play This HAARP: Advances in Tesla Technology* (Anchorage: Earthpulse, 1995).

58. Ibid., p. 136.

59. Cf. *The Unspeakable Confessions of Salvador Dalí As Told to André Parinaud*, trans. Harold J. Salemson (New York: William Morrow and Company, 1976), p. 182.

60. Ibid.

61. Salvador Dalí, *Conquest of the Irrational*, trans. David Gascoyne (New York: Julien Levy, 1935).

62. Marshall McLuhan, *Understanding Media: The Extensions of Man* (Corte Madera, CA: Gingko, 2003), p. 304.

63. André Breton, *Manifestoes of Surrealism*, trans. Richard Seaver & Helen R. Lane (Ann Arbor: University of Michigan Press, 1969), p. 125.

64. A remark by Gabriel Tarde indicates that this is connected to the "mental revolution" usually misdescribed as Enlightenment: "The habit of taking on faith one's priests and one's ancestors is superseded by the habit of repeating the words of contemporary innovators." (Tarde, *The Laws of Imitation*, p. 245)

65. The philosophical sources of the concept of the unconscious are discussed primarily in the following studies: Odo Marquard, *Transzendentaler Idealismus. Romantische Naturphilosophie. Psychoanalyse* (Cologne: J. Dinter, 1987) and Jean-Marie Vaysse, *L'inconscient des moderns. Essai sur l'origine métaphysique de la psychanalyse* (Paris: Gallimard, 1999).

66. Dalí, *Conquest of the Irrational*.

67. Cf. Thomas E. Graedel & Paul J. Crutzen, *Atmospheric Change: An Earth System Perspective* (New York: W. H. Freeman, 1995), p. 3.

68. Cf. Günter Barudio, *Tränen des Teufels. Eine Weltgeschichte des Erdöls* (Stuttgart: Klett-Cotta, 2001).

69. Cf. Heinrichs & Sloterdijk, *Neither Sun Nor Death*, pp. 330–336.

70. Cf. Rolf Peter Sieferle, *Der unterirdische Wald. Energiekrise und industrielle Revolution* (Munich: Beck, 1982).

71. Cf. Sylvie Joussaume, *Climat d'hier à demain* (Paris: CNRS éditions).

72. Carl Amery and Hermann Scheer discuss the technical and mental preconditions for the transition to a post-fossil energy civilization—and even more about the political and ideological resistance to the same—in their book *Klimawechsel. Von der fossilen zur solaren Kultur* (Munich: Kunstmann, 2001).

73. Cf. the excursus "Merdocracy: The Immune Paradox of Settled Cultures" in *Spheres II*, pp. 321–333.

74. Cf. Claudia Bölling & Rolf Horst, *Schirme. Der Himmel auf Erden* (Berlin: Transit, 1995).

75. Cf. Erich Heck, *Indoor Air Quality am Arbeitsplatz. "Sick Building Syndrome" and "Building-Related Illness": Ein deutsch-amerikanischer Rechtsvergleich* (Baden-Baden: Löw & Vorderwülbecke, 1994).

76. Luce Irigaray, *The Forgetting of Air in Martin Heidegger*, trans. Mary Beth Mader (London: Athlone, 1999), p. 166.

77. Cf. Anja Stöhr, *Air-Design als Erfolgsfaktor im Handel. Modellgestützte Erfolgsbeurteilung und strategische Empfehlung* (Wiesbaden: Deutscher Universitätsverlag, 1998).

78. Cf. Diotima von Kempski, *Raumluft-Essenzen-Zugabe. Ein kleiner Leitfaden über Grundlagen und Anwendungsmöglichkeiten* (Karlsruhe: Promotor, 1999).

79. Cf. Gerhard Schulze, *Die Erlebnisgesellschaft: Kultursoziologie der Gegenwart*, second edition (Frankfurt: Campus, 2005), Chapter 10, "Theorie der Szene," pp. 459f.

80. Walter Benjamin, *The Arcades Project*, ed. Rolf Tiedemann, trans. Howard Eiland & Kevin McLaughlin (Cambridge, MA: Harvard University Press, 1999), p. 221.

81. Concerning the concept of the collector, cf. Chapter 2, "Indoors: Architectures of Foam."

82. Elias Canetti, "Hermann Broch: Speech for His Fiftieth Birthday," in *The Conscience of Words*, p. 11.

83. Ibid., p. 8.

84. Ibid., p. 10.

85. Ibid., p. 13.

86. Cf. Paul Michael Lützeler, *Hermann Broch. Eine Biographie* (Frankfurt: Suhrkamp, 1985), p. 209; the word "gassing" [*Vergasung*] appears in a letter to Ernst Schönwiese from October 3, 1936. It is unknown whether Broch was aware of the development of the new, extremely toxic combat agents tabun (1934) and sarin (1938) at an I. G. Farben research laboratory. A number of contemporaneous authors had likewise made grim predications based on memories of gas warfare, for example Erich Kästner in his poem "Das letzte Kapitel" [The Last Chapter] from his 1930 collection *Ein Mann gibt Auskunft* [A Man Gives Information]: one day in 2003, one thousand airplanes set off from Boston carrying gas and bacteria and kill the whole of mankind, which can only attain its goal of world peace in this manner.

With peculiar concreteness, Kästner gives this death drive satire the date July 13, the eve of the holiday commemorating the Storming of the Bastille; cf. Erich Kästner, *Kästner für Erwachsene, Ausgewählte Schriften*, vol. 1 (Zurich: Atrium, 1983), pp. 219f.

87. Karl Kraus, *Briefe an Sidonie Nadherny von Borutin 1913–1936*, vol. 1 (Munich: Wallstein, 1974), p. 167.

88. Karl Kraus, *Die Fackel, Reprint* (Frankfurt: Zweitausendeins, 1977), issue 261–2, 1908, p. 1.

89. Hermann Broch, *Massenwahntheorie. Beiträge zu einer Psychologie der Politik* (Frankfurt: Suhrkamp, 1979), p. 454.

90. Tarde, *The Laws of Imitation*, p. 76.

91. Elias Canetti, *Crowds and Power*, trans. Carol Stewart (New York: Seabury Press, 1978), p. 86.

92. Broch, *Massenwahntheorie*, pp. 306f.

93. Ibid., p. 334.

94. Broch formulated the lesson as follows: "the fight is against the obsession with victory as such, and if it proves successful, this 'victory over victory' will no longer be a victory in the time-honored sense [...] one could almost say that the usual (and thus very human) rejoicing at victory should henceforth be replaced by mourning over victory [...]." (Ibid., p. 344). As Paul Valéry formulated from a related perspective in 1927: "Europe is strewn with simultaneously erected arches of triumph whose sum is zero." (*Cahiers II* [Paris: Gallimard, 1974], p. 1478) Furthermore, Broch's theses on political somnambulism, organized self-deception and states of mass delusion have been indirectly confirmed by recent American strategic science; it has produced an explicatory form of propaganda by defining the latter as a way for the state to "control public opinion," an indispensable tool to ensure American hegemony. With the outbreak of the Second Gulf War in March 2003, this hyper-sophistic cyber-war concept was tested worldwide in a large-scale media experiment. Cf. John Arquilla & David Ronfeldt, *The Emergence of Noopolitik: Toward an American Information Strategy* (Santa Monica: RAND Corporation, 1999).

95. Cf. Calvin Tomkins, *Duchamp: A Biography* (New York: Henry Holt and Company, 1998), pp. 223 & 374.

96. Ibid., p. 408. The conversation partner is Calvin Tomkins.

97. Concerning the investment of immunitary energies in habitation conditions, which is co-conditioned by this, cf. Chapter 2, "Indoors," Section A, "Where We Live, Move and Have Our Being," as well as Section B, "Cell Building, Egospheres, Self-Containers."

98. Cf. Jakob von Uexküll, *Umwelt und Innenwelt der Tiere* (Berlin: Springer, 1909; second edition 1921).

99. Cf. Esposito, *Immunitas*.

100. Concerning the individualistic tendency, cf. Norbert Bolz, *Die Konformisten des Andersseins. Ende der Kritik* (Munich: Fink, 1999); Tilman Habermas, *Geliebte Objekte: Symbole und Instrumente der Identitätsbildung* (Frankfurt: Suhrkamp, 1999); and Detlef Ax, *"Verwundete Männer": zu vaterloser Kultur und männlicher Identität in den westlichen Industriestaaten* (Stuttgart: Ibidem, 2000); on the collectivistic tendency, cf. Alois Mosser (ed.), *"Gottes auserwählte Völker": Erwählungsvorstellungen und kollektive Selbstfindung in der Geschichte* (Frankfurt, Berlin, Bern & New York: Peter Lang, 2001); Carolin Emcke, *Kollektive Identitäten: sozialphilosophische Grundlagen* (Frankfurt: Campus, 2000); Nikolaus Busse, *Die Entstehung von kollektiven Identitäten: das Beispiel der ASEAN-Staaten* (Baden-Baden: Nomos, 2000); and Günther Schlee (ed.), *Imagined Differences: Hatred and the Construction of Identity* (Münster, Hamburg & New York: LIT, 2002).

101. Cf. Gert Mattenklott, "Sondierungen. Das Verblassen der Charaktere," in *Blindgänger. Physiognomische Essays* (Frankfurt: Suhrkamp, 1986), pp. 7–40.

102. Cf. Donna J. Haraway, "The Biopolitics of Postmodern Bodies: Determinations of Self in Immune System Discourse," in *Differences* I/I (1989).

103. *Certe ignoratio futurorum malorum utilior est quam scientia*, in *De divinatione* II, 23.

104. Botho Strauss, *Die Fehler des Kopisten* (Munich: dtv, 1999), p. 102.

105. Cf. Sven Spieker, "Die Ablagekultur, oder: 'Wo Es war, soll Archiv werden.' Die historische Avantgarde im Zeitalter des Büros," in *Trajekte, Newsletter des Zentrums für Literaturforschung Berlin* 5, vol. 3, September 2002, pp. 23–28.

106. In Messina, as early as 1883, Ilya Metschnikow had already described the function of "devouring cells" (phagocytes) in warding off infiltrations of the organism.

107. Friedrich Nietzsche, *Beyond Good and Evil: Prelude to a Philosophy of the Future*, ed. Rolf-Peter Horstmann & trans. Judith Norman (Cambridge University Press, 2002), pp. 121f.

108. This view was prefigured in the work of Johann Gottfried Herder, whose work *Auch eine Philosophie der Geschichte zur Bildung der Menschheit* contains the remark: "I envy everything that is *of the same kind* as my nature and can be *assimilated* by it, I strive for it and make it my own; *furthermore*, kind nature has armed me with *emotionlessness, coldness and blindness*; it can even become *contempt* and *disgust* [...]." (p. 45)

109. *Philosophy and Truth: Selections from Nietzsche's Notebooks of the Early 1870s*, ed. & trans. Daniel Breazeale (New Jersey: Humanities Press, 1979), pp. 79–97.

110. Cf. *The Gay Science*, trans. Josefine Nauckhoff & Adrian Del Caro (Cambridge University Press, 2001), §344, "'In what way we, too, are still pious" (pp. 200f.) A more moderate version of this insight into the antithetics of life and knowledge can be found in Helmuth Plessner's theory of the "eccentric positionality" of humans. Cf. Joachim Fischer, "Androiden—Menschen—Primaten. Philosophische Anthropologie als Platzhalterin des Humanismus," in *Humanismus in Geschichte und Gegenwart*, ed. Richard Faber & Enno Rudolph (Tübingen: Mohr Siebeck, 2002), pp. 229–239. At the same time as Nietzsche, Gabriel Tarde pointed out the probability of a "sacrifice of [the] free and individualistic worship of hopeless truth to the social need for some common and, perhaps, state-imposed consoling and comforting illusion." (*The Laws of Imitation*, p. 125)

111. *Philosophy and Truth*, p. 57.

112. Nietzsche, *Beyond Good and Evil*, p. 122.

113. Cf. Ernst Benz, *Theologie der Elektrizität: Zur Begegnung u. Auseinandersetzung von Theologie und Naturwissenschaft im 17. und 18. Jahrhundert* (Mainz & Wiesbaden: Steiner, 1971).

114. Cf. "Die elektrifizierte Gesellschaft," exhibition catalogue of the Baden State Museum (Karlsruhe, 1996).

115. Concerning the way in which Pasteur's discoveries contributed to shaping the solidaristic and socio-hygienic thought of the late nineteenth century, cf. François Ewald, *L'Etat providence* (Paris: Gasset, 1986).

116. Cf. Jacques Poulain, *L'âge pragmatique ou l'expérimentation totale* (Paris: L'Harmattan, 1991). It is probably a meaningful coincidence that the most perceptive analyst of modern scientific culture, Bruno Latour, holds a professorship for the "sociology of innovation" at the Ecole des Mines in Paris.

117. Boris Groys, "Werbung für den Kommunismus. 50 Jahre nach Stalins Tod: warum schon damals die Kunst nur Lifestyle sein wollte," in *Die Zeit* 10/2003, p. 38.

118. Cf. McLuhan, *Understanding Media*, Chapter 18, "The Printed Word: Architect of Nationalism," pp. 233–244, and for a classic source, Karl Kraus, "Untergang der Welt durch schwarze Magie" (December 1912), in *Die Fackel, Reprint*, pp. 424f.

119. Tarde, *The Laws of Imitation*, p. 364.

120. Cf. Bruno Latour, *Pandora's Hope: Essays on the Reality of Science Studies* (Cambridge, MA: Harvard University Press, 1999), Chapter 5, "The Historicity of Things: Where Were Microbes Before Pasteur?," pp. 145–173.

121. Cf. Peter Fabian, *Leben im Treibhaus: Unser Klimasystem—und was wir daraus machen* (Berlin & Heidelberg: Springer, 2002).

122. Cf. concerning this Bruno Latour, "Do Scientific Objects Have a History? Pasteur and Whitehead in a Bath of Lactic Acid," in *Common Knowledge* 5, 1 (1996), pp. 76–91. Regarding the term "propositions," cf. Alfred N. Whitehead, *Adventures of Ideas* (New York: Simon & Schuster, 1967), pp. 244f.

123. Latour, *Pandora's Hope*, p. 143.

124. Ibid., p. 144.

125. Arnold Gehlen, *Urmensch und Spätkultur. Philosophische Ergebnisse und Aussagen* (Bonn: Athenäum, 1956), p. 26.

126. Ibid., p. 71.

127. Cf. Latour, *We Have Never Been Modern.*

128. Cf. Alfred N. Whitehead, *Process and Reality*, ed. David Ray Griffin & Donald W. Sherburne (New York: Simon & Schuster, 2010), p. 259.

129. Theodor W. Adorno, *Minima Moralia*, trans. E. F. N. Jephcott (London & New York: Verso, 2005), p. 50 (trans.).

130. Cf. Ernst Tugendhat, *Der Wahrheitsbegriff bei Husserl und Heidegger* (Berlin: de Gruyter, 1967); this study, which arrives at a negative result with regard to Heidegger's concept of truth [*Wahrheitsbegriff*], is a clear example of how the rituals of thoroughness can serve to prevent the better insight through the worse. Hermann Schmitz, working in critical proximity to Husserl and Heidegger, has more adequately reformulated the overly monolithic thesis of "forgetfulness of being" [*Seinsvergessenheit*] into a discrete list of fundamental "transgressions" by the occidental spirit. Unlike Husserl, who named two large-scale aberrations in *The Crisis of European Sciences and Transcendental Phenomenology*—transcendental subjectivism and objectivist physicalism—he arrives at the number four: psychologistic-reductionist, dynamist, ironist and autistic transgression. For each of these, the author outlines a culture-therapeutic correction from the spirit of renewed phenomenology.

131. Elias Canetti, *The Human Province*, trans. Joachim Neugroschel (New York: Seabury, 1978), p. 67 (translation modified).

132. Cf. Martin Heidegger, "Aletheia (Heraclitus, Fragment B 16)," in *Early Greek Thinking*, trans. Frank A. Capuzzi (New York: Harper & Row, 1975), pp. 102–123.

133. A reference to Martin Luther's hymn "Ein feste Burg ist unser Gott" [A Mighty Fortress Is Our God] (trans.).

134. The colloquial phrase *Gott und die Welt* is used to mean "all and sundry" or "anything and everything" (trans.).

135. Horace, *Odes* I.22, in *Odes and Epodes*, trans. Niall Rudd [Cambridge, MA: Harvard University Press, 2004], p. 67)

136. The quoted poem speaks first of the immutability of poetic love, which responds to the climate-independent magic of the beloved.

137. Plato, *Timaeus*, 33 a-c, in *Timaeus and Critias*, trans. Julian Waterfield (Oxford & New York: Oxford University Press, 2008), p. 21.

138. Concerning the origins, development and disaster of the metaphysics of the encompassing, cf. *Spheres II*, Chapter 5, "*Deus sive sphaera*, or: The Exploding Universal One."

139. Plato, *Phaedo*, 61 c2–69 e5.

140. *Hegel: The Letters*, trans. Clark Butler & Christine Seiler (Bloomington: Indiana University Press, 1984), p. 114.

141. The magnetopathic and proto-psychoanalytical wing of these tendencies is recalled in *Spheres I*, Chapter 3, "Humans in the Magic Circle: On the Intellectual History of the Fascination with Closeness." A comprehensive description of the movement as a whole can be found in Bertrand Méheust, *Somnambulisme et médiumnité (1784–1930)*, vols. 1 (*Le défi du magnétisme animal*) & 2 (*Le choc des sciences psychiques*) (Paris: Institut Synthélabo pour le progrès de la connaissance, 1999).

142. Cf. Walter Weiss, *Enttäuschter Pantheismus. Zur Weltgestaltung der Dichtung in der Restaurationszeit* (Dornbirn: Voralberger Verlagsanstalt, 1962).

143. Cf. the outstanding study by Wolfgang Riedel, *"Homo natura." Literarische Anthropologie um 1900* (Berlin & New York: de Gruyter, 1996).

144. Cf. Karl Joel, *Seele und Welt. Versuch einer organischen Auffassung* (Jena: Eugen Diederichs, 1923).

145. Cf. Helmut Lethen, *Verhaltenslehren der Kälte. Lebensversuche zwischen den Kriegen* (Frankfurt: Suhrkamp, 1994).

146. C. P. Snow, *The Two Cultures and the Scientific Revolution* (Cambridge University Press, 1959). Sigmund Bonk's study *Abschied von der anima mundi. Die britische Philosophie im Vorfeld der Industriellen Revolution* (Freiburg & Munich: Alber, 1999), which is instructive for the history of eighteenth-century thought in England, focuses on a period that is too short to convey the long-term opposition between mechanistics and world soul belief. —Furthermore, the two-culture view outlined here is itself lacking a dimension, as modern neo-gnosis, as a form of third culture, rejected both mechanicism and pan-psychism in order to break humans out of the world context altogether and direct them towards the entirely other. This tendency culminated in the work of Karl Barth, who could admittedly only arrive at his *totaliter aliter* theology through a one-sided treatment of tradition, not least by

ignoring cosmotheistic inclusions in the doctrine of the Holy Spirit—though it is unmistakable that a direct equation of the world soul with the third person in the trinity was unacceptable for orthodoxy (see the charges leveled at Giordano Bruno during his trial); cf. Henning Ziebritzki, *Heiliger Geist und Weltseele. Das Problem der dritten Hypostase bei Origines, Plotin und ihren Vorläufern* (Tübingen: Mohr, 1994).

147. Uexküll, *Kompositionslehre der Natur*, p. 355.

148. Cf. below, "Transition: Neither Contract Nor Growth—Approaching Spatial Pluralities, Which Are Regrettably Termed Societies."

149. Jacques Poulain shares the concern about this separation with Arnold Gehlen; cf. Jacques Poulain, *De l'homme: Eléments d'anthropobiologie philosophique du langage* (Paris: Cerf, 2001).

150. Cf. Gehlen, *Urmensch und Spätkultur*, p. 13.

151. Cf. Tarde, *The Laws of Imitation*.

152. Ibid., p. 34.

153. The "or" between "mothers" and "fathers" reminds us that in the majority of early lineage systems, children were only assigned in kinship to one half of the marital alliance—very much in contrast to the logic of kinship taken for granted today, in which every child is bilineally considered the kin of both parents.

154. Concerning the proto-institutional and highly artificial character of unilineal kinship systems, cf. Gehlen, *Urmensch und Spätkultur*, §37, "Blutsverband-Ordnungen" & §38, "Totemismus," pp. 217–230.

155. Aristotle, *Nichomachean Ethics*, ed. & trans. Robert Crisp (Cambridge University Press, 2000), Book IX, 1170 b 10 (p. 179).

156. Cf. *Spheres II*, Chapter 4, "The Ontological Proof of the Orb," pp. 335–439.

157. Cf. Jean-Pierre Vernant, *The Origins of Greek Thought* (Ithaca: Cornell University Press, 1982).

158. Plato, *The Laws*, trans. Trevor J. Saunders (London: Penguin, 1970), Book IV, 678 c (p. 77).

159. Cf. Peter Sloterdijk, "Stimmen für Tiere. Phantasie über animalische Repräsentation," in *Herausforderung Tier. Von Beuys bis Kabakov*, ed. Regina Haslinger (Munich, London & New York: Prestel, 2000), pp. 128–133.

160. Cf. Wilhelm Emil Mühlmann, "Colluvies gentium. Volksentstehung aus Asylen," in *Homo creator. Abhandlungen zur Soziologie, Anthropologie und Ethnologie* (Wiesbaden: Harrassowitz, 1962), pp. 303f. Mühlmann points, among other things, to the example of the Crimean Tartars, a new ethnic formation from the

most varied "ruins of peoples," a "mixture of genuine Tatars and Ottoman Turks, Genoese, remainders of the Crimean Goths, the Pontic Greeks, and probably also fragments of the ancient Iranian tribes of southern Russia ('Scythians')." (Ibid., p. 306) One source of the *colluvies gentium* was the system of clients and metics in the Hellenic polis, who sought to increase their followings through active asylum policies; here lies one origin of the clientelist-mafiotic "state," which can be understood as the dark double of the feudal and the post-democratic state. Mühlmann emphasizes that the *colluvies gentium* era is by no means over: he sees starting points for new forms of ethnogenetic drama in the refugee waves in the second half of the twentieth century. The "imagined communities" approaches of recent political sociology can be informally connected to these reflections.

161. Gilles Deleuze, *Desert Islands and Other Texts, 1953–1974* (Los Angeles: Semiotext(e), 2004), pp. 9f.

162. Building blocks for a critique of genealogical reason can be found in Thomas Macho, "So viele Menschen. Jenseits des genealogischen Prinzips," in *Vor der Jahrtausendwende. Berichte zur Lage der Zukunft*, ed. Peter Sloterdijk (Frankfurt: Suhrkamp, 1990), pp. 29–64; by the same author also "Stammbäume, Freiheitsbäume und Geniereligion. Anmerkungen zur Geschichte genealogischer Systeme," in *Genealogie und Genetik. Schnittstellen zwischen Biologie und Kulturgeschichte*, ed. Sigrid Weigel (Berlin: Akademie, 2002), pp. 15–43; Klaus Heinrich, "Die Funktion der Genealogie im Mythos," in *Vernunft und Mythos. Ausgewählte Texte* (Frankfurt: Stroemfeld/Roter Stern, 1992), pp. 11–26; Pierre Legendre, *L'inestimable objet de la transmission: Etude sur le principe généalogique en occident* (Paris, 1985).

163. The idea of communization through a qualitatively new form of assembly was already articulated by Cicero: "But a public is not every kind of human gathering, congregating in any manner, but a numerous gathering brought together by legal consent and community of interest." (*The Republic*, Book I, 39, in *The Republic and The Laws*, trans. Niall Rudd [Oxford & New York: Oxford University Press, 1998], p. 22).

164. Thomas Hobbes, *Leviathan*, ed. Richard Tuck (Cambridge University Press, 1996), p. 120.

165. Plato, *The Laws*, 903 b, c & 904 b (pp. 364 & 365).

166. *eudaímona theón*, in *Timaeus*, 34 b.

167. *zoon aídion* on, ibid., 37 d.

168. Marcus Aurelius, *Meditations*, trans. Martin Hammond (London: Penguin, 2006), p. 29.

169. Ibid., p. 10.

170. Jean-Jacques Rousseau, *The Social Contract and Other Later Political Writings*, ed. & trans. Victor Gourevitch (Cambridge University Press, 1997), p. 123.

171. Livy, *The History of Rome, Books 1–5*, trans. Valerie M. Warrior (Indianapolis: Hackett, 2006), Book II, 32, pp. 122f.

172. Plato, *The Republic*, ed. G. R. F. Ferrari, trans. Tom Griffith (Cambridge University Press, 2000), Book III, 414b–415d (pp. 107f.). The currentness of this argument is evident in the strong influence of the political Platonist Leo Strauss on the American neoconservatives, who follow their master in declaring the necessity of democratic illusion-management by elites with no illusions.

173. John Rawls, *A Theory of Justice*, revised edition (Cambridge, MA: Harvard University Press, 2009).

174. Ibid., p. 118.

175. Cf. Garbis Kortian, "Une philosophie première pour le dernier homme?," in *Critique*, January 1981, no. 404, pp. 3f. That a renaissance of contractualist theories could occur in recent times is, as exponents of the tendency concede, due not to the contract metaphor's richness in content but to theory-political motives, more precisely the interest in suppressing systemic approaches in sociology and revealing a model capable of carrying a not overly illusory theory of collective action. Neo-contractualism is the supply with which a certain "social philosophy" responds to the demand for an edifying theory for association functionaries and educators. That this is a theory of edification is evident in, among other things, the fact that members of negotiating professions (lawyers, diplomats, trade unionists in bargaining rounds, mediators, social workers, commanders of peacekeeping troops and so forth) can barely recognize their strategically determined practice in the speculations of contract theorists. Cf. Klaus Eder, "Der permanente Gesellschaftsvertrag. Zur kollektiven Konstruktion einer sozialen Ordnung," in Lucian Kern & Hans-Peter Müller (eds.), *Gerechtigkeit, Diskurs oder Markt? Die neuen Ansätze in der Vertragstheorie* (Opladen: Westdeutscher Verlag, 1986), pp. 67f.

176. Another way to stop using the word "social" in the theory of society is suggested by actor-network theory (ANT), which claims to deal only with associations. Cf. Latour, "Gabriel Tarde and the End of the Social."

177. Cf. Georg Simmel, *Sociology: Inquiries Into the Construction of Social Forms*, ed. & trans. Anthony J. Blasi, Anton K. Jacobs & Mathew J. Kanjirathinkal (Leiden: Brill, 2009), "Excursus on the Problem: How Is Society Possible?," pp. 40–52.

178. Ibid., p. 43.

179. Ibid., p. 50. This "as though" (italicized in the original) ensures that the author does not genuinely regress to the socio-holistic position, even if he occasionally falls back on the language game that the "unique nature" of the professional individual "will be that of playing a necessary part in the life of the whole" (ibid., p. 52).

180. Ibid., p. 45.

181. Ibid., p. 47.

182. Ibid. A more radical formulation of this idea can be found in Gabriel Tarde's essay *Monadology and Sociology* (1893), ed. & trans. Theo Lorenc (Melbourne: re.press, 2012), p. 47: "their constitutive elements [i.e. those of all great regular mechanisms] [...] always belong only by one aspect of their being to the world they constitute, and by other aspects escape it. This world would not exist without them; without the world, conversely, the elements would still be something."

183. Simmel, *Sociology*, p. 47.

184. Tarde, *Monadology and Sociology*, p. 28. With this turn of phrase, Tarde anticipates that of Whitehead, who, in *Process and Reality*, understands "society" as a self-supporting nexus between "actual entities"; thus he can speak of a "society of electromagnetic occasions"; cf. Whitehead, *Process and Reality*, pp. 89f. & 92.

185. Tarde, *Monadology and Sociology*, p. 28.

186. Concerning my reservations about the network metaphor, see pp. 235.

187. Ibid., p. 31. Let us note that in his thought experiment about the vertical nation, Tarde abandons the hypothesis of suspended gravity again (otherwise the materials for building the vertical city could not be postulated as particularly solid).

188. Vilém Flusser, "Räume," in Heidemarie Seblatnig (ed.), *aussen räume innen räume. Der Wandel des Raumbegriffs im Zeitalter der elektronischen Medien* (Vienna: WUV-Universitätsverlag, 1991), p. 78.

189. Cf. *Spheres I*, Chapter 5, "The Primal Companion: Requiem for a Discarded Organ," especially pp. 349f.

190. Cf. *Spheres I*, Introduction, especially pp. 45 & 61.

191. The original word *Gesellschaft* can refer either to society as a whole or to company in smaller groups, including pairs (trans.).

192. René Crevel, *Le bien du siècle*, quoted in *La révolution surréaliste. Ein Lesebuch*, ed. Una Pfau (Munich: dtv, 1997), p. 55.

193. Uwe Sander, *Die Bindung der Unverbindlichkeit. Mediatisierte Kommunikation in modernen Gesellschaften* (Frankfurt: Suhrkamp, 1998).

194. Georg Simmel, "The Sociology of Space," in *Simmel on Culture: Selected Writings*, ed. David Risby & Mike Featherstone (London: SAGE, 1997), p. 143.

195. Cf. Immanuel Kant, *The Metaphysics of Morals*, ed. & trans. Mary Gregor (Cambridge University Press, 1996).

196. Novalis, *Blüthenstaub*, no. 131.

197. Cf. Heiner Mühlmann's topological elucidations in his theory of instinctive architecture, in which he distinguishes between the biological systems of space and the spaces of artifacts or symbols, in *The Nature of Cultures*, pp. 47f.

Chapter 1

1. Deleuze, *Desert Islands*, p. 11.

2. Simmel, "The Sociology of Space," p. 141. Cf. also Georg Simmel, "The Picture Frame: An Aesthetic Study," in *Theory, Culture & Society*, 11, 1 (1994), pp. 11–18.

3. Robert Graves, *The Greek Myths* (London: Penguin, 1992), p. 132.

4. Cf. Ernst Messerschmidt & Reinhold Bertrand, *Space Stations: Systems and Utilization*, trans. Tanja Freyer (Berlin & Heidelberg: Springer, 1999), p. 142. The Salad Machine is a more developed version of the Svet cultivator tested aboard *Mir* from 1990 onwards. Growth experiments in weightlessness showed that the Svet plants initially only reached half the height of plants grown under comparable conditions on earth; tests with wheat yielded seeds that were edible, yet sterile—because of overly high ethylene concentrations, as was discovered in follow-up examinations. A breakthrough was made in the field of space plantation biology in the summer of 1997, with the first successful cultivation of germinable mustard plants in space; 1999 saw successful experiments with a second generation of space wheat. Cf. Marsha Freeman, *Challenges of Human Space Exploration* (Chichester: Praxis, 2000), pp. 74–79.

5. Ibid., pp. 109–148.

6. For a description of politicians as containers of collective states, cf. Thomas Macho, "Container der Aufmerksamkeit. Reflexionen über Aufrichtigkeit in der Politik," in *Opfer der Macht. Müssen Politiker ehrlich sein?*, ed. Peter Kemper (Frankfurt & Leipzig: Insel, 1993), pp. 194f.

7. Friedrich Nietzsche, *The Gay Science*, §124, "In the Horizon of the Infinite": "We have forsaken the land and gone to sea! We have destroyed the bridge behind us— more so, we have demolished the land behind us! [...] Woe, when homesickness for the land overcomes you, as if there had been more *freedom* there—and there is no more 'land'!" (p. 119)

8. The cosmonaut Sergei Krikalev in conversation with Andrei Ujică: "Schwerelos um Heimat Erde. Das Leben im All—Das All im Leben," in *Lettre international* 53 (Summer 2001), p. 75.

9. Ibid., p. 74.

10. Thus Barbara Ward's paraphrase in her Fuller-influenced book *Spaceship Earth* (New York: Columbia University Press, 1966), p. 15—the holistic basic teachings of the ingenious engineer.

11. R. Buckminster Fuller, *Operating Manual for Spaceship Earth* (Baden: Lars Müller, 2008), p. 60.

12. Ibid., p. 61.

13. Olafur Eliasson, *Surroundings Surrounded. Essays on Space and Science*, ed. Peter Weibel (Graz & Karlsruhe: ZKM, 2001). Cf. Also Olafur Eliasson, *The Weather Project*, ed. Susan May (London: Tate, 2003).

14. Oswald Spengler, *The Decline of the West*, trans. Charles Francis Atkinson, vol. 2: *Perspectives of World History* (New York: Knopf, 1961), p. 102.

15. One specimen is the camellia house built in 1823 at Wollaton Hall, Nottingham, which is also one of the oldest surviving greenhouses made of prefabricated elements.

16. Georg Kohlmaier & Barna von Sartory, *Houses of Glass: A Nineteenth-Century Building Type*, trans. John C. Harvey (Cambridge, MA: MIT Press, 1991), p. 317.

17. Ibid., p. 314.

18. Cf. Chapter 2, "Indoors: Architectures of Foam."

19. Gerald Stanhill & Herbert Zvi Enoch (eds.), *Greenhouse Ecosystems* (Amsterdam: Elsevier, 1999), pp. 9–11.

20. Bernd Zabel, technical director of *Biosphere 2*, in conversation with Florian Rötzer on September 25, 1996.

21. This scenario has, at least, been rehearsed since the 1920s in both mass culture and high culture; cf. E. M. Forster, *The Machine Stops* (1928), Arno Schmidt, *Kaff, auch Mare Crisium* (1960) or Philip K. Dick, *Total Recall* (1965).

22. A neologism combining the Greek words *ánthropos*, "human" and *nésos*, "island" (trans.).

23. One could also call it nine-layered, except that the image of the layers would suggest a superimposition of levels without any zero point; I have chosen the term "dimension" because it permits the notion that all dimensions branch out from a shared intersection or zero point (a here-now-we network).

24. Cf. Eduard Kirschmann, *Das Zeitalter der Werfer—eine neue Sicht des Menschen. Das Schimpansen-Werfer-Aasfresser-Krieger-Modell der menschlichen Evolution* (Hanover: Eduard Kirschmann, 1999) and Alfred W. Crosby, *Throwing Fire: Projectile Technology Through History* (Cambridge University Press, 2002).

25. Paul Alsberg, *Das Menschheitsrätsel* (1922), newly edited with a foreword by Dieter Claessens under the title *Der Ausbruch aus dem Gefängnis—Zu den Entstehungsbedingungen des Menschen* (Giessen: Focus, 1975).

26. Michel Serres, *Hominescence* (Paris: le Pommier, 2001).

27. G. W. F. Hegel, *Elements of the Philosophy of Right*, ed. Allen W. Wood, trans. H. B. Nisbet (Cambridge University Press, 1991), §187, addition (p. 226).

28. Cf. Arnold Gehlen, *Der Mensch. Seine Natur und seine Stellung in der Welt* (Frankfurt: Klostermann, 1993), p. 154.

29. The motif of relief is developed in greater depth below, in an examination with Arnold Gehlen's interpretation of humans as deficient beings.

30. Quoted in Frank R. Wilson, *The Hand: How Its Use Shapes the Brain, Language, and Human Culture* (New York: Random House, 1998), p. 171.

31. Cf. Wilson, *The Hand*, Chapter 9, "Bad Boys, Polyliths, and the Heterotechnic Revolution," pp. 164–181.

32. Hegel, *Elements of the Philosophy of Right*, § 189, addition (p. 228).

33. Cf. Gehlen, *Urmensch und Spätkultur*, p. 26.

34. Cf. Charles Malamoud, "Paths of the Knife: Carving up the Victim in Vedic Sacrifice," in *Indian Ritual and its Exegesis*, ed. Richard Francis Gombrich (Delhi: Oxford University Press, 1988), pp. 1–14.

35. Cf. McLuhan's media-theosophical statement, quoted on p. 22, about the audiosphere whose center is everywhere and whose circumference is nowhere; the pathos of this thesis lies in the fact that (thanks to electric and electronic media) it is no longer meant to apply tribe-sociologically, but rather world-sociologically.

36. Alongside rural traditions such as march music, the word *Volksmusik* in contemporary Germany refers largely to a more commercialized, pop-influenced variety with a substantial television presence (trans.).

37. McLuhan seriously believed that we were experiencing the rebirth of a global, paradoxically re-tribalized "closed society" that constituted itself as a "product of language, drumming and technologies that speak to the ear."

38. Cf. Adolf Portmann, "Um eine basale Anthopologie," in *Biologie und Geist* (Göttingen: Burgdorf, 2000), pp. 256f.

39. Ibid., p. 257.

40. Ibid., p. 261.

41. Friedrich Nietzsche, *The Anti-Christ*, in *The Anti-Christ, Ecce homo, Twilight of the idols, and Other Writings*, trans. Judith Norman (Cambridge University Press, 2005), p. 13.

42. "In the inward man dwells truth." St. Augustine, *Of True Religion*, ed. Louis O. Mink & trans. John H. S. Burleigh (Washington, DC: Regnery Gateway, 1991), XXXIX, 72 (p. 69).

43. Charles Baudelaire, "One O'Clock in the Morning," in *Paris Spleen*, trans. Louise Varèse (New York: New Directions, 1970), pp. 15f.

44. Cf. Peter Sloterdijk, *Das soziale Band und die Audiophonie. Anmerkungen zur Anthropologie im technischen Zeitalter*, ed. Stephan Krass (Wiesbaden: ZFS, 1994). Concerning the acoustics of the promise, cf. also *Bubbles*, Chapter 7, "The Siren Stage: On The First Sonospheric Alliance," pp. 477–520.

45. Concerning the establishment of individual phonotopes by the alliance of apartment dwelling and sound technology, cf. the section on acoustic self-augmentation in Chapter 2, "Indoors: Architectures of Foam."

46. Cf. Sarah Blaffer Hrdy, *Mother Nature: A History of Mothers, Infants, and Natural Selection* (New York: Pantheon, 1999), especially Chapter 6, "The Milky Way," pp. 121f., and *Spheres I*, Excursus 3, "The Egg Principle: Internalization and Encasement," pp. 323–331.

47. John Bowlby, *Attachment*, second edition (New York: Basic, 2008).

48. One manifestation of this, among others, is the resistance of dogmatic feminists to theories that realistically describe the maternally focused needs of infants. Concerning the incident at the awarding of an honorary doctorate to John Bowlby by the University of Cambridge in 1977, cf. Hrdy, *Mother Nature*, p. 489. Furthermore, the thesis of the occultation of early child abandonment (the "drama of the gifted child") must be qualified by observations that testify to an almost neo-Paleolithically intense mothering and pampering of infants in the First World. Cf. pp. 715–720.

49. G. W. F. Hegel, *Lectures on the Philosophy of Spirit 1827–8*, trans. Robert R. Williams (Oxford & New York: Oxford University Press, 2007), p. 126.

50. Cf. for example *Eurotaismus. Zur Kritik der politischen Kinetik* (Frankfurt: Suhrkamp, 1989), pp. 174–210, and *Nicht gerettet. Versuche nach Heidegger* (Frankfurt: Suhrkamp, 2001), especially pp. 142–234.

51. Plato, *The Republic*, Book III, 414b–415d (pp. 107f.).

52. Friedrich Heiler, *Die Religionen der Menschheit*, ed. Kurt Goldammer (Stuttgart: Reclam, 1999), p. 31.

53. Cf. the similar theses of the epistemo-irenicist Michel Serres: "Does all evil in the world come from belonging? Yes. All evil in the world comes from comparison. And from the wretched glory bestowed by entry into a noble collective elevated above the shared condition." Cf. Michel Serres, *Atlas* (Paris: Julliard, 1994), p. 213.

54. I shall refrain from explaining this perspective with possible scenarios from the current three-way intra-monotheistic struggle.

55. "Where it is well, there is the fatherland" (trans.).

56. Martin Walser, *Ohne einander* (Frankfurt: Suhrkamp, 1993), p. 80.

57. Friedrich Nietzsche, Human, *All Too Human: A Book for Free Spirits*, trans. R. J. Hollingdale (Cambridge University Press, 1996), p. 198.

58. Aeschylus, *Prometheus Bound*, 7.

59. Cf. *Spheres II*, Chapter 2, "Vascular Memories: On the Reason for Solidarity in Its Inclusive Form."

60. Charles Malamoud, *Cooking the World: Ritual and Thought in Ancient India*, trans. David White (Oxford & New York: Oxford University Press, 1996).

61. Gaston Bachelard, *The Psychoanalysis of Fire*, trans. Alan C. M. Ross (Boston: Beacon, 1964), p. 40. Bachelard speaks (referring to Novalis' praise of night) about the following dualism: light and public-superficial distribution on the one hand, and darkness and intimate-exclusive dedication on the other hand.

62. Cf. Emmanuel Todd, *After the Empire: The Breakdown of the American Order*, trans. C. Jon Delogu (New York: Columbia University Press, 2003).

63. Cf. Franz Xaver Bair, "Wärmesinn und Wärmeorganismus. Entwurf einer thermischen Ästhetik," in *Feuer. Kunst- und Ausstellungshalle der Bundesrepublik Deutschland* (Cologne: Wienand, 2001), pp. 463–470.

64. Cf. René Girard, *Deceit, Desire & the Novel: Self and Other in Literary Structure*, trans. Yvonne Freccero (Baltimore: Johns Hopkins, 1966).

65. Cf. *Spheres II*, Chapter 1, "Dawn of Long-Distance Closeness: The Thanatological Space, Paranoia and the Peace of the Realm," especially pp. 176–186.

66. Friedrich Nietzsche, *The Birth of Tragedy and Other Writings*, trans. Ronald Speirs (Cambridge University Press, 1999), p. 20.

67. The concept of the *tiers garant* comes from Pierre Legendre, who places the idea at the center of a reflection on the necessity of a positive passing on of norms—and presents it as a dogmatic anthropology. Legendre's heavily "occidentalist" and patricentric theory of institutions and norms, which can be read as a Lacanian response to Gehlen, naturally leads into a critique of his time that takes issue with the weakening of the functions of the father, the legislator, the superego, the symbolic order, the general obedience to norms and the guarantee-providing third parties in modern civilization. This corresponds to the warning about the omnipresent communicative-consumptive subject that is allowed to do anything and "knows no boundary." Cf. Pierre Legendre, *Sur la question dogmatique en occident* (Paris: Fayard,

1999). Consistently enough, Legendre charges prevailing communication theories with squandering the "symbolic capital of humanity" (p. 72).

68. Cf. René Girard, *I See Satan Fall Like Lightning*, trans. James G. Williams (Leominster: Gracewing, 2001).

69. Girard comes close with a substantial tribute to Nietzsche as the diagnostician of constitutive jealousy, but turns back before reaching the spiritual nub of Nietzsche's ethics of the gift and falls back on the usual theologians' clichés of "neopaganism"; cf. ibid., Chapter 14, "The Twofold Nietzschean Heritage," pp. 170–181. One has to admit that the immanent gamble of Nietzsche's ethical project, namely the combination of disinteresting and re-interesting within a polyvalent type of morality, has yet to be adequately reconstructed.

70. Cf. René Girard, *A Theatre of Envy: William Shakespeare* (Leominster: Gracewing, 2000).

71. William H. McNeill, *Keeping Together in Time: Dance and Drill in Human History* (Cambridge, MA: Harvard University Press, 1995).

72. Cf. the misinterpretation of drill in Siegfried Kracauer, *The Mass Ornament*, trans. Thomas Y. Levin (Cambridge, MA: Harvard University Press, 1995). Kracauer's "critical theory" of modern ballet as an emanation of capitalist conformity displays that school's typical combination of historical-anthropological ignorance and depth-hermeneutical pretension.

73. Cf. Ingomar Weiler, *Der Sport bei den Völkern der Alten Welt* (Darmstadt: Wissenschaftliche Buchgesellschaft, 1981).

74. Concerning the construction forms of the mass-cultural renaissance, cf. Chapter 2, "Indoors: Architectures of Foam," Section C, "Foam City: Macro-Interiors and Urban Assembly Buildings Explicate the Symbiotic Situations of the Masses"

75. Cf. Mühlmann, *The Nature of Cultures*, p. 34.

76. I will only outline the first three of Mühlmann's five phases: local rules, stress and relaxation. Mühlmann's fourth and fifth phases are iteration and degeneration; his treatment of the latter features an interesting reinterpretation of the fascism effect as an encroachment of hooliganism on the state.

77. Heiner Mühlmann, "Die Ökologie der Kulturen," in *Kunst und Krieg*, ed. Bazon Brock & Gerlinde Koschig (Munich: Fink, 2002), p. 52.

78. Heinrich Meier, *Carl Schmitt and Leo Strauss: The Hidden Dialogue*, trans. J. Harvey Lomax (Chicago & London: University of Chicago Press, 1995), p. 70.

79. Cf. Immanuel Kant, *Critique of the Power of Judgment*, trans. Paul Guyer & Eric Matthews (Cambridge University Press, 2000), §22 (p. 123). This leads to a systemic

definition of propaganda: it is a procedure to create the displeasure-based paranoia required for the stabilization of war cooperation groups, and this also supplies the definition of strategic adviser functions: they constitute a meta-paranoid service provided by embedded intellectuals to produce war-assisting paranoia of the first order.

80. For a recent neo-Hobbesian declaration of faith in war, cf. Robert D. Kaplan, *Warrior Politics: Why Leadership Demands a Pagan Ethos* (New York: Random House, 2002).

81. When the imperative of discreet rulership becomes ripe for explication, the concept of "soft power" appears; cf. Joseph S. Nye, Jr., *Bound to Lead: The Changing Nature of American Power* (New York: Basic, 1990). It is thus not a matter of universal inclusion, but of the willing and suitable. Concerning the phenomenon of imperial partial universalism, cf. also below, Chapter 3, Section 9, "*The Empire*—or: The Comfort Hothouse; the Upwardly Open Scale of Pampering."

82. Cf. Franz Joseph Wetz, *Die Kunst der Resignation* (Munich: dtv, 2003); elsewhere, in Daniel Bensaïd, *Le pari melancolique: Métamorphoses de la politique, politique des metamorphoses* (Paris: Fayard, 1997), p. 236, the "chamber music of resignation" and *micromorales* are discussed.

83. For outlines of a philosophical critique of the standard discourses on globalization, cf. Jacques Derrida, *Specters of Marx*, trans. Peggy Kamuf (London: Routledge, 1994); Jean-Luc Nancy, *The Creation of the World, Or, Globalization*, trans. François Raffoul & David Pettigrew (Albany: SUNY Press, 2007); Kostas Axelos, "La question de la technique planétaire," in *Ce questionnement. Approche—éloignement* (Paris: Editions de Minuit, 2001), pp. 15–35; and Sloterdijk, *In the World Interior of Capital*.

84. There are clear parallels with the "conservative revolution" of the 1920s and 30s in Germany; it too was based, among other things, on the political thought figure of a "self-abolition of liberalism" in the face of the state of emergency forced upon it by the enemy. Cf. Ian Buruma, "Revolution from Above" (review of Paul Berman, *Terror and Liberalism*), *New York Review of Books*, April 26, 2003.

85. Nietzsche, *The Birth of Tragedy*, p. 75.

86. Hans Kelsen, *What Is Justice? Justice, Law, and Politics in the Mirror of Science* (Berkeley & Los Angeles: University of California Press, 1957), p. 24.

87. Cf. Fritz K. Ringer, *The Decline of the German Mandarins: The German Academic Community, 1890–1933* (Cambridge, MA: Harvard University Press, 1967).

88. B. F. Skinner, *Walden Two* (Indianapolis: Hackett, 1974), p. 251.

89. Cf. Gernot Böhme, *Am Ende des Baconschen Zeitalters. Studien zur Wissenschaftsentwicklung* (Frankfurt: Suhrkamp, 1993).

90. Cf. Bruno Latour, *Politics of Nature*, trans. Catherine Porter (Cambridge, MA: Harvard University Press, 2009), especially Chapter 3, "A New Separation of Powers," pp. 91f., and Chapter 4, "Skills for the Collective," pp. 128f.

91. The plural of *imago* (trans.).

92. Exceptions to this rule can be observed in the ancestor cults of emigrants, which demonstrates the possibility of a deterritorialized interaction with the ancestors.

93. Émile Durkheim, *The Elementary Forms of Religious Life*, trans. Joseph Ward Swain (Mineola, NY: Dover, 2012), p. 305.

94. Concerning a complex image of the Old Testament God, cf. Bernhard Lang, *The Hebrew God: Portrait of an Ancient Deity* (New Haven: Yale University Press, 2002); on the hermeneutics of the embarrassing Old Testament psalms on enemies and revenge, cf. Erich Zenger, *A God of Vengeance? Understanding the Psalms of Divine Wrath*, trans. (Louisville: Westminster John Knox, 1996). Like the related monotheistic books, the Quran also reads *prima vista* like a litany on the extermination of the infidels, deniers and skeptics; like their Christian and Jewish colleagues, the Quran hermeneuticists have their hands full trying to explain that it is not meant the way it is written.

95. Hence there are many indications that what would later be called superstition is one of the basic forms of the religious mentality: among the Romans, *superstitio* meant something along the lines of "fearful attentiveness in religious matters"—it could be called the neurotic variant of the scrupulous conscientiousness (*religio*) with which the signs, prodigies and omens, as well as the ritual regulations, must be observed. Cf. Dieter Harmenning, *Superstitio. Überlieferungs- und theoriegeschichtliche Untersuchungen zur kirchlich-theologischen Aberglaubensliteratur des Mittelalters* (Berlin: Erich Schmidt, 1979), p. 21.

96. Cf. Johann Jakob Bachofen, *Das Mutterrecht: Eine Untersuchung über die Gynaikokratie der alten Welt nach ihrer religiösen und rechtlichen Natur; eine Auswahl* (Frankfurt: Suhrkamp, 1975), and also Michel Serres, *Statues* (Paris: Flammarion, 1987).

97. Cf. Martin Buber, *Eclipse of God: Studies in the Relation Between Religion and Philosophy* (New York: Humanity Books, 1988); Raimundo Panikkar, *The Silence of God: The Answer of the Buddha*, trans. Robert B. Barr (Maryknoll, NY: Orbis, 1989); and Klaus Schneider, *Die schweigenden Götter: Eine Studie zur Gottesvorstellung des religiösen Platonismus* (Hildesheim: Georg Olms, 1966).

98. Cf. Tarde, *The Laws of Imitation*, pp. 276–279.

99. Cf. Elisabeth von Samsonow, "Was ist der Sex-Appeal des Anorganischen wirklich? Theorie und kurze Geschichte der hypnogenen Subjekte und Objekte," Vilém Flusser Lecture at the Cologne Academy of Media, 2002.

100. Cf. Fred Hoyle, *The Origin of the Universe and the Origin of Religion* (Wakefield, RI: Moyer Bell, 1997).

101. Cf. Tarde, *The Laws of Imitation*, p. 278.

102. "Fear made the gods" (trans.).

103. In the case of popular religious culture, on the hand, one can observe that it has retained the traits of a panic culture to this day; cf. Alphonse Dupront, *Du sacré: Croisades et pélérinages—Images et languages* (Paris: Gallimard, 1987), p. 462.

104. Cf. Heinrich Meier, "Death As God: A Note on Martin Heidegger," in *Leo Strauss and the Theologico-Political Problem*, trans. Marcus Brainard (Cambridge University Press, 2006), pp. 45–51.

105. Max Horkheimer & Theodor W. Adorno, *Dialectic of Enlightenment: Philosophical Fragments*, trans. Edmund Jephcott (Stanford University Press, 2002), pp. 35–62.

106. Cf. 1 Corinthians 12:1–11 & 28–31.

107. Cf. Tobie Nathan & Taoufik Adohane, *L'Enfant ancêtre* (Paris: Pensée sauvage, 2000).

108. *The Aeneid*, Book VI, 851–853. Unfortunately, Anchises says nothing about what the Romans should do if their allies do not in turn show consideration for the hegemon's feelings in contentious matters of foreign policy.

109. That there are exceptions to this rule is shown by, among other things, the circumstances of the canonization of Sor Angela de la Cruz (1846–1932) in early May 2003 in Seville by Pope John Paul II: her body was displayed in the cathedral for several days and drew an immense crowd of people—as if the saints still had the power to stand up to the heroes of Western culture, in this case as classics of brotherly love.

110. Cf. Eric Voegelin, *Das Volk Gottes. Sektenbewegungen und der Geist der Moderne* (Munich: Fink, 1994).

111. For one of the most significant attempts at a xenotopic ethics, cf. Hand-Dieter Bahr, *Die Sprache des Gastes. Eine Metaethik* (Stuttgart: Reclam, 1994). For a critique of philosophical xenobiology, cf. François Laruelle, *Théorie des étrangers: Science des hommes, démocratie, non-psychanalyse* (Paris: Kimé, 1995).

112. Nietzsche, *Thus Spoke Zarathustra*, p. 53. Cf. Axel Honneth, *Kampf um Anerkennung. Zur moralischen Grammatik sozialer Konflikte* (Frankfurt: Suhrkamp, 1994), also Ludwig Klages, *Die psychologischen Errungenschaften Nietzsches*, second edition (Bonn: Bouvier, 1958). While the philosophers of the Thou (like the holists) claim that the I is blindly in power everywhere and has yet to learn the lesson of the other that would enable it to see, Nietzsche emphasizes the thesis that the I is a late

and improbable achievement that must be claimed from the primacy of the other, which has always been dominant—more still, that beings which could authentically say "I" have not yet appeared. What has been and still is called egotism was always the egotism of the other in me.

113. Max Scheler, *Die Wissensformen und die Gesellschaft* (Bern: Francke, 1960), p. 57.

114. Alphonso Lingis, *The Imperative* (Bloomington: Indiana University Press, 1998), p. 161.

115. Ibid., p. 192.

116. Vilém Flusser, "Motive und Grenzen der Kommunikation," in *Kommunikologie* (Mannheim: Bollmann, 1996), p. 261.

117. There are numbers for right-wing exterminism, but none for that of the left. In Hartmut Böhme's essay "Genozid im 20. Jahrhundert. Perspektiven der UN-Konvention von 1948 gegen Völkermord," in *Paragrana. Internationale Zeitschrift für Historische Anthropologie*, vol. 10 (Berlin: Forschungszentrum für Historische Anthropologie, 2001), pp. 124–148, the author cites the results of quantitative and comparative genocide research showing that in the course of the twentieth century, over 161 million people died as victims of terror, mostly as a result of extermination policies against populations by their own regimes; the numbers relating to totalitarian leftist regimes are higher by far.

118. Ludwig Wittgenstein, *Culture and Value*, ed. G. H. von Wright, trans. Peter Winch (Oxford: Blackwell, 1980), p. 83e (translation modified). Note that Wittgenstein's aphorism alludes to the Gnostic-homophilic dream of a society without reproduction, for one can only enter a monastic order, not be born into it.

119. Cf. Günther Ortmann, *Regel und Ausnahme. Paradoxien sozialer Ordnung* (Frankfurt: Suhrkamp, 2003).

120. Friedrich Nietzsche, *Daybreak*, trans. R. J. Hollingdale (Cambridge University Press, 1997), p. 10.

121. Tarde, *The Laws of Imitation*, p. 322.

122. Cicero, *The Laws*, Book I, 28, in *The Republic and The Laws*, p. 88.

123. Cf. Marc Augé, *An Anthropology for Contemporaneous Worlds*, trans. Amy Jacobs (Stanford University Press, 1999), pp. 71f.

124. Pierre Legendre, "Ce que nous appelons le droit," in *Sur la question dogmatique en occident*, pp. 123–152.

125. The German term for "structural engineering" is *Statik* (trans.).

126. Cf. Ortmann, *Regel und Ausnahme*, p. 33.

127. Edward N. Luttwak, *Strategy: The Logic of War and Peace* (Cambridge, MA: Harvard University Press, 1987), Chapter 13, "Armed Suasion," pp. 190f.

128. Cf. Hans-Georg Gadamer, *The Enigma of Health* (Stanford University Press, 1996).

129. Cf. Paul Lafargue, *The Right to be Lazy*, trans. Charles Kerr (Auckland: The Floating Press, 2012).

130. Gehlen, *Urmensch und Spätkultur*, pp. 88f.

131. Cf. Hans Urs von Balthasar, *The Glory of the Lord: A Theological Aesthetics*, 7 vols. (Edinburgh: T&T Clark, 1982–91).

132. Cf. Richard von Dülmen, *Theater des Schreckens. Gerichtspraxis und Strafrituale der frühen Neuzeit* (Munich: C. H. Beck, 1985).

133. Nietzsche, *Daybreak*, p. 19.

134. Dieter Thomä, *Unter Amerikanern: Eine Lebensart wird besichtigt* (Munich: C. H. Beck, 2000), p. 75.

135. Francis Fukuyama, *The Great Disruption: Human Nature and the Reconstitution of Social Order* (New York: Touchstone, 2000), especially Part Two, "On the Genealogy of Morals" (pp. 143–245).

136. Thomas Jefferson's well-known statement on the occasional character of the Declaration of Independence on July 4, 1776 shows that this can be literally true: "Neither aiming at originality of principle or sentiment, nor yet copied from any particular and previous writing, it was intended to be an expression of the American mind, and to give to that expression the proper tone and spirit called for *by the occasion.*"

137. Hegel, *Elements of the Philosophy of Right*, §§ 189–208 (pp. 227–239).

138. Cf. Michael Ignatieff, *The Needs of Strangers* (New York: Penguin, 1984).

139. Cf. Dieter Claessens, *Das Konkrete und das Abstrakte. Soziologische Skizzen zur Anthropologie* (Frankfurt: Suhrkamp, 1980).

140. Cf. Arnaud Spire, *Servitudes et grandeurs du cynisme: de l'impossibilité des principes et de l'impossibilité de s'en passer* (Saint-Laurent, Quebec: Fides, 1997), p. 218.

141. Michel Serres, *The Parasite*, trans. Lawrence R. Schehr (Minneapolis: University of Minnesota Press, 2007); before Serres, Gabriel Tarde spoke of the parasites of parasites (*Monadology and Sociology*, p. 7).

142. Cf. Giorgio Agamben, *The Open: Man and Animal*, trans. Kevin Attell (Stanford University Press, 2004). Gehlen too understood the lifting of the anthroposphere out of the surrounding element as the genuine culture-forming mechanism: "there, nature still has much of the anthropologically fundamental

quality of a 'field of surprise' into which successful practice has built, as it were, neutralized and habit-secured islands." (*Urmensch und Spätkultur*, p. 112)

143. Concerning this term [*Pflanzengenossenschaften*] cf. Friedrich Schnack, *Der Traum vom Paradies. Eine Kulturgeschichte des Gartens* (Hamburg: Rütten & Loening, 1962), p. 331.

144. Thus the title of a 1950 text by Buckminster Fuller on the construction of geodesic domes. Facsimile reproduction in *Your Private Sky: Discourse—R. Buckminster Fuller*, ed. Joachin Krausse & Claude Lichtenstein (Zurich: Lars Müller, 2001), pp. 177–226.

145. One should note that Bruno Latour's knowledge-sociological critique of the exclusion of the expert at an ontological level entails a complementary critique of the exclusion of nature.

146. Hegel, *Elements of the Philosophy of Right*, § 196, addition (p. 232).

147. Cf. Edward W. Said, *Culture and Imperialism* (New York: Knopf, 1993).

148. *Kultur hat weder Kern noch Schale / alles ist sie mit einem Male* (trans.).

Chapter 2

1. Paul Valéry, *Dialogues*, trans. William McCausland Stewart (Princeton University Press, 1971), p. 109.

2. Cf. Hans van der Laan, *Architectonic Space: Fifteen Lessons on the Disposition of the Human Habitat*, trans. (Leiden: Brill, 1983), p. 1.

3. Cf. Christopher Alexander, Sara Ishikawa & Murray Silverstein, *A Pattern Language: Towns, Buildings, Construction* (Oxford & New York: Oxford University Press, 1977).

4. Cf. Introduction above, and also Peter Sloterdijk, *Terror from the Air*, trans. Steve Corcoran & Amy Patton (Los Angeles: Semiotext(e), 2009).

5. E. M. Forster, *The Machine Stops and Other Stories* (London: André Deutsch, 1997), p. 100.

6. Cf. Bernhard Waldenfels, "Leibliches Wohnen im Raum," in Gerhart Schröder & Helga Breuninger (eds.), *Kulturtheorien der Gegenwart. Ansätze und Postionen* (Frankfurt: Campus, 2001), pp. 179–182.

7. Michel Foucault, "Of Other Spaces," in *Diacritics*, Spring 1986, p. 22.

8. The word *Bauer* more commonly means "farmer" (trans.).

9. Martin Heidegger, *The Fundamental Concepts of Metaphysics: World, Finitude, Solitude*, trans. William McNeill & Nicholas Walker (Bloomington: Indiana

University Press, 1996), p. 153. To understand what is meant by the length of the while, one must know that the German word for "boredom" is *Langeweile*, literally "long while"—a reference to the feeling of time passing slowly. Similarly, the adjective *kurzweilig*, literally "short-whiled," refers to an event or activity that seems to pass quickly because it is enjoyable rather than boring (trans.).

10. Cf. Vilém Flusser, "Wohnwagen," in *Von der Freiheit des Migranten. Einsprüche gegen den Nationalismus* (Bensheim: Bollmann, 1994), pp. 45–49 (this section is not contained in the English edition referenced above).

11. Cf. Manfred Sommer, *Sammeln. Ein philosophischer Versuch* (Frankfurt: Suhrkamp, 1999) and Thomas Schloz, *Die Geste des Sammelns. Eine Fundamentalspekulation, Umgriff, Anthropologie, Etymographie, Entlass* (Hamburg: Libri Books on Demand, 2000).

12. Martin Heidegger, "Building Dwelling Thinking," in *Poetry, Language, Thought*, trans. Albert Hofstadter (New York: Harper and Row, 1971), p. 149.

13. Ibid., p. 150.

14. Cf. Hans-Dieter Bahr, *Die Sprache des Gastes. Eine Metaethik* (Leipzig: Reclam, 1994).

15. Flusser, "The Challenge of the Migrant," in *The Freedom of the Migrant*, p. 12.

16. This is most explicit in the bizarre book *Adolf Hitler in der Geschichte* (Bonn: Bouvier, 1999), in which Hitler is portrayed as an installation artist and communitarian director whose talent lay in staging (deceptive) embedding situations of an ethno-communal nature. Schmitz employs the term "embedding situation" as a corrective for what he considers Husserl's and Heidegger's inadequate analyses of the sojourn in the "lifeworld" or dwelling.

17. Ilya Kabakov & Boris Groys, *Die Kunst der Installation* (Munich & Vienna: Hanser, 1996).

18. Ilya Kabakov & Boris Groys, *Die Kunst des Fliehens. Dialoge über Angst, das heilige Weiß und den sowjetischen Müll* (Munich & Vienna: Hanser, 1991), p. 61. Cf. Durs Grünbein's counterargument in his Salzburg speech: "captivity shared is by no means captivity halved; on the contrary, it is multiplied." (Durs Grünbein, *Warum schriflos leben. Aufsätze* (Frankfurt: Suhrkamp, 2003), p. 19.

19. That the zoological exhibition could lead to anthropozoological "human zoos" is shown in Nicolas Bancel, Pascal Blanchard, Gilles Boetsch, Eric Deroo & Sandrine Lemaire (eds.), *Zoos humains, XIXe et XXe siècles: De la Vénus hottentote aux reality shows* (Paris: Editions la Découverte, 2002).

20. Kabakov & Groys, *Die Kunst der Installation*, p. 137.

21. Boris Groys, *Politik der Unsterblichkeit. Vier Gespräche mit Thomas Knoefel* (Munich & Vienna: Hanser, 2002), p. 22.

22. Valéry, "Eupalinos, Or The Architect," pp. 93f.

23. Cf. Acts 17:28.

24. Valéry, "Eupalinos, Or The Architect," p. 94.

25. Ibid., pp. 94f.

26. Ibid, p. 96.

27. Cf. Boris Groys, *Gesamtkunstwerk Stalin. Die gespaltene Kultur in der Sowjetunion* (Munich & Vienna: Hanser, 1988).

28. Gaston Bachelard, *The Poetics of Space*, trans. Maria Jolas (Boston: Beacon Press, 1994), p. 104.

29. Cf. *Spheres II*, Chapter 8, Section 27, "The Great Immunological Transformation: On the Way to Thin-Walled Societies," pp. 951–959.

30. Cf. Hans Hattenhauer, *Europäische Rechtsgeschichte* (Heidelberg: C. F. Müller, 1994), p. 7.

31. Cf. Esposito, *Immunitas*.

32. Nietzsche, *Thus Spoke Zarathustra*, p. 24.

33. Ibid., p. 166.

34. McLuhan, *Understanding Media*, p. 124.

35. This is what the young Le Corbusier had in mind when he wrote in *Toward An Architecture* that "the man of initiative [...] demands that his meditation be sheltered in a space that is serene and solid, a matter essential to the health of elites." Le Corbusier, *Toward An Architecture*, trans. John Goodman (Los Angeles: Getty, 2007), p. 98.

36. Cf. Walter Benjamin's time-transcending (yet also historicizing) deduction of the interior from the intrauterine primal scene, in *The Arcades Project*, p. 220.

37. Concerning D. H. Lawrence's motif of the umbrella which humans spread out above them for their protection, and in which artists cut holes and slits to let in a "draught from chaos," cf. Gilles Deleuze & Félix Guattari, *What Is Philosophy?*, trans. Hugh Tomlinson & Graham Burchill (London & New York: Verso, 1994), pp. 203f.

38. On the phenomenology of the nest, cf. Bachelard, *The Poetics of Space*, pp. 90–104.

39. Cf. Markus Grob, *Tun der Architektur* (Stuttgart: Edition Solitude, 1997), and also Stephan Isphording, *Das kleine Haus für Singles, Paare und ältere Menschen* (Stuttgart & Munich: Deutsche Verlags-Anstalt, 2002).

40. Vilém Flusser carried out this analysis in one of his most active texts: "Das Bett," in *Dinge und Undinge. Phänomenologische Skizzen* (Munich: Hanser, 1993), pp. 89–109.

41. Ernst Bloch, *The Principle of Hope*, vol. 2, trans. Neville Plaice, Stephen Plaice & Paul Knight (Oxford: Blackwell, 1986), p. 722. According to Bloch, the two types crystal of death (pyramid) and tree of life (Gothic cathedral) constitute the extreme poles of "architectural utopias."

42. Ibid., p. 726.

43. Matthew 8:20.

44. John 16:32. "Yet I am not alone, for my Father is with me."

45. Cf. Peter Sloterdijk, "Wie rühren wir an den Schlaf der Welt? Vermutungen über das Erwachen," in *Weltfremdheit* (Frankfurt: Suhrkamp, 2002), pp. 326–381; also Ernst Bloch, *Viele Kammern im Welthaus*, ed. Friedrich Dieckmann & Jürgen Teller (Frankfurt: Suhrkamp, 1994).

46. Nietzsche, *Thus Spoke Zarathustra*, p. 166.

47. Le Corbusier, *Toward an Architecture*, p. 254.

48. Ibid., p. 262.

49. Ibid., p. 266.

50. Edgar Wedepohl, "Die Weissenhofsiedlung der Werkbundausstellung 'Die Wohnung' in Stuttgart 1927," in *Wasmuths Monatshefte für Baukunst XI* (1927), pp. 396f. The contemporaneous press's reaction to the Stuttgart exhibition was, incidentally, almost entirely positive; denunciations only began to gather momentum in 1933, and their effects remained palpable well into the post-war era.

51. Rudolf Arnheim, *The Dynamics of Architectural Form: Based on the 1975 Mary Duke Biddle Lectures at the Cooper Union* (Berkeley & Los Angeles: University of California Press, 1977), p. 146.

52. Bloch, *The Principle of Hope*, vol. 2, p. 734.

53. Georg Simmel, *The Philosophy of Money*, trans. Tom Bottomore & David Frisby (London: Routledge, 2004), p. 517 (translation modified).

54. El Lissitzky, *Russia: An Architecture for World Revolution*, trans. Eric Dluhosch (Cambridge, MA: MIT Press, 1984), pp. 64 & 66.

55. Ibid., p. 65.

56. Cf. Ulf Poschardt, *Über Sportwagen* (Berlin: Merve, 2002), pp. 29f.

57. Cf. Anthony Vidler, *The Architectural Uncanny: Essays in the Modern Unhomely* (Cambridge, MA: MIT Press, 1992).

58. Cf. Robert Kronenburg, "Moderne Architektur für variables Wohnen," in *Living in Motion. Design und Architektur für flexibles Wohnen*, exhibition catalogue of the Vitra Design Museum (Weil am Rhein, 2002).

59. Fuller, "Dymaxion House: Meeting Architectural League, New York, Tuesday, July 9, 1929," in *Your Private Sky*, p. 84.

60. Ibid.

61. Ibid., p. 85.

62. van der Laan, *Architectonic Space*, p. 2.

63. Fuller, *Your Private Sky*, p. 86.

64. Ibid., p. 92.

65. Cf. Adolf Max Vogt, *Le Corbusier, the Noble Savage: Toward an Archaeology of Modernism*, trans. Radka Donnell (Cambridge, MA: MIT Press, 2000), p. 11.

66. *Collected Works of Velimir Khlebnikov*, vol. 1: *Letters and Theoretical Writings*, ed. Charlotte Douglas & trans. Paul Schmidt (Cambridge, MA: Harvard University Press, 1987), p. 359.

67. Fuller, *Your Private Sky*, p. 96.

68. Ibid., p. 98.

69. Ibid., p. 99.

70. Jack Kerouac, *On the Road* (London: Penguin, 2011), p. 121.

71. Véronique Patteeuw, "The Conspiracy Against the City: Lieven de Cauter in Conversation with Richard Plunz," in *Een Stad in Beweging / Une ville en movement / A Moving City* (Brussels: Studio Open City, 1998), p. 230.

72. The construction type known as the "portable cottage" or colonial hut developed in England around 1830; cf. Matthias Ludwig, *Mobile Architektur. Geschichte und Entwicklung transportabler und modularer Bauten* (Stuttgart: Deutsche Verlags-Anstalt, 1998), pp. 20f.

73. Cf. David Weinberger, *Small Pieces Loosely Joined: A Unified Theory of the Web* (Cambridge, MA: Perseus, 2002), Chapter 5, "Togetherness," pp. 95–120.

74. Cf. Jeremy Rifkin, *The Age of Access: The New Culture of Hypercapitalism, Where All of Life is a Paid-for Experience* (New York: J.P. Tarcher/Putnam, 2000), Chapter 7, "Access As a Way of Life," pp. 114–135.

75. Cf. Peter Schefe, "Prolegomena zu einer Agentologie. Magie, Metapher oder Mache?," in *HyperKult. Geschichte, Theorie und Kontext digitaler Medien*, ed. Wolfgang Coy, Christoph Tholen & Martin Warnke (Basel & Frankfurt: Stroemfeld, 1997), pp. 411–432.

76. Bill Gates, *The Road Ahead*, second edition (New York: Penguin, 1996), Chapter 10, "Plugged In at Home," pp. 236–258.

77. Rifkin, *The Age of Access*, p. 121.

78. Reinhold Grether, "Sehnsucht nach Weltkultur. Grenzüberschreitung und Nichtung im zweiten ökumenischen Zeitalter"(PhD thesis, University of Constance, 1994), p. 100.

79. Cf. this volume, Chapter 1, "Insulations: For a Theory of Capsules, Islands and Hothouses," Section B,

80. David S. Landes, *The Wealth and Poverty of Nations: Why Some Are So Rich and Some So Poor* (New York: W. W. Norton, 1999), p. 7.

81. Cf. p. 836n8 above.

82. Cf. Sigfried Giedion, *Space, Time and Architecture: The Growth of a New Tradition* (Cambridge, MA: Harvard University Press, 1941).

83. Where the word "apartment" stands on its own in this section, it reflects Sloterdijk's use of the English word; though it is generally understood in modern German usage, this sets it apart from the usual native term *Wohnung* (which, more often than not, has been translated in this volume as "dwelling"). Compound terms such as "one-room apartment," on the other hand, are derived from *Wohnung* (in this case *Einzimmerwohnung*) (trans.).

84. Cf. Doris Weigel, *Die Einraumwohnung als räumliches Manifest der Moderne. Untersuchungen zum Innenraum der dreissiger Jahre* (Schliengen: Edition Argus, 1996).

85. Tarde, *The Laws of Imitation*, p. 63.

86. Concerning the shared history of serialism, standardization, engineering science and modern war, cf. Peter Berz, *08/15. Ein Standard des 20. Jahrhunderts* (Munich: Fink, 2001).

87. His original statement was: "Proun is an interchange station between painting andarchitecture."

88. Gottfried Semper, *Kleine Schriften*, ed. Manfred and Hans Semper (Berlin & Stuttgart: W. Spemann, 1884; reprint, Mittenwald: Mäander Kunstverlag, 1979), p. 422.

89. The definition of the elementary architectural unit as a cell or habitat atom has, from a constructivist perspective, more potential for development than the attempts of semioticians to understand the smallest unit in the built text as a room which, like a noun, would have to be placed into a complete architectural sentence, that is to say a building. See Frederic Jameson, *Postmodernism, or, The Cultural Logic of Late Capitalism* (Durham, NC: Duke University Press, 1991), pp. 105f.

90. Cf. *Spheres I*, pp. 61f.

91. Karl Marx, *The Eighteenth Brumaire of Louis Bonaparte*, trans. D. D. L. (New York & Berlin: Mondial, 2005), p. 83.

92. Ibid., p. 84.

93. Ibid.

94. Ibid., p. 87.

95. Hermann Broch, *The Guiltless*, trans. Ralph Manheim (Evanston: Northwestern University Press, 2000). The analogous statement: "together they played a game of fading away" (p. 247) is equally applicable to couples and larger social units, extending to the format of nations and alliances of nations.

96. "Un homme seul est toujours en mauvaise compagnie." Paul Valéry, *Idée Fixe*, trans. D. Paul (Princeton University Press, 1971), p. 108.

97. Cf. *Spheres I*, Chapter 2: "Between Faces: the Emergence of the Interfacial Intimate Sphere," especially pp. 192–205; the term "faciality" is a translation of Deleuze and Guattari's term *visagéité* (as used in *Mille Plateaux*).

98. Ibid., p. 203.

99. Canetti, *The Human Province.*

100. Vogt, *Le Corbusier, the Noble Savage*, p. 23.

101.Regarding metabolic nihilism, see Reinhold Grether, "Sehnsucht nach Weltkultur," pp. 98f.

102. Aphorisms from Hegel's wastebook (1803–1806) in G. W. F. Hegel, *Werke in 20 Bänden*, vol 2: Jenaer *Schriften 1801–1807* (Frankfurt: Suhrkamp, 1970), p. 547.

103. Concerning the connection between original high-cultural individualization and silentium, see pp. 357–361 above, and also *Spheres I*, Excursus 1, "Thought Transmission," pp. 263–268.

104. This formulation would appear to stem from Ariel Wizman, a French filmmaker influenced by Lévinas; he uses it to articulate his experiences as a DJ.

105. The term "biophony" is introduced by Avital Ronell in her work *The Telephone Book: Technology, Schizophrenia, Electric Speech* (Lincoln, NE: University of Nebraska Press, 1989), p. xxvi.

106. Cf. the reinterpretation of the Biblical story of Adam's creation in terms of a radicalized dyadics in *Spheres I*, Introduction, pp. 31–44.

107. Cf. the section on the thanatotope and its heterological conversion on pp. 411ff. above.

108. Betty Dodson, *Sex for One: The Joy of Selfloving* (New York: Three Rivers Press, 1996), p.6.

109. Volker Grasmuck, "Allein, aber nicht einsam."

110. The most important advance in this direction was made by Elias Canetti in *Crowds and Power* (the book's original title is *Masse und Macht*, but the word *Masse* has more often been translated here as "masses" [trans.]) by breaking up the concept of the masses into such manifold shadings that the word lost all uniformity of meaning. A further step was taken by Deleuze and Guattari when they introduced the difference between molar and molecular quantities. What I call foams reproduces one aspect of Deleuze's molecularity. Following on from Deleuze and Guattari, Negri and Hardt replace the "masses" with the "multitude" in their book *Empire*. In the theory-comprehending remainder of the political left too, then, the ideology of the masses should now be a thing of the past.

111. Cf. Emil Kaufmann, "Architektonische Entwürfe aus der Zeit der Französischen Revolution," in *Zeitschrift für bildende Kunst* 63 (1929/30), pp. 38–46; also Antonio Hernandez, *Grundzüge einer Ideengeschichte der französischen Architekturtheorie von 1560–1800* (PhD thesis, University of Basel, 1972). The term revolutionary architecture is misleading not only in chronological terms but also in substance, as the corresponding projects are scarcely connected to the ideas of 1789—whereas they show unmistakable traces of Masonic, Pythagorean and Platonic motifs.

112. Concerning the view among conservatives that the time should never have become ripe, cf. Hans Sedlmayer, "Die Kugel als Gebäude, oder: Das Bodenlose," in *Das Werk des Künstlers* 1 (1939/40), pp. 279–310, and also in Klaus Jan Philipp (ed.), *Revolutionsarchitektur* (Brunswick & Wiesbaden: Friedrich Vieweg & Sohn, 1990), pp. 125–154.

113. Quoted in *Proceedings of the Bunker Hill Monument Association at the Annual Meeting* (Concord, NH: The Rumford Press, 1914), p. 50.

114. Cf. Hans Christian Harten, *Transformation und Utopie des Raums in der Französischen Revolution. Von der Zerstörung der Königsstatuen zur republikanischen Idealstadt* (Brunswick & Wiesbaden: Friedrich Vieweg & Sohn, 1994), pp. 213–217.

115. Quoted in D. G. Wright, *Revolution and Terror in France 1789–1795* (London: Longman, 1990), p. 122.

116. Harten, *Transformation und Utopie des Raums in der Französischen Revolution*, pp. 20–29.

117. Cf. Mona Ozouf, *Das Pantheon, Freiheit, Gleichheit, Brüderlichkeit*, trans. Hans Thill (Berlin: Wagenbach, 1996), pp. 7–38.

118. Cf. Eduard Pommier, "Der Louvre als Ruhestätte der Kunst der Welt, " in Gottfried Fliedl, *Die Erfindung des Museums. Anfänge der bürgerlichen Museumsidee in der Französischen Revolution* (Vienna: Turia & Kant, 1996), pp. 7–25.

119. Cf. Mona Ozouf, *Das Pantheon*, p. 31.

120. Vilém Flusser connects the type "amphitheater discourses" to the concept of totalitarianism in *Kommunikologie* (cf. pp. 27f.).

121. Already on June 12, 1790, during the preparations for the Festival of the Federation, Marat had agitated against the bogus unity in his publication *L'ami du people*: "They are lulling you with the words 'peace' and 'union' while secretly preparing the war against us." The true friends of the fatherland therefore had to exclude both the indifferent and the cowards and traitors from the celebration. Marat thinks exclusively in moral and psychopolitical classes, not yet in ones defined by their "position in the production process."

122. Cf. Esteban Buch, *Beethoven's Ninth: A Political History*, trans. Richard Miller (Chicago & London: University of Chicago Press, 2003), Part 1, "The Birth of Modern Political Music," pp. 9–108.

123. The distinction between public gatherings in closed spaces and those in the "open air" remains significant both in Article 8 of the German constitution and in the law on assembly, as the principle that all Germans have the right to assemble without registration or permission if peaceful and unarmed can be legally restricted for open-air gatherings. Cf. Helmut Ridder, Michael Breitbach, Ulli Rühl & Frank Steinmeier, *Versammlungsrecht. Kommentar* (Baden-Baden: Nomos, 1992); also Martin Quilisch, *Die demokratische Versammlung. Zur Rechtsnatur der Ordnungsgewalt des Leiters öffentlicher Versammlungen—Zugleich ein Beitrag zu einer Theorie der Versammlungsfreiheit* (Berlin: Duncker & Humblot, 1970).

124. That the supporters of the early Olympic movement were aware of its renaissance character is shown by, among other sources, the text *Renaissance Physique* (Paris, 1888) by the French sports educator Philippe Daryl. Concerning the ancient circus system, cf. Karl-Wilhelm Weeber, *Panem et circenses. Massenunterhaltung als Politik im alten Rom* (Mainz: Philipp von Zabern, 1994); Paul Veyne, *Bread and Circuses: Historical Sociology and Political Pluralism*, trans. Brian Pearce (London:

Penguin, 1990); and Clemens Heucke, *Circus und Hippodrom als politischer Raum* (Hildesheim, Zurich & New York: Olms-Weidmann, 1994).

125. Gunter Gebauer, "Olypia als Utopie," in Gunter Gebauer (ed.), *Olympische Spiele—die andere Utopie der Moderne. Olympia zwischen Kult und Droge* (Frankfurt: Suhrkamp, 1996), p. 10.

126. Cf. Klaus Deinet, *Die mimetische Revolution oder Die französische Linke und die Re-Inszenierung der Französischen Revolution im neunzehnten Jahrhundert (1830–1871)* (Stuttgart: J. Thorbeke, 2001); also François Furet, *1789—Jenseits des Mythos* (Hamburg: Junius, 1989).

127. Canetti, *Crowds and Power*, pp. 49f.

128. Ibid., pp. 27f.

129. Concerning the German tradition, cf. George L. Mosse, *The Nationalization of the Masses: Political Symbolism and Mass Movements in Germany from the Napoleonic Wars Through the Third Reich* (Ithaca: Cornell University Press, 1991).

130. It has, at least, proved possible to point out that in the USA of today, going for walks, normally a somewhat un-American activity, can best be practiced in shopping malls: this is also a transformation of the flaneur. Cf. Arthur Kroker, Marilouise Kroker & David Cook, *Panic Encyclopedia: The Definitive Guide to the Postmodern Scene* (New York: St. Martin's Press, 1989).

131. The name of this festival venue literally means "rock riding school" (trans.).

132. The only notable exception: Albert Speer's plans for the German Stadium on the Nuremberg Rally grounds, which was to serve as the ultimate location for pan-Germanic Olympic games, featured a Greek-styled U-shaped complex almost 330 feet high with capacity of 400,000 seats. The construction work did not get beyond the excavation of the foundation pit, which was later turned into an artificial lake. According to Alex Scobie in *Hitler's State Architecture: The Impact of Classical Antiquity* (University Park: Pennsylvania State University Press, 1990), pp. 79f., this project too had more Roman than Greek elements. Speer's autobiography confirms this interpretation, though he also refers to his impressions of the restored Panathenaic Stadium he gathered on his trip to Greece in 1935. Cf. Speer, *Inside the Third Reich*, p. 106.

133. Concerning agonal *différance*, cf. *Spheres II*, Excursus 1, "Dying Later in the Amphitheater: On Postponement, the Roman Way," pp. 307–320.

134. Spengler, *The Decline of the West*, vol. 1: *Form and Actuality*, p. 35, note 1.

135. Cf. Thomas Schmidt, *Werner March: Architekt des Olympia-Stadions, 1894–1976* (Basel, Berlin & Boston: Birkhäuser, 1992), p. 48.

136. According to Speer, Hitler wanted to cancel the Olympic Games after being presented with March's plans because he refused to enter "such a glass box": in the original sketch, the interstices of the concrete skeleton were meant to be glazed. The Maifeld was only used on rare occasions, for example the state visit by Mussolini in September 1937, when the whole Reich Sports Field was flooded by 1 million people.

137. Cf. Thymian Bussemer, *Propaganda und Populärkultur. Konstruierte Erlebniswelten im Nationalsozialismus* (Wiesbaden: Deutscher Universitäts-Verlag, 2000), p. 133.

138. For a contextualization of the Nuremberg ensemble in terms of architectural and cult history, cf. Yvonne Karow, *Deutsches Opfer. Kultische Selbstauslöschung auf den Reichsparteitagen der NSDAP* (Berlin: Akademie, 1997), especially pp. 33–91.

139. Norman H. Baynes (ed.), *The Speeches of Adolf Hitler, 1922–1939*, vol. 1 (Oxford & New York: Oxford University Press, 1942), pp. 206f.

140. Quoted in Karow, *Deutsches Opfer*, p. 88.

141. Cf. Walter & Thomas Meyer-Bohe, *Bauten für Schulungen, Tagungen, Kongresse* (Leinfelden-Echterdingen: Alexander Koch, 1983). Cf. There are also the ideas for a theory of congress popularity: "In every period, particular building projects are in the foreground. After the Second World War it was housing construction, and this was followed in waves by hospital, school and university construction. Today the emphasis is on exhibition buildings—from museums to congress halls—and, connected to that, buildings for advanced training."

142. On pp. 1198–1244 of *Der M+A Messeplaner. Messen & Ausstellungen International, 83. Jahrgang, 2002* (Frankfurt: M+A Verlag für Messen, Ausstellungen und Kongresse, 2002), under the title "Facilitäten für Kongresse und Events," there is an overview of the facilities and services offered by 144 congress centers in 110 German-speaking cities, each with a range of 10 to 30 large halls, festival halls, conference rooms, lounges, seminar rooms, clubs, press rooms etc. with between 12 and 10,000 seats.

For an indication of how far the technical explication of conference activities in professionally administered collectors has progressed, cf. Klaus Goschmann, *Medien am Point of Interest: Arbeitslexikon Messen, Ausstellungen, Events, Kongresse, Tagungen, Incentives, Sponsoring* (Mannheim: FairCon, 2000). One learns from it, among other things, that floors in conference rooms should meet the minimum requirements of low flammability (as laid out in DIN 4102 Part 1 Class B1); that the German Society for the Support and Development of the Seminar and Conference Industry (DeGefest), an interest group of providers in the conference business (which holds its own annual meeting); that the room climate in conference rooms must follow the standards laid out in DIN 15906 for workplaces; and that in no-smoking conference rooms, a stream of outside air of at least 20 cubic meters per hour per person must be supplied.

143. Cf. Elisabeth von Samsonow, "Touch Down and Take Off. Entwurf einer Philosophie vom (Bau)Grund," inaugural lecture at the Vienna Academy of Fine Arts (Vienna, 1996), in Architektur und Bau Forum 1/1997.

144. "Another city for another life" (trans.).

145. Cf. Guy Debord, "Report on the Construction of Situations," in *Guy Debord and the Situationist International: Texts and Documents*, ed. Tom McDonough (Cambridge, MA: MIT Press, 2004), pp. 44f.

146. Mark Wigley, *Constant's New Babylon: The Hyper-Architecture of Desire* (Rotterdam: 010 Publishers, 1998), p. 13.

147. Georg Simmel, "The Concept and Tragedy of Culture," in *Simmel on Culture*, pp. 55–75.

148. Guy Debord wrote in 1957: "The most general aim must be to broaden the nonmediocre portion of life, to reduce its empty moments as much as possible. It may thus be spoken of as an enterprise of human life's quantitative increase, more serious than the biological processes currently being studied." (*Guy Debord and the Situationist International*, p. 45)

149. Concerning this triad, cf. Chapter 1, "Insulations: For a Theory of Capsules, Islands and Hothouses."

150. Lieven de Cauter, "The Capsular City," in Neil Leach (ed.), *The Hieroglyphics of Space* (London: Routledge, 2002), pp. 271–280.

Chapter 3

1. John Kenneth Galbraith, *The Affluent Society* (Boston: Houghton Mifflin, 1958), pp. 2 & 5.

2. Alexis de Tocqueville, *Democracy in America*, trans. Arthur Goldhammer (New York: Library of America, 2004).

3. Cf. Alfred Weber, *Kulturgeschichte als Kultursoziologie* (Munich: Piper, 1960), p. 415.

4. The phrase appears in the notorious "Occasional Discourse on the Negro Question," published in *Frazer's Magazine* (1849), which provoked opposition from both liberals and Christian abolitionists and cost Carlyle his friendship with John Stuart Mill.

5. Or those who could only be helped in the context of Christian charity or civil philanthropy; cf. Bronislaw Geremek, *Poverty: A History*, trans. Agnreszka Kolakowska (New York: Wiley, 1991).

6. Cf. Adorno, *Minima Moralia*, p. 15: "The melancholy science from which I make this offering to my friend relates to a region that from time immemorial was regarded as the true field of philosophy [...]: the teaching of the good life."

7. Eric Hobsbawm, *The Age of Extremes: The Short Twentieth Century, 1914–1991* (London: Michael Joseph, 1994). One should not omit to mention that the success of the catchphrase "age of extremes" stems primarily from its neutralizing tendency: it is attractive because of its utility for the self-amnesty of the left, which, after subjecting the extreme right to a just, harsh trial, forgives its own excesses without any trial—in the name of the "age of extremes."

8. Using the jargon of discontinuity theorists, Daniel Bell calls this the "revolution of rising entitlements," which is embedded in the "revolution of rising expectations"; cf. *The Cultural Contradictions of Capitalism* (New York: Basic, 1976), p. 233.

9. In the last hundred years, male life expectancy has increased from an average of 44.1 to 75.1 years, and female life expectancy from 47.6 to 80.0 years. Concerning the social implications of falling birth rates, cf. Francis Fukuyama, *The Great Disruption: Human Nature and the Reconstitution of Social Order* (New York: Touchstone, 2000), pp. 112–126; Emmanuel Todd elucidates the connection between falling birth rates, alphabetization and democratization in *After the Empire*.

10. Cf. the ambivalent key work of neo-miserablism: Pierre Bourdieu et al., *The Weight of the World: Social Suffering in Contemporary Society*, trans. Priscilla Parkhurst Ferguson, Susan Emanual, Joe Johnson & Shoggy T. Waryn (Stanford University Press, 1999). On the source of medieval Christian miserablism, cf. Lotario dei Segni (Pope Innocent III), *On the Misery of the Human Condition: De miseria humane conditionis*, trans. R. Donald Howard & Margaret Mary Dietz (Indianapolis: Bobbs-Merrill, 1969).

11. Cf. Galbraith, *The Affluent Society*.

12. German Government Poverty and Wealth Report for 2001, Appendix 1.13. For the 25–54 age group the figure is 9.6 percent, for the 7–13 age group 15.3% (!). Cf. also Rainer Geissler, *Die Sozialstruktur Deutschlands* (Opladen: Westdeutscher Verlag, 1992). In Austria, the average savings per household in 2002 were c. €85,000. For the USA, the U.S. Bureau of Census states that the poverty rate has never exceeded 15% since 1967. The concept of poverty among national economists refers to the situation of people in an affluent country whose income is 50% or less of the average per capita income. In Stephan Leibfried, Lutz Leisering et al., *Zeit der Armut* (Frankfurt: Suhrkamp, 1995), consider poverty in Germany a temporary aspect of people's employment histories: "We are not living in a two-thirds society, but rather a 70–20–10 society consisting of 70% who are never poor, 20% who are occasionally poor, and 10% who are more often poor. 'Only' 1.3% of the population were consistently poor during the sample period (1984–1992)." (p. 306)

13. The linguistic trace of thinking in ratios appears in phrases such as "four-fifths society," "three-quarter society" or "two-thirds society."

14. Simon Schama, *The Embarrassment of Riches: An Interpretation of Dutch Culture in the Golden Age* (Berkeley & Los Angeles: University of California Press, 1988).

15. John K. Galbraith, *The Culture of Contentment* (London: Sinclair-Stevenson, 1992), p. 12. Antonio Gramsci addressed something similar in his concept of the "historical block"; this was defined as a syndrome entailing a militant protection of one's vested rights and an aggressive, anti-political rejection of "general interests." In post-political "society," the sum of particularisms is a content resentment among majorities in the status quo.

16. I have tried elsewhere to show that philosophy developed more from the gestures of showing off knowledge, and from the competitive exaggeration of the striving to substantiate assertions, than from amazement; cf. *Spheres II*, pp. 13–43 and *Nicht gerettet*, pp. 255f.

17. In 1958, against the background of incipient automatization, Hannah Arendt prefaced her book *The Human Condition* (second edition, Chicago & London: University of Chicago Press, 2013) with the following diagnosis: "What we are confronted with is the prospect of a society of laborers without labor, that is, without the only activity left to them. Surely, nothing could be worse." (p. 5) This radically snobbish statement—which describes working humans as superfluous, tragic philistines—remains trapped in the conservative syndrome because it does not arrive at a positive concept of abundance, mass buying power, leisure and optional life praxis. The 1950 book *The Lonely Crowd* by David Riesman et al. (New Haven: Yale University Press, 2001), anticipates in passing the epochal subject of "uneasiness caused by the newly liberated" (p. 280).

18. In this context, one should acknowledge the devastating critique to which Deleuze and Guattari subjected familialist psychoanalysis in their work *Anti-Oedipus*: by rejecting the conventional interpretations of desire based on the drive structure of the poor and disciplined, the authors reveal the premises for a redefined unconscious that is productive, non-poor and not crippled by trauma.

19. When it is attempted, it is with a naïve culture-reforming focus, for example in John de Graaf, David Wann & Thomas H. Naylor, *Affluenza: The All-Consuming Epidemic* (San Francisco: Berrett Koehler, 2002), in which the authors recommend a life as moderate as the Franciscans and as content as the prairie Indians.

20. Concerning certain motifs in the misconceptions of personal affluence and the dissatisfaction of the saturated, cf. Gerhard Schulze, "Soziologie des Widerstands," in Ernst-Ulrich Huster (ed.), *Reichtum in Deutschland. Die Gewinner in der sozialen Polarisierung* (Frankfurt & New York: Campus, 1997), pp. 261–285.

21. *Das Unbehagen in der Kultur* [Unease in Culture] is the original title of Sigmund Freud's *Culture and Its Discontents* (trans.).

22. Cf. H. Kaelble (ed.), *Der Boom. 1948–1973. Gesellschaftliche und wirschaftliche Folgen in der Bundesrepublik Deutschland und in Europa* (Opladen: Westdeutscher Verlag, 1992).

23. Cf. Gregg Easterbrook, "Axle of Evil: America's Twisted Love Affair with Sociopathic Cars," in *The New Republic*, January 2003.

24. Michael Harrison, *The Other America: Poverty in the United States* (New York: Macmillan, 1962).

25. In 1923, Marcel Mauss spoke in his study on the gift that the French social security laws entailed an "already realized state socialism." In 1924, in his text "The Limits of Community," Plessner had uncovered the illusion management in radicalism and criticized its basis in a misguided idea of commune.

26. 1 Thessalonians 5:2.

27. Walter Benjamin, "On the Concept of History," in *Selected Writings*, vol. 4: *1938–1940* (Cambridge, MA: Harvard University Press, 2003), pp. 389–400.

28. Cf. Pascal Bruckner, *The Tears of the White Man: Compassion as Contempt* (New York: Free Press, 1986).

29. Raymond Tallis, a defender of rationalist utopianism, notes in his attack on the fashionable pessimism of the contemporary intelligentsia: "Critics need to borrow grievances since, if the world really is unprecedentedly horrid, it would be morally uncomfortable to be as unprecedentedly comfortable as the historical record would seem to suggest." (*Enemies of Hope: A Critique of Contemporary Pessimism* [London: Macmillan, 1997], p. 209)

30. Louis Bolk, "On the Problem of Anthropogenesis," in *Proc. Section Sciences Kon. Akad. Wetens. Amsterdam* 29 (1926), pp. 465–75.

31. This complex is the focus of the first part of Gehlen's central work *Der Mensch*, which deals with the special morphological status of humans (pp. 86–130).

32. Gehlen, *Der Mensch*, p. 34.

33. Ibid., p. 37.

34. Ibid., p. 45.

35. Ibid., p. 61.

36. Ibid., p. 83.

37. Cf. Terrence W. Deacon, *The Symbolic Species: The Co-Evolution of Language and the Brain* (New York: W. W. Norton, 1997).

38. Gehlen, *Der Mensch*, p. 36.

39. Ibid.

40. Concerning Gehlen's pessimism and its parallels to that of Adorno, cf. Christian Thies, *Die Krise des Individuums: zur Kritik der Moderne bei Adorno und Gehlen* (Reinbek: Rowohlt, 1997), pp. 275–285.

41. Friedrich Schiller, "A Walk Among the Linden Trees," in *The German Novelists: Tales Selected from Ancient and Modern Authors in that Language: from the Earliest Period Down to the Close of the Eighteenth Century*, vol. 3, ed. & trans. Thomas Roscoe (London: Henry Colburn, 1826), pp. 370f.

42. It treats the statements of committed facilitators with distrust; one can understand why. Was it not Stalin who declared: "Cheerfulness is the most striking characteristic of the Soviet Union?" The CPSU, the epitome of fun parties? Not quite; for the Nazi Party also knew its debt to the power that comes from joy.

43. Hegel, *Phenomenology of Spirit*, pp. 6f. (translation modified).

44. Cf. Richard Alewyn, *Das grosse Welttheater. Die Epoche der höfischen Feste* (Munich: Beck, 1989), p. 67.

45. "Light" is used here as the opposite of "heavy" (trans.).

46. Hegel, *Phenomenology of Spirit*, p. 10.

47. Ibid., p. 12.

48. Novalis, *Philosophical Writings*, ed. & trans. Margaret Mahony Stoljar (Albany: SUNY Press, 1997), p. 33.

49. Ibid.

50. Cf. Daniele Dell'Agli, "Abendländische Teleologie. Kritik einer Obsession" (MA thesis, Berlin, 1993).

51. *The End of Gravity*, film script by Dan Simmons and Andrei Ujică, in *Worlds Enough and Time—Five Tales of Speculative Fiction* (New York: Tandem, 2002).

52. Even the emergency industry in the true sense of the word has been familiar with the primacy of supply for some time: in congested urban centers in Germany, there are far too few accidents to make full use of accredited rescue services like the Red Cross, Arbeiter-Samariter-Bund [Workers-Samaritans Association] or Promedic. The state of the garbage economy is even more characteristic: as there is not nearly enough waste produced by German households and factories to make recycling profitable for the existing companies, the battle for the dirty gold has broken out

between the mostly communally funded waste disposal firms. Meanwhile, initiatives by good citizens still look for ways of reducing the amount of waste.

53. Thus Rudolf Borchardt (according to Theodor Lessing's account) said after the First World War: "This war was necessary to prove that I am not a coward." Cf. Theodor Lessing, *Einmal und nie wieder. Lebenserinnerungen* (Gütersloh: Bertelsmann, 1969), p. 319.

54. Simone Weil, *The Need for Roots: Prelude to a Declaration of Duties Towards Mankind*, trans. Arthur Wills (London: Routledge, 2002), p. 292.

55. Cf. Also Robert Pfaller, *On The Pleasure Principle In Culture: Illusions Without Owners*, trans. Lisa Rosenblatt (London & New York: Verso, 2014).

56. Nietzsche, *Human, All Too Human*, p. 74 (translation modified).

57. To interpret the phenomenon of humans devoting themselves seriously to the unserious, one should make use of Huizinga's remarks on the absorption of players by the game. A psychological theory of the fanatical position as an overcompensated decisionism might also have something to say on the matter.

58. Concerning the reflex against these observations in postmodernized psycho-analysis, cf. Charles Melman & Jean-Pierre Lebrun, *L'homme sans gravité: Jouir à tout prix* (Paris: Denoël, 2002). In diagnoses of our time by younger authors, one is struck by anti-ironism and the search for stability through one's own heaviness and density. Cf. Jedediah Purdy, For Common Things: Irony, Trust, and Commitment in America Today (New York: Vintage, 2000); Camille de Toledo, *Superhip Jolipunk: Confessions Of A Young Man Out Of Joint* (New York: Soft Skull Press, 2007)—an autobiographical book in which the search for new points of reference passes first through the ironic space-time of mass dandyism, then the schizoid space-time of Deleuzian liquefaction, before anchoring itself in an era of "new incarnations" ("I am heavy, I am dense").

59. Max Frisch, *Die Schwierigen oder J'adore ce qui me brûle* (Zurich: Atlantis, 1957), p. 269.

60. Peter Handke, "Leben ohne Poesie" (1972), in *Als das Wünschen noch geholfen hat* (Frankfurt: Suhrkamp, 1974), p. 15.

61. The closest analogy to this exercise is found in the chapter about the conscience, the beautiful soul, evil and the forgiveness thereof in Hegel's *Phenomenology of Spirit*. Here, evil must stand up as the self-knowing outrage of the individual before God can declare himself or the entrance of the subject into the service of the universally shared can take place. Hegel's great didacticism dates to assert the educational meaning of evil, and even to capture despair in a curriculum. Cf. Ernst Behler, *Klassische Ironie, Romantische Ironie, Tragische Ironie. Zum Ursprung dieser Begriffe* (Darmstadt: Wissenschaftliche Buchgesellschaft, 1972), pp. 113–115.

62. Bernhard Pörksen, *Abschied vom Absoluten. Gespräche zum Konstruktivismus* (Heidelberg: Carl-Auer-Systeme, 2001), p. 40.

63. Concerning this formulation, cf. Niklas Luhmann, "The Modern Sciences and Phenomenology," in *Theories of Distinction: Redescribing the Descriptions of Modernity*, ed. W. Rasch (Stanford University Press, 2002), pp. 52f.: "The tests of [reason's] validity are found in therapy, which attempts to attain less painful solutions and itself maintains a disengagement in matters of reality."

64. Ibid., p. 53.

65. Ibid., p. 52.

66. Robbie Williams, *Escapology* (2002).

67. Cf. Jaroslav Hašek, *The Good Soldier Švejk*, trans. Cecil Parrott (London: Heinemann, 1973).

68. Cf. Fuller, *Your Private Sky*.

69. Cf. Bölling & Horst, *Schirme*.

70. Jurek Becker, *Jacob the Liar*, trans. Leila Vennewitz (New York: Plume, 1997).

71. Cf. Reinhart G. E. Lempp, *Das Kind im Menschen. Nebenrealitäten und Regression—oder: Warum wir nie erwachsen werden* (Stuttgart: Klett-Cotta, 2003) and John S. Kafka, *Multiple Realities in Clinical Practice* (New Haven: Yale University Press, 1989).

72. In May 2003, the first inflatable PVC church, with a capacity of 60 visitors, was consecrated in Esher, near London—based on an idea (inspired by bouncy castles at fairs) by the entrepreneur Michael Gill from 1998 that enabled the practical implementation of pneumatology (Yahoo News, 05/14/2003). One hears that the Pentagon is currently working on an inflatable parliament building that can be set up in liberated rogue states as soon as the fighting is over, and can be filled by up to twenty-one rapidly appointed local representatives with discussions about democratic constitutions.

73. Sylvia Plath, "Three Women: A Poem for Three Voices," in *Collected Poems* (London: Faber & Faber, 1981), pp. 176–187.

74. The German word for "infant," *Säugling*, literally means "suckling (babe)," and that for "infancy" is accordingly *Säuglingsalter*, "suckling age" (trans.).

75. Hrdy, *Mother Nature*, pp. 121ff.

76. Concerning the function of patronage in the civilization process, cf. Claessens, *Das Konkrete und das Abstrakte*, pp. 61 & 64f.

77. Cf. *Spheres I*, Chapter 7, "The Siren Stage," p. 509.

78. I refer the reader once again to Heiner Mühlmann's work *The Nature of Cultures*, as well as *Kunst und Krieg*; one should also note that the "affluent society" creates not only an unease about wealth, but also an unease in peace, accompanied by bellicist romanticism and a nostalgic longing for harshness (Julien Benda already said what was necessary about this in 1927, in his book *The Treason of the Intellectuals*).

79. In the important Chapter 22 of *Mother Nature*, "Of Human Bondage" (pp. 485–510), Sarah Blaffer Hrdy points out the scarcity of allomothering resources in contemporary "society," which, from this perspective, would have to be described as an era of continuous, perhaps even growing poverty. I will take a different view below, extending the concept of the allomother beyond the phenomena of concrete childcare and using it to encompass all forms of care through state institutions or social services. In this elucidation, current "society" will appear as a comprehensive experiment about the prostheticization of maternalizing functions.

80. György Konrád: "What use is the wealth of the wealthy? It allows them to help, in their way, those who depend on it and deserve support. The protection of the child is a concentrated form of the defense of human rights." (György Konrád, *Vor den Toren des Reichs*, trans. Hans-Henning Paetzke [Frankfurt: Suhrkamp, 1997], p. 87)

81. Concerning the dynamics of such standardizations, cf. the section "The Nomotope—First Constitutional Doctrine" above.

82. Cf. Helmut Schulze, *Der progressiv domestizierte Mensch und seine Neurosen. Die Rolle von Entlastung und Belastung für Krankheit und Heilung* (Munich: Lehmann, 1964).

83. The German for "there is," *es gibt*, literally means "it gives" (trans.).

84. Genesis 3:16.

85. Bloch, *The Principle of Hope*, vol. 1, p. 238.

86. Quoted in Raphael Patai, *The Messiah Texts: Jewish Legends of Three Thousand Years* (Detroit: Wayne State University Press, 1988), p. 232.

87. It is augmented by those of safety without struggle and immunity without suffering.

88. Cf. Benjamin, "On the Concept of History," II: "If this is so, then there is a secret agreement between past generations and the present one. Then our coming was expected on earth. Then, like every generation that preceded us, we have been endowed with a *weak* messianic power, on which the past has a claim. Such a claim cannot be settled cheaply. The historical materialist knows this." (pp. 389f.)

89. *Maimonides' Commentary on the Mishnah, tractate Sanhedrin*, trans. Fred Rosner (New York: Sepher-Hermon Press, 1981).

90. Irenaeus, *Against Heresies*, 5.33.3, in Robert M. Grant, *Irenaeus of Lyons* (London: Routledge, 1997), pp. 178f.

91. From a philological perspective, however (and all the more from a religion-psychological one), there is every indication that the aforementioned paradisiacal-erotic fantasies simply resulted from mistranslations of obscure passages in the Quran, for example suras 44 and 52; according to Christoph Luxenberg in *The Syro-Aramaic Reading of the Koran: A Contribution to the Decoding of the Language of the Koran* (Berlin: Hans Schiler, 2007), the oft-cited *huris* (virgins) are actually merely white grapes—an image that makes far more sense in the context of the present interpretation of the oral-homeostatic dynamic of images of paradise. The grape awaiting the believer, as touched on above, is a common topos in Christian and Jewish afterlife literature that might also have been known to the authors of the Quran.

92. For example Ioan P. Couliano, *Out of this World: Otherworldly Journeys from Gilgamesh to Albert Einstein* (Boston and London: Shambhala, 1991); Pierre-Antoine Bernheim & Guy Stavrides, *Welt der Paradiese—Paradiese der Welt* (Zurich: Wissenschaftliche Buchgesellschaft, 1992); Friedrich Heer, *Abschied von Höllen und Himmeln. Vom Ende des religiösen Tertiär* (Frankfurt & Berlin: Ullstein, 1990); and Bernhard Lang & Colleen McDannell, *Heaven: A History* (New Haven: Yale University Press, 1988).

93. Deleuze & Guattari, *What Is Philosophy?*, p. 97.

94. Cf. Gotthard Günther, "Selbstdarstellung im Spiegel Amerikas," in Pongratz, Ludwig J. (ed.), *Philosophie in Selbstdarstellungen* (Hamburg: Meiner, 1975), p. 30.

95. "The History of Doctor Johann Faustus," trans. H. G. Haile, in *German Medieval Tales*, ed. Francis C. Gentry (New York: Continuum, 1983), pp. 156f.

96. Concerning total pampering as the result of the triad comprising income without work, security without struggle and immunity without suffering, cf. pp. 776ff.

97. Cf. *Spheres II*, Chapter 8, "The Last Orb: On a Philosophical History of Terrestrial Globalization," pp. 765–959, especially pp. 842f.

98. Pascal Bruckner, *The Temptation of Innocence: Living in the Age of Entitlement* (New York: Algora, 2000), p. 86.

99. Quoted in Thomas Kutsch & Günter Wiswede, *Wirtschaftssoziologie: Grundlegung, Hauptgebiete, Zusammenschau* (Stuttgart: Enke, 1986), p. 213.

100. Bernard Mandeville, *The Fable of the Bees and Other Writings*, ed. E. J. Hundert (Indianapolis: Hackett, 1997), p. 34.

101. Werner Sombart, *Luxury and Capitalism*, trans. W. R. Dittmar (Ann Arbor: University of Michigan Press, 1967), p. xxi.

102. This tradition of argumentation is still upheld by the premium brand theorist Wolfgang Reitzle ("only winners sell premium brands"), in *Luxus schafft Wohlstand. Die Zukunft der globalen Wirtschaft* (Reinbek: Rowohlt, 2001).

103. Cf. Anna Pavord, *The Tulip* (London: Bloomsbury, 1999), pp. 129–161.

104. This phenomenon has a contemporary analogy in the authoritarian capitalist countries of East Asia, most of all Singapore and China, whose state-loyal intelligentsia constantly warn *nouveau riche* "society" about the dangers of "excessive individualism"—embodied by the "decadent West"—that are immanent in affluence.

105. The term goes back to advertising texts for products of the porcelain and ceramics manufacturer Josiah Wedgewood in the 18th century; cf. Neil McKendrick, "Introduction: The Birth of a Consumer Society: The Commercialization of Eighteenth-Century England," in Neil McKendrick, John Brewer & J. H. Plumb, *The Birth of a Consumer Society: The Commercialization of Eighteenth-Century England* (Bloomington: Indiana University Press, 1982), pp. 1–8. The verbal image of infection with new needs proves that a hundred years before Gabriel Tarde, there had already been efforts towards a mental epidemiology. Even then, the actors in the modern enrichment game knew that the mimesis of luxury begins at the top. Hence, under mercantile premises, Colbert was right to encourage "the manufacture of silks and other aristrocratic industries" (Tarde, *The Laws of Imitation*, p. 335). That the critique of luxury can also be used for an outward cultural struggle is demonstrated by the Enlightenment topos of the debauched Turkish sultan. Thus one reads in the historico-philosophical study by Constantin François de Volney, *The Ruins, Or, Meditation on the Revolutions of Empires; and The Law of Nature* (Paris, 1792; reprint, Baltimore: Black Classics Press, 1991), p. 49: "He has surrounded himself with an army of women, eunuchs and satellites. [...] In imitation of their master, his servants must also have splendid houses [...] and all the riches of the empire have been swallowed up in the Serai."

106. *Surrealist Painters and Poets: An Anthology*, ed. Mary Ann Caws (Cambridge, MA: MIT Press, 2002), p. 46.

107. Hermann Burger, *Die künstliche Mutter* (Frankfurt: Fischer, 1982).

108. The term appears in Lionel Tiger, *The Decline of Males* (New York: Golden Books, 1999).

109. James L. Nolan, Jr., *The Therapeutic State: Justifying Government at Century's End* (New York: NYU Press, 1998).

110. The decline of intellectuals in postmodern culture can be explained in this context. The traditional intellectual can only exist as long as they speak out as a

spokesperson for real hardship or the real as such, which is almost the same thing. Since hardship became exotic, the intellectual is under suspicion of wanting to live off importing distant problems. The gesture of making political what were previously pre-political hardships and scandals is past its heyday in the West; it could only regain significance if the situation of the bottom quarter inside the luxury system approached a politicizable degree of impoverishment (Bourdieu bet on this effect with his research into the mute misfortune of the French in *The Weight of the World) and* if, in addition to protest energies, new visions for the politics of redistribution were also available. At present, and in the foreseeable future, both of these exist only in weak and confused forms; hence there were, understandably, no consequences when Bourdieu attempted to rename the mothering state of affluent society the "state of misery" (*Etat de misère*, in *Express*, March 16, 1993).

111. These are augmented by the socially narcissistic dimension of pampering in the star system of "mass" culture, where the longing for celebrity status without any works or achievements is rehearsed.

112. In "Seltene Erfolge, viele Fehlschläge und aufhaltsame Fortschritte. Reflexionen zu David Landes' opus magnum *The Wealth and Poverty of Nations*," in *Leviathan* 1/2001, pp. 142f., Dieter Senghaas points out the paradoxes, or rather the self-sabotaging structure, of the "development policies" with which developing nations are simultaneously called upon to join the competition and prevented from doing so.

113. "You have made us for yourself," words originally addressed by Saint Augustine to God in his Confessions (trans.).

114. Cf. Chapter 1, "Insulations: For a Theory of Capsules, Islands and Hothouses."

115. Cf. Annette Hünnekens, *Expanded Museum. Kulturelle Erinnerung und virtuelle Realitäten* (Bielefeld: Transcript, 2002).

116. Cf. the notes on Olafur Eliasson on pp. 853f. above, as well as the comments on the installation theory of Ilya Kabakov and Boris Groys on pp. 864ff. under the direction of Peter Weibel, the Karlsruhe Center of Art and Media Technology (ZKM) has become an embodiment, unique in the world, of a new type of institution: the museum as a systems knowledge machine. With their project for a dual art/war museum, Heiner Mühlmann and Bazon Brock have presented a controversial concept. "The double museum has the didactic purpose of producing cultural meta-knowledge with the help of exhibitions on the connections between war, entertainment containing war, and entertainment with cultural knowledge in which war is forbidden." (Heiner Mühlmann, "Kunst und/oder Krieg—Das Doppelmuseum," in Brock & Koschig (eds.), *Kunst und Krieg*, p. 189.

117. Concerning the theory of immersion, cf. the elaborations on the third step in the explication of dwelling through the installation and the *Gesamtkunstwerk* on pp. 488–498.

118. Concerning the term "collector," cf. pp. 584f.

119. Cf. Gerhard Schulze, *Die Erlebnisgesellschaft. Kultursoziologie der Gegenwart* (Frankfurt: Campus, 1992).

120. Tarde, *The Laws of Imitation*, p. 174.

121. Cf. Burkhard Scherer, *Auf den Inseln des Eigensinns. Eine kleine Ethnologie der Hobbywelt* (Munich: C. H. Beck, 1995).

122. Cf. Jean de Maillard, *Le marché fait sa loi: De l'usage du crime par la mondialisation* (Paris: Mille et une nuits, 2001).

123. Giorgio Agamben, *Homo Sacer: Sovereign Power and Bare Life*, trans. Daniel Heller-Roazen (Stanford University Press, 1998).

124. Compare the statement by Imre Kertész: "The West is a camp for inmates who are spared. This camp must be defended..." (*Die Zeit* 43/2002. p. 43)

125. Concerning the difference between the view of imagined globes and circumspection in the sphere of the continuous One (and the derivations from this for recent immersion art, for example spheric cinema), cf. *Spheres II*, Introduction, Section II, "The Parmenidean Moment," pp. 70–90.

126. Cf. Benjamin R. Barber, *Jihad Vs McWorld* (New York: Random House, 1995).

127. Norbert Bolz, *Das konsumistische Manifest* (Munich: Fink, 2002), p. 90.

128. Michael Hardt & Antonio Negri, *Empire* (Cambridge, MA: Harvard University Press, 2000).

129. Ibid., p. 211.

130. Ibid., p. 212.

131. This finding applies both to the Promethean-Franciscan escalation in Negri and the radicalization of pure militance in Alain Badiou's para-atheist essay *Saint Paul: The Foundation of Universalism*, trans. Ray Brassier (Stanford University Press, 2003). Daniel Bensaïd argues in favor of a melancholy-realist appropriation of the "legacy of prophetic reason" in his book *Le pari mélancholique*. The metaphysical line of defense of the principle of the left is shown in philosophical and religion-historical terms in Peter Sloterdijk & Thomas H. Mache (eds.), *Weltrevolution der Seele. Ein Lese- und Arbeitsbuch der Gnosis von der Spätantike bis zur Gegenwart* (Zurich: Artemis & Winkler, 1991); those wishing to go back to the sources in the twentieth century will reread Paul Tillich, *The Socialist Decision*, trans. Franklin Sherman (New York: Harper & Row, 1977) and Hermann Cohen, *Religion of Reason: Out of the Sources of Judaism*, trans. Simon Kaplan (Atlanta: Scholars Press, 1995), as well as the writings of Charles Péguy.

132. At most, it can reduce itself to an oppositional ideology based on misunderstandings and simplifications, as evident in recent contributions to the dispute between the poor world and the rich world in which one speaks of "confronting the Empire."

133. According to the *Fischer Weltalmanach 2003* (Frankfurt: Fischer, 2002).

134. Cf. Emmanuel Todd, *L'illusion economique* (Paris: Gallimard, 1998).

135. Hobsbawm, *The Age of Extremes*, pp. 289f.

136. In this context cf. again Schulze, "Soziologie des Widerstands."

137. Fyodor Dostoyevsky, *Notes from Underground and The Double*, trans. Jesse Coulson (London: Penguin, 1972), p. 41.

138. In the book *Ungewollte Kinder. Annäherungen, Beispiele, Hilfen* (Reinbek: Rowohlt, 1994), the editors Helga Häsing and Ludwig Janus start from the "conservative estimate" that even today, one in three children are unwanted at birth. The figure is probably too high, but would nonetheless, if correct, point to a historical first: a majority of two thirds are wanted.

139. Peter Handke, "Essay on Tiredness," in *The Jukebox and Other Essays on Storytelling*, trans. Ralph Manheim (New York: Macmillan, 1994), p. 28.

140. "I move, therefore I am" (trans.).

141. In Germany in 2002, with roughly 39 million jobs (in a population of 82 million) and 9 days of sick leave per employee per year (an unusually low quota due to crisis), there were some 350 million days of paid sick leave. This does not take into account the invisible weekend morbidity (which can spread to over 4 billion days per year) and hidden holiday morbidity (virtually 1 billion days), or indeed the illness-related behavior in the population segment that is not directly integrated into the working world.

142. Honoré de Balzac, *The Magic Skin* (1831).

143. Cf. Cynthia Fleury, *Pretium doloris: L'accident comme souci de soi* (Paris: Pouvert, 2002).

144. Cf. Walther K. Lang, *Grausame Bilder: Sadismus in der Neapolitanischen Malerei von Caravaggio bis Giordano* (Berlin: Reimer, 2001).

145. Cf. Charles T. Sykes, *A Nation of Victims: The Decay of the American Character* (New York: St. Martin's Press, 1992).

146. Cf. Lorenzo Pinna, *Fünf Hypothesen zum Untergang der Welt* (Munich: dtv, 1996).

147. Cf. Julia Kristeva, *Time and Sense: Proust and the Experience of Literature*, trans. Ross Guberman (New York: Columbia University Press, 1998).

148. The most masterful early monograph on luxury in a single culture, Chapter 11 of Ludwig Friedländer's monumental morality history of 1928 *Roman Life and Manners Under the Early Empire* (New York: Arno Press, 1979), divides the phenomena into the luxury of feasting, the luxury of dress and jewelry, the luxury of buildings, the luxury of domestic conditions, the luxury of burial and the luxury of slaves.

149. Cf. Norbert Bolz, *Das konsumistische Manifest*, pp. 102f.

150. Cf. Jonathan Crary, *Suspensions of Perception: Attention, Spectacle, and Modern Culture* (Cambridge, MA: MIT Press, 2001) and Walter Benjamin, "The Work of Art in the Age of Its Technological Reproducibility," in *Selected Writings* vol. 3: *1935–1938* (Cambridge, MA: Harvard University Press, 2002), pp. 101–133.

151. Concerning the derivation of *religio* from a verb from the *vis legendi*, cd. Cicero, *de natura deorum*, II, 28.

152. Cf. Günther Ohloff, *Earthly Scents—Heavenly Pleasures: A Cultural History of Scents* (Weinheim: Wiley-VCH, 2006). We learn that Jacques Guerlain, who possessed a perfect sense of smell, could supposedly distinguish with no context between 3,000 olfactory qualities, "an achievement that is only possible through intensive daily training."

153. Cf. Franz Sales Meyer (ed.), *Handbook of Ornament* (New York: Dover, 1957).

154. Concerning the snake motif, cf. the section "The Mole and the Snake" in Negri & Hardt, *Empire*, pp. 52–59.

155. Karl Marx & Friedrich Engels, *The Communist Manifesto*, trans. Samuel Moore (London: Penguin, 2002), p. 223.

156. In *"Society": Jeu investigatif et aventurier sur la communauté désavouable* (Paris: Tristram, 2001), pp. 239f., especially pp. 258–262, Mehdi Belhaj Kacem interprets the heterosexual-pornographic production of images in the era of liberalization in terms of the "hypervisibility" of female organs, as well as the performance of male arousal.

157. Carl Djerassi, *The Pill, Pygmy Chimps and Degas' Horse* (New York: Basic Books, 1992), pp. 49–65.

158. Ibid., p. 64.

159. Cf. Carl Christian Bry, *Verkappte Religionen. Kritik des kollektiven Wahns* (1924), ed. Martin Gregor-Dellin (Munich: Ehrenwirth, 1979), pp. 150 & 154.

Retrospect

1. "(Speak) nothing but good of the world and God" (trans.).

2. "(Speak) nothing but the best" (trans.).

Index

Böhme, Gernot, II: 976n66
Böhme, Hartmut, III: 861n117
Böhme, Jacob, II: 647
Boissard, J.-J., I: 285
Bolk, Lodewig (Louis), III: 654
Boll, Franz, II: 971n21
Bollnow, Otto Friedrich, III: 482
Bolz, Norbert, II: ; III: 768
Bombardoni, II: 326
Bonaventura, Johannes Fidanza, II: 975n57
Boniface IV (bishop), II: 428
Boniface VIII (pope), II: 754
Boniface, I: 404
Bonk, Sigmund, III: 847n146
Boran, Michael, III: 24
Borchardt, Rudolf, III: 879n53
Born, Bertran de, II: 998n19
Bosch, Hieronymus, I: 47, 80, 329
Botschuijver, Theo, III: 440
Botticelli, Sandro, III: 37, 38
Botticini, Francesco, II: 497
Bougainville, Louis Antoine de, II: 928
Boullée, Etienne-Louis, III: 567, 569, 581, 592
Bourdieu, Pierre, III: 884n110
Bourgeois, Louise, III: 806
Bovillus, Carolus, II: 86
Bowlby, John, III: 362–363, 716
Boys, Charles Vernon, I: 77; III: 47
Bramante, Donato, II: 420
Brandom, Robert B., III: 194
Brass, Ed, III: 328
Brazza, Savorgnan de, II: 904
Bréal, Michel, III: 590
Brendel, Otto, II: 30, 31
Brentano, Clemens von, I: 244
Breton, André, III: 150, 153, 748
Broch, Hermann, II: 137; III: 85, 171–177, 227, 464, 544, 837n15, 842n86
Brock, Bazon, III: 144, 389, 393, 397, 673, 886n116
Brockes, Barthold Hinrich, II: 1007n19
Bromová, Veronika, III: 71

Brower, Steven, III: 510
Bruckner, Pascal, III: 644
Brunelleschi, Filippo, II: 419, 577
Bruno, Giordano, I: 218, 633n5, 638n13 ; II: 470, 512, 525, 557, 562, 779, 855, 992n13, 1013n74; III: 847n146
Brutus, Marcus Junius, II: 607, 702
Bry, Theodor de, II: 220, 822
Buber, Martin, I: 558; II: 737; III: 432
Buchheim, Thomas, II: 973n36
Buddha, Gautama Siddhartha, I: 172, 176, 178, 180; III: 403
Buff, Charlotte, III: 684
Burch, Hal, III: 234
Burckhardt, Jacob, II: 301, 305
Burke, Edmund, II: 880
Byron, George Gordon Noel Lord, III: 670

Caerellius, I: 416
Caligula, Gaius Julius (Roman emperor), II: 682, 706, 707
Callot, Jacques, II: 924
Cambyses (Persian king), II: 679
Cameron, James, II: 154, 155, 805
Camões, Luis de, II: 874
Canetti, Elias, III: 114, 171, 173–174, 177, 212, 464, 549, 583–584
Cano, Juan Sebastian del, II: 795, 807, 811, 875, 876
Canterbury, Anselm of, II: 565
Capua, Raymond of, I: 103, 110, 115, 638n9
Capurro, Rafael, I: 655n45
Carlyle, Thomas, III: 629–630
Carreno de Miranda, Juan, I: 587
Carter, Jimmy, III: 169
Carus, Carl Gustav, I: 642n9 ; III: 156, 189
Case, John, II: 548
Cassius Dio, II: 416, 607, 702
Cellarius, Andreas, II: 767
Censurinus, I: 420
Charlemagne, I: 404, 423; II:

Charles IV, II: 59
Charles V, II: 445, 811, 812, 815, 825, 826
Charles, Jacques Alexandre César, III: 574, 667
Chase, Charles A., II: 491
Chastenet, Armand-Marie Jacques de, I: 233
Chateaubriand, Françoise René Vicomte de, II: 596
Chessman, Cheryl, III: 110
Cheswick, Bill, III: 234
Chilon of Sparta, II: 969n6
Christopher, St., II: 98, 103, 105–108, 111, 669
Churchill, Winston, II: 933; III: 128, 129
Cicero, Marcus Tullius, II: 422, 706, 991n11; III: 187, 438, 849n163, 887n151
Cimerlino, Giovanni, II: 882, 883
Cinna, Lucius Cornelius, II: 706
Cioran, Emile M., II: 619
Claessens, Dieter, II: 193–194, 985n2; III: 144, 700
Claesz, Pieter, II: 858
Clement V (pope), II: 756
Cleobulus of Lindos, II: 969n6
Cleve, Joos van, I: 158
Cloots, Anarchasis, III: 269
Cohen, Hermann, III: 885n131
Colbert, Jean-Baptiste, III: 883n105
Columbus, Christopher, I: 221; II: 111, 749, 783, 795–798, 804, 805, 807, 810, 825, 828, 839, 843, 853, 855, 865, 868, 872, 880–882, 898, 899, 904, 935
Confucius, II: 300; III: 403
Conrad, Joseph, II: 629, 632, 633
Constant (see Nieuwenhys, Constant Anton)
Constantine I, the Great, II: 40, 226, 687, 690, 711
Constantius II, II: 318
Constantini, Umberto, III: 593

Cook, Peter, III: 611
Copernicus, Nicholas, I: 20; II: 54, 387, 391, 393, 523, 525, 553, 555, 557, 808
Corbett, Harvey W., III: 515
Corbin, Henry, I: 567, 640n10
Corbusier (see Le Corbusier)
Corbusier, Le (see Le Corbusier)
Corday, Charlotte, III: 571
Cornell, Joseph, II: 336
Coronelli, Vinzenzo, II: 791
Coubertin, Pierre de, III: 588–590
Coué, Emile, I: 234
Couliano, Ioan P., I: 638n12
Courbet, Gustave, III: 71
Cox, Donna, III: 233
Coysevox, Antoine, II: 697
Cramer, Stuart, III: 169
Cranach, Lucas, II: 120
Crates of Mallus, II: 59
Crevel, René, III: 283
Crivelli, Carlo, I: 430
Cunctator, Fabius, III: 390
Curie, Marie, III: 199
Curtius, Ludwig, III: 588
Cusa, Nicholas of, I: 64, 570, 572, 575–577, 581, 599, 658n10; II: 46, 117, 276, 443, 447, 448, 451, 470, 512, 533, 534, 536–540, 542, 543, 547–549; III: 73
Cyprianus, Thaschus Caecilius, II: 664

D'Alembert, Jean-le-Rond, III: 205
d'Ascoli, Cecho, II: 446
Dalai Lama, II: 409
Dalí, Salvador, I: 211; III: 145, 146, 149–151, 157, 171
Daniel, Peter, I: 635n23
Dante Alighieri, II: 175, 176, 395, 453, 455–459, 461, 462, 475, 565, 569, 570, 572–582, 590, 592, 594–599, 601, 605, 606, 608, 609, 611, 612, 617, 620, 622–625, 631, 690, 691, 702, 765, 779; III: 16
Danton, Georges, III: 581

Euclid of Megara, I: 416
Eudes, Johannes, I: 127, 130
Eudoxus of Cnidus, II: 387
Eugenius, Flavius, II: 226
Euler, Leonhard, II: 518
Euripides, II: 342
Eusebius of Caesarea, II: 690, 711

Farnese, Elisabeth, II: 59
Fauser, Alois, II: 971n21
Fechner, Gustav Theodor, III: 225
Felicity of Carthage, II: 669
Fellini, Federico, I: 87
Fernández, Alejo, II: 913
Feuchtmayer, Johann Michael, II: 760
Fichte, Johann Gottlieb, I: 235,
251–257, 267, 643n13, 652n8; II:
533, 616, 722, 723, 994n48; III: 189,
404, 671, 682
Ficino, Marsilio, I: 103, 117–119,
121–123, 139, 141, 144, 212–218,
257; II: 348, 470
Findeisen, Andreas Leo, I: 336,
657n19
Finé, Oronce, II: 882
Fischl, Eric, III: 558, 783
Flasch, Kurt, II: 995n57, 996n74
Florensky, Pavel, I: 156, 159; III: 437
Fludd, Robert, II: 454, 467, 498
Flury, Ferdinand, III: 104
Flusser, Vilém, II: 139; III: 277, 458,
473, 474, 478, 484, 485, 488, 491,
522, 834n35, 866n40
Foerster, Heinz von, III: 682, 685, 686
Fontana, Domenico, II: 420
Forster, Edward Morgan, III: 468
Forster, Georg, II: 928, 931, 1009n34
Forster, Reinhold, II: 928
Fossati, Gaspare, II: 431
Foster, Norman, II: 438
Foucault, Michel, I: 90, 139; II: 41,
128, 252, 634, 845; III: 469
Fourier, Charles, I: 238
Fra Mauro, II: 807, 879
Francesca, Piero della, I: 55

Francis I (king), II: 915
Frank, Manfred, I: 638n15
Franz Xaver (Jesuit missionary), II:
926
Frederick II of Hohenstaufen, II: 332,
333
Frederick II of Prussia, I: 131; II: 931
Frei, Otto, II: 964; III: 49, 440, 693
Freud, Sigmund, I: 124, 197, 217,
223, 224, 250, 251, 268, 291, 292,
459, 463–465, 637n39; II: 71, 163,
197, 392, 597, 699, 741, 889–891;
III: 33, 36, 150, 156, 157, 229, 463,
514, 639, 653, 671, 689, 718, 734
Freyer, Hans, II: 866, 1014n85
Friedlaender, Salomo, I: 647n29
Friedländer, Ludwig, III: 887n148
Friedman, Yona, III: 277, 611
Frisch, Max, III: 678
Frobenius, Leo, II: 343, 981n6
Frontisi-Ducroux, Françoise, I:
640n17, 641n25
Fuchs, Peter, I: 661n52
Fugger, Anton, II: 829, 1010n46
Fugger, Raymund, II: 816
Fukuyama, Francis, III: 875n9
Fuller, Richard Buckminster, III: 312,
313, 323, 329, 440, 444, 447, 449,
515, 516, 519, 520, 611, 693,
863n144
Furtenbach, Martin, II: 816

Gabirol, Salomon ibn, II: 1024n11
Gaiser, Konrad, II: 970n10
Galbraith, John Kenneth, III: 627,
635, 638, 640
Galilei, Galileo, II: 562
Gama, Vasco da, II: 839, 840, 875,
892
Gandhi, Mohandas Karamchand
"Mahatma," III: 20
Gates, Bill, III: 523
Gay, John, II: 551
Gehlen, Arnold, III: 33, 204, 446,
447, 450, 652–656, 658–663, 674,

Heer, Friedrich, I: 59
Heerdt, Walter, III: 108
Hegel, Georg Wilhelm Friedrich, I: 56,
203, 236, 246, 276, 346, 417, 443, 498,
513, 583, 662n61; II: 23, 98, 291,
365, 383, 399, 414, 422, 523, 529,
639, 747, 770, 779, 853, 980n31,
984n35, 985n2, 993n29, 994n47,
1012n70; III: 31, 74, 83, 149, 225,
245, 345, 350, 363, 399, 403, 432,
436, 456, 460, 506, 526, 540, 552,
586, 647, 653, 663–665, 669, 670,
677, 712, 801, 836n8, 879n61
Heidegger, Martin, I: 12, 48, 89, 275,
333–335, 339, 341, 342, 539, 541,
626, 628, 629, 637n37, 649n44,
657n3; II: 23, 45, 48, 71, 79, 81, 82,
90, 138–140, 194, 196, 328, 392,
413, 445, 584, 619, 640, 769, 785,
790, 853, 862–864, 866, 869, 891,
918, 969n7, 971n14, 994n48,
1002n40, 100616; III: 14, 75, 114,
135, 137, 162, 137, 162, 166, 202,
166, 202, 205–207, 211, 211, 221,
290, 299, 341, 343, 347, 364, 365,
399–401, 422, 464, 469, 474, 476,
477, 480, 482, 484, 487, 488, 492,
534, 654, 674, 676–682, 687, 709,
835n56, 846n130
Heilmann, Alfons, I: 653n13
Heine, Heinrich, II: 953
Heinrich, Klaus, III: 235
Heinrichs, Hans-Jürgen, III: 832n18
Heinsohn, Gunnar, II: 981n2,
1009n35
Heliogabalus (Elegabalus) (see Varius
Avitus Bassianus)
Helmont, Jan Baptist van, I: 223
Helnwein, Gottfried, II: 628
Henry II, II: 716
Henry III, II: 717
Henry VII, II: 756
Heraclides Ponticus, II: 970n10
Heraclitus of Ephesus, III: 29, 84,
212, 398, 403, 813

Herder, Johann Gottfried von, II: 851,
984n35; III: 29, 84, 212, 398, 403,
813, 844n108
Herodotus, II: 266, 284
Herrhausen, Alfred, II: 831
Herron, Ron, III: 611
Herzog, Roman, II: 1011n49
Hesiod, III: 39, 41, 44, 832n20
Hesse, Eva, III: 369
Heubach, Friedrich W., I: 92
Hexham, Irvin, II: 1018n133
Heyden, Pieter van der, II: 598
Hildegard of Bingen, I: 363–367, 379,
382
Himmler, Heinrich, III: 118
Hitler, Adolf, II: 435; III: 20, 21, 88,
96, 116, 435, 594. 597–600, 602,
604, 864n16
Hobbes, Thomas, II: 701; III: 248,
251–253, 255
Hobsbawm, Eric, III: 632, 773
Hoet, Jan, III: 489
Hoffmann, E.T. A., I: 260, 261
Höhler, Gertrud, II: 831, 974n47
Hölderlin, Friedrich, I: 643n21; II:
766, 979n12; III: 483
Hollein, Hans, II: 252
Höller, Carsten, III: 514
Homer, I: 482, 483, 485, 488–490, 496,
497, 499, 508; II: 204, 205, 209, 292
Hooke, Robert, III: 534, 536
Hopper, Edward, III: 551
Horace (Quintus Horatius Flaccus), II:
63, 945; III: 711
Horn, Rebecca, III: 357, 410, 766
Hrdy, Sarah Blaffer, III: 699, 700, 702,
881n79
Hufeland, Christoph Wilhelm, I: 239
Hufeland, Friedrich, I: 239–242,
245–252, 409, 513
Huizing, Klaas, I: 641n20
Huizinga, Johan, III: 879n57
Humboldt, Alexander von, II: 774,
776, 777, 779, 780, 782, 783, 928,
1005n10

Humboldt, Wilhelm von, I: 236
Husserl, Edmund, II: 238, 324, 850, 851, 969n7; III: 34, 359, 433, 462, 534, 846n130, 864n16
Huys, Frans, II: 908
Hyre, Laurent de la, II: 860

Iamblichus, II: 489, 512, 692
Ignatius of Loyola, I: 581; III: 442
Illich, Ivan, II: 985n44
Ingres, Jean-Auguste-Dominique, III: 42
Innocent III (pope) (see Lotario de Segni)
Irigaray, Luce, III: 166
Isozaki, Arata, III: 277, 278

James, Henry, I: 421
James, William, I: 268; III: 184
Janet, Pierre, I: 268
Janus, Ludwig, I: 248; III: 886n138
Jaspers, Karl, II: 975n50; III: 215, 759
Jefferson, Thomas, I: 405; II: 898; III: 384, 862n136
Jencks, Charles, III: 539
Jesus Christ, I: 149, 154, 155, 162, 183, 308, 436, 476, 585, 619; II: 53, 54, 55, 101–103, 105, 106, 116, 117, 171, 175, 227, 232, 407, 409, 460, 462, 504, 506, 525, 539–541, 555, 556, 640, 643, 646, 651, 652, 656–660, 663, 665, 666, 687, 702, 712, 716, 720, 726, 727, 728, 730, 740, 742, 744–746, 751, 756, 757, 872, 899, 926; III: 403, 730
Jetelová, Magdalena, III: 137
Johansen, John M., III: 754
John III., II: 826
John of Bavaria, Duke, II: 534
John of Damascus, I: 597, 603, 605, 621, 627, 629
John Paul I (pope), II: 763
John Paul II (pope), II: 736, 763, 925; III: 860n109
John, Apostle, II: 175, 391, 678, 805; III: 529, 730

Jomini, Valérie, III: 486
Jon, Gee, III: 110
Jong, Erica, III: 834n35
Judas, I: 145–154; II: 607, 702
Julianus, Flavius Claudius (Roman emperor), II: 678, 689
Julius II (pope), II: 761
Jung, Carl Gustav, I: 124, 654n28
Justin, II: 652

Kabakov, Ilya, III: 488–492, 494, 498, 760, 763, 864n18
Kacem, Mehdi Belhaj, III: 887n156
Kafka, Franz, I: 55, 218, 358, 411, 412; II: 621, 752
Kafkalides, Athanassios, I: 248
Kalkar, Jan Joest van, II: 645
Kant, Immanuel, I: 12, 233, 630, 652n8, 662n60; II: 782, 852, 853, 902; III: 284, 414, 449, 454, 455, 494, 857n79
Kapoor, Anish, II: 956
Karow, Yvonne, III: 873n138
Kassner, Rudolf, I: 152, 641n20
Kästner, Erich, III: 842n86
Kazantzakis, Nikos, I: 496
Kemmer, Hans, II: 506
Kepler, Johannes, I: 20; II:
Kerner, Justinus, I: 244
Kertész, Imre, III: 885n124
Keyserling, Hermann Graf, II: 803, 804
Khlebnikov, Velimir, III: 517
Khonsu-Mes, I: 272
Khunrath, Heinrich, II: 316
Kierkegaard, Søren, II: 637, 640, 643, 648, 651, 662, 663, 669; III: 397
Kieser, Dietrich Georg von, I: 236
Kippenberger, Martin, III: 778
Kircher, Athanasius, I: 223; II: 278, 471, 480, 850
Kitasato, Schibasaburo, III: 189
Kittler, Friedrich, II: 1000n19
Klauke, Jürgen, II: 124, 846; III: 796
Klausner, Joseph, II: 738
Klee, Paul, II: 520

Klein, Melanie, I: 95
Klotz, Heinrich, II: 990n45
Knight, Thomas, III: 324
Koch, Robert, III: 181, 189, 199
Koestler, Arthur, II: 989n26
Kogelnik, Kiki, I: 202
Kohut, Pavel, I: 217
Kojève, Alexandre, II: 41, 873n32, 974n41
Kollmann, Julius III: 344, 654
König, René, III: 742
Konrad of Würzburg, II: 503
Konrád, György, III: 881n80
Koreff, Johann Ferdinand, I: 236
Kornmann, Wilhelm, I: 225
Kowalski, Piotr, III: 804
Koyré, Alexandre, I: 633n1, 633n2; II:
Kracauer, Siegfried, III: 857n72
Kraft, Heinrich, I: 653n13
Kraus, Karl, III: 176
Krikalev, Sergei, III: 304, 309, 852n8
Krishnamurti, Jiddu, I: 652n8
Kristeva, Julia, I: 528–531
Kroker, Arthur, I: 637n40
Kruckenberg, P. I: 236
Kubin, Alfred, I: 260
Kublai Khan, II: 299
Küng, Hans, II: 946
Kupka, František, III: 275
Kurokawa, Kisho, III: 531, 532
Kusama, Yayoi, III: 549

La Fayette, Marie Joseph Motier,
La Mettrie, Julien Offray de, I: 131, 133, 135–137
Laborde-Nottale, Elisabeth, I: 644n33
Lacan, Jacques, I: 197, 217, 468, 469, 470, 492, 533, 536, 537, 654n29; II: 155, 714, 743; III: 150, 396, 653
Lactantius, Lucius Caecilius Firmianus, II: 664
Lafitau, Joseph-François, II: 234
Lafontaine, Oskar, II: 1018n133
Laing, Ronald D., I: 309–316
Landau, Terry, I: 634n10

Landes, David, III: 526
Langbehn, Julius, II: 984n35
Lao Tse, III: 403
Latour, Bruno, III: 23, 201–205, 411, 835n52, 845n116, 863n145
Lavater, Johann Caspar, I: 166, 174–176
Lawrence, David Herbert, III: 865n37
Le Corbusier, II: 368; III: 61, 508, 509, 512, 515, 517, 526, 531, 538, 548, 619, 865n35
Le Goff, Jacques, II: 596
Ledoux, Claude-Nicolas-Louis, II: 360, 452
Lee, Mark, III: 300
Leeuwenhoek, Anton van, I: 325
Legendre, Pierre, III: 441, 856n67
Leibfried, Stephan, III: 875n12
Leibniz, Gottfried Wilhelm, I: 44; II: 512; III: 17, 74
Leisering, Lutz, III: 875n12
Lemaire, Sandrine, III: 864n19
Leo III (pope), II: 714
Leo VII (pope), II: 722
Leonidov, Ivan, III: 512
Leopardi, Giacomo, II: 234
Leopold II., II: 904, 1014n87
Lerner, Jean-Pierre, II: 975n56, 989n27, 996n78
Leroi-Gourhan, André, I: 171
Lesniowska, Gräfin, I: 244
Lessing, Gotthold Ephraim, II: 724
Lévi-Strauss, Claude, II: 230
Lévinas, Emmanuel, I: 150, 217, 635n17, 642n4; II: 988n24; III: 430, 869n104
Lévy, Pierre, III: 61
Libeskind, Daniel, II: 129
Licetus, Fortunius, I: 330
Licetus, Fortunius, I: 330
Lindbergh, Charles A., II: 810
Lissitzky, El (see El Lissitzky)
Livy, III: 264
Locke, John, III: 248
Löffelhardt, Pitt, II: 614

Merleau-Ponty, Maurice, II: 891
Mesmer, Franz Anton, I: 223–225,
227, 228, 230, 231, 233, 236–240,
242, 243, 252, 257, 258, 407,
409–411, 638n14, 642n9
Métraux, Alfred, II: 874
Metschnikow, Ilya, III: 844n106
Meyer-Bohe, Walter & Thomas, III:
873n141
Michaux, Henri, I: 83, 205, 477; II: 765
Michelangelo, II: 420
Mill, John Stuart, III: 874n4
Millais, Sir John Everett, I: 16
Miller, Hugh, II: 193
Minardi, Tommaso, III: 543
Molina-Pantin, Luis, III: 493
Montaigne, Michel Eyquem de, II:
324, 818
Mordacq, Jean-Jules Henry, III: 86–88
More, Henry, II: 559
More, Thomas, III: 347
Morel d'Arleux, Louis- Jean-Marie, I: 173
Moritz of Orange, III: 387
Mosebach, Martin, III: 829n3
Moses, I: 44; II: 283, 646
Mozart, Wolfgang Amadeus, II:
1003n55
Mühlmann, Heiner, I: 635n22; II:
982n13, 983n25, 1018n127; III: 144,
389, 391–394, 673, 831n10, 836n59,
848n160, 852n197, 857n76, 881n78
Müller, Christa, II: 1018n133
Müller, Klaus E., II: 194
Muraka, Yutaka, III: 446
Murakami, Haruki, III: 838n32
Murhard, Friedrich Wilhelm August, I:
228
Murillo, Bartolomé Esteban, II: 53
Musil, Robert, I: 453, 455, 456, 457,
539; III: 647
Mussolini, Benito, III: 675, 873n136

Nabokov, Vladimir, I: 448–451
Napoleon Bonaparte, II: 639, 722,
761; III: 225, 539, 575

Naylor, Thomas, III: 876n19
Nebuchadnezzar II (King of Babylon),
II: 284
Neck, Jan van, III: 364
Nefertiti, II: 677
Negri, Antonio, III: 769, 771,
870n110, 885n131, 887n154
Neher, André, II: 982n14
Neri, Filippo, I: 125
Nero, Claudius Caesar Drusus
Germanicus (Roman emperor), II:
666, 682, 686, 705, 707, 709
Neumann, Erich, I: 645n8
Newton, Isaac, I: 223, 224; II: 558;
III: 228, 298, 403
Niethammer, Friedrich Immanuel, III:
225
Nietzsche, Friedrich, I: 24, 27, 231,
251, 269, 283, 471, 473, 474, 476; II:
11, 41, 91, 115, 121, 185, 321, 331,
399, 441, 449, 450, 451, 483, 531,
553, 554, 558, 562, 594, 738, 822,
823, 854, 855, 857, 959, 981n3,
1016n108; III: 27, 33, 34, 121, 189,
190, 191, 221, 302, 357, 372, 380,
383, 383, 397, 403, 404, 422, 432,
435, 438, 451, 503, 630, 639, 642,
644, 654, 669, 677, 713, 719, 823,
839n38, 852n7, 860n112
Nieuwenhuys, Constant Anton, III:
611, 615–619, 622
Nilsson, Lennart, II: 91, 95, 314, 464,
856
Normand, Carl Peter Joseph, II: 359
Novalis (see Hardenberg, Karl August
von)
Nussbaum, Martha C., II: 1018n133

Octavian (see Augustus)
Oresme, Nicole, II: 445
Orimoto, Tatsumi, III: 482
Otto I, the Great, I: 423
Otto III (emperor), II: 716
Overbeck, Franz, III: 839n38

Ptolemy, Claudius, II: 391
Puységur, Marquis de, I: 233, 235, 236, 238, 255, 407, 409
Pythagoras, II: 499; III: 403

Qin Shi Huang (first Emperor of China), I: 35; II: 299, 983n26
Quintinye, Jean de la, III: 320
Quong Kee, Tom, III: 110

Rahner, Karl, III: 835n51
Rainer, Arnulf, II: 130
Rank, Otto, II: 201
Ranke-Graves, Robert von, III: 292
Raphael, II: 82
Rawls, John, III: 268, 269
Ray, Charles, III: 559
Ray, Man, II: 967
Redon, Odilon, I: 344; II: 492
Regan, Leo, III: 423
Reich, Wilhelm, I: 298; III: 793
Reichert, Klaus, II: 1009n37
Reinoso, Pablo, III: 15
Reisch, Gregor, II: 463
Reitzle, Wolfgang, III: 883n102
Reynolds, Peter C., III: 349
Rhodes, Cecil, II: 812, 889, 890, 904
Ribera, José de, II: 103
Ricardo, David, III: 629, 630
Richters, Christian, III: 473
Riesman, David, III: 876n17
Rihm, Wolfgang, I: 518
Rilke, Rainer Maria, I: 67, 295, 390, 636n28, 651n34; II: 585, 990n41, 1006n14
Robertson, Roland, II: 957
Rodger, George, II: 236
Rodler, Hieronymus, II: 907, 909
Rogers, Richard, II: 438
Rogozov, Leonid, III: 78
Rombach, Heinrich, II: 984n35
Romme, Gilbert, III: 581
Ronell, Avital, III: 870n105
Ronfeld, David, III: 843n94
Roosevelt, Franklin D., III: 645

Rosenkranz, Karl, II: 770
Rosenstock-Huessey, Eugen, I: 652n7; II: 743–747, 795, 1003n62; III: 144
Rosenzweig, Franz, II: 739–741, 744
Rotondi, Michel, III: 55, 237
Rötzer, Florian, III: 853n20
Rousseau, Jean-Jacques, I: 384, 385, 581; II: ; III: 264
Ruge, Arnold, III: 596
Rych, David, I: 336

Sade, Donatien Alphonse François Marquis de, I: 137; II: 608, 894
Said, Edward W., II: 1008n28
Saint Phalle, Niki de, III: 794
Saint Victor, Richard of, I: 611, 662n59
Saint-Just, Louis Antoine Léon, III: 371
Saint-Pierre, Jacques Henri Bernadin de, III: 289
Saint-Simon, Claude Henri de Rouvroy, I: 238
Salles, Evandro, I: 97
Sappho, III: 819
Sartre, Jean-Paul, I: 153, 360, 626, 645n4; II: ; III: 97, 680, 838n23
Sasaki, Yuichiro, III: 131
Scarry, Elaine, II: 998n21
Schaichet, Arkadi, III: 21
Schama, Simon III: 638
Schamberg, Morton, III: 421
Schedel, Hartmann, II: 282
Scheer, Hermann, III: 841
Scheler, Max, III: 432, 654
Schelling, Friedrich Wilhelm Joseph von, I: 234, 235, 239, 246, 250, 409; II: 115, 889; III: 156, 189
Schelling, Karl Eberhard von, I: 234
Schiepp, Christoff, II: 816
Schiller, Friedrich, II: 539, 1002n48; III: 663, 676
Schilling, Alfons, III: 59
Schipper, Kristofer, I: 304, 306
Schlamminger, Karl, II: 34
Schlemmer, Oskar, I: 198; II: 146
Schliemann, Heinrich, II: 271

Strauss, Leo, III: 850n172
Struth, Thomas, II: 145, 841
Suhrawardi, Shihaboddin Yahya, I: 567–570
Sulla, Lucius Cornelius, II: 298
Szlavik, Andreas, III: 758

Talleyrand, Charles Maurice de, III: 574, 575, 578
Tallis, Raymond, III: 877n29
Tansey, Mark, II: 280
Tape, Walter, II: 92
Tarde, Gabriel, III: 177, 196, 197, 235, 241, 273–279, 419, 438, 452, 463, 530, 576, 584, 762, 819, 841n64, 845n110, 851n182
Tatian, II: 652
Taubes, Jacob, II: 738, 739, 741
Tertullian, Quintus Septimius Florens, II: 730
Tesch, Bruno, III: 107
Tesla, Nicola, III: 141
Teuffel, Patrick, III: 284
Thales of Miletus, II: 30, 31, 37, 353, 869n6, 970n11
Thallemer, Axel, III: 442, 444
Theodosius I (Eastern Roman emperor), II: 226
Theophilus of Antioch, II: 652
Theophrastus, I: 223
Thomas Aquinas, I: 413, 428, 586, 620
Tillich, Paul, III: 885n131
Timm, Hermann, I: 641n20
Titian, I: 201; II: 832
Titus, Flavius Vespasianus (Roman emperor), II: 707, 1003n55
Tocqueville, Alexis de, III: 11, 628
Todd, Emmanuel, III: 875n9
Todorov, Tzvetan, I: 650n19
Tomatis, Alfred, I: 248, 263, 296, 501, 507, 508; II: 203
Tomkins, Walter, III: 843n95, 843n96
Toynbee, Arnold Joseph, II: 191
Trajan, Marcus Ulpius (Roman emperor), II: 411, 412, 414, 416

Transylvanus, Maximilian, II: 816
Trismegistus, Hermes, II: 512
Tristani, Jean-Luis, I: 646n18
Troyes, Chrétiens de, III: 827
Tzara, Tristan, III: 749

Uexküll, Jakob von, III: 180, 230, 231
Ujică, Andrei, III: 304, 852n8, 878n51
Urban VI (pope), I: 423

Valéry, Paul Ambroise, III: 82, 467, 488, 494,–496, 545, 843n94
Valmiki, Maharshi, III: 43
Varius Avitus Bassianus (Roman emperor), II: 686
Varro, Marcus Terentius, II: 302, 854; III: 471
Varus, Publius Quinctilius, II: 666
Vaudoyer, Léon, III: 567
Vaysse, Jean-Marie, III: 841n65
Veblen, Thorstein, III: 642
Velázquez, Diego Rodríguez de Silva y, II: 794
Verdelet, III: 789
Vermeer van Delft, Jan, II: 922
Vernant, Jean-Pierre, II: 986n11
Verne, Jules, II: 799, 801–804, 835, 854, 981n4; III: 296
Vesalius, Andreas, III: 68, 69
Vespasian, Titus Flavius (Roman emperor), II: 298, 1001n34
Vespucci, Amerigo, II: 882
Vico, Giambattista, II: 737
Vigevano, Guido da, I: 398
Vinci, Leonardo da, I: 63, 454; III: 47
Virchow, Rudolf, III: 534
Virgil, II: 280, 415, 575, 576, 599, 601, 624, 665
Vitellius, Aulus (Roman emperor), III: 789
Vizi, Béla, I: 94
Voegelin, Eric, II: 943–946; III: 759
Volkov, Vladislav Nikolayevich, III: 305
Vollmer, Gerhard, II: 989n31

PHOTOGRAPHIC CREDITS

Page 53 © Acconci Studio, New York.

Page 239 © Galerie Air de Paris, Paris.

Page 736 © akg-images, Archiv für Kunst und Geschichte, Berlin.

Page 794 © Archive Niki de Saint Phalle.

Page 78 © Arktis- und Antarktismuseum, St. Petersburg.

Pages 377, 743 © Bildarchiv Preußischer Kulturbesitz, Berlin.

Page 609 © BLG Logistics Group, Basel.

Page 440 © Pieter Boersma, Amsterdam.

Pages 558, 793 © Mary Boone Gallery, New York.

Page 24 © Michael Boran, Dublin.

Page 756 © Boxxes, www.boxxes.com.

Page 71 © Veronika Bromová, Prague.

Page 510 © Steven Brower, New York.

Pages 312, 337, 449, 516, 518 © The Estate of Buckminster Fuller, Sebastopol.

Page 684 © Charlotte Buff, concept fractal art, Berlin-Braunschweig.

Page 510 © Christoph & Friends/Nik Wheeler, Essen.

Page 329 © Columbia University Biosphere 2 Center, Oracle, USA.

Page 546 © Cordon Art B.V., Baarn, Niederlande.

Page 507 © DIZ, Süddeutscher Verlag/Bayerischer Rundfunk, München.

Page 559 © Donald Young Gallery, Chicago.

Pages 126, 305, 329, 439, 605 © Deutsche Presseagentur, Frankfurt/M.

Pages 208, 209 © Eames Office, Santa Monica, USA.

Page 473 © Eisenmann Architects, New York.

Page 623 © Elizabeth Diller & Ricardo Scofidio, New York.

Page 758 © Michael Elmgreen & Ingar Dragset, Berlin.

Page 303 © ESA, Paris.

Page 295 © Agentur Focus, Hamburg.

Page 419© Jacques Herzog and Pierre de Meuron Kabinett (Foundation), Fotosammlung Ruth and Peter Herzog, Basel.

Page 668 © Frank Frankes, Kronberg.

Page 47 © Fraunhofer IRB Verlag, Stuttgart.

Page 375 ©Peter Frey, Pernes, Frankreich.

Page 601 © Future Systems, London.

Borrowed from books:

H. P. Degischer (ed.), *Metallschäume*, Wiley-CH Verlag, Weinheim, 2000: p. 46.

Gerd Greune und Klaus Mannhardt (ed.), *Hiroshima und Nagasaki*, Pahl-Rugenstein, Bonn, 1983: p. 131.

C. G. Jung, *Der Mensch und seine Symbole*, Patmos Verlag, 1967: p. 76.

Martin Krampen and Dieter Schempp (ed.), *Glasarchitekten*, avedition GmbH, Ludwigsburg, 1999: p. 284.

Norbert Lossani, Röntgen. *Eine Entdeckung verändert unser Leben*, Motovun Book, Lucerne, 1992: p. S. 62.

Shlomo Raz, *Atlas transvaginaler Operationen*, Chapter 7, Ferdinand Enke Verlag, Stuttgart, 1995 © 2002 Elsevier, Philadelphia: p. 71.

Thomas Schmidt, *Werner March: Architekt des Olympia Stadiums*, Birkhäuser Verlag, Basel, 1986: pp. 594 & 603.

Bruce Alberts, Dennis Bray and Julian Lewis (ed.), *Molecular Biology of the Cell*, Garland Publishing, New York, 2002/Photograph © David Kirk: p. 51.

Weiss/Neumeister, Die Frommen von New York, Kehayoff Verlag, Munich, 1993: p. 430.

All other illustrations are from the personal archive of the author and of the publisher, Suhrkamp.